The Badiou Dic

The Badiou Dictionary

Edited by Steven Corcoran

EDINBURGH
University Press

Edinburgh University Press Ltd
The Tun – Holyrood Road
12(2f) Jackson's Entry
Edinburgh EH8 8PJ
www.euppublishing.com

Typeset in 11/13 Ehrhardt by
Servis Filmsetting Ltd, Stockport, Cheshire,
and printed and bound in Great Britain by
CPI Group (UK) Ltd, Croydon CR0 4YY

A CIP record for this book is available from the British Library

ISBN 978 0 7486 4097 3 (hardback)
ISBN 978 0 7486 6964 6 (webready PDF)
ISBN 978 0 7486 4096 6 (paperback)
ISBN 978 0 7486 6965 3 (epub)

Contents

Acknowledgements

I would like to thank all the contributors for their commitment, which enabled this considerable journey to take place and helped the project evolve in sometimes surprising directions. The editorial staff at Edinburgh University Press has been wonderful, and in this regard my editor, Carol Macdonald, is deserving of extra special thanks for her ultra-generous support.

As ingenious as Badiou's work is in its grasping of the existence of truth procedures, 'the point is' says Rilke, 'to live everything. Live the questions [or ideas] now. Perhaps you will then gradually, without noticing it, live along some distant day into the answer.' For the perpetual joy of ever embarking towards and returning from this distant day, my final thanks go to Joanna Kusiak.

Abbreviations

AFP	*The Adventure of French Philosophy*
Ahmed	*Tétralogie d'Ahmed*
AR	*Les années rouges*
BE	*Being and Event*
BF	'Beyond Formalism'
C	*The Century*
CCT	'Can Change be Thought?'
CD	'Casser en deux l'histoire du monde'
CH	*The Communist Hypothesis*
Cin	*Cinema*
CM	*The Concept of Model*
CS	*Conditions*
CPBT	*Can Politics be Thought?*
DCB	*Deleuze: The Clamour of Being*
DLF	'De la femme comme catégorie de l'être'
DNS	'Destruction, Negation, Subtraction'
E	*Ethics*
FB	*Badiou-Finkielkraut la face-a-face*
FP	'Fascism of the Potato'
DE	'The Democratic Emblem'
DI	*De l'Idéologie*
H	*Heidegger: Nazism, Women, Philosophy*
HI	*Handbook of Inaesthetics*
IA	*The Incident at Antioch*
IPL	*In Praise of Love*
IT	*Infinite Thought*
L	*Lacan: Antiphilosophie 3*
LW	*Logics of Worlds*
MCM	'Metaphysics and the critique of metaphysics'
MP	*Manifesto for Philosophy*
M	*Metapolitics*
ML	'Mark and Lack: On Zero'
MS	*Meaning of Sarkozy*
MT	*Mathematics of the Transcendental*
NN	*Number and Numbers*
NAA	'Does the notion of activist art still have a meaning?'

OB   *On Beckett*
OD   *Of an Obscure Disaster*
OS   'On a finally objectless subject'
PAL   'Platon et/ou Aristote-Leibniz'
PE   *Philosophy and the Event*
PM   *Philosophy for Militants*
Pol   *Polemics*
PP   *Pocket Pantheon*
Rep   *Plato's Republic: A dialogue in 16 Chapters*
RH   *The Rebirth of History*
RKHD   *The Rational Kernel of the Hegelian Dialectic*
RT   *Rhapsody for the Theatre*
SEM   Badiou's seminar series, transcriptions of which are to be found
         online at www.entretemps.asso.fr/Badiou/. References in the
         text include the year and date of the seminar (e.g. SEM 2012:
         October 24).
SG   'Sophie Germain'
SMP   *Second Manifesto for Philosophy*
SP   *Saint Paul*
TC   *Théorie de la contradiction*
TM   'Third Sketch of a Manifesto of Affirmationist Art'
TO   *Briefings on Existence: Short Treaty of Transitory Ontology*
TS   *Theory of the Subject*
TU   'Eight theses on the Universal'
TW   *Theoretical Writings*
WA   *Wittgenstein's Antiphilosophy*
Wag   *Five Lessons on Wagner*
WL   'What is Love?'
WN   'Who is Nietzsche?'

Introduction

Socrates: Someone whose life is a true life is happy, and even blessed. Someone whose life is disgraceful is unhappy. So we've finally arrived at this crucial statement: the just man is happy, the unjust man is unhappy. Now, being unhappy is not advantageous, whereas being happy is. So I can finally state it categorically: it is not true, Professor Thrasymachus, that injustice is more advantageous than justice.

Thrasymachus: Well, Professor Socrates can just go and party now till the sun comes up! And I, Thrasymachus, can just shut the hell up. I know how to keep quiet, my friends. You'll see what a virtuoso of rhetoric's silence is like. But that doesn't mean I agree.

From Badiou, *Plato's* Republic*: A dialogue in 16 Chapters*

In recent years Alain Badiou has yet again given a stunning demonstration of the timelessness of philosophy. The citation above his 'hypertranslation' of Plato's *Republic*, published in 2012, is a reworking for today of an essential philosophical text. Badiou's 'return to Plato' is well-documented, but perhaps what was not foreseeable in this return is his renewal of a Platonic *topos* to which his next book, due in French in 2015, is devoted: *happiness*. The discussion above between Socrates and Thrasymachus on the nature of justice and happiness is not a simple chat among friends. For it is essential for the philosopher to show, against the rhetorician and his apology for injustice and power, that the happy person is the just person. Showing this sometimes requires less than fair means, as both sides try to assert their ascendency and convince the youths in attendance. Why? Because such is always the case when a fundamental decision is at stake. The discussion precisely is not so much a discussion but a confrontation, a clash of heterogeneous principles in which an essential aim is at stake. The aim of the philosopher will be to uphold – to put it in Badiou's terms – the happiness of the person that participates in a truth, against all those who in all ages affirm that the tyrant, the trickster, is the happy person, in short that injustice is the way of the world and that the just are simply naïve fools. As a discourse that aspires to be more than a simple academic exercise, philosophy can win out by showing that there is an essential choice to be made here, a choice that cuts to the core of the subject. This is something that Badiou seeks to affirm: yes, philosophy, if it is good for anything, corrupts the youth, orients minds through the question of truth, promoting truth and happiness against the capitalist reduction of the world to what the Chinese call the three relations: the relation to money, the relation to social and economic success, and the relation to sex. To paraphrase Saint Paul, we might say: 'neither does success in these relations count nor lack of success in them but being a new creature'.

This latest phase of Badiou's return to Plato is something we shall hopefully soon have the pleasure to read. Badiou's initial 'return to Plato' occurred by way of the introduction of 'multiplicity' (through transfinite set theory) into key questions and a theory of the event. So it was a return, but by no means a simple one, since in order to give Platonic approaches relevance in a world that eschews truth and a philosophical milieu that has roundly declared its mission as being to break with Platonism, Badiou has had to reinvent the very means of this return. Many of the concepts that you will read about in this work articulate the key operations that have enabled this return – which, truth be told, is at once a rediscovery and a reinvention of Plato. Two words – 'rediscovery' and 'invention' – on whose ultimate undecidability Plato himself was the first to insist. These concepts – though *The Badiou Dictionary*, a product of collective work and all the contingencies that come along with it, is far from exhaustive and the harsh reader will have plenty to pick at – are those through which Badiou seeks, in a Kantian-type transcendental analysis, to lay bare the conditions of possibility of a truth. In *BE*, Badiou analyses the ontological conditions of possibility of truth, and in *LW*, their existential conditions of possibility.

One of Badiou's crucial concepts is that of conditions – philosophy is conditioned by four types of truth procedure, as one will read many times throughout this Dictionary, which it 'compossibilises', i.e. whose synthetic reception it organises. This means that for Badiou, philosophy itself receives truths; it is less a truth procedure than a quasi-transcendental organisation of thought around the 'there is' of truths. These truths are its 'real' and are that on the basis of which it organises its conceptual distinctions. But truths have the feature of being *rare*. What is philosophy thus to do when there is no present informed by procedures of truth – when the 'world' and its three relations would condemn truths, and thus philosophy itself, to inexistence? Says Badiou, it turns around the investigation: no longer is it a matter of inquiring in rational fashion into the conditions of truths, but instead, of examining the world itself from the point of view of truths. What kind of sense can we make of the world from the viewpoint of truths themselves? What can we say of the figures of the world on the basis of an exception that is immanent to that same world? Perhaps the most forceful example is that of love: anyone who has really been in love will grasp that the possibilities it opens up enable a completely other view of the world, in which such possibilities are nowhere to be found.

With this move Badiou embarks on a more classically Platonic investigation: if there are truths, what does this entail in terms of what we should or should not do? If there are truths, then is this a good or bad thing? And does one's incorporation into a body-of-truth make one happy, happier than the hedonist, than the liberal, than the fascist? Badiou thinks that this is the challenge philosophy should take up, these are the questions that its concepts should ultimately rally around.

When I took on the project of editing this book, I thought that the systematic nature of Badiou's philosophy lent itself rather well to this kind of 'encyclopedic' undertaking. Badiou is a philosopher in the classical sense and his concepts are clearly argued for and well delimited. The reader will not find definitions of a scholastic sort, as Badiou's thought is more axiomatic. The operators of his thinking and the operations that they enable one to perform are what readers will discover in the various contributions (e.g. the contribution they make to overcoming the antinomy between the dominant liberal political discourse and the post-revolutionary despair of many of Badiou's contemporaries). Notwithstanding, differences in interpretation and approach are manifest, as is inevitable in a work on a philosopher who, like Badiou, covers so many topics and who, it might be added, is not just the author of an increasingly vast array of philosophical works, but also of political and many other types of essays, theatre plays, novels and a libretto. Badiou's astonishing formalisations find in many of these works new inflections as they attempt to cope with the shifting contexts in which his work has unfolded. It is indeed Badiou's almost poetic attentiveness to shifts in sensible presentation (in the 'conjuncture'), and the inner movements of his formalisations that this generates, that I for one find among the most fascinating features of his work.

A dictionary project of this nature also runs the risk of becoming a mere conveyor of clichés on a thinker for polite dinner-time conversation, whereas the aim is of course to provide a more or less basic orientation to Badiou's concepts for those relatively new to his work, aids to the task of pursuing his ramified writings, as well as some hopefully new and challenging perspectives for more familiar readers. Thus many of the 'entries' are in fact quite long, which has permitted a more sustained engagement with certain concepts. Badiou's mature work from *Being and Event* on is generally considered to be the point at which he really develops a unique philosophical voice, but his publications for the preceding twenty-five or so years are of course more than instructive for understanding later developments. Many contributors have thus used the lengthier format to trace the permutations of certain concepts in his overall work, but also to develop a lengthier discussion between Badiou and another thinker, to delve further into Badiou's position on a given topic in the wider field, and so on. The range of approaches to what constitutes a dictionary entry is indeed diverse, but I think that the reader interested in understanding Badiou and looking to further problematise, complicate and test his thought in new directions can only consider this an advantage.

The dictionary consists of ninety-three entries that have been compiled by specialists in Badiou's work from around the world (contributor biographies can be found at the end of the book). Unlike the other dictionaries in this series by Edinburgh University Press, I have chosen not to include connector words at the end of each entry or the shorter linking entries. Instead the reader will find a general index at the back listing each entry and all the pages in the dictionary on which a given concept, key word, or position vis-à-vis a philosophical interlocutor is developed in some aspect. Badiou's works are generally only given in the abbreviated form listed in the system of abbreviations, but due to the large number of his writings, the more occasional and less utilised pieces (often able to be usually found in collections in English) are mentioned in full the first time they appear in a given article (e.g. 'The Law on the Islamic Headscarf') and are thereafter given in abbreviated form together with the collection in which they appear (e.g. IH/*Pol*). Much use has also been made of Badiou's seminar series, which first took place at the Collège International de Philosophie before moving in recent years to the École Normale Supérieure. Transcriptions of the seminars are available online, and references to them are given the abbreviation SEM followed by the year and date of the seminar in question (e.g. SEM 2012: October 24). English titles are used throughout the entries, except in the case of untranslated texts, where French will be used. Finally, references to the works of others are given with the author's name and date of publication in English, together with a chapter or page number if required (e.g. Deleuze 1990: 25).

A

ABSOLUTE

Justin Clemens

In Badiou, the term 'absolute' is not employed for the most part as a *technical terminus*, but nonetheless emerges at certain symptomatic points of his work. Certainly, the function that the 'absolute' has traditionally played in philosophy, most notably for G. W. F. Hegel, is strenuously criticised by Badiou. If Hegel is usually taken to be the most forceful and influential philosopher of the absolute, and in those precise terms – for instance, the final section of the *Phenomenology of Spirit* (1804) is titled '*Das absolute Wissen*' – then those senses of 'absolute' are absolutely *verboten* for Badiou. Why? Because 'absolute' can no longer be sustained as a predicate in regards to knowledge, time or totality. Very briefly, Badiou's post-*BE* work insists on an irreducible distinction between 'truth' and 'knowledge', for which he draws on Heidegger and Lacan: indeed, if knowledge is generated by truth processes, truth is also what makes a hole in (the existing state of) knowledges. Yet this is also why time can never be 'absolved' for Badiou: a truth process is to be identified with the construction of an 'eternal present' (see *LW* on the temporality of truths, e.g. 9–10). As such, there is no single 'Time' that can resolve or close upon itself, only the remaking of the times in a new time – and that new time always emerges among others. Regarding totality, Badiou deploys Bertrand Russell's destruction of 'the set of all sets' to show how the idea of the absolute as totality is inconsistent (see e.g. *LW* 109–13). Badiou's hostility to any thesis regarding the totalisation of Being is explicit even down to his nominations. In *BE* he writes:

I say 'void' rather than nothing, because the 'nothing' is the name of the void correlative to the *global* effect of structure (*everything* is counted); it is more accurate to indicate that not-having-been-counted is also quite *local* in its occurrence, since it is not counted *as one*. 'Void' indicates the failure of the one, the not-one, in a more primordial sense than the not-of-the-whole. (*BE* 56)

Yet something essential to the traditional signification of the term 'absolute' is implicitly retained by Badiou, for essential reasons. Let me provide two here. The first is, unsurprisingly, mathematical. As Badiou puts it in *BE*: 'It is quite characteristic that in order to designate a property or a function that remains "the same" within ontology strictly speaking and in its relativisation mathematicians employ the adjective "absolute"' (302). 'Absolute' in this technical acceptation means that, with regards to the constructible universe (in which every multiple belongs to a level of the constructible hierarchy), it 'is a predicate of those propositions which stipulates that their restriction [to that universe] does not affect their truth value' (303). One consequence of this is that 'one can actually *demonstrate* that no (constructible) multiple is evental' (304), and hence that there is an absolute non-being of the event. For Badiou, this sense of 'absolute' would be a disaster for thought: 'truth' and 'knowledge' would be one and the same thing; there would be no happening; no subject would be possible.

Badiou's second use of 'absolute' is therefore arrayed against the first. As he puts it, 'nothing is less absolute than inexistence' (308), and it is therefore on the basis of the event that exceeds ontology that Badiou will displace the signification of 'absolute'. Necessarily this will be done in a non-mathematical manner. Take Badiou's uptake of Spinoza's axiom: 'we have one true idea'. What does this mean? Above all, that there is indeed a 'foundation' for thought; or, more precisely, that we have, as Badiou puts it in an essay from *IT*: 'a fixed point . . . a point of interruption' (51). As Badiou explains: 'There is a moment when one must be able to say that this is right and that is wrong, in light of the evidence of the principle. There cannot be an infinite regression of quibbling and calculating. There must also be utterances of which it can be said they are unconditionally true' (54). Or, as Badiou puts it in *LW*: 'even if some typical expressions of the true evade us, our relation to truths is *absolute*' (71; my emphasis). This is, in a way, Badiou's version of Descartes' halting point in radical doubt. Here, however, the 'fixed point' of the absolute is not reached as and at the limit of a subjective process, but as broached by an event; that is, with the paradoxical semblance that institutes a truth process.

The absolute – here reconstructed in the absolutely minimal form of the Œfixed point – does not return as a firm foundation, but as that which threatens to undo all existing foundations for the re-establishment of a truth.

AFFIRMATIONISM

Jan Voelker

In the context of art, Badiou has made use of the concept of affirmationism primarily to denote a philosophical gesture towards certain aspects of early twentieth-century modern arts, but also to describe the works of some twenty-first-century artists.

It is mainly in his 'Third Sketch of a Manifesto of Affirmationist Art' (TM/*Pol*) that Badiou lays out the contours of a new schema of artistic production, based on the capacity of affirmation. This small but central text, being a manifesto, has to be understood as an affirmative gesture itself, indicating the minimal point in which the category of negation in modern arts is split in its destructive and its affirmative side, and highlighting the latter. Therefore, affirmationism is, first, in principal not about a supposed category of art (which would be named affirmative), but rather the methodological name of a philosophical intervention in the discourse of art, affirming the affirmative aspect in art. Secondly, this affirmative gesture finds its localised point of intervention in the twentieth century. And thirdly, Badiou makes use of the notion of affirmationism in relation to certain contemporary artists who can be said to be working towards a new, affirmative concept of art.

Given this frame, the notion of *affirmationism* is thus not only closely linked to the concepts in *HI*, but also to the analysis of the twentieth century in *C*. In *HI* Badiou unfolds the three schemata of didactics, classicism, and romanticism as modes of thinking the constellation between art and truth. The didactic schema, the paradigm of which is Plato, contends that there is no truth in art, and that therefore art may at best serve the purposes of education, but is also dangerous because of its imitations of truth. The classicist schema, whose main figure is Aristotle, does away with this problem by claiming that art has no relation to truth, and therefore its function is purely therapeutic. Finally, in the romantic schema, as a paradigm of which Badiou has often discussed Heidegger, art alone is capable of truth. Art will enter into a difficult relationship with philosophy, for philosophy will hand over some of its essential tasks to poetry. In the twentieth century these three schemas are saturated: the didactic schema has been used to connect art to the state, to an 'external imperative of the idea' (TM 135), the classicist schema 'subjects art to the natural rule of pleasing forms and [. . .] confers on it the practical virtue of tempering the passions, rather than a mission to truth' (ibid.) and thereby drops the concept of art in the last instance, and the romantic schema remained in the 'element of pure promise' (*HI* 7). The avant-gardes of the twentieth century, who attempted to find a new schema and sought to bridge the didactic and the romantic schema, were 'didactic in their desire to put an end to art' and 'romantic in their conviction that art must be reborn immediately as absolute' (8). The avant-gardes failed, because in the last instance their quest for a new schema led into the disjunctive synthesis of the century: 'creative destruction' (8; cf. also *C* 131–47). The failure of the avant-gardes to develop a new didactico-romantic schema then provides the grounds for the search of a new schema in which the two elements of the relation between art and truth – 'immanence' (as in the romantic schema) and 'singularity' (as in the didactic schema, in which art alone is capable of producing semblance; cf. *HI* 9) – could be linked in a new way. Affirmationism, then, can be conceived as a first step towards a new thinking of art: it would conceive art as an immanent truth procedure of its own and understand this truth as singular, unique to the realm of art. Differently put, affirmationism conceives of art as of a thinking of its own. But this art will also take up the theme of education again, because it 'arrange[s] the forms of knowledge in such a way that some truth may come to pierce a hole in them' (*HI* 9).

In the contemporary absence of a schema that would be able to combine immanence and singularity and to connect it to the theme of education, affirmationism answers two strands of the contemporary understanding of art: on the one hand, affirmationism is designed against pseudo-classicism, and on the other against romantic formalism. Pseudo-classicism manifests itself in the bombast of the empire, amuses itself with '[c]ircus games, the strict equivalent of which today is professional sport, and the musical and cinematic culture industry' (TM 138). Romantic formalism tries to oppose this sort of morbid art through its withdrawal from the laws of circulation. But, still, this attempt keeps acting in direct symmetry to the pseudo-classicist art, and will therefore, in seeking an expression of ego- or ethnos-related particularities, stay bound to the circulation of particularities. If the formalism of this attempt is the result of its directedness towards the expression of singularities, then its romanticism stems from its trust in the capacities of the body.

The postmodern art of romantic formalism thus revives the idea of a didactic-romantic synthesis in a poor way; it is a 'kind of avant-garde without the avant-garde' (136). In terms of the *democratic materialism*, there are only *bodies and languages*: bodily expressions and the mutual tolerance of their expressed particularity.

Against this continuation of romanticism as well as against the pseudo-classicist return, affirmationism makes reference to those artists of the twentieth century who tried to interrupt this expressionism of forms. Badiou claims that those artists 'slowly composed configurations that have become legible only today' (140). To read these configurations today, one will have to uncover and to extract the affirmationist aspects in the works of certain artists. Artists – Badiou names Malevich, Rothko, Pessoa, and Schönberg among others – who are otherwise part of the twentieth century, and in this respect belong to a constellation of active processes of thought that Badiou has summarised under the keyword of the 'passion for the real' (cf. C) – that is the opposite preference, namely for the destructive aspect of negation that predominated throughout the twentieth century.

The *Manifesto* then proceeds in 15 theses. The first three concern the relation between the sensible and the idea: Art is not understood as the 'sublime descent of the infinite into the finite', but as the 'production [. . .] of an infinite, subjective series' (TM 143). Therefore it is not the 'expression of a particularity', but an 'impersonal [. . .] truth' (ibid.), a truth that is in itself 'sensible' (144). It follows from these theses, as Badiou explains, that art consists of (finite) works and that the artist is only an intermediate instance of its process, which transforms the sensible into 'an event of the Idea' (ibid.). There is a plurality of arts (ibid., thesis 4), each of which 'comes from impure forms' (ibid., thesis 5). Art purifies these forms precisely because it starts from 'sensible evidence' (ibid.). The sixth thesis may be quoted at length: 'The subjects of artistic truths consist in the works that compose them' (ibid.). Thus, in art, the subject is defined as the body of works, which thesis 7 then explains as an 'infinite configuration' (ibid.). The configuration is a 'generic totality' because it does not affirm a completed set, but its very procedure, which keeps striving for change. Thesis 8 explains further the purification already mentioned in thesis 5: 'Art is a second formalisation of the emergence of a formless form' (ibid., 146; tm). Art transforms an impure evidence into an imperative and formalises the 'formless [. . .] into a form' (ibid.). The last 7 theses refer to art's contemporary position in the western world of democracy and capitalism. As a non-particularised – that is, universal – procedure, art cannot follow the 'Western idea of political liberty' (ibid.) today. It has 'to invent a new sensory abstraction' (ibid.), which will be addressed to anyone and is therefore 'tied to a proletarian aristocratism' (ibid., 147). '[S]olidly as a demonstration [. . .] as surprising as a nighttime ambush, and [. . .] elevated as a star' (ibid.) – a formulation that reminds us of the triad of the Symbolic, the Real and the Imaginary – contemporary art not only subtracts itself from the western form of communication, but renders visible what inexists in the western world. And the *Manifesto* closes with the final cut: 'It is better to do nothing than to work formally toward making visible what the West declares to exist' (148).

On a different occasion Badiou has developed that the question of affirmation in art is its process linked to the question of politics. As in political action, Badiou writes, 'negation is always [. . .] suspended between destruction and subtraction', where 'subtraction' is the name Badiou gives – in this lecture on Pasolini – to the 'affirmative part of negation' (DNS in Blasi et al. 2012). If negation consists of two parts, destruction and subtraction, the latter cannot be understood as the negation of the former. It exists independent of that which is negated by negation; it rather exists as an 'immanent difference' (cf. his talk on 'The Subject of Art' at www.lacan.com/symptom6_articles/badiou.html; last accessed 15 December 2014).

But even if art is thus linked to the question of politics, the truth procedure of art cannot be mixed up with that of politics. In the contemporary situation nevertheless, the risk of such identification is high. As Badiou unfolds in a talk, given in New York in 2010, the contemporary situation is characterised by the absence of any 'strong ideology' and the complete reign of the weak ideology in which differences are neglected. The consequence is that today, the distinction between a 'militant' art and an 'official art' can no longer be drawn. In the context of a strong ideology, 'official' art can be characterised as one focusing on the 'affirmative glorification of the result', as an art 'of affirmative certainty', while 'militant art' is an 'art of the contradiction between the affirmative nature of principles and the dubious result of struggles' (NAA). The ideological background to both understandings of art may be the same, but its place in the work of art changes. While official art realises ideology as power, militant art tracks a process and works on the presentation of what is becoming, and not on the statist representation of what is. Affirmationism is thus itself split, and the project of reaffirming the affirmative aspect of the avant-gardes can now even more precisely be understood as the reaffirmation of their weak, formal aspect. Viewed from the contemporary situation this is the only option, as there is no strong emancipatory ideology today to which an 'affirmative certainty' (ibid.) could relate at all. But also, one might note that the distinction of 'official' and 'militant' art finds its perverted double in the above-mentioned distinction of 'circus games' and 'romantic formalism' as paradigms of contemporary liberal art.

In the same talk, Badiou proposes four 'provisional rules' for how to think of a militant art today, in the absence of any strong ideology. Even if these points are not explicitly connected to the question of affirmationism as such, it seems legitimate to understand them in this context. The first demands of the artist to relate his or her work to 'some local political experiences'. The second requires engagement in attempts to return to a strong ideology. The sole connection to weak procedures is not enough; it is also necessary 'to go beyond the weakness' (NAA). The third point then demands to work on new forms of presentation, instead of subscribing to given forms of representation. The fourth and last point 'is to propose the possibility of synthesis of the first three points' (ibid.), that is, to present a work which combines the local, real connection with the reorganisation of the idea and the quest for new forms. This process is itself not a procedure of politics, but it can be a preparation for politics in its absence.

Among the examples for living affirmationist artists, Badiou has highlighted the films of Udi Aloni, on the occasion of which Badiou extends his definition of affirmationism: 'The doctrine according to which ideas generated by art do not so much carry a judgement upon the world as they indicate the point from which the world might be transfigured' (Aloni 2011: 193). Recently, Badiou has also discussed the works of the painter Pierre Soulages under the headword of affirmationism (cf. 'Pierre Soulages, un peintre affirmationniste?' at www.dailymotion.com/video/xc2xw4_colloque-pierre-soulages-derniere-p_creation; last accessed 7 January 2015). Affirmationist art can thus be understood as a procedure of contemporary artists, transfiguring the world by making legible the affirmationist part of negation, the creative part of negation. Thereby they close the twentieth century and its passion of the real and open up the twenty-first century as a possible affirmationist century.

ANTIPHILOSOPHY

Tzuchien Tho

In Badiou's intellectual trajectory, the theme of antiphilosophy arrives precisely at the moment of his mature emphasis on the philosophical act governed by his 'theory of conditions'. That is, it was during the period surrounding the publication of BE (1988) and its companion MP that a series of counter-figures begin to emerge as a means to think philosophy systematically as act through its internal and external relations. An important instance of this is Badiou's development of the theme of antiphilosophy. From 1992 to 1996, the years immediately following Badiou's declaration of a return to the philosophical, Badiou dedicated his lecture courses at the University of Paris VIII to four figures of antiphilosophy: Nietzsche, Wittgenstein, Lacan and Saint Paul (cf. the lecture notes written up on www.entretemps.asso.fr; last accessed 15 December 2014). A number of publications on these very authors were subsequently published on this theme and CS (1992) can be read as the enfolded kernel of reflections that slowly unfold in these seminar lectures and individual articles.

Understanding how the concept of antiphilosophy emerges in Badiou's own intellectual trajectory is important to disambiguate the functional role that this concept plays in his philosophy. For example, Badiou only once mentions antiphilosophy in *BE*, and this is in reference to Lacan's notion of antiphilosophy, from which he distances himself (*BE* 2). In this same text, his critiques of Pascal, Rousseau and Lacan (later identified as antiphilosophers) are not made along the lines of their antiphilosophy. While Badiou's readings of these same authors will eventually lead to the construction of this concept, the emergence of antiphilosophy will become significant only in the context where philosophy becomes central in his intellectual project.

While Badiou's increasing identification as philosopher is evident in *BE*, it is in *MP* that this identification is unequivocally declared. Announcing a return to a 'Platonic gesture', Badiou underlines that this philosophical act is to be coupled with a task to confront Plato's own double, the sophist. Here, Badiou argues that the necessary requirement of this act is 'to go beyond the subtle wrangling of sophistry as well as be educated by it about the essence of the questions of his time' (*MP* 98). For Badiou, this identification with philosophy immediately signals a confrontation with 'Great Modern Sophistry', an antagonism that will index philosophy to the contemporary historical horizon. Against the philosophical act, which essentially orients thought to truth, the fundamental mode of sophistry, ancient or modern, is the linguistic circumvention of any positive claims to truth (*CS* 25). In turn, the sophistic mirroring of philosophical discourse is one that must be met, once again, with a 'Platonic gesture'. As he puts it, 'Philosophy is always the breaking of a mirror. This mirror is the surface of language onto which the sophist reduces all the things that philosophy treats in its act. If the philosopher sets his gaze solely on this surface, his double, the sophist, will emerge, and he may take himself to be one' (*CS* 25). As the philosopher's doubled other, the sophist is thus philosophy's internal enemy, its immanent danger.

Underlining Badiou's treatment of the figure of the sophist is part and parcel of his treatment of the antiphilosopher. A number of Badiou's works seem to closely identify sophist and antiphilosopher. Both Nietzsche and Wittgenstein are explicitly named as sophists, but also carefully determined as antiphilosophers. Traced through Badiou's description of the sophist above, there is something that the sophist and antiphilosopher must have in common. Yet from his most recent work, his 'hyper-translation' of Plato's *Republic* from ancient Greek to contemporary colloquial French, Badiou provides a characterisation of the sophist that is far from that of the antiphilosopher. Book I of Badiou's *Republic* is titled 'Reducing the Sophist to Silence'. In his short introduction, Badiou underlines a separation between philosopher (Socrates) and sophist (Thrasymachus) as consisting in the defense of eternity and truths on the one hand, and the defense of opportunism of interests on the other. It is clear from this that Badiou aims to distinguish the sophist as cynical and worldly, a characterisation not pertaining to the antiphilosopher (*Rep* 36–56). Despite this more recent distinction, the mirroring of philosopher and sophist is clearly the original matrix of oppositions from which a number of reflections throughout the 1990s opened up the theme of antiphilosophy as a further development of the notion of the sophist.

What the antiphilosopher and sophist share is a basic but different kind of opposition to the philosopher. Both the antiphilosopher and the sophist reject the access of the subject to truth, but the antiphilosopher provides a certain kind of 'cure' to the philosopher's pretentions, an act that orients the subject towards the real. This is unequivocally underlined in his clearest presentation of the theme in *WA*, comprising two articles published in the 90s. Here he underlines that 'Each antiphilosopher chooses the philosophers whom he hopes to make into the canonical examples of the empty and vain shell of a word that for him is philosophy' (*WA* 69). Simultaneously, however, the antiphilosopher is a sort of philosopher, but one that ultimately brings to bear against his/her colleagues [*confères*], the philosophers, an extreme violence. This violence is one that is aimed against philosophical discourse as vain futility, the sort of sound and fury encrusted in self-reference and language games, but made to shine in self-importance. That is, antiphilosophical 'violence' strikes out against the vanity of philosophy as an act and seeks to depose, rather than refute, the philosopher. In turn, Wittgenstein the antiphilosopher also shares in the philosopher's struggles: those against presumptuous speech and futile repetition. The difference is that the antiphilosopher treats his/her own life as the stage upon which the historical eruptions of truth leave their mark. As such, they make their lives 'the theatre of their ideas, and their body the place of the absolute' (68). This false immediacy of the absolute and the real, at least in Wittgenstein's case, ends in a twisted mysticism (49).

It is this same approach to truth and the absolute that will characterise the thought of the veritable 'prince' of antiphilosophy (*CD* 24): Nietzsche, a thinker whose influence on Wittgenstein could be considered as constituting a 'tradition' of antiphilosophy in the twentieth century (thematically entwined with its deep anti-Platonism) (*WA* 16). Badiou's two focused discussions on Nietzsche – *Casser en deux l'histoire du monde*, and 'Who is Nietzsche?' – indeed constitute an important place for seeing how he first separated the notion of antiphilosophy from more general notions of sophistry. Almost ten years separate the former text from the latter

(1991/2001), and these years coincide with Badiou's process of refining his notion of philosophy under condition. Both texts address Nietzsche's role in underlining the actuality of modernity: the rupture between sense (*sens*) and truth. That is, Nietzsche, in his genealogical critique of philosophical 'truth', attempts to reduce truth to sense and unveils the figure of the priest that stands behind such pretensions to the universal and absolute. Here, Nietzsche's antiphilosophical gesture is his accusation of philosophy's 'theological blood', a closing in upon itself of a series of coherent but ossified realms of meaning (Nietzsche 1990: 62).

Nietzsche's critique of philosophy cast in terms of (universal and absolute) metaphysics is indeed one that Badiou will also endorse, underlining that it is precisely through engagement with antiphilosophy that philosophy is given its modern historical task to uphold the rupture between truth and sense. Upholding the disenchantment of nature, the death of God, the decentring of the subject, truth is subtracted away from sense. While Badiou insists on a philosophy oriented towards a meaningless (senseless) truth, Nietzsche takes up the other side of this rupture. That is, Nietzsche takes up the side of sense against truth. Against any renewed 'Platonic gesture', Nietzsche's antiphilosophical act takes up the grandeur of the poetic against any truth that is not the very madness of an unprecedented act. This notion of the act, mad because self-referentially circular, is precisely also that which Nietzsche takes upon himself to carry out from the philosophical position: the destruction of philosophy as philosophical *act*.

What Nietzsche demonstrates is a necessary confrontation with the rupture between sense and truth. While Nietzsche aims to destroy philosophy from within, this antiphilosophy, in its truest sense, has two important legacies. As mentioned above, the first legacy is that of a modern antiphilosophy running from Nietzsche to Wittgenstein and Lacan, who brought this sequence of antiphilosophy to its end. The other legacy is philosophy itself. As Badiou explains, 'Philosophy is always heir to antiphilosophy' (*WN* 10). Nietzsche's antiphilosophy, indeed any antiphilosophy, plays a crucial role for philosophy itself: a confrontation with a rupture that brings thinking into its own time.

Although Nietzsche is the prince of antiphilosophy, Lacan represents its most intimate and immediate reference. Despite having a historical status since the eighteenth century, it is through Lacan's own elusive use of the term that Badiou picks up the theme. As he explains, 'Lacan declared himself an "antiphilosopher". It is partly thanks to him that I began to ask myself, in a fairly systematic way, what might be declared antiphilosophical' (*E* 122). Lacan's two instances of self-identification with antiphilosophy are pertinent here. The first is his 1975 speech '. . . *peut-etre à Vincennes*', where he implores psychoanalysts to train themselves in linguistics, logic, topology and antiphilosophy (Lacan 2001: 314–35). The implication here is embedded in Lacan's difficult relationship both with academic philosophy and with the immense experimentations undertaken by his contemporaries, under the influence of (post-) structuralism within philosophy itself. Lacan distinguishes himself from philosophy, a discipline that takes discourse at once too seriously, in the sad and 'stupid' university discourse, as well as not seriously enough, myopically oriented towards the positivism of propositions. The second of Lacan's identifications with antiphilosophy was registered with the termination of his School in 1980 (Lacan 1980: 17). The worry of the psychoanalytic school turning into an institution and 'becoming a church' with its own internally guaranteed meaning no doubt provoked Lacan to effect its termination. In his famous 'Letter of dissolution' in 1980, Lacan seems to echo Nietzsche's theological criticisms of philosophy in stating that 'The stability of religion stems from the fact that meaning is always religious' (Lacan 1987: 129). As such, this antiphilosophical charge is addressed not really to philosophy, but rather to the inherent temptation of psychoanalysis to philosophise – that is, to cast the analysis of the unconscious as some sort of 'truth'.

Lacan's antiphilosophy is poised against the inertia of the production of knowledge cemented and repeated through academic authority and the institutions guaranteeing its 'meaning'. This very inertia is one that brings philosophical, qua university, discourse into the enclosure of a reality that is cut off from its disavowed real. It is precisely this distinction between reality and the real that provided the occasion of Badiou's confrontation with Lacan's antiphilosophical mirror. In the antiphilosophical legacy shared by Nietzsche and Wittgenstein, Lacan sought to think what was not already given within a horizon of language itself. Through mathemes, knots and the wider domains of topology, Lacan experimented on the edge of language in order to sustain the thinking of the slippery interplay between the effable and the ineffable. In this effort, Lacan's antiphilosophy provided, for Badiou, a crucial mirror in addressing a return to philosophy itself.

Through the three major figures of antiphilosophy that receive sustained treatment, Badiou makes clear that his initial notion of the sophist does not suffice to render the intimate connection between philosophy and its other. The antiphilosophical is not merely an enemy of philosophy's truth. The antagonism between antiphilosophy and philosophy brings about a complex relation, one that forces philosophy to confront the actuality of the non-given and the inconsistent. It is through these confrontations that philosophy can historically establish its place of enunciation. In this sense, the development of the notion of antiphilosophy should be read against Badiou's own assumption of a philosophical voice, around the late 1980s. This identification requires a number of different mirrorings. Outside of the problem of truth conditions, it is antiphilosophy that establishes the necessary moorings of a return to philosophy itself.

APPEARANCE, EXISTENCE

Steven Corcoran

If the essence of being is to appear, we might say that what *BE*'s theory of being is missing is precisely a theory of how being appears. How does being qua multiple of multiples actually appear in a world? How can pure, inconsistent multiplicity come to appear as a consistent world? Finding an answer to this question is indeed one of the primary objectives of *LW*, and the technical details of the answer are as forbidding as they are rigorous. The pure multiplicities theorised in *BE* are indifferent to, or lack the order exhibited to us by, the empirical world. Pure multiplicity is simply made up of other pure multiplicities, whereas an object of the world is a count – a pen, a wave, the moon sitting over the ocean in late afternoon, a quark. These are self-evidences of experience and of physics. In the terms of *BE*, they are all 'count for ones' and therefore based on nothing other than inconsistent multiplicity. The problem is then to understand why being does not present itself as inconsistent multiplicity, but rather un-presents itself: for the manifold things presented to us are intrinsically bound up in given, stable entities on which we could seemingly build a foundation – countries and collectivities, objects and activities, bodies and languages. These unities do not emerge entirely from an arbitrary act of a subject affixing a unity of count to them from without – they govern their own sensible donation, if not in being, then at least in appearance (cf. Meillassoux 2010).

Consequently, this presents us with a transcendental-type question: how is it possible to have an order of appearance that does not proceed from being itself? Kant argued that the a priori forms (time and space) of a constitutive subject are what underlie the phenomenal order. Badiou's materialism means that the subject cannot be constitutive but must be constituted. His theory of the subject, elaborated in *BE*, cogently shows that a subject only ever depends on the contingent occurrence of an event that it is itself unable to produce.

So, if appearance can have any consistency, it can only be by virtue of an a-subjective order and this order must be both connected with being – for it is always being that appears – and distinct from it – insofar as its order does not result from multiple-being as such. *LW* thus strives to articulate the singularity of appearing vis-à-vis being *and* the link between them (cf. Meillassoux 2010).

A first key thing to note is the contrasting logics of being and of appearing. Ontology presents us with a single classical logic. In an ontology of the multiple, which in Badiou's terms is presented only through set theory, only one of two things can be the case: either a set 'a' is an element of set 'b', or it is not, 'there is no third possibility' (*LW* 185). This statement is either veridical or not, and thus obeys the law of excluded middle. Now, appearing pays scant regard for this law. The variable intensity of the given requires judgements of the type 'x is more or less'. It implies degrees of complex differentiation and probability, the various realities of which escape the strict disjunction between affirmation and negation (184). The given, then, constrains us to add to the mathematics of being a logic of appearing able to accord with the diverse consistencies, the 'infinite nuances of qualitative intensities' (38–9), implied in our experience. For the innumerable modes of appearing possible for being, the 'infinitely diversified figures of being-there' (38), a logic able to capture them must be deployed, one that provides some sort of connection, however slight, to visible things. Now, since appearance is always an appearance of being, this logic will be a mathematised one (*LW* 37–8). This is the role that category theory plays in *LW*: it provides a mathematical logic able to theorise countless classical or non-classical worlds.

Badiou posits that a complete logical theory of appearing requires three basic operations, which govern the way in which beings appear in a world. Without entering into Badiou's formalisations here, we can nonetheless grasp the general set-up: the immutable 'being in itself' of a being (a number, a person) appears in numerous distinct worlds that are accordingly governed by very diverse logics. The logic of appearing that defines a world allows the term 'world' to be taken in a most general sense: an epoch, a battle, a state of artistic achievement, etc. The upshot of this is that a world can therefore be just as easily successive in time as synchronic, while a being can appear in a thousand ways, in a thousand different worlds at the same moment.

This sets the stage for perhaps the key question of *LW*: not as in *BE*, what is the being of a truth, but how can a truth come to appear in a world, and crucially – for otherwise it could not be a truth – how can the same truth appear across distinct worlds, that is, how 'an eternal truth [can exist] through the variations of its instances: the multiplicity of its (re)creations in distinct worlds' (10). To do so, it must be shown able to disrupt logics of appearing that are entirely heterogeneous to one another. In an innovation of the formal theory of the subject presented in *BE*, *LW* thus resolves to show how a subject of a truth can appear. That is, given that truths are not made of anything other than bodies and languages, and insist only in their effects, how it is that fidelity to an event emerges in the form of a subject-body, replete with organs able to treat the 'points' of a world. The subject-body thus defines an alternative mode of appearance, one determined by a subject that, endowed with a body, is incorporated into that world, duly reorganised around the production of a new present.

The appearing of truth

If 'truths not only are, [but also] appear, (*LW* 9), then there are two basic questions that Badiou has to answer. First, on what basis it is possible to argue, against the cultural anthropologist, for the transworldly existence of truths? And second how, given the consistency of a specific world, can a novelty appear in it? How is it possible for inconsistent multiplicity to surface in a world and bring the laws of appearing in that world to in-consist? Accordingly, there are two aspects to Badiou's elaboration of the appearing of truths that are crucial here, which we shall treat in turn. To show how it is that a truth can appear in worlds that are vastly distinct from one another, sometimes centuries apart – and thus refute the 'cultural anthropologist', who would like to relativise cultural and historical production, even in mathematics (12–16) – he elaborates the idea of transworldly invariants. And to explain how it is that truths can appear in a situation to effect a transcendental re-evaluation of a world, he elaborates the idea that a transcendental re-evaluation occurs when a 'proper inexistent of an object' (322) – i.e. something that, while 'of the world', ontologically speaking, 'is not absolutely in the world according to the strict logic of appearing' (342) – comes to exist maximally in that world, fracturing the norms of appearing. What once appeared as nothing now appears as everything (an illustrious example of this being the proletariat – 'we are nothing, let us be all').

Aiding the phenomeno-logical description of such an appearing, Badiou is able on the basis of the inexistent's passage from minimal to maximal existence to elaborate – another key innovation of *LW* – a fourfold typology of change, in which we come to see the crucial role, in the production of a truth, of a subject-body. At one end of the typology are simple *modifications* of the world of appearing – a world that contains no truth is not merely static, merely how things appear in it are fully regulated by the transcendental of that world. Badiou thus lends some credence to that well-known phrase *plus ça change, plus c'est la même chose*. For example, in its mad dance, capitalism thrives by revolutionising the conditions of its own existence; nonetheless Badiou rigorously shows that this 'revolutionising' never amounts to a revolutionary break with its transcendental of appearing, but on the contrary, is part of a transcendental of appearing.

Then come *facts* (novelties that barely leave any mark on the situation), *weak singularities* (novelties whose consequences in the world in which they emerge are feeble) and *strong singularities* (events that develop into fully-fledged truth procedures with maximal consequences). Only in the latter does the subject-body fully demonstrate its role.

To come back to the first of the aforementioned points: Badiou provides examples of such invariants from each of the four procedures in the preface to *BE*. These examples illustrate at once the multiplicity of worlds and the variations of the 'invariants' within these 'always-singular worlds' (*LW* 9). Being chance-ridden, truths, exemplified here in their appearing as bodies-of-truth, can have no necessity deduced from them. Nor do these 'bodies' (which may be poems, political organisations, etc.) appear *as such* in any way that would mark them out from mere opinion.

Yet their very existence qua universal exceptions is thereby illustrated – this is what is at stake – allowing us to counter the notion, intrinsic to the relativism of 'democratic materialism', that there is no hierarchy of ideas, but instead a 'juridical equality' among 'the plurality of languages' (ibid.), wherein every idea is fully circumscribed by the specific cultural and historical material that supports it. By contrast, the effective existence of truths, as universal exceptions, exceeds any such circumscription to comprise an 'atemporal meta-history' (ibid).

In the preface to *LW*, Badiou gives an example of an invariant concerning the features that come into play whenever a 'truly political' vision of the state is enacted (20 ff); then, in Book 1, which bears on the formal theory of the subject, he discusses another example, better for our purposes because it ties in nicely with the second key point mentioned above (the coming to maximal existence of an inexistent), namely the slave revolt in the ancient Roman world that goes by the name of Spartacus. As Badiou shows, the invariant idea of the key statement of the slave revolt, 'We slaves, we want to and *can* return home', does not remain lost after the 'subject-body' Spartacus is crushed at the hands of the Roman Imperial Army. Badiou shows that this statement's incorporation into a new present – in returning home, they are slaves no longer! – is also taken up and incorporated into contexts entirely remote from it. Then, in Haiti in 1794, the 'Black Spartacus' Toussaint-Louverture reactivated this truth about the non-naturalness of slavery and extended it further, creating the 'first state led by former black slaves' (64). Then again, in the 1910s, and in an entirely other context, Karl Liebknecht and Rosa Luxemburg ensured the truth of Spartacus would not be forgotten, restoring its maxim and creating a genuine counter-reaction through the Spartacus League. Each time the same statement of an end to slavery is at issue, and each time new presents are developed that extend the consequences through a new subject-body.

The example of Spartacus shows that after the crushing defeat, the truth that slavery is not natural reappeared. It was resurrected and deepened in its consequences in historical worlds vastly disparate from that in which it first appeared. It is indeed intrinsic to a truth that it reappear in transworldly fashion and that it do so through developing further the consequences of that truth.

We alluded above to the operations informing Badiou's account of the coming into appearance of a subject-body – its coming to exist maximally in a situation in which it had existed minimally. The basic idea involves showing how inconsistent multiplicity or being – that which was effectively nothing within a world – can come to appear in a situation as maximally existent, and thus force a transcendental re-evaluation of the laws of appearing. Badiou thus makes a distinction between the being of a thing – an individual, a number, etc. – and its appearing. A being (which thus presents itself as a mediating term between being as such and appearing) may appear in a manifold of disparate contexts. And while it is always the same being (its being, as inconsistent multiplicity, is immutable), its appearing will vary as a function of context. Such variations in the intensity of appearing define its *existence*, which ranges between maximal and minimal.

In the world of ancient Mediterranean societies, the political existence of the slaves was obviously next to inexistent. The slaves were part of the situation – as was attested by the set of laws governing them – but in such a way that they were not considered properly to belong to it as other members (legal citizens, etc.). They were included in it in such a manner as to be excluded from proper existence. Defying their inclusion in the order of things, however, they came to exist maximally as producers of a new present. If this is possible, Badiou argues, it is because the inconsistent multiplicity comprising a thing is always liable to rise up into the situation.

Indeed, it is only through the emergence of this inconsistent multiplicity into the surface of the situation that it is possible to break with the laws of appearing of that situation and appear maximally. When the context has reduced a being's existence to the edge of inexistence, only a decision, unfathomable within the laws of appearing of that situation, and the creation of a subject-body able to treat the situation point-by-point, can deal a blow to the inegalitarian organisation of existence.

Commentators have debated the connection between Being and beings in Badiou's work, and specifically the way in which the ontic level of beings figures in his account. Peter Hallward argues that Badiou does not manage to account for the fact that 'being' comes to appear (that being is also being-there), and requires a third, intervening term – the beings (a worker, a country, a work of art) that are caught in the various logics of appearing defining different worlds. The charge is that Badiou is thus unable to account for the material density of ontic reality, whose appearing in the world seems entirely contingent (cf. Hallward 2008). Against this, Slavoj Žižek argues that it is illusory to see this so-called ontic level as a separate 'reality out there', as that which is thus able to provide a material level of resistance able to disrupt the various logics of appearing in which it gets caught. The truly materialist perspective does not involve accounting for the material processes that form ontic being, but seeing that the transcendental of appearing is *immanent* to beings themselves, which are not separate from the transcendental itself. It is not the level of inconsistent ontic reality that disrupts the transcendental of appearing, he argues, but that the inconsistent 'symptomal point of torsion of a situation', out of which effects of disruption proceed, is generated by the transcendental itself, as its founding exclusion (cf. Žižek 2012: Part IV, Ch. 12).

AXIOM

Anindya Bhattacharyya

One of the most striking differences between Badiou and his contemporaries in postwar French philosophy lies in the presentational style of his work. In contrast to his peers, who typically make heavy use of the poetic resources of language to make their case, Badiou's arguments are laid out in a pristine and almost formal manner. His inspiration lies in the discourse of mathematics rather than that of poetry.

Nowhere is this more evident than in Badiou's use of axioms in *BE*. The fundamental principles of ontology are laid out as formal statements, each of which license or regulate the existence of pure multiples. He lays out just nine of these axioms, citing Aristotle's dictum that the first principles of being be as few as they are crucial (*BE* 60).

Badiou's axiomatics derives strictly from modern mathematics, as opposed to the more traditional notion of an axiom. In ordinary speech, an axiom typically means a self-evident first principle, one whose validity is so universally accepted that it does not require any kind of proof. But this is not how mathematicians use the term. When mathematicians call something an axiom, they are not claiming there is anything self-evident about it. Rather the axiom is simply posited as a starting point for logical reasoning. It marks a decision for thought to proceed in one direction and not another, and an inaugural decision at that.

The axiom of the empty set, for instance, decides the question 'is there something or nothing?' by declaring the thingness of nothing, the existence of the void. This is not a matter susceptible to proof by appeal to reason or intuition. It is simply a step that can and must be taken as a precondition of thinking pure multiple-being.

The emergence of this notion of an axiom as a decision for thought is closely bound up with the historical fate of the original axiomatic system in mathematics, Euclid's presentation of geometry. Most of Euclid's axioms (or 'postulates' as they are often known) are axioms in both senses of the term: starting points for geometrical reasoning and self-evident statements of geometric fact. A typical example would be the first postulate: between any two distinct points there is a unique straight line.

Euclid's fifth postulate, however, proved to be more controversial. It effectively states that given any line and any point not on that line, there is a unique line running through that point parallel to the given line. By the nineteenth century it had become clear that there were perfectly viable alternative geometries to that proposed by Euclid where the first four postulates were satisfied but the fifth failed. One could have no parallel lines (elliptic geometry), or multiple parallel lines (hyperbolic geometry). From this perspective Euclid's fifth axiom is about prescribing a particular kind of spatiality (strictly speaking, a curvature in space), rather that about describing a fundamental feature of spatiality as such.

The late nineteenth and early twentieth centuries saw the concept of an axiom rapidly generalise from its initial context in geometry. Axiom systems were developed for abstract algebra, propositional logic and topology. In particular, set theory was put on an axiomatic basis in an effort to rid the theory of the paradoxes discovered by Bertrand Russell, Georg Cantor and others. The most common of these axiom systems, Zermelo-Fraenkel set theory, forms the basis for the ontology Badiou lays out in *BE*.

This shift towards axiomatic foundations for mathematics has a profound ontological consequence that Badiou exploits in his philosophical appropriation of the axiom. It enacts a certain structuralist gesture: in geometry, for instance, what matters is no longer what points and lines are exactly, but rather the specifiability of the formal relations between them; in group theory, the elements are no longer necessarily permutation maps to be composed, but tokens to be formally multiplied.

Axiom systems are thus marked by a certain indifference towards their empirical reference: we talk of empirical reality modelling the axioms, rather than vice versa (cf *CM*). In particular, fundamental entities can be specified without falling into an infinite regress in explaining what they are. Sets, for instance, can be any things that entertain a formal binary relation of membership $\in$ that behaves according to the axioms of Zermelo-Fraenkel. This is how we cut through Parmenidean interdependence of the one and the multiple that opens *BE*.

'The Real is declared, instead of known', as Badiou puts it in *TO* (45).

Transposing this 'generic orientation in thought' to a philosophical register involves presenting, say, 'the masses think' as an axiom, and thereby allowing Badiou to avoid defining what the 'masses' might or might not be exactly. Axiomatics enables thinking apart from the figure of the object, thinking that does not ultimately fall into or rely upon any kind of exteriority.

Two final points should be noted concerning axioms: they are typically independent of each other, and typically incomplete. Independence here means that any particular axiom stands or falls independently of the others. One can have set theory with an axiom of infinity, or set theory without, just as one can have Euclidean or non-Euclidean geometry. In particular, the axiom of foundation is independent of the other axioms of set theory. One can suspend it and thereby admit the being of strange multiples that contain themselves as elements: events, in Badiou's terminology.

Incompleteness means that no axiom system can exhaust all mathematical questions and possibilities. Kurt Gödel proved that any tractable axiomatisation of set theory would always leave certain statements neither provable nor refutable. P. J. Cohen proved that among these 'undecidable' statements lay one of the great unsolved problems of set theory, Cantor's continuum hypothesis. For Badiou, this fundamental incompleteness testifies to the inexhaustible nature of ontology as a science. There will always be an undecidable to decide upon, and the creativity of axiomatic decision can never be exhausted.

B

BECKETT

Nina Power

Samuel Beckett occupies a curious position in Badiou's thought: depicted by Badiou in various short essays as a author midway between fiction writer and philosopher, Beckett allows Badiou to clarify some of Badiou's own key concepts, particularly those from around the time of *BE* – the void, the generic, the event (particularly under the condition of love, which Badiou picks out as a central theme of Beckett's late work). Badiou's reading of Beckett deliberately ignores the secondary material that has built up in such vast amounts around the texts, and also focuses primarily on Beckett's novels and short stories, rather than the plays. Badiou's reading of Beckett thus represents a serious attempt to reclaim Beckett from various popular characterisations of his work, while at the same time taking seriously the themes and conceptual contributions that his various writings make.

Although Beckett does not receive a meditation in *BE*, it is quite clear that Badiou sees strong parallels between Beckett's project and his own, not only in relation to the proximity of terms used, but also methodologically. When Badiou speaks of Beckett's process of literary 'subtraction', he explicitly compares Beckett's attempt to pare down prose to the phenomenological work of Edmund Husserl, to the five genres of Plato's *Sophist* (Movement, Rest, the Same, the Other, Logos) and to Descartes' attempt to identify and suspend everything doubtful before conducting an enquiry into what Badiou calls 'thinking humanity'. Badiou thus identifies Beckett as practising 'methodical ascesis' in prose – eliminating, not without humour, all that is inessential to the nature of generic humanity in order to identify better what is energetic and immortal about this humanity. Badiou is resolutely opposed to pop existential readings of Beckett, particularly if they depict him as nihilistic or revelling in the baseness of man. On the contrary, Beckett allows Badiou to describe, under the guise of Beckett's 'purified axiomatic', a particular kind of courage: the courage to persevere even, or especially, in the face of the gradual elimination of possibility.

Badiou identifies a key break in Beckett's oeuvre at around the time of *How It Is* (first published in French in 1961 and translated by Beckett himself into English three years later). Prior to this text, Badiou argues, Beckett's characters remain caught within an oscillation of being and the cogito that is expressed through the solitary voice (the ever-diminishing narrators of the so-called Trilogy of *Molloy*, *Malone Dies* and *The Unnamable*, published over the course of the 1950s). The final famous line of *The Unnamable* – 'you must go on, I can't go on, I'll go on' – followed by both the silence of the text and a crisis in Beckett's own writing, is understood by Badiou as the end of a certain approach to writing that can only be broken by something exterior. This interruption of alterity arrives with *How It Is* and Beckett's poetic description of the muddy and violent encounter between two characters, the narrator and 'Pim'. Here, love, albeit a fairly non-traditional version thereof, permits Badiou to see Beckett's work as, particularly in the later work, an opening up of narration to the possibility of the event. In this way, Badiou reads Beckett's many famous couples as allowing access to an infinite conception of the world, in which solipsism is replaced by an expansive relation to knowledge, via a relation to the other.

Beckett's work ultimately allows Badiou to expand and reflect upon categories central to his own metaontological project. Placing Beckett within Badiou's various taxonomies remains a difficult question, however, particularly when Badiou exhorts us to read Beckett as a philosopher, or at least to take seriously his conceptual and methodological explorations. Does Beckett's work thus itself constitute a truth event, as Badiou's descriptions of some artworks in *HI* might suggest, or does it merely reflect and re-describe in a poetic tenor the four truth conditions (particularly love) and the structure of the event, without actually being one itself? We could, at the same time, see in Badiou's work on Beckett the outline of an ethics: how to keep going in the midst of disaster, or following a disaster. If giving up on the truth of an event is always possible, and a permanent threat to the project, in Beckett Badiou sees a way of beginning again or keeping going even though everything is the worst it could possibly be. In Beckett's apocalyptic text *Comment c'est*, it is also possible to hear the injunction *commencez!* (begin!). Badiou's Beckett seeks to restore to Beckett the courage of the French resistance fighter, rather than the sardonic nihilist we might otherwise be tempted to see.

BEING

Fabien Tarby

'Being' is of course the primary and terminal concept of every conception of philosophy. Being is, for Badiou, multiple and void. But this affirmation is far from being enough to characterise Badiou's system. What does it mean to say that being is multiple and void? How does this assertion turn upside down both Deleuze's (the multiplicity of being) and Heidegger's (being qua being) conceptions?

1. Badiou recognises that Heidegger is the 'last universally recognisable philosopher'. This point is essential, as Badiousian ontology can be cast as a *materialist theory of 'ontico-ontological' difference* (in Heidegger's terms), and that perfectly neutralises the remainders of idealism and romanticism in Heideggerian thought. Badiou is, in this sense, in 'continental' philosophy, the materialist thinker *par excellence* concerning ontology. A clear view of this and of the confrontation with Heidegger is essential to an understanding of his system. It is here that the power of his thought is revealed.

   Heidegger turns time into the secret of being qua being. In so doing, he ties being to the indeterminate, and beings to determination. This passion for indetermination is ultimately unfolded in a poetic mystique. Against this, Badiou eliminates the theme of time. Being is not temporal, nor originally poetic, but mathematical and multiple. It is set theory, as the most accomplished form of mathematics, that for Badiou unfolds Ideas. It can of course be admitted that mathematics more exactly founds a 'discourse on being qua being' (445) and even that 'Being *does not want to be written*' (446). Badiou further specifies that: 'The thesis that I support does not in any way declare that being is mathematical, which is to say composed of mathematical objectivities. It is not a thesis about the world but about discourse. It affirms that mathematics, throughout the entirety of its historical becoming, pronounces what is expressible of being qua being' (8). In effect, if all apparent unity is in fact a multiplicity of multiplicities, and is so without assignable end, then ultimately we arrive at the void, as the first and last name of multiple-being. Set theory in fact recognises in the empty set (Ø) the sole matter of the regulated system of belonging and of sets, i.e. of multiplicities. It is thus possible to deploy the anonymous system of being by following the axioms of the Zermelo-Fraenkel system that rigorously develops and coordinates the law of pure multiplicity (for example: presentation, representation, dissemination, infinities). However, it is of course quite impossible to encouter the void as such. The void does not present itself, and the empty set, which lies at the very basis of set-theoretical mathematics, is merely its symptom, and in no way its capture or magical formula. Notwithstanding this fact, mathematics is the discourse that presents all that can be presented of being.

Heidegger's thought owes much to the equivocation of the distinction between the ontic and the ontological. If all determination is ontic, the ontological always necessarily escapes discourse. It is for this reason that Heidegger ultimately yields to the poem as that which is alone able to express being. For Badiou, on the contrary, there are always determinations of being, but multiple and lawful ones, right down to inconsistency and the void. The only discourse of a 'pure ontology' (in Heidegger's sense of it having an impossible existence) consists in the observation of an originary and terminal void. However, this problem can also be inverted by virtue of a certain ambiguity in the terms 'ontic' and 'ontological', being [*étant*] and Being. It can be stated that the exposition of mathematical determinations of the multiple is already, for Badiou, ontological and not simply ontic. In short, what Badiou shows is that the remaining idealism in Heidegger's thought can be redressed by submitting his excessive passion for a discourse that would be beyond the ontic level to a resolutely lawful field. At issue is not to know whether we – finally! – reach the ontological, *beyond* the ontic; nor when and under which conditions. The point is to unfold a sort of field that goes from apparent or phenomenal unity to ontico-ontological multiplicities, which themselves have only the void as their ultimate horizon. It is thus that Heidegger's thought can be rid of all whole series of useless or false problems (such as: is there a pure ontological field? What is this indeterminable mystery beyond determinations? What is its relation to time?)

2. With this Badiou does not only deconstruct Heidegger's thought; his theory of being is also a response to Deleuze's romanticism of being. Badiou's is a thought of the multiple that is opposed at every point to the multiplicities of which Deleuze and Guattari speak. For Badiou, the bottom of being is not Chaos or the Virtual but void and eternal. And a multiplicity is not a movement but a structure. Appearing and disappearing do not manifest an internal life of multiplicities, but only the power of our degree of analysis of the multiples engaged in a presentation.

3. What remains now is the difficult question of the relations between the global lawfulness of multiple-being and the local upsurge of an event. The event is extra-ordinary. It cannot, in particular, be thought apart from within a schema of self-belonging. Now, this schema is precisely prohibited by set theory, and thus by ontology. Ontologically speaking, then, it is not the case that a multiple can belong to itself, that is to say, self-consist. The event is therefore a transgression of a fundamental law of ontology. However, Badiousian thought is far more complex here. For, while paradoxical, it is at the same time necessary that being renders the event possible. In reality, it seems that the void of being is the key to the subversive possibility of the event. In this sense, *LW*, which ties appearing to being in a new complexity, will define the event on the basis of an appearing/disappearing and the advent of a newly maximal existence in the site under consideration. Even if that which in-exists refers to appearing and not to being, it is clearly the void power of being, such as it is expressed in its connection with appearing, that continues to be the crucial point here. There can nonetheless be no global event of being itself.

Translated from the French by Steven Corcoran

BODY

Bruno Besana

Body and identification

Depending on the inconsistency of an evanescent event, the subject for Badiou is shaped by a logic of subtraction, formal construction and generic address, which functions independently of – when not against – the limits, finitude and contingencies of the body. Badiou's concept of the subject starts from a fierce opposition to the classic theme of embodiment: not only does he not analyse the history of the mind/body or soul/body relation, but he also rejects traditions such as the phenomenological idea of the subject as internal unification of the flux of lived experiences, the existentialist analysis of the subject via reflective perception or the (Deleuzian) idea of the subject as an immanent, synthetic result of a set of anonymous bodily drives and desires.

Indeed, early on Badiou wrote 'The Fascism of the Potato' (FP/*AFP*), a polemical piece against Deleuze's and Guattari's idea of rhizome, an idea in which he perceives the will to reduce the activity of the subject to an infinite, non-structured communication between bodies. Such polemics belie more than his antipathy to the postmodern centrality of desire. For Badiou, Deleuze's position is ultimately an ideology of the 'immediacy of the body', in which 'only individuals exist, of which only counts that they can touch each other without any law' (*FP* 197; tm). Here a double problem appears: first, despite a superficial criticism of present social relations in the name of the freedom of desire, Deleuzianism is for Badiou unable to impact the order of society, as the latter largely relies on these very drives. The second and more fundamental concerns the 'ideological' core of Deleuze's position: bi-univocally linked to the body, the subject, which is apparently subtracted from social representation, appears to be nonetheless identified with an immediate, self-evident reality, a sort of 'original unity', which of course is largely the product of those same representational structures that it is supposed to undermine.

Although Badiou will largely reconsider such judgements, still he will maintain throughout the years that, for Deleuze, all subjective change is ultimately reduced to the constant variation and transformation of bodies: in Deleuze's thought – writes Badiou thirty years later – 'the event is not identical to the bodies that it affects, but neither does it transcend what happens to them or what they do. So it also cannot be said to differ (ontologically) from bodies.' Such structural homogeneity between the body and the event is fundamentally due to each body's being the expression of the unity of a 'body-life'. In Deleuze's perspective, one 'should think of the event of Life as a body without organs: its nature is [. . .] legible as the result of the actions and passions of these organisms' (*LW* 383); and bodies are the expression of the body-nature, a unique 'event of life' expressing itself in them and in their mutual relations.

By contrast, Badiou names 'event' exactly that which is subtracted from the laws upon which bodies are recognised, organised and mutually relate: thus one must 'reverse Deleuze [. . .] It is not the actions and passions of multiples which are synthesised in the event as an immanent result. It is the blow of the eventual One that magnetises multiplicities and constitutes them into subjectivisable bodies' (*LW* 385). Badiou's starting point is that the subject depends on the event and is therefore separated from any positive bodily determination; but the arrival point, as the last quote shows, is that the body can be subjectivised. We will see that such a relation between body and subject is essential to Badiou's description of the latter.

Body and subject

The first kernel of a concept of the body is constructed in *TS*. Badiou starts by criticising how Althusser, in his attempt to define change independently of all ideological modes of reproduction of the present, not only dismisses the category of humanity, but also that of the subject. Badiou remarks how Althusser's subjectless change is ultimately identical to a merely structural form of modification, a mere unfolding of a pre-given necessity – of which the masses would be the non-subjective, unconscious actor, and that the avant-garde would reveal to them. Badiou's theory of the subject, by contrast, presents change as a subjective chance, as a novelty irreducible to any structure, and identifies the proletariat as its active *subject*.

Identified with the proletariat, the subject of change is defined as 'a body' (*TS* 130). First, it appears as an unstable figure, as a point of contradiction in the rigidity of social classification, as an inconsistent element disturbing the order of the still, almost-dead social body in which each class endlessly comes to occupy the same place. But, secondly, the proletariat appears as a sort of sick part, or disease, within the social body. It appears as 'never cured' (ibid.), both in the sense of a never-cured body suffering the bourgeois condition, and of a never-cured disease undermining the stability (or rather the *rigor mortis*) of the bourgeois order. Thirdly and finally, it is presented as a sort of surviving germ capable of producing new divisions inside the dying organism of capitalist society, *divisions that the proletariat gathers in the shape of a new body*. New body, sick limb or deadly germ able to produce new life, the proletariat appears 'in internal exclusion' (ibid.) of the bourgeois organism: within the latter it is impossible to decide if it is a new healthy body appearing within the rotten flesh of the social body, or if it is the very disease of the latter.

The last part of the book names the condition on which this germ can gain a full existence: the party is here identified as a means of embodiment of the proletariat (or indeed as its very body), i.e. as that which provides the proletariat with the necessary organs or organisation. The point of course is not simply for the proletariat, via the party, to reorganise a body analogous to the precedent, but with inverted roles of domination. 'Body' rather designates here the organised form of something that remains intrinsically undecidable and that therefore constantly fractures the tendency of the new body to stabilise, hierarchise and reproduce its internal differences.

TS thus presents the body as the instrument of the appearing of the subject, and simultaneously as its condition or support: 'the party is the body of politics, in the strict sense. The fact that there is a body by no means guarantees that there is a subject, whether in the case of the animal body or in that of the institutional body. But for there to be a subject, for a subject to be found, there must be the support of a body' (*TS* 290; tm). An important point is here acquired that will remain a constant argument in Badiou: just as the subject is not an original essence, nor is the body the pre-given support of the appearing of such an essence; on the contrary, the evanescence of a subject, of a point of interruption of the situation's consistency, gains consistency when it finds the means to organise its effects in the situation in the form of a body. The body is thus certainly the 'general *hypokeimenon* of the subject-effect' but simultaneously it is also a 'bearer of the undecidable' (297): far from being an object of the world, the body appears as a contradictory stance, which at once depends on a minimal subjective point of inconsistency and supports the becoming consistent – the embodiment – of such inconsistency.

Body and event

TS presents thus the body both as the *minimal requirement* without which a subject would be nothing but an evanescent inconsistency, and, simultaneously as a *consequence* of the latter, as the organisation of such an inconsistency. *BE* develops such a concept indirectly, mainly by investigating further the status of subjective inconsistency in relation to the evanescence of the event.

In the chapter he dedicates to Rousseau, Badiou stresses how, against any possible identification of the subject with a human animal naturally inclined to association, one should not understand the 'body politics' as a natural form of association of an atomised multiplicity of individual 'political animals': political unity is not that which is constructed starting from any positive characteristic (such as wealth, origin, religion or nationality) of the elements composing it. A political *unity* is rather a synthetic result: namely, the inscription of an evental element, an event being that which makes possible an interruption of the current mode of organisation of the political body (race, religion, nationality, class, etc.), exposing how the latter is no natural reality, but relies on a *contingent* decision based on nothing substantive. The form of the political body is thus the organisation of the acts that expose and fracture the current, contingent mode of societal organisation with its internal hierarchies and inequalities.

The novelty introduced in *BE* (one which largely relies on the conceptualisation of the event as self-belonging) is that the evental element being based on no positive common character of the elements, but rather on the common negation of the commonality of this or that positive element, is nothing else but the addition to the elements of their count as a unity. The evental moment is thus identified, in this case, with the pact, and 'the pact is nothing other than *the self-belonging of the body politic to the multiple that it is*, as founding event' (*BE* 346).

In this perspective, the 'body' of a 'body politic', is any series of acts that gives consistency to the very inconsistency of the event (as based on nothing substantive, the event of the pact is inconsistent with the organisational logic of the situation, and appears in it as nothing). The subjective unity of political activity necessarily takes thus the form of an efficient *body*, which organises in and for the situation the consequences of the evental inscription of this *groundless* political event.

Body and void

The body is thus that via which a subject becomes consistent in a situation, without nonetheless becoming a normal object of the latter: it is that by which a subject exists and 'persists' by 'embodying', in a given part of the situation, the consequences of an event. *LW* develops this idea, showing that if a subject is that via which an event unfolds and 'takes place' in a situation, its body is that via which the subject exists, the extension of its existence being identical to its capacity to perform locally the fracture announced by the event.

Of note here is that *LW* nevertheless presents the body in a twofold manner: on the one hand, the bold opening statement of book, which recurs throughout ('there are only bodies and languages, except that there are truths' (*LW* 4), reaffirms Badiou's original antipathy to identifying the subject with a human body. That is, a human body characterised by an endless circulation of desires, opinions and forms of communication, each of which is perfectly representable by language and knowledge. With this opposition to the commonsensical idea of 'body', Badiou ultimately refuses any identification of the subject with a positive set of objective elements – i.e. ones that are transparent to knowledge and that can be hierarchised and used accordingly. On the other hand, further on, Badiou defines a subject as that by which the consequences of a vanished event, that addresses the whole situation, are unfolded in a given part of the latter. And he defines a body as that via which such an unfolding takes place by fracturing the evidences upon which that part of the situation is structured.

The body thus stretched between two definitions, Badiou claims the necessity to overcome the opposition between subject and body, stressing of course that the subject/body relation is not to be understood in terms of the human body as natural support of the subject. In order to elaborate his argument, Badiou starts from a criticism of Lacan. First, Badiou notices that, setting out from the necessity to 'contrast the backward physiologism of many psychologists', who deduce the property of the subject from the positive characteristic of the human being, Lacan argues 'for the signifier against the body' (*LW* 477), the body being that 'which resists in numerous ways against realising the division of the subject' (ibid.). Conversely, the subject would be an excess over the structures of knowledge, of communication and of interrelation between bodies upon which the order of the situation relies – or, more precisely, it would be a fracture in 'the inert mediation of the efficacy of (such structures)' (ibid.). Badiou concurs with this refusal of the body as natural support of the subject – which ultimately reduces the latter to its positive, animal features – but he also stresses that this should not entail an opposition of principle between the body and the subject.

Again with reference to Lacan, Badiou manages to articulate the two foregoing ideas of the body, that is, the body as object of the world, resisting subjective inscription, and the body as the essential element of incorporation of a subject into a situation. As seen, Lacan presents the body as a normal object, constantly 'affected by the structure'; but, he adds, what affects the body is first and foremost the linguistic structure, in such a way that 'the language-effect imposes itself on the body' (478). By posing a structural relation between body and language, Lacan produces a fracture with a certain phenomenological idea of 'immediate experience': the body is not that which provides consciousness with an immediate access to the world. Inhabited by language, the bodily experience of the human animal is not the result of an immediate access to the sensible world and of simple pragmatic communication between human animals; rather, it is inseparable from the inscription of a something (the Other) that constantly escapes the structural simplicity of practical knowledge and of functional communication. The unity of the body, more precisely, is even the unity itself of the metonymic chain of operations by which the first signifier, split by the inscription of Other, is reinvested in further signifiers. In this sense, 'the repetition of the primacy of the signifier over physiological data is first and foremost a polemical thesis, which in no way excludes that the body is *also* the name of the subject' (478–9).

Furthermore, in Lacan, notwithstanding the apparent opposition of the two terms, the subject not only appears to be bound to the body, but even to be directly deduced from the biological nature of the latter. That is, the opposition between the symbolic order (always pierced by the real) of the subject and the consistency of a compact and monotonous nature appears to be based upon a – largely implicit – biological claim: the existence, *within* the compactness of nature, of a region characterised by a lack. This region is that of the human animal, characterised by a lack of adaptation, a poorness of resources, constituted by a body so lacking in positive features that it has no possibility of grounding its relation to the world in a pragmatic, determined way, mirrored by the efficacy of a simple communicational system. Such a body must necessarily transform itself perpetually, articulating thus its lack and enabling its survival: lacking a specific 'place' (for instance, a specific biological niche) in which to live, humans are forced to reinvest constantly in new forms their own lack-of-being – similarly to the way in which the metonymic chain of the S1–Sn constantly articulates the cut defining the subject qua $. The subject, on this view, is a direct product of the disadapted human animal, which is twice lacking in its own place, constantly *subtracting* itself from its *lack of determination*.

The idea that the activity of the subject is fundamentally subtractive (i.e. that the subject, via its body, performs a series of actions via which it subtracts itself from a given categorical definition, be it the one identifying it with a disadaptation or lack-to-be), is of fundamental importance for Badiou. That said, Badiou rejects the notion that such subtractive activity would define the natural 'proper' of a given living species (i.e. the human animal). For Badiou there is no objective, natural hypokeimenon of the subject, be it a paradoxical body defined by its lack: if, for Lacan, 'the formal operations of incorporation . . . of splitting of the subject constitute . . . the infrastructure of the human animal', for Badiou, by contrast, the 'subjectivised body treats point by point' a situation starting from 'the occurrence – rare as it may be – of the present-process of a truth' (*LW* 480–1). The subject, if and wherever it occurs, is a groundless activity, depending on an evental fracture; it provides itself with its own body from within, the latter being simply defined as the organised tool *and* result of the actions by which the subject subtracts itself from the representational and organisational structure of the situation in which it appears. A subject *happens* to take place in a certain relation to the human animal, but a human animal is neither the sufficient, nor the necessary support for it.

It follows that the subjective split 'is then on the side of creation, not of the symptom' (481): the subjective split is not the symptom via which we recognise the natural activity of a specific being (the body of the human animal); rather, the body is that via which an evanescent split in a situation (*an event*) – a split that can occur in any part of it – manages to constitute a coherent sequence, appearing thus as a new subject that gains consistency in the situation, independently from the logic organising the objects of the situation, and thus weakening the latter. The body, it might ultimately be said, depends on the subject, but the subject's consistency, in return, relies on the body.

Body and organs

Badiou unfolds this idea by claiming that the body is 'the support for the appearing of a subject-form *whose organs treat the world point by point*' (478). Although a subject does not act as any object – i.e. according to the defining properties of a class or genus within an organised and consistent world – but on the contrary acts by creating a space of inconsistency within such a structured situation, still it does so by organising a series of functions that allow it to produce and maintain such a space of inconsistency. To this aim, the subject needs a body endowed with efficient parts, able to operate in the specific part of the situation in which it is located: otherwise put, it needs an *organ*ised body. If 'the subject, which is a situated and local configuration . . . is the incorporation of the event into the situation' (OS 28), the body is the specific and necessary tool of this incorporation: 'a body is really nothing but that which, bearing a subjective form, confers upon a truth, in a world, the phenomenal status of its objectivity' (*LW* 36). Providing consistency to the local consequence of an inconsistency (the subject in relation to the event), the body is 'this very singular type of object suited to serve as a support for a subjective formalism, and therefore to constitute, in a world, the agent of a possible truth' (451).

Performing the incorporation of an event in a specific part of the situation, a subject literally organises itself, i.e. provides itself with organs, with efficient parts. Each organ is shaped around two criteria: 'its ideal subordination to the trace' of an event, and its 'efficacy', which is proven 'locally, point by point' (470). In fact a body is, on one hand, composed 'of all the elements of the site that subordinate themselves, with maximal intensity, to that which was nothing and becomes all' (468) (i.e. the event); on the other, such a capacity to incorporate the eventally inexistent in a particular part of the situation is realised via a set of singular decisions that are rooted in the specificity of that part of the situation in which the subject operates. In sum, *a body produces an immanent organisation of its parts according to the necessity to verify the event for each given point that it encounters.*

Worthy of note is that such a 'body with organs', although literally opposed to the Deleuzian 'body without organs', shares with the latter the idea that the different parts (here named organs) constituting a body do not exist and are not organised following the definition of the species to which the body is supposed to belong, but are immanently determined by the goals of the subject (the incorporation of the inconsistency of the event) and by the contingency of the encounters, of the different elements of the situation that the subject has to deal with during this process.

More precisely, organs are for Badiou that which make it possible to produce, for a given specific part of a situation, a series of binary choices – namely, to decide if a given set of elements that is apparently consistent with the rules organising the objects of the situation can or cannot, under the conditions of the moment, be separated from such rules: in Badiou's words, an organ is that via which the subject 'is capable of treating some points of the world, those occurrences of the real that summon us to the abruptness of a decision' (451). The organ is that via which a decision is operated in a specific point, via which such a point is de-cided (separated) from the laws of the situation, and via which the event is incorporated in the part to which the point belongs. This is for instance the case of a determinate action in which a group of workers stops identifying themselves via a certain shared or common capacity, around which a regime of representation, hierarchisation and exclusion is organised, and instead starts to identify its members as having nothing in common but their complete equality, i.e. their equal capacity to undo the unequal role that each of them had been attributed to on the basis of their supposed capabilities. An organ, in this case, would be the specific instrument that the group chooses in order for such de-cision to be incorporated into the situation (for instance, the fact of no longer negotiating specific rights supposed to pertain to that group, and instead demanding something that cannot be reciprocated to any specific qualification or type of activity performed). In this perspective, a body is nothing but the organisation of a series of such organs; an organised body without which the subjective figure, which declares such an idea of equality, would be nothing but its own evanescence. A subject cannot thus but take the form of an organised body.

Finally, Badiou synthesises his idea of the subjective body by naming five requirements under which a body can take place in a world. The first is that there is 'an active and dense world, teeming with new problems' (475): without several local inconsistencies to be connected with, a hypothetical event would have no possibility of being incorporated into the situation, would thus simply not have been – pure evanescent inconsistency disappearing in its lack of consequences. The second is the existence of a 'site', i.e. a part of the situation in which are exposed the potential effects for the whole situation of the inconsistency of the event. The third is that different elements are related to the site, or to the trace of the event, and are then organised in a mutually compatible way. The fourth is that there are efficient parts, able to treat specific points according to the new value given to elements. The fifth is that something 'envelops the efficacious part and thereby defines a new organ of the body' (474): the organ, in other words, is the minimal form of organised unification of efficacious parts, able to face the emergence of new points. A body, in its turn, 'is nothing other than the set of elements that have this property'; it is a set of organs (467).

Body and the present

The body is thus characterised by the local 'embodiment' of an evental fracture – embodiment that happens via a series of operations in which a subjective position progressively takes place. Far from being a 'full body', such a body is rather 'always under erasure, since it is "marked" by the subjective formalism' (453). Cut into two by the 'evental trace (for which) it serves as material support', the body is simultaneously the being-one, or consistent manifestation, of such division. It is that in which an event takes place in the form of a decision that concerns a specific point of the situation and produces a fracture in the very place of such decision. It is here that Badiou's old dictum, 'one divides into two' recurs: the body is literally the one of a split, the consistency of an act of fracture, or of a series of them. In fact, whilst each current object of a situation presents itself as an original essence, as a simple concrete unity, but ultimately is nothing but a specimen reproducing the identifying characters of a given category, on the contrary the unique and essence-less unity of a subjective body is the making-one of a series of fractures inserted within the apparent unities of a part of the situation, and able to expose their ideological nature. In this sense its non-representational unity is ultimately for Badiou the only possible non–ideological form of unity.

Badiou argues that, because of this, such a body 'opens to a new present' (467), as it allows for the situation to escape the uniformity of a timeless time: with the singularity of its logic of appearance, the body literally fractures the homogeneous time wherein each element is nothing but the reproduction of the categories by which a class of objects is constructed, represented and hierarchised. As the formula of the faithful subject suggests (53),

$$\frac{\varepsilon}{\cancel{c}} \Rightarrow \pi$$

a new present (p), differing from the continuity of a monotonous time, is the result of the inscription of the event (e) on a body (C), the unity of which is not only split, but is an agent of the evental split, incarnating the latter for a specific part of the situation.

Nonetheless, as it relies on a fundamental inconsistency, 'the body' is always open to the possibility of 'produ(cing) its own erasure as effect of the negation of the evental trace' (454), i.e. of dissolving its own inconstancy, thus becoming a normal object of the world, identified by specific qualities and belonging to a given class of objects. This is the case of what Badiou calls the 'obscure subject', the subject for which each present is the repetition of a monotonous time, and each singular element is the local manifestation of a global sense. This figure relies on the 'invocation of a full and pure transcendent Body, an a-historical or anti-evental body (City, God, Race . . .)' (59–60), and ultimately identifies each singular element of the situation with a specific class (or 'limb' of this 'full' body), actively eliminating those elements that do not correspond to such logic. Relying on an established identity with acquired privileges, the obscure subject acts in order to erase the inconsistencies and the cuts performed by the different local embodiments of the evental trace: it acts in order that 'the trace [of the event] will be denied' (59–60). The consequence of this is the erasure of the present (meant as active fracture in a homogeneous time): what this body organises, then, is 'the descent of the present into the night of non-exposition' (59).

As the following formula suggests,

$$\frac{C \Rightarrow (\neg \, \varepsilon \Rightarrow \neg \, \mathrm{\cancel{c}})}{\pi}$$

from the affirmation of a full body – of which each object is an element identified without rest by its specific place and function – proceeds the negation of the event, and the consequent impossibility of inscribing the latter within a subjectivised body. This, then, results in the disappearance of any present novelty, and ultimately of the present itself.

The body is thus ultimately that in which the alternative is locally decided between the subjective embodiment of an event and the disappearance of the subjective fracture within the solidity of a world of normal objects.

$$\boxed{C}$$

CANTOR

Anindya Bhattacharyya

Badiou begins *BE* with a bold declaration followed immediately by a curious caveat: ontology is mathematics, but only now do we have the means to know this. The reason for this caveat is that the knowledge that ontology is mathematics depends upon, and comes in the wake of, an event: the development of the modern mathematical theory of the infinite by Georg Cantor in the 1870s.

Cantor's redefinition of the infinite ushered in a revolution in mathematics. It was fiercely controversial at the time, triggering vituperative attacks from many of Cantor's contemporaries, notably Leopold Kronecker. But it also had its champions, notably David Hilbert, who declared in 1926 that 'no one shall expel us from the paradise that Cantor has created'.

For Badiou, Cantor's theorisation of transfinite sets performed a task that previous generations of materialists had been unable to accomplish: the desacralisation of the infinite. Prior to Cantor the infinite was invariably associated with the divine beyond. It was an attribute of God, not an attribute of humanity or the material world. While humans could conceive of the infinite, this conception was necessarily bound up with mystery (due to the paradoxes associated with the infinite) and pathos (due to the fundamental inaccessibility of the infinite to our finite and limited intellects). Cantor's conception, in contrast, places the infinite on a rigorous and scientific basis, bringing it down to earth and stripping it of its divine associations.

It is unlikely that Cantor would have endorsed this reading. A deeply pious Lutheran, Cantor claimed a divine inspiration for his work and corresponded with leading theologians of his day to reassure them that his work posed no threat to religious teaching on the infinite. Whether many others found these claims plausible is moot; for it is undeniable that on at least two crucial issues, Cantor departs radically from the (Aristotelean) tradition on infinity: on the question of actual versus potential infinity, and on the question of wholes and parts.

The background to Cantor's reformulation of the infinite lay in a previous mathematical crisis: that associated with the development of calculus in the late seventeenth century by Newton and Leibniz. The development of the calculus had relied upon the controversial use of infinitesimally small numbers, famously lampooned by Berkeley as 'the ghosts of departed quantities'. Setting the calculus on a rigorous basis thus became a preoccupation of mathematicians. It was eventually accomplished through two related manoeuvres. First, the infinitesimals themselves were banished, recast as imaginary pseudo-entities that acted as notational conveniences for more cumbersome reasoning involving infinite sequences. Second, a previously intuitive conception of linear continuity was replaced by the more rigorous notion of the real line, an ordered field that possessed the crucial property of completeness: any increasing sequence of real numbers would either grow arbitrarily large or converge to a definite limit.

But the development of the real line settled one set of problems only to open up another. In particular, completeness meant that the real numbers were a far richer collection of entities than mathematicians had previously encountered. They included familiar subcollections, such as the real numbers strictly between 0 and 1, but also all manner of strange subcollections that were harder to pin down. It was the attempt to categorise these stranger subcollections that impelled Cantor to develop the theory of sets and its associated theory of transfinite numbers – actual infinities that could be added, multiplied and ordered in a manner analogous to ordinary finite quantities.

Cantor defined a set to mean 'any collection into a whole of definite, distinct objects of our intuition or of our thought'. Two sets are considered equinumerous if their elements can be put into one-to-one correspondence with each other, each element of the first relating to precisely one element of the other, and vice versa. For instance, touching the tips of one's fingers and thumbs together serves to demonstrate that we have the same number of digits on each hand. Or, if every student has a chair and every chair is occupied by a student, we can conclude that there are as many students as there are chairs.

Innocuous though this definition might seem, it already departs severely from traditional conceptions of number and size. For it means any set that can be indexed by the natural numbers $\{0, 1, 2, 3 \ldots\}$ is in fact the same size as the natural numbers. But we can easily use the natural numbers to index a part of the naturals, such as the even numbers $\{0, 2, 4, 6 \ldots\}$. So the naturals are the same size as the evens, despite the evens being part of the naturals. The venerable law that wholes were necessarily larger than their parts applied to finite numbers only, and did not hold in the more general transfinite case.

The treatment of infinities as actual, completed entities rather than as potentials banished to the beyond soon led to further complications. For while many infinite sets could be put into one-to-one correspondence with the naturals, many others, it transpired, could not. In particular Cantor used his famous 'diagonal argument' to prove that there was no way of serially enumerating the real line. The real line was an infinite set, but an uncountably infinite one, strictly larger than the set of naturals. A generalisation of this diagonal method led to what is today called Cantor's Theorem: the power set of any set is strictly larger than the original set (or in Badiou's terms, the quantity of the state always exceeds the quantity of the situation). This in turn implies that there can be no largest set, and in particular that an ultimate Whole, the collection of everything, cannot exist: the One is not. Instead we have an infinity of infinities of differing sizes, which (given certain other assumptions) can themselves be shown to lie in an ordered line.

This raises a question: if the real line is larger than the natural numbers, how much larger is it? Is it simply the next infinity up from the naturals? Or are there infinite sets that are too large to be counted, but not so large that they are the same size as the entire real line? Cantor assumed that the former of these two cases held, and spent much of the remainder of his life trying to prove this so-called Continuum Hypothesis. His final years were marked by frustration and frequent bouts of mental illness. He died in January 1918 at the age of 72. The riddle of the Continuum Hypothesis was not fully resolved until 1963, when P. J. Cohen demonstrated that it was undecidable: it could be neither proved nor refuted from the standard axioms of set theory.

CATEGORY THEORY

Tzuchien Tho

Badiou's turn to category theory

Regardless of how one interprets Badiou's relationship with the formal sciences in the development of his philosophical work since the 1960s, there is no doubt that this close relationship converges most closely in the project of mathematical ontology that is systematically outlined in the (first) two volumes of *BE* and *LW*. If the rallying call of this project is the equation 'mathematics = ontology' then we might schematically align one sort of mathematics with each of the volumes. Pertaining to the first volume, set theory, or more precisely Zermelo-Fraenkel set theory with the axiom of choice (ZFC), is the mathematics relating to ontology with respect to being-as-such. On the other hand, for the second, *LW*, it is category theory that will provide the theory of beings, or the theory of appearance. As he remarks, the first volume follows out the consequences of the Cantor event and the second pursues the 'Grothendieck-event (or of Eilenberg, or Mac Lane, or Lawvere . . .)' (*LW* 38).

Badiou's turn to category theory was first announced in *Short Treaty on Transitory Ontology* (*TO*) around the midpoint of the twenty-year gap that separates the two ontological volumes. In this text he makes his fundamental motivation for this turn clear. Simply put, while set theory allows us to localise (in a 'situation') the appearance of ontology, categories will allow us to treat localisations and appearance as such (*TO* 161). In other words, set theory is the localised treatment of what is not localisable (being) and category theory is the treatment of the local (beings including set theory itself). While this explicit motivation is here addressed to the problems inherent in his systematic ontology, the turn to categories also aims at providing an explanatory dimension that was thought to be lacking in *BE*. That is, while *BE* treated fundamental problems in the relation between being-as-such, beings, events and subjects, it did not seem to provide a concrete enough framework to deal with phenomena, objects and the world. In this turn, what Badiou aims to provide is a general *logic* (in the Hegelian sense) of appearance that is both consistent with the systematic grounds of set-theoretical ontology and concretely descriptive of ordinary 'multiples': a painting, a battle, a walk in the countryside, a meeting of activists.

Something of a vertigo strikes in attempting to sort the compatibility and distinction between these two dimensions of ontology: *onto*-logy and onto-*logy*. We commented on set-theoretical ontology being too abstract and thus insufficient to describe multiples in appearance, but this is due to the fact that its methodological minimalism can only allow us to treat multiplicity through the fundamental relation of belonging or set membership ($\in$) and its consequences. It is here abstract in the sense that it does not recognise anything outside of sets, the elements of sets and the relations therein. Infinite though these relations are, they are theoretically aimed at producing a discourse concerning multiplicity itself and far from being directly related to concrete situations, phenomena or objects. Ironically, this is the case precisely because set theory is *too concrete*. Set theory is concrete precisely in its treatment of multiples as multiples and not the different 'forms' of multiplicity (appearances, spaces, etc.). Categories, in this sense, are more abstract in that they can provide a formal treatment of sets, groups, rings, modules, topoi and a host of other mathematical objects (Mac Lane 1971). Categories, in its development, can be seen as the most abstract of mathematical formalisms in its capacity to model just about anything. For this reason it has been dubbed 'general abstract nonsense' by its very promoters (Mac Lane 2004). A dialectical twist thus arises in Badiou's work, one that aligns his mathematical ontology very closely with the relationship between sets and categories themselves. It seems that the rigid localisation of pure multiplicity in *BE* proves to be abstract with respect to beings but concrete with respect to being-as-such. The categorical treatment of all these various localisations (appearances) is (more) concrete with respect to beings but abstract with respect to the very multiplicity from which it operates. The consequences of this dialectical back-and-forth seem to be what animates this turn towards categories.

What is general abstract nonsense (categories)? Category theory developed out of abstract algebra and topology in the 1940s. Its founders, Samuel Eilenberg and Saunders Mac Lane (beginning with their founding 1945 paper, 'General Theory of Natural Equivalences'), sought to provide an abstract framework for treating structures across different mathematical forms (sets, groups, rings) as variable in a wider structure. Its theoretical aim was to provide a way to treat structures occurring across different contexts, and then to treat the structure between these different contexts as a structure, and so forth. This theoretical aim was, however, attenuated by the mode by which its founders sought to elaborate the theory. Hence, founders such as Mac Lane had a more pragmatic aim of developing categories as a tool that mathematicians from different fields could use to elaborate, simplify and unify structures ranging across as many contexts as they would care to. The idea of a mathematical foundation in categories was thus, historically speaking, a pragmatic one which aimed to provide a 'toolbox', rather than a quasi-ontological one. Much of this development pertained to what one could do with categories rather than what they 'are'. We shall see in a moment how this pragmatic aim is profoundly demonstrated in the theory itself.

Before venturing into a more direct look at categories themselves, I would like to address Badiou's use of them. Badiou's turn to categories is not a complete one, and the bottom-up construction of the relation between onto-*logy* and categories is not given such as was done in *BE* (between set theory and *onto*-logy). This is largely due to the fact that Badiou mainly takes up the theory of topoi in his development of the themes such as world, localisation, atoms, existential analysis and such. That is, Badiou enters into category theory from the point of view of sets and their logical context rather than from a ground-up categorical approach. Roughly speaking, topoi are generalisations of structures that are developed from the categorical treatment of the relations between sets with topological spaces. Before the explicit treatment of these structures through category theory, the (in)famous Alexander Grothendieck had already introduced the term and theoretical underpinnings in algebraic geometry. Importantly, Badiou defines his notion of 'world' as a Grothendieck topos, which is named after the mathematician (*LW* 295).

Due to this focus on topoi, elementary formalistic expositions in *LW* (especially in Book II) are written in (Heyting) algebraic formula that is closely related but not explicitly *categorical*. The difficulty here is that Badiou approaches categories from the aspect of topoi and hence through the door of logic and set theory (and the logical foundations of set theory). It might thus seem that many of the elementary aspects of category theory are incongruent with Badiou's use. Now categories, unlike set theory, does not refer back to a constant 'universe' (such as the universe of constructible sets V=L), and thus we should be free to consider categories as an 'approach' (a categorical approach to sets, logic, groups, etc.), rather than carrying any deep ontological commitments. Even so, while the technical sections of *LW* may seem more algebraic than categorical, Badiou's arguments no doubt refer back to a technical categorical framework that he does not develop from the ground up. This undeveloped framework leaves the reader the task of reconstructing the mathematical background approach implied in the text, and may also provide the resources to push the concepts in different directions.

Categories: the axiomatic qua mechanical basics

Categories begin with the idea of a function at its basis (f: a→b). A function sends one value to another. One might think, for example, that an activist of a certain stripe (a) goes to a certain type of meeting (b). Rosa the anarchist attends the meeting of local autonomists. Karl the environmentalist attends the working group on carbon reduction. We can add another function however (g: b→c). Here, each meeting (b) takes place in a certain building (c). The local autonomists gather in a certain bookstore and the environmentalists meet in a grocery cooperative. Now each of these functions can be combined to form a 'composition'. If we take f and g together, we can get another function h (h: a→c). Since a is sent to b and b sent to

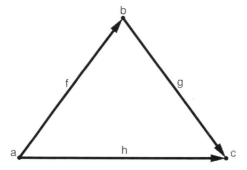

Figure 1 Redrawn from Mac Lane, *Categories for the Working Mathematician*.

c, h is the function that takes a directly to b. If Rosa forgets her keys, we know exactly where to deliver them (anarchist bookstore).

This simple example, which borrows terminology from simple algebra and may remind us of elementary discussions of set theory, gives us the basic mechanics of categories. Instead of 'functions' (f, g, h) between objects (a, b, c), category theory uses 'arrows'. Just as set theory is built up from the two elementary notions of 'set' and 'membership', category theory is built up from two notions (not analogous to set and belonging). The first are objects (or structures): a, b, c, etc. The second are arrows (or morphisms): f, g, h, etc. The first result, as seen in our example above, is that this 'map' tells us something about the arrows. For every arrow (f) there are a domain (a) and a codomain (b). For two maps such as we saw in the above where f: a → b and g: b → c, we can express a composite map with an arrow h such that h= g ∘ f and g ∘ f and so h: a → c.

The notions of objects, arrows and map composition are all axiomatic features of category theory. Another axiomatic aspect is the notion of an identity map. This is not simply the idea that every object *is* itself, but that there is an arrow (**Ida**: a → a) that takes each object to itself. Employing the terminology that we have laid out, this arrow (**Ida**) takes a → a and thus has a domain of a and a codomain of a. A related but different notion of identity reins in the compositional operations of the arrows themselves and is named the unit law. Here let us suppose that f sends a to b. We can mechanically suppose that there is an identity arrow (**Idb**) that sends b to b. This results in the identity of the composition of f and the identity mapping of b. As such, Idb ∘ f = f and f ∘ Idb = f. With this, we should also add that these arrows

$$(k \circ (g \circ f) = (k \circ g) \circ f)$$

are also associative, which can de demonstrated in the following diagram.

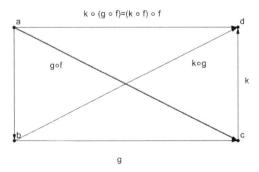

Figure 2 Redrawn from Mac Lane, *Categories for the Working Mathematician.*

We see, as with the elementary example, how working with categories can be understood as 'arrow' chasing. This pragmatic aspect of the theory is no small feature. Indeed, as Badiou himself mentions, with categories, the arrows – that is, morphisms – are central and the notion of objects are secondary (*TO* 147). We can see clearly in the above why this is so. At its basis, all objects have their identity through arrows; objects can be eliminated, leaving only arrows. This 'arrows-only' axiomatic, as Mac Lane calls it, is perhaps less intuitive but is wholly equivalent (Mac Lane 1971: 9). In either case, a category is a set of objects and arrows (or just arrows) that obeys the axiomatic outline above. To simplify the above, we can have a category of just one object and one arrow (the identity arrow). In our example of the activists, we have a category with three objects and three non-identity arrows.

A major aspect of category theory is its capacity to treat these elementary relations in a more powerful way. This capacity is concerned first and foremost with functors. Much of the origin of category theory lies in the development of functors in algebraic topology, and it was with an aim to study these in a simpler and more direct way that categories were first developed. From a historical perspective, we might understand functors as the development of the translation between the different fields of topology and algebra. A canonical and historically pertinent example in this regard is the way topological structures are studied via Abelian groups. How do we relate something that is inherently spatial and something that is inherently algebraic? By taking the relations internal to topology and relating them to relations internal to groups, we provide a 'translation': from homotopic maps to homomorphisms. The relations of these two structures are understood in categories as a functor between the category **Top** → **Ab**, the functor between the category **Top** (topological spaces) and the category **Ab** (Abelian groups). In this sense the treatment of functors in category theory aims at the structural correlation between topology and groups (Abelian or otherwise) in treating the morphisms between them.

Since we have already mentioned that sets, topological spaces, groups and rings are all categories, it is no surprise to find out that a functor is a morphism of categories themselves. The details concerning this may be an obstacle to understanding, so I will simply remark that a functor is a morphism between categories in the same way that arrows are morphisms between objects. Any functor T: C → B has the domain C and codomain B. Yet, since we are dealing here with a 'higher-order' relation, functors do not simply relate objects a and b, but the objects *and* arrows of the first category C with the objects of the second category B interpreted functorially through T.

Now the problem with functors is that they are not as straightforward as arrows. While arrows provide and preserve the structure of the maps that we examine, different kinds of functors treat the structures of the categories differently. A simple functor is no doubt the identity functor (or endofunctor). Just like the identity map, the identity functor maps a category to itself. This no doubt preserves the structure. A different sort of functor is one that maps **Top** to **Set** (topological space to sets). In this case, the mapping 'forgets' the structure of the topological space in its mappings with sets (Bell 1981: 351).

From functors to topoi

It is with the notion of functors that we can finally present something closer to the aim of the founders of category theory. As they argued in their founding paper, 'General Theory of Natural Equivalences', Eilenberg and Mac Lane remark that:

It should be observed that the whole concept of a category is essentially an aux-iliary one. Our basic concepts are essentially those of a functor and of a natural transformation [. . .] The idea of a category is required only by the precept that every functor should have a definite class as domain and a definite class as range, for the categories are provided as the domains and ranges of functors. (Eilenberg and Mac Lane 1945: 247)

In this sense, the study of categories is the study of structures mediated by functors. Here, as we saw in the remark above by Mac Lane, just as we eliminate objects and deal solely with arrows we can thus view functors as the heart of the theory. Indeed, here, functors lead us to the crucial structure that it aims to illuminate. This is what is mentioned in this original conception as the 'natural transformation'. Now, just as functors send the elements of one category to another, we can equally understand functors themselves as a category. No doubt the functor category will have as objects the functors between categories. The arrows between any two functors will be arrows that define the morphism of functors (Mac Lane 1971: 16). These morphisms are the 'natural transformations' alluded to above. The pragmatic notion at the heart of category theory thus corre-sponds to its deepest quandary. As Mac Lane remarked, ' "category" has been defined in order to define "functor" and "functor" has been defined in order to define "natural transformation" ' (Mac Lane 1971: 18).

There is no doubt that this mechanical introduction to the basic themes and aims of categories will be insufficient for *doing* any mathematics (except perhaps basic arithmetic). But to conclude, we return to a key point in Badiou's use of categories. This concerns the problem of the relation between set theory and categories. As we may perhaps already have ascertained from the above, sets and categories are not opposed and sets can be treated as a category that can be studied through its structural relationship with other categories. As Mac Lane and others have done, elementary textbooks on categories often take sets as the universe through which categories are given a first interpretation. That is, given a meta-theoretic outline of the axioms, set theory provides a convenient universe in which a model of these axioms is developed (Mac Lane 1971: 9). There are good historical and heuristic reasons for this, but it should not lead us to falsely understand categories as dependent on a set-theoretical foundation. Quite the opposite – this is one of the reasons for understanding the abstract generality of categories as a strength of the approach. Set theory ultimately still relies on some basic *reference* to sets and the universe of sets, while categories need only refer to structural relationships which are relative between any two structures.

Now, conversely, a category theoretic treatment of set theory can shed light on this. Alluding to Badiou's use of topoi, I will refer to the notion of an elementary topos that, by way of example, is a category of a model **M** of set theory which has all the sets in **M** as objects and all the mappings between sets in **M** as arrows. What is surprising in the categorical treatment of sets in this manner is that all the logical and set-theoretical operators in this model **M** can be treated as structurally internal to the topos, thus producing a model of set theory that is unhinged from its original (classical) logical scaffolding. Indeed, the treatment of sets by categories in this manner reveals an intuitionistic logic, a Heyting algebra (Bell 1986: 414). What follows from this is the treatment of propositional logic in a similar manner. In short, the categorical treatment of sets foregrounds the structural and functional dimension of sets and thus relativises the logical foundations of sets. In this sense, we may grasp a fuller understanding of 'logic' in Badiou's frequent use of the terms 'mathematised logic' and 'logic of worlds': logics can be understood as the internal structures of topoi, which ultimately refer to nothing but the arrows and objects (satisfying the axioms of category theory) that compose them.

What has been developed here, outside of rudimentary mechanical understanding of categories, is far from an adequate exposition on the importance of category theory and topos theory. In order to gain additional background to Badiou's exposition in *Logics of Worlds*, especially for the crucial passage concerning the 'complete form of the onto-logy of worlds', readers should familiarise themselves with sheaves and presheaves (different sorts of functors), which are immanently connected to the notion of topos above.

(TWENTIETH) CENTURY

Steven Corcoran

Taken objectively as an historical unity, the twentieth century can be rendered as 'The Soviet' century of the communist epic, the totalitarian century of mass state crime, or, according to its result, as a liberal century of the happy correlation of unrestricted markets and shore-less democracy. Each objectification commands its own limit dates (except for the last one, which we are not done with) and a certain attitudinal bearing – nostalgia, horror, triumphalism. Badiou himself does not take an explicit position on any one of these objects in particular, as though the philosophical task would be to judge which of them was truer, more apt. For this 'constructivist' approach to history as such is an inherently ideological one: all these positions mark narrative constructions of facts after the event. They are symbolic projections concerning the becoming of the state and the 'subjective' reactions one might take to this objective becoming.

If Badiou's work *The Century* is rather concerned to grasp the century as an Idea, it is because he wants to grasp what, from the viewpoint of the subjectivity that animated the Century, was singular about what was thought in it. The point is not to take the Century as a collection of (factual) objects, as though it were an object to be interpreted, but as a form of labour. So, if the twentieth century existed, by which Badiou means existed for philosophy, existed as the labour of an idea, what form of subjectivity invested it? And if it existed – and Badiou thinks that it did – what was thought in it 'that was previously unthought – or even unthinkable?' (*C* 3). By what means can we evaluate the century's achievements in thought? A rehabilitation of the Century is not Badiou's goal. But if we are either to prevent developments that would enable a return of certain actions (e.g. the disaster of Stalinism) or want to discern what remains in it of inherited problems still needing to be solved, it is only by seizing its movement of thought that we provide ourselves with the wherewithal to do this. In such matters, a tribunal of human rights, which involves judging historical constructions formed retroactively according to extrinsic criteria, can only be as mediocre intellectually as it is ineffectual politically.

Now, before addressing Badiou's interrogation in further detail, it is worth pointing out that his positing that the twentieth century exists means, among other things, that he thinks it – i.e. the Century – cannot be accessed hermeneutically as the reign of technological domination, etc. *à la* Heidegger, as the extension of a metaphysical nihilism with which we must be done. The point of Badiou's undertaking is decidedly not to thrust it back into an established regime of sense, not even one that is established retroactively – such that the reasons explaining what occurred are always already supplied beforehand, whether the diagnostic tool is socio-economic or philosophico-hermeneutical. Instead, the approach is more Beckettian: the twentieth century created a disturbance in the course of history, and Badiou hopes to shed light on its 'missaying' and on what in it has been 'misseen'. To *name* this twentieth century for Badiou is thus to assert some kind of allegiance to the thought of the century itself. This is why his analysis takes the form of a series of 'lessons', in which he evaluates what in this thought went wrong, and what must be retained. From this point of view, Badiou's intervention is a proper act of naming itself, in the philosophical register.

Badiou seeks to understand how, in making a break that was not pre-scribed by the foregoing situation, the actors of the century approached their tasks of breaking with it. Key here is the link between subjectifi-cation and indiscernibility. A subjective movement always involves a hypothesis on a 'that which will have been the case', provided that fidelity is maintained to an event, which is at present indiscernible. The signifi-cance of the statements that Badiou refers to in his series of lessons will indeed exist only retroactively, once an attempt is made to bring what is at present indiscernible into existence, but this will not add up to a nar-rative, or to any overall meaning. The types of documents in which these statements are to be found (poems, manifestos, plays) convey and envelop the extraordinary intensity of an active thought. For, as Badiou argues, by breaking with the world of established knowledge and opinion, the subject labours under the 'anguish of the void' (*BE* 94), seeking to vanquish this unknown real, a live lived in a present that consists partly in the gaps it produces in the known. The intelligibility of this anguish is given in the categories through which the subject of these documents relates to this indiscernible real, in the figure of the Two that it constructs in breaking with the established order.

This exercise thus demands that Badiou identify defining texts in which this thinking subjectivity emerges and travels, and it is thus no wonder that he locates it essentially in a series of poetic texts and artistic manifestos that are precisely devoted to thinking events. For Badiou, art in general and poetry in particular, notably since Mallarmé, is much con-cerned with a twofold contingency, namely the rareness of events and the world's being founded on the sole void, which it aims to expose. Poetry guards or protects the very principle of this double contingency. Love and politics might include discussions of particular events, but not of the event itself. Art, however, is unique among the truth domains for not only is it produced by events (e.g. Mandelstam's poetry itself is an event) but it is also capable of reflecting on them as such. In so doing art destabilises the object, exposing its inherent instability, which is to say the radical instability of the world of appearing, which is a condition of the emergence of the event.

In the Century, the poem is conjured not as something that necessarily comes after the event (e.g. Mandelstam's poetry after the Russian Revolution) but as the anticipation of an event that may or may not take place. Bound up in the extreme precariousness of a supposed evental fracture in a world, Mandelstam's poetry emphasises that it could well be that the event has not even taken place. The poem leaves the question in suspension. Perhaps it is precisely the absence of such an event that must be taken as the point of departure. The point would then be to meditate on the conditions that might make it possible again. Poetry does all this, which is why, in certain circumstances, it can name a real to which politics, concerned with unfolding the subjective consequences of an event, would remain closed (*PP* 31). That is why, in lieu of the event, poetry is placed to contemplate the conditions of freedom and justice themselves. Badiou's philosophy, disquisitioning on the existence of the twentieth century, takes up the challenge of both poetry and politics. It looks into poetic attempts to name the real and learns the lessons dealt by the subjective consequences of political fidelities.

Badiou's philosophical approach to the twentieth Century is thus both irreducible to the history of states and anti-humanist, insofar as the former sets out from a ready-made idea of the human or of the human search. All the above-mentioned historical takes on the twentieth Century, for example, presuppose some kind of image of human finitude (contained in each of the objects or 'historical unities'). What Badiou alerts us to is that philosophy, as conditioned by poetic statements explicitly devoted to thinking through the twentieth Century, is concerned with what is not yet known as possible within human experience, a 'humanity' that is yet to arrive, is yet to declare itself as such. This is Badiou's wager in *TC*: what is not yet human cannot be known to be destined to become human until it has done so; it is inaccessible in and of itself. But what philosophy can perhaps do is to point to the formal conditions of such an eventuality as they have already been experimented with but not yet brought to fruition. As we shall see, Badiou recognises the truth of the twentieth century not as the present reality of a nature whose explanation must be found, whose unconscious truth must be divulged, but as an ideality that is localised. Badiou's analysis thus produces a protracted series of 'finite approximations' to, or variations on, this ideality (*BE* 434–5).

The passion of the real

As he sees it, the century's key actors were driven by what he calls 'a passion for the real' – what the nineteenth century only dreamt of, or promised, was to be achieved here and now. Key to this passion was the theme of New Man – if the idea of the nineteenth century was to entrust oneself to the movement of history in the bringing about of a new humanity, then the twentieth sought to confront it, 'to master it politically'. The new world is coming, but when? The inertia of historical sediment means that history itself could not be relied on to bring about what it presages. Thus a new act would be required to discard the semblances of reality and reveal the real laying beneath them.

On Badiou's analysis, however, this passion of the real remains caught in a vitalist-voluntarist paradox. It asserts a vitalism of history, of the movement of real objects of history, but objective inertia requires the will to force this vitalist necessity to come into existence. The paradox is ultimately terrorising; it effects an undecidability between life and death. As the new was to be revealed beneath the semblances of the reality, destruction of that which history had already stamped with future obsolescence would become a sign of commitment to the new world. Death thus becomes a sign of the vitality of life. The passion for the real here is thus ultimately immersed in a fascination for destruction conceived as a prelude to creation. In its political version, it was governed by the notion that as forms of historical sediment, such as the 'obsolete' historical existence of the bourgeoisie, were swept aside, New Man would reveal itself. The Century's passion for the real thus forges a link between negation (destruction) and affirmation (creation), presupposing the idea that beneath the falsity of appearances there lay a content to be divulged. But no such content exists and the link could be achieved only by a violence that did not lead onto anything.

In his non-dialectical conjunction of a diagnostic of nihilism and regeneration, Nietzsche figures as the century's prophet. Mandelstam's poem, 'The Century', as analyzed by Badiou, reprises these two themes – on the one hand, that of renunciation, resignation, lesser evil, moderation, crisis, and end of humanity as spirituality; and on the other, a breaking apart of the history of the world into two, the bringing about of a radical new beginning. The century is traversed by a complex connection, an intertwining between end and beginning. The figure of the two at stake here is a non-dialectical, disjunctive synthesis.

The Century's problem is thus to be in the non-dialectical disjunction between end and beginning, nihilism and institution. How are they to be articulated? How is it possible to articulate an endless destruction and a perpetual peace? The entire subjective disposition of the passion for the real Badiou sees as being overdetermined by a paradigm of war. In the false peace that had merely cemented divisions after WW1, the pressing question was indeed, 'How is it possible to create a new type of war, a war to end all wars, a radical instauration and not a simple "end of war"?' Again, by contrast with the nineteenth, the stake of war was no longer Hegel's (development of national consciousness), but that of the decisive war, of the last man. The twentieth Century's idea of war, which was paradigmatic for its subjectivity, is that of a decisive combat, a combat between those who were resolute with continuing on as before and those who aimed to do away with the old ways and begin something. The passion for the real points to a combative existence aimed at obtaining something definitive, whether a definitive solution to war itself (a new kind of war to end all wars); a definitive solution to mathematical problems (Bourbaki), a refounding of relations between the sexes, and so on.

Again, the idea of the Two here is not dialectical. There are two Ones, two camps, and they are locked in a decisive battle for supremacy. Herein, according to Badiou, is the kernel of the passion for the real, namely the pathetic conviction that one is convoked to the real of the beginning; that the real, it if is to be real, is horrible and enthusing, mortifying and creative. Especially as the idea that history is on one's side involves a certain *indifference* to the price paid for beginning (i.e. for creating New Man). Badiou shows that this indifference is by no means coincidental. The intrinsic reason for it relates to the idea of the real that this passion presents.

Now, the real by definition can never be suspected of being a semblance. But what can attest that the real is really real? Nothing bar a system of fictions will do this attesting. However, it is necessary to show that something like the real indicates itself as such. As the passion for the real presumes the possibility of *de-ciding* the semblance, however, it must be that the passion of the real is a passion of destruction. It is precisely the fact that this passion cannot locate a real entirely separated from semblance that destruction of semblance becomes a show of commitment to the real of a new beginning. Ultimately the passion for the real, for the new, was unable to separate itself from destruction as a sign of the new.

Destruction vs Subtraction

But the Century throws up another response to the question of attesting to the real, of how a discourse can be produced which is delimited from that of the semblance. Here Mallarmé replaces Nietzsche as the Century's prophet. Malevich takes up this path with his attempt to 'hear the breath of a new day in the desert'. The idea of subtraction, in contrast with that of destruction, is to emphasise a minimal difference: that between the element and its place, i.e. the universal element (life, history, equality) and the place of its inscription (in representations, social institutions, etc.). That minimal difference is the difference between the universal and the 'supernumerary' particular that directly stands in for this universal. Here there is purification not as destruction but rather as the subtraction from all representation and from all identity.

Let's take Malevitch's 'white square on a white background' as an example of radical purification in art, a purification that is nevertheless not about destruction but rather subtraction. Here there is a subtraction of semblance – colour, form – but also the simultaneous maintenance of a formal indice, attesting to a vanishing difference between the place and the taking-place.

Now, Badiou's hypothesis is that subtractive thinking upholds a different protocol to that of destructive thinking, one that is still alive for us. The issue between subtraction and destruction is essentially one of whether the real is to be treated as an identity or not. When is the proletariat really the proletariat? The problem with destruction is that, taking the proletarian as one who occupies a socio-historical place, it is still too caught up in identity, and thus also in the semblance. But subtraction, by contrast, treats the real as a minimal difference where there is an undecidability between subjectivity and objectivity, between the place and the taking place – and this protocol demands a subtraction from the semblance of identity. It grasps the singularity of the proletariat as one with the production of a generic collective in indifference to identity.

To sum up, then, we see that the Century's production of the Two is itself split into two:

1. The passion of the real as destruction, wherein the real is by nature an identity. Passion here involves grasping the identity of the real, which supposes unmasking it, unmasking it beneath its copies.
2. The passion of the real as subtraction, as a differential, differentiating pattern that is devoted to constructing a minimal difference.

Badiou's diagnosis is thus that, in spite of its inventiveness, one 'new' remained too tied to identity to be really new. Only where the Century produced a Two in the form of a minimal difference (e.g. workers differ from their place not by expressing the identity of a real capacity but by detaching from that capacity and articulating their equal capacity to undo relations of domination) was the promise of genuine novelty traced.

What Badiou's evaluation of the century attempts to prolong is a certain principle of attentiveness that was in evidence in the documents he analyses. In doing so, he has a specifically philosophical view in mind: the Century's experimentation with the Two revealed the need to invert the relation between affirmation and negation. The passion of the real as destruction showed, precisely, that negativity, destruction, is no prelude to creation. As subtraction, however, this passion evinces the need to produce the affirmation of a minimal difference. Only the creation of a possibility, of the real of a minimal difference, gives rise to the new, and negation – the necessary passing of that which becomes obsolete (forms of domination, etc.) – comes after.

So Badiou's inquiry into the twentieth Century is ultimately about discerning what the century bequeathed to us in the way of subjective invention. This subjective invention is split between two ideas of the two, one destructive, one subtractive – one that revealed the limits of its conception of the real (and that continues on today, in a weak form: 'we must remain in tune with the fundamental movements of the capitalist economy, or risk being on the side of the losers of history') and another that has remained insufficiently experimented and that continues to haunt us.

CINEMA

Pietro Bianchi and Bruno Besana

The systematic nature of Badiou's theoretical edifice notwithstanding, cinema appears in his work as a spurious object, lacking proper conceptual localisation. Its status is repeatedly declared uncertain or more precisely 'impure'. This is perhaps why, contrary to his extreme systematicity of approach, Badiou's interventions on cinema are scattered over a large time span, dispersed in myriad film reviews, short articles and conferences, and for the main part are devoted to discussing one or several individual films, as evidenced by his recently published collection, *Cinema*.

At first glance Badiou seems to deal with cinema in the manner of a film critic, insofar as he discusses single problems, single films, and frequently detaches specific sequences from a film as a whole (e.g. the ending of Mizoguchi's *The Crucified Lovers* and Rossellini's *Journey to Italy*, and the scene of poetry reading in Wenders' *The Wrong Move*). What is missing in most of Badiou's texts on cinema is direct philosophical engagement with the question of cinema as a specific art form, in contrast to Deleuze's treatment of it in his two volumes on cinema in the 1980s.

Yet far from being an idiosyncratic posture, this method is consistent with a philosophical approach to art that refuses to develop a discourse *over* a generalised field. Instead, Badiou is interested in the activation of localised truth procedures made possible by specific works of art, scientific marking points or political sequences under condition of which philosophy can think. It is no accident that Badiou, given his refusal of the notion that philosophy's aim is to discuss the essence of art or what art in general should be, completely dismisses the term 'aesthetics', understood as a regional application of philosophy to the field of art. Badiou's neologism 'inaesthetics' names both the deactivation of aesthetics (understood in the aforementioned sense) and the attempt to name the intra-philosophical consequences produced by singular, specific works of art (cf. inaesthetics).

In accordance with his 'inaesthetics', art is not a understood as a field, as a general object of philosophical reflection, but rather as a condition, i.e. as a set of *singular works* able to produce intra-philosophocal consequences, and hence able to *activate* philosophy.

Yet in a few passages (see esp. *HI*, Ch. 8: 78) Badiou does come close to discussing cinema as such: if discussing the generality of the philosophical relevance of art *per se* is foreclosed, cinema as a whole nonetheless receives a description. Cinema, according to Badiou, is an *impure* art, insofar as each single film is lost in a sort of indistinction between art and non-art. This indistinction also points towards a certain necessity to decide, namely to the fact that, ultimately, art's ability to produce singular truths is decided work by work.

The possibility that truth has to appear proceeds in cinema on the basis of a qualification that runs contrary to Deleuze's definition of cinema as the immediate expression of pure movement. For Badiou, in fact, cinematic 'movement is held up, suspended, inverted, arrested' (*HI* 78), as if it were an almost *static* form of art. Cinema also does not create or manifest something within the visible; rather it 'withdraws' from the visible. Badiou's counterintuitive definition aims at understanding the very act of framing as a separation, as a cut from an already existing visible. Cinema, then, does not create a 'visible' or enhance visibility but is instead 'a controlled purge of the visible'. He clarifies the reason for this definition shortly afterwards: 'the flowers cinema displays (as in one of Visconti's sequences) [are] Mallarméan flowers [. . .] absent from every bouquet'; what is shown on the screen is 'both their singularity and their ideality' (ibid.). In a typically anti-mimetic move, Badiou believes that cinema, far from representing what is already (in the) visible, should empty out the particular concreteness of the represented image. The singularity of the object incarnates an ideal aspect exactly – as in the Mallarméan object – on account of its subtractive capacity to undo the 'naturalised' habits via which perception is normally organised.

But if painting or poetry can call on many resources to perform such an operation, the position of cinema is far more problematic:

> To write a poem you need pen and paper [. . .] To paint a picture, you also begin with an absence, a surface [. . .] But beginning a film is not at all the same. The conditions of production of the movement-image or the time-image involve a unique assemblage of materials. You need technical resources, but you also need to marshal extremely complex and, above all, heterogeneous materials. For example, you need locations, either natural or constructed ones; you need spaces; you need a text, a screenplay, dialogues, abstract ideas; you need bodies, actors; plus you'll need chemistry, and editing equipment. (*Cin* 225–6)

In contrast to other art forms, cinema is encrusted with a wide variety of elements that belong to the 'state of a particular situation', not to mention the latter's structural proximity with the capitalist entertainment industry. For cinema to isolate from these myriad elements the ideal flowers 'absent from every bouquet', far greater effort is required. Further complicating this is the fact that no single artistic agency controls any film from beginning to the end. Remaining is a confused mixture of hetero-geneous forms of art (theatre, photography, music, literature, painting) and contradictory tendencies. But this difficulty is not merely contingent. In fact, although it would technically be possible to make a film using minimal elements and resources, outside the control of big studios, the thing that gives filmmaking such a problematic standing would remain: movement itself.

For in art the idea *operates* by *fixity*: it cuts within a transient mixture of empirical elements, of confused sensations and semantic equivocity. The eternity of the idea is thus nothing but the void of a fracture that interrupts customary modes of perception and recurrent modes of organisation of sensible material. For this reason, the idea always returns as identical to itself, qua void of any positive content, qua pure capacity of subtraction in a given mode of presentation and circulation of phenomena. Hence *the* flower cannot but be the absent one, as subtractive presence in a deter-mined, situated bouquet the presence of which carves an inconsistency in the current modes of organisation and perception of what a bouquet of flowers is. If cinema, as any art, presents this operation, at the same time, being essentially inseparable from a myriad of movements, it also constantly erases such operation, and therefore constantly erases the idea. In cinema the idea is thus reduced to an ephemeral *passage*: 'cinema is an art of the perpetual past. [*It*] is visitation: the idea of what I will have seen or heard lingers on to the very extent that it passes' (*HI* 78). Cinema is the art of the temporary *transition* of the Idea, not of its specific and rigorous localisation: the permanent localisation of truth is simply contradictory to the definition of *movement*-image itself.

But this separate role of cinema is also, conversely, that which places it in a crucial position in relation to all arts: lacking a specific form of truth, the practice of filmmaking implies all the other arts. More precisely, in cinema all arts are simultaneously present and are emptied out from within ('[it] is always in a defective relation to one or several among the other arts' (86)). In Visconti's *Death of Venice*, for example, the theatrical opacity of the acting features of Dirk Bogarde is combined with the pictorial themes of Canaletto, the literary atmospheres of Proust, the echoes of the subtle uncertainty of Henry James's heroes and the melancholic flavour of Mahler's music. But if all these elements amplify each other, they also 'corrode one another in a sort of decomposition by excess'.

This means, first, that even in the most skillfully orchestrated composition of elements, as with Visconti, 'the formalist path, which leads to supposedly "pure" filmic operations' cannot but be an impasse, and leads back to 'impurity'. In the cinematographic territory stretched between art and non-art, the Idea, unable to be presentified in its absence, can only *pass through* and pass, with each film constantly falling back into impurity. But, second, it is important to note that, when Badiou acknowledges the *passage* of the Idea in some specific filmic sequences, this occurs at the very peak of art's impurity, *within* the very arrangement of a film as the *Kampfplatz* of the other various arts. Analysing the opening sequence of Visconti's rendering of Mann's *Death in Venice*, Badiou observes:

Let us suppose that, in this instance, the idea is the link between amorous melancholy, the genius of the place, and death. Visconti arranges (or 'edits') the visitation of this idea in the space within the visible that is opened up by melody. This takes place to the detriment of prose, since here nothing will be said, nothing textual. Movement subtracts the novelistic from language, keeping it on the moving edge between music and place. But music and place exchange their own values in turn, so that the music is annulled by pictorial allusions, while every pictorial stability is conversely dissolved into music. These transferences and dissolutions are the very thing that will have ultimately constituted the Real of the idea's passage. (*HI* 80)

When an art plays against another in a given sequence, the subtractive force of art emerges within the confused mixture of impure arts that operates on the screen. Here the confused, transient nature of the film is blocked by a series of subtractive operations. Hence a certain immobility – equivalent to the visitation of an idea – is produced by the very movement of cinema, which therefore exposes itself neither as mere movement, nor as mere immobilisation, but instead as 'false movement'. Such 'false movement' is the very form of the ephemeral visitation of the idea; it is that which constitutes cinema as nothing but a peripheral art (even more, an art whose movements constantly erase the ideas that perform such acts of suspension or neutralisation). But, at the same time, this 'false movement' demands the mutual conflict of all the other arts, and thus constitutes cinema as a pivotal art, that restlessly articulates the totality of the other arts by organising a series of (ephemeral) subtractive points.

Even so, for Badiou cinema remains farthest from the ideal form of a condition. When in *MP* Badiou lists philosophy's four conditions (*MP* 35), he mentions, as the model for all artistic practice, the 'poem', and more specifically Mallarmé, who occupies a rather crucial role in Badiou's philosophy. If Badiou tends to privilege art based on literality, rather than on the empirical imaginary of vision, this is not only due to its proximity with mathematics ('like mathematics, poetry is language reduced to the strict presentation of presentation' (Hallward 2003: 197)) but also to the relation that the poem entertains with the state of a situation. Against all approaches to poetry and art as a form of access to the thing-in-itself in all its sensuous plenitude, Badiou believes that poetry – and especially avant-gardist poetry, where the materiality of the signifier is the most distant from any possible signification – is able to operate a cut in the habits via which material existence is perceived and organised. Mallarmé's poetry is a model of subtraction from the confusion of experience, the poem working as an operator of separation that disjoins all relations and interrupts the continuity of the imaginary. Devoid of empirical reference, poetry detaches language from the regime of presence and maintains active or alive that 'nothing' (*BE* 192) – radically singular, pure action – which would otherwise fall back into sheer nullity.

Discussing Mallarmé's *L'Apres-midi d'un faune*, Badiou writes:

The wind and the water are nothing when compared with the power that art possesses to stir up the idea of water, the idea of wind [. . .] Through the visibility of artifice, which is also the thinking of poetic thought, the poem surpasses in power what the sensible is capable of itself. The modern poem is the opposite of mimesis. In its operation, it exhibits an Idea of which both the object and objectivity represent nothing but pale copies. (*HI* 21)

Although explicitly Platonic, this passage does not equate the empirical realm with a 'pale copy' of ideas, but with a pale copy *of what the idea is capable of*. The idea of wind is absent from any given wind not because it would be an in-se that never manifests itself, but because it is exactly the gap of fracture within any given manifestation, understanding, classification or usage of a wind. Therefore 'the classical maxim *par excellence* is: "the true is sometimes not the likely"' (ibid.). In relation to this radically antimimetic paradigm, cinema presents an unsurpassable limitation, insofar as it is too entangled with the reproduction of the sensible: cinema, because of its technical properties, reproduces reality all too well, it is strictly bound to a mimetic reproduction of reality, thus rendering the operations of subtraction from the state of the situation extremely difficult. Films cannot but fall again and again within the consistency of the situation in which they appear.

Cinema is a mass art [. . .] because it shares the social imaginary with the masses. Cinema's starting point isn't its history but the impurity of its material. This is why cinema is a shared art form: everyone recognises contemporary imagery in a film. (*Cin* 230)

But if cinema is in a way homogeneous to the empirical situation in which it takes place (hence Badiou's particular insistence on commercial films, whereas he spends little time analysing avant-garde and experimental cinema), at the same time its weakest point is inseparable from the possibility of its redemption. In fact, it is precisely the very same characteristics that make cinema a non-art (or a liminal art constantly moving or falling out of art) that ground the possibility it has to to perform a certain subtractive movement, albeit exposed in the evanescent mode of a visitation. In fact, being the most impure form of art, constantly falling again within the regularity of the (commercial, political, communicational) situation to which it belongs, cinema not only allows for the passage of an idea (via the articulation of a set of arts) but is also able to effectuate an intervention in the state of the situation in an extremely immediate and effective way: such specific, albeit thwarted localisation, is ultimately what grants it its relevance.

In the uninterrupted course of non-events that define the state of a situation, cinema is able, if not to operate a subtraction, then at least to *immobilise* the stream of non-events present at the centre of the social imaginary of the masses. Bound to a movement that refuses its permanence within the stabilised realm of art, cinema conversely performs – as the language adopted by Badiou shows – a series of arrests, interruptions, blocks: 'the impurity of the Idea is always tied to the passing of an immobility or to the immobility of a passage' (*HI* 88). Essentially bound to movement, and therefore constantly dragged out of art, *cinema is nonetheless characterised by a movement of immobilisation, which is constantly negated by the impurity of its own forms.* A twofold 'false movement' that, on the one hand, is composed by a series of acts of interruptions of the movements of the present, and, on the other, is constantly doomed to ephemerality.

In this sense one sees how the Godardian technique of 'dirty sound' – which Badiou reads as an attempt at a formal purification of the permanent rhythmic background that accompanies every activity – is obtained by producing an 'adulterated murmur', and hence an intensification of sounds (*Cin* 140). Or again, one sees how the use of long car sequences in Abbas Kiarostami's *Taste of Cherry* turns the typical Hollywood imaginary of speed and uninterrupted action into a sign of slowness, 'constraining what is an exteriority of movement to become a form of reflexive or dialogic interiority' (ibid.), and does so by reintrojecting this turned sense within the very imaginary of which it is an interruption. Or again, one sees how the re-articulation of the ideological injunction to exhibit sexualised bodies in the abstract pornographic scenes of Godard's *Sauve qui peut (la vie)* (English title *Every man for himself*) does not turn away from pornography, but rather reinjects the latter's interruption into the pornographic exhibition of bodies. It can thus be said that cinema's thwarted movement is based on ephemeral acts of interruption, acts that interrupt the movement and order of a situation only by constantly falling back into it. But this constant falling or failure both provides the place, constantly subtracting itself from art, for a subtractive relation between arts, and constantly re-inscribes this subtractive activity within the very situation from which art marks its own distance.

COMMUNISM

Frank Ruda

'Communism' may be considered one of the concepts – obviously not invented by Badiou – that has brought Badiou the most fame and the most criticism. It stands, however, as one of the most consistent points of reference right throughout Badiou's work. To illustrate the role it plays in the several stages of Badiou's work – and leaving aside too much in the way of biographical historicisation – one can distinguish four concepts in Badiou's work, listed here in terms of their chronological order of appearance: first, *communist invariants*, followed by *periodisation*, which is more historically inflected, and finally the *communist hypothesis* and its historical sequences, which comes to be supplemented by the *idea of communism*.

The concept of communist invariants, which first appears in the phrase 'ideological communist invariants' in *TC* (1975: in *AR* 76), is given its first systematic treatment in *DI*. The basic idea behind this concept is that any true emancipatory politics that interrupts and breaks with given, predominant regimes of oppression follows some sort of fundamentally invariant logic. This is what makes it possible, Badiou argues, to see that the revolutionary stance taken by Thomas Münzer, for example, had something of a communist nature, because he also aimed at 'the disparition of class-society, the end of private property and at the withering away of the state. This is a matter of an energetic egalitarian doctrine . . .' (TC/*AR* 143). Early on Badiou saw in the peasant-revolution, whose main figure Münzer was, a communist type of attempted revolution. Communist invariants are precisely invariants that align all the great popular revolts of history. Yet the precise character of the popular revolts has a specific character of its own: (1) The struggle of the oppressed is in some sense formally bound to the dominant ideology (in Münzer's case to Christian religion), because it seeks to perform a specific kind of torsion of, and within, the dominant ideology itself: the struggle emerges when it becomes clear that the dominant ideology simply cannot maintain its own standards; (2) on the level of content, the popular struggle has clear communist and invariant goals – the overcoming of exploitation and domination, and hence the end of oppression; and (3) in its historical reality, the popular struggle articulates and realises revolutionary ideas in an always specific form, such that they can become the guiding principles of emancipatory struggle. Communist invariants delineate the transition from one type of oppressive order to a new kind of order. From a classical Marxist perspective this transition also implies a period of transition, something famously articulated under the label of dictatorship of the proletariat. At the heart of all popular revolts throughout, communist invariants are at work when they articulate the forward movement of the masses – and Badiou always insists that there can be no communist content without a reference to the masses – and simultaneously allow for the anticipation of their own realisation. The struggle against oppression driving the masses enables the anticipation of an end to oppression. The invariants affirmatively help to project such a future, yet, as the driving force of the masses; they are simultaneously what make it possible to generate the very conditions of possibility of this future. Communist invariants are a paradoxical entity, because they are self-belonging: they enable that which they will have been. And as this is the precise definition Badiou gives to the concept of event, we can see that the historical emergence of communist invariants will later come to define a political event.

   In short, communist invariants are communist because they can be fulfilled only through an egalitarian reference to the masses, where egalitarian means that all are equal with regard to their political choices and are not referred back to their social positions. And they are invariant because all popular movements in history have the same aim: an end to oppression. The invariant aspects that any emancipatory, and hence communist, movement involves can be more accurately detailed as follows. They always contain: (1) a dimension of the will in which freedom is affirmed against the necessity of the given order of things; (2) a dimension of equality that is opposed to established socio-political or monetary hierarchies; (3) a dimension of confidence wherein the suspicion is overcome that the masses cannot be trusted; and (4) a dimension of authority directed against the allegedly natural free play of competition and exchange (cf. *LW* 27). These dimensions also make up the crucial cornerstones of what Badiou will later refer to as the 'communist hypothesis' (first mentioned in *MS*). It is imperative, first, to clarify the sense in which Badiou has come to refer to communism as a *hypothesis*. For this we are obliged to take a historical detour through the sequences of this communist hypothesis. The idea of an emancipatory politics, of a government of equals over equals, has found different historical articulations. According to Badiou, it received an essentially republican articulation in the eighteenth century – recall Rousseau or Kant within philosophy, and Robespierre or Saint-Just within practical politics; a '"naïvely" communist' one in the nineteenth (*RH* 63) – e.g. Saint-Simon in philosophy or the Paris Commune politically – and a statist-communist one in the twentieth (cf. ibid.). In the first two historical epochs, the idea first emerges that there can be a social and political order aiming at the continual organisation of the impossibility of inequality, i.e. an order in which equals organise themselves as equals. The crucial question linked to these first two articulations is: what concrete form could such an order take?

The first sequence of the communist hypothesis begins for Badiou with the French Revolution and lasts 80 years up until the (72 days of the) Paris Commune. It can be understood as a time marked by the attempt to provide a first formulation of the hypothesis as hypothesis. Here it also becomes clear what the expression 'hypothesis' formally refers to. The hypothesis of communism functions akin to a scientific hypothesis (from where the expression derives). Badiou gives the example of Fermat's theorem in mathematics. This theorem indicates that for the formula n>2 there can be no solution for the formula in the realm of natural whole numbers. Originally formulated in the seventeenth century, Fermat claimed to have proven it, but the proof was not passed on and it was not until Wiles and Taylor in 1995 that it was finally proven. The example shows that, despite taking about 300 years to prove, the hypothesis retained its validity as hypothesis and in the interim inspired many discoveries and instructive experiments. Similarly with the first sequence of the communist hypothesis, during which the communist hypothesis was first formulated as hypothesis, by combining the concrete form of socio-political movements – namely the mass movement that appeared histori-cally, for example, in the guise of revolts, unrest, strikes or protests – with a political idea, namely that to overthrow the state as it was. As a conse-quence, this time was led to believe that the state can only be overthrown by occupying its centre. What renders the first sequence *one* (despite its many different articulations), and gives it internal consistency, is the assumption that the state is defined by its restricting of possibilities (say, of individual freedom, of equality, etc.). Thus, according to the hypoth-esis, all that is required to counter the state is a just regime of equals. The necessary consequence of this definition of the state is that, qua state, it must be destroyed for the truly free action of equals to be attained. The supposed agent of this task, the mass movement, or, more precisely, its organised form in the worker's movement, had already appeared in action on several occasions. Revolution was precisely this: the overcoming of statist restrictions by the mass of workers. In this time, formal operators, i.e. abstract expressions like 'equals', 'organisation', etc., were generated to enable a concrete analysis of concrete historical situations. That analysis demonstrated that the Paris Commune generated two things: first, it gath-ered all the elements for this formulation of the hypothesis (a mass move-ment with a clear worker reference that seeks to abolish the state and set against it another type of organisation); and second, it demonstrated, and in a very concrete manner, the limitations of this assumption, of this con-struction. During the two months of its existence (from 18 March 1871 to 28 May 1871) the Commune was unable to verify the hypothesis of a new organisational format beyond its very limited local territory. The organi-sational model of the Commune functioned in a limited manner (only for the Commune), and was unable to be expanded. A second deficiency also emerged: the Commune was unable to secure itself against the influence and manoeuvring of its enemies, the so-called counter-revolutionary movement.

The second sequence of the communist hypothesis began with the Russian Revolution in 1917 and lasted until the mid-1970s, essentially ending for Badiou with Mao's death in 1976. Its end is marked by the end of the Cultural Revolution, on one side, and by the revolts of May '68, on the other. The crucial question of the second sequence, which also falls under the hypothesis of a just order of equals, is: given the experiences of the Paris Commune, how it is possible to attain victory, and indeed to *remain* victorious? Lenin was among the first to give a practically and theoretically influential answer by endowing a symbolic body to that which linked both sequences. He developed a symbolic body that allowed for tenacity and constancy, as well as for an expansion from the level of the local to the national, but in principle also to that of the international, and was able, moreover, to combat counter-revolutionary tendencies. This symbolic body was the Party. The second sequence was thus constituted with recourse to the unsolved problem of the first, namely in which symbolic and material form it is possible to establish, and in an enduring manner, a just community of equals. The Leninist Party was by all means capable of victory against a weakened power – in Russia against the powers of Tsarism – and even allowed for a national expansion of its model of organisation (and hence for the perpetuation of its acquired power). But it was simultaneously unable to realise precisely what it was supposed to, namely, a form of the exercise of power in which the exercise of power was ultimately abolished as such. This incapacity meant that the Party's exercise of power would become increasingly para-noid. Having acquired state power, the building of the communist party required the establishing of a bureaucratic, authoritarian and terrorist state, in which the idea of a withdrawal of the state was expurgated. In this sense, Stalin's adaption of the revolutionary idea amounted to a sort of defense reaction against the principally universalist kernel of Lenin's politics, but was able to dock on to it precisely because the construction of the second sequence, which consisted in the articulation of 'power', 'state' and 'party', made it possible. Here the specific limitation of the second sequence comes to the fore, which implied a failure (in the attempt not to fail). Even the last result of this sequence – e.g. May '68 and certain historical moments of the Chinese Cultural Revolution – sought to over-come the internal limitations that had led to authoritarian state-terrorism. In this sense the movement of '68 attempted to invent another type of organisation – and Badiou himself was politically very active during this time – that was neither syndicalist, and hence oriented towards political power, nor unified under the banner of the party. But these movements failed, because they proved incapable of breaking with the fundamental combination of 'power', 'state' and 'party'. Recall here Mao's attempts to set the Communist Party against itself and its own bureaucratic tenden-cies by establishing a new relation to the mass movements (of students and peasants). He experimented with the idea of a general transformation of the statist frame and with dissociating its constitutive elements. But the Cultural Revolution in its unfolding would highlight the limitations of such a dialectical attempt to overcome the state by statist means. The attempt from within the party-state to generate a collective organisation that exceeds it, led – contrary to Lenin's understanding of the dictator-ship of the proletariat and even to Stalin's hatred of the peasants – to previously unseen masses of people becoming involved in thinking a new, non-centralised collective form of self-organisation. This attempt did not only generate a significantly new political experience for Badiou but also came with terrific atrocities. This is *inter alia* due to the fact that the attempt of the Cultural Revolution to realise the communist hypothesis entered into a contradictory oscillation between an immanent destruction of the party-state model of organisation, for which constantly new state boundaries had to be found and generated, and the purge of all reactionary tendencies from the party and the state. Hence an infinite swaying was engendered between state destruction and reinforcement, that is, between mass integration and dynamisation of the party-model, on the one hand, and maintaining order and ensuring the bureaucratic stability of the party, on the other. The Cultural Revolution, as much as May '68, failed to prevent the second sequence from failing, and led to a strengthened return – and to a widespread naturalisation – of the state in its existing form (whose central element is the party aiming to take power).

Though all attempts to realise the communist hypothesis have hitherto failed, Badiou argues that this does not invalidate the hypothesis as hypothesis. Take the example of a sick patient visiting a doctor. That the first attempts to cure the patient fail, does not mean that efforts should be abandoned. And if, for Badiou, we are deep in the malaise of capitalism, then we need to search further for possible cures. This implies that thinking emancipation today will bring us closer to the first sequence than to the second – although it is imperative to bear in mind the experiences of the first two sequences. Accordingly, it is necessary to revamp the hypothesis of emancipation, to articulate it in completely new terms that free it from the grip of the party-power-state triad, and avoid ideas of strict military discipline, not to mention bureaucracy and terrorist violence. Attempts to realise the hypothesis to date thus not only yield negative results, but also provide a sharp contour of what must be included in its reformulation. Linking this back to the communist invariants, we see that its most crucial elements are: 1) the egalitarian idea; 2) the conviction that the state as a form of organisation separated from the masses is not necessary; and 3) that the division of labour, which stands at the basis of all social and political division, can be overcome.

If the communist hypothesis requires revamping, it should nevertheless not be conceptually conflated with what Badiou calls the idea of communism. For the latter represents the abstract totalisation of three elements that Badiou formulates with reference to Lacan's well-known triad of the real, the symbolic and the imaginary. In other words, the idea of communism requires a real dimension, i.e. a political procedure emerging from an event that inscribes its own movement in the symbolic, which is to say in a concrete historical situation. Moreover, it can only function properly via an imaginary dimension according to which any individual at all partaking in this procedure – i.e. undergoing subjectification – is able to anticipate the role that this movement will have played in the history of humanity as such. If, for Badiou, communism can thus be considered the only idea of politics, for the idea to be an idea, it needs the effectivity of an actual political procedure. In times – like ours – in which it is lacking, the only recourse possible is a reformulation of the communist hypothesis, a rethinking of emancipation. And as such a reformulation obviously cannot of itself generate a new political procedure – since events cannot simply be produced at will – communism today, for Badiou, is a task for those disciplines of thought that either are able to renew the hypothesis as hypothesis, such as philosophy, or are able to generate new forms, a new imaginary articulation for it, such as art.

COMPOSSIBILITY

Jan Voelker

Compossibility, a notion originally coined by Leibniz, refers to the possibility of thinking truths in their singularity without giving up the 'unity of thought' (*CS* 11). 'Philosophy', Badiou writes, 'sets out to think its time by putting the state of procedures conditioning it into a common place' (*MP* 37). To make truths *compossible* is philosophy's specific procedure, in which it crosses a topological concept with a concept of time, as well as heterogeneity with unity.

Compossibility, firstly, means that philosophy is defined topologically: it is cast as the creation of a *space* in which truths (of love, science, politics, art) are seized. Secondly, this space itself is defined via a special relation to *time*: by thinking the truths, philosophy thinks 'its time'. In addition, the space philosophy creates is a 'common place', which means that it is not only a created place for truths to be seized, but that it also enables the transmissibility of truths and their universal addresses. Philosophy opens a space in which truths are gathered by their names that themselves supplement the events (in the four conditions). Names like 'Mao' or 'Cantor' serve as conceptual space for a truth procedure, and philosophy is nothing other than procedure of '(re)naming' itself (*LW* 521).

As an act of thought, philosophy's claim is not to 'grasp' truths as knowledge; it does not seek to compare and combine supposed substances of real events. Instead, the aim is to think through the common of the differing truths. In so doing, philosophy is first and foremost to be distinguished from sophistry, which, by contrast, targets judgements about the given, or opinions about what happens. Philosophy, however, seeks the abstract constellation of the thoughts of differing truth procedures. Philosophy, in arranging *one* space for truth*s*, pushes the heterogeneous truths to their possible compossibility in thought. Therefore the space of philosophy is not only the space in which philosophy is able to seize truths, indeed the proper act of philosophy consists in the very creation of the space itself. As a practice that creates this singular space, philosophy is at once able to seize truths and, as Badiou puts it, to be astonished by them. The seizure of truths is also a becoming seized by truths, not by the fixed nature of knowledge.

Philosophy thereby attests to the possibility of heterogeneous truths starting from the thought that there are truths. This Badiou also calls the *singular* Truth of philosophy. Philosophy is the space in which the names of truths can be knotted together into one frame, and this one frame marks the unity of thought as an operative, undetermined category and as the Truth of philosophy. As it is nothing other than the compossibility of the truths outside of philosophy, this one Truth is in itself logically void. Philosophy does itself not produce any truth: it can start only from the axiom that 'there is truth'. In *CS*, Badiou further explains that philosophy is a discourse that uses the Truth as 'operational category [. . .] which opens up an active void in thought' (*CS* 23). In it, philosophy imitates its conditions. It combines a 'fiction of knowledge and a fiction of art' in its style of exposition, and acts in the void between these two imitations. The act is 'addressed to all' and in its 'intensity' it resembles 'a love without object' (*CS* 23).

The space of compossibility is thus a difficult construction: a fictious and a real space of a seizure of truths, and as such an act of philosophy. It is a space in thought, submitted to the unity of thought, but it is also a structure of fiction, in which the truths can be rendered compossible. But as this construction is fully dependent on truth procedures taking place outside philosophy, philosophy is only possible if the truth procedures are given. In times when truth procedures are hindered by obscure or reactive subjects, it thus falls to philosophy to work on questions about how a truth procedure can be continued.

Philosophy as a procedure of compossibility is thus bound to the historicity of its conditions, but the relation of compossibilisation to time is twofold: compossibilisation enables a system of periodisation and it periodises ruptures in time, moments of infinity. This means, first, that the philosophical conjuncture of truths creates a configuration of ruptures in time, and, second, that under the predominance of one condition, 'regime[s] of compossibility' (*MP* 44) can be distinguished. For example, a Platonic period of philosophy is characterised by the rupture of the matheme in thought, and therefore this period is dominated by science as a condition. Other periods might be characterised by the 'invariance' of a theme, such as in the modern period in which the 'theme of the subject' (*MP* 43) is predominant and operates by subsuming several constellations regardless of the condition most strongly at work in them.

As philosophy does not follow the encyclopedic interest in knowledge, but rather thinks truths, defined as that which produce 'hole(s) in knowledge' (37), the periodisation periodises ruptures. Truths being essentially subjective, we can say that philosophy periodises subjective ruptures in the objective constitution of appearances and compossibilises them. For Badiou, these ruptures are moments of eternity in concrete situations. Philosophy is bound to the historicity of its conditions, but seizes the moments of infinity that emerge in them. It is thus subtracted from time and creates a space of timelessness, in which moments are simultaneously eternal, as they can be regained by thought at any point.

Compossibilisation as the procedure of philosophy therefore determines philosophy as always coming after the event and as the thought of subjective truths. It is in this sense that philosophy for Badiou, here following Althusser's lead, has no object: there is no philosophy *of* love, politics, science or art in general. It is a space that makes breaks with time, or moments of unbinding, compossible. Through compossibilisation philosophy completes its strictly egalitarian aim: all truths are shown to be equal to one another, and as moments of unbinding they are each determined by the concrete situations in which they emerge and are formally describable. As such, they are proven by philosophy to be singular moments of infinity, accessible for all.

CONDITIONS

Justin Clemens

This concept is one of the most important in all Badiou's work, and is integral in Badiou's own 'becoming-Badiou'. Absent from his early writings, up to and including *TS*, it is finally given its canonical form following *BE* in the entire sequence of publications to the present, including the eponymous *Conditions*. For Badiou, philosophy is not an independent discourse, but requires an 'outside' for its own taking-place. The conditions constitute this outside. These conditions are the 'truth procedures' or 'generic extensions' that are science, art, politics and love. All and only these procedures are the necessary and sufficient conditions for philosophy, and have been so since Plato's establishment of philosophy. Each of these procedures thinks, and thinks in its own way, irreducible to the others; moreover, if one of them is inactive or missing from presentation, then philosophy itself becomes impossible.

The consequences for philosophy are extreme. The conditions actively produce truths, but philosophy is not itself a truth procedure. The conditions are 'truths' insofar as they are self-authorising, self-problematising, self-limiting, and self-sustaining processes. They are self-authorising because they cannot be determined in or from the situation in which they arise; indeed, they give themselves their own 'laws'. They are self-problematising insofar as, in accordance with the previous feature, they set themselves their own problems, which may then come to problematise the aforementioned laws. They are self-limiting insofar as they are, first, only involved with their own particular problems and, second, come to formalise their own limits as an integral part of their operations. Finally, they are self-sustaining, insofar as they are indefinitely extendible, insofar as they continue to be 'creative' in their own terms.

Yet the conditions can only accomplish these insofar as they 'subtract' themselves from the existing laws of a situation. For this to happen, they have something 'anonymous' about them. More technically speaking, such truths are considered to be 'generic', because the above features are formalised by Badiou using Paul Cohen's theory of forcing. This theory, as Badiou puts it in *LW*, holds that a 'generic part is identical to the whole situation in the following sense: the elements of this part – the components of a truth – have their being, or their belonging to the situation, as their only assignable property' (*LW* 36). It is precisely for this reason, too, that the truths can be rigorously thought of as at once singular (linked to a particular situation) *and* universal (they present the universality of their situation in their evasion of any predicate). Such truths are, moreover, *necessarily infinite*.

Philosophy itself is not a truth, precisely because it is not a self-authorising discourse. Rather, it is entirely authorised by its conditions – if by nothing else. If philosophy is not truth, what, then, does it do? Philosophy ensures the 'compossibility' of its conditions by constructing a new articulation of them; the category of 'Truth' is employed by philosophy to precisely this end. 'Truth' has at least a double significance. First, it is essentially 'empty', having no proper content as such (its 'content' is given entirely by its conditions); second, it is the 'seizure' or articulation of the truths in such a way as to expose their non-reductive unity. This is what philosophy, and only philosophy, does and can do. Badiou therefore can speak of *truths*, lower-case, plural, as the conditions of philosophy; and Truth, capitalised, singular, as the philosophical identification, articulation and affirmation of these conditions as compossible together. Truth is the syntax of truths. In doing so, philosophy simultaneously constructs a 'humanity function', an affirmative, non-humanist conception of what humans are capable of (see *CS*, esp. 195–8). In Badiou's own philosophy, a subject is thought of as a *punctuation within* and as a *result of* a particular truth process.

If all philosophies require these conditions, for Badiou, philosophies are also singularised by *what* they take from their conditions, and the specific *relations* that a philosophy forges between these conditions. For Badiou himself, what he takes from 'science' as a general condition is pure mathematics; from pure mathematics, he takes set theory; from set theory, a particular variant known as Zermelo–Fraenkel with Choice (ZFC); he takes ZFC to provide a contemporary ontology. From 'art', Badiou takes poetry; from poetry, he takes above all Stéphane Mallarmé (supplemented, in subsequent works, by Fernando Pessoa); from Mallarmé the revolutionary poem *Un coup de dés*; he takes *Un coup de dés* as providing the contemporary matrix of the event. Regarding politics, Badiou takes revolutionary politics as a paradigm; from revolutionary politics, above all the problematic of post-Maoism; post-Maoism entails the final separation of political militancy from the state. Regarding love, Badiou relies on psychoanalysis; from psychoanalysis, he takes above all Lacan's work; from Lacan, the recognition that love is ultimately a work of non-relation on the basis of an encounter.

It is therefore crucial to understand that, when Badiou speaks of philosophy's being 'on condition', this is not a mere *façon de parler*. On the contrary, we can see how Badiou systematically derives his philosophy from these conditions, in which mathematics = ontology, poetry gives the matrix of the event, politics entails universal emancipation without the state, and love is a continuing work of non-relation. Yet philosophy does this with a certain impassivity in regards to its conditions. In Badiou's own words, the philosophical task is to:

– envisage love solely according to the truth that hatches on the Two of sexuation, and on the Two *tout court*; but without the tension of pleasure–displeasure kept in play by the love-object
– envisage politics as truth of the infinite of collective situations, as a treatment in truth of this infinite, but without the enthusiasm or sublimity of these situations themselves
– envisage mathematics as a truth of multiple-being in and through the letter, as a power of literalisation, but without the intellectual beatitude of the resolved problem
– and finally, envisage the poem as a truth of sensible presence lodged in rhythm and image, but without the corporeal captation of rhythm and image. (*CS* 44)

Moreover, this particular configuration does not mean that Badiou does not or cannot discuss other forms of science, art, love or politics – only that he always does so *on the basis of this fundamental conditioning*. There is thus a radical self-disciplining demanded of philosophy on the basis of the conditions: once the fundamental decisions vis-à-vis conditioning have been philosophically made, then certain new problems open up, as certain other avenues of inquiry are necessarily shut down. This is, once again, why philosophy is not and cannot be totalising, and isn't so all the way down; if there is no 'whole' to think, there are also irreparable *divisions* within the parts of immanence available to philosophy that it cannot reconcile without falling into inconsistency. Yet – and this is another great counter-intuitive discovery of Badiou's that he rigorously derives as a result of his own conditioning by set theory – such singularisation, such limitation and partiality, is not an index of finitude, but of infinity, of infinite infinities!

This is where it becomes necessary to underline the accompanying motifs of contingency, decision, *polemos*, and fidelity, which in Badiou's work are argumentatively inseparable from and coherent with the concept of conditions. Every truth process begins with an event, and proceeds haphazardly within its situation, giving it a triple contingency: that an event takes place at all; that a subject decides for and supports the consequences of an event; that there is a necessarily contingent and 'disorderly' nature to the trajectory of the inquiries that a subject makes within its situation. Badiou, in various places, therefore examines the specific historicity of the conditions, the vicissitudes of their rivalry and function (see esp. *M*, *HI* and *TO*).

One can see how Badiou also treats other philosophers on the basis of their own conditioning. Gilles Deleuze is repeatedly acknowledged by Badiou as his primary contemporary *philosophical* interlocutor. Yet Badiou does so, as always, with the problematic of conditions foremost. If, for Badiou, the ontological paradigm is mathematics, Deleuze's is clearly the biological; if Badiou professes the non-sensible, separated constellations of Mallarmé in order to think the event, Deleuze prefers an implicative 'logic of sensation' that can be derived variously from Proust's *À la recherche*, Francis Bacon's paintings, or the cinema itself; if Badiou's politics is that of post-revolutionary activism, Deleuze's is that of imperceptible ethical becomings; if Badiou takes Lacan's Two seriously, Deleuze affirms diverging schizoid foldings. There is thus a real, irresolvable and serious antagonism between the two philosophies, one that must be relentlessly pursued, at least in accordance with one fundamental element of philosophical ethics. These brief remarks hardly exhaust the role of intra-philosophical engagement, but gesture towards just how much weight Badiou places on the conditions, and how he relies on them at all levels of his thought.

It is also necessary to note certain other philosophical interlocutors Badiou implicitly addresses regarding the genealogy of the concept of conditions. The most influential philosophical formulation of the concept of 'condition' is that of Immanuel Kant's. In his *Critique of Pure Reason* (1781; second edn, 1788), Kant famously poses the question of 'how is synthetic knowledge a priori possible?' It is usually accepted that part of Kant's achievement is to have made a new and rigorous distinction between two terms used relatively equivalently in medieval Scholastic philosophy, the *transcendent* and the *transcendental*. Kant redefines the transcendent as whatever exceeds *any possible experience*; the transcendental is rather what *makes possible experience in general*. For Kant, the conditions are always conditions of possible experience because, in his terms, we can only ever know representations (forms of appearing), not the thing-in-itself, which can never become an object of knowledge in its own right. Kant thereby supercharges the Cartesian placement of the subject at the centre of thought, by literally 'saving the appearances' as regulated by invariant functions of pure reason.

Badiou's own concept of conditions therefore picks up the Kantian reference, in order to overturn and extend it. Badiou retains the sense of 'conditions of possibility' crucial to Kant's transcendental idealism, but explicitly re-articulates the terms of the relation between a subject and its knowledges. Indeed, it is Kant who is invoked at the very opening of *BE*, and precisely in a context in which Badiou is drawing the immediate consequences of his own equation, mathematics = ontology: 'In a reversal of the Kantian question, it was no longer a matter of asking: "How is pure mathematics possible?" and responding: thanks to a transcendental subject. Rather: pure mathematics being the science of being, how is a subject possible?' (*BE* 5–6). As Badiou explains later in *BE*: 'Kant finds this foundation [of quantity] in the transcendental potentiality of time and space, whilst we are attempting to mathematically think multiple-presentation *irrespective* of time [. . .] and space' (*BE* 265). So Badiou's response is, as aforementioned, that the subject itself is a moment in a truth process – and therefore not a register of experience, a category of morality, an ideological fiction, a structural recurrence, etc. (cf. *LW*, esp. Book 1) – and this process is necessarily 'subtractive', i.e. evades the existing structures of knowledge.

Moreover, we immediately have to add that Badiou's truths are, unlike Kant's categorical imperative, absolutely situational and immanent (as opposed to absolutely formal) as well as being non-judgemental (in the juridical sense at least). Finally, Badiou's conditions are themselves integrally engaged in the production of novelty; precisely the opposite is the case *chez* (one dominant strand in) Kant, for whom, in the ordinary course of their functioning, the faculties are essentially liable to overflow their own proper bounds, and fall into error. This is the police function of Kantian critique, identifying 'subreptions' in the common deployment of reason, at once showing that the possibility of such subreptions is irreducible given the constitution of the subject, but also that they can be apprehended and corrected with the appropriate speculative vigilance. For Badiou, in contrast, the new knowledges produced in the contingent becoming of a truth process cannot be anticipated, apprehended or authorised by any existing logic.

But if *BE* effected this uptake and critique of the Kantian transcendental conditions at the speculative crossing of being and the subject, *LW* involves a different kind of return to Kant, who, as Badiou puts it, gave the decisive modern philosophical impetus to the thinking of objects. Now the problematic of the 'transcendental' returns explicitly, and in direct confrontation with Kant: 'Kant is without doubt the creator in philosophy of the notion of object' (*LW* 231). Badiou even provides an illuminating table of comparisons (*LW* 233):

KANT	BADIOU
Possible experience	Possible world
Unity of self-consciousness	Structural unity of the transcendental of a world
Transcendental object = x	General (or logical) form of the objectivity of appearing
Synthetic unity	Postulate of the real one (of atoms)
Empirical object	Unity of appearing in an actual world

As in *BE*, the conditions remain operative, but are in *LW* reconsidered at the level of the transformation of appearances (and not of knowledge-being). If *BE* provided an ontology without objects, *LW* provides a phenomenology without subjects. Badiou's explicit aim in the latter tome is to produce a new theory of the object and objectivity, which relies integrally upon the logics of post-WWII category theory. Yet Badiou does this in order to be able to *reintroduce* an account of the subject within appearing itself. This, as he puts it, is to 'subordinate the logic of appearing, objects and worlds to the transworldly affirmation of subjects faithful to a truth' (*LW* 37). Badiou thereby splits 'condition' (generic truths) from the 'transcendental' (logic of worlds).

It is therefore the concept of conditions that remains – and I predict will remain – primary throughout Badiou's post-*BE* work. It will also undoubtedly be one of Badiou's abiding key contributions to the future of philosophy.

CONSISTENT AND INCONSISTENT MULTIPLICITY

Christopher Norris

The distinction between consistent and inconsistent multiplicity is one that goes to the heart of Badiou's thinking about mathematics in relation to ontology and which therefore has a crucial bearing on all his philosophical, political, artistic, and other main concerns. In fact the default order 'consistent/inconsistent' should really be reversed, since it is axiomatic for Badiou that the inconsistent exceeds, transcends, or numerically surpasses the consistent as a matter of demonstrative (mathematically provable and logically necessary) truth. This truth has been known and incorporated into standard procedures of mathematical reasoning at least since Cantor and the great revolution in thinking about the infinite which came about as a result of his approaching it by way of set-theoretical concepts and methods. These offered a means not only of reckoning with an actual (as distinct from virtual or potential) order of infinity but also of conceiving how there might, indeed must, exist many such orders on a scale of increasing magnitude that rapidly outruns the utmost powers of human intuitive grasp.

Unaided intuition can just about grasp the truth that the infinite sequence of integers (natural or counting numbers) and the infinite series of even numbers must be infinites of a different cardinality or 'size'. Yet it quickly runs out of intellectual steam when confronted with the consequence, i.e. the giddying rate of expansion that occurs when set theory is brought to bear on issues of the one and the many that have puzzled philosophers from the Pre-Socratics, Plato and Aristotle down. These thinkers retreated in the face of what they saw as the inherent paradoxicality – the illogical or reason-subverting character – of any idea that infinity might truly (as distinct from just notionally) surpass the best powers of human calculation. However, that conclusion is strictly inescapable, Badiou contends, if we follow through with adequate rigour on Cantor's inaugural insight and understand what that entails for our thinking about issues both within and beyond the mathematical domain. Some idea of those further implications can be gained by considering Cantor's concept of the power-set, i.e. the set of every possible combination (subset) of members, elements, or constituent multiples within some parent set. The power-set will have a size that very quickly exceeds that of the parent set by a huge margin, and which of course outstrips any possible finite calculation as soon as the parent set includes infinite multiples.

Badiou makes this point partly by demonstrative (axiomatic-deductive) reasoning from first principles and partly, in some of the 'historical' inter-texts that punctuate *BE*, through a detailed critical-diagnostic account of how various philosophers, starting with Plato, have run into logical and conceptual problems through their insistence on treating the one as prior to the many. Only with the advent of Cantorian set theory and its techniques for 'turning paradox into concept' – that is, its way of positing the infinite as a starting-point and basis for calculation rather than a vaguely grasped *ne plus ultra* – did this legacy of philosophic baf-flement at last give way to a mathematically precise means of coping with the issue. It now became possible for mathematicians to reckon with the multiple orders of infinity and (what Badiou takes to be the single most decisive advance) to treat the finite as a special case or limiting instance of an otherwise open-ended multiplicity of infinites. On the other hand, he insists, the Cantorian breakthrough should not be taken as having reduced this wild proliferation of multiples beyond the compass of commonsense-intuitive or (finite) rational grasp to the level of a straightforward manipu-lative method or placidly procedural approach. For it is just Badiou's point that the Cantor-event marked a rupture with any such recuperative strategy since it finally showed – as a matter of formal demonstrative proof – that Plato and his like-minded successors got it wrong. Thus Plato was mistaken in opting for the one over the many, or (what this entails) for consistency over inconsistency, even though he pressed the case with such determination and rigour that his thinking was ultimately led to a stage of aporia – a sticking-point of undecidability – which, however distantly, signalled that event. What pre-Cantorians could not have foreseen was how set-theoretical concepts when deployed in this context, i.e., that of reckonings with the infinite, are such as to reverse the traditional (meta-physically sanctioned) order and establish the precedence of inconsistent over consistent multiplicity.

For Badiou, this rupture has decisive consequences not only in math-ematics and the formal sciences but also in fields – politics among them – that might seem wholly unrelated to such abstract modes of reasoning. Its relevance appears through Badiou's repeated demonstration, in differ-ent historical contexts, of the way that decisive, politically transformative events come about through an unforeseeable irruption of the inconsistent into a social order that had up to then seemed to be consistent with its own (e.g. liberal-democratic) principles or to fully contain and represent all the multiples that fell within its proper domain. The state operates through a second-order count of the 'count-as-one', that is to say, a supplementary count that steadfastly ignores (as Plato tried to ignore) the existence of the void – or the null set – as that which both subtends and constantly disrupts or destabilises any appearance of consistent multiplicity. Such is the reckoning imposed by a dominant, state-sponsored conception of social membership, civic identity, legitimate status, or (in the worst case) ethnic or racial belonging that pre-emptively excludes certain parts of the populace – like the *sans-papiers*, or mainly North African immigrant workers without documentation – but which may, at certain times, be brought flat up against the truth of that exclusion and thereby find itself thrown into crisis. Such challenges arise at 'evental sites' where some discrepant multiple is suddenly the locus of intensive activity. At first – as in periods of pre-revolutionary ferment – that activity is directed mainly towards quelling the disturbance and restoring the 'legitimate', pre-existent order. However, it may then be turned around and exerted to all the more powerfully disruptive effect by those same recalcitrant, fractious or anomalous multiples if and when they arrive at the critical point of inducing major perturbations throughout the system. These can take the form of unresolved paradoxes of the kind that have driven so many signal advances in set-theoretical thought, among them Cantor's inaugural discovery and – equally important for Badiou – Paul Cohen's concepts of 'forcing' and 'the generic' as a means of explaining how it is (as Plato framed the question in his dialogue the *Meno*) that thought can on occasion achieve such extraordinary leaps beyond anything remotely prefigured in some previous state of knowledge. Or again, they might be manifest as symptoms of minority disquiet or unrest which then, at a certain stage in the process of socially driven intensification, turn out to have heralded a major crisis in the current, ideologically sanctioned political status quo.

This latter possibility exists only insofar as the excluded, marginalised or disenfranchised group – paradigmatically the *sans-papiers* – can undergo the radical change of status vis-à-vis that political order which makes of it a visible anomaly, an 'excrescence' disregarded or passed over by the dominant count-as-one. It thus becomes a chief focus for activists opposed to all those other instances of social injustice or political oppression that had likewise remained very largely invisible owing to that same prevalent conception of what/who should properly, legitimately count as a member-multiple in good standing. This is in turn made possible – unlikely as the claim might seem – only by a cardinal truth of mathematics that Cantor was the first to enunciate clearly and that has since been the motor of every main development in set-theoretical thought, namely the priority of inconsistent over consistent multiplicity. That axiom is therefore the precondition for everything that Badiou has to say concerning the relationship of being and event. For an event is precisely what comes to pass whenever some existing ontology – mathematical, scientific, social, or political – is brought up against the limits of its power to contain and suppress that which exceeds its representational or calculative grasp.

DECISION

Dimitra Panopoulos

Decision of existence

The concept of decision applies to all four generic procedures, but holds together two dimensions that seem most remote from one another. For the militant or activist dimension of decision must, to be fully grasped, be thought on the basis of what it enables in mathematics. That is to say, with a demonstrative rigour inspired by this discipline, decision relates fidelity to duration and to the regulated consistency of the chain of consequences, as well as to the explanation of principles, premises, hypotheses, and rules of consecution. In Badiou's words: 'On the one hand, mathematics, grasped philosophically, is without a doubt tied to the question of being, from the moment thought is no longer battling against the opacity of experience, but is visibly freed from the constraints of finitude. On the other, however, it is certain that mathematics is paradigmatic in that which concerns rational sequences, consecutions, proofs. And that, in a broad sense, its logical value is eminent. This is so much so that mathematics really is distributed, in regard to the construction of the philosophical site, in the double register of decision as to the thought of being, and the formal consistency of arguments' (*PAL* 69, in Salanskis and Panza 1995).

Decision, in Badiou, does not bear on the assertion of a definitional content, but instead on a hypothesis whose validation through consequences provides a measure as to the intelligibility on which it depends and the possibility that it can be shared.

For a decision applies only if, through a subjective conviction, proofs can be produced as to the effectiveness of consequences able to be shared. Here, that which is minimally the case in love, in which a decision can only be that of a 'two', goes all the more for mathematics, politics and even art.

So, the notion of decision in Badiou, as subjective, cannot be reduced to the Sartrean existentialist conception. And yet it remains that every decision engages the existence of the one who pursues its consequences, and who posits that the object of that decision exists rather than not. Likewise with the concept of number, as Badiou argues in his book on transitory ontology (cf. *TO*). Indeed, a decision is what enables us to account for the diagonal of the square, a length that geometrical resources can construct but that Pythagorean arithmetic is unable to measure. The former consti- tutes a proportional approach that, incommensurable according to unity, is nonetheless able to enter into the equalities proposed by Eudoxus's theory of proportions, which gives rise to the following question: 'Is it necessary to bring into existence numbers whose principle is no longer the composition of units?' (*TO* 5; tm). The same, Badiou shows, holds for the decision on the infinite: 'This is because the infinite is broadly subtracted from constructive and algorithmic checks and balances. The infinite is decided' (104).

Far from being a simple contemplation of the idealities of Being, the Platonic orientation is defined as a capacity to decide on an existence: Platonism is the recognition of mathematics as a thought that is intransitive to sensible and linguistic experience, and that is dependent on a decision which makes space for the undecidable, while assuming that everything consistent exists (91). And, in a more general way, Badiou argues that 'Mathematical questions of existence refer only to the intelligible consist- ency of what is thought. Existence here must be considered as an intrinsic determination of effective thought, to the extent that it envelops being. That it does not envelop it is always attested by an inconsistency, which must be carefully distinguished from an undecidability. Being, thought and consistency are, in mathematics, one and the same thing' (PAL 66).

Immanent decision

This idea of decision ought to be related to that which can be qualified as decision in the order proper to philosophy in general, and in Badiou's philosophy in particular: a decision on the not-All (*cf.* the demonstration in *LW* 153ff), and on the multiple character of Being qua being, a decision redoubled by the statement according to which mathematics is ontology. Consequences ensue from this depending on whether one decides to adopt the hypothesis of set theory, or to adopt the hypothesis of category theory.

Badiou's philosophy involves inaugural decisions that ought also to be reinscribed as ways of putting forward a certain idea about what a Platonic philosopher is able to propose for present times. Indeed, such a philoso- phy will, *concerning its aim*, be essentially bound to reconnecting with ideas of truth and of justice – i.e. with a *decision on the possible* at the point of the real and of the supposed impossible – and, *concerning its method*, involve requirements of maximum intelligibility – a *decision on what is able to be thought* as such. However, the real meaning of the dialectical inspiration that Badiou gets from Plato is not about the contemplation of separate and transcendent mathematical idealities: 'the theme of Platonism consists precisely in rendering immanence and transcendence indiscernible. It seeks to settle in a thinking space where this distinction is inoperative [. . .] Plato is not interested in the status of the purported mathematical "objects", but in the movement of thought. That is because mathematics is summoned in the end only to identify dialectics by means of difference. Well, in the thinkable, everything is Idea' (*TO* 90; tm).

Generic decision

All decision carries with it an orientation of thought, which is to be understood in a reflexive modality: decisions lay at the origin of divergent orientations of thought. However, all decisions issue from within a similar conception of thought, which is that thought exists in the sense that it touches the real of Being qua being. As Badiou puts it, 'To my mind, it is wrong to say that two different orientations prescribe two different mathematics, or two different thoughts. It is within a single thought that the orientations clash. Not one classical mathematician has ever cast doubt upon the recognisable mathematicity of intuitionistic mathematics. In either case, it is a question of a fundamental identity between thought and being' (*TO* 54; tm).

Decision of method

Decision, insofar as it fixes an orientation of thought, bears on its different aspects, indivisibly, and 'extends not only to foundational assertions or to axioms, but also to proof protocols, as soon as their stakes are existential' (54; tm).

In this regard, a decision taken on which method to adopt for thinking is already internal to an orientation of thought. As Badiou expresses the point: 'Are we willing to grant, for example, that existence can be asserted based on the sole hypothesis that inexistence leads to a logical dead end? This is the spirit of indirect proofs, or reasoning ad absurdum. Granting it or not pertains, exemplarily, to an orientation in thought: a classical one if we grant it, an intuitionist one if we do not. The decision has to do with what thought determines in itself as a path of access to what it declares to exist. The way taken toward existence concentrates the discursive course' (ibid., tm).

From voluntarism to immanence

This gives us a conception of truth, then, that is under the condition of what is declared to exist: decision here is that which seems obliged to expose truth to the spinning wheel of the arbitrary. *LW's* reconfiguration of *BE* has the resolution of this problem as a central stake (whereby the theory of points in the former in part breaks with the theory of forcing presented in the latter).

In *BE* and in *CS*, Badiou's notion of decision seems still to presuppose a pure voluntarism. It appears to leave precisely no room for any unconscious, whether individual or collective. The question of knowing *who* decides is thus not entirely clear, since this decision is not the fact of an unconscious, bar perhaps that of the situation such that it decides in me and that I am who I am inasmuch as I have the courage to take this decision.

But in addition to the question of who decides, there is that of knowing from where the acceptance for such a power comes; for if the subject does not create the event, in which sense is it a subject? And if it is acted upon by the situation, then what is meant by decision?

In *BE*, decision still takes the form of a wager: the subject forces the decision, and it is said, in the time of the future anterior, that this decision will have been veridical if its consequences prove consistent.

However, the voluntarism that this implies leads to a new form of immanence. Badiou is thus fully aware '[t]hat mathematics is a thought means in particular that, with respect to it, the distinction of a knowing subject and a known object has no pertinence. There is a regulated movement of thought, coextensive to the being it embodies – a coextension that Plato names " Idea." It is a movement wherein discovery and invention are properly indiscernible, in the same way in which the idea and its ideatum are indiscernible' (*TO* 94).

And nevertheless, as he shows, this movement of envelopment maintains the properly dialectical dimension of rupture: 'As for the content of Plato's dialogues, the undecidable also commands the aporetic style of the dialogues: drive us to the point of the undecidable so as to show that thought must, precisely, decide as regards an event of being; that thought is not foremost a description or a construction, but a break (with opinion, with experience) and therefore a decision' (92; tm).

We might say that the paradox of decision is that if it is to be decisive, it must occur in a mode that upholds indiscernibility, indivision, inseparation. Such is exactly what is at stake in the decision on the inseparated in Brecht's play *The Measures Taken*, which Badiou discusses in *C* (cf. Ch. 10, 'Cruelties'). And it similarly participates in the Beckettian motif of being at the point of the black-grey of Being where existence is 'indistinguished' (*CS* 256). Decision thus comes to redouble the question of truth, for there is a further requirement to decide what a truth is a truth of (132). This, as Badiou shows, is the first subtractive dimension of truth: 'All thought – and therefore mathematics – engages decisions (intuitions) from the standpoint of that which is undecidable (or nondeductible)' (*TO* 95; tm). The undecidable is therefore not to be taken in a negative sense: 'It is less a matter of a "limit", as one sometimes says, than of a perpetual prompting to practice inventive intuition [. . .] Mathematics "itself" has to be constantly decided afresh' (94). This is because '[t]he word "intuition" here has no other sense than that of a decision of inventive thinking with respect to the intelligibility of axioms [. . .] Let us note that the intuitive function does not work to grasp "external" entities, but to decide clearly on a first or irreducible proposition. The comprehensive invention of axioms is what vouches for the mathematical proposition as thought and, consequently, exposes it to the truth' (93).

To initiate, to continue

In this, another dimension of decision finds itself strengthened. This dimension concerns that which assigns it to two aspects of one and the same truth procedure, namely the capacity to initiate, and the resource of its continuation.

Just as it does in Sartre, decision in Badiou's sense bears on existence. The whole question here is to understand why it seems to border on decisionism more than on existentialism. The reason is the axiomatic dimension, which forms a real point of rupture with what existentialism still concedes to phenomenology. Thus says Badiou, 'Why must one always decide as to what exists? For the whole point is that existence is in no way the first donation. Existence is precisely being itself, inasmuch as thought decides it. And that decision essentially directs thought [according to] three major orientations [. . .] able to be simultaneously identified in moments of mathematical crisis and just as well in times of conceptual reshuffling within philosophy itself. These orientations are the constructivist, transcendent and generic orientations' (PAL 55; tm).

The concept of decision Badiou thus explains as follows: 'The [generic orientation] posits that existence is without norm, save for discursive consistency. It privileges indefinite zones, multiples subtracted from all predicative recollection, points of excess and subtractive donations' (ibid.).

The conception of decision Badiou endorses here leans towards decisionism to the extent that it puts forward for agreement something that by definition escapes the consensual framework of the norm. Decision does not result from a point of view, interpretation or opinion, nor can disagreement be an object of debate, properly speaking. As Badiou writes, 'No serious quarrel between pronouncements of thought contrasts interpretations over some existence recognised by all. In fact the opposite is true: agreement is not reached on existence itself, since that there is what was decided' (56; tm). It is the generic orientation that provides the measure of the radicality of modern philosophy, which recognises itself in this first act: 'subtract the examination of truths from the simple form of judgement. This always means: decide (for) an ontology of multiplicities' (62).

Nevertheless, concerning the thought of decision, what differs or varies between *BE* and *LW* concerns more than a shift of emphasis. While the former considers the resources of a subject of decision, the latter aims simultaneously to characterise a situation in which a decision comes to be inscribed and on which it sheds light.

A decision is a decision about existence from the inside of a given world: it is not a decision on an alternative in the form of either one thing or another, but in the form of either this thing or not this thing. It is a decision in the strong philosophical sense, then, if we admit in Leibnizian terms that philosophy decides that there is something rather than nothing. Opting for nothing is not an absence of decision. It may be that it is of little consequence if inscribed in a certain world, but it does not result from an absence of decision. There is no neutrality that does not consent to an orientation, whether or not this is conscious and made explicit.

Thus can we grasp the fact that decision, for Badiou, is not about a figure of subjectivation that can simply sublimate the ordinary into the extraordinary. For if it is claimed that there is no decision to be made, then a decision is made for a nihilistic figure of the given world. This is because one is either in the element of a decision according to which there are truths or, on the contrary, in the element of a decision for which 'there are only bodies and languages', according to the maxim put forward in *LW* to identify what Badiou refers to as democratic materialism.

The decision to be an Immortal, as Badiou puts it forward in *E*, can only be given here in the figure of exception or of subtraction: 'there are only bodies and languages, *except* to understand things in the light of the Platonic dialectic'.

The concept of decision is key when is it a matter of continuing or initi-ating – a motif that governs the distinction between the various sequences of one and the same truth procedure. Between one sequence and the next of a truth, decision sheds light on the fact that it is the same inaugural idea, or principle, or orientation of thought that is at stake, rather than a transition made to something entirely different. It is the same idea but put to the test of another schema, another question. In this way, the concept of decision is able to shed light on unsuspected continuities or on evident ruptures. Take, as an example, the decision, reactivated three centuries after it was first made, to carry out the demonstration of the theorem that Fermat had first hypothesised (*CH* 6). This reactivation involved a decision that it was necessary to take up this hypothesis again, but to do so in line with other requisites, other constraints, other designs: that is what subtends the Beckettian maxim 'You must go on, I can't go on, I'll go on.' This maxim expresses not a simple voluntarism but courage in the face of truth, a courage concerning what truth imposes on the trajectory of thought.

Lastly, that decision cannot be thought on the basis of some donation in the situation is to be understood according to the dialectic put forward in *BE*. Being a matter of the undecidable and of the impossible, what is at issue is to decide on an existence – for to decide to be decisive concerning something that is in itself undecidable is not the whole difficulty. The most important decision lies further upstream still: in the capacity to decide and to declare, at the point of an impossible real, that one must decide on this impossible as on an undecidable. The decision cannot be said to be arbitrary; it takes the form of a wager. But this wager is subordinated to an imperative that forces the subject much more than the subject forces reality to yield to its desire. This is the context in which, in *CS*, Badiou refers to the thematic of continuing proper to Beckett's *Unnamable*: 'This imperative, which is indifferent to all possibility, this terrorist command-ment to have to maintain what cannot be' (261).

Thus conceived, all decision consists in an act whereby it is exempted less from neutrality than from renegation. For to renounce to decide is to renounce the idea that something is able to except itself from the state of the world such as it is governed and ordered according to the logic and the management of interests. And as a decision must be disinterested and addressed in principle to all, it further results that there is no decision that engages only a single individual.

Meta-decision

Here, something like a metaphysics of decision comes into play. This is because decision provides a basis on which it is possible to discern the multiplicity of orientations. From this viewpoint, the generic orienta-tion manifests a privileged status over the others insofar as it yields a conception of decision as a conscious operation of touching the being of that which is thought. By contrast, the other orientations seem only able to accede to a conception of thought as a logical form. This difference, Badiou maintains, is first and foremost given in the opposition between Plato and Aristotle: it is a difference between a relation to the real of a thinking decision, and a more strictly logical decision of thought via the representation of its possibilities:

What counts for a Platonist are the *principles* of rupture. What counts for an Aristotelian are the *protocols* of legitimation. This opposition, applied to the inscription of mathematics in the field of philosophy, gives the following: the Platonist's interest bears entirely on the *axioms*, wherein is decided the thinking decision. The Aristotelian's (or Leibnizien's) interest bears entirely on the *definitions*, wherein is decided the representation of possibles. (*PAL* 68)

However, the generic orientation inherits the specific aporia of the set theory that inspires it, and the structure of not being able to provide reasons for its founding axioms: 'set theory is the example-type of a theory where (axiomatic) decision prevails over (definitional) construction. The Aristotelians of our century have moreover not omitted to object to set theory that it is unable even to define or to elucidate its organic concept, that of set. A remark to which a Platonist such as Gödel will always retort that what counts are the axiomatic intuitions, which constitute a space of truth, and not the logical definition of primitive relations' (70).

A generic orientation, to the extent that it falls under the set-theoretic conception, seems necessarily to be subsumed by the theory of topos or category theory, which returns the set-theoretic conception to being but one of the available logical orientations: 'Topos theory enables the visibility of logical contraints of an ontological option [. . .] Topos theory, which thinks mathematics as logical in *immanent fashion* is certainly unable to claim to *rival* foundational theories. But it arranges these theories in a complete network of possibilities, which permits us to represent decision *as decision*, which means as a singular choice, including as the choice of a logic' (80–1).

This admitted, Badiou argues that the following remains: that by which a thought makes a truth of Being still relates to a decision concerning some existence. 'Moreover, the generic orientation seems to prevail from the fact of its ability to proceed from the possible to its consequences. While in the Aristotelian–Leibnizian constructivist orientation, there is always doubt concerning the use of the actual infinite, a restriction of existential assertions, and a pluralist perspectivism against all assertions of unicity' (cf. 69).

Concerning the concept of decision and mathematics, it is therefore necessary to understand the following: 'At bottom, that mathematics is a thought means foremost that it is not a logic. But it is no less true that there is always a logic of thought. To think mathematics as thought means, from within that thought, to forget logic in favour of a fidelity to decisions' (81).

Translated from the French by Steven Corcoran

DELEUZE

Jon Roffe

Gilles Deleuze (1925–95) is the contemporary philosopher to whom Badiou returns more than any other. His engagement with Deleuze is however neither homogeneous nor unequivocally critical, as it is often thought to be. In short, Deleuze figures in Badiou's work as his pre-eminent philosophical disputant.

Broadly speaking, Badiou's engagement with Deleuze has taken place in three stages.

The first of these – a heavily politically inflected series of rhetorical attacks – ran throughout the late 1970s. During this period, Badiou (in his own name and, on one occasion, under the pseudonym 'Georges Peyrol') attacks Deleuze's work, using what he calls 'the heavy verbal artillery of the epoch' (*DCB* 2), primarily with reference to the texts co-authored with Félix Guattari – above all *Anti-Oedipus* and the short text on rhizomes that would later take the form of the introductory chapter of *A Thousand Plateaus*. At stake for Badiou at this juncture is what he takes as the retrograde political consequences of these texts.

While Deleuze and Guattari appear committed to revolutionary activity, Badiou argues that this is only superficially so. In reality, what underlies the apparent radicalism of the philosophy of desire, flux and novelty found in these works is a commitment to the most conservative moments in the history of western philosophy: a pre-Hegelian investment in the notions of freedom, the autonomous subject, and the Good. In sum, a 'return to Kant, that's what they came up with to exorcise the Hegelian ghost' (FP/*AFP* 79). As a consequence, Badiou presents the approach of desiring-philosophy as entirely irrelevant to contemporary political struggle, adding 'saint Gilles (Deleuze), saint Félix (Guattari)' and 'saint Jean-François (Lyotard)' to Marx's Saint Max (Stirner). For Badiou, their philosophies, committed as they are to 'propulsive desire, evasive flux', to 'the heterogeneous', and to the critique of 'all organisation' and '"totalitarian" Marxist-Leninism', merely repeat 'word for word' the kind of claims that Marx and Engels' *German Ideology* needed to 'tear to pieces' in order to present a cogent revolutionary program (TC/*AR* 61). Finally, and as a result, Deleuze and Guattari's work is not just irrelevant to the political program espoused by Badiou, but deeply hostile to it: despite the rhetoric of revolution – to cite the strongest of Badiou's formulations of the period – 'Deleuze and Guattari are protofascist ideologues' (FP/*AFP* 51).

This bruising textual engagement runs alongside a series of

interruptions of Deleuze's famous seminar at Vincennes by Maoists with whom Badiou was associated, and in fact in *DCB* (2) he even notes that he led one such intervention himself.

By *TS*, however, a shift has taken place, ushering in a second, considered period of sustained engagement with the content of Deleuze's thought. There, Deleuze is presented no longer as an ideologue but rather a philosopher. To be more precise, the commitment to flux and change in Deleuze's work is taken by Badiou to be a philosophically important commitment and not just a bourgeois affectation. In *TS*, Badiou will assert that this commitment to flux, or 'dynamism', is one of the two foundational orientations of materialist thought, but that Deleuze, insofar as he privileges this at the expense of the equally important 'mechanist' hypothesis, fails to attain a rigorous materialism.

In this book, Badiou will also assert three other claims of Deleuze's philosophy. First, he argues that Deleuze's dynamist philosophy commits him, perhaps paradoxically, to a kind of naturalism. Deleuze is, on this account, 'a wandering materialist, a vagabond philosopher of natural substances' (*TS* 209). Second, Badiou argues that, by virtue of the neglect it shows to the mechanist facet of materialism, Deleuze's philosophy hypostasises novelty: it 'follows a perspective of flight. It is a radicalism of novelty. It breaks all mirrors' (*TS* 207). This latter assertion is one that *DCB*, published thirteen years later, will explicitly abandon. However, the third substantial claim made of Deleuze in *TS* remains at the heart of this most important of Badiou's texts on Deleuze: that Deleuzean philosophy is in fact not a theory of multiplicity but the elaboration of radically unified theory of Being. Badiou writes that 'There are others, like Deleuze, who posit the Multiple, which is never more than a semblance since positing the multiple amounts to presupposing the One' (22).

The central moment in Badiou's discussion of Deleuze is in keeping with this – however brief – genuine consideration. *DCB*, as Badiou notes in the first chapter, is the final entry in a long epistolary sequence he undertook with Deleuze between 1991 and 1994, whose purpose was to clarify the differences and coincidences between their respective projects.

The main thesis of *DCB* is infamous. Contrary to 'an image of Deleuze' that sees him as the proponent of 'the heterogeneous multiplicity of desires' (*DCB* 9), Badiou asserts instead that 'Deleuze's fundamental problem is most certainly not to liberate the multiple but to submit thinking to a renewed concept of the one' (11).

It is essential to see that this key text – like Badiou's review of Deleuze's *The Fold*, published in 1989 – is not in the main a *critique* of Deleuze, but an attempt at an *explication* of his position that undoes what Badiou sees as a mendacious and misleading caricature, and a particularly striking attempt to mark out their differences.

The Clamor of Being is tripartite in structure. It begins by asserting the general claim that Deleuze is a thinker of the One, and then this claim is then fleshed out in a characterisation of Deleuze's method. For Badiou, regardless of the topic under investigation (Sacher-Masoch, Leibniz, cinema, differential calculus, etc.), Deleuze always proceeds in the same way: he begins with the particulars of the case, and then moves from this instance to the primordial status of the One qua ground and source. However, this method (which Badiou calls intuition, having recourse in a broad sense to Deleuze's account of intuition in Bergson) is not an external method imposed upon particular cases, but doubles in thought the constitution of reality itself. If Deleuze begins with the action-image in the classic cinema and then thinks it as an indirect time-image, thereby reinstating its connection with the open Whole, it is because this is the ontogenetic structure that underpins the action-image as such. Likewise, if the paintings of Francis Bacon are of interest to Deleuze, it is insofar as their manifestation of the vital One can be so directly and powerfully traced. In place of the demand made by phenomenology to return to the things themselves, for Badiou Deleuze's insistence is to return *by way of things* to the ontological ground on the basis of which they arise. This is the sense in which Badiou's claim that Deleuze is an ascetic thinker must be understood. On his view, Deleuze's method only becomes available to thought by discarding the external impositions that habit imposes upon thinking itself. Finally, taking a series of key concepts in Deleuze's work as his material, Badiou then goes on to show how this methodological structure bound to the aegis of the One and its role in ontogenesis is played out in them. The concepts that Badiou examines – the virtual, the event, truth and thought – are not chosen at random, being the touchstones of Badiou's own work in the circle of publications surrounding and including *BE*: being, event, the subject and truth.

Now, while *DCB* is fundamentally explicatory in nature, it is not slavishly so. On the one hand, Badiou throughout marks his distance from Deleuze as he construes him. As he notes, both the book and his exchange of letters with Deleuze had the aim of getting 'straight to the *sensitive point* at which different conceptual creations separate' (*DCB* 5). The goal therefore is as little to critically dismiss Deleuze's work as it is to unambiguously praise it. Instead, Badiou attempts something like an inclusive disjunctive synthesis, to use a category from Deleuze's *Logic of Sense*: a bringing together of two contrasting positions in order that their differences come to light. On the other hand, Badiou does mount a single important critical argument at Deleuze's thought in *DCB*. While he sees

Deleuze as a thinker fundamentally committed to the One, Badiou argues that Deleuze's philosophy does not itself provide the requisite means to support this commitment itself. Specifically, Badiou argues that the virtual/actual couple stand at the centre of the Deleuzean edifice, but that Deleuze cannot maintain the reality of both the virtual and the actual at the same time: 'The more Deleuze attempts to wrest the virtual from irreality, indetermination, and non-objectivity, the more irreal, indeterminate, and finally non-objective the actual (or beings) becomes' (53). As a result, not only the virtual/actual pair but the entire One-multiple structure of Deleuzean philosophy comes apart on Badiou's account.

In the texts on Deleuze immediately following *DCB*, the sense of a common project pursued in two different fashions itself starts to unravel, and Badiou increasingly comes to insist on an exclusive disjunction between his philosophy and Deleuze's. The differences between the two projects, rather than their closeness, is more strongly emphasised, and the goal of obtaining the sensitive point of divergence is gradually replaced with an external opposition of two blocs of thought. Furthermore, while the genre of these more recent statements remains philosophical, some of the rhetorical flavour of the texts from the seventies begins to return. 'One, Multiple, Multiplicity', Badiou's somewhat bewildered defense and restatement of *DCB*, while beginning '*at the point of greatest proximity*' (*TW* 68) depicts Deleuze's philosophy as a 'natural mysticism' (80) which impoverishes (70) and metaphorises (75) mathematics, and neutralises formal thinking as such by subordinating it to empirical sensibility. Many of these points are also made in 'Deleuze's Vitalist Ontology', another text from the period immediately following *DCB*.

In the chapter devoted to Deleuze in *LW*, titled 'The Event in Deleuze', the disjunctive quality of Badiou's approach is even more evident. He claims there that it is possible to arrive at 'a pretty good good axiomatic for what I call "event"' (384) by inverting Deleuze's philosophy of the event. Most recently of all, in the notes which close his *Pocket Pantheon*, Badiou is to be found presenting the two respective positions in starkly opposing terms: 'I learned to love Deleuze, but from within a controversy that would not die down. At root: Platonism and anti-Platonism' (*PP* 194; tm). This is in keeping with the claim found in *LW* that 'there are only three crucial philosophers: Plato, Descartes and Hegel. Note that it is precisely these three that Deleuze could not bring himself to love' (*LW* 552; tm).

Thus at the end of this lengthy tripartite engagement, there is something of a synthesis achieved between the rejection of Deleuze's philosophy that dominated the first period, and the more considered approach that characterised the second.

DEMOCRACY

Jan Voelker

In a footnote to a text first delivered at a conference on the *Idea of Communism*, Badiou states that it is unclear whether 'the word [democracy] can so easily be salvaged, or, at any rate, I think that making a detour through the Idea of communism is unavoidable' (*CH* 249). This statement illustrates well the dialectical treatment that the concept of democracy finds in Badiou: on the one hand, it is the 'dominant emblem of contemporary political society' (*DE* 6) – i.e. it is a central term of the reigning capitalist ideology – but there is also the 'literal meaning of democracy', namely 'the power of peoples over their own existence' (15), a true meaning which a detour through communism might manage to salvage.

Thus, the word democracy is a split and intricate one, connected to different subjectivities, and it variously sets into play the relation of politics and philosophy. Broadly speaking, Badiou discusses the notion of democracy in three main relations: (a) democracy as a figure of state; (b) democracy as a philosophical notion; and (c) its adjectival use in the notion of *democratic materialism*, which Badiou understands to be a metaphysical axiom of contemporary western societies and thus the dominant ideology.

Democracy as a figure of state

In *CPBT?*, published in French in 1985, Badiou's analysis of the crisis of Marxism uncovers an even more extensive crisis, which is that of the political as such, understood as the sphere of representational state-politics. It is a crisis in which, argues Badiou, democracy and totalitarianism form a couple, inseparable in thought as two techniques of the representational social bond. Democracy refers here to a state form, in which the social bond and the form of representation are merged. In later work (cf. *M*), Badiou furthers this analysis of democracy as a state form through a discussion about whether democracy can be understood as a *philosophical* concept. The problem here is that democracy, according to Lenin's characterisation of it as a state form, seems to contradict the idea of generic communism and the withering away of the state. If philosophy conceives of genuine politics as having generic communism as its aim, then democracy cannot be a concept of philosophy. Based on the Leninist account of democracy, Badiou structures the discussion around three crucial hypotheses, one of which one will have to be abandoned if democracy is to be a concept of philosophy: the first sees the ultimate aim of politics as generic communism; the second outlines philosophy's task as being to make these aims explicit; and the third fixes democracy as a form of the state.

Were the first hypothesis to be abandoned, such that the aim of politics was not generic communism, the discussion would come to turn on the quest for the good or best (least worst) state and its norms. As the state is an 'objectivity without norm', a 'principle of sovereignty, or coercion, functioning separately', such norms are not of the state but are rather applied to it from the outside it as 'a prescription stemming from subjectifiable themes' (*M* 83). Regarding our 'present situation, or the situation of our parliamentary states', Badiou identifies three norms: 'the economy, the national question and, precisely, democracy' (ibid.). Democracy as a norm of state denotes the 'category of *a* politics' (84), establishing a subjective relation to the state. Democracy as a form of state thus presumes a specific subjective prescription related to the separated character of power. By 'form' is meant 'a particular configuration of the separate character of the state and of the formal exercise of sovereignty', where democracy's own form is posited as a 'figure of sovereignty or power' of the people (79). So, the state's main characteristic is the separate nature of its power, and democracy is understood as one form of that separation. However, if philosophy takes generic communism as the aim of politics, the state cannot be a conceptual starting point for grasping politics. The upshot is that democracy can be a concept for philosophy only if politics is thought at a *distance* from the state.

Democracy as a philosophical notion

Relinquishing the second hypothesis, the idea that philosophy is about clarifying the 'generic meaning of the ultimate aim of a politics', opens up two possibilities. The first would involve a reduction of the philosophical task to a 'formal description of instances of politics, their typology' (*M* 85), wherein democracy would again be one specific state form. According to the second, philosophy's proper task, says Badiou, would be to 'grasp politics as a singular activity of thought whose apprehension, within the historico-collective domain, itself provides a form of thought that philosophy must seize as such' (86). But if the state, as an apparatus and instance of separation, 'does not think', then democracy as 'a category of politics as thought' (87) needs to be understood at a distance from it.

Badiou offers two possibilities for how to think through this distance. In the first, democracy is understood as mass democracy, which implicitly means mass-sovereignty, or a sovereignty of the masses. Democracy is here inherently linked with mass dictatorship, a nexus philosophy cannot appropriately grasp 'under the sole concept of democracy', as mass democracy can only be legitimated not in itself but as an anti-statism. Elsewhere, Badiou also underlines that phenomena of revolutionary rupture have 'rather the form of a sudden emergence in history' (*BP* 50). To understand democracy in these terms is to accentuate the moment of event but to leave the question of its consequences in abeyance.

The second involves tying democracy to a dimension of universal prescription. '"Democracy" would be inherently bound to the universality of political prescription, or to its universal capacity, thus establishing a bond between the word "democracy" and politics as such' (*M* 90). But the universality of political prescription is necessarily tied to particular cases, so that 'democracy' comes to designate this specific character of universal prescription in its particular realisations, where the aim is essentially to render impossible statements and practices of inequality. Says Badiou, 'Democracy, as a philosophical category, is that which *presents equality*. Or again, democracy is what prevents any predicates whatsoever from circulating as political articulations, or as categories of politics which formally contradict the idea of equality' (93). Democracy thus articulates the idea that political prescription can prevent the inegalitarian distribution of subsets or identitarian determinations, that it can counteract 'separating names' (*RH* 77, 81): '"Democracy" means that "immigrant", "French", "Arab" and "Jew" cannot be political words lest there be disastrous consequences' (*M* 94).

So, if generic communism is the aim of politics, democracy can become a philosophical notion on the proviso that it is separated from the notion of state. For, otherwise it becomes a question of state politics. Similarly, if philosophy can discern no generic sense in politics, it is reduced to the typological description of state forms. The key contradiction runs between the state and politics as a generic procedure, such that the understanding of democracy depends upon the decision taken from within this contradiction. Badiou thus confirms that from a philosophical viewpoint neither of Lenin's first two hypotheses can be relinquished, but that democracy can be a concept of philosophy only if not conceived as a form of state.

Democracy can acquire a place as a philosophical name for concrete and particular presentations of political prescription. From a strictly philosophical viewpoint, however, this link can also be understood under the concept of justice. In a text called 'The Enigmatic Relationship between Philosophy and Politics' (in *PM*), Badiou takes justice to refer to the intrinsic relation of philosophy to democracy. This inner philosophical constellation, then, ties the three concepts of democracy, politics and philosophy around the notion of *truth*. Philosophy's way of thinking of truth is unique, however, and bears a twofold relation to the question of democracy: first, philosophy is 'a discourse independent of the place occupied by the one who speaks' (*PM* 26). What counts is thus not the symbolic value of the one *who* speaks; but instead *what* is said. Likewise, philosophy, whose address is both universal and independent of the position of enunciation, is also inherently democratic. Second, Badiou argues, philosophy 'opposes the unity and universality of truth to the plurality and relativity of opinions' (28). It therefore does not accept the equivalence of everything *that* is said; as a discourse it follows strict rules and cannot be carried out spontaneously.

So philosophy's objectives cannot be said to follow the principles of democracy. Within its purview, the essential 'characteristics of a valid politics' are rather the 'equality of intelligences' and the 'universality of truth' (28). The 'classical name for this', Badiou continues, is 'justice'. 'Justice means examining any situation from the point of view of an egalitarian norm vindicated as universal' (29). It means placing equality higher than individual freedom, and universality higher than particularity.

Here the 'enigmatic relationship', it becomes clear, concerns not only the presentation of a universalist politics in philosophy, but also implies a conclusion about the philosophical procedure itself. Democracy is not simply a question of politics, but a 'possible means of popular emancipation': it is 'neither a norm nor a law nor an objective' (35). As such, democracy designates a *formal* condition of philosophy and a *real* politics seized by philosophy. The combination of both senses Badiou calls 'communism', which is to say 'the hypothesis of a place of thought where the formal condition of philosophy would itself be sustained by the real condition of the existence of a democratic politics wholly different from the actual democratic State' (36). Democracy in the sense of justice denotes an internally unseparated truth procedure that, instead of denoting a separated form of power (a form of state), separates itself out from any attempt at separation. It is therefore 'much more appropriate to speak of popular *dictatorship* than democracy' (*RH* 59).

This dictatorship is both without any representative separation of power and a firm adversary of the 'impotent democracy' of today, i.e. of democracy as 'servile towards the site of real power – Capital' (40).

Democratic materialism

From the preceding discussion it is evident that Badiou's polemics against 'democracy' aim at the precise figure of democracy as a state form, or *democracy without any relation to a truth procedure*, which is to say he aims at the dominant ideological understanding of the present situation. Badiou identifies democracy as the 'dominant emblem of contemporary political society' (*DE* 6): irrespective of which political agenda one is pursuing, the only necessity is that it fit under the umbrella of democracy. This guarantees that the political agenda does not exceed the ideological frame of our contemporary western political societies. Given this prescription, Badiou argues, 'the only way to make truth out of the world we're living in is to dispel the aura of the word democracy' (7). And in recognising that the emblem's axiom is that 'everyone is democratic', it becomes evident that, qua emblem, democracy splits the world into two: on the one hand, *the world*, that of democracy; and, on the other, a leftover non-world, a 'remnant of life, a zone of war, hunger, walls and delusions' (ibid.). Democracy, it turns out, is ultimately the name of a 'conservative oligarchy' (8). It can thus be said that if democracy in its communist sense separates itself from any attempt of separation, then democracy in its contemporary sense is precisely an act of separation. Democracy is not only about the 'objective space' (ibid.) in which this democracy takes place, but also about the subjective type it produces.

In short, democracy as a figure of state not merely implies but actually is a subjective relation to the state. Here Badiou takes up Plato's criticisms of the 'democratic type' of Athenian democracy – notwithstanding the aristocratic inflection he gives to it – as an 'egoism and desire for petty enjoyments' (ibid.). For Badiou, these criticisms retain two crucial points: '(1) the democratic world isn't really a world; (2) the only thing that constitutes the democratic subject is pleasure or, more precisely, pleasure-seeking behaviour' (9). In this frame, the democratic subject takes on two central characteristics: either 'youthful Dionysian enthusiasm' or 'elderly indifference' (10). Setting out with a wild desire for everything, the democratic subject winds up indifferent thanks to the equivalence of everything it encounters – a total equivalence that gains another form in the 'monetary principle' (ibid.), the rule of which makes perceiving any world impossible, as everything becomes blurred. This democratic non-world turns on anarchic interchangeability, in which the youth predominate, and the aged are apathetic. The youth's predominance is linked to a pure presence and 'indiscipline of time' (13), a 'nihilism' in which today is the same as yesterday and already passes into tomorrow, and in which there is an 'organised death wish' (14). Accordingly, as Badiou puts it in his book on Sarkozy, the 'global perspective of democracy' is 'war' (*MS* 14). As for the question of parliamentarism, it, too, is one form of the equation that reduces everything to equal numbers, which is proof, if any were needed, that contemporary democracy is 'strictly indifferent to any content' and falls under the 'law of numbers, just as the world unified by commodities imposes the monetary law of numbers' (59). This is why, in characterising our contemporary democracies, Badiou speaks of 'capitalo-parliamentarism' (*CH* 99) and of 'parliamentary fetishism' (*MS* 7).

Democratic ideology is wont to oppose to this total equivalence of the order of circulation to the notion of 'totalitarianism', but this latter, Badiou demonstrates, is no more than a 'caricatural reversal' of the former. Instead, what stands opposite this total equivalence is 'creative affirmation' (*DE* 15; tm), which is to say communism (ibid.), or the prescription of equality constituting a truth procedure. Here, communism rejoins the 'literal meaning of democracy [. . .] [as] the power of peoples over their own existence' (ibid.), showing that communism is the true subjective stance for affirming the buried aims of democracy, ever at a distance from the state. The subjective position of communism then becomes the adversary of the contemporary proposition of democracy that produces, via the state form, the total equivalence of everything. Communism is finally the name for 'the historical and negative inscription of politics in history', i.e. the inscription of a politics that draws the consequences of an event and formulates 'democracy as a political subject' (*BP* 51).

Under today's political circumstances, it is not enough simply to point to the different possibilities of the word democracy, as 'this would ultimately put us in a defensive position' (49), rather it is necessary to uphold the affirmative position of communism, if democracy shall find its truth again, beyond the common doxa.

More broadly taken, this adversary, the contemporary doxa, Badiou refers to as '*democratic materialism*' (*LW* 1). Following the 'equation "existence = individual = body"' (2) its only accepted objective existence is that of the finite bodies, bodies and their desires. As these are living bodies, this materialism is a 'bio-materialism' (ibid.). At the same time, this materialism is democratic, because it accepts that these bodies speak a variety of languages and 'presupposes their juridical equality' (ibid.). Democratic materialism's one decisive axiom is thus: 'There are only bodies and languages' (1), such that it has only one 'global halting point for its multiform tolerance' (2), namely that at which the equality of languages (cultures, communities) gets interrupted. Tolerance then switches to the right to intervene in order to stop such 'totalitarian' tendencies. Against the doxa, Badiou prescribes what he calls a '*materialist dialectic*' (3), which again does not consist in swinging to its 'formal contrary', which would be an 'aristocratic idealism' (ibid.), but rather attempts to open up space for an exception amidst the given reality of bodies and languages. This exception is that besides bodies and languages, there are also truths. 'Democracy' here signifies the contemporary doxa. For this reason the materialist dialectic does not rely on salvaging this difficult term in the first instance. Instead, against false equality – the formal equality of numbers and of the market – the prescription of universality and equality might, in its concrete presentation, change the sense of the term democracy, that is, as a consequence of a political truth procedure at a distance from the state.

DERRIDA

Christopher Norris

Badiou shares with Jacques Derrida (1931–2006) a certain way of reading texts that brings out hitherto unnoticed complexities of sense and logic. Such 'symptomatic' readings – which also take a cue from Louis Althusser's approach to the writings of Marx and Jacques Lacan's structuralist-inflected account of Freudian psychoanalysis – very often go strongly against the grain as regards the express (author-warranted) meaning of the text or its commonly accepted import as handed down through a canonical tradition of authorised scholars and exegetes. Nevertheless Derrida's deconstructive commentaries on thinkers from Plato and Aristotle to Descartes, Rousseau, Kant, Hegel, Nietzsche, Husserl, Freud and many others can be seen to argue their case with the utmost fidelity to matters of detail and logical implication. Although Badiou doesn't go in for that kind of highly extended and meticulous close-reading, he does make a regular point, especially in *BE*, of defining his own position vis-à-vis the arguments of earlier thinkers, some of whom he subjects to a forceful critique of their basic presuppositions, while others (the majority) he treats in a mode of partial and carefully qualified approval. Indeed his practice of textual exegesis can best be seen as a further working-out of his case with respect to developments in set theory, that is to say, as showing how advances come about through a close engagement with problems or anomalies which thereby offer the critical purchase for a leap beyond received habits of thought.

This brings him close to the deconstructive standpoint adopted by those, like Derrida, who examine texts for the moments of unresolved tension between opposed orders of logic and sense which often betoken some deeper philosophic or ideological conflict of interest. Indeed it is fair to say that Badiou must have learned a good deal from Derrida's many (themselves now canonical) essays on the great thinkers of the western philosophical canon. However, it should also be noted that Badiou is dead set against what he sees (though with only very partial justification in Derrida's case) as the nexus between deconstruction and other variants of the linguistic turn – ranging all the way from post-structuralism to Wittgensteinian 'ordinary language' philosophy – that, in his view, very often deploy their obsessive concern with theories of signification or minutiae of everyday usage as a means of avoiding any deeper engagement with genuine philosophic, not to mention political issues. Here Badiou is at one with those seventeenth-century rationalists who regarded natural language as at best a relatively clear and efficient means of communication, and at worst a grossly distorting medium which philosophy should either seek to reform or (ideally) replace with a logical symbolism or conceptual language of its own devising. Moreover, he is thereby placed – to this extent at least – in the company of mainstream analytic philosophers, from Frege and Russell down, who have likewise very often tended to suppose that one of philosophy's primary tasks is to reform (i.e. clarify or disambiguate) the vagaries of 'ordinary', natural language.

However, Badiou's rationalism and consequent hostility towards most versions of the linguistic turn never goes so far as to pitch him against the basic claim – in his case chiefly of structuralist provenance – that language enters into all our dealings with the world and also into much (though not everything) that rationalists might be inclined to think of as strictly a priori and hence in no way subject to linguistic mediation or structuring. Otherwise he could scarcely find so much room – and at so deep a level of his own thinking in matters of foremost concern – for the claims of a psychoanalyst such as Lacan or a political theorist such as Althusser, both of whom made a programmatic point of reading their source-texts (Freud and Marx) through a conceptual lens informed by the insights of structural linguistics. Although Derrida doesn't loom so large among Badiou's intellectual sources, his influence does emerge clearly in his critical yet nonetheless constructive manner of engagement with philosophers from Plato to Heidegger. More specifically, it forms the basis of his frequent claim to have discovered certain crucial fault-lines in the structure of their thought – localised symptoms of a larger non-coincidence between what the author explicitly says and what the logic of their text constrains them to imply – which open the way to such a jointly diagnostic and (in Badiou's as in Derrida's case) appreciative account.

This is not to deny that Badiou is very deeply at odds with some of those thinkers whose work he passes in critical review from stage to stage in the unfolding sequence of historically, thematically and dialectically structured argument that constitutes *BE*. All the same these differences are brought out by means of a reading that is also (in the true sense) a critical encounter, that is, a coming-up against problems unlooked-for on other, more orthodox accounts. What Derrida has to say about the various deviant or paraconsistent logics of the *pharmakon* (Plato), 'supplementarity' (Rousseau), the *parergon* (Kant), *différance* (Husserl), or 'iterability' (Austin) finds a close analogue in Badiou's reading of those philosophers from Plato down whom he regards as having somehow proleptically grasped – albeit in a faltering, intermittent, or largely unconscious way – certain truths about the orders of being and event that would arrive at the point of formal expression only with the advent of Cantorian set theory. That is to say, despite being so far in advance of orthodox thinking in their time as to anticipate temporally distant conceptual advances, they were still in the grip of other powerful preconceptions that stood in the way of any conscious or deliberative means of attaining those truths.

So there is a strong case for claiming that Badiou's mode of critical engagement with his major precursors has much in common with Derrida's deconstructive exegeses of texts in the mainstream western philosophical tradition. Self-evidently any such engagement will need to argue its case through a close attentiveness to crucial or (very often) problematical passages in the works that represent those thinkers' various truth-claims, doctrinal commitments, conceptual priorities, and so forth. However what Badiou does very forcefully disown is the extreme version of this claim proposed by some post-structuralists, not to mention Wittgensteinians and adepts of the present-day 'linguistic turn' in its more extreme versions. On this view there is simply no way that thinking can get some critical, diagnostic or corrective purchase on language, since language is the very element of thought or the absolute horizon of intelligibility beyond which it cannot purport to go without falling into manifest nonsense. Such is the cultural–linguistic–relativist notion that Badiou denounces with admirable force in his reflections on the prevalence of sophistry as a substitute for genuine thought in much that nowadays passes for philosophy on both sides of the English Channel. It is one reason why he evinces an attraction to Spinoza's philosophy – despite contesting some of its most basic ontological theses – insofar as Spinoza likewise regarded thought as intrinsically prior to language, and language as a more-or-less adequate means of communicating thoughts rather than a matrix or shaper of them. It is also why Badiou can justifiably claim to read Plato, Rousseau and others in a way that respects the conceptual integrity of their work while nevertheless finding that work to signify something other and more than could plausibly be held to have figured in the authors' conscious or deliberate design. Although not a sedulously close reader or prober of textual doubts and complications in Derrida's way Badiou can be seen to raise similar questions about the sometimes divergent, even contradictory relationship between explicit (avowed or intended) meaning and what the text actually says, implies, presupposes, or logically entails.

Indeed Badiou's distinctive line of approach to these issues via mathematics is one that may help to correct those prevalent misunderstandings of Derrida which fail to recognise the formal (logico-semantic) rigour of his work and consequently treat it – whether with praise or blame – as an exercise in the 'textualist' or strong-descriptivist vein designed to show that philosophy is just one 'kind of writing' among others. To understand why Badiou is so squarely opposed to this whole way of thinking on political and social as well as on 'purely' philosophic grounds is at the same time to grasp why Derrida's thought has been so travestied by analytical detractors on the one hand and, on the other, by an appreciative company of literary-cultural theorists along with some 'post-analytic' or continentally-oriented philosophers. What links these two otherwise dissimilar thinkers is a critical impulse that takes the form of a rigorously argued undoing of certain hegemonic yet questionable truth-claims by means of a discourse that stakes its credit on the power – the logical and conceptual power – to reveal just where those claims run up against hitherto unnoticed obstacles, dilemmas, or aporias. That Badiou sets about this project *more mathematico* and Derrida seemingly *more linguistico* should not be allowed to disguise their kinship as thinkers who explore the capacity of reason to transcend the kinds of limit imposed by any in-place currency of knowledge or belief.

DIALECTICS

Steven Corcoran

The question of dialectics runs throughout Badiou's work. Early Badiou explicitly identified with the tradition known as dialectical materialism, of which Badiou's teacher, Althusser, was a great exponent (cf. 'Theorie de la Contradiction', 'De l'Ideologie', and 'La noyau rationnelle de la dialectique hegelienne' in *AR*)). He distinctly rejected the Sartrean notion that dialectical movement was neither pervasive nor caught up in a progressive, forward movement, but was rather a sporadic, intermittent occurrence wherein humanity emerged in its 'authenticity' before falling back into the massive indifference of being. The younger Badiou thought that dialectical 'negativity' worked continuously to give impetus to new phases of dynamic intervention in the movement toward communism. However, by the mid-1980s, Badiou would come to write a two-part essay called 'Six proprietés de la vérité' in which, for the first time since the events of 1968, he proposes a theory of truth as a cut in time that simultaneously breaks with 'dialectical materialist' referents. This orientation is confirmed in *CPBT*, where he registers the separation that has come to pass between these referents and Marxist theory, spelling a fully-fledged crisis of the latter. Finally, in *BE*, Badiou separates ontological discourse from all spatial or temporal reference, and develops his notion of event, the chance-ridden nature of which compels him to depart definitively with the idea that there is sublation in history or a dialectical odyssey. Instead, he replaces it with a dialectics of the void and excess whose rareness strongly resembles, as Peter Hallward points out, the Sartrean 'historical-ephemeral pessimism' he had once dismissed. Despite what henceforth appears as a rather anti-dialectical orientation (his explicit critique of traditional dialectics continues at least up until *MP* from 1998), some have argued – and his work around and including *LW* bears this out – that he always seems to have left room open for another kind of dialectics. If the key question of Badiou's later work is: how can we think an excess or a supplement to the situation that in truth is still immanent to this situation itself? – or: how does a truth emerge from an existing situation that it then works to transform? – then he came to realise that the logic of emergent truths calls for a new set of dialectical categories. In *LW*, Badiou will dub this new logic the 'materialist dialectic', which, in contradistinction to the dialectical materialism of his younger days, outlines a rare dialectical movement that he will come to call 'non-expressive' or 'affirmative'.

In no uncertain terms, today's Badiou declares that developing a new dialectics is the 'fundamental problem in the philosophical field today'. Marx took the step of developing a new logic, in the wake of Hegelian dialectics, in order to make an explicit connection to revolutionary novelty. Yet the demise of the revolutionary project, as Badiou understands it, has fundamentally revoked this connection. Badiou's diagnosis is not that of nearly all his contemporaries, who in one way or another have abandoned the idea of emancipatory politics and instead have focused on problems of power, action, life, and so on. In so doing they tend more or less explicitly also to reject the claim that the twentieth century involved much in the way of political novelty, and consign it, along with dialectics, to the dustbin of history. The upshot, according to Badiou, is that they are unable to grasp novelty and only achieve a theoretical expression that is mired in the finitude of an entirely constructible present, an ideology Badiou dubs *democratic materialism*. So Badiou opts for a different path: we must stick to the hypothesis of emancipatory or communist politics, and rather take a step further in trying to develop a new logic by which to grasp political novelty. We must counter democratic materialism with a materialist dialectic. If we are to follow in Marx's footsteps and reconnect emancipatory politics with a dialectical logic, the essential guide for this must be those moments of creativity in politics of the last century that showed up the limitations of its dialectical logic, those moments where the dialectics of the party-state pointed beyond itself.

Badiou's attempt is clearly part of the general so-called crisis of negativity. This crisis is bound up with the democratic framing of capitalist domination, which enables the system to assimilate and feed off the very critiques that aim at undermining it. Attempts to develop points of autonomy from the system for self-organisation would thus appear to be always-already bound to fail. This is what Marcuse referred to as the system's 'repressive tolerance': its ability to tolerate and absorb all forms of determinate negation of capitalist relations. If negation is the driving force of dialectical progression, its movement would seem to be countered in advance by capitalist dynamics.

Badiou repugns this negative and pessimistic conclusion. If there is one thing that did instill fear in the capitalist classes and hamper the rampancy of capitalist relations, it was indeed the existence, during the twentieth century, of a political alternative. Pace Marcuse, Badiou contends that if, today, a politics of non-domination is struggling to emerge from within the ferocity of late capitalism, it is not due to the impotence of negativity to undermine it, but instead due to a lack of affirmation. Simply, since the demise of the revolutionary project, egalitarian politics has struggled to reinvent itself, has been unable to create new possibles.

Badiou argues that what must be altered if we are to take a further step is the relation between negation and affirmation within the dialectical process. The classical dialectical framework, still clearly evident in Marx's work, posits negation as its motor. Room for creation, for the new, is opened up only after a process of determinate negation, of 'being against', of opposition to. A new form of classless society was to be opened by overthrowing bourgeois domination, by expropriating the expropriators. The glorious day of New Man was to follow the destruction of the old social forms that history was already consigning to the past. Negation came first, and was considered the effective driver of creation. But the problem is that the idea of New Man, by being tied to historical objectivity, to the identities to which it stood in opposition, did not give way to the real of creation. Creation does not emerge from the determinate negation of historical forms, under which there is nothing except the dubious fascination of destruction itself.

Now, Badiou's seemingly simple contention is that we must not dispense with either negation or affirmation, either destruction or creativity, but simply alter their relation. His approach can thus be distinguished from two other attempts at confronting this general crisis of negativity. The first, the Adornian one, sees in this classical Hegelian dialectics too much affirmativeness, an oversubordination 'to the potency of the Totality and of the One'. His well-known counter-proposal involves the hyper-negativity of 'negative dialectics'. The problem with proceeding this way, Badiou argues, is that it leads to an ethics of compassion that is entirely compatible with the current capitalist and state-democratic order. The other attempt, more affirmative, was pursued by Deleuze, Negri and Althusser, and involves reclaiming the supposedly affirmative nature of Life or History. Whereas Althusser developed a logic of dialectical expressivity (e.g. the revolution as the concentrated expression of historical contradictions), Deleuze and Negri strove to develop an affirmative logic wholly devoid of negation. Negri's analysis of contemporary capitalism follows this path. For Negri, capitalist forms are inhabited by a more affirmative force of communist creation that they will ultimately be unable to contain. In the first case, Badiou argues that Althusser leaves us unable to account for contingency, as in his expressive dialectical schema every particularity can be seen as a moment of underlying necessity. In the second, he argues that Deleuze and Negri's 'destruction of all forms of dialecticism' leaves us with an acceptance of the dominant order. The destruction of 'all forms of dialecticism' in favour of pure affirmation does not breach the impasses of finitude. It also remains necessary to struggle against things, to oppose them.

Badiou's dialectical proposal in some sense dialecticises these alternatives. Like Adorno, Badiou dismisses Totality and the One (and thus Life or History, with which an event always breaks) and insists on the irreducibility of multiplicity, but like Althusser he rejects the primacy of negation and insists that newness can only come from affirmation. So Badiou's approach is to 'reverse classical dialectical logics inside of itself', to create a logic in which creation, or at least its future anticipation, a logic in which 'something of the future precedes the present of negation'. Philosophy's task would then be to understand the conditions under which a concrete negation is possible, and for Badiou this possibility presupposes the field of affirmation. Otherwise put, it presupposes the minimal difference opened up through an event (i.e. the opening of a possible) and its unfolding (i.e. the creation of a subjective body able to change the situation), such that the negative is to be located in the consequences of that creation. Examples abound of this logic in Badiou's work, but perhaps the most elaborate description of this general orientation is contained in his book on Saint Paul. In it, Badiou demonstrates that genuine production does not occur through the logic of the negative; rather, there is first an affirmation (of the event) and then a division. The process of this division bears two key aspects: the creation of a subject-body able, first, to unfold the consequences of the evental affirmation – which is to say a series of organs that are able to maintain the independence of the (political, artistic, etc.) novelty from the old situation in which it emerges; and able, second, to deal with the inevitable encroachments that will visit it from the outside. This is the general orientation of Badiou's 'affirmative dialectics'. But in order to understand better (a) how it differs from the old conception, and

(b) how it alters our approach to the examination of things, let us take as an example the relationship between politics and power.

An affirmative dialectics registers, among other things, the seismic shifts that have occurred on the terrain of political action. In the classical conception, the directive of this action was revolution. Revolution defined the goal of political action as the seizing of power in order to destroy the machinery of state and its enemies. It was the process by which the party seized power and led the way to non-domination, or communism; however, in reality it failed to effectuate this, and where any significant non-state political initiative emerged (such as in China during the years of the Cultural Revolution), state logic and pro-capitalist practices eventually prevailed. If revolution can no longer be the order word of politics, it is because ultimately it was all too easy to define genuine socialism negatively as being all that bourgeois state democracy was not. The party of the socialist state thus enacted a negation whose identity was all too dependent upon what it negated. This strict duality is therefore not enough.

So, where classical dialectics contains three terms (negation, the negation of negation, and the totality of the process), an affirmative dialectics, in Badiou's conception, has four, and these four terms define a different topology relative to the inside/outside of the state (or logics of representation more generally). First, there is the separate existence of the state; second, the emergence of evental ruptures with the state, opening a latent possible immanent to the situation; then, there is the 'elaboration of the consequences of collective action and determination of the new political subject'; and last, there is the 'negative inscription of politics in history', which concerns process of the withering away of the state, and hence falls under the name of communism.

It is this complex of terms, then, by which Badiou proposes we rethink the problem of the relation of politics to power outside of the classic theme of revolution. It may be restated as involving three places that prescribe a different topological relation –that is, where the goal of politics is no longer to be inside the state. These three terms are the state, the event, and the creation of a new subjective body. Corresponding to them are three processes: the evental emergence, which creates a new possible in the situation, such as one that works to undermine the segregative division of labour; the engaging of repressive state machinery to quell this possibility, since, insofar as it concerns the organisation of the collective, politics enters onto the terrain of the state; and finally the moment of politics proper, the creation of a subjective body able to unfold the evental possibility and ensure the victory of popular politics. It is clear, then, that this subjective body will have two tasks. It must be able to develop the content of this new politics by making prescriptions. A politics may develop prescriptions on, say, the factory (e.g. to overcome the divisions between technical and manual work as the basis of power in the factory) but this will immediately call the state into play, for which the factory and its workers are mere economic entities without political being. The subjective body thus has to develop organs able to produce innovative ways to undo separations among the masses, to develop prescriptions that establish a relation with the state. But it must also – this is the key problem of determinate negation – 'maintain the possibility of being outside [of the state] while prescribing something that concerns [its] inside. In the development of politics, then, there is a sort of topological difficulty, namely the relation between outside and inside. Because the state is always inviting you inside and asking that you not be outside' (Badiou 2013a: 52).

To sum up, we can say that for Badiou there are two affirmations and two negations: there is the conservative proposition, and then the affirmation of the new possibility in the event; but there are two different negations also, because the reactionary negation of the new possibility has to be distinguished from the negative part of the new affirmation, which is directed precisely against the conservative position. In the end, the affirmation of people's access to politics outside the state must necessarily inscribe itself negatively as the process 'of the progressive vanishing of the state', which is manifest in 'all results that are proofs of the weakness of the state and finally of the possibility of its vanishing' (51). If people's access to politics outside the state is to be confirmed, it requires precisely a disruption of state (laws and practices) that work to prohibit this access. But it is only on the basis of a new proposition of this access that any meaningful negation can take place.

We might say that this inversion of classical dialectical logic is Badiou's answer to the failed attempts of pure affirmationism and Adornian negativity to grasp, faced with the so-called crisis of negativity, the singularity of creative processes. It takes Marx's lead in affirming that the real process of becoming (in politics) runs from the concrete movement of innovative revolt to a new proposition. Only on the basis of the worker's struggles in France, of the concrete movement of the Parisian proletariat, was Marx able to arrive at his concept of the proletariat. So the real movement is not from the concept to the movement, but precisely the other way around. As a result of this, Badiou's diagnosis is that the real discussion today is 'not about the concrete analysis of global society, but about our relation to the state'. In the framework of affirmative dialectics, in which affirmation comes first, the idea is that you must be outside the state (of the situation).

Ultimately, what Badiou is proposing is a sort of general anthropology. Today's general anthropology prescribes non-dialectical forms of (non-)thought – the ideological frame of which Badiou calls democratic materialism – wherein humanity is entirely reduced to its concrete being or, in other words, is entirely constructible. For Badiou it is an ideology of finitude, in which the capacity of being human is supposedly enveloped by the predicative power of language and affects of corporeality, without remainder. The human individual thus gets presented as being entirely inscribed within linguistic predication and bodily enjoyment, all of which is easily rendered by the general monetary equivalent (each group has its special interests, consumer products, and so on), on the basis of which we get a sort of capitalist anthropology: the human is a being before the market, with each individual locatable on the hierarchy ranging from the ultra-rich, who have great means, to the desperately poor, who are without means. Capitalist anthropology conceptualises the protection of this set up, by foreclosing all definitions of the human other than as a self-interested animal. But this foreclosure forgets precisely the capacity of this animal for truth, or for its incorporation into a procedure of thought that is entirely in excess of the perishable materiality of 'bodies and languages', 'individuals and communities'.

If Badiou's materialist dialectic is dialectical, it is because it is able to point to the forgetting of the dialectic that lies at the heart of the dualism, 'there are bodies and languages'. It is thus able to overcome this dualism by pointing to the infinity of this process of incorporation – since the affirmation of a new possibility always has infinite consequences. The dialectic recalls the exception associated with a rupturing leap of the infinite within capitalist succession (which relies on number and con-structability). In Sartrean fashion, it is this rare and ephemeral process of exception in which, for Badiou, something emerges that we can call generic humanity.

DISASTER

Ozren Pupovac

Disaster, as suggested by its lexical meaning, connotes an adverse turn of events, a dramatic failure that ruins the perspectives we maintain and annuls the projects we pursue. In Badiou's doctrine of the subject, the concept of disaster points to the foundering of the subjective unfolding of truth, witnessed when the quest of an emancipatory novelty turns into a corrupt dogma, which revels in its own exceptional nature and can think change only as tyrannical destruction. Stalin's terroristic vision of Marxism, the desire of the artistic avant-gardes to fuse art and life, the romantic ideal of love as destiny, the attempt to replace ordinary language with a formalised science – but also Heidegger's grafting of philosophy to the poem, or Plato's death sentence to sophistry – are all instances of disasters. In its essence, every disaster is a disaster of the subject: its source is not to be attributed to external or objective circumstances. A disaster is not something that befalls us from the outside, like a natural catastrophe, but concerns the internal transformation of the subject itself. More precisely still: 'Every empirical disaster originates in a disaster of thought' (*CS* 17). This means that what can be ethically determined as evil – and for Badiou, disaster is the philosophical name of evil – is not the manifestation of a sheer irrationality, but has a rational structure of its own. Disasters are to be located for Badiou not at the margins but at the very centre of thinking. His doctrine of truths implies that the possibility of disasters follows from the very essence of thought, due to its self-founding and self-affirming nature. Ultimately subtracted from any constitutive relation with either experience or an object, true thought – as opposed to opinions or knowledge – bears a relation only to itself. Summoned by the event as an exceptional and irregular occurrence, a truth is founded upon a contingent decision and finds no accord with a transcendental principle or an external norm. If this logic of pure affirmation opens up the possibility for a radical novelty, it also exposes thought to potentially disastrous consequences. What the German idealists defined as *Schwärmerei* – a fanatical thinking which is not only self-enclosed and self-determining, but proclaims its own absolute freedom through a direct negation of the existing world – describes precisely such a disastrous mode of thought, which, despite its universalistic aspirations, is only able to affirm itself through destruction and violence.

Badiou identifies three specific criteria by which we can recognise the eruption of disasters in thought: (a) an ecstasy of place; (b) a sacred name; and (c) a despotic injunction. All three imply the subordination of the essentially hypothetical and experimental nature of a truth procedure to a rigid figure of necessity, and also indicate the way in which a subject succumbs to obscurity. First, if the subjective unfolding of truth deploys a thinking that is local and always in need of inventing its own autonomous places and forms – the multiple places of politics, for example, have included factories, revolutionary parties, demonstrations, political organisations, soviets, councils – a disaster occurs when this thinking forcibly imposes a single place of truth determined in a global sense. Since truths always appear as contingent exceptions to rules, this imposition of globality is itself devoid of rules and can therefore only affirm itself through its self-absolutisation. Thought is here overwhelmed by ecstasy as truth comes to resemble religious revelation. It can be accessed only through immediate intuition, and never through reason. It is reserved exclusively for the initiated and can only be a matter of imitation, and never of invention. Secondly, if truths always appear under different names, which singularise them in time, a disastrous procedure claims for itself a name that it deems unique and sacred, that lies outside historical time and that is in most cases a proper name. Finally, disastrous thought recognises its own singular nature not as a possibility but as an absolute authority, seeking to impose its own contents on the situation without remainder and to prescribe a norm determining what is worthy of existence and what not. Thought hereby extends into terror, and enthusiasm for invention changes into a rationale for annihilation. Combining all three of these operations, every disaster is indeed an *obscure disaster* – as in Badiou's Mallarméan designation of the failure of historical socialisms (cf. *DO*). The obscurity of disastrous thought extinguishes the active and experimental dimension of truth, its very capacity to generate novelty in its infinite expansion. Instead of a living present, in which the urgency of acting goes together with the willingness incessantly to test thought against reality, the obscure subject institutes a dead time by calling for a return to a lost origin (e.g. the historical fascisms) or by declaring the future already achieved (e.g. Stalin's project of 'New Man').

As a concept, disaster displays an analytical dimension in Badiou's doctrine, allowing for a comprehension of the historical failures of thought and practice, especially those that plagued the twentieth century – from the self-destructive tendencies in artistic movements and scientific projects, to the wayward effects of emancipatory politics, all guided by the 'passion for the real' (cf. *C*). Such disastrous results, however, need to be separated out from the intrinsic universalism of the subject, as there is no inherent teleology that will lead the subject from a declaration of radical change to catastrophic violence. Disasters, while a permanent possibility of all true thought, are never necessary, and their emergence can only be determined as a drastic shift within the subjective register. This is why, when referring to politics, Badiou insists that the history of communism needs to be split into two, with its 'subjective' aspect (the militant, experimental and universalistic nature of politics) separated from its 'objective' one (in which we see politics identified with the violent operations of the state) – the latter designating a subject's passage towards obscurity. The link between Lenin and Stalin, between the prescriptions of October 1917 and the terror of a police state, can only be thought as a 'pure empirical consecution' (*OD* 28).

However, the concept of disaster also contains a normative dimension, insofar as it provides the means to set limits on any unwarranted excesses of radical thinking without demanding that it abandon its revolutionary impetus. Against the quietist ethics of the postmoderns, Badiou stays faithful to the universalism of modernity, defending the philosophical commitment to the idea of truth, even if such a commitment always carries a risk of violent disasters. From a strictly philosophical perspective, 'a disaster is better than a lack of being (*mieux vaut un désastre qu'un désêtre*)' (*CS* 159). If philosophy is capable of grasping disasters not as absolute evil, but as perversions of truth, it can also – guided by its own ethics – struggle to prevent them. Philosophy is called to do so because it itself assumes a privileged place in the register of empirical disasters, due to its resemblance to the operations of thought inherent in truth procedures. Philosophy is oriented around moments of exception, operates at a distance from experience or meaning, proceeds through axioms and affirmations and articulates truths in the universality and eternity of their being, which is why it carries an inherent potential for disasters. These occur whenever philosophy attempts to substantialise its categories and, most crucially, whenever it fills in the void of Truth as something that is to be attested as an immediate presence. Otherwise put, they occur whenever philosophy begins to consider itself not as an operation of seizing truths outside of it in their multiplicity, but as a truth procedure. Lacking the inner content required for this, philosophy must then graft itself onto one of its own truth conditions. The latent urge of such *sutures* is to demand that existing reality comply exhaustively with philosophical definitions. Reciprocally, every empirical disaster contains a philosopheme that knots together ecstasy, sacredness and terror. The Stalinist philosophy of Diamat, for example, invested in the project of 'socialism in one country', exhibits not only a complete suturing of philosophy to politics – to such an extent that even science and art are forced to profess only explicit political contents – but also a disastrous philosophical desire, according to which the realisation of thought demands drawing a clean slate with regard to existing reality, which is why the Soviet project of 'New Man' came to be constructed through a violent negation of its support in concrete individuals.

To curb the disaster of such attempts of its 'realisation', Badiou insists on philosophy's desuturing and desubstantialising of its own operations, on it assuming a disjunction with regard to the temporal procedures that it seizes and is seized by. Ultimately, this amounts to demanding that it keep its categories empty, i.e. maintain them as operations. As the sense and the force of the philosophical categories of truth and being remain out of reach, philosophy must not regard itself as a situation of truth, i.e. must refuse to posit that the Truth *is*, just as all thought immanent to truth procedures is blind to its own immediate effects and powerless to name the set that will have accomplished in its generic expansion.

$$\boxed{\text{E}}$$

ENCYCLOPEDIA

A. J. Bartlett

Badiou's use of the term 'encyclopedia' is decisive. His entire generic orientation subverts any notion of 'complete knowledge' or 'complete instruction'. Rationally, such a completeness or wholeness is demonstrably, ontologically inconsistent. That the encyclopedia conceals this inconsistency as central to its operation marks for Badiou the strategic weak point of any 'state of the situation' or function of re-presentation – terms that are interchangeable with encyclopedia. The re-presentation that the encyclopedia performs as knowledge is thereby characterised by excess; the excess of parts over elements, or representation over presentation, or the rule over the rational. The hole at the heart of knowledge is what the encyclopedia, as pure repetition, exists to conceal. As he notes, '[w]hat this means is that everything is at stake in the thought of the truth/knowledge couple' (*BE* 327).

There is an ontological predication and a consequent 'orientation in thought' that subtends this conception of encyclopedia as rule: constructivism. Ostensibly drawn from Leibniz, the rule of this rule is that the 'indiscernible' does not exist. This rule, Badiou argues, is constitutive of the knowledge of ordinary situations and as such knowledge is grounded in a prohibition, not just of that which is indiscernible but, as this implies, of the very excess itself. For Badiou, knowledge so constituted knows nothing of, or rather knows *as* nothing, the gap between presentation and representation, situation and state, the gap by which 'what happens in art, in science, in true (rare) politics, and in love (if it exists)' might come to light (16). Simply put, knowledge knows nothing of the event (329), precisely because, for knowledge, everything that is, everything that exists in a given situation or world, exists by virtue of its adequate correspondence to what Badiou calls an encyclopedic determinant, that is, a universal predicate through which existence is granted. We can assert, then, that the normal reign of the encyclopedia extends to the point of knowing not only what cannot be known (as knowledge) but to what *must* not be known. In passing, let's add that Badiou chooses this word, encyclo-paedia, not only because of its resonance with the eighteenth-century *philosophes* or with Hegel's Absolute or Whole but also because of its pedagogical conceit (cf. Bartlett 2011). All this is to say knowledge, given as encyclopedia, knows nothing of truths. In *BE*, the work wherein this conception of the encyclopedia takes shape, Badiou's central target, as noted, is the constructivist orientation of thought.

The constructivist encyclopedia, says Badiou, has three essential features: language, discernment and classification. The function of language is to indicate that this or that element of the situation contains a certain property. Language, according to Badiou, intercedes between presented elements and their representation. It expresses the criterion of the former's inclusion by the latter. Badiou calls the *capacity* language has for marking out these properties 'knowledge': 'the constitutive operations of every domain of knowledge are *discernment* (such a presented or thinkable multiple possesses such and such a property) and *classification* (I can group together, and designate by their common property, those multiples that I discern as having a nameable characteristic in common)' (*BE* 328). In the case of discernment the situation itself is supposed such that its elements present properties specific to it. If an element can be *discerned* as such, it is because this element belongs to the situation, is presented as such. Language, so the constructivist position assumes, nominates only on the basis of what exists. The assumption is that nothing external to the situation is imposed in and through such discernment. This would, after all, suggest the *existence* (and therefore the being) of that which cannot be named. (In the ancient world, naming the inexistent was considered the height of impiety and was punishable by death. Socrates is the most high-profile casualty of this subtraction from the tenets of the encyclopedia.) If such a property is discerned within the multiple the latter is immediately classifiable in the sense that via its 'common' name it can be included with others similarly discerned. Badiou notes that the capacity of language to achieve this commensurability between an existent or belonging multiple and an included rule of its 'inclusion' is the means by which language is able to police the excess inherent to the representative relation. 'It is this bond, this *proximity* that language builds between presentation and representation, which grounds the conviction that the state does not exceed the situation by *too much . . .*' (*BE* 288). To control errancy – the possible site of the void – by means of binding belonging to inclusion, elements and parts, as tightly as possible through the specification of nomination is the goal of the 'constructivist' orientation. 'Knowledge' names the coordinated movement of these three functions. The functions of discernment and classification are further grounded in capacities supposed inherent in the constructivist subject: discernment is grounded in the capacity to judge, classification in the capacity to link such judgements. To judge is not to decide (thought is not a matter of knowledge) but to speak *correctly* or to make sense insofar as what is picked out conforms to and confirms the situational order; in this case, the power of language. The point being that, for the constructivist vis-à-vis the situation, nothing else is sayable (289). 'Knowledge' does not speak of what is not presented precisely because it is impossible to ascribe to 'nothing' an existent property of the situation and to count it as such. 'If all difference is attributed on the basis of language and not on the basis of being, *presented* in-difference is impossible' (319). It is a mark of Badiou's Platonism that we can recall Plato having Protagoras put the same thing like this: 'it is impossible to judge what is not, or to judge anything other than what one is experiencing, and what one is immediately experiencing is always true' (*Theaetetus*, 167ab). It is in this way that 'knowledge is realised as encyclopedia' (*BE* 328). That is to say, the 'summation of judgements' made concerning what exists for the situation such that they are all counted, or grouped by a 'common determinant'. This 'encyclopedic' determinant organises the judged elements into parts based solely on the ascribed property. In turn, then, 'one can designate each of these parts by the property in question and thereby determine it within the language' (329). In sum, knowledge solely determines existence in the form of its nomination. A consistency is supposed at work; or rather, a law already orders the thinking of the situation such that certain (non-)attributes can have no possible means of appearing. In his critique of Leibniz on this point Badiou notes that what this orientation excludes as impossible to the formulas of a well-made language, a language in which what exists conforms to the reason of its existence, is the 'indiscernible' (320). The indiscernible is such that no reason for the existence of what it divides can be given, and thus 'language' as nomination through rule is contradicted. As Badiou notes, Leibniz himself says that '*if the void exists, language is incomplete*, for a difference is missing from it inasmuch as it allows some indifference to be' (*BE* 321; cf. Madison-Mount 2005). Constructivist thought is founded on the impossibility of the existence of the void qua situation, which is to say the indiscernible and that which presents it. As this conception of the encyclopedia suggests, not to know the void, thus the event, is not a matter of knowledge but of constitution.

ETHICS AND EVIL

Jan Voelker

Badiou's take on the question of ethics shows in a nutshell how much his philosophy is oriented against the grain of contemporary opinion. Against the conviction that ethics is above all about the tolerance for the other, and the laws to safeguard this recognition of the other, Badiousian ethics elaborates the notion of the same as its cornerstone. Against the principle of the prevention of evil as a starting point for ethics, Badiou will set the beginning of the discussion in the good. Both points – the question of the other, and the question of the existence of evil – are combined in the understanding of the finite individual as the basis for any ethical reflection. Against this anthropological grounding of ethics, Badiou will proclaim the subject's capacity to infinity.

The discussion of ethics in Badiou's oeuvre develops as early as in *TS*, where Badiou considers the question of ethics in the confines of the becoming of a political subject. This early conception of ethics shows significant differences from the principles developed later in his small book *Ethics: An Essay on the Understanding of Evil* (2001 [1993]).

In *TS* the discussion of ethics focuses on the question of how to decide in the midst of a subject-process that is inherently structured around a point of undecidability. The subject is conceived as a doubled process, combining the process of subjectivation, connected to the realm of the given, with the subjective process, connected to the impossible. Out of this structure and their respective possibilities of failure four possible types of the subjective arise: anxiety, justice, superego, courage. Like courage, anxiety is a form of excess – both interrupt: anxiety explodes into violence, but it does not really put the law into question, whereas courage seeks to go beyond it. The superego restores order by answering the chaos of anxiety, and justice then tries to relativise the law. The process of subjectivation consists of anxiety and courage, the subjective process out of superego and justice. This structure of the subject is crossed by two processes, which Badiou names α (courage/justice) and ψ (anxiety/superego). Ethics is a question of giving consistency to the becoming subject on both of its sides, the process of subjectivation and the subjective process, and all of its four elements. Between the processes of α and ψ there is undecidability, and the ethical point of view is to decide from the point of this undecidability. Badiou discusses two forms of deciding this undecidability: scepticism and dogmatism. Both lead to a morality whereby one is either guided by the law or lost in meaninglessness. Ethics, and in particular Marxist ethics, is possible because α is part of every subject-process. The solidification of this process has to be avoided by new purifications – subjectivation is an unending process, and Badiou will hold up to this. But if, in *TS*, Badiou still puts a strong emphasis on the destructive side of this process, the further development of his work will strengthen the affirmative aspect of a truth procedure, which affects the role of ethics, too.

Nonetheless, many of the elements in Badiou's early discussion of ethics can be traced in the later works. The four moments of the subject, for example, reappear slightly changed and intern to the conditions as affects in *LW*. The main question of ethics – the question of consistency in interruption – is taken up again, before the publication of *LW*, in his small book *Ethics*. Here Badiou continues the unfolding of an ethics of truths against the reign of opinions, but now in the framework of *BE*.

Ethics follows a tripartite strategy: first, Badiou starts his inquiry from the central significance ethics has in contemporary (philosophical) discourse. Second, he dismisses the commonsensical concept of ethics, built as it is on three main premises: an anthropological understanding of the human being, a consensus about the existence of the evil, and the notion of the other. Against this, Badiou proposes a plurality of ethics, bound to the primacy of truth processes in which subjects and not individuals engage.

The commonsense understanding of ethics aims at the judgement of opinions. Ethics concerns 'how we relate to "what is going on"' (*E* 2), and therefore is broadly understandable as a system that 'regulates judgements and opinions concerning evil' (33). In this sense ethics, as Badiou remarks, is today closer to a Kantian ethics of judgement than to a Hegelian ethics of decisions. The notion of evil in this conception is primary, as 'we presume a consensus regarding what is barbarian' (8). Ethics, in its return to Kant as the theoretician of radical evil, is then defined as the ability to discern evil and base one's judgements on this discernment. 'Ethical ideology' (24) thus obtains a most radical pre-eminence in the arrangement of everyday life, especially with its subordination of politics to its rules. The flipside of the notion of evil is then a conception of the human being as an animal that must defend itself against the destructive power of the negative. This animal is capable of reflecting on itself as a potentially suffering animal. The good takes its source in its defense against the negative, and the human animal shuts itself within what is called the human right 'to non-evil' (9).

Today's 'ethical ideology' is based on the notion of the Other (or others). Following Levinas, Badiou shows that the development from the acceptance and experience of the other necessarily leads to the religious notion of an 'Altogether-Other' (22). Here, ethics is conceived of as subjugating the logic of identity to a logic of the Other, to the Law of the Other. Hence the grounding of this law can only be ontological, and the experience of the other will consist in crossing this distance. Later in *C*, Badiou remarks that the notion of evil is, in the last instance, also grounded in the notion of God, who is responsible for it even though its existence has to be denied (cf. *C* 4). Thus contemporary ethics, built upon the twin notions of evil and the Other, is altogether an outcome of a weakened religion.

The theme unifying these distinctions is the *One*: the one anthropological non-evil human animal tolerates the other-one that it ultimately recognises as another-one. This is the outcome if the notion of the other is placed on an anthropological level, and its religious kernel dissimulated: the cultural ideology of differences allows difference only insofar as these differences do not become fundamental. Here resides the pivotal point of Badiou's approach to the question of ethics: 'For the real question – and it is an extraordinarily difficult one – is much more that of *recognising the Same*' (*E* 25). If cultural differences are what *is*, then the question of the *Same* is one of becoming.

Badiou's radical conception of ethics, as a plurality of ethics of truths, does not deal with what is given, but draws on what comes to be. Badiou's ethics of truths forms a point-for-point counterpart to an ethics of finitude: (1) in contradistinction to the anthropological grounds of commonsensical ethics, it upholds the anti-humanist stances of Foucault, Althusser and Lacan to resist the negative, finite definition of man. By understanding the human animal as an animal capable of thought and thus of interrupting its animality, Badiou contradicts the first principle of everyday ethics. The human animal does not live in the frame of finitude; instead, its life consists in the creation of its own infinity in truth procedures. (2) In opposition to the secularised notion of the Other, Badiou maintains that given differences are rendered insignificant in the process of a truth that affects the future. A truth's universal address opens onto the question of the same insofar as the singular truth procedures in their universality structurally amount to being the same. Only from this viewpoint of Sameness can real differences between singularities arise. So while 'commonsensical ethics' runs from alleged differences to actual similarity, the ethics of truths makes real differences possible, on the basis of sameness.

Badiou's *Ethics* was published between *BE* and *LW*. In the preface to the English edition (2000), Badiou clarifies the modifications his conception of ethics receives in the light of *LW*. In relation to the question of ethics, these essentially concern the possibility of the negative figures that can arise in a truth process. However, what is foreshadowed in the *Ethics* book is the emphasis in *LW* on the contemporary metaphysics of bodies and their differences. What Badiou later describes as *democratic materialism* is already implicit in *Ethics*: contemporary ethics is based on both a logic of the living body and one of differences that come down to one decisive difference: that is, contemporary ethics excludes the possibility of a truth procedure.

Badiou thus inverts the orientation: good is not to be understood as following from evil – rather, evil is something that can only emerge from a truth procedure. He defines ethics in this context as '*that which lends consistency to the presence of some-one in the composition of the subject induced by the process of this truth*' (*E* 44). That some*one* is the actual individual who enters in a truth procedure and its subjectivity by exceeding himself, although at the same time being caught up in the situation. So, in Badiou's terms, this some*one* is simultaneously an 'interested' animal as well as a 'disinterested' subject, i.e. disinterested in the facts of the situation. But it is a '*disinterested interest*' (49) insofar as ethical consistency is the paradox of keeping up one's perseverance in the interruption. While contemporary ethics preaches perseverance to the situation, an ethics of truths demands that we 'persevere in that which exceeds your perseverance' (47). Badiou gives this consistency the formula of '*being faithful to a fidelity*' (47).

Badiou discusses the undecidability connected to this structure of ethics under the question of 'asceticism'. If, on the one hand, ethics prescribes a break with the realm of opinions, there is an a-sociality proper to it; but on the other hand, the interested individual itself is the material for the inclusion in the truth process. From an objective point of view there is no difference between the some-one of the situation and the some-one of the truth process. So asceticism is possibly unnecessary. The second step Badiou's argument takes is to say that not all components might be needed, either in the situation, or in a truth process. And it is here that the difference between particular interests and the ethical dimension of dis-interested-interest may become visible. The process might be rearranged from some yet unnoticed component, and then 'the split' – between inter-est and disinterested interest – 'may become representable and asceticism may move on to the agenda – and, with it, its inversion: the temptation to give up, to withdraw from the subjective composition' (*E* 55). It is unde-cidable whether disinterested interest is not merely the simple interest of the subject for itself, and thus that courage remains necessary through the whole process, against all possibilities.

Badiou conceives of three forms of evil that can arise in relation to a truth procedure: *simulacrum*, *betrayal* and *disaster*. The first is the simu-lacrum of a truth process and gathers all the formal definitions of such a process. However, it aims not at the void of the situation, but at a single particularity – e.g. 'Germans' during Nazism. The void then returns under the name of the 'Jew', designating 'those people whose disappear-ance created, around that presumed German "National Socialist revolu-tion" simulacrum, a void that would suffice to identify the substance' (75). The name of the 'Jew' was a particular invention of the political sequence of Nazism. In this the singularity Nazism can be grasped, and Nazism has to be explained as a political sequence, without neglecting the 'irreducibility of the extermination' (64). In the simulacrum of a truth process, evil is not understood on the basis of the good, but on the basis of its imitation. The simulacrum draws a dividing line, like the truth process does, but the enemies of the simulacrum are precisely the stakes of truths, universality, equality, eternity. The consequence of the simulacrum is necessarily terror, a 'terror directed at everyone' (77), because it is terror against universality.

In the second place, evil takes the form of betrayal. Betrayal is a direct possible consequence of the undecidability if the disinterested interest is only a pure form of desire of the subject for itself. This point of undecidability is a 'crisis' (78) of the truth process in which the one involved is pressured by interests, either from the situation or from the truth process. As already part of the truth process, this individual will be unable to simply to withdraw from it. Rather the betrayal of a truth process is self-betrayal: 'I must betray the becoming subject in myself' (79).

The third form of evil Badiou calls disaster. Disaster consists in the re-transformation of a truth onto the knowledge of the situation. It is the attempt to transfer the 'power of a truth' (85) onto opinions with the intention of turning them into parts of the truth process. Against this danger of absolutisation of the 'subject-language' of a truth over the 'language of the situation' (85), there has to be one at least element inside the situation that resists the power of the truth to give new names to the elements. This 'unnameable' (86) – in the realm of politics, for example, the community cannot be named – resists the forcing via the subject-language. Disastrous is every attempt to name the unnameable. The possibility of the disaster is related to the undecidability of the truth process in its very beginning.

While the simulacrum is linked to the event, betrayal is related to fidelity and the disaster concerns the truth. In the context of *LW* these figures of evil could then be examined in how far they correlate – in different ways – with the three types of subjectivity: the faithful, the reactive, and the obscure subject. The obscure subject obscures the event and seeks a transcendent power instead, so it establishes a simulacrum instead of the event. The reactive subject acts in reaction to the event: it accepts the event, but wants to counteract to it. This could be understood as a case of perpetual betrayal, as the truth of the event is inscribed in the unconscious of the reactive subject. The faithful subject finally could be linked to the disaster, insofar as the disaster is the permanent risk of the faithful subject, from the beginning on. '[A] disaster is better than a lack of being', as Badiou puts it (*CS* 159). The some one has to take the risk that the fidelity to a truth might absolutise this truth.

EVENT

Christopher Norris

For Badiou, an 'event' in the proper sense is that which occurs unpredictably, has the potential to effect a momentous change in some given situation, state of knowledge, or state of affairs, and – above all – has consequences such as require unswerving fidelity or a fixed resolve to carry them through on the part of those who acknowledge its binding force. Events of this type may occur in mathematics, in the physical sciences, in politics, the arts, or in the sphere of human interpersonal relations where Badiou takes erotic love (not 'sex') as the most telling and representative instance. Events (proper) are also marked out from 'events' in the everyday, journalistic, or even the textbook historical sense by their possessing a power to radically transform received or prevailing conceptions of reality. This they do by exerting a disruptive effect on the ontology – the accredited order of being and truth – that holds sway in some given domain at some given time. Indeed it is the defining mark of events, in Badiou's highly distinctive usage of the term, that they either bring about such a drastic transformation in direct consequence of their having occurred, or else make it possible as a more-or-less remote yet still retroactively dependent future consequence.

Still, these characterisations don't quite capture the distinctiveness of Badiou's event-concept. For one thing, they ignore its rootedness in the set-theoretical reasoning that occupies so prominent a place in his project as a whole and allows him to define the event as that which is indiscernible within some given ontology or existing situation, yet which nonetheless – through procedures such as Cantor's diagonalisation or Paul Cohen's 'forcing' – can later be seen to have haunted its margins and interstices. These emerge in the form of unrecognised problems, unperceived anomalies, unresolved paradoxes or (in the socio-political sphere) 'uncounted' or disenfranchised groups such as the *sans-papiers* that likewise exert a so far ignored but at some future time decisive or transformative effect. This 'future-anterior' modality of thought is highly typical of Badiou's work across a great range of topics from mathematics, logic and the formal sciences to politics, art and (on his own very heterodox conception) ethics. In each case it involves the conjoint claims – again derived principally from developments in set theory after Cantor – that truth exceeds knowledge, that inconsistent multiplicity must always exceed its consistent (i.e. notionally countable) subset, and hence that events in the strict sense are those that take rise from some coming-to-light of truths concealed – or actively repressed – by an earlier state of knowledge or situation.

Badiou devotes a large amount of detailed exposition to the working-through of these advances in set theory and the resultant claim, *contra* post-structuralists and cultural relativists of various persuasion, that there is indeed such a thing as knowledge-advancement or progress (as distinct from mere shifts of dominant belief) in politics as well as mathematics and the sciences. This exposition has to do partly with topics – diagonalisation, power-sets, forcing, the generic and other intra-mathematical concepts

– whose bearing is primarily formal and not to be applied outside that domain by the kinds of loosely suggestive analogy too often found in popularising treatments of science. All the same, as Badiou makes clear, they are capable of other, more revealing and even revelatory uses when deployed with a due regard for the demands of precise and adequately detailed argument. What then emerges is the definition of 'event' as that which may at some future time be seen to have occurred through the prior, so far unrecognised irruption of an indiscernible or a leverage-point for generic forcing amongst yet beyond all the multiples belonging to an in-place or currently ratified count-as-one. More specifically, it is just that kind of occurrence that meets two further set-theoretically derived specifications. These are (1) that it should figure crucially within some notable event to which it stands as a proper part, and (2) that its lack of present resolution in terms of attained truth or political consequence should leave room for the faithful or 'militant' subject as the locus of its rigorous working-through. It is here – in the margin thereby preserved for subjective commitment, despite Badiou's strongly anti-relativist and anti-constructivist approach – that we can best see what is so original about his conception of the event, properly so called. What this involves is always a matter of 'deciding the undecidable', or committing to a certain investiga-tion, research-programme, path of enquiry or political cause that offers no presently available guarantees since staking its faith on a truth that exceeds their furthest remit. And in so doing it vindicates Badiou's claim that the event is always and by very definition a matter of that which overturns some existing order, whether of attainable knowledge or of socio-political justice.

Hence the title of his book *Being and Event*, where 'being' signifies whatever is taken to constitute a certain pre-constituted object domain or existent totality of some kind, while 'event' signifies whatever eludes or exceeds the scope of any such prior (ontological) specification. In other words, an event is that which occurs – which suddenly breaks out, in the case of political revolutions, or which breaks upon the largely unsuspect-ing world as a great mathematical or natural-scientific discovery – without having been predictable on the basis of any obvious build-up of social forces or any clear-cut sequence of preparatory work. In his terms, events are 'intransitive' to being, or undetermined by any pre-established logic of the situation in which they occur and from which they nonetheless arise (every event is situated, i.e. includes an event site). This is why Badiou can assert, to the astonishment (and outrage) of some, that the terrorist attacks of 11 September 2001 were not 'events' in his precise sense of the term. Despite their unprecedented scale and cataclysmic nature they must none-theless be seen to have occurred as the upshot of a prior history – notably a history of US foreign policy decisions and military campaigns – which clearly led up to them and played a motivating role in the mindset of their planners and executants, even if they could not have been predicted as taking such a form. On the other hand, certain seemingly marginal episodes – among them 'failed' revolutions like the 1871 Paris Commune – do so qualify, on Badiou's account, since, despite having been violently repressed or written out of the official great-event record, they have since come to figure as decisive markers in a history that still makes it possible for 'militants of truth' to sustain their revolutionary aims. Thus the status of event is conferred not so much by immediate impact or directly visible effect in shifting the course of world history, but rather by the way that such episodes can germinate – lie dormant, so to speak, for long periods – and come to exert a decisive force only at a crucial point when the outcome of some future revolutionary enterprise hangs in the balance.

An event in mathematics – Badiou's other main source of examples – has the same character of appearing as if from nowhere (though really in response to a sequence of accumulating problems, anomalies or failed solutions) and radically transforming the existent state of knowledge along with its range of conceptual resources for further such transformative events. His paradigm case is Cantor's achievement in ending more than two millennia of baffled speculation on the infinite by grasping how the use of set-theoretical procedures might enable mathematicians not only to conceptualise an actual (as opposed to merely virtual or potential) infinity but also to reckon with different orders of infinity, such as those consisting of all the integers and all the even numbers. What gives this discovery its special significance for Badiou is the depth and extent of its transformative effect, that is, its offering a nonpareil instance of the way that an existing ontology – i.e. the sum total of those various abstract objects, entities and functions that made up the domain of mathematical knowledge before Cantor – undergoes an event which drastically extends the powers of creative-exploratory thought. Such, for instance, was Cantor's conception of the power-set, or the set that comprises its own member-multiples plus all the various subsets or internal combinations into which they can be grouped. If those multiples are infinite then it is clear that the power-set will exceed the original set by an order of magnitude that thought can grasp – since Cantor opened this possibility – but which goes far beyond anything attainable by intuition or even by knowledge if this involves, as Kant argued, the requirement that our concepts always have fully adequate intuitive content.

Thus the Cantor-event is one that revolutionised thinking in math-ematics and which should furthermore be seen as having vast implica-tions for our thought about other fields of human endeavour such as the physical sciences, politics and art. In each of these domains a veridical event gives us the capacity – like Cantor's concept of the power-set – to break with received, intuitive or philosophically entrenched notions of the limit on human thought and action. This clearly entails a very heterodox approach to the understanding of history, an approach that places no credence on conventional (popular or academic) notions of what constitutes a 'great' event, and which insists on a full-scale revaluation of currently accepted rankings. Moreover it requires that we cease to use the term 'event' in relation to episodes, like the French Revolution, that extended over a considerable stretch of time and which encompassed many episodes – some of them events in the proper sense – the significance of which can be reckoned only through a more detailed historical account. At the same time this Badiouan version of *histoire événementielle* makes no pretence of scholarly objectivity, but conceives its task very much from the standpoint of a 'militant' who looks to those signal events as a continuing source of courage and commitment in the face of successive political defeats. All the same, this should not be taken to suggest that Badiou's is a decisionist conception of the event as somehow brought about through a unpremeditated leap of faith or a commitment undertaken on no better grounds – for no more compelling reason – than sheer force of personal conviction. That reading is ruled out not just by his frequent explicit rejections of it but also, more to the point, by his repeated demonstration in various contexts that decisions and events of the kind in question are such as can occur only through truth procedures that involve a highly disciplined activity of thought on the part of individuals and collectives. Here again the sequence set in train as a result of Cantor's breakthrough discovery is Badiou's model instance of the way that an event of this order can require both the utmost subjective commitment and also the utmost intellectual dedication or intensive exertions of thought amongst those who pursue its further consequences.

Badiou has more to say about events and their aftermath in *LW*, his second major opus and a sequel to – though in many respects a radical departure from – the arguments developed in *BE*. Now his main interest is in the phenomenology or the coming-to-appear of various agents, collectives, objects, and events whose relative degree of prominence or salience in any given situation is an index of the extent to which they are politically, socially or culturally empowered in and by that situation. Badiou ranges over an extraordinary number of historical episodes, political protests, artworks, literary texts, pastoral scenes, war-strategies and other such instances strikingly if often improbably yoked together. They all serve to make his cardinal point: that the degree of salience (or effective intra-world existence) as regards any constitutive element is governed by the situation-specific 'transcendental' that allows some elements to enjoy high visibility or foreground status while others are consigned to the margins or to outright invisibility. Much has changed in Badiou's approach since *BE*, including the particular branch of mathematics (category theory rather than set theory) chosen as the basis for a formal exposition of his thesis. However, there is still the sharp focus on events – and events of the same decisive, epochal or world-transformative character – that typifies the earlier book and which here plays a vital integrating role throughout the book's otherwise somewhat picaresque plot-line.

This comes across clearly in his choice of a line from the *Internationale* – 'nous ne sommes rien, soyons tout!' ('We are nothing, we shall become everything!') – as a kind of motto for the text as a whole. Although their primary reference is of course political, the words also bear a pointed relevance to Badiou's mathematically-based conception(s) of being, event, appearance and world. What the line so tellingly evokes is that singular conjunction of political passion with intellectual rigour that Badiou both practises and thinks prerequisite to any event properly meriting the name.

EXISTENCE/NON-EXISTENCE

Fabien Tarby

The transcendental deals with indexations between diverse multiples, and attributes to their appearing different intensities or degrees (p) in the form $\mathbf{Id}(a,b) = p$, according to which p belongs to T, the transcendental of a world. It enables the idea of considering the intensity proper to an element *a* of a world **w** (a multiple) in its 'relation' to itself as natural and possible. We thus obtain the expression $\mathbf{Id}(a,a) = p$. This expression measures precisely the existence of a multiple *a* given as an element. Badiou's shorthand notation for this is $\mathbf{E}a$.

$\mathbf{E}a = p$ clearly depends, similar to $(a,b)= p$, on a world **w**, and on the Transcendental T that is assigned to it (as a subset of this world, which nevertheless configures this world at the same time). This is to say that the notion of existence is relative, since it depends on the consideration of a world and of its Transcendental. It makes no exception to the general logic of the form $\mathbf{Id}(a,b)= p$ *in* **w** *according to* T. There is thus no absolute existence or absolute inexistence, in conformity with the strict logic of relativity that Badiou, throughout his work, applies, even as he adjusts it. As there is an infinity of worlds, 'existence' only measures these non-subjective points of view, which one can say are at once possible, real and necessary (whereby Badiou exceeds the customary classifications of metaphysics).

The word existence is saturated with meanings that come from meta-physics (*essentia/existentia*) as much as from existential and phenomeno-logical philosophies. Badiou's intention is to propose a new conception of existence that would escape both metaphysical constructions and the notions of consciousness, or the specificity of human existence, such as they are promoted in existential and phenomenological philosophies, from Kierkegaard to Sartre. Badiou conceives existence, as we shall see, in a manner that is strictly configurable and logical, that encompasses all 'being-there', without it thus becoming a theme relating to the specificity of human existence (Heidegger). Hence his conception of death (or of inexistence) is likewise able to avoid turning human death into the centre of reflection (against the finitude of *Dasein* and Heidegger's theme of 'being-for-death' in *Being and Time*): death is simply taken as an objective but multiple phenomenon among others. Lastly, when it comes to human reality, Badiou revives Epicurus's intuition about death contained in the famous *Letter to Menoeceous*, but tries in addition to show that at work in it is nothing other than a strict logic.

However, beyond the study of materialist and logico-mathematical structures that Badiou maintains in his idea of existence, the latter also comes to underpin his conception of the event.

Badiou develops two points in this regard:

1. The logic of the transcendental admits a minimal and a maximal value of appearing. All appearing thus a permits a value = p that defines its identity to itself, or the 'force' with which it appears identical to itself in a world – a transcendental – and in accordance with an object (in the strictly Badiousian sense of the term). Death is therefore logically nothing other than the passage from one given value p to a minimal value in *a determinate world*. The death of a singular appearing element is also, in a world, 'the coming to be of a total non-identity to itself', writes Badiou (*LW* 'Death', 583). More precisely still, death *is* this transition. To understand this, let's take the death of Victor Hugo as an example. Victor Hugo's biological death can be described as a pure non-identity in terms of his consciousness in the world con-stituted by those close to him, those with whom he lived and talked. All that remains is indeed his corpse, whose process of corporeal non-identity takes longer to accomplish (longer than psychological non-identity). The written oeuvre also remains, and continues to endure for the lover of literature. It literally *exists*, and yet it does not so exist for someone who has never heard of the writer. Similarly in the world constituted by Hugo's birthplace, Besançon, his statue at Place Granvelle has a real existence. In instances of death and

existence, then, everything thus depends on the world under consideration, as well as what is meant by 'Victor Hugo'. Badiou thus
manages to avoid being ensnared in any sort of romanticism; instead,
he shows the extraordinary relativity induced by the multiplicity of
worlds, a relativity that must also bear on a question such as death,
which cannot thus be considered strictly human: all multiplicities
exists more or less or else are dead, inexist, in accordance with the
world(s) under consideration. Consciousness is not that which gives,
by itself, existence or inexistence to beings, since it itself participates
in the world under consideration. The above example should not be
taken in an anthropomorphic manner.

2. However, beyond this materialist treatment, the notion of existence
   acquires another status in *LW* as Badiou comes to link it to the question of the event. This linking yields a notion of the event that is
   expressible as a transgression in accordance with a logic of existence
   or of inexistence: an event occurs when an object of the site begins to
   appear maximally, as does the site itself. To put it another way, the
   event can be described as a transition from inexistence to maximal
   existence. This 'logic' of irruption, according to which, under specific
   conditions, inexistence suddenly implies maximal existence, entails, at
   least for an instant, a transgression of the customary logical order of
   appearing.

This double use of the notion of existence recalls that Badiou's strict
materialism of structures is nonetheless sublated by an astonishing theory
of the transgressive event, which does seem to open Badiou to a certain
charge of idealism, but whose conception is seemingly unprecedented in
the history of philosophy and of materialisms.

Translated from the French by Steven Corcoran

FACTORY/WORKER

Frank Ruda

Throughout Badiou's oeuvre, his numerous reflections on political action
or organisation or emancipation in general yield multiple examples in

which a factory plays a crucial role. From the practically forgotten strikes at the Talbot-Poissy factory mentioned in *PP*, those at the Renault-Flins factory evoked in *LW* (209–10, 260), or at the Renault-Bilancourt factory referred to several times in his work, up to the references to the Chausson factory as one essential 'site' May of '68 (*CH* 58ff); the factory is and has remained the name for a paradigmatic political 'place' within Badiou's work. The most systematic comprehension of what the term 'factory' stands for can be gained from the reading of a brief text that was initially supposed to be included in *BE* but then appeared separately in the political journal *Le Perroquet* in 1986. The short piece is called 'Factory as event-site' and, as the title indicates, it was supposed to illustrate in an exemplary manner the concept of evental site that Badiou introduces in *BE*. Underlining the paradigmatic nature of the factory as political place, Badiou claims that it is one of the 'most significant evental sites of modernity' ('Factory as event-site' 176). It should nonetheless be noted that the statement the factory is an evental site is not simply an objective or historicist diagnosis but rather a thesis or even a prescription.

This points to the essential characteristics: 'factory' is the name of a specifically modern site of events. It is specifically modern as it is precisely with modernity that socio-political situations are reproduced and constituted via factory work and that at the same time these very places are depicted as being of no political relevance whatsoever. The former aspect Badiou takes up from Friedrich Engels' analyses in his early *The Condition of the Working Class in England* (Engels 1999 [1845]), in which we find a reconstruction of the crucial role of industrial labour, the concentration of human masses and their quasi-military organisation in English factories. The latter aspect, on the other hand, explains why factories can be considered (potential) evental sites, for they belong to the situation (are internal to it) but are not included in them (this is the most basic definition of an evental site, i.e. of a singular term in Badiou's sense), thus reprising in his way Marx's early theory of alienation (Marx 1988). For these sites belong to the political situation (they are for example essential for the production of goods whose circulation and distribution the political situation administers), but the elements of which they are composed do not count within the situation, do not count as belonging to it. Simply put: within the factory workers do the work, but they themselves – although they are 'there' in the factory – do not count in the situation, are not presented, as Badiou says in *BE*. This is also why sites are what Badiou calls in *BE* 'on the edge of the void'. In terms of political representation the workers are null, voided, seen as having no (not even potential) agency of any political expression or relevance. This is why factories *can* become evental sites. For when something unforeseeable, unknowable happens – that is, an event – it ultimately changes the very structure of (political) presentation and representation.

Within the political situation, such an event lifts the worker to the status of a political agent. Workers and their political claims start to count and exist as legitimate political agents and statements. This is precisely how Badiou takes up the classical Marxist linkage of a universal (yet under present conditions alienated) *subjective* capacity (of the workers that count for *nothing* and are therefore capable of organising *everything*) and of a local *objective* register (the factory as possible site for this very capacity to emerge): this linkage makes it thinkable that there can be 'a workers' one in politics' ('Factory as event-site' 171). But at the same time Badiou wants to defer from the orthodox Marxist rendering of this linkage. As he and his comrades from the *Organisation politique* never withdrew from the idea that the reference to the worker is essential for any emancipatory politics, they also insisted that it is necessary to renew the idea of how a political subject is constituted (as Badiou already attempted in his early *TS*). The subject needs to be grasped as a local (yet nonetheless universal) agent emerging at a specific (i.e. singular) site and not as a global agent, i.e. as a (preconstituted objective) class (merely lacking the proper class-consciousness). The thesis that the factory should be conceived of as an evental site thus does not prescribe any necessity of the taking place of events in the factory (there is no hidden logic of history which would immediately link the workers and their capacity to politics); it only pre-scribes that events can emerge in the factory.

There can only be an event if the consequences it yields will have been evental (i.e. strong consequences in the terms of *LW*), and there can only be a political effect if what follows from it can be qualified as political (i.e. with regards to what Badiou calls the *numericity* of a condition, cf. metapolitics). Put differently: there is politics if there will have been an event in/at a factory that generated the previously impossible possibility of a new organisational (i.e. political) consistency, one made by people who formerly did not count as having political existence or relevance. It is precisely with this complex, retroactive structure that Badiou wants to make sure that 'the thesis does not in any sense say that workers are "political". It says that they are *inevitable for politics*' (ibid.). This also implies for Badiou that neither the worker nor the factory reference can be abolished within emancipatory politics. To be precise, it should be noted that what Badiou understands by 'worker' is something as broad and inclusive as 'people' or, more precisely still, 'peoples'. The worker is thus not a sociologically determinable entity, an objective existence, but something like a universally implied existence without attributes, since it is an agency that is not deducible from objective knowledge. But the worker can only be prescribed when the place, site, the worker occupies in the given situation is also prescribed. And this is exactly what the thesis that the factory is an evental site does. For another formulation of this very thesis is: 'in the factory, there is the worker' (*M* 41).

Badiou provides an exemplary description of a factory-event he was a part of as follows: 'At the time May '68 was getting under way [. . .] So one day we organised a march to the Chausson factory [. . .] the biggest factory in town to have gone on strike [. . .] What were we going to do when we got there? We didn't know, but had a vague idea that the student revolt and the workers' strike should unite, without the intermediary of the classic organisations [. . .] We approached the barricaded factory [. . .] A few young workers came up to us, and then more and more of them. Informal discussions got under way. A sort of local fusion was taking place [. . .] This was an event in the philosophical sense of the term: something was happening but its consequences were incalculable. At that point, we realised, without really understanding it, that if a new emancipatory politics was possible, it would turn social classifications upside down. It would not consist in organising everyone in the places where they were, but in organising lightning displacements, both material and mental' (*CH* 58–60).

This biographical episode makes it paradigmatically clear that what is at stake for Badiou with thinking the 'factory' has to do with the question of political representation *tout court*. The prescriptive statement that 'in the factory, there is the worker' leads to a seeking out of the consequences of the proposed 'factory/worker pairing' (*M* 41); it relates to the factory as a political place from which new and singular political statements and organisational forms can emerge, forms that change the very structure of political representation. But it is precisely this (potential renewal of) political representation with regards to the factory/worker pairing that faces two great modern threats: (1) The state (of the situation), i.e. the domain of representation, does not count the factory 'as such' (it does not count what it is 'made of') but it 'unifies' it. This is to say that the factory is not *represented as factory* (in which there is the worker) *but* as something else. And the name for this something else is '*company*'. Such a representation of the factory as company suspends any relation to the worker (which is what the factory is composed of). It obfuscates the singularity of the factory and makes the worker disappear. 'Company' is thus the name of a *pure representation – without* any *presentation* of the workers – i.e. what Badiou calls an excrescence. The purely excrescent character of such a representation becomes even more apparent when the company itself gets represented by the 'head of the company', who bears less than no relation to the worker. (2) Unionism, which presents itself as a representation of (legitimate) workers' demands. Since it is precisely insofar as unionism involves representation in the form of *legitimate* demands that it already obeys the state and resigns to the legal, juridical domain. At the same time this representation only functions if the category of *demands* is itself represented as that which is able to represent the workers as workers (which is not the case as the capacity of the worker as political figure does not merge in a 'demand for X'). Unionism, whilst arguing that the factory is sociologically composed of workers and their representation can be erected in bio-juridical terms, leads to a representative objectification of the worker that has nothing to do with the universal dimension that the worker stands for.

Company representation and unionism are thus for Badiou two sides of the same statist and excrescent coin of representation of the factory that immanently suspends the link to the worker. For him, both are forms of parliamentary politics. But for Badiou all genuine 'politics is the work of presentation, and cannot be satisfied with the unpresentable' ('Factory as event-site' 175) or with not-presenting that of which the singular term, the factory, is composed. If this is not the case, the workers cannot be considered (potential) subjects of politics (and instead will be taken as pure labour force) and 'the figure of the worker is evacuated' (*M* 49). Against any such evacuation, Badiou systematically insists that every 'contemporary politics has the factory as its site' (ibid.), since otherwise it leads to the parliamentary, 'excrescent' suppression of this very universality or to a politics of abstraction (or grand narratives about the laws of history). Affirming the factory as (potential) evental site is tantamount to the local inscription of the capacity and the (potentially universal) subject of the worker in any historic–political situation. It nevertheless should be kept in mind that as an evental site becomes what it is by nothing but the retroactive consequences of an event, this retroactive constitution also applies to the factory. This is to say that the crucial question Badiou raises with this category (and the factory/worker pairing) is what today might be considered to be factory (what will a factory have been?) and where to localise the universal workers' capacity (of renewed political representation). This question can never be answered in advance, but what can be said is that the factory-prescription is fundamental for any emancipatory political stance siding with Badiou.

FEMINISM

Louise Burchill

Badiou's references to feminism are predominantly in the context of the battle he waged during the 1980s and 1990s against 'the cult of national, racial, sexual, religious and cultural identities seeking to undo the rights of the universal' (*SMP* 4). As a theory and practice based on the category of 'woman', broadly understood as referring to an existing identity presumed to provide a framework for political initiative, feminism is dismissed by Badiou as an 'identitarian standpoint', or communitarian particularism, whose calls for the recognition of women's rights and specificity can ultimately, whatever their importance, only amount to a demand for integration within the existing order of things. This follows from Badiou's core tenet that any authentic symbolic undertaking, such as an emancipatory politics seeking to transform society as a whole, can uniquely come about through 'subtraction' from 'identitarian predicates' referring – like 'woman' – to a pre-constituted historical group, since solely in this way does it attain a universal signification valid for one and all (*E* ch. 2; *SP* ch. 1).

Feminist theorists and philosophers who advocate a 'recognition of women's difference' are guilty, from this perspective, of the 'sophistic' claim that 'the only genuine universal prescription consists in respecting particularities' (TU/*TW* § 2). This is, of course, to deny a 'neutrality' to the universal – as is, indeed, the case in a wide spectrum of feminist analyses that argue the universal to consist, throughout history, of nothing more than the mystifying sublation of a point of view and values proper to one specific group that, whatever its other attributes, invariably proves to be male. Badiou disqualifies all such claims on the grounds that, in accordance with the necessary subtraction of identitarian predicates entailed in every truth process, 'there is no possible universal sublation of particularity' (ibid.).

Two crucial errors are imputed to feminists, along with other 'postmodernists' and 'advocates of an ethics of difference', who dispute the neutrality of the universal. First, the error of inconsistency: to contend that only an avowed respect of the plurality of particularities constitutes a genuine universal prescription amounts, all in all, to simply electing as universal norm another particular identity: namely, the western liberal democratic subject. The 'respect for differences' would, as a result, apply only to those differences consistent with the identity in question: namely, 'differences' deemed to be good democratic values, in attune with 'modernity' – such as 'the emancipation of women from patriarchal codes and constraints' (*E* 24; *SP* 11). Feminism is singled out in this context as especially inconsistent, even duplicitous. Advocating ostensibly a respect for differences, feminists reject, in fact, any value inassimilable to their own identity – even when that which is in question concerns a woman's choice in matters of her body and its attire. This is exemplified, for Badiou, by the so-called 'headscarf affair' – a lengthy public debate in France about 'cultural difference' and 'national integration' sparked off when three young Muslim women were expelled from their school in 1989 for wearing headscarves, the end result of which was a bill banning the wearing of conspicuous religious symbols (cf. 'The Law on the Islamic Headscarf' – IH). Feminists' objections to the hijab as a sign of male power over young girls and women infringing the right of all to self-determination would, for Badiou, be but a 'disguise' (*SMP* 141) dissimulating feminism's true championing of liberal demo-cratic ideology and pro-free-market rationale. Why otherwise would they so furiously decry this sign of patriarchal control over women's bodies and sexuality, yet remain silent in face of the far greater control exercised by capital's dictates that the female body be put on display and female sexual-ity maximally deployed (IH/*Pol* § 13 & 15)? In short, feminists' promotion of universal self-determination is to be deciphered as the exhortation to comply with the commoditisation of the body and the imperative to enjoy. Badiou underlines, moreover, the inseparability of this liberal democratic ideology from the coercive force of the military and juridical apparatuses: when he returns to the headscarf affair in 2009, it is to castigate feminists and intellectuals for the responsibility they bear in the anti-Islamic meas-ures voted in the wake of the ban on the hijab, and to recall feminists' support for the American bombing of Kabul (*FB* 2009).

The second error Badiou imputes to those denying the neutrality of the universal is that of inconsequentiality. Given that no truth – no universal – can be premised upon an existing situation, any position hailing a particu-larism, such as sexuated identity, as the bearer of innovation in the fields of art, science, love or politics is quite simply (for the Badiou of the eighties and nineties, at least) doomed to insignificance. For Badiou, the first to have understood that a truth process only has any real effectivity to the extent that there is a 'de-particularisation' of those adhering to this truth is Saint Paul, whose proclamation that, in respect to the event (the event-Christ), 'there is neither Jew nor Greek, neither slave nor free, neither male nor female' (Galatians 3: 28–9) constitutes a 'founding statement'. It is, then, all the more significant that Badiou privileges Paul's pronounce-ments on sexual difference when he sets out to elaborate what the 'dialec-ticisation of departicularism and trans-individual universalism' consists in (SEM 2010) – doing so, moreover, with the clearly stated objective of refuting feminist interpretations that condemn Paul as misogynist.

The Paulian prescription that women should cover their hair when they publicly pray or proclaim their faith is, for Badiou, an exemplary instance of 'universalising – departicularising and trans-individual – egalitarianism'. It would strictly set out to establish the universal's power over 'difference qua difference': insofar as a woman's long hair is in itself a sort of 'natural veil', the fact of reduplicating it by an artificial sign testifies both to women's acknowledging their sexed particularity and to the 'indifferentiation' of this identity within a symbolic process of trans-particular scope. Indeed, Badiou emphasises that the 'only reason' a woman must wear a veil is to show that the 'universality of the declaration' (i.e., the resurrection of Christ) includes '*women who confirm that they are women*' or, otherwise put, in order that the indifferentiation of sexual difference within the universal confirms the very status of the universal as such (*SP* 105). It is, then, of the utmost significance, from Badiou's perspective, that Paul addresses a 'symmetrical' prescription to men exhorting them to leave their head *uncovered* when they declare their faith or pray in public in order not to 'disavow' their sexed particularity, such as this is (in part) defined by the customs of Paul's time. Attesting in itself to an essential 'egalitarianism' of the universal, this 'symmetry' of constraints imposed upon men and women shows feminist criticisms of Paul's precepts in respect of women to be fundamentally skewed in that they take no account of the constraints Paul addresses to men. There is no disputing the massive sexual inequality of Paul's epoch, or even Paul's adhesion to the hierarchical vision of the world then prevalent, in terms of which Christ rules over man, and man rules over woman. Yet, with respect to his time, Paul proves to be progressive as concerns the status of women insofar as he conveys the universalising equality of truth by setting down constraints that apply symmetrically to men and women alike in lieu of unilateral ones in respect of women alone (*SP* 105).

That said, the objection could be made to Badiou here that, insofar as the veil is a sign of woman's subservience not only to God but also to man, stipulated to be 'the image of God' (1 Corinthians, 11: 7 and 13), Paul's 'hierarchical vision of the world' must be understood to underpin not only his so-called symmetry of constraints but the very 'truth of the declaration' since fidelity to the event-Christ entails acknowledging Christ to be 'the head of man' and, therefore, 'man the head of woman' (1 Corinthians 11: 3). Men and women are, in other words, treated equally by the law only in the *formal* sense that both are submitted to constraints, while the law itself proves to be *substantively* unequal insofar as it makes man the unmarked term (wholly in 'the image of God'), in relation to which woman is marked (both 'naturally'and 'artificially') as subservient – which is also to say, other or different. That this 'unequal difference' bears no significance for one's capacity to participate in the process of truth – truth being 'indifferent' to differences – in no way entails its not being (re-)marked within, and indeed by, the process as such.

Amounting, all in all, to claiming the inequality – or non-neutrality – of not only a law supposedly supporting the universal but the very content of a universalising truth process itself, this objection to Paul's precepts obviously runs contrary to all the claims Badiou himself makes for the latter in his 1997 book (see also McNulty 2005: 205). It is, then, all the more remarkable that, over the first decade of the twenty-first century, Badiou's thinking on the universal has taken a 'turn' whereby the non-neutrality of symbolic thought is no longer denounced as an error entertained by feminists and other postmodernist protagonists of a contemporary sophism, but affirmed as having characterised the history of 'humanity' up until today. Whence Badiou's declaration, in a lecture given in 2011 ('Figures de la femme' [Figures of Woman]), that a sexuation of symbolic and philosophical thought is inevitable once we acknowledge that the order of symbolic thought no longer depends upon the 'Name-of-the-Father' or the 'power of the One' as upheld traditionally from a masculine position (FF 10). It is not inconceivable that feminists' interrogations of Badiou's thesis on universality in the years following the publication of his book on Paul contributed to this inflection in his thought. Be this as it may, Badiou has acknowledged that questions regarding sexed universals have been made possible today because of 'the impact upon truths of the historical changes brought about by the feminist movement in the broadest sense' (personal communication, June 2011). In 2009, he equally declared twentieth-century 'feminine movements' to have influenced his 'insight' that 'a feminine perspective on political thought and action' would give rise to a new politics no longer based on power. The question today, he added, is whether 'feminine theory' is not, therefore, an essential part of a politics seeking a new way of action (cf. the 'Discussion' with Susan Spitzer in *IA*, esp. p. 6).

Badiou's speculations on the way in which sexuation would function in truth domains without God or a paternal guarantee remain – at the time of this entry's writing – strictly tentative, and formulated as such frequently in the interrogative: 'What is a woman who engages in the politics of emancipation? What is a woman artist, musician, painter or poet? A woman excelling in mathematics or physics? A woman philosopher? [. . .] And conversely, what do the fields of politics, art, science and love become once women fully participate [. . .] in the creative equality of symbols' (FF 16)? This interrogative inflection on the sexuation of truths has not, however, led Badiou to similarly 'question' his view of contemporary feminism as monolithically synonymous with liberal reformism. On the contrary, reiterating his denunciation of 'a bourgeois and domineering feminism' set solely on placing the existing order in the power of women and in no way interested in creating another world, Badiou's 2011 lecture confirms, all in all, feminism as an identitarian position, in terms of which 'woman' is now destined to become the new instance of the One, raised up on the ruins of the Name-of-the-Father (13, 15).

That admitted, Badiou's sustained hostility to 'feminism' calls for a few final remarks.

First, the 'national' or 'cultural' (and hence, political and historical) context of Badiou's relation to feminism (and 'femininity') needs to be at least mentioned here. Badiou's appraisal of contemporary feminists as aspiring solely to power and privilege shares the quasi-hegemonic view, among French intellectuals of his generation, of feminism as basically intent on reversing the power relations between the sexes and wresting phallic predicates from men. As reflected in texts written in the sixties to eighties by Badiou's philosophical peers – notably, Deleuze, Derrida, Irigaray, Kristeva and Lyotard – this view informs a twofold critique of feminism as hypostasising 'the feminine' in the figure of 'woman' and remaining, through its simple reversal of the man–woman hierarchy, within the metaphysical paradigm of binary oppositions. Moreover, as wary as one needs to be of the traps of culturalism, there is undoubtedly a different definition, and construction, of 'gender' within the specific social, historical and political contexts respectively making up 'French culture' and, say, 'Anglo-American culture'. Suffice it to say here that what seems to be a repudiation, in *The Incident at Antioch*, of 'second-wave feminists' not for any sort of 'reformist zeal' but for their eschewal of traditional forms of femininity – 'Looking ugly, wearing your hair pulled back, hiding your femininity under military fatigues or wearing shapeless dresses' is hardly required for a 'politics of hope and joy' (*IA*, Act III Scene IV) – raises the issue of an 'image of femininity' that has been less critically questioned in French culture, French feminism included, than in Anglo-American contexts.

Second, Badiou's characterisation of the feminist philosopher Luce Irigaray as 'an antiphilosopher, even the antiphilosopher *par excellence*', in that she operates 'a violent determination of philosophy on the basis of the category of "woman"' (personal communication, 2011), would seem to confirm that the category 'woman' remains for Badiou too entrenched in a 'particularism' to ever constitute the *subject* not only of an emancipatory politics but also of a philosophical enterprise. In accordance with his definition of antiphilosophy, Badiou is claiming here that Irigaray positions 'woman' as a sort of super-cognitive category that serves as the gauge of philosophical rectitude or failings. Again, Badiou concurs here with his philosophical peers who, in the sixties to eighties, objected to the hypostasis of the figure of 'woman' in feminist thought.

Third (and, as it were, *a contrario*), despite what Badiou himself states on the subject, one could argue that feminism (a *certain* feminism) fully qualifies, in Badiou's own terms, as an 'event' insofar as its declaring woman to be a 'subject' not only signals women's transformative passage from inexistence (the 'other of man'; 'the proletariat of the proletariat') to full subjective force but equally enjoins a radical change of the existing order.

Fourth, and finally, for all the disparaging predicates that Badiou attributes to the term 'feminism' – communitarian particularism and consequent reformism, a pretension to phallic predicates and the 'power of the "One"', profound collusion with reactionary forces and a reification of 'woman' as a sort of a transcendent ground – there are, throughout his work, a number of gestures that, in addition to his recent affirmation of sexed universals, can well qualify as 'feminist'. Other than including a young woman as one of Socrates' interlocutors in his 'hypertranslation' of Plato's *Republic*, Badiou has notably published three short texts on 'woman creators' – Joan of Arc, Sophie Germain and Emmy Noether – arguing that these women's surmounting the conditions of their time to participate within the truth processes of politics and mathematics constitutes exemplary proof of *woman*'s inclusion within the universal (cf. EN; SG; IJ). Such gestures, among others, show Badiou to consistently uphold women's 'right' to become subjective bodies-of-truths on an equal footing with men. That this is understood as a feminist 'fidelity' by Badiou himself is suggested by an affirmation that has all the declaratory force of a 'last word on the subject': 'Despite what people say, I am a feminist!' (personal communication, December 2011).

FIDELITY

Christopher Norris

Fidelity, in Badiou's lexicon, is a term that bears all its usual meanings – 'faithfulness, loyalty, steady allegiance, perseverance despite adverse conditions' – but also has a range of specific connotations developed throughout his work. Basically his usage can be seen to encompass the two distinct but – as he would have it – closely associated senses. The first of these has to do with truth as a matter of correctness, validity, warrant, or the match (correspondence) between truth-bearers and truth-makers, that is, between statements and whatever it is – in physical, historical, or mathematical reality – that fixes their truth-value. To this extent Badiou might be described as a realist or objectivist about truth, although that description needs qualifying in certain crucial ways. For the other main sense of 'fidelity' as Badiou deploys it has to do with those aspects that involve *truthfulness to* some idea, hypothesis, theory, project, undertaking, or political cause that requires an investment of intellectual or political faith beyond what is presently justified by the best available proof-procedures or total evidence to hand.

To most philosophers – at any rate, those within the mainstream analytic tradition – these senses would appear altogether distinct, though liable to confusion and therefore in need of periodic sorties to patrol the boundary between them. On this view the interests of truth require that it be conceived in objective terms, that is to say, as an attribute of certain statements that holds good whatever our current-best state of belief and (even more emphatically) whatever the dispositions, motives, or incentives that may induce certain seekers-after-truth to seek after certain truths. Anti-realists take a different view, holding that objectivism about truth places it forever in principle beyond human epistemic reach and hence leads inevitably to scepticism. Rather we should give up any idea of truth as recognition- or verification-transcendent, and instead make sure to avoid that undesirable upshot by treating it as epistemically constrained, i.e. as subject to the ultimate tribunal of best opinion or optimal belief amongst those best qualified to judge. However, both parties – realists and anti-realists – are agreed in upholding a firm distinction between what pertains to issues of truth and falsehood, on whatever precise understanding, and what pertains to the mindset or motivating interests of those involved in its pursuit. Thus even anti-realists who make no bones about confining truth to the scope and limits of human epistemic, perceptual, or evidential grasp will nevertheless draw what they take to be a well-defined and principled line between 'context of justification' and 'context of discovery'. That is, they will insist that questions of the former sort – whether issues of truth or of epistemic warrant – be treated as altogether separate from (and scientifically or philosophically prior to) any issue as to what may have prompted the interest or sparked the dedication of those embarked on some particular path of enquiry.

Badiou doesn't for one moment deny the importance of conserving that distinction insofar as it allows him to insist that certain paths of thought – in mathematics and elsewhere – have a genuine claim to the title of 'truth procedure' while others, lacking such orientation, must be counted beside the point for truth-evaluative purposes. Nor, for that matter, has he any quarrel with the analytic precept that we need to apply different criteria in assessing truth and truthfulness, the former involving primarily epistemological considerations while the latter takes us quickly into regions of psycho-biographical or socio-cultural-ideological research. In short, Badiou is as far out of sympathy with the advocates of 'science studies' or the 'strong' sociology of knowledge – those who would seek to annul that distinction in pursuit of their own social-science agenda – as any analytic upholder of the 'two contexts' principle. However, as I have said, his conception of fidelity is one that encompasses both truth and truthfulness-to, and which might therefore seem to run them together in a way that rides roughshod over any such boundary marker. Where this appearance misleads is by ignoring his argument that subjects of truth – 'subjects' in Badiou's very carefully specified sense of that term – are defined solely *in and through* their dedication to the truth procedure in question and not with reference to this or that aspect of their personal, professional, political, or non-truth-procedural lives. More precisely: events of that strictly extraneous character may later be seen to have a definite bearing on the subject thus defined, as for instance in the case of two notable mathematicians and members of the French wartime resistance – Jean Cavaillès and Albert Lautman – who were shot by the occupying German forces. However, it is just Badiou's point that their heroism was above all a matter of following through consistently on a certain combination of axioms (or major and minor, ethical and factual-circumstantial premises) that led them inescapably to sacrifice their lives in that cause (cf. *M* 2–8).

A further potential source of confusion here is the fact that Badiou draws a rigorous distinction between truth and 'veridicity', the latter pertaining to knowledge or what is currently (i.e., at some particular time and within some particular knowledge-community) taken to merit that title. By 'knowledge' he means what most analytic philosophers would refer to in doxastic rather than veritistic terms, that is, by talking about 'belief', 'best belief', 'expert judgement', 'qualified (best) opinion', or some other state of understanding short of – no matter how well-placed to approximate – knowledge. For them, knowledge properly speaking is a strictly factive or 'achievement' term, one that requires not merely the existence of more-or-less robust grounds for imputing truth but (as a downright definitional matter) the objective truth of what is known. For Badiou, on the other hand, 'knowledge' designates an epistemic state that falls short of truth precisely insofar as it harbours certain yet-to-be-recognised anomalies, paradoxes, aporias, or other such problems.

This is how he conceives the possibility of advancement in various fields, prototypically that of mathematics, where set-theoretical procedures like Cantor's diagonalisation and Paul Cohen's 'forcing' are able to demonstrate – albeit (necessarily) after the event – how new, sometimes epochal truths emerge through the process by which 'paradox turns into concept'. It is a process characterised by Badiou in strongly objectivist, truth-apt, and progressivist (or at any rate incremental) terms. Certainly it constitutes a standing reproof to that nowadays widespread doxa – whether post-structuralist, postmodern-pragmatist, Foucauldian, Kunhian, or (late) Wittgensteinian – according to which beliefs, items of knowledge, or truth-claims are all to be treated as relative (or 'internal') to some extant language-game or cultural life-form. That he nonetheless thinks of it as involving fidelity on the part of subjects in quest of such truths will seem contradictory or downright confused only to those who have failed to take the point of his radical redefinition of 'subject', i.e. his idea that subjects come into existence precisely in and through the commitment to some particular project or truth procedure.

So fidelity according to Badiou is an ethical as well as epistemic virtue, or rather – since he clearly rejects the distinction as traditionally drawn along with the two opposed terms in their standard usage – a name for that which transcends and confutes any treatment along those lines. In brief, it is an attribute of certain thought-procedures or kinds of action that involve both *truth* and *truthfulness* without involving the patent fallacy of collapsing the former into the latter and thereby embracing some form of naïve psychologism. Nor does it fall into the kindred error of some virtue-epistemologists who too readily suppose that talk about the ethical virtues of patience, open-mindedness, epistemic modesty, self-correction for cognitive bias, etc., can substitute for all that old philosophical talk of knowledge and truth. What renders his usage proof against any such charge is Badiou's flat-out rejection of the whole epistemological mode of thought that goes back to Plato but finds its central and defining episode in the sequence of modern European thinkers from Descartes through Kant to Husserl. In particular he has no time for the notion of 'judgement', famously a source of interpretative problems in Kant, since it has to do service as a kind of all-purpose mediating function that somehow accomplishes the passage between a number of otherwise disparate faculties such as those of sensuous intuition and conceptual understanding. However, his chief objection has to do with its tendency, in liberal thinkers from Kant to Hannah Arendt, to cast doubt on the merits of political activism – viewing it as always in some way precipitate or premature – and conversely to elevate the supposed virtue of a detached, reflective, and hence politically disengaged attitude towards great historical events such as (in Kant's case) the French Revolution.

To Badiou this appears nothing more than a philosophically evasive and politically craven retreat into the murky depths of a Kantian pseudo-faculty that offers a convenient bolt-hole for those anxious to shuck off the burden of rigorous thinking in either sphere. It is for this reason mainly that he takes such a hostile or downright dismissive line towards ethics, or the kinds of discourse – academic or popular – that tend to go under that title. What they typically do – on his diagnosis – is exploit these hyper-induced problems and complications in order to put obstacles in the way of any more direct appeal to truth, knowledge, and the rational grounds of politically motivated action. Badiou's anti-ethicist stance is not at all, as some of his detractors would have it, the product of a callous indifference to issues of moral or humanitarian concern, but a straightforward consequence of his wanting no part in the large-scale retreat from activist commitment that has been so conspicuous a feature of post-1968 French intellectual life. To eliminate the detour through judgement in its various modes – along with many of the problems that have dogged epistemology and ethics in the Kantian wake – is to encounter the utterly different order of thought that stands behind Badiou's deployment of the term 'fidelity'.

FORCING

Olivia Lucca Fraser

'Forcing' (*forçage*) is among Badiou's signature expressions. From 1968 onwards, it has traced out an axial category in his work. Despite certain shifts in meaning, it has sustained a cluster of ideas and concerns that are, throughout, invariant. The core idea seems to be this: *what Badiou calls 'forcing' is in each case a radical and systematic transformation of a situation by means of series of actions acting upon, or proceeding from, the real of the situation – that which, prior to the activity of forcing, subsists in the situation as an invisible, unoccupiable, or 'impossible' site, occluded by knowledge and cloaked by (the dominant) ideology.* Invariant too is that it is in each case *mathematics* that conditions the category of forcing.

We can split Badiou's use of the term into two periods, each of which presents a crucial variation on this central theme. The pivotal texts of each period, in which the concept of forcing is formulated or reformulated, are 'Infinitesimal Subversion' and *BE*. (For the sake of completeness, *TS* should also be mentioned, but despite the importance that a whole array of related and analogous concepts of *force*, *torsion*, etc. play in that text, the idea of *forcing* itself, appears only in a transitional capacity.)

Forcing in 'Infinitesimal Subversion'

The context of 'Infinitesimal Subversion' is the project undertaken by several members of *Le Cercle d'épistémologie* – the working group behind *Les Cahiers pour l'Analyse*, and to which Badiou belonged in the last years of the 1960s – to develop a general theory of *structural change*, informed by both Lacanian psychoanalysis and Althusserian historical materialism – a project which gave Badiou's enterprise its initial and lasting coordinates. With minimal violence, we can characterise it according to the following theses, which find their canonical expression in Jacques-Alain Miller's

'The Action of Structure' (published alongside Badiou's 'Infinitesimal Subversion', *Cahiers* vol. 9. Cf. also the recent English translations in Hallward and Peden 2012):

1. The structure of a situation always has at least one 'empty place', a place that, according to the structure, cannot be occupied. It is characterised by a certain structural impossibility, as the 'Real' of the situation. Jacques-Alain Miller calls this the '*utopic point*' of the structure. (97)
2. The empty place is, in general, indiscernible. It is a 'blind spot', unstably masked or 'sutured' by ideological or imaginary illusion.
3. 'Any activity that does not play itself out entirely in the imaginary but that is to transform the state of the structure', Miller writes, 'departs from the utopic point, the strategic post', specific to the situation. (97)

If the reader of these remarks recognises in the idea of a 'utopic point' not only an echo of Lévi-Strauss's 'floating signifier' and a fellow traveller of Deleuze's 'empty square' of structure, but a prefiguration of Badiou's later category of the 'evental site', then she is on the right track. But first we must turn to the text where the idea of *transforming a situation from the bias of its utopic point* is first thought through *under the condition* of mathematics, for it is by placing this notion under the mathematical condition that the *category of forcing* is won.

This all gets underway in 'Infinitesimal Subversion', where Badiou transports Miller's schema into the laboratory of formal mathematics and model theory, in an analysis of Abraham Robinson's invention of *non-standard analysis*. The situation's structured space of possibilities here becomes the *space of inscriptions* allowed by a formal axiomatic – the formulae that it can demonstrate. The Real, the 'utopic point', becomes the place of the *underivable*, the space unoccupiable by formulae licensed by the formalism. That every consistent formalism is punctuated by such impossibilities is an iron necessity; if every place could be occupied, and every expressible formula written down as a theorem, formalism would become 'an opaque body, a deregulated grammar, a language thick with nothing' (SI 122), which is to say, *inconsistent*. A formalism is only consistent – and so interpretable in a *model* – if there is at least one formula which it can express but not demonstrate; it is 'owing to the exclusion of certain statements, the impossibility of having the constants occupy certain constructible places, that an axiomatic system can operate as the system it is, and allow itself to be thought differentially as the discourse of a real' (122).

The demarcation of an unoccupiable place is made precise in mathematics, with its syntactical distinction between *constants* and *variables*. The system of finite arithmetic, for instance, allows no constant – no integer – to be substituted for the *y* in the expression '*For all integers n, n ≤ y*' – but by recourse to the *variable* '*y*' it is able to *mark* this inoccupiable place, without, for all that, *occupying* it. 'A variable', Badiou writes, 'ensures that impossible equations are sufficiently legible to read their impossibility'; it is the

operator of the real for a domain, it in fact authorises *within* that domain the writing of the impossible proper *to* it. The existent has as its category a being-able-not-to-be the value of a variable at the place it marks. (122)

'Forcing' is a procedure of radically transforming the structure by *occupying one or more of its real, unoccupiable places*, without for all that collapsing the structure into sheer inconsistency. It begins with an act of nomination, the definition of a *constant* that occupies an inoccupiable place, closing one of the open and formerly unsatisfiable sentences in which only variables could once be written. Robinson's intervention consists in defining a new constant α and axiomatically stipulating it to be such that for all real numbers *n*, *n* ≤ α, a gesture which, by occupying the inoccupiable, marks an intrusion of formalisation into the real that was its impasse. (Badiou calls occupation the inscription of an 'infinity-point', though the general concept is meant to apply to constants like the 'imaginary number' with which Bombelli breached the *x* in '$x^2 + 1 = 0$', which the existing algebra had declared inoccupiable.) The forcing procedure continues with a submission of the new constant to all the remaining operations of the initial system – α, for instance, can be added to, divided by, and so on, and so Robinson is able to define *infinitesimals* simply as multiples of $1/α$. In sum:

the infinity-point is the marking of something inaccessible for the domain; a marking completed by a *forcing* of procedures, constraining them to be applied to precisely that which they had excluded. Of course, this forcing entails a modification of the way in which the domain is set out, since the constructible objects in the higher domain are able to occupy places which those of the domain itself 'inoc-cupy'. The new space in which the procedures can be exercised is disconnected from that which preceded it. The models of the system are stratified. (SI 120)

This brings about not merely an extension, but a transformation of the domain in question: new patterns are unleashed, old ones often destroyed. And so Badiou goes on to identify this *forcing procedure* as a 'reforging' (*refonte*) of the structure, connecting it explicitly with the theory of *epistemological breaks*, a theory that he inherits, with modifications, from

Althusser and Bachelard – a recognisable prototype of the theory of *truths* unleashed in *BE*.

Forcing in *Being and Event*

Between the theory of forcing presented in 'Infinitesimal Subversion' and the one we find in *BE* intervenes a new and decisive condition: a technique developed by Paul J. Cohen in his proof of the independence of the Generalised Continuum Hypothesis and the Axiom of Choice from the axioms of Zermelo-Fraenkel set theory (ZF), which likewise appears under the name of 'forcing'. Before we address its incorporation into Badiou's philosophical apparatus, we will take a quick look at forcing in its native, mathematical terrain.

It is, once again, set-theoretical model theory that provides Badiou with the requisite conceptual (scientific) material. Like Robinson's procedure for the making of 'non-standard' models, Cohen's forcing technique is, at bottom, a systematic way of generating a new model from a model already given. The main thrust of Cohen's proof is to take a countable, transitive model of ZF and '*force*' the existence of a new model by supplementing it with a generic element *included* in, but not *belonging* to, the initial model – together with all the sets which can be constructed on the supplement's basis as licensed by the ZF axiomatic. Considered in its logical structure, forcing is a relation of the form 'α forces P', where α is a set and P a proposition that will hold in the generic extension of the initial model – *provided that* a turns out to *belong to the generic supplement* on which that extension is based. In this respect, forcing resembles a logical inference relation, but one that differs markedly from the inference relation of classical logic – the *law of the excluded middle*, in particular, does not hold for the forcing relation, and the logic it generates is essentially *intuitionistic* (cf. Fraser 2007).

As Cohen has shown, the consequences of this supplementation can be quite extraordinary, and go far beyond simply adding a new set's name to the census. The generic supplement, for instance, may be structured so as to induce a one-to-one correspondence between transfinite ordinals that, in the initial model/situation, counted as distinct orders of infinity, thereby collapsing them onto one another and making them effectively *equal*. Cohen exploited this possibility to great effect by taking the model that Gödel had built in order to show that the Generalised Continuum Hypothesis (GCH) – the thesis that the size of the set of subsets of any transfinite cardinal number $\aleph_n$ is equal in size to the next greatest cardinal $\aleph_{n+1}$ – is *consistent* with ZF (a model in which the continuum hypothesis *holds*), and on its basis *forcing* a generic extension in which the continuum hypothesis *fails* (the extension being a model in which the set of subsets of

$\aleph_n$ is demonstrably equal to *almost any cardinal whatsoever*, so long as it's larger than $\aleph_n$), thereby demonstrating the consistency of GCH's *negation* with the theory, and hence the *independence*, or undecidability, of GCH with respect to ZF.

BE recovers Cohen's concept and enlists it in a re-articulation of the existing category of forcing: the set underlying the model is now seized upon as the *situation* that forcing will transform, and faithful to Miller's cartography of change, Badiou adds that the whole procedure – both the articulation of the generic truth and the forcing of its consequences for the situation to come – must in every case proceed from an anomalous occurrence in the 'utopic point' of the situation in question, now rechristened 'evental site'. Though it is now Cohen rather than Robinson whose mathematics condition Badiou's theory of change, the new category of forcing preserves most of the features familiar to us from 'Infinitesimal Subversion'. One crucial difference, however, is that the whole process is now seized as a *logic of subjective action*: Forcing is now named 'the law of the subject' (*BE* 411), the form by which *a subject faithful to an event* transforms her situation into one to which a *still-unknown truth* (understood as a generic subset of the initial situation) well and truly belongs, by deriving consequences that the inscription of this new constant will have brought about.

In light of *BE's* decision to interpret ZF as the theory of *being qua being*, and *forcing* as the form of a subject's truth-bearing practice, Badiou extracts two lessons from Cohen's proof of the undecidability of GCH: first, that it demonstrates the existence of a *radical ontological gap* or 'impasse' between infinite multiplicities and the sets of their subsets (to which Badiou associated the notions of 'representation' or 'state of a situation'), the exact measure of which is indeterminate at the level of being-in-itself; second, that this ontological undecidability is nevertheless decidable *in practice*, but only through the faithful effectuation of a truth, suspended from the anomalous occurrence of an event.

GENERIC

Olivia Lucca Fraser

The concept of 'the generic', which Badiou first deploys in *TS* in an essentially metaphorical reflection on the subjectivising production of excess

(271–4), comes into full philosophical force in *BE*, where it is taken up to describe the ontological – set-theoretical – structure of a truth procedure: the total multiplicity that will have been composed of all the elements in the situation that a faithful subject positively links to the name of an event (by way of a 'fidelity operator'), from the perspective of this multiplicity's always-futural and infinite completion, takes the form of a *generic subset* of the situation in which the subject of truth operates. As a consequence of their genericity, truth procedures exhibit at least five critical traits: (1) their *indiscernible, unpredictable* and *aleatory* character; (2) their *infinitude*; (3) their *excrescence* relative to the situation; (4) their *situatedness*, and (5) their *universality*. The concept of a *generic subset* itself was first formulated by the mathematician Paul J. Cohen in his 1963 proofs of the independence of the Generalised Continuum Hypothesis (GCH) and the Axiom of Choice (AC) relative to the axioms of Zermelo-Fraenkel set theory (ZF). The problem Cohen faced was this: Kurt Gödel had already shown (in 1940) that both GCH and AC are *consistent* with ZF by showing that if ZF has a model, then a model can also be produced which satisfies ZF supplemented by GCH and AC. This means that one can never prove the *negation* of GCH or AC on the basis of ZF, but it *does not* imply that the statements themselves can be proven. To show that ZF is no more able to entail these theses than their negations, Cohen sought to construct a model in which AC and GCH fail to hold. This would show that they are independent – or *undecideable* – relative to ZF. Cohen's strategy was to alter Gödel's model S (in which GCH and AC do hold) by supplementing it with (i) a single element ♀ and (ii) everything that can be axiomatically constructed on its basis. The supplemented construction $S(♀)$ must be capable of satisfying the ZF axioms (and so remaining a model of ZF) while encoding the information needed to falsify GCH or AC (information which can be extracted by the forcing procedure). The difficulty is this: though it suffices to encode the many ZF theorems concerning *transfinite sets*, 'from the outside' (when embedded in a sufficiently rich supermodel, that is) Gödel's model-structure appears to be *countable* (it can be placed in a one-to-one correspondence with the set of natural numbers). (The surprising fact that set theory has such models, if it has any at all, is guaranteed by the Löwenheim–Skolem Theorem.) Any supplement carrying that kind of information would spoil the structure's claim to be a model of ZF, and so:

♀ must have certain special properties if $S(♀)$ is to be a model. Rather than describe it directly, it is better to examine the various properties of ♀ and determine which are desirable and which are not. The chief point is that we do not wish ♀ to contain 'special' information about S, which can only be seen from the outside [. . .] The ♀ which we construct will be referred to as a 'generic' set relative to S. The idea is that all the properties of ♀ must be 'forced' to hold merely on the basis that ♀ behaves like a 'generic' set in S. This concept of deciding when a statement about ♀ is 'forced' to hold is the key point of the construction. (cf. Cohen 1966: 111 – notation modified to parallel Badiou's in *BE*)

Leaving technical subtleties aside, the idea is to construct ♀ in such a way that *for every* predicate or 'encyclopedic determinant' restricted to S (where 'restricted' means that its constants and quantified variables range only over elements of S), ♀ contains at least one element which fails to satisfy this predicate. This suffices to determine the generic: (1) as *indiscernible*, insofar as *no predicate* can separate it from the swarming multitudes of S, and for this reason the generic must present itself in time as *unpredictable* and *aleatory*, its lawless composition impossible to forecast; (2) as *infinite*, since it remains essentially possible to determine any *finite* multiplicity by means of a complex predicate, even if this is only a *list* of its constituents (the syntactic constraints of set theory, if nothing else, prevent us from ever writing an *infinitely* long formula); (3) as *excrescent*, meaning that it is a *subset* but not an *element* of the 'situation' (the *model* in which the generic is articulated), the reason for this being that if ♀ was an *element* of S, then the predicate '$x \in$ ♀' alone would be enough to capture it; (4) as *situated* or *immanent*, since genericity is by no means an *absolute* property, but one which is relative to the model in which it is articulated; (5) as *universal*, since the generic outstrips every mark of particularity to the extent that no element of the model is excluded from entering into a generic subset by reason of the predicates it bears. Finally, though it must be connected to an essentially non-mathematical (non-ontological) *theory of the event* in order to do so, genericity helps to capture the idea that truths are effected through the work of a subject *whose existence precedes and outstrips its essence*. The 'existentialist' resonance that the concept of genericity brings to the Badiousian theory of the subject must be taken seriously, for it bears directly on obstacles accompanying trait (2): insofar as every actual truth procedure unfolds undeterministically *in time*, each procedure is at any actual moment *finite*, and can lay claim to genericity only by *projecting itself ahead of itself*, by being the future it factically is not: the infinite truth-multiple that it seeks to complete but which it cannot fully determine in advance.

HEIDEGGER

Norman Madarasz

From the outset, Badiou's thesis on ontology recognises Heidegger's importance for philosophy, as he established the need to clearly articulate a thought
on being qua being. As he writes in the introduction to *BE*, 'With Heidegger,
we defend that the requalification of philosophy must be sustained from the
angle of the ontological question' (8). More recently, Heidegger has assumed
for Badiou the position of 'greatest philosopher of the twentieth century'.
Nonetheless, Badiou's system initiates one of the most accomplished alternatives to the Heideggerian paradigm of ontology and philosophy *tout court*.
As Dominique Janicaud writes of *BE*, it is 'the first book since *Being and Time*
that again dares to ask the question, "What about being qua being?", and
brings forth an answer to it' (Janicaud 1993: 187–8).

Invariably, Badiou returns to Heidegger. In the midst of the '*affaire
Heidegger*', however, it was not his Nazism that created the drama for
philosophy, but what Badiou argued was Heidegger's 'pertinent and
legitimate diagnosis' of how the power of the poem was to 'relay thought'.
As such, philosophy rendered itself to the poem in a suture that empowered philosophy again, although at the expense of transforming it into 'the
system of its aberrations' (ES 84).

Still, the central concept of Badiou's ontological reconstruction is
the event. The latter derives in part from *Ereignis*, which was forged by
Heidegger in the 1930s, and entered the French context through the work
of Derrida and Deleuze in the semantic matrix of May 1968. The shift in
referential scope must be emphasised, however. In *LW*, Badiou considers
Ereignis as 'being as coming-to-be' (381), which is considerably different, if not radically opposed to his own definition of *événement*. Badiou's
understanding and defining of 'event' also undergoes major changes as
he moves from the ontological register to that of appearing in the world.
In the ontology, the event is defined subtractively as a rupture in a situation; it is the site of an event that gives it its character. In *LW*, the event
is but the most intensive of the four figures of change that emerge from
the appearing into a world of what once was a point of inexistence. In this
sense, Badiou asserts that the specific definition of 'existing' he uses also
has its source in Heidegger as always 'relative to a world' (208).

For all that, the nature of Badiou's ontology is to break with the diagnosis of the results of the one articulated by Heidegger (*MP* 114). Heidegger's motif of the 'end of philosophy' is identified as one of the reasons that led to the general state of malaise in which philosophy found itself in France in the 1980s (ibid., chapter 1). As a combat position, Badiou takes issue with Heidegger's belief that 'we are historically directed by the forgetting of being, and even by the forgetting of this forgetting' (ibid., 115). Thesis 2 of 'The (Re)turn of Philosophy Itself' clearly marks Badiou's disagreement with the Heideggerian school in France as he decides to turn the motif of forgetting against itself, that is, a forgetting of forgetting, in order to decide instead on a new beginning in an old matter (ibid.).

Regardless of how firmly he holds to such decisionism – after all, it would be inconsistent for a Marxist-Maoist of Badiou's calibre to forgive Heidegger's revolutionary enthusiasm for Hitler – Badiou's break with Heidegger converges on at least three questions: (1) mathematics as ontology itself, (2) the concept of subject, and (3) the locus of the poem as one in which truths are produced.

1. Mathematics as ontology: Heidegger activated the use of logical operators previously associated with sophistic reasoning. The hermeneutic circle, which he defends explicitly in *Being and Time* as a virtuous circle, is foremost amongst those operators. But given the predominance of Aristotelian logic in the onto-theological setting of Germany in the 1910s, Heidegger increasingly saw logic as an impediment to deal with the forgetting of being and the demands of non-objective thought. Heidegger cannot be said to have been ignorant of the groundbreaking work done in mathematics in the late nineteenth century, as he wrote his second published article on Frege and Russell. He may very well have been aware of Cantor's transfinite numbers, though the latter did nothing to change his mind on the unitary nature of the infinite. Heidegger's disobjectification of God, as is seen clearly in the publication of the *Gesamtausgabe*, stems from both the religious conflict within German Catholicism, of which Messkirch was a centre during Heidegger's youth, and from the implications of *Ereignis* as a formative and process concept undersigning the category of identity. For Heidegger, God is without Being – or without being 'God', as Jean-Luc Marion has argued. Whether one reads a reworking of the conception of the divine and the sacred into Heidegger's speculations on *Ereignis*, it is plain that neither logic nor mathematics, nor the multiple, are deemed by him to capture that thought. This would be a matter instead for the poetic word. Yet Badiou claims that the antinomy of the matheme and the poem Heidegger sets up is groundless:

'Heidegger constructs the antinomy of the matheme and the poem in such a way as to make it coincide with the opposition of knowledge and truth, or the subject/object couple and Being [. . .] The authentic relation of poets to mathematics is of a completely different nature. It takes the form of a relation of raveled rivalry, of heterogeneous community *occupying the same point*' (*MP* 75). Unlike Heidegger, Badiou stresses the mathematical insight encountered in the poets of philosophical relevance (Lautréamont, Rimbaud, Pessoa). On this basis, he asserts that 'poetry, thus more profound than its philosopher servant, has been altogether aware of a *sharing of thinking* with mathematics [. . .]' (ibid.).

2. Heidegger was the first philosopher to coherently expel the subject from the ontological domain. When checking that Badiou has reintroduced the subject into the ontological domain, one ought to be cautious and speak of the 'subject', for the latter is anything but a return to a previous configuration. Badiou claims that 'for Heidegger, 'subject' is a secondary elaboration of the reign of technology' (ibid.). And he maintains this idea of a secondary elaboration, albeit in complete disconnection from technology, as the subject is 'second' to the event. There is no subject independent from the event. However, the event is not warranted on an objective scale: it relies on a subjective gesture to acquire its name.

3. One of the most controversial statements in Badiou's work is found in his thesis on the 'end of the age of the poets'. This thesis is an inaugural position regarding the concept of 'suturing', which is one of the main arguments explaining philosophy's discontinuous existence since its inception in ancient Greece. Badiou does not so much criticise Heidegger here as issue the need to complete this age, which begins with Holderlin and ends in the torment and drama of Paul Celan's suicide. In recognition of the master of Todtnauberg, Badiou writes, 'until today, Heidegger's thinking has owed its persuasive power to having been the only one to pick up what was at stake in the poem, namely the destitution of object fetishism, the opposition of truth and knowledge, and lastly, the essential disorientation of our epoch' (ibid. 74). In Badiou's thought, these are some of the essential characteristics of the poetic contribution to philosophy. Nonetheless, it is of utmost importance for philosophy to free itself from the poetic suture.

More so, Badiou rejects Heidegger's diagnosis of the radical finitude of Dasein. Dasein is in the fundamental situation, but Dasein also becomes a subject, an 'immortal', when recognising, i.e. naming, the event. As becoming a subject immediately raises the question of the bounds of finitude, Heidegger's maintenance of a theological conception of the infinite makes his claim on science problematic. This is the upshot, according to Badiou, of Heidegger's sidelining of the mathematical sciences to the dominion of the essence of technology's nefarious threat to being qua being. It is the reason he parts with Heidegger's reconstruction of a fundamental ontology, as well as the entire existential analytic of Dasein.

The most detailed critique of Heidegger occurs in *MP*, chapter 4. On a point-by-point basis, then, the dynamic is as follows:

1. Badiou accepts the critique of the Subject, but rejects the expulsion of subjective forms from the ontological field.
2. Badiou accepts the diagnosis of the Earth's destiny as under constant menace, but considers it has more to do with the dynamic of Capital than technology per se (ibid. 56).
3. While Badiou recognises the poetic word has preserved Being from oblivion, he considers this to be the result of a philosophical imposition on the poem, which has led philosophy to a suture with some forms of poetry, i.e. the essential forms designated by the term 'poem' (72–3).
4. Philosophy has attained a form of completion. However, this is the form in which it has been sutured to the poem.
5. The hypothesis of a return of Gods ought to be ruled out, as it is the illusion arising from Being when captured under the equivalence of the One and the Infinite. The option of thinking Being under the concept of pure multiplicity is sufficient to maintain philosophy within an atheistic fold.

The critique of Heidegger continues to be the backdrop against which Badiou develops his ontology. In *MP*, Badiou's critique is local, or indeed an accumulation of local issues. Over the long course, Badiou is able to issue Heidegger's most notorious critique against himself. In the *SMP*, Badiou writes, that which is in question in what Heidegger calls ontological difference can be said to be the immanent gap between mathematics and logic. It would be proper then, in order to continue to follow him, to call 'metaphysical' any orientation of thought confusing mathematics and logic under the same Idea (*SMP* 42). Badiou does anything but confuse the two. As such, in terms of his own philosophical output, Badiou sets Heidegger up as a metaphysician, which means he is debarred from within ontology, although not from philosophy.

Heidegger also has the distinct privilege of setting one of the limits of the linguistic turn, the other being accomplished with Wittgenstein. According to Badiou, 'they each turn the identification [of mathematics with logic] into an appeal to the poem as that which persists in naming what is withdrawn. With Heidegger, all that remains for us is the song that names the Earth' (*TO* 109). This remains after the exhaustive effort of submerging language into an interpretative frame. Badiou concludes the *SMP* recalling how the first one was aimed against Heidegger and especially Heideggerians, whom he calls his 'enemies'. As such, the Platonic gesture is identified as a war machine to rid philosophy of Heideggerian motifs, and ontology of language-based interpretation. Mathematics is neither language, nor interpretation – although it is *logos*, *logos* as the truth of the real, just as Heidegger has speculated.

One does not rid Heidegger from ontology with ease. It should come as no surprise, then, that in the preface to the French translation of correspondence between Martin and Elfride that he co-authored with Barbara Cassin – subsequently published as a book titled *Heidegger: le Nazisme, les femmes, la philosophie* – Badiou considers Heidegger 'without a doubt, [to be] one of the most important philosophers of the twentieth century' (*H* 27–8), as well as 'a Nazi, a common Nazi, a middle-class Nazi from the provinces . . .' (30).

HISTORY/HISTORICITY

Steven Corcoran

For Badiou, the only history there is, properly speaking, is the history of truth, or rather of truth*s*. In the 1970s, Foucault also spoke of the history of truth, in a genealogical attempt to de-absolutise the notion of truth by reducing it to the always specific effects of certain epistemological and historical conditions. That is, for Foucault, the history of truth, which he calls a political history, rests upon his inscription of truth in a pragmatics of expression, and subsequent emphasis on effect (truth qua phenomenon) and efficacy (productions of knowledge-induced power differentials) (cf. Balibar 2004). Badiou's thesis about the history of truths is far from this notion of truth-effects, which he flips on its head. He does not try to dissolve the absoluteness of truth through history by showing how it is caught up in a genealogy of power, but shows that processes of truth have their own effects and efficacy, and that this is genuine history. More precisely, his positive doctrine of truths entails a seemingly paradoxical link between history and eternity: there can be a history only of the eternal, because only the eternal hinges on the chance encounter of an event. At least two key dimensions emerge from this link between history and eternity: the first is that Badiou is brought to oppose two standard positions that presuppose the diametrical opposition of history and eternity. Second, it leads him to oppose two very different but equally 'idealist' notions of history: the idea of a totalising Marxist-Hegelian History (in *TS*) and that of what he calls 'democratic materialism' (in *LW*).

According to classical metaphysics, there can be eternal truths deprived as such of their historicity, that is, of the specificity of their historical appearing. Democratic materialism turns this around, claiming that there can be no eternal truth, since all discursive statements (even those of mathematics) are irremediably inscribed in, and thus reducible to, the complex series of historico-cultural processes within which they appear. What both positions thus share is an emphasis on the mutual exclusivity of truth and history.

In *BE*, Badiou argues that neither position holds. Truths are at once the truths of historical situations, specified as such in their historical variability, and yet no less eternal for all that. He repugns the classical idea of a metaphysical system, with its emphasis on timeless, necessary truths untouched by historical variation, thanks to two novelties: the theory of the event, which provides a rigorous linkage of eternal truths to contingency; and the theory of conditions, which states that philosophy is conditioned by no less than four truth procedures (art, love, politics, science). Combining these doctrines, Badiou can argue that there are eternal truths, but that they cannot be unified in a metaphysical system (see Meillassoux 2010). This is so precisely because truths are spread across the above-mentioned singular and irreducibly heterogeneous truth procedures, and because these latter, being contingent, are immanent to a situation, unable to exist in any transcendent realm. Instead, truths insist in their effects, effects that are brought about through the chance encounter of an event and the fidelity of subjects that investigate the world in its wake. Conversely, against the historicist viewpoint – vulgar Marxism as much as democratic materialism – Badiou argues that there can be truths, which is to say localised procedures of thought, irreducible to the historical and cultural context from which they emerge.

LW adds cogency to Badiou's claims that all processes lacking truth are not historical in the true sense. The theory of appearing developed in it strives to show, on the contrary, that processes without truth amount to simple temporal modifications – 'facts' in the language of *LW* – which are governed by a transcendental of appearing, and are thus fully part of the world of their appearing. (As such a world without truth procedure is not a mere stasis but a series of governed modifications, which may secede one another rather rapidly on a phenomenological level, but without breaching the transcendental governing them. Through such means Badiou is able to show that capitalism, which is often said to exist only through continually revolutionising its conditions of existence, the production of crises etc., nonetheless in so doing does not ever breach the transcendental of appearing of the world of which it is part.)

History in the true sense is thus not a matter of asking 'What happened?' and of reconstructing a story and determining its causes (see C, esp. Ch. 1). For Badiou we cannot presume to be in human history, which, if it is to be universal – and all truly human history is universal – must depend on an event, on the contingent construction of a generic multiplicity, rather than on governance through a transcendental. As beings with bodies and languages, we can only presume to be in a world, replete with its hierarchies and formations of knowledge, e.g. in situations of political governance or at a certain state of artistic achievement, distributed into its recognised schools, and so on. Only the ontological illegality of the event (a generic multiplicity escapes the transcendental – it is indiscernible, which means that it also has all the properties of a given situation, but in a way that is undecidable and defies all procedures for the application of a law) can disturb the order of knowledge (e.g. May '68, Cubism). Undecidable in its happening, whoever subjectivates such rare and chance-ridden occurrences partakes in making a new kind of procedure prevail, which is the only kind of proof that this event really and truly occurred, and which in turn results in a radical reorganisation of knowledge.

Where history plays out, then, is (1) in the movement between the situated event, (2) the truth that, (3) provided it is subjectivated and a fidelity to it invented, might have been. This is slightly complicated in *LW* by Badiou's fourfold typology of figures of the subject – as the reactionary subject also produces novelties. Nonetheless, it is the militant discourse of the faithful subject (Cantor, the Party, and so on. See *BE* 392), not the reactionary's, that supports such truths and is able to escape the grasp of erudition (indeed, reactionary novelties can only be grasped as operations performed on the discourse of a faithful subject that attempt to undo it and render it obscure). For the erudite historian, bound to a version of history as a succession of brute facts, the eventual disappearance will always lead to claims that the novelty was merely apparent. This is because the very subtraction of the eventual name or statement from the event itself yields only a succession of complex processes entirely accessible to knowledge, which when they disappear will give rise to claims that, for example, May '68 didn't take place, nothing occurred politically, it was merely about *updating* French mores to contemporary capitalism, and so on. It is thus only the militant procedure and discourse that will ever decide whether or not these claims are true.

But how is it that such truths, whose being is generic, can be at once eternal and the bearers of history, the only genuine history? It is because a truth bears on an infinite number of consequences, a set of inquiries that is inexhaustible and capable of being extended to historical moments in vastly different contexts. The historical consequences of a particular sequence of truth will remain acquired, once and for all, but the unfolding may become saturated. Saturation does not imply failure or exhaustion, however, since a truth is *infinite*, meaning that it can and indeed must – if it is really to be counted as a truth – be reinvented in another world. The practico-theoretical movements of a truth thus comprise a history that is both profound (is continually deepened) and discontinuous (requires refounding in the particular world of its appearing).

Badiou can thus also show why it is that those bound to the discovery of new consequences of a truth simultaneously produce a genealogy of precursors. A precursor, by definition, is someone that is *retrospectively* determined as having come before. The novelty of truth, therefore, always *forces* a rediscovered, i.e. previously unknown historical depth, gathering together a series of ideas hitherto dispersed in the general intelligence (in the register of philosophy, which itself does not produce any truths, one could argue that the singularity of Badiou's position on the relation between truth and history marks out a singular, hitherto unforeseen position, replete with its series of precursors, in the field of French philosophy – on philosophy not having a history, see *PM*, Chap. 1; on Badiou's philosophical genealogy see Badiou's Preface to *AFP*).

If history is identical to the history of truth, then the historicity of a particular truth is caught between the realisation of an idea in the present and the production of a past, seen as unknown or misinterpreted, in which that idea was seminal but which the present adds a twist to. (See for example the way that the twentieth century's 'passion for the real' relates to the nineteenth century in *C*.) This production of an unseen or misinterpreted past also enables the present of an unfolding truth to be grasped as the deepening of consequences of a previously articulated truth within a new world. Hence, for example, Badiou speaks, in the light of work done by his fellow traveller Sylvain Lazarus, of the 'historical modes' of the realisation of the communist Idea (cf. *M*, 39).

The eternity of truths is thus possible because they are historical. The truths of a particular procedure carve out a history, their temporal sequences tying together across otherwise disparate worlds, as transfixed subjects unfold more deeply the infinity of their consequences. An example Badiou gives of this is the development of the mathematical truth discovered in Euclidean geometry, 'so significant that it has governed the entire development of modern abstract algebra', namely that 'prime numbers are always implicated in the multiplicative composition of a non-prime number' (*LW* 13). As we also see in Badiou's 'hypertranslation' of Plato's *Republic*, the truths of Plato's time are still truths for us, thus proving their eternal nature, but they cannot be so in the form of simple and sterile repetition, as though they were a knowledge that we'd simply forgotten to apply. Rather, they and the very means for accessing them must themselves be reinvented: each new reactivation of a truth sets new consequences in motion, further opening the revolutionary path.

So, for Badiou, the right way to relate history and truth is not to see truth as always and ever recommenced, as that which pushes history along in its becoming. Truth does not *happen to* history, nor, for that matter, history to truth. Instead, it is a truth's reactivation, which is to say its infinite capacity for redeployment within worlds that *gives rise to* history. History is only ever 'reawakened' by the rare appearance of an event that, by definition, exceeds the order of commonplace worldly appearing that governs the activities with which we ordinarily while away the hours. It is only deepened by a subject that, organising a fidelity and unfolding the event's consequences, avails itself of a possible real future, any genuine sense of which must involve a leap into the unknown, tearing us from the routine of daily work and social relations, pitting us against the arbitrariness of oppression and breaking with the ruling opinions that prop it all up.

LW, as aforementioned, gives a more rigorous form to *BE*'s thesis about historico-eternal truths by articulating a concept of world that goes further to the somewhat analogous concept of situation in *BE*. The concept of 'world' aims at formulating the context of appearance of a truth. It allows us to think through the connection between a posited truth (as the rising to the surface of a situation of immutable inconsistency) and the extraordinarily various historico-cultural contexts in which that same truth can reveal itself to subjects who would otherwise be irremediably separated from one another and thereby can attest to a common Humanity.

This is something that the relativism of democratic materialism of course denies is possible. Democratic materialism claims to be the only genuine historical materialism. It pretends that the only existing materiality is that of 'bodies and languages'. This ontological thesis pretends to a totalisation of the field of materiality, which Badiou emphasises through the suffix '-ism'. But it also irremediably commits any resultant vision of history to a cultural, linguistic and historical relativism, since, for Badiou, it repudiates the materiality of the being-there of truths which, incorporated into subject-bodies, exceeds circumscription within any knowledge–power nexus. Badiou's statement that 'there is no History' – with a capital H – thus finds two targets. The first is in *TS*, where he rails against Hegelian-Marxist totalising conceptions of History (see *TS* 92; *BE*

176–7); the second, over twenty years later, is in *LW*, namely the above-mentioned democratic materialism. Apropos the latter, Badiou does not claim that the unfolding present of truths are made of anything else other than bodies and languages, but that their consisting in transworldly effects – 'acquired once and for all' – attests to the emergence of a dimension beyond the perishable existences that form their material supports. Democratic materialism, by contrast, merely describes a world without present: the finitude of bodies and languages simply perishes. There is no other materiality that would exceed them, that would subtract itself from the present order of things. Without any immanent excess in a situation, we are simply destined to repeat a series of governed variations of appearing, a series of coordinates inscribed in past appearing. The difference between past and future collapses, then, because the latter is already inscribed in the former as foreseeable. The future thus being no more than a repetition of the past, the present is no more than a past on the way to a predictable future and lost in perdition.

It should thus be clear why, despite its infinite variability or 'complexity' – something many philosophers, vitalists, deconstructionists and the like of the past fifty years love to emphasise, but that Badiou considers unworthy of genuine thought – Badiou thinks that appearing can have no history (Meillassoux 2010). Because, as characterised by an absence of truth, of any real present, it involves the sheer repetition and maintenance of being. Changes of intensity of a being (a person, a number, a country, etc.) in various contexts do not go to making up a history, whether continuous or discontinuous. Any country will present differences in the intensity of its appearing across non-continuous worlds, but may also exhibit long periods of relative structural constancy (feudal Russia, for example). But this does not comprise a history, since the history of a country will reside essentially in the consistency forged through the productions of generic multiplicities that, in the aftermath of an event, make a truth of it (i.e., give generic expression to its elements). Last but not least, we should mention a crucial addition to Badiou's arguments: in *LW* he provides himself the wherewithal to argue against those that claim his version of the history of truth to be akin to creation *ex nihilo*: on the contrary, it involves the abrupt manifestation of something that already existed in the situation but whose existing in it was consistently thwarted. Genuine historical breakthroughs thus occur only when the 'inexistent comes to exist', when a being or beings belonging to a world, but whose intensity of existing in this world is almost nil, suddenly develop a point of autonomy that makes the norms of appearing of this world in-consist.

$$\boxed{I}$$

IDEOLOGY

Olivia Lucca Fraser

Badiou's most explicit meditations on the topic of ideology appear in a series of texts written over the course of a decade or so, stretching from the late 1960s to the late 1970s. The series divides in two: the first sequence, all composed prior to the events of May 1968, aims to think ideology as *that from which thought subtracts itself*, impurely and interminably, whether through *aesthetic process* or *epistemological break*. The second sequence, in which a faithful articulation of the uprising's consequences is at stake, and in which *political rebellion* comes to actively condition Badiou's philosophy, aims to think ideology itself as *a mode of struggle and process of scission*.

Ideology: before 1968

In 'The (Re)commencement of Dialectical Materialism' ([1967], in *AFP*), Badiou distils a highly schematic concept of ideology from Althusser's work, breaking ideology into the three imaginary functions of *repetition*, *totalisation* and *placement*, which serve:

1. to institute the repetition of immediate givens in a 'system of representations [. . .] thereby produc[ing] an effect of *recognition* [*reconnaissance*] rather than cognition [*connaissance*]' (RMD/*AFP* 449; tm);
2. to establish this repetitional system within the horizon of a totalised lifeworld, 'a normative complex that *legitimates* the phenomenal given (what Marx calls appearance)', engendering 'the *feeling* of the theoretical. The imaginary thus announces itself in the relation to the "world" as a *unifying pressure*' (450–1).
3. to interpellate both individuals and scientific concepts (crossbred with ideological notions) into the horizons of that lifeworld (450, 450 n.19).

In the background of these three functions is what any Marxist analysis must take to be the ideology's ultimate aim, which is 'to serve the needs of a class' (451 n.19) – by which is meant, however tacitly, the *dominant* class. Badiou's earliest works have little to say about this most basic function of ideology, and even less to say about Althusser's quiet conflation of ideology *tout court* with the category of *dominant* ideology. But this complacency (which, it should be noted, is not uninterrupted – *CM* (1968) marks an important, but ultimately inadequate, exception) will not survive the rebellion mounted in *Of Ideology*, to which I will return in a moment.

In his first theoretical publication, 'The Autonomy of the Aesthetic Process' (1966 – written in '65), Badiou describes how art, though it does not tear a hole in ideology as science does, nevertheless serves to subtract thought from ideological domination by capturing the latter in 'the discordant unity of a *form*: exhibited as *content*, ideology speaks of what, in itself, *it cannot speak*: its contours, its limits' (APE 80), decentring the specular relation that ideology works to preserve, and exposing the audience to the 'outside' surface of ideology's infinite enclosure:

If ideology produces the imaginary reflection of reality, the aesthetic effect responds by producing ideology as imaginary reality. One could say that art repeats, in the real, the ideological repetition of that real. Even if this reversal does not produce the real, it *realises* its reflection. (81)

If ideologies, as Badiou suggests in *CM*, play themselves out as continuous *variations on absent themes* (*CM* 7), then the point of the aesthetic process is to expose those themes in their *presence* by capturing them in their *form*.

The second mode by which thought subtracts itself from ideology is *science*, conceived as a sequence of *epistemological breaks*. Ideology confronts scientific practice in the form of what Bachelard termed *epistemological obstacles*. In 'Mark and Lack: On Zero' (1969 – written in '67; in Hallward and Peden 2012), Badiou contends that epistemological obstacles affect scientific discourse in the form of an unstable *suture* of the scientific signifier. Epistemological breaks must therefore act on structure of the signifier itself: they demand a labour of formalisation, *desuturing* and *stratifying* the scientific signifier, assembling it in an inhuman machine that tears through the fabric of ideological enclosure. The structure of the scientific signifier comes to *foreclose* every attempt at ideological recuperation, but this radical dissonance with ideology is not accidental. It is the constitutive engine of scientific practice:

it is not because it is 'open' that science has cause to deploy itself (although openness governs the *possibility* of this deployment); it is because ideology is incapable of being satisfied with this openness. Forging the impracticable image of a closed discourse and exhorting science to submit to it, ideology sees its own order returned to it in the unrecognisable form of the new concept; the reconfiguration through which science, treating its ideological interpellation as material, ceaselessly displaces the breach that it opens in the former. (ML 173)

Science thus proceeds in an endless dialectical alternation of scientific rupture and ideological recapture – a dialectic that structurally corresponds to that which Badiou will later describe as taking place between *truth* and *knowledge* (cf. *CM* VII in particular).

Ideology is the ubiquitous medium of thought and practice, within and against which art and science operate. Philosophy's task cannot, therefore, be one of *purifying* thought – whether scientific, artistic or philosophical – of ideology. Its task, as formulated in *CM*, following the direction of Althusser's 'Philosophy and the Spontaneous Philosophy of Scientists', is to draw abstract lines of demarcation between ideology and the subtractive practices it unstably envelops – but this demarcation is not an end in itself. It is carried out for the sake of *new* ideological–scientific syntheses. In fact, the Badiou of 1968 *defines* philosophy as 'the ideological recovery of science', the manufacture of 'categories, denot[ing] 'inexistent' objects in which the work of the [scientific] concept and the repetition of the [ideological] notion are combined' (*CM* 9). It is clear that this vocation is futile so long as the category of ideology itself remains undivided – subsumed, root and branch, under the category of *dominant ideology*. The philosophical necessity of this division is already legible in *CM*, whose attempt to trace 'a line of demarcation' between the scientific concept of model and its bourgeois–ideological recapture is *explicitly* oriented towards readying the concept's 'effective integration into proletarian ideology' (48). But the *theory* of this division is not yet clear, and so, for want of a clear articulation of the difference between *dominant* and *resistant* ideologies, *CM* can only end with this promissory note.

Ideology: after 1968

The reader of Badiou's post-1988 works may recognise in the *aesthetic process* and the *epistemological break* an anticipation of the later conception of art and science as *truth procedures*. Only after '68 does the third condition arrive in full force, and it is the entrance of *political uprising* onto the scene that will force the division of the category of ideology that is needed if the philosophical fabrication of categories is to be justified. This fission comes to a head in a 1976 pamphlet, coauthored with François Balmès under the title *Of Ideology*. Badiou and Balmès's first (and powerfully Sartrean) move is to insist on the transparency of ideology:

We must have done with the 'theory' of ideology 'in general' as imaginary representation and interpellation of individuals as subjects [. . .] Ideology is essentially
reflection, and in this sense, far from being an agent of dissimulation, it is *exactly
what it looks like*: it is that in which the material order (which is to say, the relations of exploitation) is effectively enunciated, in a fashion that is approximate,
but nonetheless real. (DI/*AR* 19)

Following a merciless critique of the Althusserian theory of ideology
(within which Badiou's initial reflections on the topic took shape), Balmès
and Badiou lay down the rudiments of a properly Marxist and militant
theory of ideology. They begin by drawing a line between the *ideology of
the exploiters* (the 'dominant ideology') and the *ideology of the exploited*.
There can be a 'dominant ideology' only where there are people who are
dominated, and those who are dominated will resist, whether powerfully
or weakly. It is from the standpoint of this resistance that the concept of
ideology must be formulated. In resisting domination, the exploited form
a more or less systematic representation of the real and antagonistic class
relations that exploit them. This representation contains the germ of the
ideology of the exploited class – the germ of an ideology of resistance. It is
in a resistance to the ideological resistance of domination that the *dominant
ideology* takes shape, struggling, not to deny the existence of contradictory
class relations – which could only be a product of blindness or stupidity
– but to downplay their antagonistic character. Its platform is threefold:

1. Its first move is to contend that '[e]very apparent antagonism is at best
   a difference, and at worst a non–antagonistic (and reconcilable) contradiction'. (*DI* 40)
2. Its second is to maintain that '[e]very difference is in itself inessential:
   identity is the law of being, not, of course, in real social relations, but in
   the ceremonial register of regulated comparisons before destiny, before
   God, before the municipal ballot-box' (ibid.).
3. Its 'third procedure is the externalisation of the antagonism: to the
   supposedly unified social body [*corps social*] a term "outside of class"
   [*hors-classe*] is opposed, and posited as heterogeneous: the foreigner
   (chauvinism), the Jew (anti–Semitism), the Arab (racism), etc. The
   procedures of transference are themselves riveted [*chevillées*] over an
   exasperation of the principal contradiction' (ibid., 40; n.27).

Resisting this resistance of resistance to domination, the ideology of the
exploited may become an active ideology of rebellion. To do so, 'revolt
must produce an inversion and reversal of values: for it, the differential
identity of the dominant ideology is the exception, and *antagonism* is the

rule. Equality is what is concrete, and hierarchy exists abstractly' (41). In this exponentiation of resistance the *communist invariants* take shape: *egalitarian, anti-proprietary* and *anti-statist* convictions, which, Badiou and Balmès argue, are not specific to proletarian revolt, but genuinely universal, legible in every real mass revolt against class exploitation (66–7). These invariants comprise the *contents* of resistant ideology, and not necessarily its *form*, which it as a rule inherits from the ideology of the dominant class (the communist invariants inscribed in Müntzer's peasant rebellion, for instance, were couched in a religious form inherited from the ideology of the landowning class).

This division between content and form – with the *form* of an ideology deriving from the ideology it resists, and its *contents* reflecting the real class forces that drive it – supplies Badiou and Balmès with a straightforward way of accounting for false consciousness. '*Illusion and false consciousness*', they write,

concern the form of representations, and not their content. That a small-time union boss might hold the sincere conviction that he speaks in the name of the working class, and even has the backing of a tawdry Marxism, when he bends over backwards to liquidate a mass revolt, that's false consciousness – but only so far as the formal side of the question goes. The truth is, our little revisionist is invested by the force of the bourgeois class, which his thought *quite adequately* reflects. (32)

It is here that the Marxist formation of a proletarian *party* becomes crucial to the organisation of revolt, in its function of welding the *correct ideas of the masses* – the invariant, communist *contents* of mass revolt – to the scientific *form* of Marxism. It is this that sets the proletariat – the organised proletariat – apart from the exploited classes of the past, for while it 'is not the inventor of ideological resistance, it is its first logician' (128).

INAESTHETICS

Nina Power

Badiou describes the concept of 'inaesthetics', the focus of a text originally published in French in 1998, in succinct terms in a note at the beginning of the text. Inaesthetics is, he writes,

a relation of philosophy to art that, maintaining that art itself is a producer of truths, makes no claim to turn art into an object for philosophy. Against aesthetic speculation, inaesthetics describes the strictly intraphilosophical effects produced by some works of art.

Behind Badiou's clear definition lies the historical weight of philosophy's relationship to art, particularly in its romantic mode, which sees art alone as providing a way of understanding the world, of presenting certain kinds of truth or new kinds of knowledge. In the twentieth century, Badiou sees this philosophical relation to art primarily in the work of Heideggerian hermeneutics. Badiou's concept of inaesthetics, on the other hand, seeks to understand and undo the damage that philosophy has done to art (and to itself) by untangling philosophy from artistic production, and simultaneously preserving a space for artistic 'truths' beyond philosophy's grasp.

While Badiou is emphatic that art can and does produce truth on certain rare occasions, he insists that these truths should not be taken up by philosophy as its own (a mistake he terms 'suturing'). Similarly, Plato's famous attempt to reduce art to pretence and seduction and dismiss it accordingly is described as 'didactic' by Badiou, namely, the idea that all truth is external to art. Badiou also sees the didactic schema at work in Marxist theories of art. The 'classical' reception of art which Badiou locates in Aristotle and, in the twentieth century, in psychoanalysis, which understands art's function as cathartic or therapeutic, is similarly unable to deal with the singularity of the truth produced by certain works of art. Badiou's definition of 'inaesthetics' thus attempts to avoid the pitfalls of these three significant philosophical attempts – romantic, classical and didactic – to deal with art.

To this end, Badiou proposes a fourth schema to understand art, which he describes as a relationship between artworks that is at once singular and immanent. In other words, 'Art *itself* is a truth procedure.' It produces truths of its own and as such is irreducible to philosophy. Philosophy's role with regard to the truths produced by 'certain works' of art is not to steal its truths as philosophy's own, but to show the immanent truth produced by art as it is. Just as with the other truth procedures – science, love and politics – philosophy's role, according to Badiou, is to act as the go-between, to protect and to circulate the truths specific to art. The question then becomes, what ensures the unity of art as a discipline? And furthermore, which works of art generate truths?

Badiou describes the specific status of art overall via a description of the relationship between the finite and the infinite. Artworks, he claims, are 'trebly finite', that is to say the artwork has a finite objectivity in space and time; secondly, it has a finite relation to its own limit, that is to say it has a certain kind of completion, and thirdly, 'it sets itself up as an inquiry into the question of its own finality'. The truths art is capable of generating are necessarily 'local' truths, if art is to avoid romantic or Christly invocations of revelations of the infinite in the finite. Sidestepping questions of authorial or artistic intention, and questions of historical influence, Badiou argues that ultimately the 'pertinent unit' for thinking about a work of art is neither the work nor the author but 'the artistic configuration initiated by an evental rupture'. This configuration calls into question earlier artistic configurations and re-writes, as it were, the history of art (and philosophy) up until that point. Badiou is, however, extremely careful not to reduce this conception of configuration to forms, genres or 'objective' periods in the history of art, preferring to talk of 'sequences' that unfold, and may not have finished unfolding. Art's immanence is described as 'in each and every one of its points the thinking of the thought that it itself is'.

Badiou gives several examples of artistic configurations under the 'pretexts' of poetry, theatre, cinema and dance. All of these genres 'think' or are a form of thought for Badiou, rather than expressive or spontaneous productions. Badiou thus tries to outline in each instance what form of thought is generated axiomatically or formally through each mode. Through a reading of Mallarmé and Rimbaud via certain mathematical terms, Badiou declares that every naming of an event is poetic, and that philosophy must avoid 'judging' poetry if it is to avoid Plato's famous suspicion of poetry, and the repeated attempt to dissolve its mystery. Badiou's description of the poem places it rather on the side of a formal operation, containing a universal address, much like mathematics: 'neither the poem nor the matheme take persons into account, representing instead, at the two extremes of universality, the purest universality' (*HI* 31).

Badiou then attempts to give an overview of the forms of several artistic regimes. Through a reading of Nietzsche's use of 'dance' as the opposite of gravity, Badiou understands it as a form of thought and of restraint 'immanent to movement', against the idea that dance is simply expressive or spontaneous. Dance is similarly described as a metaphor for the event, at the moment before a name for this event has been decided or fixed. In Badiou's discussion of theatre, which he describes as the 'positive opposite of dance', he invokes the idea of 'assemblage': material and immaterial qualities are gathered together in the performance which is 'an event of thought'. The assemblages of these productions produce 'theatre-ideas', which are generated from the tension between *eros* and *polis*, in the form of intrigue or catastrophe. Cinema, on the other hand, despite sharing much in common with the theatre at the level of costumes, actors and so on, has a special relation to the other arts, operating as it does as a 'plus-one', using the other arts as a starting point for its own investigations into movement and visibility. Cinema is for Badiou the organisation of the 'impossible movements' of the other artistic configurations. Cinema's impurity also accounts, thinks Badiou, for its contemporary force, because it turns every idea into its own, for the duration of its own false movement. Cinema as impurity is nevertheless a place of experimentation, of the possibilities that other 'purer' arts might be capable of, once they have passed through cinema's mish-mash of genres and techniques.

At the opposite end of this discussion of impurity lies Badiou's lengthy discussion of Samuel Beckett's work, particularly the late prose work, *Worstward Ho*. For Badiou, this text represents 'a short philosophical treatise, as a treatment in shorthand of the question of being'. Beckett's work is clearly very close to Badiou's own philosophy, or at least Badiou feels a certain kinship with Beckett's 'subtractive' method and concepts. But as with the lengthy reading of Mallarmé, Badiou's invocation of these writers is ambiguous according to his own conception of artistic events: is the work of Beckett a literary event? Mallarmé's a poetic one? Or are they closer to philosophers in different genres (prose, poetry)? (cf. *HI* ch. 4 & 5) Badiou sees in Beckett's work, for example, a method, and in Mallarmé's a description of the event, the name and fidelity, key concepts for Badiou's own thought; but the question of whether these particular writers have a kind of meta-status vis-à-vis the genres they work in is left unresolved in *HI*.

INFINITY

Anindya Bhattacharyya

Infinity plays a dual role in Badiou's work: it has an intrinsic function within his system of subtractive ontology, and an extrinsic function of situating Badiou's overall project within the wider philosophical tradition. We will consider both these aspects in turn, starting with the intrinsic.

In *BE* meditations 13 and 14, Badiou highlights three characteristics required of any multiple that we could plausibly call infinite: an initial point, a rule of passage and a second existential seal.

The initial point is simply any particular multiple, marked out and deemed as 'first'. A rule of passage is an operation that transforms one multiple into another one, deemed its 'successor'. This operation is subject to a couple of constraints: distinct inputs must produce distinct outputs; and the initial point cannot be a possible output. These constraints are sufficient to ensure that iterating the operation produces 'still more' multiples without returning to those previously produced and thereby getting locked into a finite cycle.

Nevertheless, Badiou is at pains to point out that the mere presence of an initial point and a suitable rule of passage do not by themselves guarantee the existence of an actual infinite multiple. All we get is what Hegel called a 'bad infinity': an endless succession of ones, but no means of gathering them all together or traversing them all at once. To do this requires a new principle of being – the second existential seal – that axiomatically decides a completed infinity into existence.

These three characteristics are implemented in Badiou's set-theoretical ontology as follows. The initial point is simply the name of the void, $\varnothing$. The rule of passage operates on a given multiple by uniting it with its own singleton: $\alpha \rightarrow \alpha \cup \{\alpha\}$. (The axiom of foundation ensures that this rule conforms to the constraints mentioned above.) The second existential seal is the so-called axiom of infinity: the declaration that a limit ordinal exists, a limit ordinal being defined as a non-void natural multiple that does not succeed any other natural multiple.

These definitions and axioms suffice to ensure that all the finite numbers (and nothing but the finite numbers) can be collected into a single multiple ω, also known as countable infinity. A theorem of Cantor's demonstrates that the existence of this countable infinity allows us to generate an endless series of uncountable infinities, each one strictly larger than its predecessors. We do this by repeatedly using the axiom of subsets, which ensures that every set has a power set that collates all its parts.

Badiou bases this approach to the infinite on mathematical innovations from Cantor, Peano and Von Neumann, among others. He notes that it breaks with both the Greek tradition that posits an essentially finite universe and the Christian one that supplements the Greek finite universe with an infinite beyond. Badiou's mathematical approach, by contrast, decouples infinity from the One and returns it to multiple being. The infinite is no longer transcendent, but mundane.

It follows from this that rather than the infinite supplementing the finite with a beyond, it is the finite that comes in second place, 'qualified as a *region* of being, a minor form of the latter's presence'. Subtractive ontology presents us with an infinity of infinities that proliferate upwards from ω. Being is thus *typically* infinite, with the finite persisting only as an exception to this general state of affairs.

This brings us to the extrinsic role played by infinity in Badiou's corpus – the way in which his localisation of infinity separates his philosophy from what he calls 'Romanticism'. In his 1989 paper, 'Philosophy and Mathematics: Infinity and the End of Romanticism' (cf. *CS* ch. 7), Badiou argues that the emergence of a mathematical conception of the infinite in the early modern era went hand-in-hand with a historic disjunction of philosophy and mathematics.

The crucial figure here is Hegel, whose interrogation and critique of mathematical infinity lays the basis for what Badiou terms the Romantic era in philosophy. Badiou's reponse to Hegel on this question in turn offers us the means of exiting the Romantic era, thereby inaugurating a radical materialism purged of any appeal to the divine or to a transcendent beyond.

It should be stressed that Hegel does not simply dismiss the mathematical infinite. On the contrary, following Spinoza he argues that the emerging mathematical science of the infinite is far superior to its previous metaphysical treatment. Nevertheless Hegel finds that the mathematical infinity is itself conceptually incoherent (an accurate assessment for the early 1800s when Hegel was writing). Consequently it in turn must be sublated and replaced by a superior dialectical understanding of infinity.

Mathematics and philosophy thus find themselves locked in rivalry over infinity. For Hegel this rivalry is ultimately resolved by the abasement of mathematics. Badiou takes the opposite route. Cantor's achievement, he argues, lies in developing a rigorous mathematics of the infinite that renders Hegel's objections redundant. Consequently it is philosophy that must give up its ontological pretensions and accept that the question of the infinite is henceforth decided by its scientific condition.

In particular, Badiou argues that infinity can now be fully desacralised and thought independently of any relation to theology. This in turn allows us to finally make effective Nietzsche's declaration of the death of God, and 're-entwine' philosophy and mathematics in a genuinely new configuration.

JEW, USES OF THE WORD

Elad Lapidot

The basic *topos* of Badiou's reflection on the Jewish theme is not Judaism, a word that Badiou rarely uses, but Jews, namely Jewish people. Badiou's questioning, however, does not refer directly to Jews. On the contrary, he explicitly declines what he considers to be a long intellectual tradition whose basic approach to Jews consists in putting them into question, and which would therefore require a certain solution. Instead Badiou approaches Jews fundamentally as a fact: 'there are Jews' (*Pol* 167). Jewish people are just another particular group of people, like any other. As such, for Badiou, Jews give rise to no special philosophical inquiry.

It is precisely Badiou's observation that a certain contemporary discourse does refer to Jews as a special theme, which sets in motion his inquiry, henceforth polemic in nature. Not Jews as such, but Jews in discourse, constitute the direct object of his questioning, namely the word or the name 'Jew'. The fundamental question refers not to the meaning but to the current function of this word, hence the title of Badiou's collected texts on this subject, *Uses of the Word 'Jew'* [*Portées du mot 'juif'*] (cf. *Pol*).

Originally published in 2005, Badiou's polemic, mostly refraining from naming its concrete adversaries, encountered a vigorous counter-polemic in the journal *Les Temps Modernes*, under chief editor Claude Lanzmann (cf. Marty 2005–6: 25; Milner 2005–6: 13). Over the subsequent decade, this debate has been further developed in France by various authors in various media and forms, extending to an ever broader perimeter of topics in current affairs. Providing a point of reference and conceptual framework for the formation of thematic associations and intellectual alliances, the ongoing controversy around the word 'Jew' has come to define one line of confrontation currently shaping the intellectual public sphere in France (for Badiou's perspective see his contribution, co-authored with Eric Hazan, to *Reflections on Anti-Semitism*, 2012).

For Badiou, since Jews are just particular groups of people, the name 'Jew' ultimately designates a person's adherence to this group. Jewish intellectual tradition he conceives generically as 'religion', which is 'incompatible' with 'the tradition of Enlightenment' and 'contemporary universalism' and amounts to no more than 'an identitary norm' (*CN* 92–4). On the basic level, 'Jewish' is just another 'identity predicate'. What Badiou observes in contemporary discourse is a certain use of this name as being more than that. He indicates that the name 'Jew' seems to function in specific contexts as an 'exceptional' or even 'sacred signifier', which lies 'above all usual handling of identity predicates' (*Pol* 159).

This perceived 'nominal sanctification' of the name 'Jew' constitutes for Badiou a political problem. To sanctify the name means to sanctify 'the community claiming to stand for it', namely those who call themselves Jews. This particular group of people is thus 'placed in a paradigmatic position with respect to the field of values, cultural hierarchies, and in evaluating the politics of states' (ibid.). In other words, to sanctify the name 'Jew' is to ascribe to those who identify themselves thus, the Jewish people, as such, a special status in comparison to all other particular groups. For Badiou, this idea of 'communal transcendence' contradicts what he conceives to be one of the basic categories of true politics in general, i.e. universality.

However, this use made of the name of the Jews is for Badiou not just another particular example of a problematic politics of names, but, as aforesaid, a certain exception in current discourse that deserves a special philosophical attention. Thus, according to Badiou, the alleged communal transcendence of 'the Jews' does not merely challenge the general idea of universality, but in particular 'contemporary' universalism (ibid.). His position is articulated more concretely in his evaluation of the politics carried out in practice in the name 'Jew', namely the Jewish State. It is here that Badiou later localises the fundamental problem that his intervention in this matter seeks to address (*CN* [70]). The particularistic politics of the State of Israel is not problematic just in itself, but also in comparison to the 'modern conception', which 'is an open conception: a country is made up of all the people who live and work there' (*Pol* 214). 'Truly contemporary states or countries' being 'always cosmopolitan' (163), the Jewish State appears to Badiou as 'a kind of archaism' (159). (Badiou later clarifies that his position is 'for the disappearance of States' in general, and that 'I said in my life infinitely more bad things about the French State than about the Israeli State' (*CN* 76).)

Badiou thus acknowledges the uniqueness of the very discourse that places the name Jew in a situation of exception, to which at one point he refers as a 'French exception' (*Reflections on Anti-Semitism* 45). For him, this move is unjustified: Jews are no exception. He therefore identifies the factual unjustified exception that has been *made* of the name 'Jew'. Consequently, the fundamental concept of Badiou's discussion of Jewish specificity is the unjust exclusion that has been historically made of and against Jews, namely *anti-Semitism*. The main *topos* selected by Badiou for his analysis is the concrete reality of the annihilation of the Jews: the 'extermination of the Jews by the Nazis'. It is here that Badiou finds the common ground with the discourse that he criticises. In fact, Badiou does not criticise the reference to the Nazis, which he detects at the basis of the exceptional use made of the name 'Jew'. On the contrary, refusing to see in this reference a justification for this use, he sees it as its very origin: 'it was above all the Nazis who, before anyone else [. . .] drew all the consequences from making the signifier "Jew" into a radical exception' (*Pol* 163–4).

It is in this sense that Badiou's reflection on the Jews draws on his reflection on the Nazis. Unlike the Jews, who are just another particular group, the basic object for Badiou's reflection on the Nazi theme is not the multitude of 'Nazi people' but the politics of Nazism. Badiou's criticism of the sanctification of the name 'Jew' is formally similar to his criticism of a contemporary discourse that lends Nazism transcendence as 'absolute Evil'. However, the sanctification of the Jews is criticised as an unjustified political exception made of a politically neutral reality, i.e. of mere particularity. The absolutisation of Nazism is criticised by Badiou, on the contrary, as not allowing us to think its real political singularity: 'even in the case of this Evil, which I would call extreme rather than radical, the intelligibility of its 'subjective' being [. . .] needs to be referred back to the intrinsic dimensions of the process of political truth' (*Pol* 175). For Badiou, to *think* Nazism as Evil is to acknowledge it not as non-political but rather as a negative form of politics: as 'criminal politics'. In Badiou's categories, if the epicentre of politics is a true political event, then Nazism is its exact antipode: a non-event, a 'simulated event'.

The true political event is a procedure of political truth, which is by definition universal. In a given situation, the political truth can be therefore no particular position in this situation. To apply to everyone, truth must refer to no one in particular. In contrast, the simulated political event only seems to be universal, while in fact it consists in giving 'substance' to a certain particular group and preserving it as such. This can only be done by imposing the void on everything else, universally: 'what is addressed "to everyone" [. . .] is death' (*Pol* 178). The simulated event is inherently an event of extermination.

The simulated event of Nazism referred to the particularity of the 'Germans' or 'Aryans'. In order to lend substance to the Aryans, Nazism consisted in the universal extermination of all non-Aryans. However, 'in the case of Nazism, the void made its return under one privileged name in particular, the name "Jew". There were certainly others as well: the Gypsies, the mentally ill, homosexuals, communists [. . .] But the name "Jew" was the name of names' (ibid.). When Badiou rejects the view that 'Nazi atrocities work in some way to validate [. . .] the election of the "people"' (*Pol* 161), it is therefore not because there has never been any election, but because the election that did take place was originally Nazi: 'inasmuch as it served to organise the extermination, the name "Jew" was a political creation of the Nazis, without any pre-existing referent' (179). The Nazi election has led to the sanctification of the name 'Jew' in the twentieth century: 'Once the Nazis were defeated, the name "Jew" became, like every name of the victim of a frightful sacrifice, a sacred name' (168).

This acknowledgement of the elected destiny of the Jewish people, be it through a Nazi election, itself raises the fundamental question of any election: Why? Why the Jews? What is the reason for the Nazi election of the Jews? As Badiou affirms, 'it was no accident' (ibid.).

Of course, Badiou categorically rejects the Nazi discourse. The reason the Nazis elected the Jews is not because they are in reality non-Aryan: '[b]ut the Aryan doesn't exist. It is only a tautology of Nazi discourse that says: Aryans are Aryans' (213). For Badiou, the Jews are not conceived in Nazi categories, but in the categories of his own political analysis of Nazism.

The Jews are not non-Aryan but non-Nazi. Since Nazism is the political non-event, namely the simulated event of particularity, then '[t]he choice of [the name of the Jews by the Nazis] relates, without any doubt, to its obvious link with universalism' (178–9). In this way, by conceiving the Jews as that to which negative politics is opposed, Badiou arrives, in *Uses of the Word 'Jew'*, at a use of the word Jew, wherein it does not just designate yet another particular identity predicate, but names a specific aspect or moment within the process of universal truths: 'a meaning for the word "Jew" that would have universal import' (165).

This use comes closest to a Badiouian concept of the Jew, to his conception of what has been designated since early Christianity as *Judaism*. Badiou himself never explicitly formulates this concept as such, consistently refusing to recognise in proper Jewish intellectual tradition anything other than 'religion', which supposedly lies beyond the realm of pertinent philosophical intervention. It is, however, precisely his reading of the foundational Christian text, *Saint Paul: The Foundation of Universalism*, that constitutes the second major Badiouian *topos*, other than Nazism, where the word 'Jew' comes to name an essential aspect in the event of universality. 'Jew' once again is that in relation to which the process analysed by philosophy takes place: in the formal event of the 'Christian subject' – the 'Jewish community' constitutes its 'site' (*SP* 23). Badiou emphasises that the Christian content of Paul's gospel – 'Christ died and resurrected' – insofar as it constitutes a 'fable' of 'religion', precludes the Pauline movement from constituting a genuine event of 'true universality'. What Badiou reads in Paul is rather a formal 'theory' of the event (*CN* 77). In this framework, 'Jew' names the 'evental site', if not of the real 'Foundation of Universalism' properly speaking, as the admittedly 'excessive title' of the book on Paul suggests, nonetheless of a 'powerful break (*césure*)' in its historical emergence (*SP* 115).

As the site of the Christian event, which as a Universal 'traverses and transcends' (99) all particularities, Jewish particularity has 'a kind of priority' (102) over other particularities, such as the Greek. 'Jew' is the particularity from which Christian universality may emerge. The Jewish particularity is not just a matter of indifference to universality, like all other differences of 'opinions and customs'. As particular, it is an inherent moment of universality. More precisely, it is the particular that is the yet empty place, the 'site', of the universal to come. How should we understand this? One may suggest that 'Jew' names the particular that is the absent universal, the non-universal. As absence, within which its event is to take place, the universal appears as the 'Jew', who is not yet the universal singularity of the Christian subject, but a universal particularity. On this reading, 'Jew' is the particular with 'universal import', particularity not just as a particular fact, but as a figure of the subject, i.e. the very thought of particularity.

A precise articulation of this line of thought can be found in Badiou's novel *Calme bloc ici-bas*. It is put in the words of one of the protagonists and should therefore be taken with caution, bearing in mind, however, that Badiou did choose to include the passage as an independent fragment in his collected texts on *Uses of the Word 'Jew'*. In this passage, Badiou has one of his fictional characters explicitly ask the fundamental Jewish Question: 'What is Jewish/a Jew [*juif*]?' (*Pol* 184). The answer outlines a summary Jewish theology: 'Imagine that there is a Law, which says that you are you, and that, in God's eyes, you alone are who you are. "You" is something that comes from the mother'.

The 'law' is already a central theme of *SP*. There, subscribing to Paul's operation of 'disjoining the true from the Law' (*SP* 15), Badiou explains that '[t]he law is always predicative, particular and partial' (76). Being essentially 'statist', the law is the constitutive principle of particular collectives, of 'the particularising multiplicity' (78). As a form of thought, a specific figure of the subject, '[t]he law is what constitutes the subject as powerlessness of thought' (83), as stated by the third theorem of Badiou's 'materialism of grace' (81). Constituting the subject as powerless thought, a dead thought, law is the principle of subjective life as *de facto* death. The law, like the letter, 'mortifies', it 'gives life to death' (82). Non-life under the law is precisely the site for the Pauline event of graceful 'resurrection'.

This site is specifically Jewish, because the 'Jew' is not just another particularity operating under its own particular law. Rather, vis-à-vis the universal Christian event, '[t]he Jews raise the question of the law' (28). The Jewish site is not just a contingent, factual particularity, but the particularity as a matter of principle, i.e. the principle of particularity, law as the Law. The particular Jewish law is therefore formulated in Badiou's novel as the universal Law of Particularity: 'in God's eye, you alone are who you are'. What makes Jews exceptional is that 'the Jewish discourse is a discourse of the exception' (41). The 'Jew' names the paradigm, the very thought of particular identity as universal exception. 'Jew' designates namely the universal non-universal.

Jewish discourse thus recognises and attests to universality as possible and at the same time precludes its reality. The 'Jew' is, in other words, *virtual* universality, the site of universality's potential existence, actual inexistence – the site of universality's event. The Jews who *positively* identify themselves as such – who 'only declare their identity' – are therefore *eo ipso* 'virtual Jews': '[b]ecause it must necessarily be there, that powerful and detestable identity, to enable a Jew who is more than the Jews to come' (*Pol* 186). The positive, 'actual Jew' then perfects the Jewish identity precisely by breaking it: 'What happens is that someone gets up who says: if I alone am who I am, that's because this "myself" is nothing but all the others [. . .] Let's call "Jew" the one who [. . .] grasps his own being to brake the divisive law, and thereby exposes humanity to the universal' (168).

The 'universal import' of the name 'Jew' thus leads Badiou to an operation of re-naming, strongly reminiscent of Paul: 'For he is not a Jew, which is one outwardly; neither is circumcision that which is outward in the flesh. But he is a Jew who is one inwardly; and circumcision is that which is of the heart, in the spirit, and not in the letter' (Romans 2, 28–29). The negative element of this operation, as Badiou indicates, is not of 'abolishing Jewish particularity' (*SP* 103). The universality declared by Paul requires Jewish particularity as the site for its event, as its 'principle of historicity'. 'Jew', designating community, law and book, names the absence of the subject as the universal singularity to come, the inexistence from which it is to emerge. Badiou expresses the same idea in respect of the relation between traditional Jewish communities and the State. The Jewish people, he acknowledges, was 'non statist, diasporic, transversal, and by this very fact, in its fundamental particularity, it was destined, convened to universality'. It was thus the 'localisation for a possible universality, which, at its base, is homogeneous to communism' (*CN* 76–8). It follows that 'being Jewish/the Jewish being [*l'être-juif*] in general, and the Book in particular, *can and must be resubjectivated*' (*SP* 103). This 'resubjectivation' abolishes neither book nor being. It rather renews: it transforms them into a new book, for example the New Testament, and a new subjective being, for example the Christian. The emergence of the actual Jew from the virtual Jew is less abolition than conversion.

This operation is reflected in the list of proper names that make up Badiou's short history of the actual Jews: '[f]rom the apostle Paul to Trotsky, passing through Spinoza, Marx and Freud' (*Pol* 162). These people can only be defined as 'Jews' by a radical criterion of particular identity: their mother. Indeed, in the actuality of these persons, their Jewish particularity is for Badiou nothing but the *negative* condition of possibility, the 'site', of their universal thinking. These 'actual Jews' have been universal by converting their Jewish particularity into universality, thereby creating 'new points of rupture' with Judaism: 'they are people who enjoin the thought of all to the strictest universality, and, in memorable founding acts, enacted a rupture with any and every end of the law that was somehow exclusionary or identifying. They say 'no one is elected, otherwise everyone is'. And they can say it precisely because they were the supposed bearers of the most radical election in the eye of God' (*Pol* 185). It is the same logic that ultimately leads Badiou to formulate his own announcement – personified perhaps, at least provisionally, by the proper name of Udi Aloni – of the 'Jew to come' (*Pol* 207): 'It is clear that today's equivalent of Paul's religious rupture with established Judaism, of Spinoza's rationalist rupture with the Synagogue, or of Marx's political rupture with the bourgeois integration of a part of his community of origin, is a subjective rupture with the State of Israel' as a 'Jewish State' (*Pol* 162–3).

JUSTICE

Dimitra Panopoulos

As in Plato, for Badiou justice itself is pronounced before any idea of justice as such. This is not to diminish its scope and effectivity. The point is that justice is unable to be evaluated as to its relevance on the basis of a simple consideration of the givens of the moment.

In contemporary space, this has enabled a certain idea of communism as justice to be given a renewed pertinence; for the objection that communism failed to take place in accordance with its promise can thus no longer stand. On the contrary, the idea of communism remains a name for the idea of justice (cf *CH* 5) in the manner of a not-yet-proven mathematical theorem. Badiou cites, in this vein, Socrates' question in the *Republic* concerning the coming true particular to the Platonic City: 'Do you think, then, that our words are any the less well spoken if we find ourselves unable to prove that it is possible for a state to be governed in accordance with our words?' (*CS* 152)

Prior to any discovery of its prescriptive and axiomatic dimension, Justice seems graspable only as an Idea, and negatively. Why? Because justice does not set out from a consideration of injustice, nor is it inscribed either in the figure of law or in that of the state, or even in the design of the ideal community.

Justice and injustice

Again echoing Plato, the idea of justice in Badiou is independent of the consideration of injustice: 'injustice is clear, justice is obscure' (*M* 96). Justice, being primary in the sense that it is independent of the facts of injustice, commands an affirmative logic.

Justice is not the object of a theory that would examine cases of justice. It is not of the order of a consequentialism, and does not pertain to the evaluation of the better choice. Does this mean that it necessarily proceeds here from an idealist conception? Is it really dependent on a supreme idea such as the Idea of the Good? As we shall see, Badiou's conception of justice is less idealist than axiomatic. And if it aims at the Idea of the Good, this can only be in an effective sense, which means that justice must be conceived as ordained to the creation of possibles.

Justice and law

Justice remains subtracted from all identification with any law that would govern situations on the basis of what is given in them. In its Platonic inspiration, justice is axiomatic insofar as it aims at the creation of possibles. It can give rise to the invention of new figures concerning that which can create law: 'More radically, justice names the possibility – from the standpoint of what it brings into being as subject-effect – that what is nonlaw may function as law' (*TS* 159). In addition, it provides points of passage beween ethics and politics, since politics is what an Immortal proves capable of, but does not suppose or confirm any subordination of politics to ethics, which would legislate on the idea of justice on the basis of a figure of law, as we see happening today with the international juridical reach of human rights.

Badiou's conception of justice is also implicitly opposed to the idea of it expressed in Rawls's theory of justice, where it figures as a theory of the state. Instead, 'justice' for Badiou names a fundamental gap between politics and law. This is why equality is not to be taken here as a legal category either.

Justice and state

There is an opposition between justice and law in the framework proposed by the state of right, but another relation to law or right is envisageable. This other relation is one in which the law is subordinated to political inventions and in which the uses of law are prescribed in line with considerations of emancipation: 'When our "philosophers" speak of the State of Right, they have no way of taking stock of the right without right by which a political consciousness *declares itself*. These philosophers speak of an institutional figure, and place philosophy, not under the condition of politics, but under the condition of the parliamentary state' (*CS* 294).

Veritable justice presumes that each individual is counted as one, that is to say according to the singularity of that which relates her to the situation and not according to the norms that are supposed to govern that situation, wherein is counted that which is already ordered and representable in the order of state-parts or parties. Instead of the count-for-one that a generic declaration sets out, the state of right only effects a count of the count: 'The state only ever relates to parts or subsets. Even when it deals in appearance with an individual, it is not the individual in its concrete infinity that is concerned; instead, this infinity gets *reduced to the one of the count*, that is, to the subset of which the individual is an element, what the mathematicians call a singleton. The one who votes, who is imprisoned, who contributes to social security, and so on' (*CS* 295).

Communism and community

There can be no equalising of social inequalities, or neutralisation of these latter through a fair acceptance of differences and awareness of other communities whatever they may be, or even by aiming for an ideal community, as the ideal incarnation of the Idea of Justice. As Badiou puts it:

One has too often wished for justice to found the consistency of the social bond, whereas it can only name the most extreme moments of inconsistency. For the effect of the egalitarian axiom is to undo bonds, to desocialise thought, to affirm the rights of the infinite and the immortal against the calculation of interests. Justice is a wager on the immortal against finitude, against 'being-towards-death'. For within the subjective dimension of the equality that one declares, nothing is of interest apart from the universality of this declaration and the active consequences that arise from it. 'Justice' is the philosophical name for statist and social inconsistency of all egalitarian politics. (*M* 104; tm)

This is why communism, if it is defined as aiming essentially at a production of the Same, is furthest from the consistency proposed as justice in the communitarian conception, even when ideal. For Badiou, justice remains diagonal to every social as well as state figure: 'the impossibility of community forms no objection to the imperative of emancipatory politics, whether we name it communism or otherwise' (*CS* 271); moreover, 'if just politics, in order to be, does not require any proof in terms of necessity or of possible existence, if it is first a form of thinking that brings into being the tenacity of a subject in the body of statements constituting its prescription, it follows that the community, as supposition of a real being of justice in the form of a collective that makes truth of itself, is never – either intrinsically or in its letter – a category of politics' (*CS* 273–4; tm).

Equality and declaration

Justice, according to Badiou, refers to a demand for equality far more than for freedom. Equality, for Badiou, is postulated and verifiable: it depends on statements that prescribe a reality, which comes about purely by virtue of being said and thinkable.

Despite the Platonic inspiration informing this idea, justice is processual and so does not refer to a horizon merely to be realised. So the proletarian, for example, can be said to fall under a process of emancipation from the moment that her militant subjectivation is disjoined from her condition as a worker: 'Justice is not a concept for which we would have to track down more or less approximate realisations in the empirical world. Conceived as an operator for seizing an egalitarian politics, which is the same thing as a true politics, justice indicates a subjective figure that is effective, axiomatic, immediate' (*M* 99; tm).

The prescriptive dimension of justice implies that it is justice's supposed impossibility that has instead to be proven. Badiou cites, in this regard, Beckett's phrase: 'in any case we have our being in justice, I have never heard anything to the contrary' (quote from *How It Is*, cf. *M* 99). Justice is a judgement on collective being, without any relation to a finality. It uniquely concerns the intrinsic ontological equality of the figures of the subject: 'Equality is subjective. For Saint-Just, it is equality with regard to public consciousness and, for Mao, equality of the political mass movement. Such equality is by no means a social programme. Moreover, it has nothing to do with the social. It is a political maxim, a prescription. Political equality is not what we desire or plan; it is that which one declares in the heat of the moment, here and now, as that which is and not as that ought to be' (*M* 98; tm).

Mathematical axiomatics and politics

Given this axiomatic conception, justice would thus appear to be negatively defined, but in such a way that requires a proof by contradiction and therefore on the proviso that it aims at an affirmative proposition of what effective justice is. Badiou bases his axiomatic conception on Cantor's demonstration of the infinite: 'Hence also the function of proof by contradiction. Since, there are no positive ways to demonstrate an inexistence. Existence must first be posited and then a contradiction deduced from it. This link between equality, existence and proof by contradiction forms the matrix underlying all philosophical thinking on emancipation: to show that a philosophically adverse politics is absurd, one must first suppose that it bears equality, and then show that this leads to a formal contradiction. There is no better way of doing it than to underscore that equality is not a programme, *but an axiom*' (*CS* fn. 4, 492).

But if the axiomatic dimension cannot be reduced to that of the declaration, it is because it binds one to the consequences:

equality here is an 'axiom' and not a goal [. . .] Equality must be *postulated* and not *willed*. 'Both [right-wing statements and left-wing statements] are opposed to whoever postulates equality and pursues, not the desire for equality, but the consequences of its axiom [. . .] what one is perfectly able to want and to prescribe is the universal domination, or the universal evidence, of egalitarian *postulation*. One can prescribe, case by case, situation by situation, the *impossibility of inegalitarian statements*. For this impossibility alone, inscribed in the situation through a protracted politics in the places that are peculiar to it, verifies that equality is not at all realised but *real*. (*M* 112)

Justice, truth, equality

The notion of real equality, brought about through an axiomatics of declaration and the carrying through of consequences, thus confers all its force to the demand for justice, positively taking up that which was imputed to it as a prejudicial utopian aim. What it takes up is indeed the idea that politics proceeds as truth. Against accusations that it continues the totalitarian nightmare, Badiou upholds the idea of justice as the core of politics (cf. *E* 15). Similarly for the notion of ethics, because at stake 'for the philosopher, is to tear names from that which prostitutes their usage. Long ago Plato had all the difficulties in the world to hold firm on the word *justice* against the fickle and quibbling use of it made by the sophists' (*E* 56). It is this centring of the idea of politics on the truth that is at stake and that renders justice and equality unable to be substituted, strictly speaking: 'We shall call "justice" that through which a philosophy designates the possible truth of a politics. We know that the overwhelming majority of empirical instances of politics have nothing to do with truth. They organise a mixture of power and opinions' (*M* 97).

For Badiou, justice thus designates the intra-philosophical name of the truth of politics, more exactly of the *possible* truth of *a* politics that is singular each time. It is thus at once the name that philosophy gives to one of its conditions, and also the name of the relation of this philosophy to its condition. But the relation of a philosophy to its condition is itself conditioned by its condition. Whence the fact that 'equality' is a circulating category. But justice is not equality: instead, it is the name given to a politics on account of this politics' presentation as egalitarian. A just politics always sets up a distance to the state and to law. 'Equality' names this gap, and 'justice' names the existence of this gap.

Translated from the French by Steven Corcoran

$$\boxed{\text{K}}$$

KANT

Christopher Norris

Much of what Badiou has to say about Kant is so hostile, sarcastic, dismissive, or at very least sharply critical as to raise the hackles of dedicated Kantians, not to mention more orthodox philosophers and historians of ideas. Indeed, Kant occupies a curiously privileged position in the roll-call of those who have provided Badiou with a means of steering his own philosophical course as much by productive disagreement as by seeking out kindred spirits or elective precursors. His grounds of disagreement range across all the main philosophical disciplines and subject-areas from metaphysics and ontology to epistemology, ethics, aesthetics, and politics. Moreover, they concern issues – of truth, knowledge, will, judgement, desire, agency, and finitude – that have long preoccupied Badiou and led him to some very un-Kantian conclusions. Still, there is a strong sense that this critical encounter is one of such central and abiding significance for Badiou that his thought may after all harbour certain Kantian elements, however firmly repressed or disavowed.

There is an endnote passage in *LW* that very forcefully articulates the main grounds of Badiou's antipathy and also conveys something of the relish with which he often expresses it.

Everything in him exasperates me, above all his legalism – always asking *Quid juris?* or 'Haven't you crossed the limit?' – combined, as in today's United States, with a religiosity that is all the more dismal in that it is both omnipresent and vague. The critical machinery he set up has enduringly poisoned philosophy, while giving great succour to the academy, which loves nothing better than to rap the knuckles of the overambitious – something for which the injunction 'You do not have the right!' is a constant boon. Kant is the inventor of the disastrous theme of our finitude. The solemn and sanctimonious declaration that we can have no knowledge of this or that always foreshadows some obscure devotion to the Master of the unknowable, the God of the religions or his placeholders: Being, Meaning, Life . . . To render impracticable all of Plato's shining promises – this was the task of the obsessive from Königsberg, our first *professor*.

This will give some idea of the denunciatory passion that typifies Badiou's dealings with Kant. Yet it also suggests how that attitude stems from his exasperation with the depth and extent of Kant's present-day influence, that is to say, his sense that Kant has managed to set the agenda for so many nowadays focal or basic philosophical debates that there is little choice but to join in. 'Once he broaches some particular question', Badiou continues,

you are unfailingly obliged, if this question preoccupies you, to pass through him. His relentlessness – that of a spider of the categories – is so great, his delimitation of notions so consistent, his conviction, albeit mediocre, so violent, that, whether you like it or not, you will have to run his gauntlet.

Underlying these various specific complaints is Badiou's chief objection that Kant reduces everything – epistemology, ethics, politics, art – to a matter of strictly normative *judgement* as arrived at through a process of rational negotiation in the Kantian 'parliament' of the faculties. This in turn he treats as a matter of what best accords with truth-claims, standards, values, or criteria that must have their ultimate justification either in the a priori tribunal of what is, supposedly, self-evident to reason or else in the *sensus communis* of received (presumptively enlightened) belief.

Badiou has many reasons for objecting to this Kantian way of setting things up so that judgement plays such a prominent role, albeit one whose function or mode of employment is left very obscure in the First *Critique*. For one thing, it goes along all too readily with the ethos of 'liberal-parliamentarian' (pseudo-)democracy, that is to say, the idea that liberty of opinion plus the exercise of electoral choice is enough to safeguard the collective best interest. For another, it annuls the cardinal distinction between truth and belief (including best belief as reckoned by any, no matter how 'enlightened' consensus) that furnishes the linchpin of all Badiou's thinking about mathematics, politics, and art. More specifically, it reduces issues of ontology to issues of epistemology, thus contriving to foreclose the various symptomatic gaps – as between presentation and representation, situation and state of the situation, or ultimately being and event – that alone afford a rigorous understanding of how change (real change as distinct from its simulated versions) comes about in each of those domains. That is, it excludes any thought of the void as a presently unknown or unrecognised source of the various unresolved anomalies, paradoxes, contradictions, or aporias which are latent within any given situation or state of knowledge, and which therefore (in Badiou's preferred future-anterior tense) will subsequently prove to have been the crucial precipitating factor. What is precluded by the Kantian emphasis on epistemology, judgement, and consensus – the three main components of his finitist thinking – is the ubiquity of the void and, by the same token, that of the infinitely multiple orders of infinity.

This is why Badiou is so insistent that the Cantor event has radically altered the scope of human thinking or conceptualisation not only in the formal sciences but equally across those other disciplines that make up the operative 'conditions' of all valid philosophical thought. Infinity is no longer an idea to be shunned or feared (as by many philosophers from the ancient Greeks down) or regarded with quasi-religious awe (as by mystics and irrationalists of various persuasion). Rather it has a necessary place in any adequately-informed process of reasoning whether with regard to mathematics, science, politics, or art. To continue in those old ways of thought is not only to regress to a stage of pre-Cantorian ignorance or mystery-mongering but also, as concerns the wider context, to embrace a deeply conservative conception of the scope and limits of achievable change. Kant belongs squarely with the conservative party by reason of his emphasis on normative judgement, his demotion of ontology vis-à-vis epistemology, his subjugation of politics to ethics, his highly restrictive idea of what befits us mortal knowers, and – subsuming all these – his outlook of resolute finitism with respect to the powers of human intellect and the prospects for human emancipation. For Badiou, this is nothing but a secular (or quasi-secular) equivalent of the theological veto on any attempted exercise of human understanding that thinks to exceed its proper remit. Hence its confinement to a realm – as defined by the elaborate policing-operation of Kant's First *Critique* – where sensuous intuitions are 'brought under' corresponding concepts, but where concepts are required to possess some cognate phenomenal content and thereby have anchorage in the sensuous domain. Otherwise they will be prone to overstep the limits of human cognitive grasp and venture into the sphere of metaphysical or speculative thought, a sphere in which pure reason is properly at home – since rightfully concerned with issues of a supersensible import such as God, freedom, or the immortality of the soul – but which sets all manner of snares and temptations for seekers after knowledge of a more earthbound, i.e., everyday or scientific sort.

Chief among them is the risk that it will mistake speculative ideas for concepts of understanding with determinate or empirically verifiable reference to this or that item of knowledge. Whence Kant's famous image of the dove thinking to soar high and free in regions where its wings will encounter less resistance or drag from the rarefied air, but failing to realise that it is just that resistance that supplies its only source of lift and forward propulsion. Badiou has nothing but contempt for this Kantian idea of philosophy's main task as a matter of constantly beating the bounds between the various human faculties or laying down limits for the exercise of thought in its various legitimate domains. His antipathy is reinforced by Kant's strong aversion – shared by a great many philosophers from the ancient Greeks down – towards that specific deployment of speculative reason which has to do with the infinite, or with that which inherently transcends the limits of straightforward cognitive-intuitive grasp. This goes clean against Badiou's cardinal claim that the history of truly epochal discoveries in mathematics and the sciences or transformative events in the political, ethical, or artistic spheres is precisely that of breakthrough moments when thought acquires the power – and the courage – to give up its reliance on received ideas of intuitive self-evidence. Instead it should trust to a process of rigorously logical, axiomatic-deductive reasoning that may involve a downright affront to any number of deep-grained common-sense beliefs but does so in the interests of truth rather than the interests of compliance with existing (whether common-sense or ideologically conditioned) habits of mind. Of course his prime instance here is the great revolution in mathematical thought through which it became possible – after two millennia of flat refusals or failed attempts – to conceive the existence of an actual as distinct from merely virtual or potential infinite. More than that, Cantor proved that there must exist a series of progressively 'larger' orders of infinity on a scale of magnitudes that far exceeded the utmost powers of intuitive grasp but were nonetheless capable of rigorous treatment by thought in its axiomatic-deductive mode. For Badiou, this stands as a perfect illustration of the way that such advances come about through thought's capacity to 'turn paradox into concept', or transform what had once been perceived as an obstacle on its path into the source of a radically new perspective on its future scope and possibilities.

Beyond mathematics, logic, and the formal sciences, it also provides him with a more-than-suggestive analogy for what transpires at moments of decisive (revolutionary) change in the socio-political sphere. Here again it is Kant – along with his followers in the broadly liberal tradition down to thinkers like Hannah Arendt – whom Badiou holds squarely responsible for that preemptive closing-down of the prospects for genuine change that has produced such a widespread sense of exhaustion in the various (nominally) liberal-democratic or social-democratic states of the new millennium. In particular his ire is directed at Kant's response to the French Revolution, an event that Kant greeted at first with open enthusiasm but then in sober retrospect advised should be taken as a sign, a portent, or a spectacle the sheer sublimity of which might serve to dissuade its viewers from any too actively participant a role. In this regard Kant's political theory is very much of a piece with his cautionary approach to the scope and limits of human knowledge when confronted with those metaphysical questions which – despite their great importance for our super-sensible lives as moral agents – we should learn to treat as incapable of finding any determinate (conceptually adequate) answer. Nothing could be further from Badiou's ethico-political as well as his onto-metaphysical and epistemo-critical outlook. That Kant, in company with many present-day liberals, arrives at this position on the basis of a theory of judgement – judgement, for him, as a mysterious yet strictly indispensable power whose office is to mediate between the various faculties and hence to restrain as much as to enable our carrying of thoughts into action – is yet further reason for Badiou's determination to demote it from any such privileged role.

Thus when he summons up examples of moral courage and political commitment his choice falls on figures like the two eminent mathematicians and members of the French resistance, Cavaillès and Lautman, who were shot by the occupying German forces and whose heroism – Badiou maintains – was primarily a matter of their following through with the utmost rigour on premises (both general and context-specific) which required exactly that consequence. His point is that such actions or commitments are not of the kind that typically follows upon judgement in the Kantian reflective, act-impeding or moderating mode but are rather of the kind that typically issue from fidelity to certain basic and ultimately act-determining principles. Kant's doctrine of judgement is such as systematically to downgrade the human capacity for change, and especially for change of the radical kind typified by political revolutions or by major advances in the formal and natural sciences. Not that Badiou rejects the very notion of judgement, any more than he denies the quality of moral courage – and that in the highest measure – to the mathematicians-*résistants*. Rather he considers its over-centrality, along with the other above-mentioned aspects of Kant's legacy, as having lent the weight of philosophical edict to ideas that have often – during the past two centuries – been put to highly conservative uses despite their seemingly liberal character.

Hence the great pains that Badiou has taken not only to place a large (sometimes polemical) distance between his own thinking and Kant's but also to specify just those respects in which any apparent resemblance between their projects is really no such thing. Thus it might be thought that Badiou's 'communist hypothesis' has much in common with Kant's 'regulative ideas', these latter defined – in impeccably liberal-democratic terms – as belonging to an ideal or limit-point conception of the communal good that cannot rightfully be held accountable to the sorts of dismissive verdict often pronounced upon them by way of a hard-headed appeal to 'the evidence' of failures up to now. As Badiou makes clear, his communist 'ideal' is in truth no such thing but rather in the strict sense a *hypothesis* to be advanced, extended, developed, refined, and tested by subjects whose very existence *as* subjects – in his distinctive usage of the term – is sustained and itself put to the test by their faithful upholding of it. All the same it is clear, despite these emphatic distancing efforts, that Badiou's relationship to Kant is (to adopt his own terminology) that of philosopher to antiphilosopher in the sense of a thinker who demands to be taken on frontally or at full intellectual stretch rather than dispatched to the sidelines of sophistical or quasi-philosophical debate. Although he never explicitly places Kant among the antiphilosophers – along with Saint Paul, Pascal, Rousseau, Kierkegaard, Lacan, and (on his lately revised estimate) Wittgenstein – this would seem an accurate characterisation of the adversary role that Kant occupies in relation to Badiou's own intellectual trajectory.

KIERKEGAARD

Dominiek Hoens

Badiou's work is characterised by a tension between two opposite philosophical programs. On the one hand, there is the determining influence of a structuralist approach that aims at an analysis and formalisation of configurations and processes without any reference to a 'subject', let alone subjectivity or consciousness. On the other, like his master Jacques Lacan, Badiou continues to use a notion of 'subject' and grants it a central role in his theory of post-evental truth procedures. This tension is repeated on a metaphilosophical level, for Badiou identifies himself clearly as a philosopher, but also holds in high respect a series of 'antiphilosophers', including Søren Kierkegaard (1813–55). Whereas philosophy tends to abstract from the subjective and articulate general, desubjectivised theses, antiphilosophers such as Kierkegaard take subjectivity, or the simple fact of human existence, both as the starting and the end point of all reflective activity. It is no exaggeration to claim that Kierkegaard's writings as a whole circle around the question of *den Enkelte*, the singular individual. It is this question that he addresses to the Hegelian System, understood as the philosophical Concept that pretends to be able to grasp anything without leaving a remainder. Kierkegaard's name regularly appears in Badiou's writings, although his work is nowhere discussed in detail, with one notable exception in *LW*. Before turning to this, it pays to note the formal resemblance between the works of both thinkers. (For more on Badiou as a reader of Kierkegaard, see: 'Le penseur vient témoigner en personne. Entretien avec Alain Badiou', *Europe: Revue littéraire men-suelle*, no. 972, April 2010, 92–8; and 'Alain Badiou, L'antiphilosophe', *Magazine Littéraire*, no. 463, April 2007, 50–2.)

The most obvious difference regards Kierkegaard's clearly Christian project and Badiou's atheism. Similar to what is argued when discussing Paul, Pascal and other Christian thinkers, Badiou considers divine inter-vention or grace as analogous to what he has in mind with the notion of event. As truth and becoming the subject of a truth procedure are post-evental, this implies that there is no truth without an event. This event, however minimal and evanescent it may be, is not created or chosen by an autonomous individual. Rather, it is the other way around: the event befalls the individual. For the Christian, the experience of an alterity within the daily confines of one's existence is an act of divine grace. In Badiou's theory of the event, the latter functions analogously, as it occurs, and 'causes' the faithful subject to go beyond any personal or par-ticular individuality. This, however, does not happen automatically, but demands an active choice by the subject. One could just as well ignore or betray the event. Here Kierkegaard, too, emphasises the importance of choice, which he elaborates in terms of three distinct stages: the aesthetic, the ethical and the religious. What he names the aesthetic refers to a life of non-choice, or the choice against choice, as the aesthete is distracted by all the refined, interesting and colourful things life has to offer. His main enemy is boredom. The ethical stage starts from the moment the aesthete makes a choice, more precisely, chooses to choose, and turns one of his interests into a profession and prefers one woman above all others and marries her. The religious and last stage implies a return to one's individuality, for despite all the stable qualities the individual chose by entering the realm of ethical life, the problem of the self remains untouched. The man of ethics starts to despair. This is where the reli-gious comes into play and the individual starts to struggle with what preceded and created him, namely God, who, as eternity, manifested himself via Christ *within* time.

The analogy of the religious stage with Badiou's program is striking, for to become a subject of an event also implies a break with the normal (read: ethical) order of things. The event does not entirely separate one from an existing situation, but demands that one reconsider and actively re-create the situation from the standpoint of the event. Neither the Knight of Faith (Kierkegaard) nor the militant of truth (Badiou) can rely on the event (of God) as a positive element – a law, an insight, a dogma, etc. – that makes it clear what one should do. Yet, they are nonetheless called on to explore the consequences of being a subject only through the encounter with an alterity that comes to inhabit one's existence. There is a twofold difference between these thinkers, however. For Badiou the subject is a subject of a political, scientific, amorous or artistic event, while religion is explicitly rejected as a fifth domain. For Kierkegaard, however, religion alone is able to force the individual to confront its singularity. In addition, the affective tonality of the two authors is quite different. Whereas Badiou emphasises the post-evental truth procedure and the courage, discipline, patience and tenacity it requires, Kierkegaard stresses the anxiety and despair the Christian experiences when set the task of leaving behind the comfortable security of *being* a Christian, provided for by the Church one belongs to, and actually to *become* a Christian. As with the event, one does not know what the Christ-event means, but whereas Badiou puts the emphasis on the post-evental truth procedure, Kierkegaard devotes much more attention to the impossibility of what is demanded from the Christian: I should become a Christian without knowing what this means and without ever attaining the certainty that I am what I think I should become. Badiou, to be sure, includes the category of the unnameable in any truth procedure and is aware of the different positions a subject can occupy within it – fidelity, but also betrayal, obscurity, and fatigue – but is less interested in individual despair and anxiety, for the individual qua subject of a truth procedure is only part of a larger subject, along with pamphlets, strategic choices, party organisation, and so on (to use only the example of politics). The difference, briefly put, is that between a conception of subjectivity as individuality and one as non-individual support (*subjectum*) of a truth procedure.

This may explain why Badiou's only discussion of Kierkegaard of some length does not concern the latter's reflections on boredom, the anxiety provoked by the abyss of one's own existence, or the 'fear and trembling' that accompanies the religious suspension of the ethical, but the central place given to choice. In Book VI, Section 2 of *LW* (425–35), Badiou explains that truth is tested in a point, with the alternative of an either/or. This means that truth is neither a given, nor a promise (eventually given to the one who chooses the right option), but experienced as a choice. It forces the subject to make a choice, or to choose to choose. Here Badiou is not so much interested in the subjective interiority and religious despair accompanying this impossible task, but is congenial with Kierkegaard when the latter argues that the infinite complexity of the world sometimes can be reduced to the alternative of an either/or. For Badiou this alternative is named the Two, which saves the world from atony and allows – but also demands – the subject to be localised in the element of truth, that is to say, through choice a relation is established between one's subjective, finite time and eternity.

$$\boxed{\text{L}}$$

LINGUISTIC TURN

Christopher Norris

The 'linguistic turn' is a phrase first put into wide circulation by the neo-pragmatist philosopher (or post-philosopher) Richard Rorty, who used it as the title of a 1967 anthology of essays representing various schools of thought – 'continental' and 'analytic' alike – that had taken one or another version of the turn towards philosophy of language as *prima philosophia*. These included the tradition of logico-semantic analysis descending from Frege and Russell; the reactive appeal to 'ordinary language', with its main sources in the later Wittgenstein and J. L. Austin; and on the continental side, hermeneutics (from Heidegger to Gadamer), structuralism, post-structuralism, Foucauldian discourse theory, and assorted strains of post-modernism including some (like Lyotard's variations on Wittgensteinian themes) that had a foot in both camps. Then there was Rorty's own syn-thesis – essayed obliquely in his 1967 Foreword, then developed through a lengthy series of books – which brought together elements of all these except the Frege–Russell analytic mode which he took them jointly to have rendered pretty much obsolete. That is, they had shown that there was no point going halfway with the turn – stopping at the point where language was still held subject to logical analysis – since this was just a throwback to old ideas of philosophy as a constructive, problem-solving discourse with its own distinctive methods and truth-telling prerogatives.

What was needed if philosophers were to have any voice in a 'post-philosophical' culture was that they should give up such pretensions of intellectual grandeur and take the lesson provided by Wittgenstein, Heidegger (minus all the depth-ontological stuff), post-structuralism and some of the less zany postmodernists. This cheerful eclecticism was stretched a bit further to embrace the American pragmatists, Dewey especially, as a down-to-earth reminder of their social role as promot-ers of the ongoing 'cultural conversation'. Such was at any rate Rorty's prescription for the best way forward once philosophy had absorbed the news – delivered in regular instalments by his books over the next thirty years – of its no longer having anything distinctive (or at any rate anything distinctively philosophical) to say. It is a doctrine that Badiou finds alto-gether repellent and to which he has devoted a good deal of passionate and eloquent counter-argument. His chief objection has to do with the close link between this language-first idea and the highly conservative precept – one with its source in the later Wittgenstein – that thinking cannot make any kind of sense outside the context of some given 'language-game' or communal 'form of life'. In which case, so the argument goes, we must always be wrong (self-deluded) and at risk of committing an injustice if we presume to criticise practices or beliefs that have their communal habitat in a life-form other than our own.

Badiou sees this, rightly enough, as a form of cultural relativism with disabling (indeed disastrous) implications for any project – like his own – which takes a critical stance on many issues (from politics to mathematics, science, philosophy, psychoanalysis, and the arts) and does so on the strength of arguments that claim validity across languages and cultures. Such is his other main grievance: that the turn towards language has all too often been a turn towards languages in the plural, or towards what he (in company with many analytic philosophers) would deem the strictly nonsensical idea that different languages are 'incommensurable' and hence incapable of inter-translation or mutual intelligibility. This line of thought can very easily end by offering support for those currently fashionable notions – of 'difference', 'alterity', 'heterogeneity', 'absolute otherness', and so forth – which Badiou rejects as philosophically obtuse and politically divisive. Against it he asserts the strong universalism of an outlook, decidedly unfashionable nowadays, which takes human beings to be capable of achieving a real community of interest and purpose – across even the apparently deepest socio-cultural-linguistic divides – once freed of the false understandings that currently set them apart. Along with this goes the equally firm conviction that different languages can articulate identical thoughts, and moreover that thought is prior to language both in the sense 'preceding its particular mode of verbal articulation' and also in the sense 'properly the chief object of philosophic attention'. For otherwise Badiou would be in no good position to assert his various far-reaching claims for mathematics – especially modern set theory – as a source of insight into matters way outside its technical domain, including issues of political representation and the status of those, like 'illegal' immigrants, who count for nothing in the state of the situation.

Where the linguistic turn, especially in its continental, e.g. post-structuralist variants, has encouraged an emphasis on cultural difference and heterogeneity, the appeal to mathematics has the opposite effect of pointing us back to those basic commonalties that unite human beings across such potential (and exploitable) distinctions. It can therefore be seen that Badiou's case for mathematics, rather than language, as our best source of guidance in other domains is closely tied up with his universalist ethic and his vigorous rebuttal of difference-thinking – or cultural particularism – in its various forms. That case is further strengthened by the way that post-Cantorian set theory, especially in its dealing with orders of infinity, made possible a drastic and unprecedented break with those habitual or intuitive perceptions which tend to reinforce existing habits of thought. This is why Badiou makes a point of selecting a set-theoretical system or ontology that avoids the liability of natural language, i.e. that defines sets, members and membership conditions in strictly extensional (object-related) rather than intensional (meaning-dependent) terms. What qualifies a multiple for membership is purely and simply its belonging to the set in question, rather than any particular feature – any membership-bestowing property or attribute – that sets it apart from others that are not so qualified.

This commitment at the logico-semantic level has large implications for Badiou's political thought, falling square as it does with his universalist principles and – more specifically – his work with the *sans-papiers* or workers without and hence deprived of all civic, legal and constitutional rights. It is also a leading consideration in his work on major episodes in the history of ideas, as with the sections on thinkers from Plato to Heidegger that intersperse the passages of intensive mathematico–philosophical commentary in *BE*. Thus despite taking issue with Leibniz and Spinoza as regards their commitment to a closed or immobile ontology that leaves no room for genuine change, or for the irruption of world-transformative events into the realm of plenary being, Badiou is very much in agreement with them concerning the priority of thought over language and hence the need for philosophy to seek a degree of conceptual sharpness and precision beyond that attainable by ordinary language. So far from rejecting analytic philosophy *tout court* he declares a strong allegiance to certain select parts of it, notably that *echt*-analytic line of descent that took its main bearings from mathematics and logic rather than from reflection on the nature of language. These philosophers held out against the late-Wittgensteinian or other such wholesale versions of the 'turn', and continued to insist on the capacity of thought to surpass and correct the deliverances of naïve sense-certainty, unaided intuition, or everyday verbal usage. By so doing they continued to honour philosophy's age-old imperative to resist that power of 'bewitchment by language' that Socrates denounced in the sophists of his day and that Wittgenstein professedly sought to cure but which has lately got a hold in many quarters of debate through his own, highly infectious version of it.

LOVE

Louise Burchill

One of the four fundamental truth procedures comprising the conditions of philosophy, love is, for Badiou, that which alone furnishes a universal ground on which sexual difference can be thought. The truth love produces bears precisely on what it is to be two and not one: 'the amorous scene is the only genuine scene in which a universal singularity pertaining to the Two of the sexes – and ultimately pertaining to difference as such – is proclaimed. This is where an undivided subjective experience of absolute difference takes place' (TU/*TW* § 3). Such a claim – that sexual difference finds the conditions of its determination in the category of love, as defined, in this instance, in philosophy – directly challenges the pronouncement of Lacanian psychoanalysis that philosophy, as a will to systematisation, is constitutively demarcated by its *foreclosing*, or refusing to acknowledge, sexual difference. Yet, while Badiou refutes Lacan on this point, and indeed proceeds to a major revision of the latter's formulae of sexuation from the perspective of 'love as the guarantee of the universal', he nonetheless credits Lacan's psychoanalytic teaching as constituting an event – *the* 'modern' event – in the order of thought dealing with love's contribution to truth (*MP* 81). No philosophical category of love is possible today then, on Badiou's understanding, unless it is compatible, or compossible, with the psychoanalytic concept qua event and requisite condition. This is to say that the dialogue – or perhaps, more strictly speaking, *différend* – Badiou entertains with Lacan must be understood to veritably structure his entire axiomatics relative to love and sexual difference.

That which makes Lacan, in Badiou's view, the most profound 'theoretician of love' since the Plato of the *Symposium* or the *Phaedrus* is his differentiating love from desire on the basis of 'the specifically ontological function' it would fulfil (82–3). 'Love approaches being as such in the encounter' is a declaration from Lacan's famed seminar XX (Lacan 1998: 145) that Badiou systematically adduces whenever he expounds his own thinking on love, placing it at times in tandem with the assertion of Plato's *Republic* that 'in love you cannot love in a piecemeal manner but must love all of the loved being' (*PE* 52, 64; *IP* 19). As defined in terms of its striving towards the totality of the other, and not, as is the case with desire, some 'part', 'trait' or 'object' – be this a partial object lodged in the body of the other – love is revealed, on Badiou's reading, as an existential process that conveys individuals beyond a merely solipsistic, or narcissistic, experience of the world. Before the chance encounter that inaugurates the amorous procedure, there would be nothing, as it were, but 'monads' or 'ones', each enclosed in its singular narcissistic sphere: a egoistic unity or 'dominance of the One' (*MP* 83) that love precisely fractures by opening onto an experience of the world that is taken on as an experience of 'Two'. This experience or, as Badiou puts it, 'scene of the Two', involves, as such, a 'revaluation' of everything that is given in the situation, with each fragment of the world henceforth to be investigated and invested through a *material* procedure of construction – rigorously distinguished from the fusional, oblative or sceptical conceptions of love (WL/*CS* 181–2) – that is carried out from the perspective no longer of One but of Two. Not only is this process of construction infinite in nature in terms of its investigation of the world but it equally entails the progressive, inexhaustible discovery of the infinity of different strata and alterities that make up the 'totality of the other'; this being the twofold sense in which Badiou characterises love as an undivided subjective experience of absolute difference. Conducted in fidelity to the declaration 'I love you' that seals 'the evental encounter', this passage from one to two, introducing difference into the same, is 'the first opening-up of finitude – the smallest but, undoubtedly, also the most radical' (*PE* 54). Whence the numerical schema of 'One, Two, Infinity' that structures love's production of the truth that two separate, or disjunct, positions exist in the situation (WL/CS 189; *SI* 304). The subject of this procedure – the two of the lovers, qua a wholly immanent Two – is, as such, the smallest possible kernel of universality, yet one that pre-eminently attests to there being a common humanity, universally valid for all.

Love's functioning as a guarantee of 'humanity's universality' is, for Badiou, strictly inseparable from its status as the sole field in which sexual difference can be thought. Lacan is, in this instance again, the indispensable interlocutor, though less in his capacity as an exemplary theoretician of love than as a thinker of desire, whose formulae of sexuation are to be subjected, on Badiou's part, to relentless rectification. A preliminary point of agreement between the two thinkers on the question of sexual difference needs, however, to be recalled: namely, the sexuate positions 'man' and 'woman' can in no way be distributed universally on the grounds of biology, sociology, or any other form of knowledge that takes as its object the simple facticity of the human animal. In Badiou's terms, such forms of knowledge fail to cross through the configuration of 'what is given' to attain the truth of that presented in an existing situation. Indeed, while two sexuated positions can be said to be 'given' in the field of experience, these positions are in a state of total disjunction such that neither position can know anything of the experience of the other, nor, moreover, have any experience or direct knowledge of the disjunction as such. It's in this sense that Lacan's tenet of the impossibility of a relationship between the

sexes is one that Badiou readily embraces, though ultimately with a qualification that will prove to be the decisive point of divergence between his
understanding of sexual difference and that of Lacan.

What Badiou essentially objects to is Lacan's defining sexual difference
in terms of the phallic function – the 'universal quantifier' that divides
all speaking beings on either side of an unary trait: having or being the
phallus – whereas he himself considers this function to govern the dimension of desire or *jouissance* (sexual enjoyment) alone, with sexual difference
requiring, for its truth to be revealed, a supplementary function introduced by love, which Badiou precisely names the 'humanity' function.
For Badiou, sexual difference simply does not exist on the level of desire
or jouissance: any and all sexual 'interaction' that is non-amorous engages
each participant solely within her or his particular position or narcissistic
sphere and is, thereby, 'strictly masturbatory'. Sex without love is a com-
putation, in other words, of '1' plus '1', without this yielding any '2' (WL/
CS 187). Stipulating Lacan's proclamation 'there is no sexual relation' to
hold solely, thereby, in the realm of desire, Badiou specifies that, insofar as
desire is always desire of an object borne by the body – a partial object or
'object *a*' in Lacan's terminology – and neither the body as such nor, much
less, the 'other' as subject, this equally entails that desire is essentially
finite in nature (*PE* 64). The fact that Lacan, for his part, restricts such a
definition of desire to what he names 'phallic jouissance' (Lacan 1998: 8)
and posits that, for those who occupy the feminine sexuate position, there
is a 'supplementary jouissance' – a jouissance 'beyond the phallus' – at
the basis of which 'something other than the object *a* is involved in the
attempt to supplement the sexual relation that doesn't exist' (63), only
confirms for Badiou the failure of Lacan's schema to ground sexual difference within a universalising truth that holds in strictly the same way for
both 'man' and 'woman'. Condemning Lacan's theory of sexual difference
as 'segregative' (cf. woman), Badiou sets down that, while there is no relation between the sexes, there has, nonetheless, to be at least one term with
which both sexuate positions entertain a relation. This is, of course, the
element introduced by love. An amorous encounter gives rise, in fact, to
a *disjunctive synthesis* of sexuated positions (TU/*TW* §3) since woman and
man now share a common, if unanalysable, term—the indefinable element
at the basis of their love—that, by manifesting the non-substantial, or
non-ontological, nature of the positions' disjunction, establishes them as
belonging to a single humanity. Badiou effects, in this way, a 'twist', or
'turn of the screw' (WL/*CS* 198), in respect of Lacan's formulae of sexuation since the element operative in the 'humanity function' reveals itself to
consist in what might be termed a *sublimatory* transmutation of the object
a, whereby this no longer circulates purely in the sensible sphere of the

sexual non-relation but acquires the supplementary and 'more essential' function of assuring an approach to the being of the other (*PE* 52).

Indeed, with an amorous encounter, the object *a* is veritably transposed, in Badiou's terms, within a 'different topology' (*SD* 54) where it now serves as the point of intersection on the basis of which the sexes compose an immanent figure of the Two. Insofar as the 'relation' of the sexes is shown thereby to depend not on the object–cause of desire alone but also on the being as such of the sexuate positions, Badiou renames the element in play the 'atom *u*', by way of marking not only its 'ubiquity', blind 'usage' and non-decomposable, unanalysable 'unicity', but also the 'universality' to which it attests (*SD* 48; *PE* 58). The atom *u* must be understood to animate the 'non-sexual matter' of the scene of the Two: it is what founds the external 'expansion' of the Two of the lovers in their shared investigation of the world, in contrast with the movement of 'contraction' back upon the 'obscure core' of the sexual non-relation fuelled by the illusion of the object. While both of these 'sublimatory' and 'sexual' movements are necessary to the amorous procedure, it is, of course, the former that properly defines love, for Badiou, as a truth process of universalising scope. Any and every love proposes, in fact, a new experience of truth concerning what it is to be Two and not One – a truth, in other words, of the nature of the disjunction or difference as such insofar as love establishes that sexual difference is a law of one, shared situation and not of a duality, or plurality, of situations grounded in a separation in being. Desire or *jouissance*, for their part, are incapable of yielding any such truth of the Two precisely because of their alignment on the object relation that imprisons each position in its particularity. This '*excess*' of love over the object (*SD* 54) is, then, what makes of it a 'guardian of the universality of truth' (*WL* 190).

This admitted, there is still a further twist that Badiou imparts to Lacan's formulae of sexuation by transposing them within the 'topology' of his axiomatics of love. Let us recall here that Badiou defines 'humanity' as the space of thought comprised by the four truth procedures, art, science, politics and love itself; a definition roughly analogous to what others – including Lacan – name the 'symbolic'. While 'love's truth' is that a common humanity is shared by the two sexes, the latter do not relate to this 'shared symbolic' in the same way. Not only does the disjunction of the sexes remain operative in the field of love but their disjunction in respect of the humanity function is precisely the 'content' of one of the axiomatic definitions of sexual difference Badiou sets down on the basis of the amorous procedure (*WL* 193–7). Succinctly put, all those who take up the position 'man' view the symbolic sphere as a composite of the different truth procedures, such that each type of truth can stand for all the others, whereas 'woman', on the contrary, privileges love as the truth procedure that would knot all the others together and without which the symbolic sphere as a totality simply does not exist. Thus defining 'woman' as the position that upholds love as the guarantee of a universality to humanity – as what ensures that this is indeed *shared* – Badiou's axiomatics of love assign the 'universal quantifier' to the feminine position and not, in contrast with Lacan's sexual formulae premised upon the 'universality' of the phallic function, to 'man'. Reciprocally, while Lacan defines 'woman' as 'not-all', or 'not-whole', under the phallic function in virtue of feminine jouissance's opening onto an infinite 'beyond', in Badiou's transposition it is 'man' who is situated as *not wholly* under the humanity function insofar as truths, for the masculine position, are mutually independent, all while each 'metaphorically' stands for the totality of one and all.

Badiou's revisions, we might say, thus 'transmute' the *exceptionality* that Lacan attributes to feminine 'supplementary jouissance' into woman's *singularly* upholding 'love's excess' over desire. This returns us to Lacan's diagnosis of philosophy's constitutive foreclusion of sexual difference – at least insofar as this is more strictly formulated as philosophy's impossibility to countenance the question of sexual jouissance, linked as this is to the absolutely unsymbolisable 'Thing', or maternal body. There is no doubting that, from the perspective of psychoanalysis, Badiou's 'twisting' of Lacan's sexual formulae can but still seem set on circumventing the 'real' of the drives. Acknowledging, for his part, that philosophy does exclude the question of jouissance, Badiou nevertheless states that this is necessary in order to seize what is at stake in sexual identity, with jouissance then becoming an issue to which philosophy can return (WL/*CS* 179; SEM 2002).

MAOIST POLITICS

Dhruv Jain

Alain Badiou's relationship to Maoist politics is both biographical and philosophical. Badiou, like many French activists in the late 1960s, was attracted to the Great Proletarian Cultural Revolution (GPCR) and helped to form the Maoist groupuscule, the Union of Communists of France Marxist-Leninist (UCFML). Furthermore, Badiou's relationship to Mao Zedong bears precisely on the event of the GPCR and the 'thought of Mao Zedong' or Maoism (see the publication by the Groupe pour la Fondation de l'Union des Communistes Francais (Marxiste-Leniniste), *La Revolution Proletarienne en France – Comment Edifier le Parti de l'Epoque de la Pensee de Mao Tse Toung*). Thus, one must actually 'divide one into two' and see that Badiou's relationship to Mao has little to do with him as a figure of state, but instead pertains to the political 'thought of Mao Zedong', evidenced in his reading of the GPCR. Effectively, Badiou's own account of the GPCR speaks to a fundamental tension between Mao qua figure of state and the 'thought of Mao Zedong' as it pertains to the worker and student political organisations in the Cultural Revolution that exceeded state functioning, and rendered a return to the previous state organisation inoperable. Mao Zedong remains an important figure in Badiou's thought and politics, despite his break with Maoism in particular and Marxism more generally in the early 1980s (cf. Marxism), because (1) Mao's thought placed a great emphasis on the role of antagonism for the production of politics; (2) Mao's emphasis on 'trusting the masses' allowed Badiou to recognise the gap between presentation and representation in politics; and (3) Mao's thought permitted Badiou, in both his Maoist and post-Maoist modes of thought, to apprehend the facts under a different set of political axioms, and hence articulate a new 'communist hypothesis'.

Badiou writes that the twentieth century 'declared that its law was the Two, antagonism; in this respect, the end of the cold war (American imperialism versus the socialist camp), as the last total figure of the Two, also signals the end of the century' (*C* 59). The twentieth century is marked by a sharp antagonism between a series of contradictions that cannot be synthesised, but wherein one side is victorious through annihilating/suppressing the other side (ibid.). This particular analysis of contradiction, which grounds antagonism as a necessary condition for politics, arose from a philosophical debate in China and guided Leftists during the GPCR and their activities. For Badiou the operation of One dividing into Two is best expressed in the GPCR slogan that it is 'right to rebel against the reactionaries'. Badiou, in fidelity to the 'leftists', argues against any attempt to fuse the Two into One, as this One is but the old One masquerading under the 'cover of synthesis' (60). It is this very procedure of dividing One into Two that Badiou utilises in analysing Mao and the GPCR.

Badiou does not shy away from criticising Mao and does not completely reject critical narratives about Mao and the GPCR, but remains sympathetic to many aspects of Mao's political programme while simultaneously drawing his own lessons from the failures of Mao and the Cultural Revolution (*Pol* 293–5). Badiou provides a particularly nuanced analysis of

Mao's role during the Cultural Revolution. On the one hand, he applauds Mao for launching the Cultural Revolution against the bureaucratisation of the party-state through an emphasis on political mass mobilisation, revolt and organisation uncontrolled by the state, but on the other he simultaneously sought to internalise all new organisational forms into the party-state itself (297). Indeed, this is why Badiou refers to the name of 'Mao' as a paradox. Mao is both the head of the bureaucratic party-state and a representative of that element – the Red Guards and other leftists – that wished to be victorious by smashing the very same state. As Badiou writes, 'We can clearly see that Mao, by bringing in the workers, wanted to avoid the situation turning into one of "military control". He wanted to protect those who had been his initial allies and had been the carriers of enthusiasm and political innovation. But Mao is also a man of the party-state. He wants its renovation, even a violent one, but not its destruction' (317). It is this last point regarding the renovation and destruction of the state on which Badiou comes to distance himself most from Mao (and the party-state).

Due to Badiou's emphasis on this paradox, his sympathies are less vested in Mao's official positions within the Communist Party of China and more in the specific kinds of political procedures that were produced by Mao's thought. Badiou distances himself from the cult of personality and argues that such a cult of personality was tied to the party and a conception of the party according to which it is the hegemonic site of politics (318). Badiou notes that the personhood of Mao serves as guarantee of the party's infallible capacity to represent the masses, when there is in fact nothing that can 'guarantee any such representation' (ibid.). It is this impossibility of guaranteeing representation upon which Badiou's contemporary post-Maoism rests. Badiou explains, 'More generally, the Cultural Revolution showed that it was no longer possible to assign either the revolutionary mass actions or the organisational phenomena to the strict logic of class representation. That is why it remains a political episode of the highest importance' (299). This political truth allows Badiou to discern another from Mao and the Cultural Revolution, namely the complete 'saturation' of the party-state (292). If there is no guarantee of representation, the party's claim to act as the state is undermined and allows for the development of a 'politics without a party'.

Furthermore, this division of Mao into Two, state figure and name for the thought of a political procedure to be thought in the future anterior (the splitting of the name Mao into two is precisely this split between the time of the state and the time of the truth procedure) allows Badiou not to simply limit the truth procedure of politics to statements of condemnation or support for any given action of Mao, but rather allows greater emphasis to be placed on what was thought, on the political problems that we have been bequeathed and that need reinventing today. For example, Badiou argues that the Great Leap Forward, a policy put forward by Mao in 1958, was a failure, but a failure in a different sense than is ascribed to it by most commentators. Badiou points out that Mao's attempts to promote development in the countryside and reconcile the relationship between the countryside and city were an attempt to avoid the mistakes made by J. V. Stalin during the forced collectivisation of 1928–40, by shifting the emphasis to economic autonomy and small-scale industrial production in the countryside (*Pol* 295). The failure of the Great Leap Forward was thus of a different kind than Stalin's own errors, insofar as this failure was a political one. As Badiou himself writes, in regard to the difference between Stalin and Mao's failure, 'we should affirm that the same abstract description of facts by no means leads to the same mode of thinking, when it operates under different political axioms' (ibid.). It is this affirmation of the capacity for modes of thinking to operate differently upon 'the same abstract description of facts' under new political axioms that Badiou employs in his own immanent reading of the GPCR and Mao. Thus, Mao's thought remains at the centre of Badiou's philosophical system and contemporary communist metapolitics.

MARXIST POLITICS

Dhruv Jain

Badiou's relationship to Marxism remains one of the most contentious aspects of his theoretical and political production, especially his call for a renewed communist politics. He defines Marxism as 'the organised knowledge of the political means required to undo existing society and finally realise an egalitarian, rational figure of collective organisation for which the name is communism' (*RH* 8–9). However, Badiou's Marxism rejects key aspects, political and philosophical, of Marxist orthodoxy, especially as regards his wariness of suturing philosophy to politics. His relationship to Marxism will be explored through four fundamental concepts that he outlines both in the period marking his 'red years' and during and after the publication of *BE*. However, Badiou's Marxism remains consistent throughout his oeuvre in two regards: 1) the necessity of a politics of non-domination that is irreducible to the state; and 2) the designation of the maximal sites of singularity, or the need to discern the weakest links in a given system.

The four fundamental concepts of Marxism in *TS*

In *TS*, Badiou notes that there are 'four fundamental concepts of Marxism': the party, the class struggle, the dictatorship of the proletariat, and communism (282). Each of these concepts has been deeply transformed by each subsequent mode of Marxist politics, of which there are three. These three stages, for Badiou and his comrades in the Group for the Foundation of the Union of Communists of France Marxist-Leninist (UCFML), are Marxism, Leninism and finally Maoism. The UCFML's, and similarly Badiou's, Marxism was thus not simply a form of post-Marxism but also a post-Leninism in its recognition of the newest 'stage' of Marxism, Maoism (Groupe pour la Fondation de l'Union des Communistes Francais (Marxiste-Leniniste) 2005: 527). Thus, when discussing Badiou's Marxism one must necessarily be attuned to the constant refurbishing of these four concepts. Furthermore, one must note that Badiou's Marxism remains consistently distant from, and in sharp opposition to, the French Communist Party (PCF). This distance and opposition results in the 'combative' form of Marxism that Badiou espouses being in part shaped by the PCF's form of Marxism (*TS* 9). Badiou and his comrades were concerned by a form of Marxism that is specific and homogeneous in its content, while being adapted to the working class as a means by which to include it in bourgeois and imperialist 'space' (*TS* 9). Controversially, Badiou and the UCFML understood this bourgeois and imperialist space, which the working class occupied, as including trade unions and electoral politics. This resulted in Badiou's boycotting of both trade unions and electoral politics as spaces in which one could practise Marxist politics.

Marxism, for Badiou, initially served as a referential point that allows for the subjectivisation of the workers' movement (*TS* 44). Badiou and his compatriots argued that workers could only become a revolutionary subject through being organised into an instrument, or apparatus, capable of unifying the masses into collective action through recognition of a politics not simply guided by specific interests. This need for organisation is because, Badiou argues, the working class is incapable of resolving the division between its social immediacy and the political project that produced it. Thus, there needed to be an apparatus through which this division could be fully comprehended and overcome. However, this apparatus must be less interested in surviving as an apparatus and more interested in achieving the political goal of communism, which would require the apparatuses' self-destruction. During the 1970s, for Badiou and the UCFML this apparatus remained the party. Thus, the UCFML consistently advocated for the formation of a 'party of a new type' based on Marxism-Leninism-Maoism.

However, Badiou's reframing of the concepts of Marxism was not limited to his redefinition of the party but also included that of class. Badiou's definition of class contravenes orthodox Marxist definitions of class and class struggle due to its avoidance both of a sociological definition of class, which is grounded in the relations of production, and as a 'concentration of all antagonism to the bourgeoisie'. Rather, it favours the recognition of class as 'partisan political action' that is anchored in the capacity of the masses to produce history (*TS* 26–7). For Badiou the bourgeoisie is no longer simply reducible either to control over the State apparatuses or to the logic of economic profit, but rather is also capable of leading the class struggle and the production of a subject able to intervene in the class struggle (42). Indeed, unlike other Marxists, Badiou recognises that the bourgeoisie itself is able to organise its own political project and subjectivise the working class around such a project.

The final project for Badiou is communism. Badiou equates the content of this communism with that of another main concept of Marxism, the dictatorship of the proletariat (282). Communism and the dictatorship for Badiou was the 'same thing', with the former being the part that was concerned with justice, whereas the latter was concerned with the capacity to regulate society through its function as a superego of society (ibid.). Indeed, this equating of communism and justice is something that Badiou continues to uphold today, although he has rejected the needed for the superegoistic function of the dictatorship of the proletariat.

The 'post-Maoism' of post-*BE*

BE marks a discernible difference in Badiou's relationship to Marxism, and this differential relationship has perceptively been referred to as 'post-Maoism' (Bosteels 2005). In *MP*, Badiou writes: 'In its dominant canonical form, Marxism itself has proposed a suture, the suture of philosophy to its political condition' (*MP* 62). This suturing of philosophy to its political condition results in the incapacity of philosophy to appreciate and internalise new 'truths' from the other conditions with sufficient rigour (63). Due to the suturing of philosophy to politics, philosophy itself is suppressed and is unable to incorporate new truths into its theoretical system (ibid.). Instead, Badiou limits Marxism to its place in the political condition. Thus, a philosophical operation is also accompanied by Badiou's reformulation of the four fundamental concepts of Marxism discussed above. Badiou no longer advocates for the Maoist party, but rather for a 'politics without a party', while also rejecting the concepts of class and class struggle that animated *TS*. Furthermore, although Badiou continues to advocate for communism, he now does so through maintenance of a 'distance from the state' rather than through the capture of the state.

In *BE* Badiou argues that the subject 'is no longer the founding subject, centred and reflexive, whose theme runs from Descartes to Hegel and which remains legible in Marx and Freud (in fact, in Husserl and Sartre). The contemporary Subject is void, cleaved, a-substantial, and ir-reflexive' (*BE* 3). Indeed, rather than a founding subject like the proletariat and the party, Badiou argues for a subject that is no longer fixed through substantialist categories like those provided by sociology or economics, but one that is produced through fidelity to an event and the 'truth' that is produced by the said fidelity. This new subject is no longer organised in a party, but rather in a politics without a party. Badiou explains that '"Politics without party" means that politics does not spring from or originate in the party . . . Politics springs from real situations, from what we can say and do in these situations. And so in reality there are political sequences, political processes, but these are not totalised by a party that would be simultaneously the representation of certain social forces and the source of politics itself' (*E* 95–6).

This rejection of the party parallels the rejection of the working class as a specific socio-economic category determined by its production relations. Badiou writes, 'it is "class" that is an analytical and descriptive concept, a "cold" concept, and "masses" that is the concept with which the active principle of the riots, real change, is designated' (*RH* 91). However, simultaneously, the figure of the worker does remain central to his political project. Badiou argues that there was an attempt by the State to erase the political figure of the worker by juxtaposing the 'French worker' against those strikers that were in fact 'immigrants', and later 'illegal aliens' (*E* 9). Thus, the figure of the worker is not a sociological category but a political one. In this way Badiou remains dedicated to a kind of worker politics that does not seek to name and represent the worker. It is in this context that the *Organisation Politique* and Badiou placed emphasis on the figure of the *sans-papier*, or worker without papers.

Another profound change in Badiou's theoretical corpus is his advocating a 'distance from the state', instead of the 'dictatorship of the proletariat'. In *BE* he defines politics as an assault, violent or peaceful, against the State (*BE* 110). Unlike the Marxist tradition, then, which calls for the capture of the State, Badiou believes that the party-state, or dictatorship of the proletariat, became a saturated experience as evidenced by the Cultural Revolution (Mao recognised very early on that this key Marxist political concept had been rendered indeterminate by the GPCR and thus lacked content, since even the Chinese socialist state was traversed by contradictions between workers and a red bourgeois). However, this does not

mean that there should be a non-relation to the State. The point is rather
that authority must not be invested in an organisation designed to take
over the state, but on one that operates at a distance by making prescriptions to the State. As a matter of fact, Badiou does not altogether abandon
the notion of dictatorship, but instead of talking of a dictatorship of the
proletariat he speaks of a 'popular dictatorship' qua a form of authority
adequate to the presentative power of a popular movement, so one that
is opposed to all forms of state dictatorship (*RH* 45, 59). So Badiou does
not reject emancipatory politics by any means, considering simply that the
party-state cannot be oriented towards communism.

The formal definition of communism as 'justice' for Badiou remains
unchanged throughout his oeuvre, and is deeply related to the concepts of
emancipation and equality. Furthermore, communism is now articulated
as an Idea, which 'is the subjectivisation of an interplay between the singularity of a truth procedure and a representation of History' (*CH* 235).
Indeed, the Idea of Communism involves precisely a subject's unfolding
of the consequences of an event and its articulation with a representation
of universal humanity.

MATHEME

Samo Tomšič

A key concept in Badiou's reaffirmation of philosophy and its contemporaneity, the matheme's importance is twofold: first, it sums up Badiou's
position on the mathematical foundation of ontology, serving as a tool of
formalisation able to push the limits of linguistic enunciation; second,
it establishes philosophy's polemical positioning in the discursive field,
helping it to delimit itself from sophistic discourse by thinking the real of
being beyond its symbolic interplays. In this latter respect, the matheme
functions as a conceptual tool enabling philosophy to reject the double
linguistic turn in analytic philosophy and hermeneutics, both of which
emphasise the primacy of discourse. Badiou's twofold use of the matheme
affirms his fidelity to Lacan's own conceptualisation of this term, which,
Badiou claims, is firmly inscribed in the Platonic tradition. In his late
teaching, Lacan introduced the matheme as a tool for the integral transmission of knowledge, whereby the integrality of transmission is conditioned
by the foreclosure of sense at the level of mathematical letters. Mathemes
are not simply univocal but stand outside the opposition of univocity and
polivocity. They are, as Badiou points out in reference to Lacan, figures of
ab-sense, of the absence of sense. Yet Lacan and Badiou's use of mathemes

bear some differences. Before discussing them, let us understand why this concept is crucial for the renaissance of philosophy.

One of Badiou's main philosophical gestures in *BE* consists in positing a system of conditions for philosophy. In addition, this work also affirms a fundamental philosophical tension not unrelated to the system of conditions and intimately linked to the dimension of language. This tension or contradiction concerns language in its formal and dynamic aspects or, simply, the difference between mathematical and poetic language. What these two aspects of language share is their thwarting of all attempts to reduce language to its communicative or utilitarian function. Yet the matheme and the poem point in clearly opposite directions, the latter towards the realm of equivocity and the production of meaning, and the former towards univocity and signification. Now, since it is back to Plato and his self-proclaimed 'murder of father Parmenides' that the fundamental break in the history of philosophy needs to be traced, Plato could be said to have committed a double patricide. Not only did he question the fundamental Parmenidian axiom 'Being is, non-Being is not', he also produced a rupture that disrupted the primacy of the poem in philosophy. By referring philosophy to mathematics, Plato situated philosophy as a movement of thinking between the matheme and the poem: 'The Platonic *matheme* must be thought here precisely as a *disposition* which is separated from and forgetful of the preplatonic *poem*, of Parmenides' poem' (*BE* 125); and further: 'Philosophy can only establish itself through the contrasting play of the poem and the matheme, which form its two primordial conditions' (*CS* 38).

By introducing the matheme Plato thus produced a fundamental split in philosophy, conditioning all of its future developments. Philosophy thus appears as a specific discursive expression of the fundamental tension *in* language between matheme and poem. Plato stands right at the end of a specific historical movement in ancient Greek thought that produced what Badiou calls the interruption of the poem: 'The Greeks did not invent the poem. Rather, they *interrupted* the poem with the matheme. In doing so, in the exercise of deduction, which is fidelity to being such as named by the void [. . .] the Greeks opened up the infinite possibility of an ontological text' (*BE* 126). A double patricide, this interruption also figures as a double birth: of philosophy and of ontology.

The importance of this interruption can be fully evaluated only from the perspective of 'the end of philosophy' in Heidegger's work, a claim that grounded his purportedly 'post-philosophical' (or post-metaphysical) thinking on the very idea of a 'return to Parmenides', a return to the state extant before the Platonic interruption of poetic language by 'the language of pure matheme' (Lacan). Naturally the significance of Platonic interruption is linked with Plato's being the first to recognise mathematics as ontological thinking. This is where the expression 'ontological text' and the connection of this text to infinity derive from. The matheme brings together the infinite and the letter, the real and the symbolic, articulating their immanent connection. This is why at issue here is not the romanticism of 'the infinite in the finite' but the text or the texture of the infinite.

Badiou's returning to the matheme, which ultimately also separates ontology from philosophy (the equation: mathematics = ontology), clearly has its polemical value as a rejoinder to the anti-Platonism marking philosophical thinking since the emergence of Romanticism. The tension between the matheme and the poem can be represented by two historical extremes: Plato as the beginning of philosophy, and Hegel as its self-proclaimed end and as 'inventor of the romantic gesture in philosophy, the thinker of mathematics' abasement' (*CS* 100). Hegel therefore initiated the historical sequence that would come, via Nietzsche, Heidegger, Lyotard, Derrida and others, to decide the intra-philosophical tension in favour of the poem. Modern anti-Platonism therefore names the exclusion of the matheme from the field of philosophy, an effort to 'heal the wound' and abolish the conflictuality that has defined philosophy from Plato onwards. In relation to this anti-Platonism, the matheme doctrine in Lacan, who proclaimed himself as antiphilosopher, plays an important role, since it accentuates precisely what philosophical modernity (since Hegel) has rejected: the philosophical significance of mathematical formalisation.

Badiou even claims that Lacan's matheme doctrine amounts to a contemporary Platonism, a modern translation of Plato's theory of Ideas: 'Mathematics has always been the place-holder of the Idea as Idea, the Idea as Idea to which Lacan gave the name of matheme' (*CS* 207). Right as the association of Lacan's use of the matheme with Plato undoubtedly is, it occurs in a slightly different way. Indeed, the function of matheme in psychoanalysis relates to the question of teaching, of the transmission of knowledge independent of all reference to the figure of the teacher (or 'master'; the French word *maître* carries both meanings). Founding transmission on the matheme entails rejecting another form of transmission well known both to philosophy and psychoanalysis, one inscribed in the very name of philosophy: transmission through *philia*, or love. Love-based knowledge transmission presupposes a subject of knowledge, the 'subject-supposed-to-know' (Lacan), and thus includes the symbolic position of the speaker and of his or her enunciation, which is, however, strictly irrelevant to the transmitted knowledge. Beyond the dichotomy of mathematical and poetic language, an opposition thus appears between transmission via formalisation and transmission via transference. On this view the matheme can undoubtedly be seen as a suspension of transference and of the 'master's discourse' (in both meanings of the term), the aim of which is to produce a strict formalisation of the real. But the problem emerges at the point where formalisation touches the real: while for Badiou this touching affirms the classical philosophical equivalence between thinking and being, for Lacan it demonstrates their discrepancy, gap or even non-relation.

Badiou often quotes Lacan's claims that 'mathematical formalisation is our aim, our ideal' and that 'the real is the impasse of formalisation'. The use of matheme aims to formalise the real as impossible, as the impasse of thinking, a claim that Lacan adopted from Koyré. This is why the doctrine of matheme is antiphilosophical: it separates not only thinking and being but also being and the real, something with which Badiou would undoubtedly agree. For Lacan what matters is the *impasse* of formalisation, which should be understood in two ways: as the point where formalisation fails, encounters an impasse – which is also where formalisation encounters the real – and formalisation *as* impasse, as that which resists the production of meaning without drifting back to simple univocity. Here the matheme is that which does not 'make sense', and so figures as the opposite of meaning. Badiou openly acknowledges these features of the matheme, with the important difference that he relates them back to the philosophical question of Being.

Another important difference is that in Lacan the matheme is not the opposite of poetic equivocity but its conceptual flipside, so that despite all appearances the matheme and poem are not construed as describing an external opposition between two languages but as a contradiction or split internal to language as such. To repeat Badiou's formulation, the tension between mathematical and poetic language such as it marks the history of philosophy is a tension within language itself.

The final question raised by the matheme concerns the nature of the formalised. Badiou suggests that matheme is 'a proposition of univocity so absolute that its literal universality is immediate' (Badiou 2010). However, another look at Lacan's use of mathemes reveals that this universality is intimately related to the impasse of formalisation. For instance, Lacan's famous formulas of sexuation, the only mathemes proper in his teaching, formalise the masculine and feminine positions but also demonstrate the inexistence of a sexual relation. Mathemes thus formalise something that does not exist but nevertheless has material consequences. This function of the matheme clearly features in the most important segment of Badiou, which is precisely the question of inexistence and the way an event breaks with a given symbolic regime.

METAPHYSICS

Jan Voelker

Given Badiou's priority orientation against the regime(s) of the One, it might be irritating that in the beginning of *LW* 'the ideological space [. . .] of a contemporary metaphysics' against 'dominant sophistry' is deemed necessary (34). Metaphysics is here understood as to proceed 'as though physics already existed' (37), a 'subjective metaphysics' (40) in which the formal distinctions between different types of subjectivity are analysed. Thus, metaphysics is here established, while the question of existence is yet undecided. To get to this 'metaphysics without metaphysics', as Badiou has called it elsewhere (MCM 190), a difficult path through the development of metaphysics has to be reconstructed. Historically, at least since Kant, philosophy seeks again and again to put an end to metaphysics, but these attempts are 'answered by the interminable and uncertain history of the perpetual reconstitution of metaphysics' (174). Structurally, Badiou's main argument constructs a constellation between Plato and Heidegger, and it hinges on the question of mathematics. While on the one hand, '[f]or Heidegger, science, from which mathematics is not distinguished, constitutes the hard kernel of metaphysics', abolished in the loss of being itself, on the other the 'Platonic institution of metaphysics is accompanied by the institution of mathematics as paradigm' on the other hand (*BE* 9). While the negation of metaphysics leads to nihilism, metaphysics and its institution of the regime of the one was built on the grounds of mathematics. Of course, neither nihilism nor the regime of the one can be the conclusion of a 'metaphysics without metaphysics', and thus, a *contemporary* examination of metaphysics will seek to uphold 'the absoluteness of the concept' (MCM 190), while avoiding recourse, in its construction, to some undetermined existence vis-à vis a finite subject. While Heidegger 'still remains enslaved, even in the doctrine of the withdrawal and the un-veiling, to [. . .] the essence of metaphysics; that is, the figure of being as endowment and gift, as presence and opening', Badiou 'will oppose the radically subtractive dimension of being, foreclosed not only from representation but from all presentation' (*BE* 9–10).

In an article on 'Metaphysics and the Critique of Metaphysics', in which Badiou unfolds the constellation of metaphysics in great detail, Badiou thus begins with the discernment of four modern criticisms of metaphysics. Badiou distinguishes the following four types: 'critique, positivism, dialectics, and hermeneutics' (MCM 175). All of these prove to react upon the same structural point of metaphysics: they criticise the false knowledge metaphysics gains out of a point of indeterminacy. But by substituting this structural point with alternative conceptions of an indeterminacy beyond knowledge, three of these strands – namely the critical, the positivist and the hermeneutical – prove to actually re-enforce metaphysics into an 'archi-metaphysics' (181). Against this background, Badiou then sharpens the edifice of classical, dogmatic metaphysics and finally contrasts another line of critique – both criticising classical metaphysics and not falling into an archi-metaphysics – which is the dialectical critique.

Badiou at first only indicates Kant's radical critical destitution of metaphysics, and then directly moves on to Auguste Comte, another paradigmatic figure, who recognises in metaphysics a state of mind transferred onto a social power, 'a conservative force that blocks a strategic passage: the passage between philosophy and social order' (177). In Heidegger then, this power of metaphysics reappears under changed circumstances as the 'ontological machination' (178). In both, Comte and Heidegger, metaphysics is thus a name of a 'corrosive power', and in it 'the true nature of what is' is left 'undetermined' (ibid.). Wittgenstein finally understands by metaphysics 'the void in signification', or 'statements devoid of sense' (180). But in all these cases, the recognition of something undetermined to be acknowledged prevails. For Wittgenstein it is the existence of the mystical side of things that cannot be said, but rather expresses itself. In Comte the question of metaphysics reappears in the question of the social religion, and in Heidegger in the question of the 'God'. Critique (Kant), positivism (under the sign of science, as in Comte, the early Wittgenstein, and Carnap), and hermeneutics (Heidegger) then unite in the contention that metaphysics created a false knowledge of the undetermined, whereas the undetermined has to be affirmed as undetermined and 'one must have recourse to a higher indeterminacy' (181). Thus, by replacing the 'necessary undetermined with a contingent one' (ibid.), the critique of metaphysics establishes what Badiou calls 'archi-metaphysics', which includes an ethical turn as a consequence of its 'indistinct promise' (ibid.).

For this reason, Badiou follows Hegel in underlining the 'native superiority of dogmatic metaphysics over critical archi-metaphysics' (ibid.), because the former situated the undetermined being in a rational framework, while the latter links thought to an undetermined point, which cannot be grasped by thought at all. Here the 'subtle balancing act' (183) of classical metaphysics is to be recognised: already Aristotle proclaimed being to proceed 'towards the One' (ibid.). Metaphysics has to organise its knowledge in terms of the One, while at its centre is organised around something undetermined. 'For metaphysics is, and this is its shortest definition, that which makes a predicate of the impredicable' (ibid.). Classical metaphysics attempted to demonstrate the existence of a being that empirically cannot be grasped and escapes thought by rational means. Thereby classical metaphysics built a bridge between the undetermined and the determined, between the infinite and the finite via the question of existence (of something undetermined). And this is the decisive point for Badiou: Metaphysics is actually 'a mode of subsumption of the existential by the rational' (184) and thus an anti-dualist stance that prevents an onto-logical rupture between being and thought. Thus, in classical metaphysics, the absolute is still rationally conceivable, while archi-metaphysics 'brings us back to finitude' (ibid.), because the infinite is rejected as a possibility for our capacities.

The exception from the repetition of metaphysics as archi-metaphysics then is critical dialectics. Hegel, Marx, Freud and Lacan are here the decisive names. Hegel, while following the Kantian critique of dogmatic metaphysics, holds against Kant that the categories by which metaphysics proceeds 'are in fact names for the becoming of the determination of this presumed indeterminacy' (187). If the determinations are to be understood as a becoming themselves, then the absolute itself is the process of these becomings, and the indeterminacy dissolves. This is what Hegel, again following Kant, calls 'logics' (ibid.). Dialectical metaphysics thus takes position against classical metaphysics as well as against archi-metaphysics. Against classical metaphysics it proves that 'every undetermined comes to determination' (188), against archi-metaphysics that determinations are not only subjective, but objective and subjective. 'It is this coextensivity *in actu* of conceptual invention and of a reality-effect that is called the abso-lute, and it is this that is the sole stake of philosophy' (189). Hegel follows Kant in the critique of dogmatic metaphysics but shows at the same time that Kant and his 'fear of the object' in the end turns out to have 'created an even more radical indeterminacy than the one he denounced in classi-cal metaphysics' (MCM 188). That the view on Kant becomes sharpened from the Hegelian perspective in Badiou's account can be linked to an intrinsic motive of metaphysics, to which Badiou alludes several times in his reconstruction: fear. Badiou understands the criticisms against metaphysics, especially Kant's, to react with great 'violence' (175) against metaphysical dogmatism, and to react in this manner precisely out of fear of the 'apparent weakness of its content' (178), namely the indeterminate-ness of true being – even if this fear does not prevent the criticisms from radicalising metaphysics (rather, the radicalisation could be understood as a consequence). The necessary 'courage of thought' is then 'with which, in Hegel's eyes, Kant was insufficiently endowed' and which Plato originally conceived as 'philosophy's cross' (188). But Hegel, for Badiou, did not pay sufficient attention to 'the link between finitude, infinity, and exist-ence within a mathematical paradigm' (190). And thus a different starting point, necessary to attack the current archi-metaphysical positions, would rely on the question of mathematics. Mathematics would allow for the thinking of the infinity of being without the need to create an indeterminate being as its source. The name Badiou proposes is a 'metaphysics without metaphysics', in which it would be affirmed 'that for everything which is exposed to the thinkable there is an idea, and that to link this idea to thought it suffices to decide upon the appropriate axioms' (ibid.).

At this point, one can return to the constellation of Plato and Heidegger: For Heidegger, the forgetting of being begins with the substitution of the true character of being as physis by the understanding of being as idea. Appearing then is no longer the appearing of physis as such, but rather of the 'cut-out of the Idea' (*BE* 125). In other words, in Heidegger's critique, Plato substitutes the ontology of presence by a metaphysics of subtraction. The 'lack' and the 'poem' will thus become the 'two orientations' that 'command the entire destiny of thought in the West' (125). Heidegger sides with the *poem* as the originary beginning of being's presence, while Badiou affirms with Plato the *matheme* as the authentic Greek break between being and appearing. The rupture of the poem via the *matheme* enabled to think change, and thus, against the recurring temptation (cf. *BE* 126) of metaphysics, a different understanding of being, appearing, and existence under the mathematical paradigm would refute the orientation of the poem and enable to think existence without the relation to the One, to finitude. Mathematics thus changes its relation to thought: while for Aristotle, and later for Leibniz, mathematics 'is woven only of purely ideal, if not fictitious, relations', it is '(f)or the Platonist [. . .] a science of the Real' (*TO* 102). The difference runs between the virtual status of mathematics and its real status: on the one side, mathematics analyses possibilities, possible beings; on the other, mathematics distinguishes real ruptures. In the Aristotelian or Leibnizian variant, mathematics is conceived as 'a logic of the possible' (103), while in the Platonist variant, 'mathematics enlightens philosophy regarding how every truth has an interventional dimension' (105). In Badiou's account, mathematics is 'freed from the constraints of finitude' and not bound to the 'opacity of experience' any longer (ibid.), while still being a paradigm for the rational discourse of philosophy. Mathematics becomes 'simultaneously ontological and logical' (ibid.). From this angle, metaphysics without metaphysics proves to be not a simple return to the Platonist account, 'not an overturning' of the constellation of metaphysics, but 'another disposition' of the two basic orientations (*BE* 125). It marks a different intervention into the recurrent temptation of metaphysics, namely the courage to think the real in its weakness, instead of its representation as one. Badiou splits metaphysics and while upholding its attempt to think the absolute, the temptation to organise it under the law of an indeterminable One has to be rejected, and therefore essential terms of metaphysics – infinity, finitude, existence – have to be set into a new disposition, via a different situating of mathematics.

METAPOLITICS

Steven Corcoran and Agon Hamza

Badiou's work *On Metapolitics* is his first major attempt to theorise the relation between politics and philosophy post-*BE*, in which he develops two key innovations: a theory of the event, which rigorously ties politics to contingency, and a theory of the conditions of philosophy, according to which philosophical conceptuality is conditioned by four procedures of thought, the only ones that Badiou thinks count as truths. If politics constitutes one of those procedures, then the task of metapolitics will be to name it as truth (which itself is not a political category). The question thus arises of how it is possible to determine politics as thought and about how to construct a positive relation to it. (A further question for this metapolitics, is covered in the entry on politics: if politics is a singular truth procedure, different from those of love, science, art, then in what does this singularity reside?)

Much of the thrust of Badiou's arguments about politics as thought in *M* is not entirely new and can be seen in his early work, up to and including *TS*. However, in this latter work the figure of thought, by Badiou's own admission, is still too tied to a vision of the historical agency of the proletariat as bearer of politics. *BE's* doctrine of the event breaks with any such historical determination of political agency, and grasps the subject as the local point of a generic procedure in rupture with the situation. Moreover, from *TS* to *M*, philosophy for Badiou ceases to be conditioned solely by politics – whereas in *TS* the only subject is a political one, post-*BE* Badiou considers there to be four such subjects, so that philosophical rationality will no longer be so rigidly tied a single condition. Nonetheless, there is a consistency in the target of Badiou's polemics: figures of theory that obscure the nature of politics as thought. In the conjuncture in which TS is written, that of the crisis of Marxist politics, attempts spring up to save Marxism by giving it a new foundation (say, via a psychology), as if its theoretical foundation were lacking, as if or as if something was missing from its 'programme'. Then, in *M*, published some 15 years later in a context in which the concepts of liberal political philosophy are hegemonic and structure the field, he engages in a critique of the 'return to political philosophy' (which overlaps with a massive 'return to Kant'). Despite the vast difference between these two approaches, what they both share is a common attempt to found politics, to supply the messy contingency of the real with a solid basis.

But if philosophical conceptuality, like the Owl of Minerva, flies only at night after the truths of day that it names have passed; and if these truths are irreducibly multiple, then philosophy cannot pretend to found politics or supply it with its missing theory of justice. What the name metapolitics designates is an attempt to uphold the irreducible multiplicity of political truths and to take innovations with respect to such truths as a condition for conceptuality. To do this, it must draw a line to separate itself out from that which, pretending to found politics, obscures its nature.

Against political philosophy

Political philosophy is defined by Badiou 'a formal apprehension of states and instances of politics [that works] by exposing and pre-elaborating the types in question in accordance with possible norms'. The three characteristics of political philosophy as Badiou delineates them are: 1) that it arrogates to itself the privilege of thinking through the messy confusion of events on the ground. Political philosophy rests on the supposition that there is a universal dimension of human experience, a clear and distinct idea of 'the political', an invariable instance or realm separate from the economic, social and so on; 2) that it determines the principles of good politics, with the post-modernist inflection that they be subject to the demands of ethics. It then goes on to weigh up the pros and cons of various state forms (aristocracy, monarchy, democracy, or rather democracy or totalitarianism, or democracy or fundamentalism) and their ability or otherwise to regulate or be regulated by the supposed invariant instance of politics; and 3) it assumes that this can be done in the modality of judgement, thus without ever having to take sides with any real political processes, from the point of view of an outside spectator. The most infamous example here is probably Kant, who, from a distance admired the French Revolution as a world-historical event and yet held nothing but contempt for its actors. Badiou thus rightly asks, 'How is it that such a gap, between spectator and actor, has been able to emerge?'

Indeed, this gap is applauded in much political philosophy. Kant's theory, for example, is explicitly praised by Arendt and others for pointing to the contradiction of principle between how we take others into account in the modality of judgement and the maxims by which we might join up with others for action. This gap between the maxim of the spectator and that of the actor is the heart of political philosophy.

To clarify this point, we could see this gap in relation to a problem that 'antiphilosophers' like to point up, that of philosophical mastery. The objection is variously voiced that the price philosophy pays for its mastery is the constitutive exclusion of some singular aspect of existence. In the domain of politics, Jacques Rancière, for example, has convincingly argued that the basic project of 'political philosophy' is predicated on the exclusion of instances of real politics. His thesis is that political philosophy, conceived as a particular domain of theorisation of politics, is invariably a response to and usurpation of the emergence of what he calls a 'part of those without part', a part that having no part, separates speech out from social function and its hierarchy, and thereby demonstrates a fundamental equality. In other words, the singularity of this part is directly connected to its universality, and in such a way that it disrupts at once the projection of a hierarchical order into the space of politics and the notion that philosophy bears the privilege of thinking through political universalism.

So this gap turns out to be an exclusion: it is enabled only through a prior negation of any localisation of politics in the contingency of that which happens – precisely in the rare and unpredictable occurrence of a part of those without part. The above-mentioned role that political philosophy arrogates to itself can be achieved only through the relegation of 'that which happens' to the status of matter for an invariable judgement on whether or not a phenomenal occurrence accords with a given norm. The price it pays for this is that the democratic multiplicity it is intent on upholding gets subordinated to a figure of the one, a figure of judgement that subjects the predicative distribution of the multiplicity (of opinions) to a judgement concerning the being-in-common of the community. Only, in thus reneging on multiplicity, the idea of an emergent and non-totalisable universality subtracted from the regime of predication becomes strictly unthinkable. And for Badiou the decision on the existence of such a multiple is arguably the central question of politics today.

The gap between spectator and actor, Badiou argues, is ultimately the exclusion by philosophical judgement of politics as a form of *thought*. Political philosophy, notably in this Kantian-Arendtian version, grasps politics as a kind of debate over the plurality of opinions issuing from recognised parts of the community. Judgement reigns in essence over a space of opinions; it presupposes a totalising regime of constructability that precludes the very possibility of any immanent exception to it. From the outset, then, it negates any definition of politics as an activity involving either truth or transformative action. From the viewpoint of political philosophy, politics can be neither about making statements bearing on the being of the collective, or about the conducting of actions by people to uncover latent possibilities within a situation, possibilities that emerge with the construction of a 'new singular collective aiming for the control or the transformation of what is' (M 16). Political philosophy thus precludes any identification of politics as that which can be localised in the realm of phenomenal appearing as 'a *thinkable* modification of public space'. We shall return to this point below.

Badiousian metapolitics, by contrast, argues that politics, if it is to be of any value to philosophy, is precisely such: a militant form of thought and practice. So whereas political philosophy, by denying this dimension, amounts to no less than an attempt to usurp the thought and practice of politics, if we are to think the singularity of a generic collective, of that which subtracts itself from all predication, a different style of philosophising is required. This style must break with such basic propositions of political philosophy as 'politics is the art of directing the life of communities, democracy is the style of people of the multiple', or 'politics is the art of transforming the law of the democratic multiple into a principle of community life'. In short, it must break with the idea that politics is based on a donation of sense, on forms of life, which it is philosophy's task to think through.

To sum up, then, political philosophy, which operates entirely in the realm between constructible existence and transcendent norms, ultimately subordinates plurality to the one. Plurality is merely simulated. In so doing, political philosophy may appeal to the existence of that which is, of that which appears within a given world, but it remains blind to that which inexists in this world and which from time to time can emerge to fracture the self-evidence of what is. Despite its alleged neutrality, political philosophy does in fact issue a subjective maxim for action: maintain what there is! What political philosophy's alleged neutrality – and apology of constructability – masks, then, is that it is but the abstract promotion of a form: parliamentary democracy and its cherished liberty of opinion. In other words, this Kantian-type political philosophy is merely the abstract promotion of *a* politics. It is incapable of thinking any modification to public space that would negate the form of parliamentarism itself, which is not simply a neutral space filled with various contents, but which structurally excludes the idea of another politics: in Badiou's terms, a politics of truth that is unfolded in fidelity to an event, in which a generic collective emerges that acts as a direct stand in for universality itself. Under the cover of a neutral determination of politics, then, what political philosophy shelters are the prescriptions of the parliamentary organisation of our 'democratic societies', in thrall as they are to the supposed necessity of the capitalist economy, which is the real site of power. Moreover, as Badiou points out, we know from experience that the plurality of contemporary parliamentarism continually gives rise to *the same politics*. The gap thus proves to be the short circuit of a suture: political philosophy's promotion of opinion over truth and subordination of plurality to the one shows that it is conditioned by the sole logic of parliamentarism.

Metapolitics thus shows that only by connecting politics to the theme of truth, to that which subtracts itself from opinion and particularity, can philosophy uphold the irreducible plurality of instances of politics against its sole conditioning by – and thus suturing to – the politics of parliamentary democracy. It reveals that only by connecting politics to the theme of truth can philosophy identify the hidden subjective prescriptions tying a philosophy (in this case: liberal political philosophy) to its political condition.

Jacques Lacan identified this operation of suturing philosophy to politics by saying that philosophy works 'to plug the hole of politics'. What political philosophy refuses to see is that politics implies a radical act, a wager that can receive no objective justification from within the terms of the situation, but that can only be retroactively justified from the viewpoint of the new situation this act brings about. The effects of such an act are, moreover, always able to be reinvented and thus it implies an open-ended set of practices.

Lacan argues that, among other things, the real function of this plugging is to shore up a subject (e.g. the Party, or the West) (*Lac* 51ff), an imaginary effect of group whose maintenance prohibits such open-endedness. But political practice is irreducible to the attempt simply to maintain the supposed existence of a group. This was also Marxism's idea: revolutionary practice and theory operate by creating holes in the dominant ideology. Instead, political philosophy plugs the hole of politics by trying to found politics, to establish a figure of the good politics, the one in which everything is in its place. But as the radicality of the political act pierces through discursively presentable imaginary coalescences, for Lacan the problem becomes one of how it is possible to affirm the existence of politics, which is to say, the radical impossibility of ever regulating the problem of places. How can one operate in an ex-centred and autonomous fashion with respect to the imaginary effects of group coalescence and with respect to adhesion to the status quo? How can we avoid the philosopher's ideal politics? (This covering up of the precariousness of politics is indeed the function of fashionable ideas that politics is essentially about 'discussion', 'communication', 'consensus', etc., all of which imply a unity, or some sort of coordination between abstract formal principles and sensible donation, between 'the political', the 'community' and the ways of the world.)

Our question is thus: if politics is this incompletable and unfillable gap, how can theory grasp its act? Badiou finds Lacan's proposal wanting:

to the philosophical tendency to plug all the holes, Lacan opposes an antiphilosophical proposition of hyperdemocracy: the effect of group is to be countered by a sort of atomistic egalitarianism – politics is posited as a field of turbulence in which anyone associates with anyone. To avoid the effect of group and uphold the immanent precariousness of politics, then, Lacan seems to advocate a radical detotalisation, in which all is provisional adjustment. Crucially, Badiou argues that the effective maxim for ensuring this can only be a maxim of dissolution, as that which ultimately wards off the danger of any effect of group. But does this radical act of dissolution not simply posit a space without place, a space of inaction, of incessant dissolution (*Lac* 151)?

Badiou concludes that Lacan simply opts for a figure of radical detotalisation that is merely the symmetrical inverse of what it opposes. Instead of the consistency of group duration, Lacan proposes a figure of the lability and mobility of everything, in which, rather than plugging the holes, all there is, is holes. He essentially tells us nothing that hasn't already been put forward by well-known anarchist theories.

But this seems to miss the central point of politics. Politics is not an ideal space in which everything finds its place, or one in which there is no space of places. Instead, it always contains a proposition about a displacement of the distribution of places, in accordance with a variable principle of what a dis-placement is. (See, for example, Badiou's discussion in *LW* about the various politics associated with the name Spartacus.) What Lacan's hyperdemocratism misses is that the entire question is one about organisation: how is it possible to maintain the duration of the procedure, the duration not of an imaginary group effect but of the production of a generic collective? Or: how can one remain faithful to the event by continually and creatively unfolding its consequences? Now, it is also clear that for there to be duration, *there must be a certain unity* of thought. The thought of politics is not a theory awaiting implementation of the ideal city, but an experimentation of prescriptions. Political thought is immediately its localisation, as Badiou puts it. It is an active figure of unity of theory and practice.

Philosophy *and* Politics

In order to construct a positive relation to politics as thought, Badiou posits two basic statements, both of which are rejected by political philosophy: statement 1 is that philosophy must suppose the equality of intelligences. This axiom points to philosophy's democratic condition, since philosophy necessarily presupposes that what counts is not the *position* from which a statement is enunciated but the statement's objective content. Statement

2 stipulates the subordination of the variety of opinions to the universality
of truths. Politics must be connected to the theme of truth, for it is only if
a statement carries with it a rational obligation to accept 'the existence of
a universal logic, as formal condition of the equality of intelligences' (*PM*
37), that it is valid for philosophy. The question here is about recognising
the validity of arguments. In other words, the axiom of the equality of
intelligences does not entail that all opinions are of equal worth. Although
philosophy has a democratic condition it does not have a democratic
destination (in the sense of the liberty of opinion): there is a freedom of
address, but also the necessity for a strict rule for discussion. 'Philosophy
must maintain a strict rule of consequences' (ibid.).

Badiou argues that only by taking these two statements together can
philosophy identify politics as thought and as that which is capable
of forming a condition for philosophy itself. Both statements must be
posited, if we are to view politics as that which involves an always singular
proposition about dis-placement that fractures the regime of organisation
and representation, and is able to fold back onto this situation with a view
to transforming it. These statements mark a positive relation between
philosophy and politics, while necessarily insisting on their separation
qua two dimensions of thought. Suppressing them is the core of political
philosophy, which performs a suture that can lead to the worst.

Thus 'people think', 'people are capable of truth'. Badiou's summoning
of Plato to help construct this axiom may seem odd. But what is of interest is precisely Plato's insight into political thought, against all notions of
politics as a sort of *phronesis*, i.e. a kind of practical wisdom for making
strategic judgements in the pursuit of predetermined ends. Plato's 'ideal
city', as he makes clear, does not attain legitimacy on the basis of what is,
of the ways of the world. Indeed Plato's insistence is that political thought
involves a prescriptive dimension that makes it intransitive to objectivity.
That politics is a form of thought thus means that every politics involves
an unconditioned prescription, i.e. a statement that does not have to
establish the proof of its possibility with reference to objective reality.
For Badiou, the fundamental being of politics is axiomatic. It involves
deciding on the fundamental statements that inform political thought and
action and is measurable not in terms of pre-established, i.e. objectively
determinable, possibility, but purely in terms of the consistency of its
effects. A political prescription is like a 'writing-forward' – it aims to
create the conditions that retroactively justify it. It is first and foremost a
commitment to the consequences, i.e. a wager on the egalitarian strength
of these consequences.

For Badiou, every genuinely emancipatory politics rests on an axiom
of the equality of all elements within the situation, without requiring a

prior determination of the terms on which it operates. In this way, situation specific prescriptions based on this axiom do not demand any prior definition of, say, the citizens of a polis to whom rights and duties are to be distributed. Equality has nothing to do with the liberal topos of how we might approach the ideal of a government treating all its citizens with equal respect. Equality is not a goal and it is not objectivisable. This is so for the simple reason that it is not the objective of action but its axiom. The logic of equality here is perfectly classical: equality is in the here and now of an unfolding political procedure, or it is not. It follows that the only material guarantee of a politics is the effects of equality it is able to inscribe into the situation of its emergence.

Metapolitics posits, first, the irreducible multiplicity of political instances, against the notion that there is any such thing as 'the political' or 'politics as such'. Second, it states that politics is precarious, indicating that there is something that is never filled, that it is incompletable. Sequences of egalitarian politics can also become frozen, unable to keep unfolding themselves in the situation (see saturation), and inevitably generate reactive forms of subjectivity that attempt to halt the consequences of egalitarianism in the guise of working for it. Conversely, an egalitarian political sequence is itself never closed: metapolitics grasps such instances from the point of view of their hypothetical completion (from the future anterior of their having been true on the proviso that fidelity to an event is maintained) but on the political level they are never finished, since the consequences of a truth procedure are infinite and liable to be further developed in a different situation or world. Lastly, the very occurrence of egalitarian politics is entirely contingent, able to come about in chance-ridden and improbable conditions.

The metapolitical task thus cannot be the traditional one of finding comprehensive, timeless rules for the administering of justice and plugging the holes of politics. This is essentially because justice is the *achievement* of a fidelity: a rigorous adherence to prescriptions and the tenacious organisation of a body politic capable of developing an autonomous political capacity and thus shedding light on the fact that the regime of representation and organisation into which it erupts as excess was geared to privileging the maintenance of a given world, henceforth seen in its contingency. To grasp the singularity of each political procedure, philosophy must seize the categories inherent in these prescriptions about the situation, categories that are necessarily in excess of the language of the situation with which they rupture (Virtue and Corruption for Saint Just, Revolutionary Consciousness for Lenin, and so on).

A metapolitics thus has two tasks: 1) to examine political statements along with their prescriptions, and to draw from them their egalitarian kernel of universal signification; and 2) to transform the generic category of 'justice' by putting it to the test of these singular statements, according to the always irreducible mode through which they carry and inscribe the egalitarian axiom in action'. The metapolitical task is to show that, the category of justice thus transformed, it designates the contemporary figure of a political subject, e.g. citizen, 'professional revolutionary', 'grassroots militant' – egalitarian figures without borders. Metapolitics thus seeks to think the singularity of historical modes of what Badiou calls 'militant' politics – the subject of politics is not involved in making judgements about social phenomena, but rather is a militant that makes a resolute decision to develop the immediately practicable consequences subsequent to an event, a prescription that has no other justification than the insubstantial, inconsistent being – the empty equality – of the collective.

So, what is metapolitics? Is it that which relates the essence of politics back to the singularity of the event, to a decision on the event that prescribes a universal possible. It is, says Badiou, what 'a philosophy declares with its own effects in mind to be worthy of the name "politics"'. Or: it is 'what a thought declares to be a thought and under whose condition it thinks what a thought is' (*M* 152).

MODEL

Olivia Lucca Fraser

CM is the first book Badiou published in philosophy, and in it he initiates a lifelong concern not only with mathematics and mathematical logic, but also with the ways in which philosophy can receive these disciplines as a condition for the philosophical thinking of truth and change. The concept of model, itself, will go on to occupy a pivotal position in Badiou's work, orienting in productive and problematic ways his later use of mathematical set theory, and, as Oliver Feltham has argued, giving him an apparatus by which to think the compossibilisation and interaction between various truth procedures in addition to mathematics. But what is a model?

The simplest, and least adequate, answer is that a model is a pair, consisting of (1) a *structure* that a given formal theory can be taken to be theory 'about', and (2) an *interpretation* that systematically, and functionally, links the terms of the theory to the structure in question, in such a way that we can say that the axioms of the theory are 'true' or 'valid' for the model, and in such a way that the rules by which the theory transforms its axioms into theorems '*preserve truth*'. This simple idea can give rise to numerous misapprehensions, so it is best to go over things more carefully.

First, we should resist any temptation to view the model/theory distinction as the distinction between an object and its discursive representation. This, by Badiou's lights, is the error of the *empiricist epistemology of models* (*CM* 18–22). It is inadequate on two counts: to begin with, the model/theory distinction is, strictly speaking, *internal to mathematical practice*: both a formal theory and its models are mathematical constructions, and no structure can 'deploy a domain of interpretation' for a mathematical theory if it is not already embedded 'within a *mathematical envelopment*, which preordains the former to the latter' (42). The point of interpreting a structure as a model for a theory (or interpreting a theory as the theory *of* a structure) is not to *mathematically represent* something already given outside of mathematics, but to generate a *productive interaction between already-mathematical constructions*, opening each to new, essentially experimental techniques of verification and variation: determining the relative intrications and independences among concepts, establishing the extent of a concept's mobility and applicability, sounding out unseen harmonies between apparently heterogeneous domains, and exposing what the logician Girard has called 'disturbances' and points of 'leakage', the 'cracks in the building' which 'indicate what to search and what to modify' (Girard 1987: 14; 2001: 441 and 485). Freeing it from the doublet that binds representations to their objects, Badiou proposes

to call *model* the ordinance that, in the historical process of a science, retrospectively assigns to the science's previous practical instances their experimental transformation by a definite formal apparatus [. . .] The problem is not, and cannot be, that of the representational relations between the model and the concrete, or between the formal and the models. The problem is that of *the history of formalisation*. 'Model' designates the network traversed by the retroactions and anticipations that weave this history: whether it be designated, in anticipation, as break, or in retrospect, as reforging. (*CM* 54–5; tm)

That it is indeed a *network* of relations that are at stake in the concept of model, and not the bilateral mirror-play of object and representation, is pressed on us by the fact that, *in general*, no privileged relation obtains between a syntactically formulated theory and a structure interpreted as its model: more often than not, a theory admits of a vast *multiplicity* of models, which only in the rarest of cases map on to one another in any strict sense (where a strict mapping – or, precisely, an *isomorphism* – exists between all the models of a theory, that theory is said to be *categorical*, but this is quite uncommon); similarly, a given structure can in most cases be equipped with distinct interpretations, each of which makes of it a model for quite different formal theories. It is even possible, with a bit of tinkering, *to interpret the literal structure of a formal theory as a model for the theory itself* – a technique that often proves useful in logic (an example of this technique is given in the Appendix to *CM*).

The ('ideologically' motivated) intuitions that push us to see the mirror-play of object and representation in the model/theory distinction are strong ones. It is instructive to learn that even Paul Cohen – to whom we owe some of the most significant proofs that have ever been written regarding the relation between Zermelo-Fraenkel set theory and its models, including his *proof of the independence of the continuum hypothesis*, in which the concepts of *forcing* and the *generic*, so decisive for Badiou's philosophy, first see the light of day – would confess that

The existence of *many* possible models of mathematics is difficult to accept upon first encounter [. . .] I can assure you that, in my own work, one of the most difficult parts of proving independence results was to overcome the psychological fear of thinking about the existence of various models of set theory as being natural objects in mathematics about which one could use natural mathematical intuition. (Cohen 2002: 1072)

An avatar of this prejudice – which Cohen magnificently overcame – is the distinction between *standard* and *non-standard* models, which is even today commonplace in mathematical literature. The 'standard' model of a theory, in a nutshell, is simply *the structure that the theory is intended to describe*, together with an interpretation that puts things together in the expected manner. A 'non-standard' model is a structure and interpretation that deviates, often wildly, from these educated expectations. (To put it another way, a 'standard interpretation' obeys the *spirit* of the law; a 'non-standard' one adheres only to its *letter*.) Though he rarely addresses this distinction head-on, ever since his remarkable study of Abraham Robinson's *non-standard analysis* (the non-standard model that Robinson constructed for the infinitesimal calculus), Badiou has engaged with mathematics in such a way that the distinction between the standard and the non-standard can confront his readers only as an obstacle to understanding. Nowhere is this distinction less pertinent than in *set theory*, and no single insight does a better job of linking Badiou's ontological use of set theory with his pronouncement that 'the One is not' than the realisation that, in all rigour, *a standard model for set theory does not exist*. If there is anything that set theory is expected to be a theory *about*, it is the 'universe of all sets', but it was a theorem already known to (and considered to be of tremendous importance by) Georg Cantor that *the set of all sets cannot exist*, on pain of inconsistency.

If set theory is ontology, but an ontology that, ungrounded by the annulment of the One, has no standard model, then there is every reason to expect that the rules for its interpretation cannot be given in one stroke – a fact which has caused no end of frustration for Badiou's exegetes – and that they must (within strict but underdetermining constraints) be reinvented situation by situation. The difficulty that remains, of course, is that of escaping the iron strictures of *CM*, which forcefully argues that *only an already mathematical structure can model a mathematical theory*. This may be true for mathematics qua mathematics, but it cannot (on pain of philosophical suture) be maintained for mathematics *qua condition for philosophy*. The *philosophical* category of model, conditioned by the mathematical concept, cannot remain (as it does in '68), a purely *epistemological* category. What is needed, as Oliver Feltham has forcefully argued, is a category of 'modelling' that

is the inverse of the procedure of conditioning. In modelling the syntax is constructed in philosophy and then tested in diverse semantic fields such as revolutionary politics or Mallarmé's poetry. In contrast, with conditioning it is a particular generic procedure such as set theory that provides the syntax and philosophy provides the semantic domain: hence 'metaontology' is a model of set theory. (Feltham 2008: 132)

This inverse operation is not contrary to, but *demanded by*, philosophy's mandate to compossibilise radically heterogeneous conditions, for

if it must circulate between a multiplicity of artistic, scientific, political and amorous conditions, [philosophy] can never be perfectly faithful to one truth procedure alone. Thus, with regard to the comparison between modelling and conditioning, one cannot simply assert that it is always a truth procedure alone that furnishes the syntax for the model; sometimes it is also philosophy that provides part of the syntax, based on its encounters with other conditions. (ibid.)

It is in this light that we should see in the concept of model the *first condition*, issuing from the truth procedure of mathematics, of Badiou's philosophy, the philosophical effects of which make it possible for Badiou, many years later, to put into practice a full and unsutured *philosophy under conditions*.

MULTIPLICITY

Bruno Besana

At the origins of the concept of pure multiplicity

'They are, then, other to each others as multiplicity (κατὰ πλήθη); for they cannot be so as unity (κατὰ ἕν), if the one does not exist. But each one, as it seems, is a set (ὄγκος) infinite in multiplicity (ἄπειρός πλήθει)' (*cf.* Plato 1926 & 1997: 164 c–d. Translation modified in line with the Italian edition *Platone. Tutti gli scritti* 2000)

With these words, which will linger between the lines of philosophy, cyclically reappearing in them as a disturbing dream, Plato starts the conclusions of his *Parmenides*. The dialogue begins with the necessity to define what it means that *a* thing *is*. If a thing is – so it seems – it must be one: it would otherwise be impossible to attribute to it something (from a banal attribute up to the fact of being) in a clear, univocal manner.

Plato brings the problem to its purest abstraction, dividing it as follows: what does it mean 'the one is', and what does it mean 'the one is not'? If the one is, then by 'multiple' we will mean either a multiplicity of unities, or also a multiplicity of attributes which can be predicated of a given being, which is by essence one; if the one is not, then what 'is' will be by definition a multiplicity, but this multiplicity will not be the collection of several primary elements, but will be a pure multiplicity of multiplicity. This second hypothesis is difficult to grasp, but Plato does not prove it to be false. The dialogue in fact unfolds both hypotheses: the one claiming that 'that which is' is a unity that appears as a multiplicity (an idea appearing in a multiplicity of concrete 'copies', but also a being which has one specific essence and a multiplicity of accidental characters – as Aristotle will argue in the *Metaphysics*), and the opposite one, according to which what appears as 'one' is not a 'thing', but rather a 'set' consisting in a multiplicity of elements, each one of which is a set, and so on. In this last case, 'there will be many sets, each of which appears to be one, but is not one, given that one does not exist' (Plato 164d 1997; tm). We see here a 'reversal of Platonism' taking place inside Plato's text itself. For such a reversal, phenomena are not the multiple presentation of an idea that properly 'is', but 'being' is a multiplicity that appears on a phenomenal level as the unity of a thing.

The 'reversal of Platonism' is a crucial theme in late-1960s French philosophy, in which the young Badiou develops his thought. On the one hand, Gilles Deleuze makes of this topic the very goal of philosophy: 'to reverse Platonism [. . .] the formula seems to mean the abolition of the world of essences and of the world of appearances' (Deleuze 1990: 253).

But more precisely, for Deleuze the bottom of the problem is not the relation between 'being' and 'phenomena' (in fact, after Kant, the questioning around the difference between noumena and phenomena loses its legitimacy – at least at the theoretical level): the object of the reversal of Platonism becomes rather the opposition between the unity of a term that essentially constitutes a given *res*, and the multiplicity of the accidental characters defining its becoming. This reversal is thus also a reversal of Aristotle, who considers accidents (*sumbebekota*) 'akin to non-being' (Aristotle, *Metaphysics*, VI, 2, 1026 b 20), given that their cause is that unstable, changing, multiple matter which after all is nothing but a potentiality to be determined by the unity of a form. This is the crucial point informing the idea according to which 'being is being united and one, and not being is being not united but more than one' (Aristotle, *Metaphysics*, IX, 10, 1051 b 10).

On the other hand, Badiou, via Althusser, embraces the idea that the transformations, the accidents that constitute the material, effective becoming of a given being are essential to the definition of the latter. In his reading of Marx, Althusser (Badiou took part in his seminar at the École Normale in Paris) conceives every relevant fact as the condensation of the heterogeneous contradictions – with no common denominator – that constitute the real movement of a given situation (Althusser 2010: part 2, ch. 6 § 'Structure in Dominance: Contradiction and Overdetermination').

At the same time such a relevant fact is overdetermined in relation to these contradictions, it is therefore a new element which retroacts *as an event* on the whole situation, provoking a radical change in it. In this sense, from the very first pages of one of his earlier texts, Badiou starts from the assumption that to understand what a given being is, one needs to start from its modes of transformation – which are thus the central object of inquiry of philosophy. So, in *Théorie de la contradiction* he writes that 'the internal nature of things, their essence, is nothing other than the law of their transformation', and this constitutes 'what one can call a Heraclitian line of dialectics' (cf. TC/*AR* 39–40). The book stresses nonetheless how such coincidence between being and becoming shouldn't be framed as a teleological movement unfolding of a unitary sense: quite the contrary, 'truth only exists in a process of scission' (21), strictly opposed to the idea of the unfolding of a unifying, teleological sense of history. And in fact, 'philosophical revisionism consists precisely in this: to pretend to acknowledge that each reality is process, but fixing at the same time the concept of process, which converts the laws of transformation that regulate it into a new type of metaphysical invariants' (41). The real is rational, but it does not have the rationality of the progressive unfolding of a unified sense; it rather has the rationality of an always contingent set of relations that on the one hand appear as unified phenomena and on the other act by constantly breaking the evidence of the supposed essential nature of the latter. Reason, in other words, is on the side of division, of splitting, and not on the side of a supposed essential nature of the actual state of fact of things. This is why, quoting Mao, Badiou stresses in several passages that 'it is *right* to rebel' (*on a* raison *de se révolter*): thought does not adequate to being via a process of unification of sense that will reveal what the object of inquiry 'is'; on the contrary it seizes being by finding how, by which means, by which connections, 'one divides into two' (42).

Such a primacy of relation over essence implies a primacy of materiality and of contingency: what is removed is the idea that in order to seize what a given situation is, one should start from supposed original, simple elements, and from principles supposed to regulate the mutual relation of these elements (but unaffected by the contradictions and changes acting in the situation); what is on the contrary claimed, is the necessity to start from the middle, from the relations materially acting in the situation, determining the regime of transformation of the phenomena of the situation. The principle at stake is therefore that the set of transformations of the infinite, accidental, determinations which constitute a given being is something more essential than the unity of the form, constituting its mode of presentation in an actual, given situation.

'Nevertheless, this simple and violent principle is nowadays menaced, it is a principle that needs to be constantly re-conquered in a drastic class struggle, because it is this very principle that draws the principal line of separation with the antagonist tendency: the metaphysical tendency' (40). Opposed to the metaphysical tendency, it is posed as a materialist principle. It is materialist, because it is opposed to the idea itself that a given situation might have original elements of principles regulating it, but subtracted from the material, contingent contradictions immanent to the situation; and it is a principle because it cannot be deduced: exactly as in the case of Plato's *Parmenides*, the idea of the primacy of multiplicity and of relations cannot be deduced from a further principle, but is the object of a philosophical decision. Even more, such a decision is rooted in a context of struggle: first, this struggle is informed by 'the critique of the metaphysical principle of identity', a critique for which '*the being of a transitory state of reality is transition itself*' (49): not only is 'one' that which, structured according to a given law of organisation of a situation, appears as unity, but also such a unity is constantly exposed to the transformative action of those forces of which it is the manifestation. Secondly, this struggle exposes the contingency of the structures of the present, by manifesting them as the product of a set of relations of force, which might be changed. Thus 'the essence of this principle consists in the affirmation that [. . .] the law of things is neither balance, nor structure, but the rupture of all balance, and, by consequence, the necessary development of the destruction of the current state of things' (40).

In more abstract terms, one might say that each individual being is not only the collection of a multiplicity of elements, but is also the actual state of fact of a process of division: in this sense, Badiou will stress in *BE* that each individual being is the manifestation of something infinitely divisible, i.e. of a multiplicity such that, no matter how small a part of it one might consider, it will be always possible to divide this part in further smaller parts, of which it will be possible to describe an immanent criterion of composition. Via such an identity between an individual being and the infinite multiplicity composing it, it can be grasped that there is an excess of being over its own actual mode of presentation. Each thing is identical to itself only inasmuch as it differs from itself: a thing is in fact identical to a multiplicity that constantly divides itself, a multiplicity that is difficult to grasp, because it both divides itself into smaller parts, and it is larger than itself, exceeds itself.

Pure multiplicity

Here we again come across the central theme of the second part of the *Parmenides*: the idea of a multiplicity that is in excess over its own presentation, an excessive multiplicity such that 'if you take what seems to be the smallest bit, it suddenly changes; like something in a dream, that which seemed to be one is seen to be many, and instead of very small it is seen to be very great' (Parmenides, 164d). Such a multiplicity cannot be reduced to a numerable series of units, of which it would be either the multiplication or the copy; it is rather a pure multiplicity of multiplicity, a 'multiplicity deprived of any limit to its multiple-deployment': a multiplicity whose 'essence [. . .] is to multiply itself in an immanent manner', a multiplicity which multiplies by dividing itself (*BE* 33).

It is in relation to these considerations that Badiou declares: 'the point of depature of my speculative project is to "detach the one from being", to break with the metaphysical boarding of being by the one' (*TO* 34; tm), to affirm thus 'the non-being of the one': as in Plato, this choice is not supported by any further proof, but relies on the 'inacceptability' of the opposite thesis (which nonetheless is not proved false). Plato, facing both options (the one is; the one is not, and being is thus pure multiplicity) finally chooses the first one, because multiplicity appears as an abyss, as a vertigo or a nightmare; in an analogue but opposite fashion, Badiou explains: 'if being is one, then one must posit that what is not one, the multiple, *is not*. But this is unacceptable for thought (*répugne la pensée*), because what is presented is multiple [. . .] if presentation is, then the multiple necessarily is. It follows that being is no longer reciprocal with the one' (*BE* 23). The consequences of the equivalence of being and one are unacceptable, even disgusting, because that which is always appears as multiple, composed; and further still, in an abstract manner, and without any criteria of choice, it would be impossible to determine the unity of one being. It would be impossible to find any limit to the proliferation of its parts (to determine, for instance, if I have in front of me a train, ten wagons, or a hundred tons of several different materials).

Deleuze, too, formulates the perspective of such a reversal of Plato's choice: as he writes in *Difference and repetition*, the equivalence of being and multiplicity breaks the equivocity of being, i.e. its division (following *Metaphysics* Delta) in an essential sense, and in an accidental one: if being is essentially multiplicity, one cannot rely any more on an a-priori criterion allowing to discriminate between the unity of the essence and the multiplicity of its accidental affections. The rejection of the *en kai on*, of the reciprocity of being and one, exposes being-as-multiplicity as essentially univocal: 'being' is said always and only of an infinity of terms which do not exist actually as such, but which, ontologically, 'are' exclusively in their mutual relation. Each 'actual' being is then an internal, expressive point of view, which actualises the totality of such present, past and future (near or distant) relations, relations which all together constitute the virtual multiplicity of everything which 'is'. From this it follows that there is no accidental, external, relation between beings, but only correspondences between different modes to express the same infinite multiplicity.

Concerning Deleuze's position, Badiou remarks that if each being is simply an expression of the same unique multiplicity, then difference between beings is purely formal, inessential: each being is nothing but a mode, a manifestation of the same being-multiplicity, which is thus essentially a unity. Deleuze's ontology would thus ultimately reintroduce a hidden idea of the One, of being as virtual, of which each actual being is an internal expression; and the effect of this would be to reduce any form of change to an inessential new expression of the same virtual. Against this, 'it is necessary to follow the thread of the multiple-without-oneness [. . .] *purely actual*, haunted by the *internal excess* of its parts' ('One, multiple, multiplicities', *TW* 79). For Badiou, only mathematics, via set theory, is able to fulfil such a double condition: excess and complete actuality. For set theory, the unity of an element is not a self-sufficient datum: an element is rather that to which it is possible to attribute 'one time' the identifying criterion of the set itself. From this it follows that there is no difference between the pure multiplicity constituting a given being and its appearance as *an* element, there is no such thing as the relation to a pure multiplicity, extensively infinite and functioning as other-than-actual, other than the actuality of the considered being. On the contrary, the set 'is entirely contained in the actuality of its own determination', and therefore the thought of the multiple 'manages to remain entirely faithful to a principle of immanence' (72–3).

Badiou explains the excess of such a multiplicity by referring once again to the platonic text. Plato remarks that each term, considered as a multiplicity, is non-identical to itself: given that the unity of that which is 'one' is not original, then each unity cannot be reflexively identical to itself, and different from the multiplicity of the others, but on the contrary is identical to that other-than-itself, which is itself considered as a multiplicity infinitely composed of further multiplicities. Each unity is identical to that multiplicity which, having no ground, constantly exceeds it, constantly becomes other, the multiplicity considered as 'heterogeneous dissemination [. . .] total dissemination of self' (*BE* 33); it is identical to that multiplicity the essence of which is 'to multiply itself in an immanent manner' (ibid.), and which thus constitutes that very principle of transformation that – as aforementioned – is the very essence of each being.

Nonetheless, each being, in order to be grasped, simultaneously needs to have, and even to be, a certain unity. This is why 'there is Oneness (*il y a de l'un*)' is the reciprocal term of 'the one is not'. Pure multiplicity, which, as multiplicity of no original element, is 'multiple of nothing' (58) (and in fact its proper name for Badiou is 'the void'), does not appear as such, and cannot even be thought of as an origin or a principle, which would come 'before' things as they appear, structured in thinkable and perceptible unities: pure multiplicity is, on the contrary, always retroactively apprehended as composition *of* a given being, which is then always at once *multiplicity* and *one*.

NATURE

Frank Ruda

Nature is the name for absolutely stable, unchangeable multiplicities, and yet it simultaneously does not exist. This may be considered the most succinct statement on Badiou's concept of nature, first elaborated in contrast with his conception of history in *BE* and further developed in *NN*. However, to the astonishment of many readers, the concept is largely absent from any of Badiou's later writings (for example, in *LW*), and, as shall become clear, has no reason to appear in his phenomenology. In a first approach, it is possible to distinguish between nature and history, on the grounds that natural multiplicities are fundamentally stable, while historical multiplicities are the most unstable. This is one way of rendering the thesis that events can take place in history but not in nature, since any event structurally needs an eventual site and hence implies some degree of instability with regard to the multiplicity to which it happens. Technically this can also be formulated by stating that history implies a gap between presentation and representation (i.e. not all elements of an element belonging to the situation themselves also belong to it), whereas nature contains a maximum level of correlation between presentation and representation, such that all elements of the elements of a multiple are elements of the latter multiple. Badiou initially defines nature, in a first and still abstract manner, as 'the recurrent form-multiple of a special equilibrium between belonging and inclusion, structure and metastructure [. . .] Naturalness is the intrinsic normality of a situation' (*BE* 128). 'Nature is normal' – this thesis relies on Badiou's distinction between singular, excrescent and normal terms, of which only the latter are characterised by a full transitive relation between belonging and inclusion. In terms of Badiou's metaontological, or set-theoretical, account this implies that nature is composed of transitive sets, as only in transitive sets does it always hold that for any $\beta \in \alpha$ it is equally true that $\beta \subset \alpha$, which in turn implies that: $(\gamma \in \beta) \rightarrow (\gamma \in \alpha)$. The elements of the elements of a given set are thus also elements of the set. This is the basic defining feature of what is called an ordinal, which bears the characteristic of transitivity because all its elements are themselves ordinals for which the indicated correlation between belonging and inclusion – or, in other terms: between the first presentation as an element and the second (re-)presentation as part – holds. So we can perhaps conclude from this that there is nothing un-natural in nature. Nature is even if it infinitely disseminates natural elements. Nature is all (of) the same.

For Badiou, '[t]his concept literally provides the backbone of all ontology, because it is the very concept of nature' (*BE* 133), which he relates back to his interpretation of the Greek term *physis*. Why is this so? Because the transitive relationship between sets and elements (and their elements) introduces the idea of an order: any element of a transitive set (whose elements are hence also elements of it) is smaller than the set of which it is an element. It is thus possible to generate the idea of a stable order, 'yet this order [. . .] is nothing but the order of presentation, marked by the sign $\in$' (135). That is, the set-theoretical concept of nature, of absolutely stable, transitive ordinal sets provides an account of the one and only operation on which set theory relies, namely belonging. Belonging can thus be understood as implying a relation of order. This should already clarify why, for Badiou, '"Nature"[. . .] refers to nothing sensible, to no experience'; it is 'an ontological category, a category of thought, of the pure multiple or set theory' (*NN* 69). The very concept of nature presents an ordered account of the same (i.e. of ordinals). Against this background, it is important to mention two essential aspects of nature as ontological category depicting the very ordering structure of belonging: (1) nature is atomic – this is what Badiou calls the principle of minimality (*BE* 135f.); and (2) nature is globally connected. (1) Nature is atomic because one is able to find, for whatever property, that an ordinal might have one (and only one) smallest ordinal possessing this property. If nature is stable and ordered – by being composed of smaller and bigger ordinals – 'there will always exist an *ultimate* natural element with this property' (135). This implies that for whatever property (of an ordinal) there is an atom of this property in nature. This is what Badiou refers to as 'natural "atomism"' (ibid.), for it is precisely those transitive sets that are the minimal. The sets that possess a certain property are ultimately unique, as they do not share the fact that they possess this or that property with any other ordinal. This is why for any property there is a smallest ordinal, i.e. a transitive set, which means that for any property there is 'a unique halting point' (139). (2) If there is a relation of order between natural multiplicities, then it is at the same time equally true that any ordinal – precisely because ordinals are transitive – either presents or is presented by another ordinal. Otherwise the very idea of ordinality could not be upheld. Nature is atomic and simultaneously globally connected. For this reason there is 'an abundant diversity and, at the same time, a mute monotony' (*NN* 184). What is at stake in nature, then, is a general concept not of action but of 'life' (*BE* 177). Both points can be synthesised through making sense of Badiou's claim that 'an ordinal is the number of its name' (140). This is to say, that any ordinal is composed of other ordinals, but that what defines this particular ordinal in difference to all others is its place within the order of ordinals. This place can be determined by accessing what this ordinal includes. If an ordinal includes seven ordinals, the number seven indicates precisely its position in the order of ordinals. This is why '"nature" and "number" are substitutable' (ibid.). In Badiou, nature is another name for number, as any number implies a positioning in an ordered set. But as will also become clear, number 'is that through which being organises thought' (*NN* 92). This is because thought requires presentation and is hence dependent on the very ordered structure of presentation, namely of belonging.

But why does nature not exist? Put simply, because there is no set of all ordinals (no set of all sets). Nature never comes to form a whole, and hence does not exist: 'Nature is not-all, just as being-qua-being, since no set of all sets exists either' (83). So what exists then? This question refers back to what Badiou calls the two existential seals of his metaontology. To constitute a consistent set-theoretical approach, it needs to be assumed that there is (1) the empty set ('The empty set being an ordinal, and therefore a natural multiple, we might say: the point of being of every situation is natural. Materialism is founded upon this statement' (83)). That is to say, it has to be axiomatically decided that the empty set – the unique multiple of nothing – exists. Containing no elements whatsoever, it cannot not be an ordinal. In accordance with the power-set axiom, it is possible to generate from the empty set infinitely many sets (e.g. given $\{\emptyset\}$ and it is possible to generate $\{\emptyset, \{\emptyset\}\}$ and so on *ad infinitum*). So, through the power-set axiom not only does one assert an existence, the existence of the empty set – which is not a substantial existence, but instead one that entails that what exists bears no marks of existence, because existence means to be *an element of* – but one also has a rule for generating infinitely many new multiples. However, in addition to this, we also need (2) another decision. Why? Because while infinitely many more ordinals can be generated, we never leave the proper space of the finite (as if one would generate infinitely many new whole natural numbers). It is only through the assertion of what, in technical terms, is called the 'limit ordinal' that the spell of the finite is broken and it can be properly assumed that nature does not exist. Otherwise, it is simply not impossible that the very rule by which infinitely many new ordinals are generated itself becomes the very totalisation of the series of ordinals. It is therefore necessary to assert that there is a limit-ordinal, which limits the construction of infinitely many ordinals and hence de-totalises the whole of all ordinals. Without these two existential seals, nature would exist – but it should be clear that the second seal is a derivative of the first.

Ultimately this makes it possible to account for two further implications of Badiou's notion of nature: (1) the distinction of nature and history is his rendering of what Martin Heidegger called the ontic-ontological difference. For, in ontology – which refers to being-qua-being, and hence nature – a multiplicity is natural 'if it is founded by the void alone [. . .] It is a *void-foundation of void-foundation*' (*BE* 189). The same does not go for history. Nature is derived from the void; history constitutively obfuscates this fact and so never directly addresses the void as the name of being. If the void appears in history following an event, it always appears under a different name (say, proletariat). (2) Being fundamentally stable, nature is not historical and is thus absolute, while history as such is relative. This leads Badiou to claim that 'history can be naturalised, but nature cannot be historicised' (176). Why it is that nature cannot be historicised should be clear. Why, however, can history be naturalised? Because while nature is on the side of being-qua-being, and history is on the side of ontic beings, if something happens (i.e. an event) within a historical multiplicity, it becomes possible to measure what was previously immeasurable, namely the excess of the state. History can be naturalised because it can be measured, where measure is an effect of evental happenings that make it possible to relate a historical situation to the well-structured order of belonging that is established in the thought of nature. For Badiou, without nature there could be no orientation in history; nature is that which organises thought because it orients thought and provides it with a measure.

NIETZSCHE

Alenka Zupancic

The importance of Nietzsche in Badiou's philosophy could best be summarised, albeit not exhausted, by Nietzsche's 'antiphilosophy'. The latter constitutes one of the key categories in relation to which Badiou develops his own philosophical project. To be sure, this relation is not simply that of opposition, but has a far more complex structure. Discussed at many different points of his work, Nietzsche gains a more sustained attention in the context of Badiou's severe polemical debate with the *nouveaux philosophes*. In their advocacy of liberalism, strongly related to their attack on *la pensée '68*, the latter published what Badiou calls their 'manifesto' under the title *Pourquoi nous ne sommes pas nietzschéens* (*Why we are not Nietzscheans*, Boyer et al. 1991). Badiou's rejoinder to the text consists in a conference paper published as a tiny booklet titled: 'Casser en deux l'histoire du monde' (To break the history of the world in two) (*CD*). Under this Maoist-sounding title, taken from one of Nietzsche's letters to Brandes (1888), Badiou deploys a very incisive reading of Nietzsche, and of what constitutes the core of his philosophical stance. This text also constitutes the summary of the annual seminar that Badiou has dedicated to Nietzsche (1992–3, followed by seminars dedicated to other major 'antiphilosophers' – Wittgenstein, Lacan, Saint Paul). Nietzsche's singularity, Badiou argues, consists in his conception of a philosophical act, which coincides with the philosophy declaring it. This act is not an overcoming; it is an event. According to Badiou, both Heidegger and Deleuze missed this crucial point, which is related to the *power* of the act. Deleuze missed it through his focus on the question of sense, whereas the essence of an act is precisely that it has no sense, is sense-less. Nietzsche's philosophy is thus not about introducing (new) concepts. Rather, what Nietzsche's singular use of proper names points to is that the name of a philosophical event can only be a figure or a proper name. Hence the network of them in his work: Christ or the Crucified, Dionysus, Ariadna, Saint Paul, Socrates, Wagner, Zarathustra, and finally Nietzsche himself. These names are not simply codified types that could be fully written out using other words (e.g. Saint Paul as the preacher, the genius of hatred and of negation, the will to power driven by Nothing . . .). If this were the case, 'the network of proper names, constitutive of the naming of an act, would be reduced to what is the general aspect of sense, and Nietzsche would be caught in the parade of interpretation. This way, I think, we lose the opacity of the proper as that with which Nietzsche builds his category of truth [. . .] We could say that proper name expresses the philosophical act in the sense in which the power of life in it cannot be evaluated [. . .] In order to approach Nietzsche one thus has to keep to the point where the evaluation, the values, the sense all fail in the test of the act' (*CD* 8–9). It is this aspect of Nietzsche that gets most of Badiou's attention, since it is clearly related to some of his own fundamental preoccupations, especially the issue of the relationship between the event and its declaration/naming. The other side of Nietzsche, the genealogical, philological and critical part of his writing, gets rather rapidly dismissed as a paradigmatically 'sophistical' proceeding, divided between a philological investigation of statements and a reference to the register of power; though in the same essay Badiou also describes Nietzsche as the 'Prince of contemporary antiphilosophy', due to his assigning philosophy the singular task of renewing the question of truth in its function of breaking with sense. This last point remains crucial, however, in that which concerns, in the complex configuration of (philosophical) act, event, subjectivity and truth, both the proximity and the distance between Nietzsche's and Badiou's conceptions. Their proximity bears on the eventual origin of any truth, which accounts for what in it is irreducible to positive knowledge or sense, but remains necessarily opaque (what marks this breaking of the chain of reasons in Badiou is the notion of 'fidelity'). Moreover, Badiou reactivates, so to speak, the Nietzschean use of proper names in his more recent work on the idea of communism, in which he accentuates the importance of the 'glorious Pantheon' of names (Spartacus, Thomas Münzer, Robespierre, Toussaint-Louverture, Blanqui, Marx, Lenin, Rosa Luxemburg, Mao, Che Guevara . . .) for the Idea of communism and for political subjectivation as such. Nietzsche is not mentioned here, but his contemporary enemies are: 'the abstract critique of the role of proper names in political subjectivation', related to the criticism of the 'cult of personality', is the perfect soil in which the 'new philosophers of reactive humanism' can flourish (*CH* 249–51). However, Badiou insists on keeping both the Idea of communism and the logic of the event separated from the functioning of proper names. While the latter symbolise 'heroic exceptions' from the ordinary that make it possible for us to relate to the event, they are not constitutive of, or essential to, the event as such. In Nietzsche, on the other hand, the two are indistinguishable. Moreover, in his conceiving of an act/event as essentially philosophical act/event, Nietzsche firmly adopts, according to Badiou, the paradigmatic antiphilosophical position which blurs the difference between philosophy as composition of truths and the realm of their production (politics, mathematics, poetry, love). In Nietzsche's case this has further and very palpable consequences for the philosopher himself. Since Nietzsche refuses to posit the event as the (external) cause or inaugurating point of thought and its subsequent generic procedure of truth, the event appears as immanent to the 'speculative principle of declaration'. Consequently, the statement 'I am preparing the event' is indistinguishable from the event itself. This statement will break the world in two, while simultaneously declaring precisely this: that it will break the world in two. The declaration lacks the Real (the event itself), and this is why 'Nietzsche will have to make himself appear at the point of this Real which is lacking and in relation with which it is impossible to distinguish between its presence and its announcement. This is precisely what will be called Nietzsche's madness' (*CD* 15). In other words, Badiou doesn't hesitate to establish a direct link between Nietzsche's breakdown and his philosophical position, with the former appearing as heroically (to the point of 'saintliness') sustained consequence of the latter.

Badiou also takes up the Nietzschean declaration of the death of God, in order to differentiate between three kinds of gods, or divinities:

1. The properly religious God as God of the encounter, that is, God as part of the evental horizon of Christianity (resurrection), God as real and as life ('Only a God that was once alive can die'). Badiou repeats the declaration of His death: this particular event is over, its consequences exhausted. Contemporary rise or return of religion and of religious fundamentalism are not the sign of the opposite – rather the contrary, Badiou recognises in them 'obscure subjectivations' of the death of God itself.
2. The metaphysical god of philosophers, which becomes inoperative the moment we undo the suture that sustains it, namely the suture between the infinite and the One.
3. The God of poets, recognisable in Heidegger's exclamation, 'Only a God can save us!' At this level true atheism aims at 'disencumbering

language, cutting from it the constellation of loss and return. For we have lost nothing, and nothing comes back. The chance of a truth is a supplementation and, something, then, comes upon us' (*TO* 31).

Nietzsche is not discussed by Badiou only in his office of antiphilosopher, but also as part of a specific philosophical tradition, based on vitalist ontology (together with Bergson and of course Deleuze). Here, Badiou's main point of disagreement is twofold: vitalism relies on the constituent power of One (the One-term which has the power to transcend the states that deploy or unfold it), while the guarantee of the One as constituent power comes from the mortality or finitude of the multiple: death alone is proof of life. This aligns, perhaps unexpectedly, phenomenology and vitalisms, and separates them from the Badiouian project: 'To unshackle existence down here from its mortal correlation requires that it should be axiomatically wrested from the phenomenological constitution of experience as well as from the Nietzschean naming of being as life' (*LW* 268).

NOUVEAUX PHILOSOPHES

Joseph Litvak

Most prominently represented by such figures as André Glucksmann and Bernard-Henry Levy, the *nouveaux philosophes* are a group of former leftists who have made names for themselves as 'media intellectuals' by spectacularly repudiating the supposed totalitarianism of revolutionary politics in favour of a reactionary reduction of philosophy to morality. Badiou's polemic against them, beginning with their emergence in the 1970s and continuing into his most recent texts, has been a recurrent and emblematic feature of his work. As Nina Power and Alberto Toscano have suggested, the *nouveaux philosophes* exemplify the problem of *betrayal* that – somewhat surprisingly, given Badiou's emphasis on a 'purifying subtraction from worldly entanglements' (Power and Toscano 2009: 34) – impels Badiou's thought: as the symptomatic reactionary or reactive subject, the *nouveau philosophe* stands in a highly revealing relation to the faithful or revolutionary subject around whom Badiou's philosophy turns.

Both in his shorter, obviously polemical writings and in his major philosophical works, Badiou has consistently directed his most withering satire at the *nouveaux philosophes*, for their rise to fame bespeaks the descent of post-1976 France from the *années rouges* into the counter-revolutionary *années noires*. And since this descent is also a return – to the *pétainisme* or collaborationism that Badiou sees as France's 'transcendental' (*MS*

103–15) – the complicity of the *nouveaux philosophes* in this latest restoration has understandably earned them Badiou's special scorn. And yet,
there is something in the 'new' philosophy's very claim to novelty that
nonetheless fascinates Badiou, and that has occasioned some of his most
intriguing philosophical reflections. Although it is tempting to dismiss the
'*nouveaux*' in '*nouveaux philosophes*' as merely the most blatant evidence
that their celebrity is nothing more than another abject triumph of market-
ing, Badiou more interestingly juxtaposes the ostentatious 'newness' of the
nouveaux philosophes with the newness of the *event*, that radical transformation to which the faithful subject remains faithful. In *LW*, he has this
to say about the *nouveaux philosophes*, and specifically about Glucksmann:

I [. . .] shared for a long time the conviction that what resists the new is the old
[. . .] But this view of things underestimates what I think we must term *reactionary novelties*. In order to resist the call of the new, it is still necessary to create
arguments of resistance appropriate to the novelty itself. From this point of view,
every reactive disposition is the contemporary of the present to which it reacts.
Of course, it categorically refuses to incorporate itself to this present. It sees the
body – [as] a conservative slave sees the army of Spartacus – and refuses to be one
of its elements. But it is caught up in a subjective formalism that is not, and cannot
be, the pure permanence of the old. (54)

Where the faithful subject affirms an *active* present, the reactive subject
epitomised by the *nouveau philosophe* seeks to produce an *extinguished*
present. In order to do so, however, the *nouveau philosophe* must still bind
himself, at the level of form, to the active present he would extinguish.
'It is not in the least irrelevant', Badiou writes, 'to note that almost thirty
years after the irruption of the *nouvelle philosophie*, Glucksmann has
rushed to defend the invasion of Iraq by Bush's troops in singularly violent
tones. In his own way, he is devoted to the present: in order to deny its
creative virtue, he must daily nourish journalism with new sophisms' (55).

In his frenzy of denial, that is, the renegade pays tribute to what he
denies. The '*nouveaux*' in '*nouveaux philosophes*' is not merely the mark
of trendiness: it signifies an unwitting attachment to the transformative
newness that the *nouveau philosophe* once desired and would now negate.
Or, as Badiou puts it, 'the form of the faithful subject nonetheless remains
the unconscious of the reactive subject' (56). In the long-running *trahison
des clercs* that the *nouveaux philosophes* are driven to keep re-enacting,
these conservative slaves prove themselves to be masters of denunciation,
indeed of the whole repertoire of sycophantic practices developed by
informers and collaborators before them, from the time of Spartacus to
Vichy France to the United States of the McCarthyite 1950s. Like their

predecessors in betrayal, however, these conservative slaves have hidden within themselves, and *from* themselves, the revolutionary slaves whom they betray, but to whom they remain attached. To reveal this attachment is to betray the betrayers: to disclose what their treachery would keep concealed. And, for Badiou, this second betrayal – this bringing to light of the reactionary unconscious – is precisely the task of philosophy. Now that the moralistic melancholia of the *nouveaux philosophes* has succeeded in passing itself off, in France, as philosophy *tout court*, what is necessary is to 'demoralise philosophy' (*SMP* 83), for it is only by demoralising it, only by betraying the *nouveaux philosophes*, that we can arrive at a philosophy that is truly new.

NUMBERS

Jon Roffe

While Badiou discusses the nature of number on occasion in passing, his most extended reflection is found in *NN*. His motivation for directly considering this topic arises on the basis of two concerns. On the one hand, the contemporary use of numbers in the governance and regulation of capitalism has rendered them ubiquitous while subordinating their deployment to the regime of brute calculation. The scope of human possibility has likewise been yoked to this same regime.

On the other hand, the status of the concept of number as such has been radically problematised by developments within mathematics itself, to the extent that a unified theory of Number has been serially voided throughout mathematics' history. Badiou notes three in particular, emphases that are also elaborated in *BE* in the context of Badiou's metaontological construal of set theory: the demise of the figure of the One, the advent of zero, and the Cantorian innovations around the infinite. In addition, then, to the impetus provided by the blind ubiquity of number in contemporary society, there is a conceptual requirement to think the being of number in the wake of these cataclysmic shifts in the history of mathematics.

Badiou makes use of two previous conceptions of number in his account, drawn respectively from John Conway and Richard Dedekind. From Conway (and the more formal presentation of the same approach by Harry Gonshor), Badiou takes a great deal of the detail of his own account, noting that he essentially only parts ways with Conway's version on 'poetic' grounds (*NN* 107). While the latter speaks of a theory of surreal numbers, Badiou contends that the word is misleading, because of the specific colour of the word 'surreal', which gives the impression that the development in question is only an extension of pre-existing accounts. In fact, what is involved is 'a complete reinterpretation of the very idea of number [. . .] the possibility of finally thinking number as a unified figure of multiple-being' (ibid.).

On the other hand, the essential concept put into play in Badiou's account, drawn from Dedekind (who was also an influence on Conway's account, albeit an occasional one on his own admission), is that of the *cut*. For Badiou, the concept of the cut is 'the heart of the maths of Number' (144). The number series, he notes, is densely ordered, that is, 'between two Numbers there always exists a third, and thus an infinity of Numbers' (155). What is required to identify a particular number is a means to rationally think such a cut – and the same requirement underlies the definition of Number as such.

Badiou's account begins on the terrain of the ordinals, which he explicates in a way that closely follows the fourteenth meditation of *BE*. Having established ordinals as fully ordered and each possessing a minimal element allowing them to be identified in their singularity, Badiou provides his first definition of Number: 'A Number is the conjoint givenness of an ordinal and a part of that ordinal' (102). The given ordinal is termed the *matter* of the number, while the part of the ordinal (a part that need not be unified or even non-void, but which can clearly be no larger than the whole ordinal) that qualifies it is termed the number's *form*. Badiou then demonstrates that such a definition provides the means to distinguish numbers from each other and define a total order over the number system (that is, locate any number in relation to any other in terms of size). Furthermore, a crucial point, the discrete, well-ordered character of numbers is not the result of any activity on the part of an agent, but is *intrinsic*.

The next, more detailed definition relies upon a further intra-structural specification of numbers: each number is defined on the basis of its two *sub-numbers*. More specifically, every number can be uniquely defined on the basis of a cut within its *form*. What lies above the cut in the form will be termed the number's high set – $Hi(N)$ – and what lies below it the low set – $Lo(N)$. On the basis of the earlier account of the uniqueness of the ordinals, Badiou shows that, for every paired set of subnumbers, a unique number exists. We are led as a result to the *canonical presentation* of Number: the number N_1 is defined by the cut $Lo(N_1)/Hi(N_1)$, or again by the ordered set $<Lo(N_1), Hi(N_1)>$. Generally then, a number is 'a structure localisable in thought as a point of articulation of its substructures' (138).

It is clear, as Badiou himself notes on several occasions, that such an account bears little relation to the numbers we are familiar with in everyday life – even though the operations that we take to be part and parcel of 'everyday mathematics' can be straightforwardly defined on these terms, and even though this definition includes not only the natural numbers, but negative numbers, rationals, the reals, infinitesimals and transfinites.

Badiou's theory of Number is thus, in general terms, set-theoretical. Beginning from the account of minimality furnished by the ordinals, and through to the canonical presentation, set theory underpins the entire account. This distinguishes his position from a number of important alternatives, including those of Frege, Dedekind and Peano (discussed in the opening chapters of *NN*).

Correlatively, Badiou's is a *Platonic* account of number. This is because number needs no agency of constitution, but insists in being as such. No activity, whether operational (Peano), intuitive (Dedekind) or axiomatic-deductive (Cantor) is required to bring them into being. However, he also departs from the traditional form of mathematical Platonism insofar as numbers are not conceived to be eternal *objects*, discrete self-identical beings. Instead, as we have seen, a number is an intrinsically determined and rationally apprehensible set-theoretical structure.

OBJECT

Tzuchien Tho

Not until *LW* (2006) does Badiou give the concept of object a direct treatment. However, since the term 'object' does have a certain lineage in the philosophical vocabulary that Badiou inherits, it is necessary to address briefly how he uses it in his work up to *LW*.

The problem of object or objectivity concerns determination. Determination is what distinguishes an object from a thing. Some vagueness surrounds how to distinguish 'thing' from 'object', but the general direction is from the minimal determination of a thing to the maximal determination of an object. Let us say, then, that one is thirsty and hence seeks to quench one's thirst. We might start by looking around the environment for some 'thing' that might quench the thirst. Of course we are selecting among the things of the world that might be liquid. But of course the leftover wine from last week's party, by now sour and stale, won't do for the moment. After searching further, we arrive at more and more criteria until this 'thing' is refined into a determinate object: cold apple juice in the fridge opened just yesterday.

From another perspective a long cognitive tradition is handed down through the Kantian tradition that distinguishes between the object of cognition and the thing-in-itself. The object is localised in space and time and it is determined by the quantities attributed to it in relation to the cognitive subject (consciousness). Yet this same object has a pre-cognitive existence and a certain independence from the subject's relation to it. The Kantian tradition famously designates the thing-in-itself as unknowable. Yet all acts of knowing are forms of judgement and hence any objectivity relies on an explicit relation between a knowing subject and an object to be known. The concept of thing remains crucial here insofar as it provides a transcendental background against which a knowing subject determines a 'thing' qua object. In the Kantian form, the genesis of object and objectivity relies on the logical formation of an 'object $= x$' or a variable empty placeholder in the form of judgement to regulate the unification of various sense impressions into a coherent judgement (Kant 1996: CPR, A109, 160). Kant famously relates the scenario of viewing a house from different points of view, the form of judgement synthetically unites these sense impressions into the judgement that this 'x' is a house: a determination (Kant 1996: CPR, B235–B237, 261–3).

From the apple juice to the house, we have a general introduction to the philosophy of the object. That is, in the first place, we have object as a determination of the will. The thirsty person desires an object to fulfill that thirst. In the second place, we have object as a determination of cognition. This is the determination of an object given to knowledge and to which a subject stands in a relation through judgement. This relation is actualised by attributing to this place-holder 'x' the object's relation to the subject or its relation to other objects. In Badiou's philosophical trajectory, we find both modes of this problem of object. In the earlier parts of Badiou's work, most notably *TS*, he understands the object along the lines of will or desire. With *LW*, we find a treatment of object that follows more along the model of cognitive determination, although Badiou would essentially reject the cognitive aspects for a theory of the object.

Badiou makes no significant mention of the concept of object until *TS*, and even in this latter work, references to it are few and far between. Given that Badiou drew heavily, albeit critically, on Lacanian sources in this period, the notion of the object at work here is that of the Lacanian '*objet a*'. The '*objet a*' is an analytic concept that allows us to treat the framing of desire in a particular field or, in other words, the 'object-cause' of desire. A concrete object like apple juice may be the particular demand of fulfilling desire at a particular cause, but once it is consumed, the desiring subject moves towards another concrete object, and so on down the line. In the case of the apple juice, we stated that the subject was thirsty. But the Lacanian subject is *always* 'thirsty'. The subject's desire is, for Lacan, *caused* by the '*objet a*' insofar as it retroactively (via an *a posteori* analysis) orients the subject towards a particular direction.

Badiou's use of the Lacanian object in *TS* is largely analogical. The Lacanian problem is first developed in the second part of the book through an extended analysis of Mallarmé's poetics, and then later employed in a more explicitly political setting. There is no engagement with clinical psychoanalysis as such, but the treatment of the object intentionally echoes the structuralist period of Lacan and the concept employed is clearly that of the object as the absent cause of the subject. In the case of Mallarmé, Badiou sees poetry as a means to present a 'subtracted object' or 'null-object reducible to the sonorous void of the signifier' (*TS* 101). The 'null-object' here is not the object understood directly but, because it is 'empty', such a null-object discloses the grounds for the 'objectivity' of the object: the vanishing object reveals the 'placements' that governs any given object's *meaning*: an index that underlies the capacity of an object to enter into relations with other objects.

The formal relation between the 'subtracted' object, objects and their object-places reveals the interplay between objects and their placements. From this, Badiou will develop a reading of the limitations of this perspective in politics. From a Maoist perspective, the problem of proletarian politics was the double front of economism and reformism. In both cases, the antagonism of proletarian politics gets reduced to resolution or the reproduction of the state. That is, the antagonism of class struggle was reduced to the endless revolution around the lack immanent to the state itself. Against this, he argues for the non-existence of class relations in the sense that proletarian politics could not have an existence with respect to its 'object', the bourgeois state. On the one hand, class antagonism prevents proletarian politics from 'existing' with respect to the bourgeois state, so it is always 'outside' of it. On the other hand, this same antagonism is its 'cause'. Badiou's general answer to this problem at this point is to insist on the existence of proletarian politics through the continuous 'purging' of its bourgeois content. Ultimately, through this model, Badiou will point out the inadequacy of the Lacanian conception that had aided him thus far. Badiou argues that even though the dynamics between placement, lack and cause opens up an analysis of the relation subject-object, 'It is not an empty place, not even that of power, that conjures the emergence, in the political disorder, of the subject of its occupation' (*TS* 131). Recalling his earlier treatment of Mallarmé, Badiou argues here that it is only the *destruction* of the place, rather than merely attending to it, that constitutes the protracted labour of political subjectivity.

From this analysis of the object in *TS*, Badiou establishes the basic themes of what he will later call an 'objectless subject', a term that might be misleading without the dialectical inflections mentioned above (cf. OS). We move into the period of Badiou's work around *BE*, where the object is rarely discussed. Badiou's ontology developed in *BE* casts a basic distinction between an analysis of being-as-such and beings, but does not develop these questions towards the relation between being and object. Yet insofar as the subject constitutes an existence that radically breaks with the order of being, one could maintain a rough characterisation of the being-subject distinction with its earlier instantiation in *TS*.

We should reiterate here that the theme concerning the object that we have been discussing remains rather thin and relies on a Lacanian background rather than a direct account. All this changes in *LW* (2006) when the object will occupy a central place in the development of his ontological system from a set-theoretical or 'mathematical' language into what he calls a 'logic'. This move schematically translates into a move from the earlier treatment of being-as-such through set theory, an ontological level, to a treatment of beings as they appear, with the resources of category theory, an ontic level. As such, the appearance of beings, the being-there of being, comes to the fore in *LW*. At the same time, this might be understood as a shift from the register of objects as the determination of will to the treatment of objects on the register of the determination of cognition. Badiou makes clear that his treatment of appearance does not rely on traditional subject–object relation such as we have them in the empiricist, cognitive or phenomenological traditions. Appearances, as it were, are taken independently of the perceiving or cognitive subject and have a value independent of their being perceived or cognised. Instead appearances form a 'world' taken with respect to a transcendental structure of the multiplicity of the world. The concept of object, in this case, is not simply appearance but a 'count as one' that brings together the multiplicity of appearance with the formal mapping of the structure of difference in a world.

The Kantian flavour of the 'transcendental' here, along with Badiou's characterisation of his theory of objects as a 'phenomenology', might be misleading. Indeed Badiou does understand himself to be echoing the conditions of possibility treated in the *Critique of Pure Reason* (*LW* 233). Nonetheless, the theory of object here is without a subject and the nature of appearance is developed as the immanent relations between existences localised in a world rather than due to the synthetic work of apperception (231). For Badiou, the structure given by the 'transcendental', a mapping of identity and difference *relative* to the mutual relations between the elements in a world, occurs locally and immanently. In short, for any given world, the transcendental indexes the world by assigning values of relative difference (or identity) to every pair of elements in the world. If we take, say, the two most different elements in a given world, we will be taking the 'minimum' value μ of the world, the bare consistency of what it is to appear in the same world. Conversely, the two most identical elements render the greatest value, the 'maximum' value M of the world. Of course any two elements of the world can be evaluated according to some value ranging from μ to M (from minimum to maximum according to the transcendental). As such the values μ to M define the limits of the world and, depending on the world, appearances will range somewhere between these two values mapped onto types: the same type of appearance will share the same value within the world. But at the same time, this mapping will allow us to distinguish between appearances such that appearances at the limits of the transcendental index can be distinguished as 'absolutely' distinct relative to a given world. This distinction allows us to define an atom: an absolutely distinct unity evaluated against the transcendental index of the world. This atomic status is also the evaluation of its reality (*LW* 250).

So what, finally, is an object? An object is simply a collection of real atoms (251). We need not think of atoms as those point-particles defined in classical physics, but those would certainly provide a suitable *representation* according to a certain world (spherical charged atoms in a Bohr-world, for example). The crucial point here is to see that the multiplicities unified under the concept of object are *real* atomic elements. Of course these real atomic constituents of the object are defined formally, through the application of the transcendental index on appearances, rather than through a given empirical unity. As such, Badiou's theory of objects here does not correspond to any particular empirical thing; it is a formal means to account for the unit-structure of appearance in his transcendental algebra. It is important also to note that Badiou's object here is constituted immanently, 'bottom-up' from formal atoms, rather than imposed 'from above' by a traditional mode of transcendental synthesis. Badiou is here keen to reject a (neo)vitalist notion of objectivity where an excessive preponderance of the virtual is merely 'tamed' by a cognitive sequestering of multiples into determined and unit-objects. Rather, in Badiou's case, there are certainly an infinite number of appearances, virtual and real, that can be evaluated against the transcendental index in a world. However, objects and objective reality are constituted by the irreducible atoms of that evaluation. Hence just as being-as-such is inconsistent multiplicity but being is presented as consistent, so in turn, appearances are multiple in the world but objectivity is constituted as the product of appearances with irreducible unity with respect to the transcendental index of the world.

Much of what is continuous in Badiou's thinking about the object in his work until now, despite the lack of a direct treatment in earlier works, is consonant with the non-relation between the subject, the active mode of rupture, destruction or invention, and being. That is, across his work, the non-subjective mode, whether understood as being, thing, object, remains essentially a dynamics of the reproduction of a given order where the subject simply does not figure. As such, the figures of the subject exist in a mode that is distinct from being (or object). Since *BE*, Badiou has attempted a radical recasting of his theory of the subject insofar as the consistency and continuation of the subject must *exist* in some way and hence must dialectically draw from the very fabric of being against which it is determined. As such, in both *BE* and *LW*, the subject exists as a transontological being, an existence that breaks with the structure of being while participating in the formal syntax of being or world. In other words, determination of the object logically precludes the subject, but the subject nonetheless formally exists. In turn, the object would simply provide the existential anchor of Badiou's ultimate aim. In *LW* the subject acquires consistency, that is, a body, insofar as it migrates between worlds, but the very composition of this body requires a formal reference to those non-subjective (objective) elements that constitute its localisation in a world. The theory of object is thus that of a formal exposition of the consistency of any given world independent of the subject. Yet the ultimate aim of Badiou's systematic exposition remains, echoing a similar argumentative strategy in *BE*, to provide an ontological background for the theory of the subject that makes use of the exclusion of the subject in the world in order to present its paradoxical existence.

THE ONE

Olivia Lucca Fraser

BE begins with an announcement of the book's inaugural decision: that 'the one *is not*' (23). There is no One, no self-sustaining unity in being, but only the *count-as-one*, the non-self-sufficient operation of unification. There is no unity-in-itself, because every unity is a unity *of* something, something that differs from the *operation* of unification. This decision is no less fundamental for Badiou's philosophy than his well-known equation of mathematics with ontology, and their metaontological meanings are deeply entangled; any attempt to isolate one from the other would mutilate the sense that Badiou gives its twin.

Through the prism of set theory, the non-being of the One refracts into three distinct ontological bans: (1) the prohibition of an 'All', or a *set of all sets* (by the ZF axioms, the supposition of such a set's existence leads directly into the embrace of the Russell paradox) – an important corollary of this ban is that there is no 'set-theoretical universe' against which the various models of set theory can be measured, and so *every* coherent interpretation of the axioms will be pathological or 'non-standard' to some extent – there is no such thing as *the* standard model of set theory – a fact we must bear in mind when grappling with Cohen's results, among others; (2) the ban on *atomic* elements, or units that are not themselves sets (ZF makes no provisions for unities that are not unities-of-something – with the possible exception of the void, into which the axiom of extensionality would collapse any putative 'atoms'); and, we could add, (3) a self-unifying unity, a set that counts-as-one itself alone; schematically, the set Ω such that $\Omega = \{\Omega\}$ (this set, which would in any case evade identification by the axiom of extensionality, is expressly forbidden by the axiom of foundation).

Note that there exist axiomatisations of set theory that violate *each* of the three impossibilities by which we have translated, 'the One is not'. There are set theories with a *universal set* V, such that for all e, $e \in V$ (the One as All, as *set of all sets*); there are set theories with *urelements*, elements u such that no element e belongs to u, but which are nevertheless distinct from the empty set (the One as atom, as a unity that is not a unity-of-something) (cf. Zermelo 1967); and there are set theories with *hypersets*, sets X such that $X \in X$, or $X \in A_1 \in \ldots \in A_n \in X$ (the One as counting-itself-as-one, as self-presentation) (cf. Azcel 1988).

It is the identification of ontology not simply with mathematics but with a *particular version* of set theory (ZF) that therefore helps to motivate the decision that the One is not. Observing the existence of other One-affirming set theories emphasises the particularity of this decision. The converse motivation – of the decision to identify mathematics with ontology by the decision on the non-being of the one – is somewhat murkier, but Badiou insists upon it. It is because the One is not, Badiou argues, that we must resist any temptation to subject being qua being to the unity of a *concept*. Subtracted from unity, ontology can articulate the sayable of being only by means of a non-conceptual regime of *axioms*, which regulate the construction of pure multiplicities without having recourse to any *definition* of multiplicity (*BE* 29). But why insist that concepts cannot deploy themselves axiomatically, by way of definitions that are purely implicit? Even if this is granted, nothing prevents a reversal of the argument. What, for instance, keeps an opponent from objecting to the placement of being-without-oneness under the 'formal unity' of an *axiomatic*, rather than submitting it to 'the mobile multiplicity of the concept'?

ONTOLOGY, METAONTOLOGY

Christopher Norris

The term 'ontology' has traditionally been used to denote that particular branch of philosophy – though one always open to contributions from other disciplines such as the natural sciences – which concerned itself with certain very fundamental questions. These were questions such as: What (objectively speaking) exists? How (objectively) did it come to exist? What is (must be) its fundamental nature? What – as a matter of objective necessity – must we take to be its properties, structures, causal dispositions, modal attributes, and so forth? It is thereby distinguished from epistemology, defined as having to do with questions like: What precisely is knowledge? What are its scope and limits? What is its relation to objective truth? How (if at all) can we distinguish epistemological from ontological issues since – as appears self-evident to some – any claim to a knowledge or understanding of ontology will *ipso facto* be a claim founded on (what else?) our knowledge or understanding.

This latter line of argument has typically been pressed by those, anti-realists of varying strength, who would deny that it can possibly make sense to posit the existence of recognition-transcendent or knowledge-surpassing truths. Realists just as typically respond that we cannot make sense of the history of science, or indeed the everyday course of human experience, except on the premise that knowledge can always fall short of truth and is always subject to refinement, revision, correction, expansion, updating, or (at times) radical overhaul on precisely that account. Then again there are those – notably W. V. Quine – who nowadays use the term 'ontology' (or the plural 'ontologies') in a relativistic sense that is almost completely divorced from that traditional conception of reality as existing quite apart from the scope and limits of human cognition. This usage has been widely picked up by social constructivists and 'strong' sociologists of knowledge, and also finds its continental equivalent in the various, e.g. post-structuralist, postmodernist and Foucauldian theories that would relativise 'truth' and 'reality' to this or that culture-specific language, discourse or signifying practice.

Badiou stakes out his distance from both schools of thought: from the objectivist view that tends to immobilise ontology by conceiving it as that which entirely transcends the shaping power of human activity, and the relativist/constructivist view according to which ontologies are as many and varied as the conceptual schemes, paradigms, frameworks, discourses, or Wittgensteinian language-games within which alone they possess some intelligible content. For him, the term 'ontology' most properly denotes just those parts, attributes, properties, aspects, or features of reality that current-best knowledge is able to encompass at some given stage in its development. He is at one with the realists in holding that truth is always potentially recognition-transcendent but all the same agrees with constructivists of a moderate, i.e. non-anti-realist sort that human knowledge makes progress and, moreover, that it does so by working constructively to find out means by which a seemingly consistent because sutured reality can be forced to confront an inconsistent real. The real in question may be physical as with the natural sciences, or socio-political as with various revolutionary initiatives, or even artistic as with the kinds of breakthrough achievement that mark a new stage in the ongoing exploration of formal and expressive resources. However, to Badiou's way of thinking, this process is best exemplified by the instance of a formal science such as mathematics and, in particular, by the sorts of advance that have typified the development of set theory from Cantor to the present. What then emerges with great clarity is the sequence of conjectures, proofs (or refutations), proposal of further, more adventurous conjectures, discovery of new, more powerful or rigorously formalised proof-procedures, and so forth, which he captures most succinctly in the book title *Being and Event*.

The term 'being' is here used in its traditional (ontological) sense and denotes that range of entities – multiples, sets, classes, parts, members, etc. – that make up the set-theoretical object domain and thus place certain jointly constraining and enabling conditions on the further conduct of enquiry. Thus, quite simply, 'mathematics is ontology' insofar as post-Cantorian set theory with its infinitely numerous orders or 'sizes' of infinity provides us with the most abstract but also (and for just that reason) the perfect or exemplary instance of how reality intrinsically exceeds any present-best power of human cognitive grasp. This is why mathematical thought is never capable of ranging over more than a tiny, indeed infinitesimal portion of the infinite domain that it is given to explore. It is also why Badiou comes out in such passionate opposition to those various trends in present-day philosophy of mathematics – anti-realist, intuitionist, fictionalist, or Wittgensteinian – which have in common the basically finitist idea that mathematical truth can extend only so far as the currently available stock of methods, proof-procedures, or operative concepts. Where they go wrong, he maintains, is in mistaking the above-mentioned (undeniable) fact that mathematical *knowledge* at any given time can only encompass some tiny portion of reality and truth for the more contentious (in fact insupportable) idea that mathematical truth is itself subject to the scope and limits of human knowledge.

To Badiou this seems a perversion of reason and a failure to grasp the significance of Cantor's revolution, namely his having opened the way to a radically expanded sense of the unknown regions – the ontological *terra incognita* – that await future exploration. This is why Badiou specifies his as a 'metaontological' project, that is to say, one that takes as its task the analysis of those first-order ontologies (or ontological commitments) that constitute some specific object-domain, such as – prototypically – numbers, sets and classes in mathematics. However, his usage of the term is pointedly different from the way it is deployed by analytic (or post-analytic) philosophers after Quine, for whom it signals a framework-relativist conception according to which the question 'what exists?' is equivalent to the question 'what has a place in this or that ontological scheme?', be it gods and centaurs in Homer's scheme or leptons and muons in that of present-day physics. Although it makes sense, from Badiou's standpoint, to pluralise 'ontologies' in keeping with various, more or less informed states of knowledge, there is still the signal case of mathematical discovery – of breakthrough events like those of Cantor and Cohen – to block any slide towards other, intellectually disabling forms of scheme-relativism.

So there is a great deal at stake when Badiou berates finitist thinkers for selling mathematics short, or for holding it within some ready-made enclosure – whether that of intuition, pre-existing knowledge, agreed-upon method, or communal warrant – which effectively negates the vital tension between knowledge and truth. More precisely, it is the tension between what is presently known concerning some limited region of an infinite object-domain and what is yet to be discovered in the quest for truth. Only insofar as that tension exists can thought harbour a motivating sense of unfulfilled potential or unrealised possibility, a sense periodically sharpened by the emergence of hitherto unlooked-for problems and paradoxes. It is at times like these – as in the years before Cantor's epochal discovery – that there is the greatest likelihood of thought undergoing the impact of some decisive 'event' that brings about a drastic shift in its range of ontological commitments, or (most strikingly in this case) a huge expansion in its scope for ontological research. In mathematics as in politics, the problems accrue and find a focus or point of maximal intensity – what Badiou terms an 'evental site' – where the existing state (whether state of knowledge or political state) comes up against a singular challenge to its power of comprehension or legitimate rule. Indeed the analogy is pressed yet further: just as the history of politics is one of successive failed or suppressed revolutions, like the 1872 Paris Commune, that nonetheless leave a indelible mark and look forward to some future event by which they might retroactively be redeemed, so likewise mathematics offers many examples (among them the history of efforts to cope with the idea of infinity, or attempts to find a proof-procedure for long-standing puzzles like Fermat's Last Theorem) of repeated endeavours that assume their true significance only with the advent of some later breakthrough discovery. Above all, for Badiou, the event that should have wrought a full-scale revolution in our sense of ontological possibility across every domain of thought was Cantor's discovery of a way to deploy the resources of set theory as a means not only of conceiving infinity but – what had seemed altogether absurd to thinkers from Galileo down – of reckoning with its various 'sizes' or cardinalities.

Thus Cantor truly revolutionised our powers of thought when he managed to 'turn paradox into concept', that is, when he transformed the topic of infinity from a source of philosophical disquiet and bafflement to the immensely productive source of new ideas that David Hilbert described as a 'mathematician's paradise'. Such was Cantor's famous 'diagonal' proof of the existence of multiple infinities, a proof that Badiou takes to have established once and for all that thought is capable of making advances beyond anything contained within or directly entailed by some existing state of knowledge. So when Badiou issues his much-discussed and much-criticised claim that 'mathematics is ontology' he means – quite literally – that only by thinking these issues through in the terms provided by a strict (extensionally defined) set-theoretical approach can we adequately address ontological questions, whether of a global or a regional character. Furthermore, the discourse that explains and 'applies' all this – Badiou's own discourse, or the purely expository parts thereof – must be counted as belonging to the genre of metaontology since it has the primary function of locating the specific situations in which some particular ontology is manifest and then drawing out the concealed problematic that portends a situation-transforming event.

The distinction between knowledge and thought – like that between knowledge and truth – is absolutely crucial to Badiou's account of what occurs at those breakthrough moments when a standing anomaly or obstacle to progress (such as prevented earlier thinkers from conceiving the existence of 'actual' as opposed to merely 'virtual' infinities) suddenly becomes a spur to renewed speculation and thereby the means of making a discovery quite beyond anything previously envisaged. This is Badiou's cardinal claim with regard to the 'future-anterior' modality of truth-oriented thought, i.e. its dependence on the prospect of eventually *having been* brought to the point of discovery or proof through a procedure that *would not* have been possible in the absence of just that prerequisite stage in the often long-drawn process of enquiry through which truths emerge. That is to say, if it is the case (*contra* anti-realists and intuitionists) that truth might always surpass knowledge in any given situation – that there exist verification-transcendent or recognition-transcendent truths such that a conjecture is warranted by them even though that warrant cannot yet be known through any available method of proof – then this will require that there should also exist some potential but so far unutilised analogue to the procedure of Cantorian 'diagonalisation' that would, if applied, yield just that sought-after result.

Hence Badiou's stress on the indiscernible, on whatever cannot be discerned, or – as he more paradoxically puts it – whatever may be 'indiscerned' within some given situation. Its effects become manifest, though only later on, through further engagement with the problems, contradictions, anomalies, discrepancies, excesses of inclusion over belonging, of inconsistent over consistent multiplicity, and so forth, which constitute an intrinsic (even if so far unrecognised) feature of that same situation. It is here that we can see the most original aspect of Badiou's ontology, namely its ability to make full allowance for the recognition-transcendent character of truth while also – via the open-ended dialectic of being and event – allowing for the ways in which thought can undergo some unforeseen and thus genuinely epochal or breakthrough event. Where ontology has to do with a certain situation – some given state of being or correlative state of knowledge concerning it – metaontology is the discipline of thought that draws our attention to what's thereby concealed, obscured, or repressed concerning the 'state of the situation'. For it is precisely by reflecting on the difference between them, or (via the resources of set theory) the extent to which the latter exceeds the former, that philosophy finds its Badiou-appointed role as a metaontological means of accounting for transformative or epochal events.

P

PASCAL

Dominiek Hoens

In Badiou's work, Blaise Pascal (1623–1662) belongs to a series of names that also includes Kierkegaard, Nietzsche, Wittgenstein and Lacan. These authors are qualified as antiphilosophers, meaning that their main polemical target is the philosophy of their time. In the case of Pascal, it is Descartes who is considered 'to deplete in the concept the most precious aspect of existence, which is interiority' (*LW* 425). As Pascal finds in interiority and existence the starting point for much of his writing, his arguments against Cartesian rationalism and apology for Christianity cannot avoid a subjective point of enunciation (541). Badiou's only text on Pascal, 'Mediation 21' of *BE*, expresses a profound sympathy for Pascal's antiphilosophical intervention. Not only does Pascal dare to think against the grain of his time, but his articulation of what the 'miracle' of Christianity stands for resembles, in a formal yet profound way, Badiou's theory of the event and the subjective, militant fidelity to it.

This becomes clear in Badiou's analysis of Pascal's *pensée*: 'Except in Jesus Christ, we do not know the meaning of life, or death, or God, or ourselves.' In this statement one finds all the parameters of the doctrine of the event. If the death of God is an event, it does not consist in an account of the circumstances and details of the death of Christ on the cross, but in the claim that an incarnated God is subjected to death. This entails that the divine One is divided into a Two, Father *and* Son, into a Two that cannot be reduced to the simplicity of a self-identical presence. From the perspective of the Roman state, this event is deemed non-existent and foolish, signalled, among other instances, by the description that Pliny the Younger gives of it as 'extravagant superstition' in a letter (AD 112) to Emperor Trajan. Equally important for Badiou is the role of the Church, qualified as 'the first institution in human history to pretend to universality' (*BE* 214), consisting in the organising of a fidelity to the Christ-event. The importance of the Church is underlined by the Pascal quote that Badiou uses as a motto for this particular chapter: 'The history of the Church should, properly speaking, be called the history of truth.' (For more on Badiou as a reader of Kierkegaard, see the 2010 interview with Badiou in *Europe: Revue littéraire mensuelle*, and that in 2007 published in *Magazine Littéraire*.)

This can be directly related to Badiou's idea that truth is post-evental, which requires an organisation of the faithful within a party, or a church, in order to be the support (*subjectum*) of the generic or post-evental truth procedure.

The history of this Church, however, is traversed by discussions about the way the event of Christ should be understood and related to. In *SP*, Chapter 4, Badiou points out the differences that separate Pascal from the more radical Saint Paul. First, Christ is conceived by Pascal as a medium, an instance mediating between Christians and God. Despite our dereliction and ignorance, we know God thanks to Christ and are called upon to observe rules and laws that stem from the Old Testament. Paul, on the contrary, considers the event of Christ as an advent that breaks with the hierarchical relation between God and human beings: it annuls the law and installs a universal equality (cf. *SP*). A second and more decisive difference regards the status of Christian discourse. Whereas Paul emphasises the 'lunacy' of Christian thought, Pascal argues that the non-believer of the Christian truth can be persuaded otherwise by referring to miracles

and to the Prophets that predicted Christ's coming. This attempt at providing solid proof for belief in Christ goes hand-in-hand with the reliance
on a mystical intimacy filled with ineffable words. In this aspect, too, Paul
is closer to Badiou than is Pascal, for the latter tends to equate truth with
divine suggestion, while the former understood that truth can only be
elaborated in a procedure, that is, a preaching with a universal address,
and hence does not refer to any incommunicable revelation.

Pascal's emphasis on persuasion should be situated in the historical
context of his intervention. The emergence of modern science in particular provoked two new ways of thinking and defending Christianity. One
consists in trying to bring Christianity to accord with scientific thought;
the other separates the realm of the religious from the domain of science.
Whereas the first leads to the idea of an abstract, clock-maker God, the
second establishes a sphere beyond the reach of science and which is ultimately indifferent to it. In this sphere, a different God appears: 'the God
of Abraham, the God of Isaac, God of Jacob, not of the philosophers and
the scholars' (*Pensées*, frag. 177 [23 November 1654]). This God is different, for he confronts the Christian with the question of belief and trust
in the absence of a proof that any such God exists, and demands that the
believer rely on God's grace even though this grace cannot be calculated,
provoked or bargained with.

It is no accident that this God occupies a central place in some of the
antiphilosophers Badiou is interested in: Pascal, Kierkegaard and Lacan.
Badiou will reformulate the questions and theses provoked by such a
divine yet opaque supplement to our finite, earthly life in a more formal
and explicitly atheist manner. Grace gets 'banalised' through its mathematical description and the argument demonstrating it as an immanent
occurrence, to wit an event. Comparable to divine grace, this event is rare
and cannot be calculated, predicted, or simply stated; however, rather than
a transcendent, divine intervention into the finite realm of humanity, the
event is simply a supplement emerging within and going beyond a given
situation. Whether Badiou completely succeeds in secularising divine
grace and avoids any Christian implications when arguing in favour of a
supernumerary event that breaks with the normal ordering of a situation
should be discussed in closer detail elsewhere. Of special interest would
be to compare two readings of Pascal, one by the philosopher Badiou and
the other by the antiphilosopher Jacques Lacan. (Lacan discusses Pascal's
notorious wager in two of his seminars, unpublished in English: *The Object
of Psychoanalysis* (1965–6) and *From an Other to the other* (1968–9).) This
would answer the question as to how and to what extent the event separates Badiou's philosophy from one of his main sources of inspiration, i.e.
(Christian) antiphilosophy.

PHILOSOPHICAL SITUATION

Steven Corcoran

The idea that philosophy should come out of its ivory tower and descend from the cold abstraction of its concepts into the real world always begs the question: what exactly is the real life in which the philosopher is called to intervene? We can give a first answer to this question by looking at two sorts of supposedly philosophical books. First, there is the veritable phenomenon of bestsellers like Alain de Botton's *Consolations of Philosophy*. In the latter, for example, Socrates is called upon to teach us how, in the face of our unpopularity, we can learn to find unexpected pleasures; how Schopenhauer can help us to deal with our love pains, and so on – in short, we are shown how we might relativise our experiences and see that, faced with our suffering and feelings of insignificance, philosophy gives us the wisdom to grasp what real life is actually about – a life freed from the media-propagated ideals of the rich and famous that obscure it. This is one way of rendering an image of philosophy as restored to its function: namely, to change the lives of those who dedicate themselves to it.

Critics of such books often rightly complain that philosophy would thus be about confining us to our existential problems. For them, the wisdom of philosophy does much more than afford us such private consolations: it has a special role to play in tackling broader issues of human dignity and freedom in the modern world. For this demand there are books, not as blessed with sales, whose authors claim that philosophy can be consulted for the unique perspective it sheds on contemporary ethical problems: much ink has been spilt, for example, on the apparent moral crisis provoked by biogenetics as regards human autonomy and dignity, as it has on the crisis of an open democracy in the face of 'Islamic' extremism. To the potentially explosive results of the former, a certain neo-Kantianism replies, while tacitly accepting such research, that limits must nonetheless be set on the temptation to 'go too far', to transgress human nature. As for the latter, the question of whether or not to maintain our liberal 'openness', at the risk of losing ourselves in the face of modern 'extremism', and those who hate 'us', or assert our identity more strongly (cf. *FB*), is a not a radical choice but conceals the real question. The postmodern ethics of otherness that regulates this debate – and emphasises, for example, the need to adopt a form of communication that respects the other qua other – is ultimately inseparable from the intolerance against those 'inhuman' others who do not display this same respect for otherness. It is thus inseparable from the current forms of state intervention, both at home and abroad, that are justified on the basis of the need to protect our 'good' democratic values against 'evil' others. In both cases philosophy is reduced 'to conserving, spreading and consolidating the established model of humanity', rather than being attentive to the signs that compel us to alter our philosophical preconceptions and ethical world picture.

What philosophy should strive to make clear is that these debates present false alternatives, which both point to and conceal the sign of a real problem. Badiou is adamant that philosophy, if it is worth anything, must be about the invention of such new problems, which are 'irreducible to any preconceived idea of human nature' (*PP* 73) or to the state of things. If the philosopher merely takes a detour through the concept to illuminate and return us to real life, slightly modified, consoled, justified, then he or she becomes indistinguishable from the swarm of consultants, doctors, psychologists, sociologists, and other experts daily informing us how to act and live, how to enjoy life more, within a given horizon of the possible. The essential point of all great philosophers consists, says Badiou, in the theme of the singular universal, of an excessive point beyond particularity that is also directly universal, beyond all the particularities on which are based the ready-made problems that 'society', which is generally to say powerful interests, throws up. Only this presupposes not that universality is a directly human experience (i.e. something that pertains to our fundamental finitude), but that it contains an element of the inhuman, or infinity in Badiou's language – in short, a human capacity for the infinite.

Badiou's view of the conditions under which these new problems 'for everyone' are constructed gives considerable direction to this singular philosophical commitment. At its most generic level, we might sum up this task of intervening in the present by paraphrasing something the German poet Rilke is reported to have said: the philosopher aims not to help you change *your* life, but to live your *change* – i.e. to draw the consequences of something, of an event, of a problem, that exceeds you.

So when does a situation become philosophical for Badiou? Under what circumstances does philosophy have something to say to us about life, or rather its transformation? A situation is *for* philosophy, or indicates that a problem needs inventing, when it displays the following three characteristics.

First, when it involves a fundamental encounter. Badiou's example is the discussion between Socrates and Callicles in Plato's *Gorgias*. But this discussion is not one: between Callicles arguing that 'might is right', that the happy man is a tyrant, and Socrates claiming that the man of truth is happy (or just), there is no real dialogue, but instead a struggle between two irreconcilable types of thought. Between the ideas that the powerful are just and that justice is thought, there is no common measure. Plato's staging of the encounter, Badiou argues, is one in which neither side could be said to have engaged in the discussion in a fair or 'amicable' way. What this staging thus means to show, according to Badiou, is precisely the stakes of having two radically different types of thought. It is to show that between two such types of thought it is necessary to choose, that we must choose and that this is a choice of existence. Philosophy's task is to shed light on the choice. Consequently, philosophy does not concern itself with apparent struggles that are actually well-regulated and simply part of the normal running of things. The philosopher, says Badiou, does not give one advice, for example, on how to vote in an election, the common norm of which, being democratic alternation, is grounded in the consensus on the market economy, such that the politics of the parties voted in are generally the same. As such there is nothing in elections that points, says Badiou, to the need to invent a new problem.

Badiou illustrates the second characteristic of a philosophical situation with the example of the death of the great Greek mathematician Archimedes. Here we have another encounter which is precisely a clash over a choice of existence that ends in the use of state violence. As that mathematical genius, Archimedes, pondered the mathematical figures he had been drawing in the sand on a Sicilian beach, a soldier arrived, sent by the conquering Roman general Marcellus. The soldier had come to tell him that the general wanted to see him. Archimedes' refusal to interrupt his demonstrations immediately upon this summons elicited first incomprehension and then the fury of the soldier, who was unable to believe that someone could refuse to obey an order from General Marcellus. Repeated refusals became too much for the soldier, who drew his sword and slayed Archimedes, leaving him to die slumped over his demonstrations in the sand. The example is a perfect illustration of the gap without common measure between the right of state and a process of creative thought. Philosophy's task is to think about this gap, to shed light on the distance between the blind and routine power of state and irreducibly singular processes of creative thought. This distance is today usually carefully administered by the state (which considers mathematics only from the viewpoint of its practical applicability), but sometimes the encounter is direct, and often ends in a violent act that is symptomatic of this gap.

The third aspect of a situation that is for philosophy, in which philosophy proposes a new problem for everyone, is the exceptional character of any process of thought. This is beautifully illustrated, for Badiou, by Mizoguchi's film *The Crucified Lovers*. Set in medieval Japan, the film depicts the love encounter between a married woman and a worker of the woman's husband, the wealthy owner of a scroll manufactory. Accused of adultery, an offense punishable by death in these times, they flee but are eventually captured. The hint of a 'smile' on the lovers' faces as they are led to their death creates a philosophical situation, says Badiou. Far from being the sign of a desire for romantic fusion in death – and further still from any liberal notion of love as a mutually advantageous contract – the smile indicates that the lovers did not desire to die, but instead that love is what resists death, in indifference to established custom. Philosophy here shows again that between the event of love and the rules of ordinary life, 'one must choose'. It says that 'we must know what we have to say about what is not ordinary', that we must think through the event's transformation of life.

The philosopher is thus someone who thinks a paradoxical 'relation without relation', who invents a problem to show that this paradoxical relation can be thought. This sets Badiou at odds with more postmodern notions of philosophical commitment that equate it with critique. Postmodernism, in the guise of a 'deep' ethics of the other, tells us something like: we live in an imperfect world, and any attempt at 'changing its foundation' will lead to catastrophe. It is the epitome of a 'philosophical commitment' that lies in saying, negatively, what is false, unacceptable, evil, causes suffering, etc. On the political level, it is perfectly compatible with a 'leftist' stance that vents its indignation at the blatant injustices of capitalism, while vigorously defending parliamentary democracy as the guarantee of difference – with the idea that any attempt to impose a hierarchy of ideas amounts to a kind of ethical violence against an original plurality. But this merely serves as a way to defend the alternation of political parties in power, i.e., a perfectly well-regulated systemic functioning. If philosophy is to intervene in the present in an affirmative way, to propose to us a way of thinking the paradox of a relation without relation, it can only do so on the basis of another political proposition, of an incommensurability that demands a choice. The philosopher does not intervene on the side of the particular (state), but on the side of the universal exception to the rule – if there is a choice to be clarified, it lies between representative democracy *and* another proposition on democracy at a distance from the state.

PLATONISM/ANTI-PLATONISM

A. J. Bartlett

The history of philosophy has maintained an ambiguous relationship to Plato. This ambiguity, marked on the one hand by fidelity to what he founds, and on the other, the recovery of what this foundation conceals, leaves a complex mark on the contemporary philosophical scene such that Badiou sees it fit to label all the major strands of philosophy since Nietzsche as 'anti-Platonist' (the so-called mathematical Platonists included, cf. *TW* 3–58). For Badiou, it is from this anti-Platonism, whose condition is 'Platonic', that 'Plato must be restored'. In his seminar from 2007 to 2010, significantly titled 'Plato *for* Today', Badiou repeats and extends the six categories of anti-Platonism he identified in *MP* in 1989: the vitalist (Nietzsche, Bergson, Deleuze), the analytic (Russell, Wittgenstein, Carnap), the Marxist, the existentialist (Kierkegaard, Sartre), the Heideggerian, and that of the 'political philosophers' (Arendt and Popper). He says that 'ultimately the twentieth century reveals a constellation of multiple and heteroclite anti-Platonisms'. Taken together, 'their anti-Platonism is incoherent', but what unites them is that each ostensibly accuses Plato of being ignorant of something essential to philosophy, and 'this something is identified with the real itself' (change for the vitalists, language for the analytics, concrete social relations for the Marxists, negation for the existentialists, thought in as much as it is other than understanding for Heidegger, democracy for the political philosophers). In *DCB*, Badiou gives the most succinct formulation of this 'Platonism', noting that it is a common figure that circulates 'from Heidegger to Deleuze, from Nietzsche to Bergson, but also from Marxists to positivists, and that is still used by the counterrevolutionary new philosophers as well as by neo-Kantian moralists'. For all these figures, this term of insult, Platonism, 'is the great fallacious construction of modernity and postmodernity alike. It serves as a type of general negative prop: it only exists to legitimate the new under the heading of anti-Platonism' (101–2).

As with the generalised sophistry in Plato's Athens, the influence of contemporary (anti-)Platonism (which is not necessarily sophistic in this same way) extends across the contemporary 'system of reference' into the fields of politics, love, mathematics, art. In both *CS* and *IT*, Badiou elaborates three predominant 'philosophical' tendencies derived from this anti-Platonist collective: (1) the hermeneutic tendency, whose central concept is interpretation; (2) the analytic one, whose concept is the 'rule'; and (3) the postmodern one, concerned with the deconstruction of totalities in favour of the diverse and the multiple. To these three tendencies could certainly be added an 'aristocratic Platonism', recognisable in the work of figures such as Leo Strauss and Alan Bloom. The virtue of this latter tendency is its recognition of the category of truth, but its conception of justice remains decidedly pedagogical. Nevertheless, with regard to the predominant three, Badiou shows that what they have in common is a commitment to language, its capacities, rules and diversity such that language is the 'great historical transcendental of our times' (*IT* 46). Contemporary anti-Platonism, he says, effectively 'puts the category of truth on trial' (ibid.), where truth involves the emergence of an exception to contemporary 'democratic materialism', which the linguistic turn reduces to being; that of the exhaustion of knowledge as 'bodies and languages'. The genericity and the singularity of a truth means, as in the *Apology*, that it has no place in the contemporary polis. If it appears there, immanent to the axiom of bodies and languages, it is as an exception to it. In other words, truths are not submitted to the demands of the contemporary transcendental but constitute an exception to it. As in the *Apology*, what must not be is what is in exception.

Badiou agrees with two claims that arise from this anti-Platonism qua contemporary Platonism: 'Being is essentially multiple' (which at first glance seems to mark a challenge to the Platonic idea of truth, given its apparent indexation to the One) (*MP* 103), and the claim that Plato does mark a singular and decisive point in the history of thought. Here Deleuze (*LW* 386) as much as Heidegger (*BE* 125) are central figures of reference. However, concerning the first point of agreement, to say today that being is multiple is to say it falls under the regime of mathematics qua ontology and not that of 'language' – which is entirely consistent with Plato's strategy and conditioning of philosophy. As regards the second point, Plato is to be understood as an *incitement to thought*, he through whom thought is given 'the means to refer to itself as philosophical' and thus 'independently of any total contemplation of the universe or any intuition of the virtual' (*DCB* 102). Plato is decidedly not the moment at which thought turns to despair (an attitude which, ironically, turns on a decision that negates the affirmative and detouring force of Platonic aporia). For Badiou, the rejection of the linguistic (re)turn is predicated on the existence 'of a regime of the thinkable that is inaccessible to this total jurisdiction of language'. This thinking is mathematics and it is 'foundational'. In 'one and the same gesture [it] breaks with the sensible and posits the intelligible', denying, *by* its formal existence, the right of doxa to elevate its knowledge into the 'truth of [an] era' (*TW* 30). Badiou claims that with Plato mathematics is the discourse that 'thinks' the situation, that grasps, beyond what logically constrains it, the form of its being, thus elaborating its consistency without recourse to the vicissitudes of language. For Badiou, then, what is required today against doxa is a 'Platonic gesture', the condition of which is a 'Platonism of the multiple' (*MP* 97–109). Badiou even notes that Plato himself determined the core problem of the latter in the *Parmenides* where the discussion turns on the distinction between *plethos* and *polla*: inconsistent multiplicity and 'consistent' or 'structured' multiplicity. In *LW*, Badiou reaffirms the need for such a gesture in order to 'overcome democratic sophistry by detecting every Subject which participates in an exceptional truth-process' and in *SMP* where, rehearsing *LW*, he elaborates for a Platonic materialism, a materialism of the Idea. 'Plato's problem', he argues, 'which is still ours, is how our experience of a particular world (that which we are given to know, the "knowable") can open up access to eternal, universal – and in this sense – transmundane truths' (*LW* 10). In this work, the Platonic gesture involves the question of denoting the formal distinction of, and the rigorous relation between, Same and Other. In Badiou's terms: of 'being-there'.

Platonism, in Badiou's reinvigorated sense, affirms 'an ontology of the pure multiple without renouncing truth' or, in other words, it declares that the universality of the true is 'transmitted outside of sense' and as such requires that one 'mathematise by hook or by crook' (*LW* 522). The consequences of this for Badiou's philosophy are extensive, involving, as Badiou notes, the Platonic institution of the speculative and formal divisions between being and appearing, truth and opinion, philosophy and sophistry, mathematics and poetry, but also, more implicitly, the orientation of Badiou's own practice, which revolves around Plato's formal demonstration of what constitutes philosophical discourse as a *practice* of separation, division *and* invention. Philosophy is *subtractive* of all forms of 'sophistic' knowledge, thereby holding in abeyance both 'the tutelary figure of the One' (*TW* 37) and the resigned conservatism of the 'rhetoric of instants' (*LW* 511).

That Plato's dialogues are concerned with mathematics, art, love and politics confirms for Badiou the generic importance of Plato for philosophy. Plato's dialogues work through these conditions; his central figure, Socrates, interrogates rhetoricians, orators, businessmen, men of the law courts and so on – all the good men of the state who represent these conditions to the state itself, as to their truth. He effectively subtracts a non-knowledge of this sophistical knowledge in order to begin to think *through* what it is these good men propose as knowledge, in order to make it possible that this knowledge be thought otherwise: specifically, with regard to its *form*. In a parallel move, Badiou notes that to return philosophy to itself *today*, one must take from Heidegger the importance of the ontological question *devoid of its poetic vocation*; from the analytics the 'mathematico-logical revolution of Frege-Cantor' *devoid of their reflexivity to the rule*; from deconstructive-postmodernism (wherein Nietzsche lives posthumously) the inexistence of the one of totality *without recourse to the ineffable*; and from Lacan's antiphilosophy, a modern doctrine of the subject *subtracted from its psycho-sexual topologisation* (*BE* 2). Badiou, as with Plato before him, seeks to free what is essential in these discourses from the linguistic, theological, hermeneutic and logical predicates constraining them, in order to compose a new philosophical form contemporary to its time but ultimately concerned with what philosophy 'had for a long time decided to be, that is, a search for truth' (*IT* 47). As a Platonist, the practice of philosophy for Badiou is not concerned primarily with definition or interpretation but with transformation: it is the discourse of the possibility of transformation – that truths are real, that truth is possible. Philosophy, since Plato and with Plato, composes the *form* of transformation, of thinking, precisely, the 'universal part of a sensible object [as] its participation in the Idea' (*LW* 301–2). For Badiou, Platonism is a matter of the subjective constitution of philosophy: which is simply to think the truths of its time.

POLITICS

Steven Corcoran

The problem of how philosophy is to approach the word politics is especially difficult, as it is itself a stake of political struggle and thus steeped in equivocity. When nineteenth-century workers and feminist movements considered themselves to be engaging in politics it was to demonstrate against their 'de-politicisation', against their relegation to the status of non-political beings that existed in the social or private sphere. It was to show that the very designation by the powers that be of such spheres as non-political was itself a political act. In short, the question of just who is and who is not considered political, and what objects are part or are not part of political consideration, is itself always intrinsic to politics. Philosophy thus encounters the word politics as inherently equivocal or, in Badiou's terms, as a 'split word'.

Badiou's treatment bears out this 'inherently split' aspect, which, he maintains is a key feature of politics, singling it out from the other domains in which truth is in question. Contrary to art, science or love, a political procedure is always determined, within itself, according to a schema that pits one politics against another. One can thus say that in order for politics to exist, the word politics must necessarily designate heterogeneous things. For there is no politics that is not obliged to name as 'politics' something that is adverse to it. As Badiou puts it: 'Politics is an immanent procedure [based on an unconditioned decision], but a procedure that among its names includes the name politics in such a way that it is never its proper name' (SEM 1991: October 24).

The upshot of this is that the name politics remains intrinsically equivocal within politics itself. If politics is thus a genuine concept, as Badiou contends that it is, it falls to philosophy to define it. Against the background of this equivocation, philosophy thus generally starts with a definition of politics. The difficulty in defining it is that, as aforementioned, this equivocation has to be grasped via the scission of the word: a scission that involves something that has no concern with truth, and which is intimately tied to the conflictual, equivocal ordeal of politics. So, if philosophy is constrained to seize politics in the element of truth, this entails the ineluctable purification of the name in philosophy, the history of which one can trace in all the great thinkers.

If political philosophy's approach to this definition remains essentially tied to the question of why it is that people come together in a community, and seeks the ground for politics in sense, or in history, Badiou argues, by contrast, that we can only grasp politics as a radical subtraction from sense or history. This argument is, however, not without historical backing. As the historical mediations that were supposed to open onto communism lost all consistency, under the pressure of historical fluctuation and the evolution of political truth-procedures, Badiou drew the key lesson: history does not bear political subjects. For the philosopher, it thus became crucial to define the conditions for politics as a process of subtraction from history.

His notion of event, that Mallarméan throw of the dice that never abolishes chance, first introduced in *CPBT*, is a key part of his answer to this problematic. If politics is to be of interest for philosophy, if it is something other than games of power, state regulation, the management of desires, and so on, it must depend upon an exception to the formal rules of the state of the situation. As this exception can no longer be that of revolution, in which the party representing the working class aims to destroy the old state order in order to bring about a classless society – for reasons that are not essentially historical but that have to do with ontology and with politics as a procedure of thought – Badiou argues that the evental exception must be configured as a subtraction from the state.

It is his understanding of radical subtraction that enables Badiou to account for the split nature of the word politics. Grasping the word politics from the point of view of its scission means understanding it as designating both the immanent process of the unfolding of an egalitarian political prescription in fidelity to an event, i.e. the emergence of a possibility proscribed by the state of the situation, *and* practices of state, i.e. practices entirely removed from the immanence of truth. (Cf. Badiou's distinction in M between the different – 'interior' and 'exterior' – modes of politics.)

Throughout his work, Badiou has maintained the key importance for philosophy of egalitarian politics as a procedure of thought in its own right. This has culminated in the idea that politics is thus not an object but a condition of philosophy (cf. *BE*, *CS*). Understanding politics as thought implies breaking with traditional identifications of politics, whether as that which is localised in the form of state, the community, or even in emancipation. Identifying politics with the figure of state sovereignty, political philosophy classically presents us with a typology of states, which it subjects to a normative evaluation, with the idea being to discern the good figure of sovereignty compatible with the good figures of the community. More revolutionary identifications of politics have in turn construed it as a form of organisation and consciousness through which people become emancipated from the figures of sovereignty or of the community. This was the core of the revolutionary model, wherein politics is identified with the historical movement of collective being such as it liberates itself through collective operations to de-link itself, through and in revolution, from such figures and affirm its generic nature.

Badiou's understanding of politics as a condition owes much to this latter version of politics. It can indeed be read as the result of his working through of the operations by which the revolutionary identification of politics has, through its immanent problems and deadlocks, failed and called for greater attentiveness. Indeed, the idea that politics is not an object of philosophy but instead a singular procedure of thought that conditions philosophy is explicitly raised as a means to maintain philosophy's alertness to singular and exceptional political occurrences and what they present that is new in thought.

So, understanding politics as a split word means grasping it in its subtraction from history, as a process of thought that cannot be reduced to the form of a unified object of philosophical speculation. Trying to produce a unified philosophical definition of it thus forgets that politics comes before philosophy – politics is not the practice that implements a philosophical theory. Politics itself is thought. If so, then it is crucial to maintain its immanence: political choice can be referred only back to the choice itself, nothing divine or transcendent prescribes the political subject.

Second, the name by which philosophy grasps this process is always anticipatory: it always relates to a 'there will have been' of the truth at stake in the procedure, i.e. it proceeds as if there was a being of political truth, as if the being at stake in political truth has come, will have come, to its being, whereas the infinite procedure of politics itself, forever caught in its incompletion, weaves its being from this process but without being coextensive with it. The philosophical name is an anticipation of the genericity of a politics, which is to say the surmise that, if it remains faithful to its axioms, it will have been true, it will have brought about a generic collective. In reality, however, a politics of emancipation does not bring about such a collective, but instead works within the framework of this genericity thanks to its always specific categories and practices. Its grasping by philosophy cuts straight toward the infinite, by giving a name to the infinity of the procedure, which is its being indeed, but its being forever yet to have come.

So, if it falls to philosophy to define politics, it also falls to it to maintain the separation between these registers. It must be upheld that the philosophical determination of politics is not itself political, since the naming of any collective that bears the political truth courts the risk of disaster. Philosophy must always desist from superposing its temporality, which points to the infinite, the eternal, onto the sequential temporality of politics. The result of not doing so is the projection of an intrinsic destiny or overarching history onto politics and its name, the price of which is that philosophy yields on the irreducible multiplicity of names and places of politics. There can be no projection onto the real of the procedure of the philosophical anticipation of the truth finally come. If politics is a philosophical category, it is only because there are singular political sequences, which is to say, rare, or discontinuous ones that are given in a heterogeneity of places and times through always unique categories. Otherwise it is a category of the state.

The question thus arises of philosophical nomination, of the name by which philosophy, in its anticipation, grasps the multiplicity of political names (e.g. Mao, Lenin, Spartacus. . .). Badiou surveys and mostly rejects the traditional names by which philosophy has received politics, notably since the French Revolution: community, liberty, fraternity, revolution, and so on. All are compromised in one way or another. The one he retains, equality, does not escape this: its particular problem is that it is itself hampered by a sort of economism, such that its philosophical use comes at the price of a threefold operation: 1) a desubstantialisation of the name: equality does not designate any delimitable figure of the collective, does not prescribe any social grouping. However, it does have the virtue of a kind of mathematical abstraction: equality is given in an axiomatic presentation. Without defining any of the terms, one can simply posit that 'all people are equal among themselves', and draw the consequences of this statement. If history can no longer be called upon to support political procedures, the breach must be filled with an axiomatisation that defines the criteria proper of the political event. The essential presupposition here is that every politics supposes an unconditioned prescription, i.e. that a politics stems from an event and relies on a prescription of equality not as that which is to be realised equality, not that which is to be realised, but that whose existence is to be postulated and its consequences created in the here and now (SEM 1991: October 24). 2) An indifferentiation of sense: under this axiomatic presentation, equality finds no guarantor in the register of sense, since it does not prescribe any sense (a sense that the opponents of equality could object to). Its abstraction allows it to play freely outside all hermeneutics in regard to the philosophical nominations of politics. 3) Equality has to be rendered adequate to the infinite, that is, appropriated for infinite situations.

By virtue of these features, argues Badiou, equality can and therefore must be legitimated as the category apt to manifest in the field of politics, what it means that only an egalitarian politics, from the viewpoint of philosophy, can authorise that our time turns toward eternity.

In company with Plato and Marx, what Badiou thus refuses is the idea that the state forms the transcendental of politics, that it organises in advance the pregiven domain of political action. The state (of the situation) relies on a logic of representation such that it infinitely exceeds the presentation of the situation. That is to say that it is impossible to measure the gap between the presentation of the situation (say, the count of all citizens, of those deemed to belong to the political situation) and its representation (the state's ways of grouping this count into taxpayers, income brackets, ethnic identities, religious professions, and so on). This is because (in line with the axioms of transfinite set theory) the number of ways of grouping the initial set is infinitely larger than the initial set itself. Now, combined with the logic of the capitalist economy, a key norm of today's state, an ideology of complexity emerges that is key to the prevailing vision of our 'democratic materialist' world – that there exists an immense complexity of groups and sub-groups, whose contradictions need to be regulated according to strategic insights; that the postmodern situation is so complex that it is impossible to find clear and universal principles of justice and instead it is necessary to find always new rules, technocratic or ethical, for negotiating between groups. But the postmodern state thrives on the idea of the necessary administration of complexity, which it presents as a bulwark against the old blood-soaked dreams of emancipation. What it thrives on in particular is the *indetermination* of this errancy, the indetermination of its superpower over the situation.

Far from making strategic judgements about the infinite complexities and complicities of history, far from engaging in interminable negotiations of culture and psychology, a genuinely political procedure will cut through this in order to make visible the inexistent element excluded by the state regulation of the normal order of things. For Badiou, defining politics in an adequate way involves eight different aspects, which we shall now go through. (1) Politics is a process of producing a generic collective that breaks through the knowledge of the 'political culture' of a given time and its established hierarchy. It 'makes truth of the situation as infinity and as virtually subtracted from the necessary existence of the state'. The specific impossibility of this truth, its real, is pure presentation (i.e.

something like the realisation of a society of free association without state), or, in a word, communism. Why? Because the unachievable real of such politics is the withering away of the state.

Politics has the precise effect of simplifying this infinite complexity, of suspending its efficacy. Its process involves an appeal to clear and universal principles of justice that prescribe a stark alternative based on a radical exception to this order, an exception that always emerges in one site (since truth is always *of* a situation). The site of the political event is that which in presentation is the most withdrawn from representation, that which counts least for the state.

Politics also always involves (2) a nominal question: what is the name of those that occupy this site, which Badiou refers to as 'the edge of the void'? For Marx, this site was the celebrated proletariat, those who had nothing to lose but their chains and whose interests could thus be identified with the becoming of generic humanity. Similarly, for Badiou, the evental site is 'the worker without papers' – a new possible can be created in the situation, or an event can emerge, only when, to put it in the terms of *LW*, that which is inexistent in it comes to have a maximal existence, an existence for which the state of the situation cannot account: either it is affirmed that this previously inexistent element also belongs to the situation politically speaking, and then we are in justice, or this upheaval of the prevailing order is discounted as a mere chaotic disturbance by foreign elements, and we are not.

The eclipse of the event leaves as a trace an indexation or a measure of the excess of the power of the state. In other words, an event measures the indetermination by leaving a trace (a name, a statement) that remains as a stigma in the situation (3). This statement or prescription will set a limit on state representation, which itself will be determined as upholding specific interests within the situation (the event enables a perspective on the state as that which essentially cares for the conditions of existence of specific groups to the exclusion of generic humanity).

Politics (4) is thus nothing but the 'organized collective action which, in conformity with some principles, aims to unfold in the real the consequences of this new possibility' (M 12). This unfolding thus interrupts the indetermination of state power, putting the state itself at a distance. A politics proceeds in this situation within this distance, i.e. it proceeds *as if* the situation had no state structure of representation, with all the hierarchies and exclusions this entails. The 'as if' dimension is crucial here, as the situation remains in the state, but politics exists in the practicable distance carved out on the basis of the prescription – this is its specific freedom.

Badiou's concept of politics thus sets forth a logic that runs directly counter to the ethical turn predicated on respect for the other. Politics can only carry out this maxim of a distance from the state through practicing a logic of the Same and of the impredicable, i.e. through the becoming of the egalitarian norm (5). If differences are *what there are*, and comprise the stuff of state biopolitical administration, then only by the interruption and measuring of the state's indetermination – its superpower over this presentative network of differences – can the practicability of the egalitarian logic be ascertained. In other words, it is essential to measure the state's power – state power is not the goal of egalitarian politics, but it must be gauged in order for an egalitarian politics to be effective (cf. *M* 144).

From this viewpoint, the organisation of egalitarian politics can no longer operate within a finite horizon of state takeover. Any politics of non-domination is properly interminable: while, empirically, a given politics is sequential and finite, its intrinsic character is to be unending, since a generic truth gathers the infinite set of egalitarian acts, or set of consequences, of the event (6). A politics will accordingly work within the situation with the aim of rendering all inegalitarian statements impossible (7). An egalitarian prescription is not simply an egalitarian judgement that opposes the idea of inequality – it is not simply a question of combating inequality by implementing more egalitarian policies. Contrary to the reformist stance, an egalitarian prescription works in the situation directly to combat the very possibility of making inegalitarian statements, to render inequality *impossible*.

Politics, according to Badiou, has its own specific numericality (8), being that which singularises it among the truth procedures. It starts out with a determinate infinite, i.e. the situation or world, and the gap between this infinite and the indeterminate infinite of the state. Then comes the evental emergence enabling this latter to be determined, and lastly the egalitarian norm. If politics thus has an unnameable, a point that cannot be forced in the situation, it is the subjective substantial existence of a communitarian type. This is because whenever politics gives up on its refusal to predicate, and designates a positively existing group that would be the bearer of political truth, it forgoes equality and terroristically marks out that which is not so predicated for annihilation. Crucially, then, an intrinsic part of the definition of politics includes stating the specific evil of which it is capable: the forcing of such an existent, the supposition – rampant today – that communitarian predicates can be political categories. Disaster strikes as the inevitable outcome, in the symbolic and in the real, as the reduction of the other to nothing in the name of the Same.

PRESCRIPTION

Frank Ruda

The term 'prescription' takes its systematic place in Badiou's work with regards to three different dimensions: (1) it delineates the basic operation of the State (of the situation) or of the transcendental of a world (its objective dimension); (2) it plays a crucial role within generic truth procedures (its subjective dimension); and (3) it marks something peculiar for philosophy.

(1) One of the most fundamental non-technical definitions of what Badiou calls 'the state' reads as follows: it is 'that which prescribes what, in a given situation, is the impossibility specific to that situation, from the perspective of the formal prescription of what is possible' (*CH* 243). That is, every state prescribes what is possible within a historical situation. The state thus includes certain things (forms of practice, actions, elements, parts) that it considers impossible. For any regime of the possible sets limits, or boundaries. Prescription on the level of the state installs and constitutes these very limitations (whose abstract rendering can be exemplified by the distinction between a regime of the possible and its specific impossibility) within a specific situation. So, prescription in this first 'objective' sense is what defines a historical situation and its limits. Its limits are included in it only by being excluded from it: the impossibility of a historical situation is singularly specific to it (this is what makes it historical), but is nonetheless included in it, as therein is also delineated all that which (actions, etc.) is excluded from what is presented as being possible (or normal, in the terminology of *BE*). Statist prescription delineates both what is represented in a situation as possible parts of it and the limits of this very possibility (i.e. the elements whose elements do not belong to the situation and are therefore singular). Badiou himself gives a simple example of this logic (outlining some of the implications):

Suppose you have a dish [. . .] full of delicious fruits: apples, pears, strawberries, plums [. . .] But one day, we don't know why, the dish is completely changed. We find apples [. . .] in it, but also, like a vile mixture, stones, snails, pieces of dried mud, dead frogs, and prickles [. . .] [I]t's the beginning of a demand for order: immediate separation of what is good from what is disgusting. The problem here is the problem of classification [. . .] On one side, we have some parts which have a clear name. Take for example the part of the dish including all the strawberries, it's a part of the dish, it's a clear part [. . .] You can also have a bigger part, a more general part, for example all the fruits [. . .] It's also a part that has a clear name

[. . .] But [. . .] you have some very strange multiplicities. What can we say about a part composed of two apples, three prickles, one dead frog, one strawberry and seven pieces of dried mud? Certainly it's a part of the contents of the dish. But, certainly too, it's a part without a name, without a clear name [. . .] Generally speaking, a law – what we call a law – is the prescription of reasonable order in that sort of situation [. . .] A law is a decision to accept as really existing only some parts of the dish of collective life [. . .] And it's very important to notice that finally a law is always a decision about existence. (Badiou 2011f: 14–15)

The state – the instance which installs a law in the aforementioned sense – prescribes what is possible, which is to say it frames what a possible exist-ence (a possible part of a situation) is. It does so, in keeping with the above example, by inscribing a reasonable order that relies on the distinction between legitimate and illegitimate existences. This becomes even more intelligible by moving from this ontological perspective to a phenomeno-logical one. For such a prescription, in the terminology of LW, inscribes a specific way of ordering the elements of a given situation: it prescribes what appears with maximal intensity and what appears with the least possible intensity in a world (therein opening the realm of intermediary intensities of appearance). And Badiou claims that to appear in a world is to exist in it.

It can be inferred, then, that a prescription in this first sense also always includes an 'objective' prescription of existence within a specific world. Hence, existence is conceptually bound to a structure of order: something exists minimally, there are intermediary existences and there is a maximal degree of existence within a given world (of appearances). These differen-tiations of existence (via intensity or degree) make it possible to conceptu-alise them within an order-structure. A prescription of such a historically specific regime of what is possible (and thus also impossible), then, can be read as that which depicts the transcendental coordinates of what appears in a world, of what exists and of what is inexistent in it.

In this sense prescription is linked to the possible and impossible as much as to the existence–inexistence distinction. Badiou takes up these two levels (ontological and phenomenological) with the claim that: 'The state is a transcendental which represents itself in the form of a pre-scription but is itself subtracted from this prescription' (SEM 2007–8). The state prescribes a regime of the possible, therein delineating the transcendental order of a world, but the very locus of the state, of this transcendental prescription (of existence), is itself subtracted from this very prescription. This means that the (transcendental) order itself is not part of the transcendental order. In non-technical terms, it can be inferred that this is one (transcendental) argument for why there is a 'measureless'

(*M*, 146) excess of state power (this is easily applicable to political situations in which it is never clear how much power the state really has). There
is an excess of state power, it might be argued – in leaving aside the proper
set-theoretical argument behind it – because the transcendental and existential order it constructs cannot itself be located within that very order. It
lies somewhere 'beyond' it. It is non-localisable, i.e. immeasurable on the
given scale. And this necessarily leads to the second systematic dimension
of 'prescription' in Badiou's work. This shift implies a transition from the
'objective dimension' to the 'subjective':

(2) The immediate remainder – one might say the immediate consequence – of an event is a trace. To use an example: after something unforeseen happens in the realm of, say, politics, such an event remains as a trace,
which usually takes the form of a prescription. 'The trace of the event
[. . .] consists of a statement in the form of prescription [. . .]' (*LW* 80).
'Prescription' here means that something new arises that takes the form
of what might be best understood as a historicised categorical imperative,
in the Kantian sense. It is a trace of an event, as it fulfils the function
of 'seeing' the given situation/world from the 'perspective of this very
event'. It is therefore grounded on something formerly impossible. From
the perspective of the state the trace is founded on something that does not
exist, as an event is marked by an indistinguishability between being and
nothing, of appearance and disappearance. Its trace, i.e. a prescription, can
thus be characterised as a newly emerged axiomatic (in politics: militant)
judgement. The prescription in this sense is thus always localised within
a specific situation. But it is also axiomatic, as it is 'a prescription that
nothing came to found' (*CS* 156). It is not simply another transcendental
order – rather something like a local perturbation, a local mutation of the
given order (of existences and appearance). It is founded on nothing, since
the event in itself is not a substance; it is nothing but the consequences it
will have yielded. But such a 'nothing', such a void of the situation, converts a previous impossibility into a new possibility. And its 'place', that
is, the when and where of the eventual occurrence, is radically contingent
and unforeseeable. As much as the trace of such an unforeseen happening,
a prescription is marked by contingency. Prescriptions are thus 'namings
of this very void' (*CS* 156), which emerge within a world and convert a
specific impossibility into a new possibility.

The first effect of an emergence of a prescription is that the state of the
situation becomes measurable. Why? Because something formerly impossible becomes a new possibility (this is an event) and thus changes the very
transcendental coordinates of the world, the very regime of the possible
installed by the state. This means that the state then has to show its face,

as it cannot continue to govern the situation in the same manner it did before. The state has to intervene, aiming and preventing any change from happening, and thereby it enters the scene of history. Simply put: it has to demonstrate its power by attempting to prevent any change from happening. The means which necessitate that it does so is precisely such an historical imperative, a prescription touching upon something real (as that which is left over 'after' an event). For example, the slogan 'all proletarians unite' exemplifies the emergence of such an imperative in a historically specific situation. It is historically specific as it has not existed since time immemorial, and thus takes a singular form. But it is also an imperative both because it demands that all actions of the historically specific 'agents' that commit to it – for 'the militant[s] of an unconditioned prescription' (*CS* 152) – attempt to act in accordance with it; and because it is voided of all concrete content such that it does not indicate 'how' one can act within the situation in a way that action accords with this axiom. A prescription never prescribes how it should be followed: this very structure explains why it touches upon something real. It does not delineate a regime of the possible; indeed, to continue the unfolding of the consequences of the event it can be necessary to do what, from the perspective of the given order, seems impossible. This is to say that at the most fundamental layer with regard to the 'subjective dimension', a prescription demands that one continues in fidelity to the event (with the unfolding of its consequences) even if it seems impossible. This is the very basic structure of a subjective prescription within a truth procedure.

Such subjective prescriptions fulfil multiple functions within a post-evental truth procedure: for such historicised imperatives enable the perpetuated unfolding of the consequences of an event (i.e. the fidelity to the procedure) by perpetuating the contingency of its own emergence (i.e., the event). If a truth procedure traverses a given situation, it does so by investigating, one element after another, whether it is connected positively or negatively to the event (thus building up a new body of elements). After the Russian Revolution, for example, there were elements of the given situation that stood in a positive relation to this event (supporting or partaking in it) and others that had a negative relation to it (remaining indifferent to what happened or even fighting against it). Although the trajectory of the truth procedure that generates a diagonal through the situation is completely aleatory, there is a certain regulatory momentum in it. The prescription ('all proletarians unite') prescribes that only those for whom it has a meaning (who want to live and act accordingly) stand in a positive relation to the event that generated it. All others stand in a negative relation to it. But a prescription does not prescribe which terms or elements are investigated first or second, and so on. What is prescribed is only that an arbitrarily chosen element of the situation is positively or negatively connected to the event. A prescription introduces a division within any world or situation.

This is why '[t]he faithful connection operator prescribes if one or another term of the situation is linked or not to the supernumerary name of the event. It in no way prescribes, however, that we examine one term before, or rather than, another' (OS 28). This also implies that prescriptions instruct the process of unfolding consequences (that is, the re-grouping of elements of the situation with regards to their positive/negative connection to the event). But if this process assembles elements that do not share a common property (except for standing in a positive relation to the event), it constructs what Badiou calls a truth (or generic set). To rephrase this within the phenomenological domain of appearance: a prescription does not prescribe how one has to treat points (a specific decision as to how to continue the unfolding of a truth) within a world, only that one has to continue.

It is important to note that just as an event is only what it will have been after the consequences it yields have been unfolded, so too the prescription. For it can never be known in advance which elements can be assembled by such a historicised imperative. A prescription becomes what it is when it becomes intelligible what it will have been. It can never be known in advance if the militant prescription 'all proletarians unite!' will make it possible to sustain a process of unfolding consequences or not. Here it can be seen why 'a truth [. . .] is deployed qua the immanent thought of its prescription and its possible effects' (CS 153). To conceive of the immanence of truth is to conceive of the prescriptions and the effects it will have generated. But here it is crucial that the consequences of an event can only be unfolded within a concrete situation, a given world, and following a prescription if there also is a subject. A subject is – ontologically speaking – a local fragment of a truth, the agent of unfolding, bringing what the event will have been into the world. This is why Badiou claims: 'every truth procedure prescribes a Subject of this truth [. . .]' (CH 232). Phenomenologically speaking this means: a subject appears within a world as a new (subjective) body, e.g. the twofold body of a couple as result of a love encounter. An event leaves a trace within a given world, i.e. a prescription, which instructs a subject in its unfolding of the consequences of an event, i.e. a truth, and this truth itself prescribes the rigorous activity of a subject.

Thus a subject is 'sustained only by its own prescription' (Badiou 1991: 21). The term 'prescription' thus also has a subjective dimension: it is that which, as trace of an event, instructs the agent deploying a truth within a situation or world; it thereby allows for conceiving of the immanence of this procedure and only by following such a historicised imperative can a subject sustain itself, uphold its fidelity to the event and perpetuate its (own) consistency. On this subjective level prescription is thus one of the most crucial momentums for the deployment of generic truth procedure. This leads to:

(3) The historically specific shape of philosophy (its concept of truth or subject, for example) depends on what Badiou calls conditions. Although, for him, philosophy always has one and the same task – to state that there are truths, since truth procedures take place within the conditions – it has to reshape its guise, the very means by which it articulates this claim. This is why, on the one hand, philosophy remains the same (its future is its past, so to speak), but on the other, it encounters an extra-philosophical prescription that it must follow. These prescriptions arise from singular truth procedures, or conditions, and force philosophy to remodel itself, its concepts and thus its means. The extra-philosophical prescription that philosophy encounters is constitutive for it. Though philosophy for Badiou does not generate truths, it still has to be contemporaneous with the truths unfolded in the concrete worlds of its conditions. Otherwise, it would not be able properly to fulfil its main task (to articulate that there are truths). This is to say, the prescription that conditions philosophy (and stems from truth procedures within the conditions) is a prescription of the contemporaneity of philosophy with the new present established and inaugurated by the new truth procedures. This is the reason Badiou claims: 'There is something unchanging in the form of a gesture, a gesture of division' that is proper to philosophy (a division, for example, between truth and opinion, democratic materialism and materialist dialectics, etc.), '[a]nd there is, with the pressure of some events and their consequences' the necessity for transforming some aspects of the philosophical gesture' (Badiou 2007e). Philosophy, then, stands under conditions and one way of comprehending philosophy's being-conditioned is to render it in the form of a prescription (of contemporaneity). This prescription enables philosophy to perpetuate its old business in a renewed, contemporary form.

At the same time, the very practice of philosophy also includes a pre-scriptive stance. For, the claim that there are truths (in whatever histori-cally specific manner articulated) is also a prescription. It is not anything that can be deduced from given knowledge, neither is this claim itself a truth: it prescribes that within worlds, or the historical situation, there can be an exception (an event) that forces a decision (to be in a positive or negative relationship with an event) and thus delineates the space for possible subjectivisations. To articulate this prescription adequately, i.e., in a contemporary form, this prescription has to follow the prescription of contemporaneity. Philosophy is thus enabled to prescribe always anew the 'impossible possibility' of exceptions, decisions and thus subjects (within the conditions).

PRESENTATION

Olivia Lucca Fraser

From the thesis that the One is not, Badiou infers that being qua being cannot, itself, be understood as a being. What is it, then, that ontology speaks of? Badiou's solution is that it speaks of the basic form of the 'there is'; the name he gives to this 'there is', taken as an object of discourse, is 'presentation'. The idea of presentation, however, is torturously obscure. What does it mean to speak of a presentation, to speak of an instance of the 'there is'? The 'Dictionary' Badiou appends to *BE* isn't much help: 'presentation', it tells us, is the 'primitive word of metaontology (or of philosophy). Presentation is multiple-being such as it is effectively deployed. "Presentation" is reciprocal with "inconsistent multiplicity". The One is not presented, it results, thus making the multiple consist' (*BE* 519) – a definition which refers us, ultimately, to the mathematical figure of the set – a figure which, by Badiou's lights, is necessarily without a concept. Now, even if ontology proper can do without concepts (and the argument for this is weak), this cannot be said of philosophical metaontology. The extreme conceptual poverty of the figure of 'presentation' in *BE*, in fact, has left Badiou's metaontology open to interpretations which, though rigorously justified with respect to the letter of the text, are nevertheless crippling. The withering critique that Brassier delivers in *Nihil Unbound*, for instance, shows us how the entire philosophical edifice of *BE* plunges unwillingly into a 'black hole of subtraction' precisely insofar as the word 'presentation' fails to find any purchase beyond the austere inscriptions of set theory. (The only alternative, as Brassier keenly observes, is to rescind the exile of concept and evidence from ontology.)

It's well known that the explicit mission of *LW* is to supplement the conceptual poverty of 'presentation' in order to avoid this fate, by deploying a richer notion of 'appearing'. But it is worth asking whether there are any clues in *BE* from which a more robust concept of presentation could be reconstructed.

One such clue is Badiou's remark that he has borrowed the concept of presentation from Lyotard's *Differend* – a text whose encounter with Badiou seems to have dissonantly catalysed his identity axiom. What does

Lyotard say about presentation that could be relevant for us here? The most salient point appears to be that Lyotard introduces the concept of presentation in order to untether the notion of the given from its anchorage in the phenomenological subject. 'The idea of [an immediate] given', he writes, 'is a way of receiving and censuring the idea of a presentation. A presentation does not present a universe to someone; it is the event of its (inapprehensible) presence' (Lyotard 1988: 61). Givenness, argues Lyotard, presupposes an I to whom the given is given; 'presentation' is what remains once this presupposition is annulled. In order for there to be an I, rather, a presentation must already be in effect: 'what resists absolutely the radical doubt is not, as Descartes believed, the "I think", but the "There has been [il y a eu] this phrase: I doubt"' (Lyotard, quoted in Badiou 1984: 853). With this, Lyotard echoes no one so much as Sartre, who insists that

the transcendent I must fall before the stroke of the phenomenological reduction. The Cogito affirms too much. The certain content of the pseudo-'Cogito' is not 'I have consciousness of this chair,' but 'There is [il y a] consciousness of this chair'. (Sartre 1957: 53–4)

What Lyotard calls 'presentation' seems to be just what Sartre calls 'absolutely impersonal consciousness' (Sartre 1957: 37), each distilling the muddied notion of givenness by neutralising the supposition of an I to whom the given would be given.

But this is not quite exact. It is in fact not the same proposition of which Sartre and Lyotard are certain. Sartre affirms the certainty of the 'there is', while Lyotard affirms the certainty of the 'there has been' (the 'il y a' and the 'il y a eu', respectively). The reason for this slight difference has already been suggested in Lyotard's characterisation of presentation as 'inapprehensible'. Presentation, for Lyotard, has, in every case, already occurred by the time that one can be certain of it, whereas for Sartre consciousness apprehends the presentation that is its very occurrence. The inapprehensibility of presentation may lead one to think that 'presence' is not quite the word we're after; Lyotard agrees: 'The There is [Il y a] takes place, it is an occurrence (Ereignis), but it does not present anything to anyone, it does not present itself, and it is not the present, nor is it presence' (Lyotard 75). When one can finally say that one is certain of a presentation having taken place, the presentation of which one speaks is no longer the presentation in which that speech is presented: 'the phrase that presents the presentation itself entails a presentation which it does not present' (ibid., 70). We're always too late.

Does this imperfect analogy with Sartrean consciousness allow us to break open Badiou's opaque claim that 'presence is the exact contrary of presentation'? It will indeed do this if we give the term 'presence' the explicit, Sartrean, definition it lacks in both *BE* and *The Differend*: presence is nothing other than a (non-thetic) reflexivity in presentation. It is because consciousness is consciousness of being conscious of something that we may say that it is a presence (specifically, a presence to something). What would block the importation of this definition of presence into Badiou's edifice, of course, would be any indication that presentation – the exact contrary of presence – admitted of such reflexivity. Does Badiou's set-theoretic ontology permit us to declare the possibility of a presentation that presents itself presenting? Given Badiou's mapping of 'presentation' onto the figure of the 'set', the question becomes: Does Zermelo-Fraenkel set theory allow us to declare the existence of a set a such that $\alpha \in \alpha$?

The answer, in brief, is that such multiplicities, or forms of presentation, are prohibited by the axiom of foundation – and this is the decisive formal difference between the Badiousian theory of presentation and the Sartrean theory of consciousness. If this interpretation is sound, we should expect from it a remarkable consequence: the conceptual tissue of Badiou's philosophy should be such that a violation of the axiom of foundation would unleash structures analogous to what Sartre called 'the immediate structures of the for-itself'. Without going any further in this direction here, I will claim that this is exactly what happens in the Badiousian theory of reflexive presentation – the theory of the event, a theory which can find itself remarkably enriched by this strange, Sartrean experiment.

PSYCHOANALYSIS AND FREUD

Samo Tomšič

In a chapter of *TC* titled 'Sex in Crisis', Badiou pays one of his most systematic homages to Freud. The title itself can be understood as describing Freud's invention as provoking a destabilisation in the field of sexuality. Indeed, Freud himself made precisely this point by associating his epistemological revolution with the respective revolutions of Copernicus and of Darwin. At issue here is a series of destabilisations or decentralisations. The name Copernicus stands for the decentralisation of the universe through modern physics, Darwin for that of life through biology, and Freud for that of thinking. In the field of psychoanalysis, two main achievements set us before a double conceptual break: the conceptualisation of the unconscious in *Interpretation of Dreams* (1900) and the theory of sexuality elaborated in *Three Essays on the Theory of Sexuality* (1905). Both Freudian breaks can be brought together in the notion of *Trieb*, drive.

Badiou points out the importance of this Freudian notion by declaring Freud 'the logician of drives' (*TC* 77) – logician and not biologist, despite his numerous attempts to provide a biological foundation for his theory of drives. At first glance Badiou's characterisation of Freud seems unusual, insofar as his claim combines the procedure of formalisation with the register of that which is 'impossible to formalise'. It is known that in Freud the concept of drive assumes a limit position. It is situated on the very border between the bodily and the psychic, in the grey zone of their obscure and enigmatic interactions. Following Badiou's suggestion, and keeping in mind Lacan's efforts to establish the link between psychoanalysis and mathematics, one could claim that what Freud aims at in his theory of drives concerns the articulation of a conflict inscribed in the very core of the constitution of the subject. This is also why, as Badiou points out in *C*, Freud underlines that, in contrast to the gynecologist, who merely relates to sexuality as a field of dry biological and anatomical facts, psychoanalysts are concerned with sexuality as an immanently inconsistent field of being. If *parlêtre* is sexuated, if its Being is 'Being-towards-sex' (Lacan 2001: 365), then Freud seems to be the one of the rare thinkers to have articulated the strict necessity of thinking Being in terms of non-relation rather than of relation. This was also the core of his (rather problematic) critique of philosophy as *Weltanschauung* in his *New Introductory Lessons on Psychoanalysis*. Reading the corresponding passages we cannot help but notice that Freud has a rather 'anachronistic' or 'classical' image of philosophy, but his point can nevertheless be validated by the persistence of certain philosophies (notably hermeneutics and analytic philosophy, which come under heavy criticism from Badiou) in engaging in the production of meaning. In this respect both Badiou's and Freud's critiques of philosophy could be said to have an underlying affinity.

Freud's theory of sexuality and his discovery of the unconscious have implications for the 'thinking of Being' and in this regard Freud indeed invented a new philosophical condition. In fact, Badiou remains undecided when it comes to the status of psychoanalysis with respect to his philosophy. On the one hand he situates its philosophical relevance as pertaining to the 'love condition', while on the other he sometimes expresses a tendency to attribute to psychoanalysis the status of a fifth condition. Indeed, if we consider the wide-reaching implications of notions such as 'unconscious' and 'drive', then their truths reach well beyond the field of love.

Accentuating the logical aspect of Freudian theory of drives raises a further point, namely the question of materialism, whereby it points to a certain affinity between psychoanalysis and the field opened up by Marx. In *TS*, Badiou strives to establish this connection beyond the problematic contexts of Freudo–Marxism. He implicitly suggests that both Freud and Marx are part of the same epistemological revolution, thereby explicitly following similar suggestions made by Althusser, Foucault and Lacan. Yet he also implies that Freud's invention of psychoanalysis needs to be considered not only in its epistemological but also in its political implications. The connection of both names has continued to remain present in his work for several decades and in a recent debate he defended the Freudian and Marxian breaks against the so-called contemporary obscurantism of the *nouveaux philosophes*. The reactionary critique of psychoanalysis strives to demonstrate that it is a false science, whereas official government policies try to regulate psychoanalytic practice by subjecting it to the 'law of the market' and to its efforts to economise time. According to market logic, the task of psychoanalysis should be to reintegrate pathological cases into existing ideological frames, making of individuals good consumers, ideal workers and compliant voters.

Psychoanalysis also entails another battle with 'contemporary obscurantism', the basis of which is Freud's unprecedented claim, in opposition to the entrepreneurial understanding of the subject as *homo oeconomicus* – the economic subject of cognition – and the idea that everyone should realise his or her 'creative potential', that the mental apparatus and human subjectivity are articulated around an irreducible conflict rather than around a supposedly synthetic Ego, Soul, or cerebral processes. Freud negated the ideological fetishisation and the essentialism of the self, and revealed that the core of the subject consists in *Spaltung*, splitting. He also showed that sexuality is not grounded on a biological or anatomical normative but on a radical absence of any 'sexual relation', just as, following Marx, one could say 'there is no social relation'. In other words, Freud revealed that 'psychic conflict' exhibits the same logic in relation to the individual as the 'social conflict' or 'class struggle' does in relation to society: 'It is beyond doubt that Freud's unconscious and Marx's proletariat have the same epistemological status with regard to the break they introduce in the dominant conception of the subject' (*TS* 280). One can also say, following Lacan's suggestion, that the proletarian is the subject of the unconscious.

As Badiou himself puts it, again in *TS*, the antagonism that is the object of Freud and Marx can also be formulated in terms of the following homology: 'there are two sexes and there are two classes'. And between them there is only the void of non-relation. In this split the Freudian realism of drives converges with the Marxian call for a materialism that would include the field of human practice, the field of subjectivity (see, for instance *TS* 197: 'Freud's materialism finds its foothold in the scission of the ego and the I').

For Badiou one of the fundamental points of Freudian psychoanalysis consists in revealing the fact that 'there is no soul, whose formation would always be moralising' (2010f). In other words, there is no thinking that would be grounded in an underlying self-identity and self-transparency. Or to repeat again Freud's own understanding of his gesture, psychoanalysis introduces a radical decentralisation of thinking, which follows the same logical movement as the decentralisation of the universe in modern physics ('There is no Cosmos', 'There is no universal divine Order') and the decentralisation of life in biology ('There is no Immortality', 'There is no Life beyond life').

PSYCHOANALYSIS AND LACAN

Justin Clemens

It can still come as a surprise to the long-term reader of Badiou just how much his philosophical work – from beginning to end – has been forged out of a confrontation with psychoanalysis and, above all, with Lacanian psychoanalysis. If Badiou's expertise is staggeringly immense, ranging over the history of philosophy, mathematics, political thought, and art, his most consistent interlocutor has proven to be not Plato, but Lacan. If Badiou does discuss Sigmund Freud, the founder of psychoanalysis, in some important pages (see *CS*), it is Lacan who is key. From the moment his teacher, Louis Althusser, sent him to report on the psychoanalyst's seminar in 1959, right up to the present day (therefore for more than fifty years!), Lacan has marked Badiou's thought explicitly and implicitly. Badiou extracts from him doctrines regarding the status of love, science, art, and even of philosophy itself. Of importance to him, in other words, is a very particular part of Lacan's work: above all, the relation it entertains to logic and mathematics, the real as impossible, and the formalisation of the subject.

If this influence is therefore too great to be adequately tracked in a dictionary entry, we should still begin by noting that Lacan crops up in both of Badiou's *Cahiers pour l'analyse* articles of the late 1960s, 'La subversion infinitésimal' (1968) and 'Marque et manque' (1969) (for the English translations, see Hallward and Knox 2012). In the first of these, Badiou invokes three key propositions of Lacan's which will return throughout the former's work in a variety of guises: that the 'impossible characterises the real', that there is an exclusion of the infinite, and that what is excluded from the symbolic returns in the real. In the second, although Badiou is concerned to criticise the 'logic of the signifier' as an ideological metaphysics in regards to the scientific order, he nonetheless provides the following footnote: 'By "logic of the Signifier", we mean here the system of concepts through which the articulation of the subject is conceived: Lack, Place, Placeholder, Suture, Foreclosure, Splitting. These concepts have been produced by Jacques Lacan and we acknowledge a definitive debt to him even as we engage in the process that circumscribes their use: this is the critical procedure' (ibid., 389). Already, in this juvenilia, we are able to discern the lineaments of a long-term engagement: for Badiou, Lacan is a crucial thinker whose propositions must be taken seriously, as they must be subjected to critique on the basis of a logico–mathematical investigation.

Lacan's presence is even legible in the political commentaries of the Maoist period. In *The Rational Kernel of the Hegelian Dialectic* we find Lacan being discussed at key moments of Badiou's commentary, and in terms that would later become familiar from TS (whose seminars date from the same period). In fact, it is extraordinary, in a Maoist text dedicated to the rereading of Hegel's theory of knowledge, that Lacan has become a privileged opponent: 'On the common terrain (Hegelian) of dialectical topology which destroys the representative opposition of the interior/exterior, we need to oppose Lacan's subject-cut [*sujet-coupure*], for which lack is a fixed cause, with the subject-scission of dialectical materialism, for which the disorganisation of force and place is a mobile cause' (RKHD 59). Note here that a similar structure is at play, if the critique this time is not launched from a mathematical perspective but an essentially political one.

TS consecrates this situation, in far more detail and depth: indeed, Lacan is such a significant point of reference that, along with Hegel, Mallarmé, Mao and Marx (and a couple of others), he receives no index listing. The very form of the book 'is that of a seminar, a genre to which Lacan has given a definitive dignity' (*TS* xxxix), and Lacan is praised in the Preface as one of 'the two great modern French dialecticians', Mallarmé being the other (xl). For Badiou, still politicised, it is nonetheless the case that 'Lacan is ahead of the current state of Marxism' (115), precisely because the analyst is 'the theoretician of true scission' (113): Lacan provides a materialist theory of the real as novelty, and as a novelty whose essence is division. Perhaps just as notably, the Lacanian themes that I have already mentioned – the real as impossible, the attempt to treat the real with the symbolic, the torsion of an immanent inassimilable exterior – are once again explicitly on show. Above all, the problem of a militant subject – whether 'the proletariat' or 'the unconscious'; that is, a non-psychological, anti-economic formalisation of the subject as praxis – has moved to the fore.

Lacan therefore survives the break that is *BE* in Badiou's work. While so many other references melt away, are downgraded or emerge, Lacan continues to remain prominent. Badiou will go so far as to announce in his 'Introduction' to *BE* that: 'no conceptual apparatus is adequate unless it is homogeneous with the theoretico-practical orientations of the modern doctrine of the subject, itself internal to practical processes (clinical or political)' (2). The 'clinical or political' is explicitly meant to encompass both Freud and Lacan, on the one hand, and Marx and Lenin on the other. It is not that the psychoanalytic revolution is being illicitly rendered consistent with political revolution, but rather submitted to a double move. The concepts of the psychoanalysts and political activists must be able to be sustained simultaneously, but without reduction. Badiou later provides one brief rule of thumb: 'politics is the inverse of love. Or: love begins where politics ends' (*M* 151; tm).

We need to emphasise that, in *BE*, Badiou's relationship to Lacan hasn't really changed insofar as the latter remains a crucial reference to be critiqued: Lacan points out to Badiou the current limits of thought, the places to pinpoint, and is therefore the guide to be overtaken through a kind of radical philosophical *emulatio*. The Introduction says nothing else: in speaking of how he arrived at his own radical thesis regarding the proposition mathematics = ontology, Badiou remarks of his earlier failures: 'None of this was consistent with the clear Lacanian doctrine according to which the real is the impasse of formalisation' (5). Lacan is at once the guide and the obstacle, above all in the thinking of the relations between the real, formalisation and the subject.

What is different here is that Badiou has finally become Badiou: that is, produced a new philosophy and a new theory of the subject. And he has done this by overgoing Lacan, on the latter's own terms. The very last 'Meditation' in *BE* is titled 'Descartes/Lacan', and contains the following (admittedly compressed and syntactically overwrought) statement: 'What Lacan lacked – despite this lack being legible for us solely after having read what, in his texts, far from lacking, founded the very possibility of a modern regime of the true – is the radical suspension of truth from the supplementation of a being-in-situation by an event which is a separator of the void' (434).

What does this mean? It means that Lacan brought to its limit the modern thought of the subject that emerged with Descartes: a subject that was, as befits such a limit subject, the evacuated substrate of a logical process. In doing so, however, Lacan had to consider the subject as a local structural recurrence, eccentric and void. What Badiou, by contrast, develops in *BE* is a theory of the subject as part of a truth process in the wake of an event that separates that subject from the void. The void for Lacan was the void of the subject; the void for Badiou becomes the void of being; the matheme for Lacan is a local moment of analytic knowledge; the matheme for Badiou is a global paradigm of knowledge in general, and so on. Badiou pursues these developments in a sequence of stunning essays republished in *CS*. What makes these essays different in kind from Badiou's pre-*BE* takes on Lacan is that they are no longer struggling with the analyst as a blocking agent; on the contrary, they now magisterially place psychoanalysis in a perspective that enables new insights for philosophy on the basis of seeing Lacan's limits, for example, vis-à-vis the latter's failure to think the infinite. In this context, two new post-*BE* themes receive their most critical impetus: love and antiphilosophy. The first of these, love, is obviously one of Badiou's four truth conditions, and therefore of critical importance for his own theory. In line with his usual practice, Badiou confronts Lacan regarding the alleged dominance of the phallic function, supplementing the analyst's theory of the sexual non-relation with a theory of the 'Humanity Function' guaranteed by the non-relation of 'Man' and 'Woman'. Regarding antiphilosophy, this term – which has quite a long and strange conceptual history – is picked up directly from Lacan by Badiou, and is formalised as a category of thought in the mid-1990s. What it means is that Badiou can now separate his own project absolutely from that of psychoanalysis, by giving a deeper account of the different modes of philosophy and its others.

Since the essays in *CS*, Badiou has continued to write extensively on Lacan, through *LW* and beyond. However, and despite the supplementation of his own ontology accomplished in *LW*, Badiou's position on Lacan has not significantly changed since the mid-1990s. If we will always find new insights in Badiou's ongoing engagements with the psychoanalyst, the song remains the same: Lacan is the antiphilosopher whose propositions have enabled a return to philosophy by way of the most stringent critique possible.

R

RANCIÈRE AND EQUALITY

Bruno Besana

A common polemics

Since the late 1960s, Alain Badiou and Jacques Rancière have been engaged in a reciprocal polemic, after setting out from a common critique of Althusser. In *DI*, Badiou argues that Althusser's 'scientistic' conception of dialectic materialism forecloses an understanding of mass struggle as a subjective moment. Althusser is charged with reducing the masses to the object of bourgeois ideology, which ultimately insists in them as a false consciousness, and with positing that the possible overcoming of such objectification must pass through scientific knowledge only (that held by the avant-garde of an organised party), knowledge that allows the masses to act without reproducing bourgeois ideology. The masses are thus doubly objectified: first, by the role they perform within bourgeois ideology, and second by 'science', which produces knowledge about the process of their liberation *from outside this* process. The result is that Althusser's thesis 'leads to the foreclosure of the essential point, which is that the proletariat is precisely the first exploited class to constitute itself as a subject' (*DI* 7).

Against Althusser, Badiou claims that it is not true that each 'immediate' action of the masses is pervaded by the mediation of bourgeois ideology, or that only external knowledge provided by a party avant-garde can dismantle the mystifying power of this ideology and restore to the masses their ability to change history. On the contrary, the masses do think and are able to produce an autonomous class ideology. More precisely, a proletarian ideology is that via which a new subject is produced, starting from *within* the specificity of a given moment of confrontation. So, for example, 'even if we are ignorant of the philosophy of Spartacus, we can make a safe bet that its First Article would be the liberation of slaves, from which we will infer that the theory of 'animate tools' found few takers among slaves' (*DI* 4). This example shows how a new ideology arises from within the reality of a given opposition, making it possible to transform the latter into open conflict with the dominant ideology. This is the starting point from which the constitution of a class subjectivity can take place: if the bourgeoisie 'knows perfectly well what to expect from its ideology', (*DI* 3) so, too, does the proletariat.

After thirty years of reciprocal polemic, of 'storm' (cf. 'Jacques Rancière's Lessons: Knowledge and Power After the Storm', in *AFP*), Badiou retraces how, in order to break with the idea that 'politics can be dependent on science, and thus on an institutional transmission' in which 'consciousness comes to the workers from the outside' (*AFP* 114–15), a fundamental element has been Rancière's critique of 'the relationship between the theoreticism of Althusser, his defence of science and the reactionary political authority of the French Communist Party' (102). Badiou notes that Rancière – who was writing under condition of the political sequences of May '68 and of the Cultural Revolution – shows that a new subjectivity appears by acting *under the condition of* a political sequence, and by producing a new knowledge that is not necessarily the reproduction of a dominant ideology. More precisely, Rancière identifies the subject as that which, by its extreme singularity, interrupts the false evidence according to which power and knowledge should have the same source, and, on the contrary, places the production of knowledge under the condition of an act of radical fracture (103–4). Such a conception, Badiou notes, surpasses Foucault's analysis of the knowledge/power relationship on at least one essential aspect: where Foucault focuses on dysfunctional characters whose singularity, problematic for knowledge, produces a shift in the modes of exercise of power, Rancière investigates those who, supposedly silent, stupid or speechless, prove their capacity to articulate a discourse, as in the case of the proletarian who spends his nights awake writing critical essays on literature and politics, when they are supposed to be used for the functions of rest, reproduction or amuse-ment (cf. Rancière's *Proletarian Nights*). In such actions, thought arises in the form of a production of knowledge at a distance from the articulation of power, and the subject appears thus as 'the relation of a non-relation, or [as] the non-relation conceived as a relation' (*AFP* 103).

Equality and thought

Such acts – which show that those who are not in a power position, or have no access to the means of reproduction of knowledge, can think – reveal the idea that thought is produced not only at a distance from power, but also as a fracture within power. Through such acts, knowledge is produced *and* something singular, irregular emerges, something that knowledge ultimately cannot account for. Furthermore, such excessive acts appear to be inseparable from a performative declaration of equality: in fact, by producing knowledge at a distance from power, they remove the inegalitarian criteria that demarcate who is able to produce knowledge and who not.

There is in fact a strict relation between equality and the emergence of novelty in thought. First of all, Rancière claims, thought cannot be bound to inequality: 'inequality cannot think itself [. . .] those who explain domination by superiority fall into the old aporia: the superior ceases being that when he ceases dominating' (1991: 87–8). Inequality – being the hypostatisation of a contingent state of fact – is a merely reproductive form of thought, endlessly positing as a principle the very contingent form of privilege it is supposed to explain. Thus lost in the endless reproduction of a self-fulfilling prophecy, and founded on the slippery terrain of merely contingent state of facts, inequality proves unable to produce novelty in thought. Inequality is thus an absence of novelty (i.e. it is a reproductive system) and an absence of thought (i.e. it relies upon a logical loop).

But if inequality is absence of thought, equality as such is not directly 'thinkable'. As a principle, it cannot be proved and is not an object of knowledge. As Rancière explains: 'it is true that we don't know that men are equal. This is our opinion, and we are trying . . . to verify it' (*IS* 73). In fact equality, being a principle, resists its inscription into an existing form of knowledge; but, at the same time, it implies consequences and verifications, in which a new knowledge is produced. Such knowledge is under condition of a principle, and resists its inscription into established knowledge: so, what Rancière shows, according to Badiou, is that 'knowledge, when it is thought under the condition of an egalitarian maxim [. . .] is clearly displaced with respect to the institution. In my own jargon, this would mean that we obtain a form of knowledge that is *equal to the status of at least one truth*' (*AFP* 124). The knowledge thus produced, more precisely, is a verification, that is, a construction of the consistency of the postulated principle. The verification of equality is thus productive; it has a proper 'intelligence': 'intelligence [. . .] is the power to make oneself understood through another's verification. And only an equal understands an equal. *Equality* and *intelligence* are synonymous terms' (*IS* 72–3). Equality is thus twice bound to thought: first, because its opposite, inequality, is based on a foreclosure of thought, being founded on a logical loop; second, because it is a necessary principle for producing new knowledge, although it is not as such an object of knowledge. Declared as a principle escaping knowledge, equality is verified (made true) in the application of its consequences, i.e. via the construction of specific situations in which the removal of a given inequality allows for new knowledge to arise. Finally, equality is conceived as a formal *principle* (rather than as an ethical *goal*), founded on the exclusion of its contrary, and verified by the unfolding in its consequences: and such a construction of equality is what constitutes, as Badiou remarks, 'Rancière's true abstract passion' (*M* 110).

As a first consequence of this, Badiou identifies Rancière's two fundamental theses concerning the transmission of knowledge under condition
of equality. First, that 'all mastery is an imposture' (ibid.), founded as it
is on a difference in status, on an inequality that it endlessly reproduces.
Second, that 'every bond presumes a master' (ibid.): thought, under condition of equality, appears as an *interruption*, as the removal of the 'bonds'
that support, via a position of mastery, the transmission of knowledge and
the reproduction of a hierarchical structure of power. This double point
identifies at once the maximal proximity between Badiou and Rancière
and their fundamental point of difference.

The axiomatic or procedural status of equality

In sum, Badiou explicitly indicates a double point of proximity with
Rancière: first, the 'fundamental reversal [. . .] introduced into the contemporary conceptual field [by Rancière] [. . .] is that equality is declared
rather than programmatic' (*AFP* 116); second, the idea that, as a result,
'the exercise of equality is always of the order of consequences' (122; tm):
equality, as a principle, appears – to put it in Badiou's terminology – as
an evental truth that interrupts knowledge, and that is verified by a set of
consequences, thus producing a new knowledge. It is exactly here that, in
the third place, a profound disagreement arises concerning the regime of
such consequences. As Badiou puts it, 'Rancière and I are in agreement
on the declared dimension of equality, but we do not share the same
hermeneutics with respect to it. For me, that equality is declared rather
than programmatic means that equality is, in reality, the invariant axiom
of all real sequences of the politics of emancipation' (116). For Badiou,
then, equality is not only a declaration that interrupts a contingent mode
of organisation of inequality, but functions as an axiom that unfolds in a
structured sequence of consequences, while Rancière, as mentioned above,
equates transmission and inequality: the transmission going from a declaration of equality to a moment of construction of consequences implies a
position of mastery, and therefore of inequality. Thus rejecting the idea
of a procedure connecting a declaration and its consequences, Rancière
– Badiou argues – reduces equality to the evanescent moment of a declaration. Consequently, the production of equality is reduced to a series
of declarations, of moments of disconnection, which are disconnected
with respect to each other, rather than structured in a sequence. Given
this refusal of transmission, the productivity of equality is reduced to the
sole declarative moment: equality becomes thus '*simultaneously* condition
and production' (117; tm). Bound to an egalitarianism of principle *and*
of production (what Badiou calls his 'hyperdemocratism'), it becomes

impossible for Rancière to determine any extension of a political action and, more generally, to unfold the consequences of a declarative moment via which new separations and fractures are generated. The problem for Badiou thus becomes: 'what is ultimately, in Rancière's thought, the system of *consequences*?' (*M* 112; tm).

Badiou, paradoxically, subscribes to Rancière's analysis: the consequences of the declaration of equality are of a different nature, and transmission does entangle inequality. But, Badiou adds, the consequences of an axiom do not necessarily have to be of the same nature as the axiom itself. Indeed, equality can, and even has to, proceed by means of inequality. That is, the process of transmission from an initial moment of fracture to a further one can be assured only by an agent that, concentrating the contradictions present in the forces that have produced such a fracture, can lead them towards a further act of fracture: concretely, in the aftermath of an egalitarian declaration, what is necessary is a 'proletarian aristocracy', able to separate the avant-garde forces from the reactionary ones, thus producing a distinction, a transitional inequality. Only such a procedure – following the principle of 'one divides into two' – allows the declarative moment of equality to work as a principle, by determining a constant *Aufhebung* of its results. As Badiou puts it, 'the emergence of a new transmission, for me, presupposes a post-evental constitution of the effects of a heterogeneous body. This heterogeneous body is not immediately democratic because its heterogeneity affects the multiplicity – the demos – at the heart of which it constitutes itself in an immanent but separating manner' (*AFP* 109).

This divergence between Rancière and Badiou begins in DI, where Badiou points out that the possibility of the masses to produce thought – and namely an autonomous class ideology – is realised through the intervention of an avant-garde that allows for 'the penetration into the masses of their own ideas, in a condensed "class-form"', (DI 89) via a process of which 'the general schema is [. . .] mass/class; party; class/mass' (ibid.). Badiou's position in this regard will progressively change over the decades, namely via abandoning the idea of the party as the pivotal point of this schematism; he will nonetheless maintain the idea that novelty can only come about when the contradictions and the ideas that the masses produce are elaborated in a conscious form and offered to the masses by the work of a structured avant-garde, which makes it possible to produce a further moment of division and of change *inside* the masses.

Contrary to this, Rancière has always refused the idea that a transitional moment of inequality, regulated by an 'extrainstitutional master', would be necessary. For him, the (Maoist) idea of a 'master of the movement that aims to depose the masters' (*AFP* 106) inevitably produces 'the subsumption of a bursting, infinite revolt under the transcendence of a personal name' (ibid.; tm). This is why Rancière 'sticks closely to the collective process in its operation to undo the established forms of transmission rather than going further along in the investigation of the very means of the material organisation of consequences' (110), thus foreclosing, for Badiou, the possibility of thinking the temporal consistency of an interruption, its 'taking place'.

Accordingly, Rancière's and Badiou's divorces from the Communist party (and from the idea of the Party) happen in quite different fashions: 'Rancière's departure from the party was a decision made outside of the consideration of the question of organisation: he left that in suspense' (118), while for Badiou, even without the Party, 'political continuity is always something necessarily organised' (ibid.).

Subject and sequence

This political difference is doubled by a different conceptual understanding of equality. Posited by both authors as a logical principle, Badiou understands equality as a truth, which has the strength of an axiom and is verified by a series of actions that incorporate it into a situation by dividing the latter constantly into two (and therefore, as seen, by producing a transitional inequality). For Rancière, by contrast, equality is neither truth nor axiom, but instead inseparably a principle and a gesture that fractures the relation between an established form of knowledge and the power it relies upon. Rather than a truth, equality is thus the emergence of an opinion (*IS* 72–3), one disconnected from all forms of reproduction of consensus, one that cannot be characterised either as a shared or consensual form of knowledge, or as something bearing the imaginary authority of a truth.

Finally, equality is, for Rancière, *a universal principle indiscernible from the absolute singularity of an opinion, which appears as an inconsistency in a well-organised structure of knowledge.* Purely disconnective, it can then only be continued via discontinuity, via another moment of interruption, via the emergence of another opinion, one bearing no connection to the previous one by a structured form of transmission: only in the non-connection between two disconnective moments it is possible to avoid the paradoxes of the constitution of a transitional position of mastery. Thus, while for Badiou equality – qua axiom verified by heterogeneous means – is fundamentally an *an-historical* truth, for Rancière it is a principle coextensive with singular fractures *in history*. This entails that for Rancière there is no dialectic between the universality of the principle and the singularity of the procedure, as they are strictly identified. Thus reducing thought and politics to a purely negative dimension of interruption – as states Badiou at the peak of their polemics – 'Rancière (might be doing) nothing but repeating the essence of our times' (*M* 111), i.e. not concluding, not prescribing anything. Refusing the axiomatic form of truth and its prescriptive character, and reducing politics to evanescent interruptions, Rancière thus maintains that politics cannot be *real*, i.e. cannot perform a constant 'universalisation of its postulate' (113). Furthermore, the *coincidence* of the universal principle and the singularity of the action means that it is not possible to realise the former as a structured sequence. Rendering thus impossible the *construction* of equality, Rancière's position is ultimately 'deceptive' (111) as it forecloses the possibility of *unfolding in a structured sequence* 'the problem that defines contemporary philosophy: what is exactly a universal singularity?' (*TW* 80).

REPRESENTATION

Fabien Tarby

Mathematical meaning

The concept of representation is one of the most important in *BE*. It is a perfectly mathematical concept since its consistency is governed by a fundamental operation of axiomatised set theory, namely inclusion ($\subset$). This operation introduces into the mathematical thought of sets the need for a multiplication of already presented multiplicities. Through inclusion, a presented set reveals all the resources of internal combination particular to it. Representation thus transcends presentation, whose immediately proven excess it is, but in a rigorously deductive and ruled sense, since representation introduces no operator other than the belonging of a presentation ($\in$); in this sense, it is a natural consequence of the regime of pure multiplicity introduced by set theory. Its sign ($\subset$), 'can be defined on the basis of $\in$' writes Badiou, as it is a 'derived sign' (*BE* 102). Given a situation (a presented multiple) it will be said that the state of this situation, or precisely its 'representation', the 'count of the count', the 'metastructure', is defined thus: 'There exists a set of all the subsets of a given set a. It is written p(α)' (102).

Let's take an example. Given the presentation of a multiple defined thus: $\{\beta,\chi,\delta\}$. Its representation p(α) is the following: $\{\varnothing,\beta,\chi,\delta$ $\{\beta,\chi\},\{\beta,\delta\},\{\chi,\delta\},\{\beta,\chi,\delta\}\}$. The rule for finite sets is the following: the cardinal of p(α) corresponds to cardinal a^2. In our example, the cardinal of the presentation a is 3; the cardinal of the representation is therefore 2^3, which is 8.

We write, for example: $\beta \subset \alpha, \{\chi,\delta\} \subset \alpha, \{\beta,\chi,\delta\} \subset \alpha$.

And then: $\beta \in p(\alpha), \{\chi,\delta\} \in p(\alpha), \{\beta,\chi,\delta\} \in p(\alpha)$

Some remarks:

— A more intuitive understanding would consist, for example, in considering all the groups of possible pieces (representation) of the 32 pieces
(presentation) of a chess game. The cardinal of the representation is
thus the following: 2^{32}, which is $4294,967\ 296$.

— With infinite sets, the question of representation becomes opaque.
According to the Easton theorem, the cardinal of an infinite (i.e. of an
aleph), is indeterminable, or even allows any cardinal at all of a successor as a solution, meaning that Cantor's problem of the continuum has
no solution (this problem is the following: is the cardinal of the set of
subject of aleph-zero, the first infinite, equal to its successor, aleph-1?)

Philosophical meaning

Representation is a concept of the multiple that is mechanically vertigi-
nous, and thus runs counter to Deleuze's concept of the Virtual, which is
supposedly unsayable, incalculable. By contrast, the excess and infinity of
all multiplicities are proven, and in a law-governed fashion that is devoid
of mysticism. It thus deconstructs the Deleuzian Virtual in the name of an
actual infinity. Deleuze's error, on this view, consists in his taking infinite
calculus to be an ungraspable force or temporality.

It is important to understand that a representation is not engendered
by anything else but the law of belonging, and, nevertheless, that the
representation of a multiplicity is another set than the presentation of
this multiplicity. Writes Badiou, 'Belonging and inclusion, with regard to
the multiple a, concern two distinct operators of counting, and not two
different ways to think the being of the multiple'. However, 'this second
count, despite being related to a, is absolutely distinct from a itself' (*BE*
83).

The consequence of the existence of a metastructure for every structure
is profound: 'There is an immediate consequence of this decision: the
gap between structure and metastructure, between element and subset,
between belonging and inclusion, is a permanent question for thought, an
intellectual provocation of being [. . .] This point, apparently technical,
will lead us all the way to the Subject and to truth' (84).

To understand what this gap leads to, and how it concerns the subject
and truth itself, it is first necessary to grasp its fundamental ambiguity:
'Meditation Eight' of *BE* presents its intricacies (93–101): the void is evi-
dently itself multiple, multiplicity taken back to its status as a multiplicity
of multiplicities – inconsistency, and thus the void, is the 'last' term of any

given multiple, and were it not for this, Unity would be reintroduced; as a result, 'All multiple-presentation is exposed to the danger of the void: the void is its being' (93). It can be inferred from this that a presentation is 'doubled by a metastructure', representation, which gives back some multiplicity to the given multiplicity by multiplying it, through the excess of effective possibilities of recombination of representation. In this first sense, representation is 'parrying in the void'. The structuring of structure (the representation of presentation) in fact aims at establishing a totality. Representation assuages the Heideggerian care of being, or peril of the underlying void.

On the other hand (and this inversion is fundamental), the multiplication of presentation is also the evident sign of the void, which, as being qua being, here roams within and haunts all structure or presentation. Otherwise why would structure admit a meta-structure? It would be primary and terminal, definitive, One. But as it is not so, its duplication through the operation of representation furnishes the proof that it is not One, and that it endures, as every multiplicity, the effect of the void in it, or of the ontological (in Heidegerrian terms). The universal inclusion of the empty set in the set of subsets of any set is, moreover, the mathematical symptom of this ambiguity.

Furthermore, we can thus consider that 'the degree of connection between the native structure of a situation and its statist metastructure is variable. This question of a *gap* is key to the analysis of being (*BE* 99). This is obvious since, as 'the last universally recognisable philosopher' (1), Heidegger's question, which is the question of being qua being in its relation to the ontic level, is literally diffracted in the infinitely open play between presentations and representations.

Three sorts of cases are thus possible, which Badiou sharply identifies:

I will call *normal* a term which is both presented and represented. I will call *excrescence* a term that is represented, but not presented. I will call *singular* a term that is presented but not represented. (*BE* 99)

Normality is the attribute of natural being, of a maximal equilibrium between presentation and representation, whereas excrescence opens onto the excess of representation over presentation. Lastly, singularity furnishes the form of the eventual site since it can deliver a multiple whose own elements are not represented. We are thus provided with a veritable typology of being.

Translated from the French by Steven Corcoran

ROMANTICISM

Justin Clemens

Between 1989 and 1998, 'Romanticism' becomes a highly significant polemical tag for Badiou, denominating a particular philosophical situation that is at once historically circumscribed and still dominant – and which, therefore, is to be polemically confronted, its presuppositions exposed and critiqued, and its closure effected. Romanticism's hallmarks include: the exclusion or relegation of mathematics as a secondary or degraded form of knowledge; the establishment of the subject as constitutive foundational agency of thought (including such apparently antithetical variations as the nihilation or dissolution of the subject); the elevation of the arts (especially poetry) as the pilot instance for thought; the turn towards time and history as dominating agencies; and, perhaps above all, the profound conviction that philosophy itself is in some way finished, or to be finished.

In terms of his philosophical self-situation vis-à-vis Romanticism, Badiou relies heavily upon the extraordinary work by Philippe Lacoue-Labarthe and Jean-Luc Nancy, translated into English as *The Literary Absolute* (Lacoue-Labarthe and Nancy 1988). Several interrelated propositions are particularly relevant here, and bear not only upon Badiou's specific account of Romanticism, but also illuminate more general aspects of his work. First, Lacoue-Labarthe and Nancy make the claim that 'we' remain in the grip of the Romantic unconscious today, that 'we still belong to the era which it opened up' (15). Second, they claim that Romanticism is only properly comprehensible on a *philosophical* basis. Third, they claim that Romanticism's singularity (its uniqueness and novelty) derives from its rendering of philosophy-as-literature, 'in other words, literature producing itself as it produces its own theory' (12). Fourth, this auto-production of the 'literary absolute' is 'perhaps above all, this absolute *literary operation*' (ibid.). Fifth, that 'Kant opens up the possibility of romanticism [. . .] it is because an entirely new and unforeseeable relation between aesthetics and philosophy will be articulated in Kant that a 'passage' to romanticism will become possible' (29).

Badiou, as is usual in his practice, takes up these key propositions, from which he learns precisely in order to counter them. Moreover – and if this holds true in general for Badiou's writing, it is worth reiterating here – his own construction of the 'concept' of Romanticism is integrally dedicated to enabling a redescription of apparently heterogeneous phenomena in such a way as to discern heretofore-unexpected continuities between them (I will give examples of this shortly). In doing so, Badiou has, as always, his eye on *the implications for philosophy per se*. Regarding Romanticism, two conditions in particular prove crucial: 'science' and 'art', or, more precisely, 'mathematics' and 'poetry'. In taking up the challenge to break with Romanticism, Badiou displaces the former's elevation of poetry over mathematics, in order to reassign their operations and import for philosophy's continuation itself.

In the important essay 'Philosophy and Mathematics', (cf. *CS*) Badiou identifies three historically significant philosophical positions on the relationship between the eponymous forms: (1) mathematics is the principal propaedeutic to real philosophical knowledge (the 'ontological' modality); (2) mathematics is inserted in a general taxonomic division of the sciences, and examines the truth conditions of other disciplines (the 'epistemological' modality); (3) mathematics is a degraded rival to true philosophical knowledge and, indeed, cannot be properly considered a form of thought at all (the 'Romantic' modality).

Since, following Lacoue-Labarthe and Nancy, Badiou maintains that the Romantic modality remains dominant if not determining today, Badiou spends some effort on its operations and implications. He first underlines that 'the disjunction with mathematics' is 'philosophically constitutive of Romanticism' (*CS* 94), and that 'Hegel is decisive in this matter' (95; see also *BE* Ch. 15 on Hegel; also *TO*). As Badiou notes, 'Hegel proposes to establish that mathematics, in comparison to the concept, represents a state of thought which is "defective in and for-itself," and that its "procedure is non-scientific"' (*BE* 161). The upshot of this dissociation is that 'Romantic speculation opposes time and life as temporal ecstasies to the abstract and empty eternity of mathematics' (*CS* 97); as such, the essence of the Romantic gesture is to de-ontologise by means of the elevation of *poesis*, and consequently consider finitude the essence of man. Moreover, the abiding force of this dissociation still governs 'our modernity' to the point that even the apparent contemporary restitution of the priority of scientific conceptuality retains various forms of symptomatic denegation of the ontological destiny of mathematics. Above all, such a denegation has the effect of making philosophy appear finite, finished.

As Badiou notes, citing the polemic between Heidegger and Carnap:

Empiricist and positivist attitudes, which have been highly influential for the last two centuries, merely invert the Romantic speculative gesture. The claim that science constitutes the one and only paradigm of the positivity of knowledge can only be made from within a complete disentwining of science and philosophy. The antiphilosophical verdict of positivism reverses the anti-scientific verdict of romantic philosophy, but without altering its fundamental principles. (*CS* 95)

Finally, as Badiou notes, the Romantic disentwining of mathematics and philosophy emerged with respect to a very particular content: that of the *infinite*. It is therefore with respect to the thinking of the infinite in and by set theory that Badiou proposes to go beyond the Romantic dispensation. Mathematics will once again, *à la* Plato, rediscover its ontological vocation, if on the basis of an entirely modern development.

Paradoxically, this reconfiguration means retaining something absolutely crucial to Romanticism – its recognition of the centrality of the literary condition as a unique kind of operation – but by giving it an entirely different status. If Plato famously excludes poets from his ideal Republic, Badiou relies integrally on poetry *to formalise his theory of the event*. This somewhat a-Platonic reliance is linked to something essential that Romanticism did indeed recognise and accomplish: that if poetry and mathematics are, first, irreconcilable rivals in the ontological domain (see also *BE* Ch. 11), philosophy requires a relation to both in order to remain philosophy at all. After Romanticism, Plato's banishment must be modified, given that it cannot be denied that poetry itself really *thinks*. Hence Badiou writes that philosophy 'will recognise that [. . .] every naming of an event or of the eventual presence is in its essence poetic' (*HI* 26). The Platonic–Romantic antithesis is thereby resolved in a non-dialectical division of tasks: mathematics = ontology, poetry = eventing. Or: maths is the pure thinking of consistency without content; poetry is the pure thinking of the inconsistency of happening.

This means that the injunction to be post-romantic opens an analysis of the post-Romantic fate of philosophy in regards to *suture* (see esp. *M* Ch. 6). Badiou investigates the vicissitudes of philosophical sutures most directly in his first *Manifesto*. He holds that philosophy is only possible if all its four conditions – science, art, love and politics – are simultaneously operative in a situation without reduction to one another, and without philosophy itself arrogating what's proper to its conditions to itself. The genius of the *Manifesto*, then, is to show how, following the Romantic expulsion of mathematics from thought, philosophy between Hegel and Heidegger fell into desuetude, precisely because it sutured itself to one or another of its conditions, above all science or politics (e.g. Marx sutured philosophy to politics, etc.). Partially as a result of this – given that it wasn't being instrumentalised by the positivist and politicised 'philosophies' of the epoch – it was poetry, above all, that became crucial. Badiou even goes so far as to call this epoch 'The Age of Poets'. This leads Badiou to another fundamental lesson about philosophy and its conditions: when philosophy proper disappears, its own proper functions may be picked up by one or another of its own conditions, which thereby transform themselves radically. In the age of poets, this was of course done by poetry itself, which, above all, accomplished 'the *destitution of the category of object*' (*M* 72). In doing so, poetry took on the necessary job of detaching ontology from objectivity (in a way that 'philosophy' was unable to discern), but at the cost of misconceiving the infinite (which mathematics was refounding at the time, at the cost of its discoveries being precisely misunderstood by a still too-Romantic 'philosophy'). Badiou, then, doesn't entirely junk the lessons of Romanticism; but he does circumscribe and re-inscribe Romanticism in such a way as to exceed it without inadvertently extending it.

It is in such terms that Badiou – at once affirming and critiquing the *Literary Absolute* – reconstructs a rebirth for philosophy that requires a surpassing of Romanticism.

$$\boxed{S}$$

SAINT PAUL

Bruno Besana

If Paul appears throughout Badiou's work as the example *par excellence* of the subject, it is mainly because of how he appears to be stretched in two opposite directions. On the one hand, Paul is the archetypal faithful subject, as one who constructs locally the consequences of the having-taken-place of an event. Indeed, he is presented as the archetype of the *first* subject, i.e. the one that, after an event, first names it, that decides without any proof and in unprecedented fashion that what happened was indeed an event. On the other, Paul is one able to sustain the consequences of such a decision only by organising them into a rigid, hierarchical structure (the Church), that is, by organising the universal address of the event within a structure that clearly separates those belonging to it from those that do not. Thus stretched between fidelity to an event addressing everyone independently of hierarchy or mode of representation, and the need to solidify the event's consequences through a rigid mode of organisation, Paul embodies the contradictions structuring the idea not only of the militant but also of the subject more generally.

TS provides an early indication of Badiou's fascination for the figure of Paul. In it, Badiou makes a (limited) parallelism between early Christianity and Marxism in order to highlight the fact that there can be no subjective, post-eventual figure without an organisation that articulates the consequences of the event. Badiou stresses how not only the subject but

also the event itself is 'under condition' of such an organised unfolding
of consequences. This is because an event, qua inconsistency that cuts
within the consistency of a situation, cannot be proved or determined
from within the logic of the situation in and for which it appears: any event
thus begins only from within the consequences drawn from it. As Badiou
puts it: 'without the founding militant activity of Saint Paul [. . .] what
would have become of this millenary power (i.e. the Church) [. . .] The
political time of the universal Church, of which Saint Paul is the brilliant
and ill-humoured Lenin, retroactively grounds the incarnation as fact.'
And again: 'organisation alone can make an event into an origin' (cf. *TS*
125–6). Paul appears here as the first subject, one that connects, via the
paradigm of universality, subjects to come with an event that will have
existed through the acts of these subjects.

But, as Badiou will later make clear in *BE*, such action of foundation
is not without contradictions. As he remarks, the Church, as founded
by Paul, 'is literally the history of truth' (*BE* 392). 'History' stands for a
finite set of actions and speeches unfolding and retrospectively realising a
truth that appears eventually, i.e. in excess over the logic upon which the
elements of a given situation are structured and represented. Irrelative to
divisions and classifications, truth is addressed to all the elements of a situation: here, salvation as addressed to everyone regardless of nationality,
race, gender, wealth or education. The twist here is that Badiou identifies
this history of a universally addressed truth with the Church, i.e. a structure that is internally hierarchised and that functions via a clear distinction
between its interiority and its exteriority (*extra Ecclesiam, nulla salus*, as it
will later be said).

Paul and the subjective consequences of the event

The full unfolding of this contradiction occurs first in *SP*. Paul is identified through two main conceptual elements: he is the point of the event's
announcement, and he is the point starting with which a consistent set of
consequences is drawn from the announcement.

Badiou emphasises that Paul's predication presents the resurrection as a
'pure event, opening of an epoch, transformation of the relations between
the possible and the impossible' (*SP* 45), that is, as a 'pure beginning'
(49) dividing history into two. Further, Christ's resurrection implies that
the possibility of defeating death is potentially given to all, regardless of
all positive criteria by which individuals may be defined, including those
of recompense for acts accomplished. The truth announced by the event
is 'indifferent to differences', and thereby exposes the contingency of the
laws organising such differences within a situation.

As Badiou stresses, that grace is posited *for all* entails that it operates *twice* outside the law's reach. First, it operates regardless of the damnation implied by our original sin (which has the force of law); but also it 'is the opposite of law insofar as it is what comes without being due' (*SP* 76–7). Grace is in fact out of proportion to the law determining our salvation or damnation based on our acts: 'a man is justified by faith apart from works of law' (Rom. 3:28, Revised Standard Version). 'Paul's revolutionary kernel', then, simply consists in declaring that not only grace, but also 'the One (of monotheism)' more generally, is 'for all' (76; see also 81). Hence, 'the universal is the only possible correlate for the One' (76): otherwise said, the One of monotheism is inseparable from the universal address of grace, which is evental inasmuch as it is radically outside of law, 'always nondenumerable, impredicable, uncontrollable'. Grace is 'translegal, [it] happens to everyone without an assignable reason' (76–7). And salvation is 'for all' (it addresses everyone, although not everyone will be saved) precisely because it is groundless, because it acts independently of all determinations: it cannot be connected to a specific cause, fact or even substantive or factual difference among humans. Thus 'there is for Paul an essential link between the "for all" of the universal and the "without cause". There is an address for all, only according to that which is without cause. Only what is absolutely gratuitous can be addressed to all' (77).

So, given his definition of the subject as the local function through which the consequences of an event are realised for a specific part of a situation, Badiou can describe Paul as a sort of 'first subject' (in relation to the event of resurrection): acting always within specific conditions, Paul nonetheless immediately addresses the entire situation, and works to constitute a set of active subjects. In this sense, he aims to inscribe the consequences of the 'illegality' or 'excess' of grace within the totality of his contemporaneity (the Roman Empire, but also the Jew/gentile divide, the Greek/barbarian divide, and a series of other gender, class and power divides), that is, to investigate the universalism of his announcement (grace's being for all) in each situation in which he preaches.

Paul and 'the present'

In keeping with his being active in many diverse situations, Paul's preaching is characterised by a mimetic attitude: he not only respects local laws, but also adapts his preaching to each audience, acting as a Jew among Jews, a pagan among pagans. If such mimetism is not incompatible with his universalism, it is because it allows him to 'traverse *all* differences' (SP 102 ff.), i.e. to merge with the specificities of a given situation, while behaving *as if* such differences were non-existent, thus unveiling the universal address of his message. More precisely, as the first letter to the Corinthians shows, his mode of relation with a situation is a sort of *negative mimetism*: he appears as *ignorant* among the Greeks, for whom knowledge is the highest value; and as a *scandal* among Jews, the people of the law. He further addresses the Romans, administrators of justice in the Empire, by stressing the idea of grace as a gift in excess of all justice and retribution (Rom. 4, 1 ff.). Crucially, Paul does not act *against* knowledge, justice or the law, he does not relate to a specific situation by positing a determinate negation – for instance, by entering into conflict with institutions. Rather, he adds to each situation a specific element that functions as a hole or inconsistency that cannot be eliminated: his words, his announcement of gratuitous salvation, appear as stupid within the realm of knowledge, yet they are also able to nullify the law without negating it, without accepting a common terrain of encounter with that which is negated. The idea that 'the righteousness of God has been manifested *apart* from law' (Rom. 3, 21; my italics) functions as a negative supplement, which he drags with him from place to place, from institution to institution, on his pastoral journey, thus undoing the fabric of each situation from within. Finally, universalism is not constructed by negating particularities, but by adding to those an empty supplement, an in-actual element, a no-thing that consumes particularities. To put it in Paul's words, 'God chose [. . .] things that are not, to reduce to nothing things that are' (I Cor. 1, 27–8).

Two consequences ensue: first, through this irrelational relation to his own present, Paul appears as a sort of formal figure that can be active in and against any situation or time. From this perspective Badiou discusses Pasolini's script for a film in which Paul's life is transposed into the twentieth century, noting that it centres on the idea of Paul's 'constant contemporaneity'. 'Paul is our fictional contemporary', says Badiou, 'because the universal content of his preaching, obstacles and failures included, remains absolutely real' (*SP* 37). Paul's 'fictive contemporaneity' to us resides not in any series of factual or positive data (e.g. an analogy between our time and the Roman Empire), but instead, in 'the universal content of his preaching', and more specifically in his ability to be in each present by 'making a hole in [it]' (37). What is contemporary to us is that which eludes both the symbolic order of Paul's time and the symbolic order of our present. It is something that, like the Lacanian real, 'is not a qualification of knowledge', but rather 'pierces a hole' in the knowledge organising the present – a certain *singularity* of his message that is able to puncture the consistency of the situation, and directly address everyone, no matter the position occupied in the situation (*OS* 25).

Second, Paul's message, by piercing a hole in the knowledge organising the present, ultimately takes the form of 'the holy will to destruction'

(*SP* 37). Truth's hole piercing 'is *diagonal* relative to every communitarian subset; it does not depend upon any given identity, nor [. . .] does it constitute any. It is offered to all, or addressed to everyone, without a condition of belonging being able to limit this offer, or this address' (14; tm): it ultimately creates a zone of indifference that destroys the fabric of a situation, but without proceeding via direct negation. It is an evental novelty that 'implies negation, but must affirm its identity regardless of the negativity of negation'. It is thus something like an 'affirmative part of the negation' (*DNS* 269).

The antinomies of militancy

The above quote is from an essay in which Badiou comments on Pasolini's poem 'Vittoria', which stages the desperation of the ghosts of dead communist partisans, due to their perception of the deadlock of their successors – the post-WWII generation. The problem this essay and Paul's figure share is: if an event is inconsistent within the logic of the situation in which it appears, then in order to overcome its evanescence, to continue on despite its 'inconsistent' nature, the evental moment has to produce a series of further acts of 'hole piercing' in different parts of the situation. A double bind seems to ensue: such fractures can either simply 'pierce holes', thus continuing in a purely destructive attitude (the partisan struggle of liberation could have continued after the war, endlessly refusing any political compromise), or they can progressively enter into a dialectical relationship with the present (such as the communist resistance that, after the war, entered the frame of parliamentary dialectics). In the first case, the event as radical fracture is maintained, but no positive consequences are forged from it, so that it consumes itself perpetually in a series of evanescent, destructive acts. In the second case, a solid edifice of consequences is apparently built, but the radicality of the interruption is lost through the very fact of accepting a common terrain of dialogue with the forces of the status quo. In one case a pure action of destruction results in 'the impossibility of politics [. . .] a sort of nihilistic suicide, which is without thinking or destination' (*DNS* 274); in the other the acceptance of a common terrain entails 'the death of negation, and it is the death of political hope' (276).

The problem Paul and the post-WWII generation share is how to escape this double bind. It is how to construct, positively, a present that is *at a distance from*, or indifferent to, the logic organising the present. Novelty requires what he calls the 'affirmative part of a negation'. ' "Negation", because if something new happens, it cannot be reduced to the objectivity of the situation where it happens [. . .] But "affirmation", "affirmative part of the negation", because if a creation is reducible to a negation of the common laws of objectivity, it completely depends on them with respect to its identity' (269). Paul's attempt is precisely to construct a novelty that can affirm 'its identity apart from the negativity of negation' (ibid.), and thus escape the double bind. But, although he tries to avoid both determinate negation and evanescent outbursts, he constantly appears to fall either into an impossible purity, or into the trap of a dialectical relation with the present. As Badiou puts it, Paul's pastoral journey 'charts the trajectory of saintliness within an actuality' (*SP* 37), and 'is located at the exact point where the nexus between faith and the law is to be decided and is otherwise complicated' (*CS* 7). The complication of his task is structural, and is due to the fact that salvation – grace as overcoming of the necessity of the law – is an inconsistency, almost a nonsense or an evanescent hope, unless its consequences are constructed, namely by the disciplined, militant form of a Church, built in its turn around a structured set of laws. By overcoming law with law, by forcing truth in the situation and discarding all differences via the construction of the closed, hierarchical structure of the Church, 'the principal aspect in this trajectory gradually becomes that of betrayal, its wellspring being that what Paul creates (the Church, the Organisation, the Party) turns against his own inner saintliness'. The Church, as well as 'the Party, is what, little by little, inverts saintliness into priesthood through the narrow requirements of militantism' (*SP* 38).

Resurrection

Paul is thus 'stuck' between the event's announcement and the Church's foundation. As Pasolini's Paul says: our situation 'is a limbo [. . .] We are not redemption, but a promise of redemption. We are founding the Church' (Pasolini 2014: 82; tm). Trapped in this limbo, the revolutionary subject can survive only by believing that the revolution, internally doomed to failure, will be renewed. This is probably why the theme of *parousia*, the second coming, is so central in Paul. Indeed, for Badiou, a revolutionary subject is never only the subject of one event, but is always between two events. Literally speaking, there is no event without a second one that re-activates the first: 'for there to be an event, one must be able to situate oneself within the consequences of another' (*BE* 210). In fact an event as such has an infinity of consequences and a universal address, but each subjective sequence developing such consequences is finite (given the *almost* necessary internal contradictions leading to its darkening). Thus an event *will have been* only when reactivated by a second one and its subjective sequence. Further, the existence of an evental sequence is possible only from the standpoint of one that is current, open (cf. *LW* 63ff.):

Spartacus exists only through Müntzer, and the Commune only through the October Revolution. With clear resonance to Paul's theme of *parousia*, Badiou calls this aspect 'resurrection'. In Paul's case, this logic implies that the constitution of the Church, the creation of laws and rules of exclusion, and the identification of internal enemies form a sort of new dialectical engine, which, on the one side, extinguishes the previous event, but, on the other, accelerates the coming of the next one. As Paul writes in the Second Letter to the Thessalonians, the construction of the Church will produce fractures, reactions, and persecutions, and this increasing evil is what will accelerate the second coming. In political terms, the organisation of a revolution (its darkening) extinguishes universalism by producing new fractures and contradictions, but this harshening of contradictions is also what might accelerate a new revolutionary process, a new event.

SANS-PAPIERS

Christopher Norris

Sans-papiers ('without-papers') is the label commonly attached in the French press to those mainly North African immigrant workers – including many unemployed job-seekers – who possess no documents and therefore lack any kind of legal or civic status. Their plight was brought forcibly to public attention by a series of headline events, such as the occupation of the church of St Bernard in 1996, which served to emphasise the fact of their extreme social exclusion and the scandal that they represented to a self-styled liberal-democratic polity. Despite being part of a global phenomenon – since undocumented immigrant workers exist and are subject to harassment, abuse and exploitation in every major industrialised country – there are certain distinctive aspects of the French case that make it particularly well suited to count as an 'event' in Badiou's more specific sense. That is, it first sees light as an altogether startling and unlooked-for occurrence that comes about as if 'out of the blue' but which can then be seen, not so much 'in the wisdom' but more in the reconfigured knowledge of hindsight, as having been the upshot of a complex, powerful and massively over-determined socio-political 'state of the situation'. What sets the French instance apart from e.g. its near-contemporaneous US analogue is on the one hand its well-organised and notably sustained character (in the US the protests petered out after a brief albeit high-profile emergence) and on the other its intransigent radicalism (in the US they tended to adopt a kind of 'alternative patriotic' mode of presentation).

So the revolt of the *sans-papiers* emerged with the kind of evental force that, according to Badiou, typifies all and only those occurrences that possess this aspect of apparent radical contingency along with the potential – whether realised or not – to galvanise action on a larger, potentially world-transformative scale through their exemplary character. One measure of that power is the response among mainstream politicians and media pundits in their chorus of support for the self-ascribed values of liberal-democracy and their failure, or refusal, to perceive its limits in the drastically consensus-challenging case at hand. Badiou has no time for either of the stock responses, namely on the one hand conservative calls that immigrants should show more respect and loyalty to their host culture, that the state should enforce law and order more effectively, etc., and on the other left-liberal calls for greater tolerance, social-welfare reforms, multicultural education, or expanded provision for 'minority' religious beliefs. These he considers the merest of sticking-plaster remedies designed to head off what might otherwise constitute a far more radical challenge to the political status quo. It is above all their drastically marginalised status, that is, their exclusion from the socially administered and state-sponsored institutional 'count-as-one', that gives the *sans-papiers* a crucial role in Badiou's political thought. They stand as a highly visible symptom of the massive confidence-trick pulled off by various European governments and parliamentary parties across the whole range of nominal left-to-right distinctions and the various shades of likewise nominal social-democratic allegiance.

Hence Badiou's stalwart insistence over the past four decades – throughout and despite such a giddying succession of national and global political events – on the need for those with an activist conscience to align themselves with extra-parliamentary movements, pressure groups, or protest campaigns and thereby avoid the corrupting effects of a pseudo-democratic manufactured 'consensus'. Hence also his scepticism (some would say cynicism, though recent events tend to bear out the former view) with regard to talk of 'human rights' or – what often goes along with it – of 'free-world', liberal-democratic values *versus* some currently touted threat to those values. Such talk contrives to draw a discreet veil over the manifold injustices, acts of aggression, and war crimes committed in its name. Indeed some of Badiou's most powerful and ethically as well as politically charged polemics are directed against this smokescreen use of a fraudulent self-justifying rhetoric on the part of governments whose record in office bears witness to their cynical abandonment of all such principles. Badiou therefore has good reason for endorsing the kinds of 'micropolitical' activism – the resistance to particular forms of social injustice through locally targeted, often street-level campaigns – which offer at least a reasonable hope of producing some worthwhile result.

That commitment has been strikingly borne out by the accession to power of Nicolas Sarkozy, a President whose reference to the *sans-papiers* as 'scum' was among the many features of his rise to high office that inspired Badiou to publish a hard-hitting and witty polemic that took his political career apart with positively Swiftian *saeva indignatio*. For Badiou – here writing very much in the tradition of Marx's likewise Swiftian *Eighteenth Brumaire* – this stands as a flagrant instance of the distortions to which 'liberal democracy' is subject when yoked to a global capitalist economic order with the financial clout to dictate its terms to any government wishing to retain nominal power. Even more depressingly, it is something that often occurs when individuals or groups who may have started out well – at the prompting of ethical-political conscience in face of some particular injustice – thereafter come to power and then very soon, in the name of political 'realism', resume pretty much where the others left off. This is why Badiou has so strongly and eloquently championed the cause of various movements on the (so-called) far left of French extra-parliamentary politics, especially those concerned with the treatment of the *sans-papiers* or 'illegal' immigrants. For it falls to these movements alone, in present circumstances, to maintain that vital degree of autonomy that allows them to resist co-option by the structures of state or institutional power.

Moreover there is a close (indeed structural) link between this activist commitment and Badiou's project of developing a social ontology – an account of the various possible modes of human communal existence, agency, and transformative praxis – that would in turn find its model in the way that post-Cantorian set theory has opened up hitherto uncharted regions of discovery for mathematical thought. In the latter case it is a question of paying maximal regard to those problematic stages in the conduct of a proof-procedure or other such extended piece of formal reasoning that resists incorporation into the current state of mathematical knowledge. When confronted with presumptive anomalies of this kind – moments of unlooked-for blockage or resistance – thought may find itself propelled towards some future advance that exceeds all the bounds of present-best knowledge (since the means are still lacking for its adequate formulation) yet can later be discerned as latent or obliquely prefigured within that same problematic. In the former case likewise it is a matter of focusing attention and bringing maximum pressure to bear at just those stress-points in the current social-political situation where the self-image of the liberal-democratic state and its prevailing rhetoric of freedom, dignity, justice, equality under the law, and so forth, come most starkly into conflict with reality.

The *sans-papiers* are Badiou's prime example of that which, no matter how forcibly repressed, remains not only as a standing reproach but as a massive, symptomatic and *rationally unignorable* threat to the claim of inclusive representation that defines the grossly deceptive self-image of liberal-democratic justice. In mathematical terms, they embody that stubbornly recalcitrant remainder that exceeds or eludes any currently accepted reckoning and which therefore cannot be reconciled to the dominant (socio-politically authorised) 'count-as-one'. To that extent they constitute an 'excrescence' – a strictly inassimilable quantity – which may (or may not – for there are no guarantees) come to mark the location of an 'evental site', that is to say, a troubled or turbulent region within the existing socio-political order where the strains are such as to portend some radically transformative event. Thus the *sans-papiers* have a central role in Badiou's pedagogy of the oppressed, and also – more theoretically speaking – a crucial part in his articulation of the link between politics, philosophy, and mathematics.

SARTRE

Christopher Norris

Badiou has never gone along with the periodic bouts of Sartre-bashing that have typified various post-1970 movements of 'advanced' French thought from structuralism, via post-structuralism and Foucauldian archaeology/ genealogy, to postmodernism and its sundry latter-day derivatives. This is partly, no doubt, because those movements shared a programmatic commitment to three axioms – the 'death of the subject', the obsolescence of truth, and the eclipse of Marxism as a living source of political inspiration – which Badiou, like Sartre, emphatically rejects. To be sure, he has his own differences with Sartre on ethico-political as well as metaphysical and (especially) ontological grounds, differences that must strike any reader who comes to *BE* with a good working knowledge of Sartre's *Being and Nothingness*. Indeed the two thinkers have radically divergent ideas of what is required by way of conceptual revision if the countervailing positive theses – on the role of the subject, the imperative of truth, and the continued vitality of Marxist thought – are to have the right valence. Nevertheless Badiou can be seen to have developed his understanding of them through a long-sustained critical engagement with Sartre, evidence of which is there to be seen in numerous passages of his own work.

One thing that plainly unites them is their shared opposition to that company of postwar French intellectuals, from Camus to Foucault and beyond, who have taken an overtly anti-Marxist or 'post-Marxist' political stance. These thinkers have most often defined their various projects against what they perceive as the fatefully inverted Marxist dialectic whereby erstwhile revolutionary or emancipatory movements are transformed into a brutal parody of all that they once stood for. Badiou is very far from endorsing either Camus' stance of intransigently individualist 'rebellion' *contra* the claims of collective revolutionary praxis or Foucault's idea of micro-political activism as the sole means by which to escape from the otherwise ubiquitous nexus of power/knowledge. On the contrary, Badiou sees absolutely no hope for progressive social and political change unless brought about through organised collective activity amongst militant groups, on whatever numerical scale, with the requisite discipline and strength of shared purposive commitment. By far the most relevant comparison among figures of an earlier French generation is with the post-1960 Sartre whose great project in the *Critique of Dialectical Reason* was to explain – very much in response to unbelievers like Camus – how revolutionary praxis *could* under certain untoward historical conditions, yet *need not* in accordance with some supposed grim law of historical inevitability, be turned back against the motives, principles and interests of those who had embarked upon it. Indeed there is a sense in which *BE* can be seen as a radical reworking of themes that Sartre developed not only in his later Marxist-inspired work but also, despite their very different inflection, in the various treatments of existential authenticity and bad faith that make up *Being and Nothingness*.

What Badiou inherits from these two Sartrean projects is a keen awareness of the need for philosophy to think its way through the unresolved antinomy that makes them appear so sharply opposed. This is the problematical disjunction between issues of personal good faith, moral conscience or authenticity and issues of a wider, i.e. collective or shared ethico-political concern. Here Badiou introduces his single most striking innovation, that is, a mathematically-based ontology with its proximate source in post-Cantorian set theory and its point of departure in certain long-standing philosophic problems regarding the one and the many. It permits him to move beyond a number of disabling and misconceived dualisms, among them the drastic Sartrean split between self and other that is visible not only in the kinds of predicament anatomised in *Being and Nothingness* but also in the drastic shift of priorities from his early to his later work. Sartre sought a way beyond this antinomy in the idea of a Marxist-inspired dialectical reason that would at once surpass the limits of formal logic and find room for the subject as source or locus of a power to transcend the conditions of some given, historically specified socio-political order. His early work *The Transcendence of the Ego* can be seen as a kindred, phenomenologically-based attempt to explain how the subject can project itself beyond any set of putative defining attributes that would reduce it to some kind of fixed essence or – looking forward to his Marxist period – mere product of passive ideological interpellation. Badiou's *TS* occupies something like the corresponding position in the development of his own work, albeit one that already shows clearly how his thinking contrasts with Sartre's in its preference for formal procedures and (after Lacan) for theorising subjectivity in terms remote from the register of first-person phenomenological experience. All the same their early writings have this much in common: that they seek to articulate a mode of transcendence whereby the subject can be thought of as always potentially eluding or surpassing any limit placed upon it by received (whether externally imposed or self-assumed) notions of selfhood.

Where Badiou most decisively breaks with Sartrean precedent is in conceiving that moment of transcendence primarily in formal, i.e. set-theoretical terms. When he sets out to specify the character of great historical events – revolutions in the socio-political sphere as well as in the natural sciences, the arts, and philosophy – he does so not merely by loose analogy with breakthrough moments in the history of mathematics but by way of a precise structural equivalence between these seemingly disparate domains. Moreover, again in sharp contrast to Sartre, he thinks of the subject as an agent whose very identity or the condition of whose existence qua subject is defined solely by their crucial role in discovering, devising, inventing, refining, or actively/creatively sustaining some potential source of revolutionary change. The subject as theorised by Badiou is the locus of those specific truth procedures that mark out a path of thought sufficiently detached from preconceived ideas or foregone investments to achieve some major advance in knowledge or some equivalent transformation in the powers of collective, politically motivated praxis. Again there are suggestive parallels with Sartre, although here with a paradigm 'early' work like *Being and Nothingness* in the notion of a project that transcends every limit laid down by pre-existing (objective or subjective) conditions and thereby creates a realm of absolute freedom or autonomous choice that defines the authentically human. However, to push this comparison too hard would plainly be to get Badiou wrong, since he places far greater weight on the circumstantial factors that not only set certain limits to this exercise of human autonomy but which also constitute the necessary background – the conditions of possibility – for any meaningful idea of freedom.

Of course Sartre came around to something more like this position in the *Critique of Dialectical Reason*, where he fully acknowledged the role of material, historical and socio-political circumstance in setting just such jointly enabling and limiting conditions on the scope for human emancipative praxis. But he did so still very much in the Hegelian-Marxist mode that located the chief engine of historical change in the various orders of conflictual relationship between subject and object, mind and world, praxis and the practico-inert, or the actively coordinated group-in-fusion and the inertly 'serial' collective. These in turn had their source and their constant implicit point of reference in Sartre's earlier cardinal distinction between the *pour soi* of human consciousness (locus of absolute freedom and choice) and the *en soi* of a stubborn, project-thwarting material world. Badiou's is a wholly different conception of the subject, and one that goes a long way towards endorsing those structuralist and post-structuralist critiques of Sartre – from Lévi-Strauss to Foucault and especially Lacan – that denounced what they saw (albeit with scant justice) as his attachment to a philosophically naïve as well as ideologically suspect humanist/essentialist metaphysics of the self. It is clear enough from Badiou's high regard for Lacanian psychoanalysis – and even more so from his vigorous defence of Lacan's cryptic topological and quasi-mathematical formalisms – that he shares at least something of this strong reaction, visible from the late 1950s on, against any version (no matter how elaborately qualified) of the Hegelian 'subject-presumed-to-know'.

On the other hand he is equally critical of that new orthodoxy that grew up around the tenets of post-structuralism and which simply took for the granted the consignment of the subject, along with its usual surrogate 'the author', via Lacan's and Althusser's jointly developed theory of 'imaginary' misrecognition to its rightful place on the scrapheap of bourgeois-humanist ideology. On this dogmatic account there is simply no room for any viable conception of human agency or of the purposes, motives, and incentives that take shape in some particular project of thought or activist commitment. The latter may be a punctual intervention that decisively changes the course of events or, in certain cases, a centuries-long process of working-through whereby what perhaps started out as a marginal event – a failed revolution, unproven and discarded hypothesis in mathematics, scientific theory proposed 'before its time' – is then taken up and developed to the point where it exerts a transformative effect on the currency of thought or makes way for some hitherto scarcely conceivable change in the socio-political order. What this involves is a capacity to grasp those as-yet strictly 'indiscernible' elements that reveal the constant (and at times critical) excess of inconsistent over consistent multiplicity, subsets over sets, parts over members, inclusion over belonging, or the 'state of the situation' over the state as that which maintains – which exists only by maintaining – the dominant count-as-one.

It would therefore be wrong to claim Badiou exclusively for either

side in the quarrel between 'humanism' and 'anti-humanism' that has
periodically occupied stage-centre in so much French philosophical
debate from Sartre down. To be sure, he is very far from endorsing that
faculty-based notion of the thinking, acting, willing, and judging subject
whose various incarnations from Descartes to Kant and Husserl have rung
so many changes on the theme of transcendental constitution. Indeed one
of the few things that Badiou shares with his long-term philosophic spar-
ring partner Gilles Deleuze is a deep, at times almost visceral dislike for
Kantian talk of 'judgement' in its supposed multi-purpose mediating role
between various otherwise dissociated faculties such as intuition and conceptual understanding (in epistemology) or pure practical reason and the
art of sound case-by-case adjudication (in ethics). To this extent Badiou
is very much aligned with that anti-humanist current of thought that can
be seen to have gained its chief impetus from the structuralist turn against
Sartrean existentialism and also against any version of Marxism, like
Sartre's, with strongly-marked humanist leanings. All the same, his debt
to Sartre is often and handsomely acknowledged, not least with respect to
precisely this question – so central to Sartre's later writings – of how one
can wrest sufficient room for the exercise of human discovery, invention,
creativity, and socio-political praxis from the strongly determinist implications of a full-scale or doctrinaire structuralist approach.

As concerns politics, Badiou's working premise, again like Sartre's
before him, is captured well enough by the famous passage from the *German
Ideology* where Marx and Engels write that human beings 'make their own
history, but do not make it as they please; they do not make it under self-
selected circumstances, but under circumstances existing already, given
and transmitted from the past'. While he presses that insight in a very
different direction – towards a formally articulated, set-theoretically based
account of how it is that certain epochal events can intervene to disrupt
and transform some existing ontological order – Badiou is nonetheless at
one with Sartre in seeking to explain more precisely the dynamics of socio-
historical change under just such restrictive though potentially enabling,
even world-transformative conditions. This involves further argument
by way of mathematics and, more specifically, his inventive use of the
set-theoretical concept of 'forcing' – taken from the mathematician Paul
Cohen – as the basis for a rigorously formal yet historically grounded and
context-specific account of the processes involved. So it is that Badiou is
able to assert the double and, as it might seem, contradictory claim that
truth is (1) 'forced' to emerge through a procedure that develops according to its own, strictly formal and hence recognition-transcendent logic,
yet also (2) discovered by subjects whose fidelity, commitment or *truth
to* the inaugural event in question enables them to press that procedure

through to its ultimate conclusion. At any rate it is clear that the 'subject' as by defined Badiou in relation to the formal, physical, and even (certain branches of) the social and human sciences is by no means synonymous with 'the subject' as conceived in psychological or subjectivist terms.

One can find a good number of passages where Badiou's formulation of the case runs close to denying – or seeming to deny – any role for the subject in a more than purely nominal or place-holder role. Such is his assertion that '[a] term forces a statement if its positive connection to the event forces the statement to be veridical in the new situation (the situation supplemented by an indiscernible truth)' (*BE* 403). Yet this claim is by no means incompatible with the ascription of a genuine, indeed a decisive role for the subject just so long as the latter is construed in such a way as to respect Badiou's crucial point about the strictly indissoluble tie *in this particular context of enquiry* between the subject and the 'post-evental' project to which they are committed. Thus if '[t]he opening of a generic procedure founds, on its horizon, the assemblage of a truth', nevertheless 'subjectivisation is that through which a truth is possible', since it 'turns the event towards the truth of the situation for which the event is an event' (393). Only on this latter condition can one make sense of Badiou's declaration that 'I will term *forcing* the relation implied in the fundamental law of the subject' (403), and his yet more rigorously formalist or objectivist-sounding pronouncement that '[g]rasped in its being, the subject is solely the finitude of the generic procedure, the local effects of an evental fidelity' (406).

This may all seem pretty remote from Sartre's trademark emphasis, early and late, on the subject as locus of a freedom essentially untrammelled – even if (for the Marxist Sartre) in various ways materially constrained – by the pressures of historical circumstance. However, what we should keep in mind, if struck by Badiou's apparently very un-Sartrean insistence on themes of forcing and finitude, is his strong countervailing insistence that recent philosophy has sold itself short – betrayed its true vocation – by espousing a 'finitist', i.e. prescriptively limiting, conception of the subject and therefore of the human potential for change. Nor is this in any way self-contradictory since we here have to do with 'finitude' in two quite distinct, indeed flatly opposed senses of the term. The first (positive) sense refers to those historically located and temporally indexed procedures by which some given mathematical theorem, scientific hypothesis, or declaration of political faith sets in train a sequence of later attempts to prove, corroborate, or actively carry through the project announced by that inaugural wager. The second (bad) sense, contrary to this, is that which enjoins thought to maintain a strict regard for the limits – the temporal and intellectual finitude – of human being, and which thereby works to preempt and foreclose any possibility of radical change. For both thinkers, it is a grasp of that crucial distinction – whether in terms of Sartrean 'transcendence' or Badiou's appeal to the multiple orders of infinity, itself a truth knowable only as the outcome of a finite proof-procedure – that opens a perspective strongly at odds with the premises of most present-day philosophy.

SATURATION

Frank Ruda

Badiou adopts the concept of 'saturation' from his comrade, Sylvain Lazarus, with whom he was *inter alia* a long-time member of the 'organisation politique'. Lazarus developed what he calls a 'method of saturation' in his *Anthroplogie du nom* (1996), defining it as follows: 'I call "method of saturation" the examination, from the interior of a work or a thought, of the expiry of one of its fundamental categories. It is thus a matter of questioning the work from the point of the expiry of the category and of re-identifying it in this new conjuncture' (Lazarus 1996: 37). Lazarus's book mainly deals with political actions and organisations, which are referred to above as work or thought. It is thus possible to attempt a first definition: saturation names a way of conceiving of the end of a work of thought from an interior perspective. It takes its place as a category within an immanent analysis (of a termination) of actions or (of a withering away) of organisations of universal address. Badiou thus refers to Lazarus's concept of saturation when, for example, the stake is to grasp the reasons for the termination of a sequence of true political actions or of emancipatory forms of political organisation. For it has to be thought in a way that takes into account only those causes that can be grasped in starting from these very actions or forms of organisations. Against this background it is intelligible that Badiou can apodictically claim: 'a political sequence does not terminate or come to an end because of external causes, or contradictions between its essence and its means, but through the strictly immanent effect of its capacities being exhausted [. . .] In other words, failure is not relevant here' (*M* 127). Badiou thus introduces the notion of saturation to avoid any external evaluation of a sequence of emancipatory political actions, for example, one possibly communist in nature, and hence shun thinking of the true stakes of such a sequence. Saturation names a counter-category against the reactionary category of failure – which always tends swiftly to condemn, for example, communist politics as simple criminal wrongdoing – whose systematicity can be grasped by considering its most fundamental ingredients: saturation is conceptually situated as part of an immanent analysis of a sequence of thought, making possible an under-standing of its termination.

But as Badiou is an acknowledged thinker of infinity, of (potentially) infinite truth procedures and eternity, and surely cannot be considered as obsessed with endings or other such categories bound to finitude, the intuition behind the notion of saturation seems to take a somewhat contradictory position in his philosophical system. Indeed, Badiou has repeatedly and violently attacked all proponents of grand narratives of finitude – for example, advocates of the narrative of the end of all narra-tives, which became highly influential under what has been called 'post-modernity' – and on different occasions has even suggested putting an end to the idea of end *tout court*. This already indicates that the notion of saturation is nothing short of a highly difficult concept in Badiou's overall *oeuvre*, and its difficulty lies in the fact that it conceptualises the termina-tion of 'something' which, at least potentially, needs have no end: a generic truth procedure. Badiou takes up this point from Lazarus, who outlines the idea by stating that the end of a truth procedure – which he calls a 'political mode' – consists in the transition from its 'historicity' (i.e., its historical effectivity) to its 'intellectuality' (Lazarus 1996: 41). As long as a political mode has a historicity, i.e., is effective and operating, it cannot be adequately and conceptually thought. For Lazarus, a politics' effective-ness, in the material form of actions and organisations, is performed by subjects and, as he specifies, subjects think. This is why politics is a matter of thought. But what they think cannot be conceptually grasped as long as these subjects act and think – because when thought is in actu and is itself changing it cannot be grasped adequately. Only with the end of a political mode does it become intelligible as to what was immanently at stake, what effects certain actions had and what the people involved in it thought – this marks the transition from historicity to intellectuality. What has thus been thought immanently only becomes thinkable with the – abrupt or slow – disappearance of these actions, organisations and subjects. And as this ter-mination is a consequence of the actions of the thinking subjects involved, it can only be thoroughly grasped by thinking what they thought.

It might be said that the concept of saturation, in both Lazarus and Badiou, is a rephrasing of a famous Hegelian insight, namely that 'the owl of Minerva takes its flight only when the shades of the night are gathering'. Saturation is needed to conceive of what has been thought and thus bequeathed to those who think what has been thought. As Lazarus puts it: 'The method of saturation distinguishes between what is thought in a thinking in the moment where it has taken place and on the other hand, between what has been thought in thought when the mode is closed' (Lazarus 1996: 42). As the immanent way of conceiving the end of subjective actions or organisations, able to be thought properly only once saturated, it also names that which needs to be thought to understand the present circumstances precisely as situated *after* a sequence of subjective thought – e.g. of collective political actions – has ended. Saturation in Badiou's work presents a way of explaining the disappearing, dis-activation or termination of a truth procedure. This is also why it lies at the heart of and more precisely constitutes what the later Badiou calls a 'sequence'. Every sequence ends with saturation, which is what makes it a sequence.

Another way of framing the essential insight behind this concept, as regards sequences of generic truth procedures, is again a Hegelian one: All that exists deserves to perish. Or in Badiou's phrasing: 'Nobody can escape saturation' (*TS* 299). This is, although it is rarely taken into account, also valid for truth procedures – this is why they are sequential – and even if Badiou also states that 'of no truth can it be said, under the pretext that its historical world has disintegrated, that it is lost forever' (*LW* 66). Truths can never be lost forever, but their effectivity, or *generic reality*, can be weakened; they can disappear and disintegrate by becoming saturated. Saturation names the termination of something which can never be lost as it is eternal. The complex question is how to understand this concatenation of eternity and termination. If actions in any procedure of fidelity – whether a political debate, a late-night conversation between two lovers, the development of a theorem from scientific axioms or a stylistic transformation within playwriting – changes the situation in which it takes place, it can be said that new means have to be found by which to remain faithful in order to maintain this very procedure in the changed situation. Fidelity always immanently raises the question of how to continue, since there can be no law or rule that could indicate once and for all how to remain faithful under changed circumstances. This is, on the one hand, why a procedure of fidelity is immanently (potentially) infinite – there is no internal reason as to why it should terminate; but on the other, this is why it can end. It can end, because it can become increasingly difficult to find new means to maintain fidelity. The cause for saturation, then, is that failure invents new means for the continuation of a procedure of fidelity. Saturation names a lack of means of fidelity – an immanent failure of a procedure with regards the norms with which it started. It refers thus not to a spontaneous rupture – e.g. a betrayal – but to the progressive difficulty of remaining one (subject) who remains (faithful).

An example from politics, Badiou has formulated with regards to the sequences of the communist hypothesis, can clarify this point (though the same can be said of each of the four conditions): since the mid-1970s there has been a saturation of revolutionary politics in its traditional framework (of the logic of class representation by parties). Badiou even claims that the word 'revolution' itself has become saturated, or unintelligible. This is to say that, within the party-state apparatus it became increasingly difficult to find new means to remain faithful to the idea of revolution, as seen notably with the various failure(s) of the Russian and Chinese Revolutions. It became increasingly difficult, since the statist means employed by Russian and Chinese revolutionaries did not prevent the violation of their own universalist commitments.

This was precisely due to central operators of these specific truth procedures (the linkage of politics to power, of power to the state, of the state to the idea of its withering away). On the level of this 'first fidelity' for the (Russian or Chinese) subject(s) attempting to remain faithful to the idea of emancipatory and revolutionary politics, these procedures became saturated. More precisely, the saturation that befell the first two sequences of the communist hypothesis materialised as follows: the first sequence (stretching from the French Revolution of 1792 to the Paris Commune of 1871) combined, under the label 'communist' mass movements, the idea of overthrowing the state and taking power. The Paris Commune materialised the strictly immanent limitations of this first sequence, unable as it was to sustain this exercise against counter-revolutionary tendencies. The second sequence (from the Russian Revolution of 1917 through to the Cultural Revolution, up to 1976) tried to solve the problems of the first by proposing the form of the revolutionary class-party to organise the newly gained power in a more stable manner. The second sequence solved problems bequeathed to it by the first, but was unable to resolve the impasses that originated as a consequence of its own construction. The Communist party was unable to organise the transition to the dictatorship of the proletariat as it led to a state which became both authoritarian and terrorist by withdrawing from the idea of the state's withering away. From this perspective, Badiou is thus able to claim that what happened with the last events of the second sequence – May '68 and the GCPR – were precisely attempts to overcome these immanent limitations. But they failed internally in being unable to loosen the knot between party, power and state. They bear witness to the immanent impossibility of freeing politics from the frame of the party-state in which it was limited, even imprisoned. The two sequences can thus be read as a saturation of the party-state model concerning any form of emancipatory, i.e. communist, political action.

However, saturation indicates not merely the unavoidable and saddening outcome of a universalist procedure; it marks something new. To paraphrase Badiou, without the saturation of the political condition in the sixties and seventies, nothing would as yet be thinkable outside the party-state model, outside the classical Marxist framework. Saturation marks an irreplaceable experience of immense significance, insofar as it conditions the ensuing situation. A saturated sequence always leaves us with a choice: either one advocates a negative interpretation of saturation (claiming that 'nothing is possible which might be linked to what happened and what was experimented on in the saturated sequence'), one espouses a dogmatic interpretation (remaining faithful in an abstract and nostalgic way to lifeless and obsolete ideas, ignoring the changed historical setting, something that the early Badiou attacked as 'old Marxist' (Badiou 1983) or one champions an affirmative interpretation (claiming that 'with the help of new events one can find a fidelity to the – first – fidelity'). Fidelity to a fidelity is neither simply a continuation of the first procedure of fidelity nor a complete break with it. Rather, it consists in an insistence on the fact that to remain faithful to what has been thought in the saturated sequence, which will always have been a truth, and thus eternal by definition, new means and fundamentally renewed and reworked operators of fidelity are required. The affirmative interpretation thus leads to a renewed concept of what, for example, emancipatory politics could be today. It can do so by starting negatively: the saturation of the last sequence demonstrates that political emancipation cannot begin with questions of power, the state or party-like organisation (but only at a distance from the state). The category of saturation implies not the least bit of pessimism. Instead, it leads from the immanent thought of a subjective termination of a historically specific truth sequence – a singular truth is saturated by its own norms– to the affirmation that, although this saturated procedure will have unfolded eternally universal consequences, the situation has changed and new means of fidelity to fidelity are needed. Saturation, required for thinking the end of a truth, thus implies the exigency to think the new (condition of art, politics, love or science).

SCHOENBERG

François Nicolas

For the philosophy of Badiou, *Schoenberg* is the name of a musical event, the initiator of a subject-process of truth (called the *Vienna School* and then *serialism*), but for all that it does not operate as a condition *for his philosophy*.

This particular relation to a non-conditioning event emerges from a properly philosophical orientation: we know that, for Badiou's philosophy, every event internal to a truth procedure does not *ipso facto* constitute a condition for every philosophy, such that a given philosophy is constituted by *philosophical* (and not musical, mathematical or political) choices as to which of the available events will constitute for it a network of conditions apt to be philosophically contemporised. Such is not the case, in Badiou's philosophy, for the Schoenberg event.

How are we to understand such a philosophical relation?

And for starters, does this relation properly speaking involve a (philosophical) decision? Does it hang on the logic of decision emphasised by Sartre in *Being and Nothingness*: that which opens up to a deliberation of its consequences rather than proceed to a prior deliberation (a *constituting* decision, then, rather than a constituted one – on the basis of a calculation that would account for it)?

In our case, *any* such type of *philosophical* decision on the Schoenberg-event should measure up to its immanent philosophical effects, and not to the specific musical interest the philosopher has or does not have for this particular music: Alain Badiou may like Schoenberg's music as he declares to like Haydn's; yet neither of them will come to be a condition for his philosophy (cf. *LW* where he speaks of a Haydn-event (84–5)).

But how can we measure the properly philsophical effects of a decision that would be *negative* ('*philosophically*', not to retain the *Schoenberg*-event as condition')?

In this point, let's adopt the hypothesis that there is an absence of decision rather than a decision of an absence: this philosophy, like every other, is not liable to be convoked *in an exogenous manner* (that is to say, a non-philosophical one) to have to decide on every event that occurs, here or there, in the teeming set of truth procedures (to have thus to measure itself – affirmatively or negatively – against the Einstein or Planck events or against the Schoenberg or Cunningham events . . .).

If we are thus dealing not with a (negative) philosophical decision properly speaking but rather with a simple choice, how can we take stock of the properly philosophical effects of any such absence of conditioning?

Let's recall, first up, that if *Schoenberg*-music is not one of the conditions of this philosophy, neither is any other music of the twentieth century, so much so that, in a certain sense, in Badiou's philosophy, the twentieth century turns out to be a century 'without music' (in a sense partly similar to Hegel's speaking of a death of art *for Spirit*: the latter admitted of course that art could continue its own life but considered that it was no longer liable to summons thought and to condition the life of the Spirit).

A contrario, we can observe that, in Badiou's philosophy, Wagner happens to name a prior musical event that, as for it, *is* apt to condition it.

Hence the following assessment: if, since the Wagner-singularity, which is apt to influence Badiou's philosophy, there have been no conditioning musical events, then what can we make of this philosophy's properly musical fidelity to the Wagner-event, that is to say, all in all, to the effective production of a *Wagner* musical truth? If the Schoenberg-event comes to be philosophically disjoined from the prior Wagner-event, then correlatively the Wagner-singularity is, in Badiou's philosophy, deprived of musical genealogy that creates truth, such that the *Schoenberg* question is retroactively projected as a Wagner question.

Let us punctuate all this with the following hypothesis: the negative decision according to which '*Schoenberg names a non-conditioning musical event*' must be explained by an affirmative decision on *Wagner*: it is the very way in which Badiou's philosophy unfolds, in musical matters, in the shadow cast by a *Wagner*-singularity that incites it, philosophically, to circumvent the *Schoenberg*-event. In sum, the key of the relation of Badiou's philosophy to the *Schoenberg-event* is to be found in this philosophy's relation to Wagner.

So the question arises: since the name *Schoenberg* does appear at different occasions in Badiou's philosophy as the name of a non-conditioning event, on what grounds does this name appear in it? What is, in this philosophy, the specific status of such an event when it happens to be mentioned in it?

In this philosophy, *Schoenberg* appears clearly as the name of an example: thus, in *LW*, *Schoenberg* becomes the name of a detailed example of a subject-process (cf. the scholia of the Book I: 'A musical variant of the metaphysics of the subject').

There are many other proper names that have such an exemplifying function in *LW*, including the names of musical works or artists: for example, we find the name of *Bluebeard* (by Paul Dukas) but also those of painter Hubert Robert and architect Oscar Niemeyer.

Does this type of exemplification arise, then, from a purely contingent correlation between that which exemplifies and that which is exemplified? In our case, is the exemplifying correlation between the musical subject born of the *Schoenberg*-event and the Badiousian concept of the subject strictly contingent (governed by considerations to do with the specific construction of the book – for example, to diversify examples in order to cover a broad spectrum of procedures) and might it have something possibly necessary, or at least compelling, about it?

This question would involve an examination of what *example* means for a properly philosophical discourse, of what *philosophical example* means in its own right: what is the specific status of the example in philosophical discourse? Of what is it an example, on what grounds can it function thus, to which discursive end is the example employed, etc.?

A few remarks. In the first instance I maintain that, concerning Schoenberg, this correlation pertains to contingency (specific to the moment of explanation) rather than to necessity (that of the philosophical system). The very idea of *example* is distinct from that of *condition* at the very least thanks to this specific trait: a condition is necessary (its necessity proceeds, as we saw, from a specific decision, and in no way from a state of fact, a decision that thus transforms some available event into a necessary condition), whereas an example remains irreducibly contingent. An example is by definition something that can always be replaced by another one (an example that would be irreducibly unique would no longer be an example strictly speaking: it would designate more than it would exemplify); by contrast, a 'condition' in Badiou's sense is in no way able to be replaced by another condition.

In the second place, it pays to look at the particular place that the *Schoenberg* example has in the general network of examples that this philosophy privileges.

Here I suggest the outline of such an inquiry in a few broad brushstrokes.

1. The *Schoenberg* example, used a great deal in *LW*, ought to be considered in the light of its surprising absence in the very place that one would expect to find it, namely in *C*, a work that is precisely devoted to the twentieth century. Thus we have an example that is more philosophically amenable *as example* for being without any properly philosophical consequences on its century.

2. The developments of the example of *Schoenberg* in *LW* suggest an argument that Badiou puts forwards on different occasions but that is never entirely tackled head-on (it is true that there is hardly any properly philosophical reason for doing so): the thesis of an intrinsic musical fidelity of serialism to the *Schoenberg* event, a fidelity that then authorises the inscription of dodecaphonism and serialism within the schema of a periodised continuity.

3. The condition of possibility of all this is that *Schoenberg* is essentially treated as the name of a musical constructivism (the musical names of which were *dodecaphonism* followed by *serialism*) without this doing any detailed justice to the other dimensions, without doubt more musically decisive, of *Schoenberg's* oeuvre.

4. What the name *Schoenberg* may thus have that is exemplifying for Badiou's philosophy must therefore be contrasted with the wholly other status that the name *Wagner* enjoys. Brusquely put, if *Schoenberg* names the constructivist dimension of twentieth-century music, it cannot in fact be the name of a possible fidelity to the event named

Wagner, and thus becomes the name of an event that comes to be replaceable with many others *as a simple example*.

One is thus left with the impression that the choice of an example does not clarify Badiou's philosophical system as such (as the affirmative decision of a condition can) but instead characterises its system, its immanent mode of explanation.

Translated from the French by Steven Corcoran

SEXUALITY

Samo Tomšič

In Badiou's philosophy sexuality is addressed from two basic sides: the register of love, and the teachings of psychoanalysis. Despite Badiou's recurring claim that psychoanalytic teachings should be placed above all on the level of the love-condition, we can note an important differentiation between truths concerning love and truths of sexuality. If psychoanalysis indeed confronts us with the metamorphosis of sexuality in the twentieth century (cf. *TC* 68), it is because it detaches sexuality from the exclusive realm of knowledge and links it to the register of truth. It is precisely this connection of sexuality and truth that needs to be detected in the Freudian idea of sexual etiology of neuroses, where Freud demonstrates that neurotic disorders turn around a deadlock of sexuality, thereby addressing the Two of sexuation on a different level than merely love.

Lacan later formulated this sexual deadlock in the well-known, simple axiom, which is supposed to sum up the real of sexuality: 'There is no sexual relation.' Two immediate conclusions follow from this axiom: (1) sexuality is not harmonic, that is, it is not centralised around a supposed form, be it biological or anatomical; and (2) sexuality does not exist, precisely because it does not represent a self-enclosed and constituted field of human experience. This is also what Badiou claims to be the truth addressed by the love condition. Both lessons can be traced back to Freud's famous extension of sexuality beyond its normative biological and anatomical frames, where sexuality remains reducible to the register of knowledge. The striking novelty of Freud's *Three Essays* is that they no longer explore sexuality in exclusive reference to the already constituted sexual difference but in relation to the child, where sexual difference and sexual identification are still in the process of constitution. Freud was the first one to think sexuality, not as something that simply gets 'activated' in puberty, as some sort of real knowledge inscribed in the body, but as the birthplace of the subject or as a process of subjectivation that introduces an anomaly in the biological or anatomic real. When Freud introduces the child as the 'third figure' of sexuated being, wherein it is actually possible to observe the formation of sexuality, he rejects the normative and normalised understanding of sexuality, which takes the primacy of anatomy for granted. Sexuality is not centralised by anatomical frames but instead decentralised in its historical development: hence the idea of the child's 'polymorphous perversion' and of the two-phased sexual development. And one can say that sexuality is here linked with the dimension of truth precisely because it appears in its immanent antagonism between biological body and libidinal body.

Sexuality intersects with the field of love, insofar as they both raise the question of the Two, of the non-relation between sexes. For Badiou love as truth procedure always already subordinates sexuality to itself. The claim does not hide its polemical character, aiming as it does at the place of sexuality in the ideology of democratic materialism. Here the relation between love and sexuality is inverted, since the affirmation of the exclusive existence of bodies and languages negates love as a possible register of truths, thereby reducing it to narcissism. Yet this ideological turn does not only affect love but also sexuality. Democratic materialism mistakenly identifies sexuality with sex, thereby making it a source of pleasure (rather than of *jouissance*). And since for democratic materialism all objects of pleasure assume the commodity form, the logical consequence is the foreclosure of sexual non-relation.

The commodification and fetishisation of sexual pleasure can in fact be detected even in theoretical contexts where the problem of sexual difference is thought in terms of multiplicity of gender identities. Badiou makes this very clear when he rejects the 'genderisation' of sexuality: 'To "deconstruct" sexual difference as a binary opposition, to replace it with a quasi-continuous multiple of constructions of gender – this is the ideal of a sexuality finally freed from metaphysics' (*LW* 420). The idea of sexual liberation produced a fundamental misunderstanding regarding the relation between sexuality and culture. Attempts to liberate sexuality ended up in conformism with the capitalist 'market of *jouissance*' (Lacan). We might think that democratic materialism thus turns out to be compatible with the Freudian notion of 'polymorphous perversion'. But this supposed compatibility is won only at the price of a deep misunderstanding. In Freud the lesson of polymorphous perversion remains linked to the irreducible conflict between the biological and the libidinal – another binary opposition that might link sexuality to metaphysics – whereas the capitalo-parliamentary version strives to think sexuality without its immanent conflictuality. One can say that gender promotes sex without truth.

In psychoanalysis sexuality is still linked with the register of love but this link remains problematic because sexuality is not entirely reducible to sexual difference. It finds its additional complexity in the division between the anatomical and libidinal body, which found its conceptual condensation in the Freudian notion of the drive. The structure and the paradoxes of the drive that Freud discusses notably in 'Drives and their vicissitudes' (1915) point towards a different dimension than the nexus of love and sexuality (or what Freud called sublimation). Love does appear as a specific enunciation of the truth of sexuality, but only of sexuality as it has already been constituted around the non-relation between the sexuated positions. For Badiou, the Lacanian axiom 'There is no sexual relation' remains the fundamental lesson of psychoanalysis, since it not only goes against the traditional anatomic-reductionist understanding of sexuality but also rejects the classical understanding of love in fusional terms. With the inexistence of sexuality, love becomes nothing less than the visibility of sexual non-relation. In this respect the Freudian conception of sexuality also modifies classical understandings of love.

Lacan's claim 'there is no sexual relation' comes suspiciously close to Lenin's motto 'One divides into Two'. Badiou addresses this proximity in *TS*, when he points out the homology of the psychoanalytic 'there are two sexes' and the Marxist 'there are two classes'. Lacan's axiom demonstrates that the opposition between 'split' and 'fusion' is fundamentally false, because sexuality can only be constituted on the background of inexistence. There is no preceding sexual 'One', to which the sexual 'Two' could be traced back. Sexuality thus exposes a difference without any presupposable or constructible unity. The axiom 'There is no sexual relation' also suggests that sexuality assumes a real status, exhibiting the following (negative) features: foreclosure of sense (sexuality does not 'make sense'), absence of law (sexuality does not include a normative model) and non-all (its consistency is not biological or anatomic but symptomatic).

For psychoanalysis, sexuality entails not only a rejection of the opposition between the One and the Two, but also between the One and the Multiple. The 'polymorphous perversion' of infantile sexuality is not some originary creative potential of gender multiplicity that would be later suppressed by the phallic One and castration. On the contrary, it presents sexuality as negativity 'in movement', which can be polymorphous precisely because sexuality is not grounded on a positive normative model or sexual relation. The basic claim of psychoanalysis is that sexuality essentially *is* deviation from the void of non-relation. Further, the sexuated Two is not simply the initial multiplication of the One but an irreducible split that, on the one hand, cannot be traced back on a preceding unity and, on the other, cannot be simply multiplied further into a proliferation of differences that would constitute a multiplicity of heterogeneities. Badiou is therefore entirely right to point out that the field of sexuality involves a lesson in metaphysics, notably concerning the persistence of negativity. Contemporary attempts at deconstructing sexuality tend to reject this lesson in the name of gender multiplicity.

SITE

A. J. Bartlett

'The theory of the site', Badiou admits, 'is fairly complex' (CCT 254). The reason for this complexity is that the site is a *marker* of immanent transition and, as Deleuze remarked early on, is thus essential to Badiou's key philosophical concern, which is to think the new in situations. Even as the site first appears as a concept in its own right in *BE* (and in essays that lead directly into this foundational work), it is possible to identify its nascent form as early as 1968's *Infinitesimal Subversion*, in which Badiou, in dialogue with Hegel, seeks to articulate the proper 'additional inscription' of the 'empty place' that thinking through the finite demands in terms of its 'iterative transgression of its own limit'. This text prefigures the wider engagement with artistic, mathematical, political and psychoanalytic conditions of later works and also the development of key terms in *TS* in 1982, terms such as out(side)-place, displacement, retroaction, coupled with a mathematically informed interest in the infinite and inscription. All in all, it is possible to identify three instances of the site in Badiou's oeuvre: one that is early though unformulated in *TS*; one that is central to the articulation of being *and* event in *BE*; and another articulated as the reflexive space through which the new comes to pass in appearance in *LW* in 2007. In each instance, this 'element' plays a fundamental role in organising Badiou's philosophical conception of how the new 'happens' or 'appears' in situations as *immanent* and *singular*, and coincidently how *being* is situated therein.

One of the central concerns of *TS* is the possibility of *new* knowledge, particularly from within the conjuncture of a revolutionary politics. For Badiou, the question was and remains: 'Can the subject displace the state'? It is at this point that the concept of site makes its initial appearance, where it is articulated in terms of the place of a *scission* and/or an effect of *torsion*. A *torsion* is a forced effect of the disjunction between what Badiou calls the *'splace'* (*esplace*) and the elements or 'outplaces' (*horlieux*) of this situation.

The *splace* is the work of structure, its attempt to *place* the *outplaces* within its determinate *space*. The *outplace* as elements of this situation, of its 'proper interiority' (*TS* 11), maintain an integral *force* as such and so the 'splacement' of these elements meets not so much with opposition but with the immanent lack of splace qua 'space of placements'. In this very movement of placing, the elements reveal themselves, so to speak, as 'outplaced': 'place', Badiou says, 'finds itself altered' (*TS* 54, see also *BST* 35). The structure can never finally place these elements 'where' it determines because as elements already *there* so to speak, and integrally so, any placement by structure produces a literally *void* 'site' of *torsion*. There is an integral disjunction between structure and element and this serves as the reservoir of force of the *outplace*. Torsion, which in *TS* is a name of truth, occurs when the placed element forces its place as outplace. Force, Badiou notes, denotes the 'topological side' (*TS* 10). It is not mere opposition to the state's placement but a forceful, and thus subjective, affirmation of that place as *its* place and not the place of the *splace*. This situation becomes 'historical', which is to say, 'periodically heterogeneous', when the subjective force of the outplace insists on the non-determination, the *scission*, of structure or splace. Badiou says, 'it is a process of *torsion*, by which a force reapplies itself to that from which it conflictingly emerges' (11; tm). And further, 'everything that belongs to a place returns to that part of itself which is determined by it in order to displace the place, to determine the determination, to cross the limit' (12; tm). Objectively speaking, torsion (which is a nascent term for event) has for its site an ambivalent 'element': one that is determinately there, certainly, but which escapes its determination. In effect, it already constitutes the immanence of a rupture with the 'space of placements', and a determination of the determination that, properly subjectivised, might displace the place of structure entirely. In the terms of *BE*, this element exceeds the normality of the situation, or is entirely 'abnormal', since while it might be 'determined' or presented, none of its elements (outplaces as such) in turn are presented. Relative to an event, these unpresented elements may be mobilised in the situation in such a way as to produce an 'unforeseeable beginning', a possible that ruptures with the given structure ('Logic of the Site' 143; cf. *LW* 365).

It is in *BE* that 'site' acquires its formal concept, on the basis of an ontological articulation that provides greater precision. By denoting that which 'presents what is unpresented', or indeed that which is nothing to the situation, 'site' stands as the literal transcription into the metaontological lexicon of the ontological name of 'void'. The singular outcome of ZFC, adopted by Badiou, is to show that the *one* of every appearing is only an effect, and that what is is intrinsically *multiple*. This authorises Badiou's fundamental claim according to which the 'one is not' and, as such, *the nothing is* (*BE* 35). 'Nothing', for Badiou, is the general regime of non-presentation. Given that it cannot be one, nothing can only *appear* as the one of the multiplicity that it is: 'It is thus ruled out that the nothing – which here names the pure will-have-been-counted as distinguishable from the effect of the count, and thus distinguishable from presentation – be taken as a term. There is not a-nothing, there is "nothing", phantom of inconsistency' (*BE* 54–5). Set theory assigns inconsistency or pure multiplicity or nothing, a mark of itself. This name or mark Ø refers uniquely to 'nothing' as such, in other words, to being-qua-being as pure inconsistency; thus making 'being' thinkable in situations. Ø renders consistent for thought (ontology) the pure inconsistency that it marks. Accordingly, set theory draws its entire form from this presentation of the multiple, from this inscription of that which is not.

The site, then, marks the point where ontology – the thinking of being as being – gives way to the thinking of truth as conditioned by an event. The site is ontologically consistent since it belongs to a given situation, yet it simultaneously constitutes the material form of the event – that which ruptures with all situational consistency. The question the site raises might be construed as follows: 'how can one multiple be ontologically consistent while at the same time being that which exposes the situation to the perils of inconsistency?' The site in *BE*, and the texts which Badiou writes after this reformulation of the place of transition, carries two qualifications. It is referred to as both 'void-site' and 'evental-site' (translator's intro, *IT* 37, fn. 26). Both these designations designate the same 'place'. 'Void-site' describes a particularity of the site in terms of how it appears in a situation. The site is an element presented by a situation, none of whose elements are in turn presented. What the site presents is void for the situation. For this reason Badiou describes it as an abnormal multiple or element, because in a normal situation all presented elements, or sets, of the situation have the elements they present re-presented. If any such abnormal multiple exists in a situation, the situation in turn cannot be a normal (or natural) situation. The existence of a 'site', Badiou argues, determines the situation as 'historical'.

It is an evental-site because for there to be an event a situation must present a site, it must include within it at least one element, or one multiple that presents nothing. The event, whose occurring is the contingent necessity for a truth procedure, Badiou says, 'indexes the void'. That is, it marks the elemental existence of that which the situation does not present. These elements, those which the situation 'does not know', but which appear there as 'void', as unknown to the state, will condition the production of the generic or truth procedure. These unpresented elements make up the very matter of the event. This is not to say that the existence of the site determines the occurrence of the event. '[I]t serves [only] to circumscribe and qualify it' (*BE* 203). Nevertheless, the importance of this singular element for thinking *historical situations*, for thinking change, is established when we consider that as a term which is not represented, a term that must not be, it allows us to say in affirmative terms that it is the site which guards the lack of the rule of the state. This 'lack', given that every element includes the void, is a capacity common to all situated elements (inhabitants). The site, then, harbouring the capacity to a-void the state, is a singular-universal – both counted as one and that which is for all. It is both aporetic and foundational.

Unlike in *BE*, in *LW* the event 'fuses' with the site –'as far as place fuses with a beyond'. In its way, it is reminiscent of the reflexive and topological depiction of the force of the *horlieu* upon its *esplace* in *TS*. In *LW*, working again through the example of the Paris Commune (and Rousseau), and under the new condition of the mathematised logic of category theory (thus making it *merely* reminiscent of that described in *TS*), Badiou determines the site to be the place of being-appearing (*LW* 113). The immanent gap insistent in the coupling of the notions of place and force, being and appearing, site and event whose *being BE* exposes, is here rearticulated. Fundamentally, that is, ontologically, things remain the same but from the perspective of a Greater Logic, wherein relation is the key concept driving all articulation – all knowledge of the being-there of any element – the site, determinedly existing in a world and still foundational to change, is reckoned in terms of intensity rather than of inscription. In thinking how the new appears at a site, it is the extensive force of what takes place that matters. At the same time, since it remains resolutely singular, the site cannot be reduced to the worldly logic of variation. In short, and precisely because it marks transition as such, it is circumscribable neither by ontology nor by logic, yet it is not, for all that, unthinkable. Indeed, in *LW*, Badiou is again constrained to think the site as double, abnormal, paradoxical, as that self-belonging multiple 'exposed to its own transcendental indexing', but this time in terms of (but not strictly speaking *as*) the logic of appearing (360–1). The site, logically annexed to the evental multiple (rather than merely providing the being of the latter), continues to mark transition, discontinuity, or real change (as opposed to 'modification'), but the register of the latter *in a world* becomes a matter of existence. For this reason, the effect is measured by the intensity of this existence, which, in the case of the site, goes from nothing as such – that which to the transcendental of the world in-exists – to the point where the world itself – the transcendental that indexes it as such – is no longer. The transcendental organisation of a world articulates existence relationally, thus somewhat constructively, in terms of predicates or objects (themselves 'transcendentally' situated). In relation to a specified object, then, those elements that make up the site, which in essence singularise it, do not exist for that world. Their relation to an object of that world, thus their transcendental or logical articulation, is 'lacking' or indeed minimal. The site is itself an object for that world, but its appearance as such is weak, to the point, as we said, of (indexing) inexistence. Yet, precisely, that what it marks *inexists*, that it is the mark of that which for the transcendental of a world is nothing, *is* what determines it to be a site for that world. However, this determination, while a fact of the world as such is determined to be a site if and only if the appearance of its elements – for the Commune, 'worker-beings' vis-à-vis the 'Thiers government' (*LW* 365) – takes a specifically 'illogical' configuration – the existence of the inexistent – i.e. the worker appears as a political force, as the realisation of an unheralded capacity, as, in their singular configuration, 'an element of the object that it is' (366). In *LW*, then, the site guarantees the appearing-there of that which, to the world, is nothing. It comes to be there at the site, to exist despite the transcendental of said world. 'It is through the existence of the inexistent that the subversion of appearing by being, which underlies it, unfolds within appearing itself' (378). Yet that which gives this multiple in appearance does not guarantee what it promises: the reconfiguration of the transcendental of the world for which it appears. The consequences – the relations of intensity between existences in a given world – are conditioned by the site but are beyond its determination. Rather, it is the effective production of these consequences that retroactively makes the site appear intensely, as, in effect, an event-site, which is a singularity and thus neither a 'fact' (a site lacking intensity) nor a modification (change subject to predication) (372). As always with Badiou, it all depends on the subject, the compositional, transversal figure whose points of articulation vis-à-vis the site are singularity, fact and modification. It is the subject holding fast to the former, whose extensive force it effectively realises and whose trace it is, that recomposes the singular-universality marked by the site and so makes truth of *evental* disorder, and thus, insofar as it simultaneously destroys a subjective incapacity, all the difference in the world.

SOPHISTRY

Samo Tomšič

Every affirmation of philosophy always already affirms its alienating double. This gesture is intimately related to the old problem of the category of truth in the quarrel against opinion: is truth merely a convention,

an adequate relation between words and things and truth-values; or is
its structure more complex, able to reach beyond the particularism of
opinions towards a concrete articulation of the singular with the universal? By virtue of its constitutive departure with the regime of opinion, a
definition of philosophy will in the same movement imply a definition of
sophistry.

Badiou's philosophy indeed engages in the most systematic confrontation with sophistry since Plato and Aristotle. As a figure of doxa that
rejects the philosophical striving for true knowledge, the sophist in
Badiou's thought is localised exactly where Plato had discerned him, in
a field where truths are rejected in favour of the multitude of opinions.
Little wonder, then, that for Badiou the principal image of contemporary
sophistry is bound to the ideological context of what Badiou in *LW* calls
'democratic materialism'. The fundamental axiom of this orientation is
that 'there are only bodies and languages', which is tantamount to saying,
'there are only pleasures and opinions', or 'there is only multiplicity'.
Language and democracy, or rather, the multitude of subjective dialects
and of personal opinions, is the ideological environment of contemporary
sophistry. Unsurprisingly, then, the postmodern condition creates a
situation in which Heidegger's idea of an end of philosophy is necessarily
accompanied by the triumph of sophistry.

LW suggests a further definition of sophistry as the 'appearing of the
negative' (*LW* 105). Referring back to Plato's *Sophist*, Badiou accentuates
the fact that the realm of sophistry is that of imaginary and discursive
indistinctness. Plato famously concludes his dialogue with the 'murder
of father Parmenides', that is, he questions the fundamental principles
of philosophy: 'being is non-being is not' and the 'sameness of thinking
and being'. By focusing on language rather than truth the sophist links
the signifier with non-being and treats the latter as something positive.
As the philosopher's double the sophist becomes something like a non-
being appearing as a being, a fake being or a semblance, a lie appearing
as truth. This is the philosophical lesson of ancient sophistry, which can
be summed up as follows: sophistry is a form of deceiving with the signifier. Upon closer inspection, and in line with the lessons of structuralism,
language precisely is non-being that constantly produces effects of being.
The sophists will consequently be masters in rhetoric and their *savoir-faire*
will concern nothing other than language.

Badiou underlines the intimate connection between sophistry and language by linking it with the so-called linguistic turn in philosophy. Two
modern figures will then symbolise contemporary images of sophistry and
its two paradigms: Nietzsche and Wittgenstein, names that Badiou also
associates with antiphilosophy. This ambiguity does not seem to mark the

ancient sophists and the two names seem to be standing both within and without sophistry. On the one hand their position contains a radical affirmation of the real against the philosophical category of truth: Nietzsche's archi-political act in *The Will to Power*, Wittgenstein's archi-aesthetic act in *Tractatus Logico-Philosophicus*. On the other, Nietzsche and Wittgenstein also articulate a rejection of truth in favour, respectively, of rhetorics and logic respectively. Here one will recall Nietzsche's praise of the ancient sophists against Plato and Aristotle, or Wittgenstein's rejection of 'speculative' philosophical problems in favour of logicism and language games. In both cases, the absolutisation of language dismisses the philosophical category of truth. Moreover, language is also all that remains after the failed antiphilosophical act: Nietzsche's poetic aphorisms, Wittgenstein's axioms, language games and aporias.

Nietzsche and Wittgenstein undoubtedly share the affirmation of the primacy of language over truth, thus making truth an imaginary effect of language. If Nietzsche is declared to be the prince of modern sophistry, its principal and inventor, this is because he was the first to privilege poetic language, language games, the power of anecdotes or linguistic metaphors over the real of truth procedures, the *jouissance* of language over mathematical formalisation.

Yet it is Wittgenstein who appears more crucial to Badiou's philosophical definition of modern sophistry:

Modern sophists are those who maintain, in the school of the great Wittgenstein, that thought is caught in the following alternative: that it either consists in effects of discourse, in language games, or that it consists in silent indication, in the pure 'showing' of that which is subtracted from language's grasp. Sophists are those for whom the fundamental opposition is not between truth and error, or errancy, but between speech and silence, that is, between that which can be said and that which it is impossible to say. Or again: between meaningful and meaningless statements. (*CS* 6)

Modern sophistry, then, appears split between the therapeutics of language and the mysticism of the unsayable, caught in the fundamental dilemma that pushed Wittgenstein's thinking into a deadlock. The two aspects are in fact logically linked in the ethical imperative that concludes Wittgenstein's *Tractatus*, this 'manifesto' of modern sophistry. If logic is the therapeutics of language and the privileged orientation in thinking, then philosophical language ought to be constituted on the delimitation of sense from non-sense. This therapy then reduces truth to the value of constructible sentences, making it inseparable from the production of meaning. This is where modern sophistry is compatible with religion.

Hence the supplement of mysticism in Wittgenstein's logical regulation of language.

Now the question is, how should philosophy confront its sophistic adversary? For Badiou this confrontation is always both ethical and political. It is political because it opposes to democratic materialism the 'affirmationism' of materialist dialectics: 'there are truths'. The political significance of this affirmation has become most evident in recent years, as Badiou has openly associated his conception of communism with Plato's foundation of philosophy and with the philosophical category of truth. And it is ethical because the confrontation with the sophist should not amount to the annihilation of the philosophical double, but merely to its proper placing. Delimitation of the two seemingly indiscernible discourses implies that the sophist is neutralised *within* the field of philosophy, but not annihilated as its timeless Other, as something that 'ought not be' (*CS* 19). For together with the annihilation of the sophist, philosophy also abolishes itself in its immanent dogmatic catastrophe.

The figure of the sophist thus serves as a reminder to philosophy: 'The sophist is the one that reminds us of the emptiness of the category of Truth' (ibid.). As a timeless Other, sophistry is the necessary polemical counterpart through which philosophy deploys its own affirmationism. In other words, the negative figure of the sophist prevents philosophy from becoming self-enclosed and mistaking itself for a meta-discourse that consequently substantialises the empty category of truth as a privileged access to the real. The singular but empty category of Truth serves as a philosophical tool to gather and hence to affirm the heterogeneous truths of the four conditions around a void that serves as a topological support of their compossibility. But in this situation philosophy remains at distance from truths precisely because of the alienating effect of the dialectical *polemos* with the sophist. In the end, sophistry reminds philosophy that there is no meta-position and that the scandal of language needs to be a subject of philosophical consideration.

SPINOZA

Christopher Norris

Baruch Spinoza (1632–1677) is one of those thinkers – 'strong precursors', in the useful phrase of Harold Bloom – with whom Badiou has long been engaged in a dialogue that is nonetheless close and intense for its critical-diagnostic character. In some respects Spinoza must surely be counted Badiou's most valuable ally among the various philosophers, from Plato to Heidegger, who figure as points of reference from episode to episode of his own developing argument in *BE*. After all, Spinoza (like Badiou) was a rationalist who believed that the human mind was capable of grasping truths – quintessentially the truths of mathematics – that led beyond the limits of present-best or even presently conceivable future-best knowledge. Then again, Spinoza (like Badiou) was a radical in politics who steadfastly refused the road taken by other, less courageous or clear-sighted thinkers of his time – those seeking a compromise settlement with the forces of political and religious reaction – and who insisted on thinking right through with his critique of monarchical power (in however 'constitutional' a form) and theological dogma. Moreover he shared with Badiou a rejection of that whole epistemological way of thought which conceived the so-called 'problem of knowledge' as a matter of somehow securing or establishing the match between subject and object, knower and known, or mind and world. For Spinoza this series of vexing dualisms was the problem bequeathed by his near-contemporary Descartes, and one that could be solved – or rendered illusory – only by adopting a resolutely monist or naturalistic approach. In the Spinozist conception, mind and body were two 'attributes' of the self-same substance and held to be distinct not by any kind of metaphysical (Cartesian) necessity but simply on account of our limited understanding.

To this extent Badiou is very much of Spinoza's party, albeit with a strong bias towards placing the corrective (anti-Cartesian) emphasis on the rationalist rather than the naturalistic side of that nowadays widely discredited dualist paradigm. He shares not only the Spinozist desire to have done with such false dichotomies but also the Spinozist trust in the power of autonomous rational thought to lift itself above the deliverances of commonsense belief. For Badiou, as for Spinoza, advances of this kind – whether in mathematics, the natural sciences, philosophy, politics, or art – can come about only through an exercise of reason or critical-reflective intelligence that marks a decisive break with existing ideas of what properly counts as veridical knowledge. Moreover they are united in deeming mathematics the paradigm case of a discipline that exemplifies just such moments of transformative insight or conceptual breakthrough. In Spinoza this takes the form of a theory of knowledge modelled on the way that the post-Galilean physical sciences have deployed mathematics as a means of overcoming those obstacles to truth put up by the natural human attachment to naïve sense-certainty or intuitive self-evidence. It is also evident in Spinoza's having structured his chief work, the *Ethics*, as a sequence of numbered definitions, axioms, propositions, corollaries and scholia laid out *more geometrico*, or after the Euclidean axiomatic-deductive mode of reasoning. Although Badiou eschews this latter, somewhat notional device he does follow Spinoza in according a central role to mathematics – more specifically, post-Cantorian set theory and its impact on conceptions of the infinite – as witnessing the power of thought to open up previously unexplored realms of conceptual possibility.

There is also a close kinship between Spinoza's remarkably prescient critique of religion in the *Tractatus Theologico-Politicus*, focused on the nexus of political power with claims to authority through grace of divine revelation, and Badiou's political writings with their combined force of theoretical grasp and practical-activist commitment. However, these points of resemblance have to be set against the fact of Badiou's taking issue with Spinoza when it comes to certain basic philosophical questions. These chiefly concern the relationship between being and event, or the extent to which some given ontology – whether mathematical, scientific, or social – may be subject to the kind of irruptive force that brings about a radical change in the pre-existent order of things. The main problem, as Badiou sees it, is not that Spinoza constructs an elaborate ontology on the basis of certain highly speculative theses – a charge, after all, that might plausibly be laid at his own door. Rather it is the strong metaphysical-determinist doctrine that Spinoza shares with Leibniz: the idea that all events have their preordained place in an absolute, exceptionless, all-embracing order of jointly causal and logical necessity, including those events which – owing to our limited knowledge or powers of explanation – we are unable to trace back through the entire concatenated chain of causes and effects. For this would leave no room for the event as Badiou conceives it, that is, for the emergence of utterly singular, anomalous, or aberrant parts of some given situation which don't count as elements thereof – or as members 'in good standing' – since they occupy a marginal region of the site where it confronts the inherently destabilising force of whatever is excluded by the count-as-one.

Badiou is thus fundamentally out of sympathy with Spinoza's dogged attempt – like that of Aristotle before him, and with similar problematical results – to conceive a plenist ontology that excludes any thought of the void, or any allowance for that which eludes specification in positive terms. This is further reinforced by his outright rejection of Cartesian mind/body dualism and consequent stress on the error of supposing that mental powers could be exerted to any effect except insofar as they corresponded to (more exactly: were identical with) some bodily affect or capacity. Badiou is very far from endorsing dualism or any of those present-day substitute doctrines that try to stake out a workable middle-ground position. However, he does take vigorous issue with Spinoza's argument from a thoroughgoing monist position in that regard to a likewise thoroughgoing determinist creed. This results from taking the mind/body identity thesis – along with the Spinozist case against traditional (typically religious) voluntarist conceptions of freewill – as one that inherently leaves no room for those events that would signal the exercise of thought or effective agency and an irruption of the void into the plenary order of being. In fact, Badiou argues, Spinoza is unable to carry this programme through and is compelled to resort at crucial points to the paradoxical (or downright contradictory) notion of 'infinite mode' in order to avoid that unacceptable consequence (cf. Spinoza's Closed Ontology, in *TW*). Thus Spinoza stands alongside Parmenides, Plato, Aristotle, and Leibniz as a thinker whom Badiou regards as exemplary not for advancing a doctrine that he finds altogether congenial, but rather for having pressed to the limit with a line of thought that is instructive precisely on account of its problematic character.

SUBJECT, FIGURES OF THE

Bruno Besana

Editor's note: This dictionary does not contain a specific entry on the subject as such, which would entail explaining some different features to the present entry. However, given concerns of space and the fact that much has already been written about the subject in Badiou, it seemed more judicious to provide readers with an extended elaboration of 'figures of the subject' instead.

Subject as sequence

In opposition to post-structuralist deconstruction, Badiou argues for the centrality of the subject as a philosophical category and distinguishes it from an empirical human being or an invariable transcendental function. More precisely, he defines the subject as 'the *local* status of a procedure, a configuration that exceeds the situation' (OS 27). It is exactly these concepts of *local procedure* and *excess over the situation* that articulate not only Badiou's concept of the subject, but also its categorisation into different figures. A subject is in fact definable as a formal sequence of operations that takes place under specific given conditions, and via which a synthetic effect – and, what is more, a novelty – is produced.

Always specific to a given situation of which it is a material element, a subject simultaneously exceeds this situation: 'every subject', Badiou states, 'is a forced exception, always coming in the second place' (*TS* 84). More precisely, a subject is defined as a series of actions that progressively unfold the consequences of an event according to the specificity of the given situation, the order of which is interrupted by the exposition of the truth claimed by the event. The truth exposed by the event is for Badiou nothing but 'the metonymy of the situation's very being' (OS 26): it exposes a certain excess of the situation over a given specific mode of representation of its elements; it exposes, for instance, the fact that the law of a situation – the manner in which the elements of the situation are structured and hierarchised – is not a necessary reality, but a contingent construction. As such truth concerns all the elements of the situation, and is therefore infinite, a subject will be both 'the local or finite status' (25) of this same truth, and 'in excess of the law' (*SP* 78) of the situation.

'Suspended to a truth' (*BE* 406), and in excess over the situation, a subject is never alone, but acts amongst a multiplicity of figures that, in different manners, unfold the infinity of the consequences of the truth exposed by the event, which addresses the whole situation. Consistently with this, in *LW* Badiou elaborates a model of articulation of four different types of positions in front of an event: such figures compose the geography of subjective space, and give a temporal scansion to the subjective embodiment of an event into a situation.

The faithful subject

The first and fundamental figure is the *faithful* subject (in previous texts, most notably *TS* and *BE*, identified with the subject *tout court*), which, by betting on the fact that an event has taken place, 'realises itself in the production of consequences' (*LW* 53). This demands a triple operation:

First, a decision. The faithful subject claims that an event, interrupting the ordinary logic of facts, has taken place. But it is impossible to prove, from within the situation, whether what occurred was an event or a simple ordinary fact. This is because the event is by definition in excess over the established criteria of judgement of facts (criteria that the event precisely aims to render operative). In the absence of valid criteria upon which one can evaluate it, the event cannot, then, be the object of a proof, but only of a radical decision, which ultimately relies upon a wager. By wagering and deciding that what happened was an event, the event starts to exist as such, as in the case of an insurrection that becomes retroactively a revolution because of the acts that extend its consequences. The faithful figure is therefore at once a consequence of the event and a necessary condition of it.

Second, the faithful subject *connects* the decision on the event to a series of singular points of the situation, for instance, by applying the equality declared by an event to a *specific* situation of inequality that declares equality impossible or utopian. Such acts of connection of a point to the event are real *decisions*, in which 'the totality of the world is at stake in a game of heads or tails' (*LW* 400). In fact, each act confronts the whole situation, in a local point, with a contradiction between the law that states and organises the unequal role of the elements of the situation and an equality that interrupts such a mode of representation by positing itself as a truth. Each of these acts 'is essentially illegal, in that it cannot conform to any *law* of representation' (*BE* 205). These acts of *connection* thus multiply the sense of decision: they *separate* (Latin: *decido*) each element from the current law of the situation, decide retrospectively that what took place was effectively an event, and realise it by performing the consequences of the declaration of its existence. Such operations constitute the proper materiality of the subject: in fact, in order to unfold the consequences of the event for the specificity of the situation (what Badiou calls a treatment of the points) the subject needs to provide itself with 'organs', i.e. with the material structures necessary to organise, to connect amongst them, the different points disconnected from the law of the situation. This operation of connection of disconnections connects the event and the contingencies of the situation (OS 29): 'fidelity is conjointly defined by a situation [. . .] by the event [. . .] and by a rule of connection which allows one to evaluate the dependency of any particular multiple with respect to the event' (*BE* 234).

Third, faithfulness, although always proceeding by acts which are specific to, or rather for, the situation, has a *generic* address and content, i.e. it exists by addressing each element of the situation, independently from their positive content, and by claiming that the truth at stake concerns singularly each element. Via such generic address, a subject shows that 'no event can be the event of a particularity' and that 'the universal is the only possible correlate to the event' (*SP* 75). A faithful subject is thus the 'local configuration of a generic procedure from which a truth is supported' (*BE* 391).

For Badiou the proper of an event is to interrupt the apparent naturality of the rules organising the elements of a situation, and therefore to interrupt a homogeneous time in which everything is a regular fact, and no novelty can appear. By organising the consequences of such interruption, the faithful subject produces a distinctive sequence of time, a new present: 'we will call present, and write π, the set of consequences of the evental trace, as realised by the successive treatment of points' (*LW* 52). This Badiou summarises in the following formula:

$$\frac{\varepsilon}{\mathvarnothing} \Rightarrow \pi$$

Here we can read that the present (π) is the result of the inscription of the event (ε) on a body (¢), the unity of which is disrupted by the removal of evidences, upon which it is represented in the situation. The faithful figure is thus at once the production of a new specific body and the organisation of a new present in which the event is exposed in its universal address.

The reactive subject

Given an event, other attitudes may spring up in relation to it, e.g. active denial and violent opposition. There are in fact several modes of relation to the event, and such modes constitute for Badiou a veritable schematism of 'typical forms' (*LW* 57), or figures. Badiou underlines that the reasons and the modes of emergence of these figures and of their relations are always contingent: for instance, a fidelity to the event does not necessarily produce an external reaction, or necessarily transform itself into a reaction (as in the case of the revolutionary person turning into a renegade or into a bureaucrat). Nonetheless, the modes of reaction to the event are always logically dependent on the emergence of a fidelity, without which they are not possible (cf. below). In other words, the different figures form a transcendental schematism, although the activation of each of these figures remains contingent.

In the wake of an event, some will of course decide to ignore it, but others will declare that, in order to obtain the present being unfolded by the action of a faithful subject, it is not necessary to posit the event's having taken place. This specific relation to the event, which Badiou names reactive, has a classical double example: given the October Revolution, one reactive figure is the reformist left wing, which declared equality to be possible without a revolution and without the destruction of the state; the other is socialist bureaucracy, which declared that, given that all the consequences of the revolutionary event had been realised, the need to 'construct' the revolution was no longer there. The former, declaring that equality is progressively obtained through reforms, reduces the revolution to a simple moment of revolt within the 'natural' order of parliamentary democracy (and it simultaneously substitutes equality with some *ersatz*, such as equal opportunity or the equal possibility to compete in a 'free market'). The latter also reduces revolution to a fact: by declaring that its consequences are fully realised, it subverts its evental nature, which is to have infinite consequences. The outcome is normalisation: there is nothing left to do, so it suffices to leave 'a subset (class, its Party) maintain privileged relations with the truth' (*OD* 83; tm).

In both cases what is denied is the necessity of *continuing*, the necessity of a further series of acts of decision. The reactive subject produces an 'extinguished present' (*LW* 55), a present in which each 'now' is the mere continuation of the previous moments. The formula of the reactive subject is:

$$\frac{\neg\,\varepsilon}{\dfrac{\varepsilon}{\cancel{c}} \Rightarrow \pi} \Rightarrow \pi$$

What it shows is how the affirmation of an event as a 'non-event' pushes the procedure of fidelity under the bar of consciousness, thus producing a present that is crossed out, cancelled in its specific capacity to be present, to produce a difference. The further consequence is that 'the body is held at the furthest distance from the (negative) declaration that founds the reactive subject' (*LW* 56): in fact the bodies of the inhabitants of such a present are more similar to normal objects than to subjective tools to change the present.

The obscure subject

The appearing of a faithful procedure also leads to a more frontal reaction that aims directly at 'an abolition of the new present' (*LW* 58–9). This third figure Badiou calls 'obscure'. It denies the present as a *kampfplatz* – as a point of division between a state of fact and an event that has interrupted its mechanisms – and actively seeks to abolish it. On the contrary, it conceives each present as the local manifestation of a global sense, and it bases this claim on 'the invocation of a full and pure transcendent Body, an ahistorical or anti-evental body (City, God, Race . . .)' (59–60). From this perspective, which is typically one of the defense of established identities with acquired privileges, the obscure subject seeks to eliminate those bodies that do not correspond to the logic of the 'full Body', thus fighting against both revolutionary procedures and those who do not participate to its own privileges. At the same time, the obscure subject sustains its operations by appealing to all those who the present situation affects, those who can be seduced by the idea of the return to a mythical original unity – such being, for instance, the case of the subproletarian that joins an ultranationalist racist party.

The aim of the obscure subject is to make it so that 'the trace [of the event] will be denied' (59–60), therefore producing the retroactive obscuration of the event itself. This figure organises thus 'the descent of [the] present into the night of non-exposition' (59), as posited in its formula

$$\frac{C \Rightarrow (\neg\,\varepsilon \Rightarrow \neg\,\cancel{c})}{\pi}$$

The formula states that from the affirmation of a transcendent full body what proceeds is both the negation of the event, and of the possibility of its inscription in a subjectified body. This has as a final result the disappearance of the present under the bar. The obscuration has as its primary goal the negation of the truth exposed by the event, and the negation of the subjective activity that interrupts the endless reproduction of the inequalities of the situation. But the effect of this is the obscuration of the present itself, which becomes the mere reproduction of the given, and the place of foreclosure both of novelty and of thought.

Resurrection

In their attempt either to make the evental novelty conform to the objective present state of facts, or to obscure both the event and the production of a new present, the reactive and the obscure figures depend 'on the minimal production of a present by a faithful figure' (*LW* 62) (production of present that they work to reduce to a mere state of fact, inserted within a linear, changeless time). As Badiou says, 'from a subjective point of view, it is not because there is a reaction that there is revolution, it is because there is revolution that there is reaction' (ibid.). By claiming this, Badiou aims at turning on its head 'the whole "left-wing" tradition which believes a progressive politics "fights against oppression" ' (ibid.).

Not only do these figures depend on the event they try to reduce, but, should they succeed, they are still unable to prevent the possible reactivation of the truth exposed by the event: in fact a truth – being essentially infinite and unaffected by the contingencies of the sequence which exposes it – can always be reactivated. What is more, such reactivation is not only factually possible but even theoretically necessary. In fact the truth of an event is equivalent to the infinite unfolding of its consequences, but every sequence is finite and therefore no event will be completely verified by a single sequence. From this Badiou concludes that 'for there to be an event, one must be able to situate oneself within the consequences of another' (*BE* 210). For instance, in order to name what an hypothetical first egalitarian event is, one must be able to name the existence of a second one, without which, properly speaking, the first one would have never occurred. More precisely, the existence of a previous evental sequence is only possible from the standpoint of a currently open one.

Reactivation, or resurrection, thus constitutes a fourth figure of the present. This fourth figure is 'a fragment of truth inserted under the bar by the machinery of the obscure (and that) can be extracted from it at any instant' (*LW* 63). And, Badiou adds, 'we will call this destination, which reactivates a subject in another logic . . . *resurrection*' (65). This last subjective figure being the one of the sudden appearance of something radically 'out of place and time' in a situation that is completely normalised, stable, is ultimately nothing but the figure of the event itself.

An evental moment of resurrection has thus always three aspects: it is the beginning of a new subjective sequence, it is the retrospective confirmation of the evental nature of a previous one, and it is the reactivation of a truth which, being infinite, passes unaffected from the finitude of a subjective sequence to the finitude of another (figure below from *LW* 67).

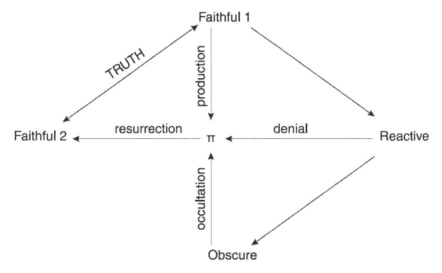

Figure 3 From Badiou, *Logics of Worlds*, p. 67.

Caught between two events, the different subjective figures articulate the mode in which a new present is created as a contradiction in its own time, and the way in which this present is normalised and eventually obscured. But, even more, the architecture of these figures exposes such logic both in its contingence and in its infinitude, showing the capacity of a subject to be the finite and organised mode of existence of the infinite capability to undo all finitude.

SUBTRACTION – UNDECIDABLE, INDISCERNIBLE, GENERIC, UNNAMEABLE

Frank Ruda

Subtraction is one of the central categories of Alain Badiou's oeuvre. To grasp its centrality we can begin with the fact that, for Badiou, philosophy itself is essentially subtractive. The particular intricacy of the concept must thus be seen as deriving from its reverberation at all levels of Badiou's thinking. An understanding of philosophy as subtractive implies that all its most crucial categories need to be conceived of in a subtractive way, including the most central one, namely truth. This is where a proper systematic elaboration of subtraction can begin. For, from the viewpoint of philosophy, truth can in the first instance be characterised in a simple and somewhat abstract manner as something that is irreducible to, or logically uninferrable from, knowledge. To say that philosophy has to 'subtract Truth from the labyrinth of meaning' (*CS* 13), means that it must insist on the distinction between the truth and meaning, truth and sense, truth and opinion and, first and foremost, between truth and knowledge. If there are truths, they are irreducible to knowledge; this fundamental claim is a subtractive claim and it necessitates that philosophy cease to identify truth with any of the above categories. Were it not to do so, truth would be posited as objectively knowable and thus would not stand in a consequential relation to an unforeseeable event.

But what does it mean for philosophy that truth is subtracted from knowledge? First of all, that what holds for truths holds equally for subtraction: as truths are procedures, so subtraction has also to be immanently related to practice. Badiou further specifies four modalities by which philosophy can account for the subtractive nature of truth procedures. This fourfold specification concerns the category of subtraction as much as constitution of truth procedures; it indicates why truth procedures fall outside of knowledge, and ultimately makes it possible to identify subtraction with truth procedures, thus providing an account of what may be called Badiou's conception of thought-practice. The four modalities include: (1) the undecidable; (2) the indiscernible; (3) the generic; and (4) the unnameable (*CS* 113–29). The concatenation of these four terms may be summarily rendered as follows: the subtractive nature of truths is marked by a contingent and unforeseeable emergence in an *event* (1), which generates, after a subject affirms it and hence commits to it, a contingent and aleatory path that traverses a given historical situation (fidelity) and is thus the effect of a newly grounded actuality of *freedom* (2); this path, by reworking the 'entire' situation, is immanently infinite, and constructs a set that no unifying predicate can be used to construct, and is therefore *singular* (3). It is on this basis that Badiou can provide a systematic account of an *ethics* of truths (4), and indeed claim that only a subtractive process allows us to think through a consistent notion of good and evil, ethical disaster, and so on. What this brief outline describes is Badiou's philosophical doctrine of truth as subtracted from knowledge. If truths are the manifestations of post-evental consequences unfolded by faithful subjects, they are universal because they are subtractive. As such, they are neither knowable nor constructible by recourse to the predicates and attributes that describe the particularities of the situation of which a truth is a truth. Because truths are subtractive they are not grounded in particularities or in one specific particularity of the situation, but have to be conceived as related to a singularity. This is because particularities can be discerned by means of predicates; singularities, on the contrary, can only be identified and named, but escape all unified predication.

However, to overcome abbreviated formalism and to account properly for the category of subtraction, a more detailed version of Badiou's four modalities of subtraction is needed.

The undecidable

Undecidables are utterances, declarations or statements unable to be evaluated according to the distinction of true or false (a distinction in and of knowledge). Take the example of a declaration of love ('I love you'), with which, for Badiou, any true love procedure begins. Such a declaration cannot be objectively either falsified or verified using the given means of the situation. It would be impossible to argue, for example, that a given man simply cannot be in love because the supposed beloved loves horses, while he hates them. There are no objective criteria at one's disposal by means of which a declaration of love can be objectively verified or falsified. What triggered and caused it, or, more precisely, what made it possible in the first place – all this remains inscribed in a solely subjective register. For only the subjects involved in the practice are authorised *through their labour itself* to decide whether or not the declared love will have been true. In other words, only the subject, namely the newly arisen love-subject, will prove the declaration to have been either a true declaration or a mere simulacrum thereof. This is how Badiou qualifies the response to an event: an individual has, say, to make decision about whether what happened is or is not worth changing his or her life for, without any objective criteria on which to do so. The event remains, strictly speaking, undecidable. It nonetheless has to be decided by an individual who, via the act of forced decision – forced, because an individual cannot not decide; even not deciding implies a negative decision – becomes a subject. Exactly this argument is to be found in the history of philosophy, although this time unrelated to subjectivisation, namely the old liar's paradox. If a liar claims to be feeling well and is known to be a liar, it cannot be objectively verified or falsified whether or not he lied. A decision is needed, and only the consequences of this decision will verify or falsify it. Undecidability thus formally indicates the limit of a given language (of evaluation) and therefore of its objectivity.

It is a formal characteristic of the event because it de-naturalises, de-objectifies the situation, opening up space for a purely subjective procedure. 'The undecidable', says Badiou, 'is therefore that which is subtracted from a supposedly exhaustive classification of statements realised according to a norm that allots statements values. The undecidable statement cannot be ascribed any value, although the norm of attribution only exists on the assumption of its complete efficacy' (*CS* 114).

The indiscernible

The second modality of subtraction is the indiscernible, a differential, relational concept that depicts what immediately follows the decision of the undecidable. A term (something) is for Badiou (formally) indiscernible if at least another term (another something) is indiscernible from it. Indiscernibility, hence, always marks a relation between terms, one that obtains when a property attributable to one of them cannot but be attributed to both of them, such that no property allows them to be distinguished from one another. Although objectively indiscernible, it is nevertheless assumed that there is more than just one term involved. Indiscernibility is not analogous to identification. Simply, unable to be discriminated, one cannot name their difference by recourse to objective criteria (properties, attributes, etc.). For example, a couple in love may be said to be acting and talking crazily, but this specific madness is thus attributed not to one but to both individuals concerned. It is impossible to give an account of their practice of love and not attribute the same thing to both of them. Simultaneously, however, it is clear that these two individuals are not simply one individual – love is not a fusion of two individuals into a new one. Both of them act as though they are mad, but they are not identical. Yet the way they act (say, by not caring about the world around them, etc.) makes them – their difference – indiscernible. This is to say, that the indiscernible depicts a specific kind of relational function between terms actively involved in a specific kind of (truth) practice that results from an event. 'The indiscernible subtracts the two from duality' (*CS* 116). This is to say that the indiscernible is what makes the procedure grounded in an event indifferent to differences (that are ascribed to the terms objectively), because it manifests a kind of relation between terms that cannot be conceptually grasped. It is impossible, then, to articulate their practice by recourse to the properties of language, since it is subtracted from them.

The generic

The third modality of subtraction, the generic, is the name of a multiple established as a consequence of an event by the subject (the indiscernible agent). For a generic multiple, no unifying property can be found that belongs to all of its elements and that would therefore be able to totalise them. The generic is an untotalisable multiple, meaning that the consequences of an event are immanently infinite. If the indiscernible indicates that some attribute becomes common to all members of a practice (all elements of the established set), the generic stipulates that no attribute is intrinsically common to all its members, from which it could be constructed (as its minimal common essence, so to speak). This also means that such a set cannot be presented in a predicative manner. It is generic, as it presents nothing but (a) multiplicity as such (it generates an indistinguishability between presentation and representation). Otherwise put, we might say that the generic abolishes all distinction between the real and the symbolic, as the symbolic itself takes the formal structure of the real. Or we might again say, with another reference to psychoanalysis, that with the generic, ego and id become indistinguishable.

The unnameable

Lastly, the unnameable, the fourth modality of subtraction, indicates that the whole procedure relies on a unique term, one so unique it cannot even be named. It is the only one that, within the unfolding of the consequences, can never be validated or falsified – it is its proper real (the necessarily impossible point of its emergence). Every truth procedure has an immediate effect on the situation of its emergence, that is, it changes the latter's objective constitution, transforms the knowledge of and within the situation. This is why any generic procedure that is effective immediately also implies a dimension of forcing (new terms into knowledge). If forcing is the anticipation of an end of the immanently infinite procedure, an anticipation of the totalisation of a set by definition untotalisable (in love, for example, the statement "I will always love you" manifests this), the unnameable indicates that there will always be a unique term to ensure this fundamental untotalisability and hence the contingency of evental emergence. With regard to the loving couple, it is possible to see that the practice of love has objective effects on the situation – namely, people know that there is a new couple who move in together, have a common postal address, etc. But there remains something that can never become an element of knowledge (can never be forced into knowledge). This is to say that one can never force the very encounter of the two (the event) into

knowledge such that one may be able to interpret it as an effect of destiny
or such that the whole procedure itself could be derived from terms that
are interior to knowledge. The unnameable is the 'proper of the proper
. . . the absolutely singular, which is thus also absolutely subtracted'
(SEM 1990–1). It is in precisely this sense that the unnameable indicates
the place for ethics. Why? Because only from within a truth procedure
can you distinguish between good and evil. In other terms, we can see
here that thought is subtracted from opinion, since it is – as stated above
– indifferent to whatever is external to it. Thought is, properly speaking,
beyond good and bad (this is why it may appear scandalous to the realm
of current opinion) and escapes conventional nominations (this is why it
is related to the unnameable). It might be said, for example, that as soon
as an immanently generic orientation of a thought-practice renounces its
own subtractive nature and immanently transforms itself into a constructible orientation, this very conversion can be called evil. The good, on
the other hand, consists in the constant reaffirmation of the contingent
encounter (say, of the loving couple) under changed conditions, hence in
the unfolding of generic consequences and in avoiding the always reoccur-
ring temptation to translate it into a non-contingent, i.e. simply possible
or necessary and thereby constructible occurrence. Doing so would imply
a shift of emphasis to stating that the event simply happened in an objective space and time. From a generic perspective, however, it is the event
itself that will have generated a new space and time (the new time of the
new subject, which is why couples, for example, have their own common
history). As soon as the move is made to infer the evental occurrence retroactively from the consequences of an event, the procedure attempts to
force that which contingently enabled these very consequences and hence
cannot be forced. What is thereby lost is what is proper to the properties
immanently established by the procedure itself. Evil is related to a forcing
of the unnameable – of that which will ever remain contingent as that
which engendered the whole procedure – because it implies a transition
from a generic to a constructible orientation. In more technical terms, the
unnameable marks the point that has to remain forever impossible, as it
indicates that something previously impossible happened – two people
met, thus converting a previous impossibility into a hitherto unseen possibility. If the whole procedure is simply converted into the actualisation
of a given objective possibility, this actualisation becomes itself necessary
and hence the contingent 'ground' of the subject is denied, as are the
subject itself and the consequences it unfolds. For Badiou, there is thus no
ethics that is not grounded in subtraction, no good and evil, so to speak,
not related to truths. He thereby repudiates (subtracts) every transcendental fundament of ethics (all Kantianism) by insisting that ethics can only

have as its transcendental the very break of the transcendental, the cut that is an event.

Subtraction: affirmation and negation

With reference to these modalities, subtraction is, however, only depicted in a purely negative manner. There is also a positive, affirmative part to subtraction, because it can also be said to name the affirmative part of negation. Badiou once stated that 'subtraction is not a negation' (*TS* 93). Contrary to many of Badiou's critics, however, it is imperative to see that neither can subtraction be rendered as completely detached from negation. Rather, it is crucial to insist on the fact that Badiou introduces subtraction to overcome all conceptions of thought that solely rely on one (negative) type of negation (this informs his criticism of Hegel and Hegelian Marxism, for example) but without falling into the position of simply embracing pure affirmation (which informs his criticism of Deleuze and vitalism *tout court*). Why is it a part of negation? Because subtraction is a category of post-evental practice and any event can only appear from the perspective of the current state of things, from the perspective of the situation as negation, as breaking with this very state. Why? Because a genuine evental occurrence challenges the way things are – the situation and its state – and thus logically functions in a negative manner. Subtraction cannot thereby be fully identified with and reduced to negation, because an event in the strong sense also creates something that materialises the modalities of subtraction outlined above. There is also a creative dimension to such practice, that is, the procedure of unfolding the consequences of an event, which thus brings about what the event will have been. If subtraction were completely reducible to negation, the transformation would depend on that which it negates. Hence the eventual novelty could in some way be derived from the situation itself. This is why Badiou calls it 'the affirmative part of negation' (cf. DNS). In other words, the negative part of negating a given state of things can be rendered in terms of destruction, where the proper creative power of the novelty that is generated, the affirmative part of negating the state of things, is subtractive. In political terms, we can make this distinction by pointing out that the mere destruction of the existing state does not achieve anything new. The proper newness of a political event has to lead to a new type of organisation, one that exceeds the pure destruction of what seems to be given. Adapting a Kantian slogan, Badiou's linking of subtraction and destruction might be summed up as follows: destruction without subtraction is blind (and ends in nihilism), subtraction without destruction is impotent (and ends in despair, since one directly seeks to attain something

without negating anything, and thus endorses something like a pure creation). So for subtraction to be concretely effective it needs to be linked to
destruction, and both of these terms have to be conceived of as the two
formal sides of negation. This means that any negation proper implies for
Badiou a determinate negation (destruction) and a determinate affirmation
(subtraction). Subtracting, it might be said, is not simply taking something
away (the natural given state of things with its specific horizon of im/
possibility), but adding something to the latter, namely the very act (or
practice) of subtraction.

If Badiou's philosophical concept of truth can essentially be qualified as
subtractive, this classification pertains to all the extra-philosophical forms
of practice in which truths emerge and evental consequences are unfolded.
We can say that subtraction is a metaontological, a metapolitical, an inaes-
thetic and, in some sense, also a psychoanalytical category. In other words,
any truth qua procedure relies on the four subtractive modalities (from a
philosophical point of view), regardless of whether it is artistic, political or
otherwise. It is precisely due to this that the proper historical dimension of
subtraction also comes to the fore. This is because, for Badiou, subtraction
was not a category of philosophy right from the start, but instead is historically linked to 'that which, from within the previous sequence, as early as
the start of the twentieth century, presents itself as a possible path that
differs from the dominant one' (BF 119). That is, for Badiou something
happened in a specific historical setting (the twentieth century) within the
conditions of philosophy that had an effect on philosophy's conceptual
means. Subtraction has an historical index, which also has to be accounted
for.

As Badiou analyses it in *C*, the twentieth century was torn between
two main strands. There was a conflict between two figures, two types
of subjective orientation of what he calls a 'passion for the real': a dominant, destructive one, and a subtractive one (*C* 54 ff.). This rendering
of the century also takes on importance in relation to the development
of Badiou's own philosophical undertaking, since some of his own work
thereby becomes a proper document of the century, also torn between
these two sides: in *TS*, which was partially devoted to the creative power
of lack and destruction, he still approvingly quotes a letter from Mallarmé
to Lefébure, in which he states 'Destruction was my Beatrice' (*TS* 87).
Yet Badiou is critical of this embrace of destruction in his later work, in
which he instead insists on the affirmative elements of negation, i.e. on
subtraction. The historical reference is of more than passing biographical
interest, insofar as it sharpens the concept of subtraction, making possible
a more consistent differentiation between subtraction and destruction.
As the passion for the real first relied solely on a negative model of how

to negate the given state of things, it tried to generate novelty by means of purification: only thereby, it was assumed, was it possible to get to that 'something' real behind the semblances and appearances, thereby presupposing that there is something like 'a real identity', something truly 'authentic' (*C* 57). Against the means of maximal used to unravel this authentic real (transhistorical) identity beneath the historical reality, the subtractive passion for the real was devoted to a different conception of the real, one that works on and through the concept of difference. The idea of minimal difference that is its characteristic defines a difference that comes close to indifference, a difference so minimal it makes difference itself appear and disappear at the same time. For Badiou, the paradigmatic embodiment of this orientation is Malevich's *White on White*, but so also is the event, which is precisely characterised by an appearance of disappearance and a disappearance of appearance (an identity of being and nothing). If the destructive passion for the real sought to attain that which could never deceive, it did so to generate an exception to the rule of deception, a transcendent exception. The subtractive passion for the real, by creating a minimal difference, rather sought 'to invent content at the very place of the minimal difference' (ibid. 58), meaning that it brought about the conception of an immanent exception that creatively produces consequences in the situation to which it is an exception. If Badiou's philosophical thought has a necessary and intrinsic historical dimension, then it is from the perspective of the concept of subtraction that it can be discerned. The reader may recall that for Badiou an immanent exception is just another name for an event, from whose trace consequences arise, the development of which only the four subtractive modalities depicted above can render. For Badiou, philosophy is subtractive because it implies an act of insisting on the impossible possibility of immanent exceptions from which truths can emerge. This is philosophy's own creative part of negation (of the simple givenness of the state of things).

SURREAL NUMBERS

Tzuchien Tho

Badiou's programme of mathematical ontology provokes a number of immediate questions. Seeing that Badiou proceeds in this project, as in *BE*, by using set theory as a protocol for the mathematical in his historical understanding that 'mathematics = ontology', we could legitimately ask the question: 'But what about numbers?' (*BE* 10). Far from holding any form of a Pythagorean position, Badiou treats numbers as one among many different sorts of beings that should receive ontological treatment. Of course the very intellectual revolutions that engendered the Cantorian 'event', the historical shift that allows Badiou to hold this convergence between mathematical thought and ontology, also brought about an upheaval in thinking number. In this, Badiou is nonetheless clear that number should receive its own treatment as a sort of being, a particular region of multiplicity, to be thought under a univocal concept of number.

This univocal treatment of the concept of number is precisely what Badiou undertakes in *NN*. This text, which could be read as an additional prolonged meditation on the being of numbers published just two years after *BE*, contains a set-theoretically inspired doctrine on the concept of number and a series of reflections on contemporary significations of number in their social and political contexts. This doctrine, Badiou himself underlines, does not originate with him and is indebted to the field of mathematical research known as 'surreal numbers', first coined by Donald Knuth after the work of John Horton Conway.

What makes surreal numbers so surreal? Badiou remarks that the adjective 'surreal' in this case is a misnaming which has the appearance of designating a new field where other numbers apparently reside. Badiou, for his part, prefers naming them simply 'Numbers' with the capital 'N' (*NN* 107). As he notes, the surreal as a 'continuity through successive widenings', an 'over-arching' opening up of the 'reals', is a misleading understanding of what surreal numbers actually designate (ibid.). Indeed, Conway, the mathematican to whose work this approach to numbers is due, simply calls them 'numbers' (Conway 1976: 3).

In this sense, surreal numbers more appropriately designates an approach to numbers rather than designating a 'form' of number like the 'natural' 'rational' or 'complex' numbers. The approach consists in the attempt to conceptually unify the different number forms in a post-set-theoretical context (cardinal, ordinal, real numbers, infinite and infinitesimal numbers). On this point Badiou argues that the post-set-theoretical situation is a chaotic one; an 'anarchy' in the thinking of number (*NN* 12). It is this 'surreal' approach that will allow us to cut through this indeterminacy by means of a 'nomination' that will pursue the being of number in the post-evental situation left behind by Cantor and Dedekind. In the same spirit, I suggest another way of treating the adjective 'surreal' from Knuth's original coining of the term. In Knuth's elegant and deceptively simple book, he writes a dialogue between two former students, tired of mathematics pedagogy, who are stranded on a deserted island. On the island they discover an (apparently) ancient tablet that provides a quasi-biblical account of the creation of numbers (Conway is God and his disembodied voice makes an appearance). If this is not surreal enough, I might add that the author's rather unique presentation provides an occasion for discovering numbers as if for the first time (which is in effect what occurs in Knuth's text). In this context we should understand the book's title as a performative: 'Surreal! Numbers!'

So what are (surreal) numbers? For his position on numbers, Badiou relies on the three major texts in this field: the original text by D. E. Knuth, *Surreal Numbers* (1974), J. H. Conway's subsequent publication *On Numbers and Games* (1976) and Harry Gonshor's *An Introduction to the Theory of Surreal Numbers* (1986). While Knuth's and Conway's texts are the original references, it is Gonshor's work that Badiou relies on most. In *NN*, Badiou's presentation on the doctrine of number and especially his use of the form/matter distinction is drawn almost directly from Gonshor's text. An important issue here is that Conway developed his theory of numbers from gaming (treating players, turns, outcomes and recursive series of games) and this important dimension is not mentioned by Badiou. Indeed, despite this discrepancy, what Badiou finds in Knuth's and Conway's arguments is their deep indebtedness to Dedekind.

Knuth's treatment of surreal numbers implicitly refers to the Dedekind cut (in a set-theoretical interpretation) where a number is determined by a pair of left and right elements (generalised from the number line) where all the elements of the left are neither greater nor equal to the elements of the right (Knuth 1974). Working from a quasi-axiomatic approach, Knuth's reference to the Dedekind cut provides the 'first commandment' of numbers. Any determination of number will be determined by this left–right cut. In turn, to give some idea of how these cuts will determine a first pass at the natural numbers, a first element, the empty set, can be determined by the pairing of a left void and right void: since neither left nor right have elements, no element in the left is equal to or greater than any element from the right. With the empty set, a number 1 can be determined by the pair of the empty set on the left and numbers greater than the empty set on the right. Following from a procedure that mirrors Dedekind's construction of real numbers from rationals, progressive pairings of this sort can get us a denumerable infinite set of numbers.

As mentioned above, Knuth's coinage of the 'surreal numbers' is due to J. H. Conway's previous work on games. While it is explicit that Knuth developed his book under Conway's tutelage, Conway's own presentation of the issue came a few years after Knuth's work. In Conway's *On Numbers and Games*, he presented his earlier work (referring back to Knuth at moments) by means of the relation between a two-player game (a left and right player). A game, $G=\{G^L \mid G^R\}$, is determined by a left and right game, G^L (left game) and G^R (right game), as sets of games and G the set of sets of games. To simplify, in a single partisan game where both left and right players have the same set of possible moves, and where the losing player is the one who is left with no remaining plays, the player to play second (or last) will win if the game is played correctly by both sides. In this case, the value of the game is zero, $G=0$. If we continue by assuming that there is only one game taking place between G^L and G^R and taking the same sort of simple partisan game, if the left starts with five more possible moves, then the value of the game is 5, $G=5$. If the right starts with five more possible moves, then the value of the game is -5, $G=-5$. With more complex games, the sets of games in G^L and G^R can take on, with recursion, different factors and build in numerical complexity towards the rational, irrational and transfinite (Conway 1976: 71–80). It is easy to see how this game-theoretic division between left and right and the ordinal-based idea behind assigning numbers to games can conveniently appropriate Dedekind's famous cuts. In this conception, a game-theoretic pair of sequential turns (by the left and right players) will generate a schema of branching terms as sets of turns, sets of games, and sets of sets of games, which can be used to model the branching division of initial unities into ω-infinite sets of numbers. In this model, the standard set of operators in arithmetic such as addition, division, multiplication, positive and negative numbers can be represented. What is interesting about Conway's presentation is that numbers are subsumed under the structure of games, which may take many different forms (and not all games are not numbers). The standard chess game and Tic-Tac-Toe are, for example, similar but not equivalent to the sort of partisan game that can produce the number tree since it admits tie games.

The power that the 'surreal' approach to numbers represents for Badiou is its overcoming of the traditional approaches, filtered through set theory, of quality and order: cardinality and ordinality. This numerical unbinding from the standard order or quantity concepts is precisely what Badiou employs in his work. In his own presentation, *Numbers*, with a capital 'N', are composed of sets of sets and are not identical to the various number 'forms' such as ordinal or cardinal. He uses a form/matter distinction immanent to the concept of a number. In this context, an ordinal is the 'matter' of number that, together with a 'form' (a set of sets), constitutes a number. While Badiou interprets this conception in *NN* through the standard number line (the continuum), it may be misleading to think that the ultimate horizon of the project is the numbering of the continuum. Indeed Knuth's and Conway's original project was devised from games and their recursive properties. Numbering the continuum would be an outcome, and not the concrete aim. Gonshor, for his part, generalises this approach in a way that more directly pertains to number theory: he formalises the notion of (surreal) numbers as a field (in the mathematical sense) which contain the various other numbers 'forms': rational, real, infinitesimal, etc. (Gonshor 1986: 22).

As such, Gonshor's work is what concretely pertains to Badiou's idea that number is not merely what counts or quantifies, but rather a being-multiple that constitutes a 'form of being' (*NN* 211). What Badiou finds of particular interest here is the idea that 'the being of Number precedes operations, that Number is above all a thinking, on the basis of Nature, of a section that extracts a form from a natural unity thinkable as the matter of Number' (111). Here he underlines that the aim is to instruct a thinking of number where 'no one would *believe* that Number is a number' (ibid., emphasis added). This would perhaps be Badiou's own meaning of the 'surreal'.

SUTURE

Olivia Lucca Fraser

The word 'suture' takes on three distinct meanings in Badiou's texts. These do not mark distinct periods in the evolution of a single category so much as three *different* categories whose association under the same name perhaps signals nothing more interesting than synonymy – though some hesitation in accepting this conclusion is no doubt appropriate. To keep things as clear as possible, we will label these categories *ideological suture*, *ontological suture*, and *philosophical suture*, and we will deal with them in turn.

Ideological suture

The word 'suture', in a sense that Badiou will diagnose as exclusively ideological in scope, first appears in Badiou's work in the late 1960s. It was the subject of an intense debate amongst the members of *le Cercle d'épistémologie* (the working group behind *Les Cahiers pour l'Analyse*), which was polarised by the positions of Jacques-Alain Miller on one side and Alain Badiou on the other. Miller made the first move. In his contribution to the first issue of *Les Cahiers pour l'Analyse*, 'Suture (Elements of the Logic of the Signifier)', he sought to extract the concept of suture from the implicit state it enjoyed in Lacan's teachings. (For a detailed account of the concept of suture and the role it plays both in Lacan's work and in the *Cahiers pour l'Analyse*, see the remarkable entry on 'Suture' on the CRMEP website, cahiers.kingston.ac.uk (last accessed 8 January 2015), and the English translation of Miller's paper in Hallward and Peden 2012.)

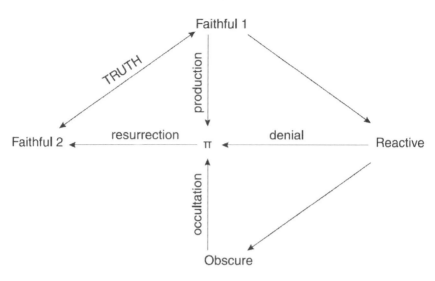

Figure 4 From Badiou, *Logics of Worlds*, p. 67.

On Miller's reading, Lacan had recourse to the word 'suture' on a handful of occasions to name the covering of an essential lack in discourse by way of a short-circuiting of heterogeneous orders (the *imaginary* and the *symbolic*, for instance), an operation that serves to constitute the subject by installing it in a chain of signifiers. Miller's gambit, above and beyond his effort at exegesis, is to show that the operation of suture is at work even in those discourses where we expect it least: indeed, he claims to detect it in Gottlob Frege's rigorously anti-psychologistic attempt to derive the laws of arithmetic from the foundations of *pure logic*. The focus of the article is Frege's definition of *zero* as 'the Number which belongs to the concept "not identical with itself"' (Frege 1960: §76, 87) which, according to Frege's earlier definition of a Number as *a set of concepts whose extensions are equal*, comes down to defining zero as the set of concepts F whose objects can be put in a one-to-one correspondence with the objects describable as 'not identical to themselves'. According to Miller, it is the exigency to preserve 'the field of truth' in which arithmetic must be inscribed that forces Frege to consider the extension of the concept 'not identical to itself' to be empty, for this field would suffer 'absolute subversion' if a term, being non-self-identical, *could not be substituted for itself* in the signifying chain (Miller 2012: 209). (This slippage from an *object* to *the mark that indicates it* goes unnoticed by Miller – a thread that Badiou will later seize upon in both *MM* and *NN*.) This definition, Miller claims, 'summons and rejects' (212) the non-self-identical *subject*, whose unconscious effects can be detected in the Fregean operation of succession (the 'plus one') that takes us from one number to another. That operation, Miller argues, functions only insofar as it is possible for the non-identical (the subject), lacking from the field of truth, to be 'noted 0 and counted for 1' (ibid.). He grounds this argument on Frege's definitions of *one* and *the successor*: Frege defines *one* as 'the number of the extension of the concept: identical with zero' (Frege 1960: §77, 90), and defines the *successor of n* as the Number of the concept 'member of the series of natural numbers ending with *n*' (Frege 1960: §79, 92) – a definition which could only yield *n* itself if the zero which belongs to each of these series were not, again and again, *counted as one*. But this 'counting of zero for one', by Miller's lights, depends entirely on the suturing of the subject that engenders the field of logical truth. It is therefore the subject that makes succession tick – but a subject manifested only in the suturation of its lack and so condemned to miscognition on logic's behalf.

Badiou will have none of this. The counterargument he delivers in 'Mark and Lack: On Zero' (published in the *Cahiers*' tenth and final volume) can be condensed as follows:

1. Scientific discourse in general, and mathematical logic in particular, is not a *unitary* field of discourse or 'field of truth' at all. It must be conceived, instead, in terms of multiple *stratified* apparatuses of inscription.

2. At no point does *any* discursive operation in *any* of these strata have any occasion or need to invoke a radical, unthinkable 'outside'. What looks like an invocation of 'lack' – the statement that the concept 'not-identical-to-itself', for example, has an empty extension – is nothing but a referral to an anterior stratum of the discourse. No scientific inscription enjoys the paradoxical status of 'cancelling itself out', as Miller supposed to take place in the Fregean invocation of the 'non-self-identical'. Analysing Frege's definition of zero, for instance, we should see the inscription, on a particular stratum (which Badiou terms the 'mechanism of concatenation', or 'M_2', and whose task is merely to assemble grammatical expressions), of the predicate '*x is not identical to x*' as a perfectly stable inscription (which indeed presupposes the self-identity of the *mark* '*x*' in a perfectly consistent fashion and without the slightest ambiguity). It is only on *another* stratum (M_3, the 'mechanism of derivation', which sorts the output of M_2 into theorems and non-theorems) that the system 'rejects' the existential quantification of '*x is not identical to x*' as a non-theorem. In no sense does M_3 cancel out the productions of M_2, or summon them only to reject them: it receives these productions as its *raw material*, and operates on them in a fashion altogether different what we find in M_2.

On a subsequent stratum (M_4), the predicate 0 can then be defined in terms of the predicate whose extension was shown to be empty, and so on. What transpires in all of this is not, and cannot be, the ephemeral invocation of the non-self-identical subject, or a wound in discourse obscured by the scar of the letter, but a stable relay between fully positive strata the assemblage of which 'lacks nothing it does not produce elsewhere' (ML 341–2), a rule which, Badiou affirms, holds good for all of science.

3. Not only does the stratification of the scientific signifier exclude suture from science, it suffices to *foreclose the subject* from scientific discourse altogether, and this is the secret of science's *universality*: Science is a 'psychosis of no subject, and hence of all: congenitally universal, shared delirium, one has only to maintain oneself within it in order to be no-one, anonymously dispersed in the hierarchy of orders' (361–2).

4. Rigorous stratification and foreclosure of subjective suturation are not just accidental features of science, but what *constitute science as science*. It is they that give form to the notion of the *epistemological break*, the continuous struggle by which science separates itself from ideology.

5. 'The concept of suture', therefore, 'is not a concept of the signifier in general, but rather the characteristic property of the signifying order wherein the subject comes to be barred – namely, ideology' (363).

This is not to say that suturation never happens when scientists speak. It occurs repeatedly – but these occurrences are nevertheless *extrinsic* to science in itself. The suturing of scientific discourse is what occurs in the continual establishment of *epistemological obstacles*, the destruction of which is the sciences' incessant task. This dialectic of stratification and suturation, or of science and ideology, is elaborated in the appendix to 'Mark and Lack', in a detailed case study of Gödel's first incompleteness theorem—a study which implicitly attacks Lacan's attempt to exploit this theorem in 'Science and Truth'.

Ontological suture

With mathematics' ontological baptism, at the beginning of *BE*, the word 'suture' makes a prominent return. It comes to serve two functions: to name the empty umbilicus that links each situation to being by way of the void that haunts it ('I term *void* of a situation this suture to being' (*BE* 55)), and to christen being with the 'proper name' Ø, the mathematical sign of the empty set. Given the rigour and severity of his attack on Miller's application of the notion of suture to mathematical discourse, Badiou's abrupt decision to declare Ø set theory's 'suture-to-being' (66) – in a sense 'which will always remain enigmatic' (59) – may strike the reader as surprising. More surprising still is that no link, positive or negative, is drawn between the then-falsified Millerian thesis that the *subject's* inconsistency is sutured by the arithmetical 0, and the now-affirmed thesis that *being's* inconsistency is sutured by the set-theoretical Ø. Even in *NN*, where Miller's thesis comes in for a second round of attacks, we find the new *metaontological* suture-thesis affirmed with innocence throughout the book (cf. *NN* Ch. 3).

When pressed on this point, Badiou replies that between these two theses, the word 'suture' 'changes its meaning': it is no longer a question of invoking the void of the (Lacanian) *subject*, but the void of *being* as radical inconsistency. This was not in doubt. But the argument deployed in 'Mark and Lack' against applicability of the notion of suture to the Fregean 0 *nowhere depends on the identification of lack, or radical inconsistency, with the subject*. If the argument is sound then it will remain so under the uniform substitution of 'being' for 'subject', and one cannot use this substitution to flee the difficulties encountered by Miller: we cannot avoid seeing that 'the torch which lights the abyss, and seals it up, is itself an abyss' (Dupin 1992: 5). If the meaning of 'suture' in *BE* differs from the meaning of 'suture' in 'ML' only with respect to the terms it relates – subject then, being now – then the Badiou of 1988 and after remains hostage to the Badiou of '69, and the stratified psychosis of mathematics will absolve itself from ontology as relentlessly as it does from ideology, foreclosing being as radically as it does subjectivity.

Philosophical suture

There is a third sense in which Badiou uses the word 'suture', which is not so obscurely entangled nor obviously connected with its older usage, though certain structural similarities can still be observed: here, it names a particular – potentially disastrous – way in which philosophy may relate itself to one of its conditions. The relation of *conditioning* that the philosopher is charged with maintaining between extra-philosophical disciplines (truth procedures) and her own collapses into a relation of *suture* when, by way of destratification, the philosopher confuses these two disciplines with one another. It is helpful to make a distinction here, according to which partner in the suture achieves dominance. The dominance of the condition – such as the poetic condition dominates the late Heidegger and his pupil, Gadamer, the political condition dominates certain strains of Marxist thought, the scientific condition dominates Carnap and Hempel, and the amorous condition dominates Levinas and Irigaray – is indicated by its hegemony over the philosophical category of truth and its capture of philosophical rationality. No other modes of truth but those of the condition, sutured in dominance, are recognised, and the philosopher measures her reasoning by strictures proper to the conditioning discipline. This renders philosophy incapable of fulfilling its mandate, which is *to construct a systematic compossibilisation of heterogeneous truths.* The dominant position in a suture may also be occupied by philosophy. When this occurs, philosophy takes itself as producer of truths – the kind of truths, moreover, that ought to be entrusted to an external condition. When this takes place, the threat of disaster looms large.

SYSTEM

Norman Madarasz

Whatever the idea of system might have been prior to the publication of *BE*, it loses importance when faced with the accomplishment of the book's proposal. However, the defense of the systematic character of philosophy really only begins with *MP*.

Amongst the many counter-currents present in Badiou's work at the time, e.g. establishing truth as the central category of philosophy, reinitiating a theory of subject, calling for an end to the 'age of the poets', or giving value to love over lust, perhaps the most surprising is the doctrine of the system. After all, only a few decades had passed since the initial assertions of existential philosophy were formulated in a bid to undermine the systematic vocation inherited from German Idealism. Still, it ought to be clear that by system, Badiou does not seek to put back what solid and varied criticism had expelled from philosophy's perimeters. As he writes, 'if by "system" we understand an encyclopedic figure, itself endowed with a keystone or governed by some supreme signifier, I would gladly accept that modern desacralisation forbid its deployment [. . .] If by "systematicity", we understand, as we must do, the prerequisite of a complete configuration of the four generic conditions of philosophy (which, once again, in no way demands that the *results* of these conditions be displayed or even mentioned), by means of an exposition that also exposes its expository rule, then it is of the essence of philosophy to be systematic, and no philosopher has ever doubted this, from Plato to Hegel' (*MP* 65).

Nonetheless, the notion of system summoned in 1989 is still a far cry from the tested shape it would later acquire. In 1989, the system consists basically of:

An ontology, predicated upon the argument that ontology is mathematics, as expressed by set theory;

An internal historical description of philosophy as emerging from four distinct discourses in which truths are produced (matheme, poem, love and political invention), and whose compossible coexistence gives rise to philosophy;

The extraction of the ontology as the common set of an evental subject whose process is to produce truth amongst the conditions;

A non-ontological theory of the event: that is, the event is a contingent rupturing forth of non-being;

An ontological theory of ethics, whose task is to understand what the event comes to mean for the subject who named it and lives through it, and for the condition in which what is manifest as conveying the good ends up producing evil;

An explanation, immanent to each condition, of the various condition-specific productions of 'truth';

A delimitation of the sphere of being from existence, still in a Heideggerian vein.

With these characteristics, Badiou's system already begins to take on a specific determination that is not found amongst his system-creating predecessors in German idealist philosophy. It is worth recalling that Hegel considered the system to be the organic counterpart of his scientific conception of philosophy, as portrayed in the *Encyclopedia*. The system is a process articulated through inclusion of different streams and branches of thought through which *Geist* unfolds on its path to absolute knowledge. Hegel's system is self-inclusive and universal in its determination. The same cannot be said of Badiou's.

One of the tasks of *MP* is to right what Badiou perceived to be various philosophical wrongs. The return to system accompanies a 'Platonic gesture' that rejects Heidegger's critique of technology and gives value to Marx at a time of rapid divestment in Gorbachev's era and the impeding collapse of the Soviet Empire, as well as reintegrating mathematics and logic into the philosophical mainstream. As such, Badiou tacitly accepts the varied critiques made since Hegel's death to the idea of system. Among these, the Hegelian system was criticised for claiming to account for the entire Universe, when the scientific revolutions of the early twentieth century proved that at the distant perimeters of the Universe, we simply do not understand exactly what phenomena occur. By contrast, the upshot of the event theory makes sense not only of the Big Bang, but of the conjecture that there may have been several Big Bangs insofar as event is always contextualised in a condition.

Still, in *MP*, Badiou remains at a defensive stage in his claim for a system in the Nietzschean age. To the criticism that the system is too restrictive a model for the Universe, Badiou replies by integrating the versatility of the Axiom of Choice and Paul Cohen's invention of 'forcing' an extension of the situation-U. To the claim that the Hegelian system is merely recapitulative instead of prospective, and therefore falsely postulating a determinist universe prior to the contingent surprise of naming carried out by free human agency, Badiou rejects any connection between his extension of the situation and the end of History. History is not a unitary process in his thought. To the criticism that all systems are the creation of individual philosophical authors, Badiou has relentlessly submitted the theses to demonstrations and to the objections from various sectors of scientific activity. Finally, to the question of the multiplicity of truth as being unanswerable from within the system alone, Badiou establishes the existence of an external generic set, which includes a suspension of the classical bivalent logic that organises the Situation as a given presentation of multiplicities that simply are.

The way in which philosophy returns to its systemic vocation is through recognition of its conditions as being the local setting for the production of (relative) truths. Philosophy does not produce truth. What it does, as part of its systemic operation, is allow analysis of the truth-production process through inspection of the commonalities to the four conditions. As part of a natural desire within philosophy, however, there often occurs a drive to identify truth as a philosophical production. This desire leads philosophy to become sutured to one of its conditions, or more, if not all. In such circumstances, it is manifest that philosophy fails to show itself according to its systemic structure.

A definitive moment for the construction of the system comes in 1990 with Jean-Toussaint Desanti's critique of set theory as the preferred model for the 'intrinsic' ontology (*TO* 110–11). These reflections contribute to the opening of yet another space in the system, devoted to the phenomenology of incorporated truths. In reply Badiou drafted an unpublished manuscript to present category theory in relation to set theory to his students. As such the growth of the system results partly as a response to some of his critiques. In 1987–90, that is, at the time of writing *BE* and presenting its consequences in public, there does not seem to be an indication that Badiou had envisioned the possibility, let alone necessity, of formalising the existential sphere into his ontological thesis and that this would be the task of category theory to formalise.

Still, he made the system clash with the conceptual persona of the antiphilosopher in a bid to both specify his claim on ontology and demonstrate that his system did not reduce philosophy to mathematics. The antiphilosopher, contrary to the sophist, is a figure seeking to occupy centre stage to prompt the event. The conceptual position emerges as a stepping-stone from Lacan back into philosophy for Badiou, initially articulated in *TS*. In contrast with that work, the *antiphilosopher* becomes a necessary component for a contemporary concept of system in the post-*BE* period. The antiphilosopher typically seeks to create, or recreate, the event singlehandedly – instead of the generic set projecting the truth of the event in the displaced temporality of the future perfect. As such, the antiphilosopher offers a vantage point that could potentially be separate from the system. Such is the case with Saint Paul, Nietzsche and Lacan, among others. And it is a position Badiou insists on occupying intermittently as he reinforces the novelties of the system he creates.

Throughout the post-*BE* period, observations arose as to two fundamental absences in the ontology: the body and language. The subject as an ontological category materialised in the conditions as a trace or figure. The specificity and pain a body brings to existence, however, were only obliquely elucidated. Formally and in terms of its destiny, the subject belonged to mathematics. The entire critical mass of 'human animals', as Badiou puts it in *E*, became the repository for an innovative subjective eruption, albeit the materialisation of its truth *in situ* would never be complete – save for a violent forcing akin to an act of terror. In *LW*, a body is defined as the existential support for the *subjective* appearance of a truth, which in turn is manifest as either the faithful, reactive or obscure subject (*LW* 451). The body undergoes three operations, as it evolves from appearing to co-apparition to infinite synthesis.

Here is a point where the two planes of the ontological and the existential converge in the evental site. In sum, the body carries the subjective formalism, an eventuality that was never a mystery. The question was: how would Badiou accomplish its formalisation? His literal reading of mathematical conceptuality bore more fruits. Galois's theory of groups leading to the notion of *corps* and Grotendiek's work on space based on the categorical logic are the model references here, as Badiou uses the latter's derivation of an identity (**id**) in world (**m**) to found the body as well as the notion of organ. The aim is to formalise the argument according to which the degree of identity of an element of the event site, evaluated not in the ontology but in the phenomenology of truths, is equal to this element's degree of existence (ibid., 290). This is the basis on which Badiou grounds the process of incorporation.

On the other hand, the phenomenology of incorporated truth in multiple possible worlds is an immersion into the field of language. This language is not hermeneutical, communicative or deconstructive in its philosophy projection. Badiou's reception of language is predicated upon the reductive use to which it is placed in the context of 'democratic materialism'. For bodies and languages to be of philosophical relevance to the ontology, they must be bound to truths and recognise the fundamental claim of truth: 'a truth affirms the infinite right of its consequences, with no regard for what opposes them'. With such principles, the system moves on to incorporate a new theory of object. In his ultimate bid to absorb and move beyond Gilles Deleuze's philosophy, Badiou introduces a new theory of life, rid of its vitalism and submitted to formalism. Such is the state of the system in 2013.

$$T$$

THEATRE

Joseph Litvak

It would be difficult to overstate the importance of theatre for Badiou. Not only has he written passionately and extensively about it: he is also the author a series of remarkable plays, which stand in a close and complex relation to his philosophy. 'Every philosopher is an actor', Badiou has said (*IPL* 91). And if philosophy is a kind of theatre, theatre is itself a 'particularly active form of thought, an action of thought' (*Ahmed* 21). In view of Badiou's Platonism, of course, the relationship between theatre and philosophy in his work can hardly be unproblematic. In Badiou's *Rhapsody for the Theatre* (*RT*) – a text as theatrical as it is philosophical – he writes:

Theatre: the putting-into-bodies of the Idea. From the point of desire, it is its life; from the point of the Idea, it is its tomb. Whence the anathema and the disputes. Theatre as bastard philosophy, or philosophical bastardy: principled impurity, diverted lesson, all-too-serious analysis, all-too-ludic truth to be assured. A revolving door. (227)

Yet theatre's principled impurity has been an object of enduring fascination for Badiou the philosopher and a richly generative matrix for Badiou the playwright. Much as Badiou may aspire to a 'pure' or even Platonic theatre, he delights in and draws intellectual energy from the resources of theatrical impurity.

'Of all the arts,' Badiou claims, 'theatre is the one that most insistently stands *next to* (or supposes) politics' (200). If theatre is intimately implicated in the State, it is by no means merely an agent of the State. Indeed, it has the potential to produce a Badiousian *event*. And when it does so, 'theatre makes it known to you that you will not be able innocently to remain *in your place*' (199). Badiou's plays themselves thus seek to make the spectator 'feel the hardness of his seat' (ibid.).

Badiou's writing for the theatre consists of *L'Écharpe rouge* (*The Red Scarf*), a 'romanopéra', written between 1972 and 1978, published in 1979, and performed as an opera in 1984, directed by Antoine Vitez and with music by Georges Aperghis; *L'Incident d'Antioche* (*The Incident at Antioch*), written between 1982 and 1984; and the four 'Ahmed' plays, written between 1984 and 1996, staged frequently in France, republished in one volume in 2010, and comprising *Ahmed le Subtil* (*Ahmed the Subtle*), *Ahmed philosophe* (*Ahmed the Philosopher*), *Ahmed se fâche* (*Ahmed Gets Angry*), and *Les Citrouilles* (*The Pumpkins*).

Badiou's version of Aristophanes' *The Frogs* (*Les Grenouilles*), *Les Citrouilles* restages the competition between Aeschylus and Euripides as a contest between Brecht and Claudel. Although a superficial acquaintance with Badiou's politics might lead one to expect the revolutionary Brecht to triumph over the reactionary Claudel, Ahmed ends the play by celebrating both authors: 'The genius of Brecht and Claudel was to make circulate on the narrow space of the stage [. . .] a global summons and strife. The former put there all the frontal resources of dialectical cynicism. The latter, all the density of language and mythologies. So that, with them, there are no more barriers, no more compartments, no more limited exercises!' (*Ahmed* 105). And just as *The Frogs* recognises Sophocles alongside Aeschylus and Euripides, so too Ahmed proposes a theatrical triumvirate, with Brecht and Claudel being joined by Pirandello, 'the man for whom everything, beginning with the theatre, exists only insofar as it's haunted by what isn't it and by what, however, will perhaps turn into it' (ibid., 106).

Brecht's dialectical force, Claudel's poetic density and epic range, Pirandello's virtuosic metatheatre: these influences loom large in Badiou's plays, along with his own distinctive concerns and literary innovations. Frankly rewriting plays by these and other authors (*The Frogs*, of course, but also, in *Ahmed le Subtil*, Molière's *Fourberies de Scapin*), Badiou puts his theatrical models to work breaking down the barriers and compartments of a theatre and of a political scene that, since the 1970s, have seemed more and more static and constricting.

As a work of the 1970s, and thus of the 'red years' to which its title alludes, *L'Écharpe rouge* revises Claudel's *Satin Slipper*, with its theme of religious faith, as a teeming, many-voiced reflection on the conditions of *political* fidelity. Depicting an insurrection and its consequences in a fictional country, alternating trenchant political debate with aria-like interludes of Mallarméan opacity, this aptly termed opera-novel at once expresses its era's optimism about the revolutionary possibilities of the Party and places that optimism under dialectical pressure.

By the time of *The Incident*, the 'red years' had given way to the 'black years' of reaction epitomised by the Mittérand regime. This play, based on Claudel's *La Ville* (*The City*), and taking as its occasion the conflict between the apostles Paul and Peter over the concept of universality, articulates a disenchantment with the Party, but it also explores the question, as Badiou puts it, of 'how to go from order to disorder, how to find a new disorder' ('Interview with Badiou', *IA* 144). As Susan Spitzer argues, it dramatises various modes of what Badiou calls subtraction from State and Party, revealing, in the subjective trajectory of a female Paul (Paula), how subtraction works as the affirmative part of negation.

Highly elliptical in its language, *The Incident*, although a tragedy, refuses a merely melancholic relation to the red years. The refusal becomes even more pronounced in the Ahmed plays, which overflow with comic exuberance, not despite but because of the increasingly sclerotic state of France in the 1990s. In these satirical farces, Ahmed, a treacherous philosophical servant – a contemporary Scapin – cuts a diagonal path through a social square defined by capitalo-parliamentarianism, a 'left' reduced to ethics and multiculturalism, a xenophobic *petite bourgeoisie* and the alienated but not entirely hopeless young people and immigrants of the *banlieues*. Enacting the new as it breaks out of deadly repetition, Ahmed is Badiou's faithful subject at his most joyously inventive, and a name for what is most revitalising in Badiou's theatre. 'Debout, les morts!' ('Hey, you dead people, get up!' (Ahmed 297), cries Ahmed to the other characters in *Ahmed the Philosopher*. With the same words, Badiou the playwright summons the spectators out of their seats and towards a new life.

THERMIDORIAN

Steven Corcoran

Badiou's philosophical interest in the French Revolution lies in its production and sustaining of a thought of the collective, of immediately universalisable prescriptions that command assent not on the basis of social belonging but of a disinterested *volonté générale*. As Badiou shows throughout much of his work, the strictly incalculable occurrence of an event such as the French Revolution, of the emergence of a collectivity irreducible to the group belonging comprising the situation (here: that of the French Monarchy, which, after the cut, tellingly came to be known as the *ancien régime*), forms an excess whose latent and infinite possibilities overflow the situation on all sides. But how is one to move forward, to orient oneself according to the general will, to properly invent consequences that nothing in the situation, bar the equal belonging of all to it, validates in advance? And how is one to do so when counter-revolution is raging inside and outside the country?

Or to put it in Saint-Just's terms: 'What do those who want neither Virtue nor Terror really want?' His answer: the end of the revolution and the restoration of the order of proprietors. What, then, is virtue? Virtue here is opposed to corruption, but far from being a general moral category (moralisation will be a feature of Thermidorian discourse, as we shall see), it must be understood as a political one that is specific to the French Revolution qua political sequence. In the wake of its advent, to uphold virtue meant to persist in the subjective conviction in Republican power, namely in the possibility, here and now, of prescribing radical equality, and of living, on the basis of these prescriptions, in view of a world to come. The consequences of this new power were immense and, as we know, vigorously opposed by pro-monarchists everywhere but also ultimately by the ascendant bourgeoisie.

Virtue is precisely about upholding the prescriptions that, with no grounding in objective givens, are able to rally people around a positive Idea. It indicates a form of thought that is at once self-legitimating and self-sustaining and therefore intrinsically precarious. Hence the reason that, for Robespierre, while virtue formed the basis of any popular government during peacetime, it could take no effect without terror. In his words: 'virtue, without which terror is baneful; terror, without which virtue is powerless. Terror is nothing more than speedy, severe and inflexible justice; it is thus an emanation of virtue; it is less a principle in itself, than a consequence of the general principle of democracy, applied to the most pressing needs of the patrie'.

The Thermidorian reaction to the Revolution proper began on 9 Thermidor Year II (1794), marked by the putting to death of Robespierre, Saint-Just and Couthon. With the sequence of virtue effectively over, Thermidor gets underway, 'opening', writes Badiou, 'a sequence in which constitutional repression is backed up by an anti-popular vision of the State' (*M* 126). Legitimacy is sought no longer in political virtue, but instead in an objective figure, the authority of the wealthy. And an explicitly avowed dimension of repressive terror is maintained to protect that wealth. Indeed, as Badiou points out, the facts show that state terror remained unabated and even increased in intensity after the death of Robespierre. Contrary to a popular liberal narrative, what was not at stake in Thermidor was the idea that terror should not be exercised. The point was to proceed to a very anti-Jacobin disjoining of terror from Virtue, and instead to articulate it with (propertied) Interest, thus bringing about a shift in the source and target of terror. As a consequence, the Thermidorian Convention would proceed to ban the 1793 Constitution, the most egalitarian of the entire Revolution, and replace it first with the Constitution of 1795 and then that of 1799, the latter outdoing the former in terms of explicitly repressive, anti-popular maxims. The Thermidorian reaction would come down vengefully on political activism at home – i.e. against the Jacobins and the sans-culottes, who considered it a duty to rise up against government injustice – and abroad – though they would eventually lose out in Haiti, where the slave revolt of 1791, led by Toussaint Louverture, would result in the country's independence in 1804, sending shock waves through the system of colonial property and slavery.

But for Badiou, a Thermidorian is more than just a term to designate former French revolutionaries who accomplished the counter-revolution in the guise of continuing it. It defines an invariant subjective figure of reaction, liable to arise after any genuine political sequence, which simultaneously makes this figure possible – but not necessary: pace Marxist-inflected historiography, Badiou does not subscribe to the notion that this revolutionary period necessarily led to Thermidorian reaction, that Stalin was the outcome of Lenin, etc. More precisely, the concept of Thermidorian is Badiou's part answer to the paradox of *reactionary novelties*: that is, of the emergence of figures that, while having been participants in an event, ultimately turn and go clean against the thrust of its radical egalitarianism, but in such a way that they cannot simply be dismissed as proponents of the former regime (against which they have also fought) and are often seen as maintaining a certain – albeit illusory – radicality. For Badiou, such a figure always arises in reaction to and not as the necessary outcome of a political event, as if the truth of the event lay in a heterogeneous future.

Badiou fleshes the concept out in Chapter 5 of *MP*, providing two main examples of Thermidorian reaction (after the French Revolution and after May '68; cf. *M*). Other key examples might include Stalin's notion of 'Socialism in one country' and Deng Xiaoping's anti-Maoist putsch. The concept is the political version of what Badiou formalises in *LW* as the reactionary subject (a figure that arises in all four truth procedures), in its twofold difference from the political subject proper and the obscure subject.

The Thermidorian: a problem of renegacy

The problem, to name it baldly, is that of renegacy, and it is one Badiou has struggled with ever since after May '68, when the so-called new philosophers, French Maoists of the day before, emerged on the scene, shamelessly trading all for which they had struggled for a place of privilege in the system (just as the Thermidorians were part of the Montagnard Convention and voted for the 1793 Constitution before turning on Robespierre and siding with propertied interest). These ex-militants would explain their turnabout in terms of error and youthful folly: older, wiser, they see they were wrong and now repent for their militant words and deeds. However, the Thermidorian is no nostalgic and does not want to return to the previous situation – which, he knows, political events have consigned to the past (the rigid stuffiness of 1960s French society, colonial wars, etc.).

A similar problem of Thermidorian backlash occurred after the Cultural Revolution in China, and Mao was fully aware it was occurring. In the mid-1970s, he warned those interested in the future of communism in China that 'it is very easy to make capitalism in China today'. Today, when the mainstream media continues, misleadingly, to refer to China as a 'communist' state, it is hard to see what he meant. Essentially, he acknowledged that the advent of Party-independent organisations of workers and intellectuals had unequivocally shown that this socialist one-party state, far from representing them, afforded special privileges to the 'red' bourgeoisie. The choice, as Mao saw perfectly clearly, was either to reinvent the notion of a worker power (a key aim of the Cultural Revolution) and therefore a communist movement, or else to continue on with affording special privileges to the bourgeoisie in commodity production and to the party elite in decision-making. These were the conditions that made it ripe for the full-blown shift to capitalism that would occur with Deng Xiaoping after Mao's death. However, upholding equality is a precarious matter – contingent as it is on a number of internal and external factors – and the Thermidorian Xiaoping will prey on this evidence, essentially by claiming that nothing else except state order and economic objectivity comprise the country – all else being fanciful and dangerous.

We see, then, that the crucial subjective issue of renegacy is not one of error, of wayward youth, but of subjective *corruption* – namely, the denial of the once-shared conviction that *virtue has a political force*. This corruption may take on many contingent empirical forms (pocketing large sums from the English in 1794; acquiring a position as a – repentant – media star after 1968), but it is first and foremost the *subjective* element of corruption that is essential. Weariness comes over the Thermidorian in the face of the task of political thought, and he opts instead to rally to the order of property.

Invariant traits of Thermidorian subjectivity

On the basis of this brief sketch, we can already glimpse what Badiou sees as the above-mentioned invariant features of Thermidorian subjectivity, of which there are three: (1) *statification*, i.e. a referring of political consciousness not to the latent emancipatory possibilities within a situation, but instead to the state order – there is either state order and injustice or disorder; (2) *interestedness*, i.e. a rejection of unconditioned political prescription in favour of an objective figure of *calculable interest* – furthermore, at a more formal level, the supposition of *interestedness* ultimately amounts to the sophistical claim that all subjective demand is *interested*; and (3) *situational placement*: the Thermidorian abhors the dissolution of hierarchy that goes with the 'aleatory trajectory of a truth' and instead seeks for a *place* – his trajectory is one of *inclusion* in an objective order.

Dislocating Virtue from terror through Interest, whose purported 'necessity' it is the function of the state to propagate, effects a series of displacements. Here, there is absolutely no difference between the original Thermidorians and former '68ers who sold out for a place in the neo-liberal order in the mid-1970s: the country will be seen not as a place for the exercise of political virtue, but as an economic objectivity; law will be viewed not as a maxim derived from the relation between principles and the situation, but as that which provides protection for property, and whose function is therefore paramount and its universality only ancillary; and the Jacobin notion that insurrection is a sacred duty of unconditioned subjective virtue in the face of injustice will be opposed, and instead legitimacy will be sought in the objective measure of property, for which ordered peace is required.

Based on this coupling of state and interest, the Thermidorian's constitutive trajectory can be determined not as traversal movement, but as situational placement. But the desire for situational placement is not a simple return to a 'natural order' coupling state and interest, in contrast with the folly of egalitarian dreams of perpetual displacement based on the void. The lack of any such natural order catches the Thermidorian in a vicious cycle: what founds Thermidorian activity is not the natural order, against which revolutionary desires of virtue can be presented as unnatural and imaginary. Instead, the Thermodorian's place and activity is wholly situated in the space opened up by the disarticulation of the political procedure. Hence, the Thermidorian will spend a great deal of energy attempting to render invisible the very materiality or consequences of that which he claims does not exist – political virtue. The essence of this subjectivity, that upon which it is based, is thus its pact with the order of power to return the idea of political virtue to the void.

The crucial operation performed by the Thermidorian is thus, along-side the connection of state and interest, the disarticulation of egalitarian political prescriptions from the situations in which they are applied, an operation invariably masked by moralising *judgements* on the political sequence in question. The well-known moralising of all renegades – their explicit recourse to abstract (in the sense of non-localised) moral catego-ries of good and evil – is merely the mask of the concrete operations they perform.

Thermidorian subjectivity – which must always be reinvented anew, as a reaction to political sequence – is thus singularised by the way in which the three above-mentioned formal features are invested to form a specific process of disarticulation. In our own time, it was the *nouveaux philosophes* in France, all of them Maoists of the day before, who elaborated most clearly the post-'68 Thermidorian stance. Glucksmann, in *Les maitres penseurs*, was the first to articulate the general theme: there can be no posi-tive vision of the Good – i.e. no political virtue – around which to bring people together. People can only be unified via a critique of evil, which it is the job of the 'new philosopher' to root out. The Thermidorian will thus first act to make separate militant statements unreadable, i.e. to sever them from the situations that give them content, and then to provide a re-reading of them: for Glucksmann, desire for Revolution would amount to nothing other than a simply perverse *interest* in wielding power, in short, to a totalitarian desire, against which all must rally to eradicate. In so doing, the Thermidorian effects a double negation: first, of the situa-tion of revolt, deemed no more than an irrational convulsion (e.g. terror, sexual self-indulgence), one which is always liable to recur and against which one must remain vigilant; and second, of its protagonists, who are henceforth seen as being merely dangerous: having no objective interests, they flout the laws of the economy and morality and precipitate the ruin of the entire country. Badiou rightly points out the absurdity that results from this operation of double negation: in the case of May '68, it allowed some ex-militants to claim that May involved the same longing for 'totali-tarian' control operative in Stalinist Russia of the 1930s. Setting aside the dubious category of 'totalitarianism', what relation is there between this Stalinism of the 1930s and the multiform practices and forms of organisa-tion emergent in this period of activism? The renegade 'new philosopher' thus engages in the construction of a non-relation, designed to render what is there to be thought through – i.e. the political sequence and its termina-tion – *unthinkable*. By contrast, if the philosopher's task rather consists in

thinking through evental statements in their specificity, that is, relating the
rare and disruptive emergence of events to the situations with which they
break (or more abstractly, to think through the relation of a non-relation
(cf. *PP*) and thereby to expose the event's face of eternity), then the philosopher is precisely the opposite of a renegade 'new philosopher'.

TOPOLOGY

Norman Madarasz

When used mathematically, topology is the study of space, and especially
of the space of a being, its neighbourhood, borders, etc. (*LW* 596). Ever
since *TS*, Badiou has maintained that the 'mathematical dialectic is that
of algebra and topology, or if one is Greek, arithmetic and geometry'
(Mackay 2007: 24). Yet topology does not receive a thorough systematisation in Badiou's system until *LW*. This tardiness has contributed to
ambiguous tendencies in reading the way Badiou conceives of its import
to philosophy. As with the general existential field laid out in *LW*, it is
important to understand the patience demanded by Badiou regarding
conceptual placing and unfolding. Still, in the aftermath of the publication of *BE*, and the association of topology to the work of René Thom,
Jean Petitot and Gilles Deleuze, all of whom are partial to topology as
fundamental mathematics, Badiou seldom asserts its value to ontology,
i.e. to mathematics, i.e. set theory. This would have to await its algebraic
formalisation in the Heyting algebra and philosophical systematisation as
the science of beings in terms of their objective appearing, whose purpose
is designated as pertaining to *LW*.

   As opposed to the ontology, *LW* is steeped within being-in-the-world,
or the formal albeit corporal localisation of being-there. However one
might like to put it, *LW* is devoted to analysing the relationship of appearing and spatial localisation. The Heyting algebra proves to nominally
converge with the relationship as its key operator is the *locale*. The strictly
topological constitution of a world is made up of points. Book Six of *LW*,
following the exposition of the three logics, is devoted to this task. It is the
condition sine qua non to begin the formalisation of what it is to be a body.
In Badiou's system, the point carries the nuances of a world as well as the
intensity of a body's intensity.

   What is the relationship between subject and body? As *BE* stresses,
but in the formal terminology devoted to analysing the conditions for the
general advent of subjective processes, there is no subject prior to the act
of naming the event. This advent is unfolded in what Badiou refers to

as one of two rationalities, i.e. mathematical rationality. Topology is the other side of the leaf, the phenomenological rationality in which a new concept of object is presented, which is adequate to including the body in a post-Nietzschean conceptuality. We are no longer in the register of mechanical objectification as with Newton or Descartes, not any more than in the melancholic post-Romantic rant of the body's depreciation as in Nietzsche, or indeed Foucault and Irigaray. The new theory of object stipulates an array of body conceptions set in a general theory of appearing. What that theory demonstrates is how the logics of topology are conducive to its creative variations. In the case of *LW*, there is no body from without the instance of the Two, and the transforming drive of a *no* into a *yes*. These are the minimal conditions for a novel conception of object based on a reconstructed conception of the body. As Badiou asserts, 'a faithful subject is the form of a body whose organs treat a worldly situation "point by point"' (*LW* 399). A point is a trial on the transcendental plane of a truth's appearing.

Given that body and world constantly revolve around spatial interiority as well as exteriority, topology as a heuristic field is a key operator in the post-Heideggerian school of contemporary French philosophy. Understanding the philosophical nature of this field has generated considerable discussion as to its conceptual uses. Topology has a natural inclination for metaphorical application. However, many philosophers will use topological concepts in a non-metaphorical fashion. Badiou himself has ventured back and forth on the specific relationship between philosophy and topology.

Apart from its obvious fundament in Kantian philosophy, space is a concept in Heidegger. It is the very fundament upon which occurs the unveiling of being qua being. The *Lichtung*, or clearing, is its descriptive motif instead of ground. In that regard, one is required to venture into the specific spatial interpretation of *logos* that Heidegger provides.

Another specific diagrammatic usage of topology in the background of Badiou's work is Jacques Lacan's. Lacan went as far as to claim that topological space is structure itself. He asserted this to refer to the structural arrangement that epistemologically grounds his claim about the unconscious being structured like a language. Topology is particularly versatile as an applied mathematical study insofar as it allows the analyst to deal with autistic space, which in the clinical setting is determined by the impossibility of asserting the existence of units. This audacious scanning of undifferentiated realms belies the mathematical ontology at work in topology, i.e. continuity. Lacan first introduces topological models in the early 1960s, in the 'Identification' seminar. The use of topology intensifies in his conceptualisation of the unconscious in the S-I-R figure. This application is what eventually propelled topology as the real presentation of subject (cf. Lacan 2007).

Badiou's mathematical universe does not recognise continuity in its ontological structure. The ontology is motivated by the event. As such, it is discrete in mathematical terms – at least as far as his reading is in *BE*. In *LW*, however, despite Badiou's attempts at maintaining an irreducible divide between mathematics and logic in the theory of the double rationalities, it is precisely topology in the form of Alexander Groethedieck's concept of *topos* that redesigns *LW*'s original purpose.

The initial application of topology in Badiou's philosophical reflection is found in his early work, *TS*. As Badiou was directly confronting Lacan's legacy in that work, the application is referential, instead of inscriptional. This changes in his later work, although Badiou celebrates Lacan's theory of body as one that refutes the appearance of its subjective unity as an illusion. The subject would have two bodies, and this reality lies within the subject's grasp to discover. As Badiou asserts, 'it is by its affect that the human animal recognises that it participates, through its incorporated body, in some subject of truth' (*LW* 480). The subject may recognise this duality; however, as Lacan stresses, she cannot transform the second body, namely the mark of the Other, into the natural body. As such, the body is not originary. As in Lacan's famous dictum: what *is* is the Other's desire. In Badiou's terms, the Other's desire is to appear. Topology as a general theory of space, put through a phenomenological mold, becomes the general theory of appearing.

From a mathematical perspective, a topological space may be defined as follows:

A set X along with a collection T of subsets of it is said to be a topology if the subsets in T obey the following properties:

1. The (trivial) subsets X and the empty set $\varnothing$ are in T.
2. Whenever sets A and B are in T, then so is $A \cap B$.
3. Whenever two or more sets are in T, then so is their union.

Note that the standard mathematical definition, here taken from Wolfram's MathWorld, is couched in set-theoretic operational terms. This convention goes in the direction of Badiou's argument regarding the set-theoretical nature of the ontological realm, or of the primordial realm of being. However, Badiou's specific task is to discriminate between the intrinsic ontology, i.e. the set-theoretic understanding of space as 'being an element of', and the strictly *topological* understanding of interiority.

Let us then use the terminology of 'opens', specific to a non-set-theoretic topology:

A topological space, S, may be defined as the set of the bodies in a delimited space:

1. A topological space is defined as an open.
2. The intersection of two opens forms an open.
3. The union of two opens forms an open.

Badiou's definition of topological space includes the correlation of an 'Int function' with the set E, i.e. the 'interior of' set E in topological terms. Key to sustaining this distinction, then, are the four fundamental topological axioms, with no set-theoretic overlap:

1. The interior of A is included in A
2. The interior of the interior of A is none other than the interior of A
3. The interior of E is E itself
4. The interior of the intersection of two parts A and B are precisely the intersection of its interiors. (*LW* 599)

Now, Lacan determined topology to be the specific science of the subject. Badiou does not uphold this view. If Badiou considers ontology to be without representation, then topology indeed has no purpose in discrete mathematics. If, however, existence is coextensive of subjectivity, then topology contains a non-subjective coefficient. This non-subjective coefficient is the sense that the term 'logic' acquires in Badiou's system.

More than set theory, it is category theory that provides Badiou with his strongest topological theorems. In *LW*, Badiou develops both a technical and descriptive dimension of topology in his theory of points. It is in this section that Badiou makes the claim that the 'logic of appearing is topo-logic'.

What this means structurally is that the notion of the transcendental of a point of a world accepts a correlation with the topological notion of an interior/inside. In Badiou's conception, E is a topological space when a function 'Int' is defined on the parts of *E*: 'A topological space is a power of localisation in the following specific sense: it distinguishes, in whatever subset of a referential space, the interior of that subset from its multiple-being as such' (ibid.). Topology thus allows one to leave the register of ontology in other to distinguish 'interior' from 'belonging to'.

The consequences of this discrimination lead directly to Proposition 50: The set of points of a transcendental has the structure of a topological space (463, 601). The transcendental of any world, save for atonal worlds (*mondes atones*), may be taken to be topological spaces. As Badiou puts it, 'it is a way of saying again that a world is the being-there of an infinite set of multiples' (463). It is also a formal demonstration of the intrinsic bound between appearing and localisation. The range of worlds may be plural, but

Badiou's topological reconstruction underscores how decision-making, i.e. the body in act, is inescapably binary in any world, i.e. Kierkegaard's either/or. Not that making a decision is simple, but rather that decision-making is fundamentally ethical insofar as staying firm with respect to its consequences is what defines the subject's bound to the Good. The theory of points is thus the formal inscription of choice. A world without points is thus one without tension. There is no place without a choice. Or rather, where there is a choice, there is a place.

TRANSCENDENTAL REGIME

Fabien Tarby

The transcendental is the key concept of *LW*. Its introduction, in Volume 2 of *BE*, consummates Badiou's thought by conceptualising a specifically Badiousian creation: a post-Heideggerian ontico-ontological materialism. In *BE* Badiou describes ontology as such, that is, the regime in itself of set-theoretical multiples. Ontology thus comes to signify the composition and decomposition of the 'play' of sets, independently of every other conception. In particular, such an ontology has no need either of the conception of relation or of variations or intensities between multiples, of their diverse relations. The operation of belonging (or not) to a set is an absolute, and is perfectly articulated with classical logic (it obeys the laws of non-contradiction and excluded middle). The world of ontology is indeed a classical one. It obeys a Boolean logic wherein one multiple either does or does not belong to another multiple. It therefore describes a global regime of multiplicities, on the basis of the Zermelo-Fraenkel system of axioms.

However, following the publication of *BE*, Badiou was faced with two questions. The first is as follows: if ultimate reality is set-theoretical, how are we to explain the fact that, in its density, being (*étant*) seems to us to be related, that is, signifying? This problem is decisive: in an atheist and materialist perspective, it is still necessary to account for the fact that the anti-foundation of a set-theoretical ontology can, despite it all, make sense. And the general response can come only from a logical mechanics of connections between multiples that the all-too-pure, too-Boolean world of ontology could not yet express. The second question thus: if the name of these possible connections between set-theoretic matters is 'transcendental', how can we account for the latter?

So, just as *BE* gave us a mathematics of being, *LW* provides a logic of the transcendental, which accounts for all the possibilities, or perspectives, between multiples.

A study of Badiou's works between the publication of *BE* (1988) and *LW* (2006) shows the insistence of this problematic in the progression of his thinking (e.g. *MT*).

The transcendental regime must first of all remain faithful to the rigorous materialism that Badiou formulates. The transcendental is neither Kantian, nor phenomenological. Its goal is to overturn all conceptions of the transcendental based on a subject, and to extricate, in the very logic of that which appears – independently of any consciousness (which is purely secondary) – the infinity of possibilities of appearing and of co-appearing between multiplicities. Technically, Heyting algebra in fact has achieved such results. It conceives a subset T of w worlds, with T designating thus relations of order (or of intensity, of degree, of the more or less between a minimum and a maximum) that express the transcendental indexations between the elements considered. The expression $Id(a,b) = p$, with p belonging to T, thus measures the degree of identity and/or difference between a and b, elements considered not on the basis of being – the atom is ultimately real and not virtual – but according to their reciprocal appearing. By managing both to understand the infinity of possibilities, but also to master their matrix on the basis of the relation of order (which supposes that it is always possible to articulate a and b – or Same and Other – through p's going from μ to M, from the minimal to the maximal), Badiou manages both to show the power but also the strictly logical necessity of possibilities. The binary structure (a,b) – a remarkable and simultaneously problematic fact – acts as a sufficient and ultimate structure for unfolding, via indexation and the measure p, all the possible relations between appearing beings.

An important consequence of this theory resides in the difference between what Badiou calls the small and the great logics. A possibly abiding question, after the end of *BE*, pertained to the logical fragments necessarily but strangely included in the set theory (for example, implications, the quantifiers). It was crucial for the ZF axioms to be articulated on the basis of notions of logic as fundamental as implication. So what were these inscriptions, relatively independent from the problem of sets? It was a crucial question. For example: what link is to be established between implication, on the one hand, and, on the other, belonging – a fundamental connector of ontology – insofar as the ontological formulas require such logical implications from the outset in their explanations, that is, as part of the expression of the axioms of the ZF system?

LW resolves it by showing that the main logical connectors are deduced from a deeper logical analysis than that of the simple inscription of key terms of logic in a symbolic formula; this analysis is set out in Badiou's concept of the transcendental regime and of the deployment of intensities

(p) that it renders possible. The 'small logic' is directly transcribed by the use (as unthought) of symbols such as implication, such that negation depends in fact on the 'grand logic' that unfolds in Book 2, Section 4 of *LW*, and which constitutes its underlying structure.

With this, Badiou shows that he is able to introduce into this thought results that do not come solely from a strictly anti-intuitionist logic, something that was not done in *BE* in the name of Badiou's repeated assertions that he is a philosopher of Platonist mathematics. Nevertheless the perspective that he adopts is not thereby an intuitionist one, if this is taken to mean promoting its sense of subjectivism. Ontology continues to remain no less Boolean, or classical.

The fundamental problem of Badiou's otherwise magnificent conception is the following: there must of necessity be a final surface of inscription of the relation between being and appearing, and it can only take place in being. Appearing is inferred from the very posibilities of being: there is no appearing without being to start with. Appearing is the very consequence of being; but being is not the consequence of a primary appearing, a notion without sense, since there must be something-multiples in order for the question of their 'thereness' to arise in the first place. There is no opening in itself, either of totality, or of the pure virtual, which for Badiou are phenomenological-vitalist phantoms. The postulate of the real atom demonstrates this; it is a postulate that, in fact, dissolves Deleuze's vitalist romanticism (*LW* is, in secret, a complete and exhaustive refutation of the Deleuzian virtual and of vitalist conceptions in general). But there is a price to pay for this: it is necessary to assert that appearing 'is' itself a being. It is necessary to screw the transcendental into being, as a type of being. With this the Aristotelian question arises of knowing what there is that is common, in being, between the lively fly, the mathematical structure of the sphere and the transcendental of relations between the two. It is a question that will not be easily resolved without Badiou's exposing himself, in the manner of Kant, *mutatis mutandis*, to a third critique, which it can be hoped that Badiou will write, after his own fashion.

Translated from the French by Steven Corcoran

TRUTH

Steven Corcoran

As Lacan points out the whole history of philosophy is inscribed in this question [of truth] from Plato's aporias of essence '. . . to the radical

ambiguity Heidegger points to in it, insofar as truth signifies revelation'
(Lacan 2006: 166). 'Truth' has always been a central category of philosophy, and the history of philosophy is itself marked by various concepts of
truth. These range from the 'correspondence theory' of truth to be found
in Aristotelian Scholasticism, wherein truth is a matter of thought's ability
to correspond adequately with a putatively external reality, to a 'coherence
theory' of truth, common to rationalists such as Spinoza and Leibniz,
wherein the truth of a theory is a matter of how well its constituent axioms
and propositions accord with, and mutually support, one another. Forms
of a 'constructivist theory' of truth have tended to dominate the recent
modern and post-modern period, wherein truth is claimed to result from
an anterior process that generates what counts as true. Constructivists
insist, in one way or another, that truth is never a 'given' but is always in
some sense produced or constructed in a historical or scientific sequence
by which it is circumscribed. Today's mood concerning truth is indeed
one of relativism.

Badiou sees two sources for this prevailing mood. The first is the
Nietzschean 'death of God'. Nietzsche sought to dislocate the infinite
from its location in the Supreme Being, as the ultimate guarantor of truth,
and reduced truth to the register of sense. For Nietzsche truth is an effect
of sense. When it comes to the truth one must always ask the question
'who speaks?', i.e. discern the particularity of a position or set of forces
that claims to truth cloak. The death of God is thus, in the Nietzschean
outlook, the checkmate of truth in its coupling with being. Second, as
truth is a central category of philosophy, this warbling of its notion has
allowed a further tendency to reinforce the Nietzschean checkmate: the
anthropologisation of philosophy itself, a process that aims to show that
philosophy is relative to the cultural and linguistic organisation of thought
in which it finds itself.

The question of truth is defining of philosophy and for this reason a
bewildering amount has been said about truth for thousands of years.
In *BE* Badiou adds to this story what he believes is a new chapter in the
modern conception of truth, articulated in a triplet along with the subject
and being, that attempts to undo the deleterious attack on the philosophical category of truth and the anthropologisation of philosophy. This triplet
of being, the subject and truth presents a renewed attempt to rigorously
distinguish philosophy in its specificity, at a time when the absoluteness of
truth has been variously attacked from analytic, Marxist, and postmodern
points of view.

What Badiou shares with more familiar conceptions of truth is the
claim that 'there is truth', or rather that 'there are truths'. Truths are,
as Badiou puts it, the real of philosophy, the 'thing' of thought, and as

is well-known his theory of conditions posits that there are four domains in which such truths occur: love, politics, science and art. As the real of philosophy, Badiou gives an account of these truths, which is to say, a description of what truths are and what it is that makes them true. *BE* gives an account of the being of truths, while *LW* provides one of their transworldly appearing (see *LW* 1–40). But in so doing he differs from correspondence, coherence and pragmatist theories of truth on crucial points. For, as we shall see, truths are the real of philosophy in something like the Lacanian sense: truths for philosophy are 'impossible' insofar as they can never be symbolised but nonetheless form that around which philosophical discursiveness revolves. As such, it is impossible to give a full account of truths, whose appearing is irreducibly contingent, as is the want of traditional theories. Or, in accordance with Lacan's dictum: there can be no truth of truth. Such attempts at philosophical mastery invariably fail to grasp truth as a procedure that is absolute and thus able to engender genuine novelty.

Badiou's own doctrine of truth might be partially seen as an axiomatic theory. We might approach this first by stating what it is not. First, it is not a semantic theory of truth. For such a theory the object-language for which a truth-predicate is defined requires a metalanguage to define that truth. Hence semantic approaches usually necessitate the use of a metalanguage that is more powerful (i.e. has more resources) than the object-language for which it provides a semantics. An axiomatic notion of truth requires far fewer resources and avoids the need for a strong metalanguage and metatheory. It has no need to define the substantive conditions of truth, as is the case in the neo-Aristotelian tradition. For the latter, by contrast, as substance has ontological primacy, 'definition is the linguistic mode of the establishment of the pre-eminence of the existent' (*TO* 31). But according to Badiou's doctrine, the existent has no such pre-eminence, precisely because 'there can be no definition of the multiple' (ibid.). What is primary is the inconsistency of the pure multiple (of being qua being). There is therefore no need for Badiou to produce a definition of existence and a metaphysics for a substantive account of truth. Having established, through subtractive means, that inconsistency is primary over the consistency of the existent (of the count-for-one), all Badiou needs to show is that this inconsistency can emerge in a situation and how this occurrence connects with an equally non-substantive or subtractive notion of truth.

For Badiou, in the wake of Gödel's second incompleteness theorem, there is a fundamental link between truth and lack of consistency or provability. A truth, that is, says more than that which can be proved or defined. It is in excess over knowledge. The necessity of claims of truth, in other words, cannot be proven. Badiou's axiomatic approach cannot seek any kind of foundation for truth, other than subtractive. In contrast to the substantive (or constructivist) approaches to truth, Badiou's axiomatic approach has no need to provide a metaphysics of truth (e.g. define the primitive terms that obtain in a relation of correspondence). Truth, viewed axiomatically, depends upon nothing outside its own consistency. This self-supporting aspect of truth – the fact that it is based on nothing other than its own integrity – is enabled because the primitive terms are subtracted from any objective definition or description of this integrity. The primitive terms in set theory, for example, are not defined. They are inscribed not as a 'nomination whose referent would have to be represented but . . . as a series of dispositions, where the term is nothing outside the regulated game of its founding connections' (CT 32). (Badiou is of course not the first to propose an axiomatic theory of truth, but in most axiomatic theories truth is conceived as a predicate of object – such as the structure of sentence types. The theory that describes the properties of the objects to which truth can be attributed is called the base theory, something for which Badiou has no need.)

This lack of definition of primitive terms is a condition of axiomatic thought, the condition required for its absoluteness: the criteria for truth cannot be referred to anything objective outside thought but instead are entirely internal to thought itself. An individual must accept to be subjectivised by the event without reference to any eternal objective criteria, such that the criteria of thought will lie in the operation of thought itself (i.e. in the consistency of its operation) (Hallward 2003: 156). Badiou maintains that the consistency of this operation can only be maintained through an internal limit to thought, which is that it respect a certain unnameable limit (the community is the unnameable of politics, enjoyment of love, and so on).

It is this self-relating and self-supporting character of truth – i.e. the fact that it includes in itself its own nomination and is buoyed only through the consistent elaboration of its own consequences – that lends it its eternal aspect. What a truth prescribes is rigorously indifferent to the forms of knowledge (with their classifications, definitions, etc.) governing the situation of which it is the truth (conversely, knowledge is deaf to the event). Only as subtracted from all non-thought (knowledge, established opinion, interest), that is, from constructed reality, does a truth as such become impermeable to corruption and the vicissitudes of history. Early Badiou conceived truth as the emergence of a revolutionary unity that came about through the cumulative historical development of the proletariat. But the precise problem with Marxism was that its truth was merged with the development of the historical encyclopaedia. With his adoption of a strictly timeless mathematical ontology in *BE*, truth itself becomes at once more punctual and eternal, or endless. A truth's validity exceeds chronological time as such (the forgetting of a truth never hinders its revival within another world). Its effects are not to be located within the specific order of knowledge, in which it 'punches holes', nor are its effects containable within any subsequent order of knowledge. A truth will always have been true . . .

What guarantees the eternity of a truth, says Badiou, is its infinity, its being endlessly re-subjectivisable, able to be experimented over and over again in disparate worlds and thus reinscribed anew. We can now see how Badiou's truth differs from the substantive desire to reduce truth to knowledge, to have it come as close as possible to absolute certainty – a truth designates that productive dimension of the real that always acts to disrupt the certainties of knowledge.

Of what is there truth for Badiou? First, there is no such thing as truth in general (say, of human nature); if there is truth, it is only of particular situations, or worlds. The inconsistency of pure multiplicity emerges within a consistent situation only in exceptional and unpredictable circumstances. Each such occurrence can come to form a truth, which is precisely the truth of that situation. Against the hierarchies, evaluations, privileges, interests, and so on informing that situation, a truth, in its essential inconsistency, exposes the sameness of being. A situation counts its elements (e.g. in the political situation, a country will count its citizens), and its state counts groups of these elements as one (citizens are divided into taxpayers, welfare recipients, 'free' citizens and inmates, full-time employees and precarious contract workers, and so on). Only a generic procedure, by contrast, exposes the truth of what is counted in a situation, that is, its inconsistent being. Generic procedures reveal that which is counted or presented 'in the indifferent and anonymous equality of its presentation' (*CS* 248). As Badiou puts it, 'Since the being of the situation is its inconsistency, a truth of this being will present itself as indifferent multiplicity, anonymous part, consistency reduced to presentation as such, without predicate. [. . .] A truth is this minimal consistency (a part, an immanence without concept) which indicates in the situation the inconsistency that it is' (*MP* 90).

What, then, is a truth? It is a process that is 'chance-ridden as to its possibility, subjective in its duration, particular in its materials, universal in its address or its result, infinite in its being and is deployed according to four distinct types of processes' (SEM 2014: October 24).

THE TWO

Alenka Zupancic

The concept of the Two appears at a crucial junction of Badiou's theory of the event, at the point that links the event to the possible concreteness of its circulating within the situation, that is, the point that links the event to its existence. For the latter doesn't per se belong to the event, which remains absolutely undecidable: 'It will therefore always remain doubtful whether there has been an event or not, except to those who intervene, who decide its belonging to the situation' (*BE* 207). Intervention is thus a crucial point in the life of an event, yet it is in itself a paradoxical notion, combining two seemingly contradictory gestures: that of identifying that there has been some undecidability, and that of deciding its belonging to the situation – whereby the latter would seem to cancel out the former. It is impossible to separate these two aspects of the intervention, and it is here that the properly Badiouian concept of the Two starts to take shape. It aims to circumscribe a link between two heteroclite terms in the very absence of any (lawful) relation between them. (And it is already here that one can detect the proximity with the Lacanian two of the non-existing sexual relation, which is central for Badiou's later redeployment of the concept of the Two in the context of love.) Badiou first deploys the Two as involved in interventional nomination of the event. No presented term of the situation can furnish its name. What the situation proposes as a base for the nomination can only be what it *un*presents, and not what it presents. This is why the inaugural axiom of intervention is '*not tied to the one, but to the two*. As one, the element of the site that indexes the event does not exist, being unpresented. What induces its existence is the decision by which it occurs as two, as itself absent and as supernumerary name' (*BE* 205). Or: the excess of one is also beneath one. In contrast to the law of the count, an intervention only establishes the one of the event as a non-one. The other name for this non-one one (of the Event) is the ultra-one, the essence of which is precisely the Two. For the event can be also seen as an interval rather than a term: 'it establishes itself, in the interventional retroaction, between the empty anonymity bordered on by the site, and the addition of a name'. In this respect, the event is ultra-one 'because the maxim "there is Twoness" is founded upon it [. . .] The Two thereby invoked is not the reduplication of the one of the count, the repetition of the effects of the law. It is an originary Two, an interval of suspense, the divided effect of a decision' (206). What this 'Twoness' ultimately means becomes more specific in Badiou's concluding articulation of the difficult relationship between intervention and event. As already emphasised, the existence of the event depends entirely on the intervention that declares it. Yet at the same time Badiou firmly upholds another axiom according to which the event alone founds the possibility of intervention, or constitutes 'the real of the conditions of possibility of an intervention'. In order to avoid the circularity involved in this mirroring of the event and the intervention, Badiou responds by splitting the side of the event: 'the possibility of the intervention must be assigned to the consequences of another event' (209). The Two of an intervention now becomes an evental between-two, 'an intervention is what presents an event for the occurrence of another'. Two thus reveals itself to be essentially linked to the notion of time. Time is the requirement of the Two: 'for there to be an event, one must be able to situate oneself within the consequences of another' (210). This prerogative of the two also shifts the accent away from the event itself: 'what the doctrine of the event teaches us is rather that the entire effort lies in following the event's consequences, not in glorifying its occurrence'. However, the consequences of an event cannot be discerned as such, and the event is only possible if special procedures conserve the evental nature of its consequences. This leads to the necessity of the discipline of time, and Badiou calls this organised control of time, as deployment of the Two, fidelity.

The Two thus refers to keeping related, in the absence of any law, that what of an event gets submitted to the structure (and can be said to be), and its fundamental undecidability. One could also say: the two refers to the constellation where an event *counts*, without counting as one (nor as two ones), for the latter would precisely erase it as event. The 'between-two-events' does not mean that each of them now counts as one, or that the two events constitute stable points between which the uncertain labour of fidelity is situated. On the contrary, the only stability (or structure) belongs to this space in between, to the work of fidelity, and the latter alone is what the two events are suspended upon from the point of view of their existence.

Against the background of this elaboration of the concept of the Two as an uncountable count of the event in general, it might come as a surprise to see this same notion elaborated as constitutive of one of the four generic procedures, that is, as pertaining specifically to the amorous event. And yet, Badiou's most elaborated and well-known concept of the Two comes from his writing on love, starting with 'What is love?' (cf. *CS*), continuing with the central piece 'The Scene of Two', and followed by the most recent *In Praise of Love*. In the singular context of love, as based on the encounter, Badiou deploys all crucial accents of the Two as formulated in *BE*.

1. Its evental origin: two (in this case, two sexual positions) only emerge as two in the aftermath of the event, and only exist as the labour of its consequences.

2. Its being uncountable: since there is no neutral stance or third position, the two positions can precisely not count as two. Badiou writes '[a]s a consequence of an encounter, what is the possibility of a Two which counts neither as one, not as the sum of one plus one? A Two counted as two in an immanent way? Such is the problem of a scenario in which the Two is neither fusion nor summation. In which, consequently, the Two is in excess of that which composes it, without, for all that, annexing the Three' ('Scene of Two' 43).

3. Its existence in the very absence of any lawful relation: 'A real Two, since what composes it is only, in itself or in its being, a non-rapport . . .'

4. Its being essentially a process, a duration, a construction of a scene: this accent on duration, with which Badiou counters the artistic, mostly literary treatment of love which fails in this respect, corresponds precisely to the accent on how 'the entire effort lies in following the event's consequences', and to the intervention (in this case the declaration of love) conceived as Time itself. Hence the importance of fidelity, conceived in terms of such an 'organised control of time', rather than as a 'promise not to sleep with someone else' (*IPL* 45).

How are we to think the relation between the two levels on which the concept of Two appears in Badiou's theory, that is, the level of the event as such and the level of a more specific event of love, which leads to and provides its most elaborate form? Is love something like a repetition, in form of independent existence, of the logic of the Two involved in the evental dimension as such? Or does every evental occurrence, in order to be thought as evental, presuppose something like minimal structure of love? Whatever way one turns this question, it seems that the Two, defined as the immanent count-for-two, also needs to be counted-for-two.

UNIVERSALITY

Steven Corcoran

Badiou's philosophy, under the void of the category of Truth, strives to think the universality of truths, in terms of their being (*BE*) and of their appearing (*LW*). His determination of truths as procedures is perhaps the most novel and far-reaching answer to a question that has occupied much of contemporary French philosophy, namely, 'What is a universal singularity?' On this question Badiou considers his key interlocutor to be Deleuze, the discussion bearing essentially on the conditions under which a singular universal may be thought as a vector of radical change. Deleuze is, he says, the 'only contemporary philosopher to have made of the intuition of change . . . the key to a renewed metaphysical proposition' (*LW* 382). For Badiou, however, Deleuze's answer to this problem falls short, the reason being the relation he posits between being and event. Deleuze's vitalist ontology commits him to grasping the event as the virtual component of being, but this then situates the event in a continuity with being. Badiou argues, however, that 'the generic form of being can never welcome the event within itself as a virtual component; but on the contrary, the event itself takes place by a rare and incalculable supplementation' (see Badiou's arguments in *DCB*). For Badiou, what must be thought through is *discontinuity* itself. Only then can we find an adequate answer to the question of singular universality.

Truth, qua singular universality, begins with the cut of the event. This evental supplementation is not yet a truth but instead, within its situation of appearing, an undecidable multiple. For the situation itself, the event-multiple is simply void: it is unpresented and unpresentable, which is to say that it belongs to no already existent sets that would allow it to be accounted for within the knowledge available. What it presents are in fact elements of the situation (workers, students, intellectuals, etc.). But it presents them in such a way that their belonging to the situation, in excess of knowedge, cannot be decided. The multiplicity of the event is ontologically peculiar: by its composition it is at once the most generic part of the situation and the most singular. Why? Because ontologically speaking, belonging to no existent set, it can only appear as self-founding, and thus illegal. Or to put it another way: the event presents elements of the situation under consideration, but does so in such a way that thwarts all procedures for the application of a law. Does the autonomous capacity of political speech shown by these workers, who have no titles to govern, really belong to the situation? What is this fervour joining intellectuals, students and workers?

For those in power who evaluate the situation from the viewpoint of the existing order, an event will appear as no more than a contingent occurrence, a local disturbance to this order or moment of irrationality. Are not the statements of the servants of the order and entrenched privilege in reaction to the event always of the type: the insurgents don't understand the complexity of things; what they are doing is illegal; they should curb their youthful enthusiasm, and so on. But what such ideological references to complexity, illegality, and so on mask is that there is genuine undecidability here: according to the situation's modes of inclusion and knowledges, these workers are not entitled to take political decisions, or only minimally so (they are allowed to vote in elections that reinforce their subordination), and yet through the political autonomy that they invent, they demonstrate their equal belonging of all elements to the situation, a presentation that belies their subordinate mode of inclusion in it. What is thus encountered in an event is precisely a truth of the situation, insofar as for the latter to continue operating, it must exclude the very capacity that emerges in the event. (This is incidentally why established power will always demand what it is exactly that the demonstrators want. The attempt is to reduce the emergence of this autonomous capacity and its potentially subversive consequences to a simple demand for X – e.g. a pay increase.) Given this undecidability, however, this belonging to the situation can only be decided, pure and simple.

Badiou's subjective universalism emerges precisely through this figure of radical choice, at the point where this excess over knowledge is converted into the recognition that there has been some undecidability and that it figures not as a simple chaos or void but as a generic expression, a hitherto unexplored part, of the situation. Subjective universalism thus requires the invention of a subjective fidelity, which is a profoundly egalitarian gesture: investigating the situation must be undertaken in line with the axiom of equality of all in the situation, without regard to the rules of inclusion, and at a distance from the application of available knowledge. A truth then unfolds through the patient and laborious enquiries that a subject undertakes in order to establish the set of elements in the situation that maintain a positive relation to the event; it is nothing but the collection of consequences that result from so enquiring into the situation (e.g. the rendering compatible of elements that were supposed incompatible, such as workers or intellectuals, etc.).

The result is what Badiou calls an indiscernible generic extension to the situation. It is one whose 'wandering excess' is, however, always situated. The intervening subject operates, from the point of view of a truth, in the field of situated knowledges, which are displaced or reorganised in a determinate fashion. There are two things to indicate here. Firstly, this truth 'punches' holes in the knowledge in which it emerges, in the sense that it shows the radical incompletion of that knowledge. Existing knowledge is indeed unable to account for the belonging of the event to the situation. Secondly, this subject, which as an operator is fully impersonal, faithfully if haphazardly investigates the belonging of the event to the situation, forcing a series of consequences that are irreducible to such knowledge. This investigation will not negate the order of knowledge or law, since as

Badiou argues, it would thus rely too much on the identity of that which it is negating, and would cease to be generic, but will posit the supplementary existence of something that renders this knowledge incomplete (see *SP*, for example, and the way in which 'grace' acts as a supplementary category that suspends the effects of Jewish and Greek discourse).

This notion of the subject as the operator of singular universality, as that which takes the illegality of the event as bearing consequence *for all* and, through the invention of prescriptions, patiently constructs it as a truth, is first argued for in *BE*. In the wake of this groundbreaking work, Badiou then provides an elaborate account of the militant discourse, through the example of *Saint Paul*, an elaborate account of the unfolding of a truth procedure. The distilled version of his thoughts on the concept of universality are given in 'Eight theses of the Universal (cf. TU/*TW* 143–52), which I list briefly below.

In *LW*, Badiou further gives himself the means to argue that universality designates the fact that a truth can be intelligible (i.e. understood as a truth) and deployed (i.e. continued, reorganised) in a world other than the one in which it has emerged. Every truth, whether an ancient play by Aeschlyus or a procedure developed in the wake of the Paris Commune, is available to us to subjectivise. This argument runs counter to the deposition of the universal and general 'anthropologisation of philosophy' prevalent today, according to which philosophy would deal with more or less heterogeneous linguistic and/or cultural organisations of thought, and is itself the result or production of one such organisation.

But this movement of anthropologisation, which obviously entails relativism, is one that Badiou vigorously refutes. In *LW* Badiou avails himself of the means to argue what it is that the universality of truth presumes: namely, that a truth, for being able to traverse many heterogeneous worlds, is in exception to its era, and qua exception marks a fundamental discontinuity. Were this not so, were a truth entirely circumscribed by the world of its emergence, we would no longer be able to understand it. Badiou provides many examples to show that this is not the case, and in each one we see that at issue is real universality, a concrete universality of real things – works of art, political processes, scientific theories, exceptional loves. Truths are things of thought and practice that traverse the centuries and are available to everyone to grasp.

A further motivation for Badiou's recasting of universality is the challenge to our situation thrown up by capital. The workings of monetary abstraction bear certain formal similarities to the ambitions of emancipatory politics. As Marx perfectly saw, the power of such abstraction lies in its dissolution of every transcendent one, in its indifference to communitarian, identitarian predicates. However, these similarities are just that, purely formal: in contrast with the genuine universality of a truth procedure, whose being is fundamentally generic, market universality is false, precisely because its condition of existence is not the elimination of communitarian differences but, on the contrary, their multiplication and systematic differentiation (*SP* 7–10). The struggle thus cannot be one of particularism against the globality of the market; there is 'no earlier territoriality calling for protection or recovery'. The only way to counter the twin processes of monetary homogenisation and the production of 'closed identities, and the culturalist and relativist ideology accompanying this fragmentation', is through the construction of another universalism.

Badiou's eight theses on universality are as follows:

1. 'Thought is the proper medium of the universal.' The universal is not a matter of the universal quantifier, but pertains to genuine leaps in thought, the affirmation of an evental supplementation to the situation as having consequences 'for all'. Consequently truth cannot be reduced to a neutral, linguistic act of judgement. Instead, truth is 'anobjective', or subjective, which also means that it is something in which individuals must actively participate, for which they must take sides, in a leap of thought that is irreducible to the situation. This they can do only by deciding to draw the consequences of an undecidable event, or by re-subjectivating a body of truth – whether this involves performing a mathematical demonstration, enacting the consequences for a situation of the egalitarian maxim, etc. The subject does not precede this universal process but emerges only through the process contained in this local point, outside of all describable structures.

2. 'Every universal is singular, or is a singularity.' Universality necessarily starts in a singular point outside of the particularities circumscribed by a situation. This means that universality does not play a regulative role with regard to the particularities or differences of a situation, which, like all situations, is entirely contingent. It is inherently anti-identitarian.

3. 'Every universal originates in an event, and the event is intransitive to the particularity of the situation.' Universality as a process is only ever generated by a fidelity to an event, which ever shows the positivist coupling between the general and the particular to be merely regulative of the materiality on which the universal is at once based and which it exceeds.

4. 'A universal initially presents itself as a decision about an undecidable.' Universality emerges when a statement about which the encyclopedia enjoins undecidability (the existence of God, the belonging of illegal immigrants to the situation, etc.) is decided. 'Yes, these workers

without papers do belong to the situation!' This decision decides on a part of encyclopedic undecidability and makes truth out of it.

5. 'The universal has an implicative structure.' Against the hermeneu-tical perspectivalism that refers all universals to the supposed forces or interests sustaining them, Badiou insists that the universal exists only in the network of consequences that are actively pursued in the wake of the decision that such and such an evental statement is true.

6. 'The universal is univocal.' Univocity relates not to the meaning of the statement itself but to the act that decides it. Whereas its valence was previously intermediate, undecidable, it is conferred, through the act of decision and the implicative results drawn from it, a significance that is exceptional.

7. 'Every universal singularity remains incomplete or open.' A universal singularity is necessarily connected, as we mentioned above, to the infinite. To be properly universal, its process must engage a transfinite dimension.

8. 'Universality is nothing other than the faithful construction of an infi-nite generic multiple.' The universal is one and the same thing as the constructing in a situation of a subset of that situation that is entirely irreducible to the predicative structure of the encyclopedia governing that situation. If a universal is to be for all, one's inscription within this universal cannot be due to one's particularity.

More recently Badiou has come to consider his characterisation in *BE* and *LW* of the singular universality of the subject to be too objective. In each case, the subject is the protocol of orientation of truth – in the first, the subject is that local point which investigates the universal truth of the event, which forces the evental consequences in which that truth insists. He establishes in it the generic being of a truth, which is negatively determined as that which is *irreducible* to the knowledge available in the situation. Then, in *LW*, the subject is posited as that which operates the protocol of construction of the body of truth. The concept of this protocol is *compatibility*: the subject operates a relation of compatibility in order to construct this truth, which is to say that within a truth 'there is a relation of compatibility between all its elements'. Unsatisfied with the objective and negative nature of these determinations, Badiou has been concerned in his recent seminars with an analysis of truth not from the point of view of being, or from that of appearing, but from the point of view of the subject of truth itself. Thus the question informing his current work is: How it is possible to think through truths in their immanence, from the point of view of the process of subjectivisation?

VOID

Olivia Lucca Fraser

The word 'void' is surprisingly equivocal in Badiou's writings. It operates, to begin with, on two distinct registers: there is a methodological register, according to which philosophy, which can produce no truths of its own, hollows out the 'void' of Truth in its own discourse, so as to receive and assemble the disparate *truths* of its time (see 'Definition of Philosophy', in *MP* 142). More prominently, and more frequently, the term occurs on an ontological register – which is the one I deal with in what follows – whereby 'void' is the name of being qua being. The latter can further be parsed into four distinct but interwoven senses, each, to varying degrees, 'sutured' to the empty set of set theory, Ø, the unique set to which nothing belongs.

1. *The void as pure, non-self-identical, inconsistent multiplicity.*
2. *The void as the ultimate ground of ontological identity.*
3. *The void as the emptiness of the count-as-one, itself.*
4. *The void as the 'gap' between presentation and what-is-presented.*

The first sense, which, through the name of the void, equates being-qua-being with inconsistent multiplicity, is best approached in terms of a dictum that Badiou adopts from Leibniz: '*ce qui n'est pas* un *être n'est pas un* être', or, 'what is not *a* being is not a *being*': entity implies unity. But unity, for Badiou, is never anything other than the effect of an operation, which he calls the 'count-as-one': every unity is a unity *of* something, something not *in itself* unitary. Ultimately, therefore, the unity of each *being* is grounded in the non-unity of being-qua-being, understood as a sheer chaos of inconsistent multiplicity – the *plethos* of being-without-unity that appears in the 'dream' evoked at the end of Plato's *Parmenides*. It is this void, which without unity and therefore without entity, but which is nevertheless supposed but every positing of entity or unity, that Badiou's identification of set theory as ontology 'sutures' to the symbol, Ø, taken up by mathematics as the name of the empty set (*l'ensemble vide*) – converting, by sheer decree, non-ontic, non-unitary being into the primordial unit of ontology. And so it is that, 'with the inconsistency (of the void), we are at the point where it is equivocally consistent and inconsistent [. . .] the question of knowing whether it consists or not is split by the pure mark (Ø)' (Badiou and Tho 2011: 99).

The void, in this sense, is the non-unitary, non-existing remainder of every count-as-one, every consistent 'situation' of beings. It is that aspect of every situation that is still-uncounted, and which inheres in every presentation as the invisible but inexpugnable residuum of inconsistency, a 'yet-to-be-counted, which causes the structured presentation to waver towards the phantom of inconsistency' (*BE* 66). The mathematical witness of this notion, in light of Badiou's metaontology, is the inclusion of Ø in every set as a subset, mirroring the inherence of the void in every situation. To this reflection, too, there is a remainder, however, for Ø is, mathematically speaking, a perfectly *consistent* set, neither eluding identification nor threatening the stability of the sets in which it inheres. Badiou responds to this disparity by taking the *mathematical* consistency of Ø to be uniquely characteristic of the ontological situation: through it, alone, we can think the void consistently.

Passing through that 'ontological situation', however, the metaontological notion of the void acquires a second sense: rather than the name of absolute multiplicity and chaos, the void is now the foundation of identity. The identity between any two sets, in ZF set theory, is determined by the axiom of extensionality, which states that 'two' sets are identical if and only if they have all the same elements. Since a set is never anything but a set of sets, this implies a regress: before the identity of a set can be established, we must first establish the identity of its elements by looking at *its* elements, and so on. The only stopping point to this regress is Ø, whose existence is asserted by the axiom of the empty set, and which, alone, is *immediately* self-identical, for there is simply no point at which two supposedly empty sets could differ from one another. Combining these two aspects of the void, we could say that the One meets with the Same only to the extent that it is rooted in the non-One, the void. The void is thus something like the substance of every situation, every situation being conceived as 'a modality-according-to-the-one [*selon-de-l'un*] of the void itself' (*BE* 57).

While these first two senses of 'void' seem capable of enjoying a certain harmony as interpretations of the empty set, Sense 3 seems to speak of something somewhat different. A set-theoretic counterpart to the notion of 'the emptiness of the count-as-one' might be found, however, by turning again to the axiom of extensionality. What this axiom says, after all, is that the 'act' of assembling elements into a set has, in itself, no qualities whatsoever, that it contributes nothing to the identity of the set so formed. Once we know all of the elements of a set, we know all there is to know about the set in question. There is no 'substance', no ontic 'thickness', to the operation of the count itself.

This gives us a clue to the interpretation of Badiou's remark that

it comes down to exactly the same thing to say that the nothing [the void] is the operation of the count – which, as source of the one, is not itself counted [Sense 3] – and to say that the nothing is the pure multiple upon which the count operates – which 'in itself', as non-counted, is quite distinct from how it turns out according to the count [Sense 1].

– a remark that seems to knot together the three senses surveyed so far into a coherent whole, even if the structure of that knot is not immediately clear. The key, here, seems to be to reflect on the axiom of extensionality, which strips unity of substance while grounding identity in the void.

Badiou's text becomes increasingly mysterious as it proceeds, however. Taking up just where we left off, we read that

The nothing [the void] names that undecidable of presentation which is its unpresentable, distributed *between* the pure inertia of the domain of the multiple, and the pure transparency of the operation thanks to which there is oneness [*d'où procède qu'il y ait de l'un*]. The nothing is as much that of structure, thus of consistency, as that of the pure multiple, thus of inconsistency. (*BE* 55; emphasis added)

Here, yet another thought of the void emerges, equivocating, perhaps, on the word, '*between*': the void is now understood not just through the unity of the first three senses, but as 'the imperceptible *gap*, cancelled then renewed, between presentation as structure and presentation as structured-presentation, between the one as result and the one as opera-tion, between presented consistency and inconsistency as what-will-have-been-presented' (54; tm): this is Sense 4 in our list.

It is not immediately clear how this conception of the void is related to the empty set. Here, Badiou seems to be naming something like the sheer moment of *differentiation* that must be supposed to hold sway between a set and its elements – a moment which, structurally, recalls nothing so much as the *nothingness* that, to Sartre's eyes, interposes itself between impersonal consciousness and its objects, and which arises as an 'impal-pable fissure' that arises in the heart of consciousness in the event of its reflexive presentation (Sartre 1956: 77–8).

I would argue that it is *this* notion of the void that allows us to make productive and non-trivial sense of Badiou's thesis that

for the void to become localisable at the level of presentation, and thus for a certain type of intrasituational assumption of being qua being to occur, there must be a dysfunction of the count, resulting from an excess-of-one. The event will be this ultra-one of chance, on the basis of which the void of a situation may be retroactively discerned. (*BE* 56; tm)

Later on, in the same vein, Badiou writes of an event's tendency to 'let forth, from inconsistent being and the interrupted count, the incandescent non-being of an existence' (*BE* 183). These gnomic proclamations can be elaborated by showing how an 'event', a moment when the count-as-one folds back on itself, breaking with the axiom of foundation and foiling the extensional regime of ontological identity, formally replicates what Sartre called 'the immediate structures of the for-itself' (Sartre 1956: esp. Part II, Ch. I, § I). The void, the 'nothingness' which erupts in such circumstances is not described by a set-theoretical ontology, but a Sartrean one, which would articulate the relation between the 'void' exposed by an event and the form of subjectivity to which an event gives rise (including its dimensions of temporality, possibility, normativity and liberty). Indeed, the basic outlines of such an existential ontology can already be found in the rudimentary theory of the subject with which *BE* concludes.

Naming both the inconsistent being of the in-itself, and the contradictory eruptions of the for-itself, 'the void' is the equivocal medium of Badiou's mathematical existentialism, the hollow in which Being and Event communicate.

WAGNER

François Nicolas

In Badiou's philosophy, Wagner is the name of a singularity more than of an event properly speaking: there is, for this philosophy, the *Wagner*-singularity more than a *Wagner*-event (which would then be liable to condition this philosophy as Mallarmé's poetry or Cantor's set theory has done).

Concerning the French version of the book of lessons he devoted to Wagner, this singularity is announced with some strangeness, since, despite not being made up of interviews, Badiou declares that it wasn't written by him and, stranger still, that it was routed, to and fro, through another language – English – before returning to French, in which it was finally thought through and presented.

Of what singularity is such a symptom an avowal?

Let's note that with Badiou's first book – a novel titled *Almagestes*, published in 1964 – music advances in privileged fashion under the proper name *Wagner* (associated in this case with the opera *Parsifal*) and that *Wagner's* music is endowed in it with a singular power of nomination that permits us to conceive of it as the secret prayer of things:

'What name are we to give to things, one that accords them?' (*Almagestes* 199)

'Music, that perfect music able to name everything, since it is hardly a sign, but you might say, but the secret of things, their prayer.' (101)

In this way, from the start of Badiou's oeuvre, music is credited, under the name Wagner, with containing a secret that the philosopher, fifty years later, will undertake to avow by presenting it in the above-mentioned *lessons* on Wagner.

In Badiou's philosophy, Wagner becomes the name of a singularity with different statuses. First, Wagner comes to name music as a fundamental operator of contemporary ideology (*Wag* 1), and, this doing, nothing less than the name of a new situation in relations between philosophy and music (71).

Second, Wagner comes to name a music vested with four different possibilities (cf. Lesson 4):

First of all, it is music that, having had great art as its ambition, prefigures the possibility of a new type of artistic grandeur: a grandeur that no longer proceeds from the completeness of a supposed total art, but that affirms itself locally as well as globablly, a grandeur that affirms itself in all moments and not solely in conclusive grand finales;

Second, music that, treating a tragically split subject, gives rise to a new type of development: a development that is not ordained towards a resolute ending, to a synthetic conclusion, but unfolds under the law of the multiple such as it is invented, for example, within a networks of leitmotifs conceived not as a list of frozen signifiers but as a collective capacity of metamorphosis;

Third, music that is able to attack the question of a new ceremonial capable of self-representing the collective as such, and that therein announces those new-type ceremonies of which generic humanity has need in its long communist march;

Fourth, music that can go beyond Christianity, which exceeds (rather than deconstructs) the latter by affirming fidelities of a new type, the necessity of which Wagner this time was only able to sense.

Note that for Badiou's philosophy these four musical dimensions (a great art, a tragic subject, a communist self-ceremonial of generic humanity, an affirmation beyond Christianity) constitute projects far more than closed effectuations. Wagner thus becomes for music the name of an opening and of a future rather than of a closure and of an advent. If, with Wagner, there really is completion and saturation as much as prefiguration, what is of interest to Badiou under the name *Wagner* is what this signifier advances as a possibility, as a motif that is still secret but already there, as the promise of a future anterior, as the announcing of a moment in which the Wagner-possibility will have come. Wherein we see that the name *Wagner* has here become a philosophical name for music.

At this point, music appears as a specific type of condition for Badiou's philosophy, one that differs not only from the scientific, political and love conditions but also from the other artistic conditions.

This specificity touches on five points.

1. Wagner's music *affects* the philosophical field more than it *conditions* it.
2. This action is an *intervention* less into philosophy as such than into the relations that music and philosophy entertain with one another (and therefore into what *condition* means in these relations).
3. In the face of this action, Badiou's philosophy will effect a *retroaction* on this music that is liable to condition it. This retroaction will operate *upstream* of any possible musical conditioning, and not in strict reversal of Wagnerian action – we will return to this.

Figure 5

4. This retroaction will give itself as a (philosophical) avowal of a (musical) secret, an avowal that endeavours to designate, under the (philosophical) name *Wagner*, an unperceived musical capacity.

In sum, *Wagner* thus becomes the philosophical name of a capacity specific to music, a capacity hitherto secret rather than musically effectuated, a capacity that has secretly remained confined to the folds of music, a capacity that Badiou's philosophy undertakes to bring to light as a sort of prescription addressed upstream of actually existing sorts of music.

This retroactive prescription thus takes the form of a prophecy that concerns less future music as such than music as a possible condition for philosophy: it is by accepting to be great art, a communist self-ceremonial of generic humanity, etc. (see the four aforementioned dimensions) that music to come will be able to re-engage its power of conditioning on philosophy.

By philosophically avowing the secrets of a possible musical conditioning, Badiou's philosophy intervenes here upstream of its own upstream, as it were, in such a way that it is a matter for it of prophesising about what music, under the name *Wagner*, is already capable of (without this being really known in music or by musicians), which means: capable of *for philosophy*.

In short, at issue is to forge a philosophical Idea of music apt to inspire the philosopher's confidence in music that, as is, is unable to condition this philosophy.

Whence a second trait of the retroactive relation of Badiou's philosophy to music such as it is engaged under the name *Wagner*: this philosophy seems to recognise music as having a pre-eminence in different capacities that it would share with philosophy:

> First, in terms of power of nomination: music would name things by exposing their specific time (122); thus, Wagner's music names the contrast of worlds in accordance with the time specific to transitions (124), it similarly names the uncertainty of periods (125) or the tragicness of a paradoxical appearing of things (126–7) in accordance with a time of equivocation or of an unfillable rift;
>
> Second, in terms of avowal: music, able to expose the appearance of things while preserving their underlying nutritive thickness and the intertwining specific to their temporality, is more able than any other form of discourse to avow the secret of things without squandering them;
>
> Lastly, in terms of address: music would have a singular power of address, which is precisely why it has become a privileged ideological operator today; music would be the prayer of things insofar as things named musically according to their own time would *ipso facto* be addressed to anyone at all as a generically addressed prayer (in the sense of a secular act by which a subject prays you to listen to it).

Wagner thus happens to name, in Badiou's philosophy, this properly musical pre-eminence in the matter of nomination according to time, of avowal according to the preserved secret, and of generic address according to prayer. Music would be endowed with this singular power of nomination that, by holding itself at a distance from language, would authorise avowing the secret of things in the form of a generic address.

Now, of these different traits, philosophy also claims to be the agent: it strives to name the contemporary, therefore to name according to time; it prophesies by avowing the secrets of the day; it, too, strives to address this nomination generically – for this it uses all the available means, mingling, at leisure, different regimes of discursivity.

Thus, Badiou's philosophy schools itself in music all the while enveloping it in accordance with its future. It promotes that which music is capable of (without music being able to know it) and it encourages this music with a gentle poke in the back, all the while listening directly to its possible lessons.

More precisely, philosophy retroacts here on the thinking musician (rather than on music directly, which can of course do nothing in this philosophical affair but) whose intellectuality of music is developed more or less explicitly in the shadow of a given philosophy.

Thus the formal – not content-based – likeness between the prophetic gesture of philosophy and what this philosophy attributes as music's proper power under the proper name *Wagner* leads philosophy to decipher its own act in the very music apt to condition it. Admittedly, the philosophical idea of music upholds the philosopher's confidence in his own (philosophical) understanding of music.

We see here that, if Badiou's philosophy endeavours – incidentally – to avow the secrets of some music that, since Wagner – refuting the Hegelian diagnostic of the death of art – maintains another relation with philosophy than one of strict conditioning, this constitutes the Wagner-secret as specifically philosophical.

Besides, there are scarcely any musicians that, to name music, would elect Wagner; their preference would rather land on Bach or Beethoven, Schumann or Chopin, Debussy or Stravinsky, Monk or Coltrane . . .

For Badiou's philosophy, Wagner would thus be the name (since Hegel and Kierkegaard?) of an indiscernability between a possibility that has not been of a musical conditioning and the necessity of a philosophical prophecy on this possibility to configure it. Ultimately, *Wagner* would be, in Badiou's philosophy, the singular name of a secret undecidability relating, *for the individual Alain Badiou*, this philosophy to music.

Translated from the French by Steven Corcoran

WITTGENSTEIN

Christopher Norris

Badiou distinguishes *philosophers* from *antiphilosophers*, and these in turn from a third class of thinkers – very much a 'third class', philosophically speaking – to whom he applies the label *sophists*. The original sophists were a group of ancient Greek thinkers, orators, professional rhetoricians and teachers who specialised in the arts of public discourse and oral communication. If we are to believe Socrates as reported by Plato then they were basically teachers with nothing to teach, or bumptious types with the gift of the gab who made up for their lack of knowledge by holding forth about any and every topic with well-practised fluency and assurance.

Though once placed squarely in the camp of sophists (cf. *CS*), Badiou then came to consider Ludwig Wittgenstein one of the three main modern antiphilosophers, in a lineage stretching from Nietzsche to Lacan (cf. *WA*). The 'sophist' label was applied very much with the term's pejorative associations in mind. 'Antiphilosophers' are those – for instance Saint Paul and Pascal – who define their vocation expressly against the aims, priorities and values that philosophers typically espouse but who for that very reason may provoke philosophers into thinking against their habitual grain and thereby doing better, more creative and self-critical philosophy.

Yet Wittgenstein is undoubtedly the single most influential and oft-cited thinker in the analytic tradition, taking this to range more widely than the hard-line or *echt*-analytic approach that came down from Frege and Russell and had its main impact on work in philosophy of logic and 'logic-first' approaches to philosophy of language. By looking briefly at the two distinct periods or phases of Wittgenstein's thought we can better understand Badiou's early claim that he – actually the later Wittgenstein – belongs to the history of sophistry rather than that of philosophy proper. And we can also better grasp why his later switch to treating Wittgenstein as an antiphilosopher rather than a sophist is not so much a sheer recantation or major shift of ground on Badiou's part as a perfectly explicit switch of focus from one to another period of Wittgenstein's thought. In short, it corresponds to the radical change of priorities that led him from the ultra-logicist conception of truth, sense and reference espoused in his early *Tractatus Logico-Philosophicus* to the contrary doctrine put forward in *Philosophical Investigations* and other posthumously edited texts.

The *Tractatus* is an austere, tightly constructed and (to all appearances at least) rigorously argued work laid out *more geometrico* in a sequence of elaborately numbered sections and sub-sections. It puts the case – again to all appearances, since commentators differ sharply about this – for a view of language as properly meaningful just so long as its constituent parts (or the parts of its constituent 'atomic' propositions) match up with real-world, i.e. factual or empirically verifiable states of affairs. It can also, he allows, make a different kind of sense in articulating logical truths or the structure of logically valid propositions, although here it has to do with

self-evident, tautologous and hence strictly meaningless since empirically vacuous statements. Thus it is hardly surprising that Wittgenstein's
Tractatus theory of language, logic and truth was picked up by the
Viennese logical positivists as a striking since powerfully compressed and
gnomic rendition of doctrines that they were in process of devising at
just that time. It seemed to state in crystalline form their basic tenet that
empirical verifiability was the criterion of meaningful or contentful language, since aside from that there existed only two kinds of statement: the
tautologies of logic and the nonsense (strictly so called) of 'metaphysical'
utterances like those of theology, ethics, aesthetics, and other such purely
'emotive' topic areas.

The logical positivists famously ran into trouble with the fact that this
verification-principle failed to live up to its own requirement – being
neither logically self-evident nor empirically verifiable – and hence turned
out to be a non-starter. There were also large interpretative problems
with Wittgenstein's *Tractatus* which contained some rather cryptic (some
would say murkily portentous) passages towards the close where he distinguished what could be *said*, i.e. explicitly and perspicuously stated, from
that which could only be *shown*, i.e. somehow conveyed, implied, or put
across by oblique or non-propositional means. Besides, by the time the
positivists' attention was drawn to these recalcitrant passages Wittgenstein
was already at work on the various fragments, aphorisms, self-addressed
memos, imaginary dialogues, dramatic vignettes, scenes of instruction, quasi-allegorical episodes, etc., which made up the *Philosophical
Investigations* and other items of the *Nachlass*. Here he renounced the
extreme logicist approach of the *Tractatus* and maintained, on the contrary, that logic was just one – and a strictly non-privileged one – of the
manifold 'language-games', together with the sundry associated 'forms
of life' that coexisted at any given time within any given community and
which required that each be interpreted on its own terms or according to
its own sense-making criteria. There could be no possible justification
for treating certain modes of discourse – say those of logic, mathematics,
or the physical sciences – as enjoying some special status or some truth-
telling power denied to others on account of their failing to meet standards
that were simply not applicable to them.

In which case, according to late Wittgenstein, it was time to give up
not only that false logicist ideal but also the other main positivist doctrine
that went along with it. This was the rigidly hierarchical 'unity of science'
programme which decreed a top-down scale with physics, chemistry and
biology in pride of place and, at the bottom of the scale, pseudo-disciplines
such as ethics or aesthetics that could either make terms with their lowly
status by accepting that their statements were merely emotive, or else be

dismissed as sheer 'metaphysical' nonsense. Late Wittgenstein not only repudiates this doctrine in its hard-line logical-positivist form, but carries that repudiation to the point of maintaining that every kind of language-game is acceptable by its own evaluative lights or on its own criterial terms. It is not hard to see why Badiou takes so strongly against late Wittgenstein and moreover sees fit to count him amongst the company of latter-day 'sophists'. Despite the best efforts of some Wittgensteinians to argue a contrary case – that the master's whole aim in this later phase was thera-peutically to coax philosophers down from their absurdly hyper-cultivated qualms about truth, knowledge, reality, other minds, and so forth – still there is an unmistakable sense in which that description is borne out by his appeal to language-games and life-forms as the furthest we can get by way of veridical or justificatory warrant. If the only relevant criteria for ascrip-tions of truth or falsehood are those that have their place in some given language-game which in turn has its place (and its legitimate role) in some given communal life-form then truth and knowledge *just are* coextensive with whatever counts as such by the cultural lights of that particular belief-community at that particular time.

In which case it is merely a piece of philosophical legerdemain for his advocates to say that Wittgenstein's later philosophy 'leaves everything as it is' with regard to our ordinary, everyday modes of thought and speech, including those that express an outlook of commonsense 'pre-philosophical' realism vis-à-vis the normal run of objects and events. Though it offers us a licence for going on talking in that routine way, it renders such talk nothing more than a matter of unthinking habit or com-monplace usage and thus denies the single most basic tenet of realism, i.e. the claim that truth is objective and (in the current analytic parlance) non-epistemic or verification-transcendent. Truth can come apart from truth-talk just as knowledge in the proper, non-Wittgenstenian sense of the term can come apart from any present-best state of belief, no matter how deep its communal roots. It should anyway be clear why Badiou takes issue with that whole movement of thought – the so-called linguistic turn – of which Wittgenstein stands as a paradigm instance.

Such thinking leaves absolutely no room for those various truth pro-cedures whether in mathematics, the physical sciences, politics, ethics or the arts that require something more than the existence of a language-game that finds room for truth-talk of the relevant kind. What they also require is the existence of a practice, a research programme, an investiga-tive protocol or artistic endeavour such that the condition of its possibly achieving truth is the possibility (in modal-logical terms, the necessary possibility) that it may fall short of that aim. The sophist – whether Protagoras as depicted by Socrates/Plato or the later Wittgenstein as cast in that role by Badiou – is one who rejects any such claim and instead reduces truth to the level of currently accredited best judgement or optimal belief. Worse still, when Wittgenstein addressed himself to issues in mathematics – very much Badiou's home ground – he did so in order to drive this lesson home (as he thought) to maximum effect by showing, through the supposed paradox about rule-following, that even here communal warrant was the most one could have by way of truth, knowledge, or bottom-line justification. Again this sets him totally at odds with Badiou's insistence on the power of mathematical thought to make the kinds of breakthrough discovery that could not be conceived – much less achieved – unless on the assumption that truth might always transcend or surpass the furthest extent of current-best knowledge. Moreover it requires a recognition that knowledge may harbour signs – gaps, anomalies, tensions, paradoxes, the excess of inconsistent over consistent multiplicity – which themselves obliquely herald some future advance beyond its present power to articulate clearly or put up as a well-formed theorem for proof or refutation.

One measure of the distance between these thinkers is the fact that Badiou devotes a large amount of detailed working-through to some pretty demanding topics in the history, development and technical aspects of set theory. This makes a striking contrast with the way that Wittgenstein – in pursuit of his generalised sceptical-communitarian case – sticks entirely to schoolbook maths examples such as simple addition or the straightforward following of recursive rules. Indeed Badiou deems it yet another symptom of the later Wittgenstein's unwholesome influence that so much philosophy of mathematics in the mainstream analytic tradition has been given over to endless wrangling about a narrowly defined range of issues that are of interest solely to philosophers and not to working mathematicians. However his chief quarrel with Wittgenstein has to do with that inertly consensus-based conception of knowledge and truth that, according to Badiou, finds a kind of *reductio ad absurdum* in this thoroughly inadequate idea of how mathematical thinking proceeds. That it also has dire implications for politics – revoking any prospect of radical change by cutting away the grounds of oppositional critique and thus confining praxis to a passive compliance with communally sanctioned values and beliefs – is yet further reason for Badiou's placing of the later Wittgenstein squarely among the sophists rather than the more usefully provocative antiphilosophers.

All the same it might be asked: even if the switch of focus from late to early Wittgenstein gets Badiou off the hook of self-contradiction, isn't there still something odd about this very marked shift of emphasis? The likeliest answer is that he now places even greater value than previously on the kinds of challenge, provocation, and stimulus to intellectual and creative self-renewal that the antiphilosopher is able to provide. Badiou doesn't choose to take a stand on the somewhat absurd debate currently raging between different factions of the Wittgensteinian faithful as to whether, in light of its cryptic closing remarks, the *Tractatus* should be treated as part-nonsense, all nonsense, 'deep' nonsense, trivial nonsense, or some other sort of nonsense altogether. What he finds in it, rather, is a strong statement (or showing) of the antiphilosophical desire to have done with all the constative protocols of reasoning, argument, consistency, logical entailment, demonstrative or probative warrant, etc. Should anything be needed by way of replacement – which Wittgenstein seems inclined to doubt – then it will surely be something more akin to poetry than philosophy, or to action rather than conceptual enquiry, or religious conversion rather than endorsing some given proposition on grounds of its rational accountability.

So *Tractatus* Wittgenstein joins those antiphilosophers, notably Saint Paul and Pascal, who adopt a strongly fideist outlook according to which the dictates of faith or existential commitment must always trump the values of logical, demonstrative, or (in certain crucially relevant senses) philosophical thought. Moreover, this finds him in agreement – or at any rate partial sympathy – with others of the same (admittedly broad) stripe, such as Nietzsche and Kierkegaard, who either attack the pretensions of western post-Socratic rationality or gesture towards a realm of ineffable since non-articulable truth. And it also brings him close in certain respects to thinkers like Rousseau whose placement among the antiphilosophers has to do chiefly with his counter-Enlightenment or proto-Romantic crusade and his elevation of passion and sentiment above the 'purely' intellectual virtues. Badiou's revised estimate of (early) Wittgenstein must therefore count as a promotion in so far as it reckons him one of philosophy's small company of worthy antagonists rather than, like the sophists ancient and modern, one of those who have sought refuge from philosophy's rigours in the appeal to language, rhetoric, or discourse.

Still it is something of a kick upstairs – or a deft backhander – because the various modes of antiphilosophy are united in evading that vital part of philosophy's task which requires that it think through the obstacles that arise when some particular instance of the count-as-one is confronted with some particular instance of inconsistent multiplicity. Thus the reader is left to infer, although Badiou doesn't make the point, that it was Wittgenstein's Tractarian avoidance of this task – and his own way of seeking such refuge – that left his later thinking exposed to the sophistical seductions of a cultural-relativist or wholesale language-first doctrine.

WOMAN, THE FEMININE, SEXUAL DIFFERENCE

Louise Burchill

'Woman' and 'the feminine' are categories that, in the context of Badiou's corpus, can be understood only in relation to the universal and generic dimension of truths as these operate in the fields of politics, love, science or art. Indeed, "woman's relation to the universal" constitutes not only the formal content of *all* Badiou's various axiomatic, logical or speculative definitions of woman and the feminine, but equally the subplot of the profusion of phenomenological narrations, polemical stances, literary or dramatic personae and declarative propositions pertaining to these categories within both his philosophical treatises narrowly defined, and his work as a whole (novels, plays, circumstantial political and critical essays, etc.). That this is the case follows quite simply from Badiou's positioning the category of truth or the universal – for they are one and the same – as pre-eminent within philosophy as a locus of thinking that knots together within itself the system of the truth procedures by which the world can be grasped for what it really is. Only that which displays a universalism of content and address is of interest to genuine thought, and woman as such stands or falls as a category according to its capacity to be taken up into, or welcome, the universal – be this at the price of its self-negation.

That admitted, woman's adventures with the universal over the course of Badiou's work may be seen to display three main modalities, designated here as follows:

1. *Subtraction*: Woman is taken up within a universalising truth procedure on the condition that sexed being is discounted or 'excised'. In this sense, 'woman' is disqualified here as a category, being but one instance, amongst an infinity of others, of the existing differences comprising humankind which the universal crosses through in its assertion of that which is the Same for everyone.
2. *Sublimation*: 'Woman' not only holds as a category taken up within a truth procedure but functions as the guarantee or, indeed, 'guardian', of universal totality on the condition of sexuate specificity as established in the field of love and marked, thereby, procedurally, by the 'capacity to pass from the sensible to something more essential' (*PE* 52).
3. *Sublation*: 'Woman' is a category marked in the universal, such that there is sexuation of thought, under the condition of sexuate/sexed specificity as established by a logic of 'the passage between Two', in terms of which the feminine is not a position but a process affirming

the non-being of the One. Hence the 'speculative definition' proposed by Badiou in 2011: 'Woman is the going-beyond of the One in the form of passing-between-Two' (*FF* 11–12).

These modalities of woman's relation to the universal are imbricated in a (quasi-dialectical) variety of ways. As a category of sexuation that is first and foremost established in the field of love, for example, woman's relation to the universal is pre-eminently in the modality of sublimation: the feminine position upholds love's very status as a process that, passing through and beyond desire with its economy of the object, aims at the 'being of the other' and is of the order of the infinite. Yet love involves, at the same time, a subtraction from sexual difference insofar as 'woman' and 'man' relate to something in common that attests their belonging to a single humanity – their being (in a non-fusional sense) 'the same'. Under other conditions, sublimation also opens onto the modality of sublation insofar as woman defined as requiring a guarantee of universality for humanity can, in itself, be considered to mark a sexuation, if not altogether *of*, at least *in respect of* the universal, such that it is then but a matter of taking 'another step' in order to arrive at the sexuation of thought.

Subtraction: woman as particularity

As an 'identitarian predicate' or 'particularity', sex, like race, religion, nation and culture, simply refers to the multiplicity of humankind, and is destined to be dissolved qua *différence* within any authentic symbolic initiative, which necessarily asserts the truth – qua *truth* – of that which is the Same for all.

Badiou's equating 'subtraction from sexed particularity' with the affirmation of a universal, *trans-particular* value should not be confused with the 'postmodernist thesis' of a multiplication of sexes or gender indistinction (SEM 2010; *LW* 420–1). To the contrary, subtraction from identitarian sexuate predicates involves the 're-marking' of dyadic sexual difference from the standpoint of the very universal value in respect of which, and by which, this difference is, strictly speaking, rendered insignificant. While Badiou most explicitly thematises this 're-marking' with respect to love, a number of his texts show that subtraction from sexed particularity equally leads – via its dual, constitutive processes of negation and affirmative incorporation – to a new determination of woman's 'sexuate position' in the fields of politics, science and art. *The Incident at Antioch* offers, for example, a dramatic representation of the subtraction from particularity that is brought about by exposure to the universalising force of an 'evental' truth in the field of emancipatory politics. In the course of her 'conversion' to the revolutionary process, the play's main protagonist, Paula – an avatar of Saint Paul, the 'founder' of universalism – is led to 'internally' negate all the worldly determinations, such as 'sister' and 'lover', that defined her up until then as a woman. By wresting herself from the predicates of sexed identity as set down by her epoch and becoming incorporated within a truth procedure – an incorporation that amounts, for Badiou, to an affirmation of a universal value, or universalisation *tout court* – Paula is 'symbolically' re-marked as a 'new' woman: i.e., a woman fully engaged in the creation of symbolic value. She becomes, in the words of the play's chorus, 'the woman of the instant' who takes the place of 'the eternal woman' (*IA*, Act 1 Scene IV). The same logic equally informs Badiou's text on Sophie Germain, who won the grand prize from the French Academy for her work on the problem of elastic surfaces at a time when women's access to any form of intellectual endeavour – much less that of 'stern mathematics' – was barred by a myriad of obstacles. ' "Woman" names here the dazzling universality of mathematics', states Badiou; Germain's victory is a 'victory of humanity' (SG 12).

In short, in the terms of Badiou's *subtractive* understanding of 'woman' as an identitarian predicate that must lose any subjective effectivity for individuals if they are to become subjects of a truth process, the ultimate signification of a woman's becoming engaged in the creation of symbolic values, and hence a 'new woman', lies in the exemplary proof this proffers of the indifferentiation of sexual difference within the universal (*SP* 112 sq.; EM 1–4; IJ, passim).

Sublimation: woman as a guarantee of universality for humanity

Woman holds first and foremost as a category relative to the universal in the field of love. One of the four fundamental truth procedures, love alone – and neither biology nor sociology, nor any other form of knowledge – furnishes a universal ground on which sexual difference can be thought. While two sexuated positions can be said to be 'given' in the field of experience, these positions are in a state of total disjunction such that neither position can know anything of the experience of the other, nor have any experience or direct knowledge of the disjunction as such. It follows that, for the sexuated positions to be defined in the disjunction of their experience, the situation needs to be supplemented by an *event* (WL 183–4), which is precisely in what the encounter initiating an amorous procedure consists, an encounter that manifests the non-substantial, or non-ontological, nature of the positions' disjunction, and establishes them as belonging to a single humanity.

The new subject – the Two of the lovers – that comes into being with

the amorous encounter is premised on a subtraction from sexuate particularity, for the two positions, man and woman, are no longer confined to
their singular, narcissistic experience of the world. Sexual difference is,
however, re-marked within the 'wholly immanent Two' of the lovers, such
that, while love is the scene in which the truth of the sexual disjunction
is produced, what each of the positions knows about love or the other sex
remains distinct from the knowledge of the other.

As (axiomatically) defined within the process of love, 'woman' and
'man' are distinguished in terms of how they *function* in love, the *knowledge* they hold in respect of love, and their relation to the space of thought
comprised by the four truth procedures, which Badiou names *humanity*
but which could also be called 'the symbolic'. (1) 'Woman' is she (or he)
who is concerned with ensuring that love is ongoing and reaffirmed; 'man'
is he (or she) who considers that, once named, love no longer needs to be
proved. (2) 'Woman' professes the Two to endure throughout life's vicissitudes, such that what 'she' knows of love is ontological in scope, being
focused on the existence of the Two, or being as such; 'man' focuses on
the split within the Two that re-marks the void of the disjunction, such
that 'his' is an essentially logical knowledge, concerned with the numerical change between One and Two. (3) 'Woman' requires love to exist
for the symbolic configuration of truth procedures to hold and to have
value; 'man' views each type of truth procedure to be in itself a gauge of
humanity, such that each is a metaphor for the others (WL 192–7).

Badiou fully acknowledges that these axiomatic definitions coincide
with the most common of clichés or gender stereotypes concerning the
difference between the sexes – 'man' ostensibly does nothing for and
in the name of love, 'woman' is the being-for-love; 'man' is silent and
violent, 'woman' is talkative and makes demands (193, 195). Describing
such commonplaces as the empirical material that love works through in
order to establish the truth of the sexual disjunction, he judges the 'staging
of sexual roles' within a dyadic gender system to have the merit, not of
expressing the disjunction per se, but of rendering this visible as a 'law'
of the situation. The 'constitutive Two' being strictly irreducible, love
is 'hetero' in its very principle insofar as it brings into play two strictly
heterogeneous sexuate positions, whatever the biological sex of the parties
involved.

This latter premise is one Badiou shares with Lacan. Yet, while
embracing Lacan's proclamation 'there is no sexual relation', Badiou
deems Lacan to have erred by making the phallic function (under which
all speaking beings fall) the 'universal quantifier' by which sexual difference is decided – with the feminine thereby becoming an 'objection to the
universal' on the basis of women's being 'not whole' or 'not-all' under this

function (Lacan 1998: 102–3). Relegating, for his part, the phallic function to the strict register of desire – or *jouissance* (enjoyment) – alone, Badiou stipulates sexual difference as such not to exist on this level. Woman and man alike, in the pure disjunction of their respective experience, are 'wholly' subject to the intrinsic finitude accruing to desire and its economy of the object: there is, in other words, no specific 'feminine jouissance', opening onto the 'infinite', that women would have access to by virtue of their being 'not-all' under the phallic order. Indeed, for Badiou, Lacan's very claims for such a jouissance reveal him to adhere to the 'segregative thesis of sexual difference', in terms of which there is no element whatso-ever common to the two sexes, and accordingly no knowledge whatsoever of the space occupied by the other. Only from the masculine position as defined within such an integral disjunction can the 'fantasy' or 'fiction' of an infinite, inaccessible, feminine jouissance be entertained (*SD* 47–8, 50; *SI* 219). Lacan's formulae of sexuation lend themselves to this insofar as, by defining the phallic function in terms of that which strictly holds universally in respect of the masculine position alone, they situate the function always-already *within* the disjunction of the sexes, and render it, as such, unsuitable as a support for the universal.

There has to be at least one term with which both sexuate positions entertain a relation: namely, the common – if indefinable – element introduced by love, which, in a final modification to Lacan's formulae of sexuation, consists, all in all, in a *sublimatory* transmutation of the object *a* (object of desire). (See also entry on love.) Since love thereby functions as a 'guarantee of the universal', the fact that the feminine position is itself defined in the process of love as 'singularly charged with the relation of love to humanity' (WL 195; tm) amounts to accrediting this position 'to require a guarantee of universality for humanity', with Badiou thereby 'returning' to women (pace Lacan) the universal quantifier within the sphere of symbolic value or 'the complete range of truth procedures'. A certain 'feminine exceptionality' would, then, still seem to haunt Badiou's '*sublimatory*' understanding of woman: an exceptionality displaced from the field of jouissance to that of love.

Sublation: woman as the going-beyond of the One

There are several indices from the very end of the 1990s of a major inflec-tion in Badiou's stance on sexuation and the universal, with this being linked more broadly to the question of the 'immanence of truths' insofar as that which is basically involved here is a truth's relation to its originating site – which is, of necessity, a 'particularity'.

In 1999, in a short text titled 'Of Woman as a Category of Being', Badiou first acknowledges the validity of thinking 'sexuated being', stating this to entail 'taking another step in the universal' (DLF 11). In 2009, Badiou again gestures to the necessity of rethinking the thesis of universality's neutrality when, in the context of a discussion bearing on why *The Incident at Antioch* has a woman as its main protagonist, he declares that the 'old vision' of sexual difference, casting religious or political theory and political action in masculine terms, is a thing of the past, and presages a 'feminine perspective' on political thought and action to take on a 'new importance' today ('Discussion', *IA*, 6). Then, in 2011, Badiou decisively sets out the 'inevitability' of a sexuation of symbolic and philosophical thought in a paper taking as its subject the 'figures of femininity in the contemporary world'. 'Symbolic thought cast in masculine terms' is now more formally characterised as a 'logic of the One', encapsulated in the 'Name of the Father' or the absolute unity of symbolic power – a power that, in contemporary capitalist societies, no longer governs the entire order of the Law or of symbolic creation. 'Woman' could, in this perspective, become the emblem of the new One, in accordance not only with the rationale of Capital but also the aspirations of a 'bourgeois and domineering feminism'. This is not the only possible scenario, however, for reasons that have to do with the very nature of femininity as Badiou now defines this. Femininity, he states, consists in a 'logic of the Two', or 'a passage-between-Two', that has traditionally 'undone' the One of the masculine position. 'Woman' designates, as a result, less a position than a process: a process consisting, precisely, in an affirmation of the non-being of the One, or, as Badiou puts it in a more dialectical formulation, 'the non-being that constitutes the whole being of the One'. Whence his 'speculative definition' of femininity: 'Woman is the going-beyond of the One in the form of a passing-between-Two'.

It follows from women's passing-beyond the absolute One of masculine logic that new forms of symbolic creation will emerge – with this attesting, from the perspective of Badiou's *sublatory* understanding of 'woman', to 'the feminine being linked, for the first time in history, to a philosophical gesture' (a transcript of this talk is to be found at le-voyage-a-geneve. over-blog.com/article-badiou-sur-les-fils-et-les-filles-70312383.html, last accessed 3 January 2015).

WORLDS

Steven Corcoran

In the *Timaeus*, Plato, astonished by the beauty and order of the universe, gives an account of the creation of the world, which he ascribes to the deeds of a Demiurge imposing a mathematical order on a pre-existent chaos, in the manner of a sculptor sculpting clay. With its obsolete motifs of the finitude of the universe and its being the result of a purposive, rational and beneficent agency acting on a matter as if from outside, the story is the prototype of idealist accounts of the universe – its ordering according to a transcendent rational model. But the story is more than just 'a fabulous and eccentric narration'. What Badiou discerns in it is a first attempt at constructing a transcendental of appearing.

But in forging a transcendental logic of worlds (which concerns the appearing of being or being-there insofar as a being can only be thought as being-there) Badiou's attempt at a materialist conception of worlds diverges from Plato's idealist cosmology, the main characteristic of which is that the universe is fashioned after an intelligible transcendent model. For starters, for Badiou there is no whole world of beings, and therefore no universe, but instead an irreducible multiplicity of worlds, each of which is identified with its own logic of appearing. Second, he impugns all transcendence. The arrangement of a world does not come from 'above' or 'without'; the parts of a being that appears within a world are also part of that world, as is the transcendental that regulates their appearing. And being contingent and discontinuous, nor do these heterogeneous worlds form part of any kind of underlying teleological movement.

In the process of grasping the being-there of multiplicities in a world, perhaps the best place to start from is the question of the whole, or the lack thereof. Says Badiou, since there is no whole, 'there is no uniform procedure of identification and differentiation of what is' – i.e. no predicative separation that would uniformly determine multiplicities through their identification and differentiation within the Whole, qua universal place of multiple-beings on the basis of which 'both the existence of what is and the relations between what is would be set out' (112). For this reason, the 'thinking of any multiple whatever is always local, inasmuch as it is derived from singular multiples and is not inscribed in any multiple whose referential value would be absolutely general' (112). The 'identifications and relations of multiples are always local' (never capable of being folded back onto a singular (Other or Whole)), always enveloped in ever larger multiples.

Badiou will call this 'local site of the identification of beings', precisely 'a world'. It is a site in which, 'in the context of operations of thought', 'the identity of a multiple is identified on the basis of its relations with other multiples' – of the being thus identified.

The world, as the local site of the identification of beings, is thus a place, since the operation of identification presumes a place of the local, but this place is only ever the place at which the 'operation operates' (113). While the place indicates the operation that takes place, from a guaranteed point, in order to reach the identity of the new being, the operation is localised by a world, which is a world for that operation. World is the place on the basis of which it is possible to think a being as necessarily situated.

'World' is a recasting of Badiou's primitive notion of situation from *BE*. Instead of viewing situations (worlds) from the viewpoint of 'their strict multiple-neutrality', they are now envisaged as 'the site of the being-there of beings'. Being-there qua appearing in the world has a relational consistency. Badiou speaks of 'a' world as 'a situation of being' – 'a' situation since is it obvious that there is no intrinsic link between a being-multiple and a given world, and that any such multiple can appear in different worlds. The irreducible multiplicity of worlds means that a multiple-being can exist in many different worlds either synchronically or diachronically. What permits this is that 'The "worlding" of a (formal) being, which its being-there or appearing, is ultimately a logical operation: the access to a local guarantee of its identity' (114). It is an operation that may be produced in many different ways, such that one and the same formal being, ontologically speaking, may co-belong to different worlds (114).

A world is, moreover, not the whole of beings, or universe, since as Badiou demonstrates the whole or universe is not. It belongs to the essence of the world that there are several worlds, since if there were only one it would be the universe (102). A being comes to be 'in' a world – but this metaphor is obviously inadequate, 'in' indicates that at issue is a localisation of multiples. The world is no container 'in' which a being is placed. It is nothing but a logic of being-there, and its singularity is identified with the singularity of its logic. What the concept of world thus does is to articulate the cohesion of multiples around a structured operator (the transcendental).

Badiou's concept of world thus aims to give us an operational phenomenology that identifies the condition of possibility for the worldliness of a world, or the logic of localisation of the being-there of any being whatever. Against Kant, then, he posits that access to thinking the world is not resolved via a transcendental subject, but through an a-subjective transcendental of appearing. The inaccessible infinity of a world is absolutely inaccessible from within the world itself, and 'any "world" that pretended to less would not be a world' (353). Second, 'this impossibility is what ensures that a world is closed, without for all that being representable as a Whole' (326). Now, this ontological closure also ensures logical completeness, such that any relation in the world must be universally exposed, objectively available.

Worldliness and Capitalism

Some of Badiou's recent remarks seem to present his work on worlds with a problem. The problem revolves around the interrelation between three terms: world, democracy (as a state form) and capitalism. Badiou's elaboration of the notion of worlds is, as we've said, based on a transcendental logic that accounts for the way in which beings appear in a world. The apparent paradox is that Badiou has also described our time as being worldless, as devoid of any world, insofar as the overwhelming majority of people are devoid of a 'name' in this world. Capitalism provides no inclusive space for meaningful engagement in a situation, no way by which we can cognitively map reality. On his account, even Nazi anti-Semitism, was a world, a criminal one, but a world nonetheless insofar as it described the present critical situation, named the goal (the Jewish conspiracy) and the means to achieve it. By contrast, on account of its economic neutrality toward all hitherto existing civilisations, capitalism has been able to become truly global, standing therein as a name not for a specific culture-symbolic world but as a neutral economic framework that operates with all particular cultural values, at the same time as it undermines them. Insofar as it undermines such specific socio-cultural values, Badiou, after Marx, considers capitalism as something to be applauded. Yet attaching itself to these values in appearance it manages to bring about 'generalized atomism, recurrent individualism and, finally, the abasement of thought into mere practices of administration, of the government of things or of technical manipulation' (Žižek 2009: 318).

Capitalism's specific danger is that it does not promote any particular values and is necessarily, on account of its being global, able to sustain a worldless ideological constellation. The inconsistency or paradox in Badiou's theory thus appears to reside in the following: 'whilst in Badiou's theoretical writings on the appearance of worlds he cogently argues that events engender the dysfunction of worlds and their transcendental regimes, in his "ontology of the present" Badiou advocates the necessity, in our "intervallic" or worldless times, of *constructing* a world, such that those now excluded can come to invent new names, names capable of sustaining new truth procedures' (Žižek 2009: 319).

The paradox is thus that capitalism's specific world is subtracted from the very idea of world. This formula of an x that is subtracted from the very idea of x is something we find often in Badiou's interventions on the present (that the Iraq war is subtracted from the very idea of war, his Genet-inspired characterisation of the present as a non-present present etc.). Today's world is subtracted from the very idea of world in that its regime of appearing is structurally awry. The idea of a present subtracted

from the idea of a present, or of a non-present present, involves the collapsing of the past into the future, thus eliding any present of action and
consequences: because no fundamental change is possible, the future is a
mere repetition of the past – and the name of this lack is Democracy. That
is, democracy is the phallic name embodying the lack of present wherein
people, knowing full well that the real site of power lies outside democratic
forms in the hands of a tiny oligarchy, continue to act as if they do live in
a democracy. What this generates is a specific kind of subjective corruption (corruption of thought) and a concomitant impossibility, namely the
impossibility of ever reaching the democracy's proclaimed standards – of
equity, justice, and so on). Does this mean that if we were to turn things
around and take democratic standards seriously, by, say, subjecting all
instances organising social life – from the state to the World Bank – to
democratic norms, i.e. by transferring democratic norms to the entire level
of state, we would finally be able to live up to democratic standards. But
the whole point is that Marx already argued that the gulf between direct
democracy and the state is so large that it is strictly impossible to do this.
Between the blind, repressive and repetitive operations of state, which
operates on the basis of modern bourgeois society, with its division of
labour, wage exploitation, and so on, and the process of direct democracy
the gap is unbridgeable.

Capitalism, we know, functions differently to previous eras. Whereas
pre-capitalist societies functioned according to a dominant representation that included an exceptional element through excluding it, capitalist
dynamism functions precisely through undermining every stable system
of representation. As Žižek again says: 'In pre capitalist formations, every
state, every representational totalization, implies a founding exclusion,
a point of "symptomal torsion", a "part of no part", an element that,
although part of the system, does not have a proper place within it–and
emancipatory politics had to intervene from this excessive ("supernumerary") element that, although part of the situation, cannot be *accounted for*
in its terms' (Žižek 2009: 318). It was the event that served as an infinite-
point by which the system in its finitude would be disrupted'. Thus, he
claims 'Badiou seems to be caught in an inconsistency': in a worldless
world (one with no total system of representation) the aim of emancipatory
politics should be the precise opposite of its 'traditional' modus operandi–
the task today is to form a new world, to propose a new Master-Signifier
that would provide cognitive mapping.

Bibliography

Badiou, Alain (1991 [1989]), 'On a Finally Objectless Subject', in E. Cadava (ed.), *Who Comes After the Subject?*, London: Routledge, pp. 24–32.

Badiou, Alain (1991), 'L'être, l'événément et la militance', *Futur antérieur* 8, p. 21.

Badiou, Alain (1992), 'Emmy Noether', *Lettres sur tous les sujets*, November.

Badiou, Alain (1993), 'Sophie Germain', *Lettres sur tous les sujets*, June.

Badiou, Alain (1995), 'Platon et/ou Aristote-Leibniz: Théorie des ensembles et théorie des topos sous l'œil du philosophe', in Marco Panza and Jean-Michel Salanskis (eds), *L'objectivité mathématique: Platonismes et structures formelles*, Paris: Masson, pp. 61–83.

Badiou, Alain (1997), 'L'insoumission de Jeanne', *Esprit*, 238 (December), 26–33.

Badiou, Alain (1999a), 'De la femme comme catégorie de l'être', preface to Danièle Moatti-Gornet, *Qu'est-ce qu'une femme? Traité d'ontologie*, Paris: L'Harmattan, pp. 11–14.

Badiou, Alain (1999b [1989]), *Manifesto for Philosophy: Followed by Two Essays: 'The (re)turn of Philosophy Itself' and 'Definition of Philosophy'*, trans. Norman Madarasz, Albany: State University of New York Press.

Badiou, Alain (2000a [1997]), *Deleuze: The Clamor of Being*, trans. Louise Burchill, Minneapolis: University of Minnesota Press.

Badiou, Alain (2000b), 'Metaphysics and the Critique of Metaphysics', *Pli*, 10: 174–90.

Badiou, Alain (2002), 'Esquisse pour un premier manifeste de l'affirmationisme', in Ciro Giordano Bruni (ed.), *La question de l'art au 3e millénaire: généalogie critique et axiomatique minimale*, Proceedings of the International Symposium, Germs, pp. 13–32.

Badiou, Alain (2003a [1997]), *Saint Paul: The Foundation of Universalism*, trans. Ray Brassier, Stanford: Stanford University Press.

Badiou, Alain (2003b), 'Beyond Formalisation', in Peter Hallward (issue ed.), *Angelaki*, Vol. 8, No. 2 (August), pp. 115–34.

Badiou, Alain (2004 [1995]), *On Beckett*, trans. Alberto Toscano, Manchester: Clinamen Press.

Badiou, Alain (2005a [1998]), *Handbook of Inaesthetics*, trans. Alberto Toscano, Stanford: Stanford University Press.

Badiou, Alain (2005b [1998]), *Metapolitics*, trans. Jason Barker, London and New York: Verso.

Badiou, Alain (2006a), 'Five Remarks on the Contemporary Significance of the Middle Ages,' trans. Simone Pinet, *Diacritics*, 36 (3): 156–7.

Badiou, Alain (2006b [1986]), 'The Factory as Event-Site', trans. Alberto Toscano, *Prelom: Journal for Images and Politics*, 8: 171–6.

Badiou, Alain (2006c), *Theoretical Writings*, ed. Ray Brassier and Alberto Toscano, London and New York: Continuum.

Badiou, Alain (2006d [1998]), *Briefings on Existence: A Short Treatise on Transitory Ontology*, trans. Norman Madarasz, Albany: State University of New York Press.

Badiou, Alain (2007a [1988]), *Being and Event*, trans. Oliver Feltham, London and New York: Continuum.

Badiou, Alain (2007b [2005]), *The Century*, trans. Alberto Toscano, Cambridge: Polity Press.

Badiou, Alain (2007c), 'L'antiphilosophe', *Magazine Littéraire*, April.

Badiou, Alain (2007d [1967]), *The Concept of Model: An Introduction to the Materialist Epistemology of Mathematics*, trans. L. Z. Fraser and Tzuchien Tho, Melbourne: re.press.

Badiou, Alain (2007e), 'Philosophy as Creative Repetition', *The Symptom*, 8: Winter 2007, www.lacan.com/badrepeat.html (last accessed 8 January 2015).

Badiou, Alain (2008a [1992]), *Conditions*, trans. Steven Corcoran, London and New York: Continuum.

Badiou, Alain (2008b [1990]), *Number and Numbers*, trans. Robin Mackay, Cambridge: Polity Press.

Badiou, Alain (2008c [2007]), *The Meaning of Sarkozy*, trans. David Fernbach, London and New York: Verso.

Badiou, Alain (2009a [2006]), *Logics of Worlds: Being and Event, 2*, trans. Alberto Toscano, London and New York: Continuum.

Badiou, Alain (2009b [1982]), *Theory of the Subject*, trans. Bruno Bosteels, London and New York: Continuum.

Badiou, Alain (2009c [1990]), *Of an Obscure Disaster: On the End of State-Truth*, Maastricht and Zagreb: Jan van Eyck Academie and Arkzin.

Badiou, Alain (2009d [2008]), *Pocket Pantheon: Figures of Postwar Philosophy*, trans. David Macey, London and New York: Verso.

Badiou, Alain (2010a), *La tétralogie d'Ahmed*, Paris: Actes Sud.

Badiou, Alain (2010b), *The Communist Hypothesis*, London and New York: Verso.

Badiou, Alain (2010c), 'The Formulas of "L'Etourdit"', *Symptom*, 11, online at www.lacan.com/symptom11/?p=385 (last accessed 11 December 2014).

Badiou, Alain (2010d), 'Le penseur vient en personne: entretien avec Alain Badiou', *Europe: Revue Littéraire Mensuelle*, 972 (April): 92–8.

Badiou, Alain (2010e), 'Does the Notion of Activist Art Still Have a Meaning? A Lacanian Ink Event', http://www.lacan.com/symptom6_articles/badiou.html (last accessed 11 December 2014).

Badiou, Alain (2010f), 'Point de vue: Le courage du présent', *Le Monde*, 13 February 2010.

Badiou, Alain (2011a), *Polemics*, ed. and trans. Steven Corcoran, London and New York: Verso.

Badiou, Alain (2011b [2009]), *Second Manifesto for Philosophy*, trans. Louise Burchill, Cambridge and Malden, MA: Polity Press.

Badiou, Alain (2011c [2009]), 'The Democratic Emblem', in Giorgio Agamben (ed.), *Democracy in What State?* trans. William McCuaig, New York: Columbia University Press, pp. 6–15.

Badiou, Alain (2011d [2009]), *Wittgenstein's Antiphilosophy*, trans. Bruno Bosteels, London and New York: Verso.

Badiou, Alain (2011e), 'Figures de la féminité dans le monde contemporain', unpublished conference paper delivered in Athens, Greece.

Badiou, Alain (2011f), 'Politics: A Non-Expressive Dialectics', in Mark Potocnik, Frank Ruda and Jan Völker (eds), *Beyond Potentialities? Politics between the Possible and the Impossible*, Zurich: diaphanes, pp. 14–15.

Badiou, Alain (2012a), *Plato's Republic: A Dialogue in 16 Chapters*, trans. Susan Spitzer, New York: Columbia University Press.

Badiou, Alain (2012b [1993]), *Ethics: An Essay on the Understanding of Evil*, trans. Peter Hallward, London and New York: Verso.

Badiou, Alain (2012c), *Les années rouges*, Paris: Les Prairies Ordinaires.

Badiou, Alain (2012d [2011]), *Philosophy for Militants*, ed. Bruno Bosteels, London and New York: Verso.

Badiou, Alain (2012e), *The Adventure of French Philosophy*, ed. Bruno Bosteels, London and New York: Verso.

Badiou, Alain (2012f [2011]), *The Rebirth of History*, trans. Gregory Elliott, London and New York: Verso.

Badiou, Alain (2012g), 'Destruction, Negation, Subtraction: On Pier Paolo Pasolini', in Luca di Blasi, Manuele Gragnolati, and Christoph F. E. Holzhey (eds), *The Scandal of Self-Contradiction: Pasolini's Multistable Subjectivities, Traditions, Geographies*, Vienna: Turia + Kant.

Badiou, Alain, 'Mark and Lack: On Zero' (2012h [1967]), in Peter Hallward and Knox Peden (eds), *Concept and Form*, London and New York: Verso, pp. 340–94.

Badiou, Alain, 'Infinitesimal Subversion' (2012i [1967]), in Peter Hallward and Knox Peden (eds), *Concept and Form*, London and New York: Verso, pp. 395–441.

Badiou, Alain (2013a), 'Affirmative Dialectics', in Marios Constantinou (ed.), *Badiou and the Political Condition*, Edinburgh: Edinburgh University Press, pp. 44–55.

Badiou, Alain (2013b), *Ahmed the Philosopher: Thirty-Four Short Plays for Children and Everyone Else*, New York: Columbia University Press.

Badiou, Alain (2013c), *Badiou and the Philosophers: Interrogating 1960s French Philosophy*, London and New York: Bloomsbury Academic.

Badiou, Alain (2013d [2010]), *Cinema*, Cambridge: Polity Press.

Badiou, Alain (2013e), *Le Séminaire – Lacan: L'antiphilosophie 3 (1994–1995)*, Paris: Fayard.

Badiou, Alain (2013f), ed. Duane Rousselle, *The Subject of Change: Lessons from the European Graduate School, 2012*, New York and Dresden: Atropos Press.

Badiou, Alain (2013g), *Le Séminaire – Malebranche: L'Être 2 - Figure théologique* (1986), Paris: Fayard.

Badiou, Alain (2013h [2011]), *Reflections on Anti-Semitism*, trans. David Fernbach, London and New York: Verso.

Badiou, Alain (2013i), *The Incident at Antioch: A Tragedy in Three Acts*, New York: Columbia University Press.

Badiou, Alain (2013j [1990]), *Rhapsody for the Theatre*, trans. and with an introduction by Bruno Bosteels, London and New York: Verso.

Badiou, Alain (2014a), *Mathematics of the Transcendental*, trans. A. J. Bartlett and Alex Ling, New York: Bloomsbury.

Badiou, Alain (2014b), *Images du temps présent 2001–2004*, Paris: Fayard.

Badiou, Alain, and Bruno Bosteels (2005), 'Can Change Be Thought? A Dialogue with Alain Badiou', in Gabriel Riera (ed.), *Philosophy and Its Conditions*, New York: State University of New York Press.

Badiou, Alain, and Barbara Cassin (2010), *Heidegger: Le nazisme, les femmes, la philosophie*, Paris: Fayard/Ouvertures.

Badiou, Alain, and Alain Finkielkraut (2014 [2010]), *Confrontation: A Conversation with Aude Lancelin*, trans. Susan Spitzer, London and New York: Polity Press.

Badiou, Alain, and Elisabeth Roudinesco (2014 [2012]), *Jacques Lacan, Past and Present: A Dialogue*, trans. Jason E. Smith, New York: Columbia University Press.

Badiou, Alain, and Fabien Tarby (2013 [2010]), *Philosophy and the Event*, trans. Louise Burchill, Cambridge: Polity Press.

Badiou, Alain, and Tzuchien Tho (2007), 'The Concept of Model Forty Years Later: An Interview with Alain Badiou', in *The Concept of Model*.

Badiou, Alain, and Tzuchien Tho (2011 [1972]), *The Rational Kernel of the Hegelian Dialectic*, Melbourne: re.press.

Badiou, Alain, and Nicolas Truong (2012 [2011]), *In Praise of Love*, New York: New Press.

Badiou, Alain, and Slavoj Žižek (2010), *Five Lessons on Wagner*, trans. Susan Spitzer, London and New York: Verso.

Groupe pour la Fondation de l'Union des Communistes Francais (Marxiste-Leniniste) (1970), *La Revolution Proletarienne En France – Comment Edifier Le Parti de l'Epoque de La Pensee de Mao Tse Toung*, Paris: Librairie du livre rouge.

Group for the Foundation of the Union of Communists of France Marxist-Leninist (2005), 'Maoism, Marxism of Our Time', trans. Bruno Bosteels, in *Positions*, 13:3 (2005): p. 527.

BOOKS ON BADIOU

Ashton, Paul, A. J. Bartlett, and Justin Clemens (eds) (2006), *The Praxis of Alain Badiou*, Melbourne: re.press.

Balibar, Etienne (2004), 'The History of Truth: Alain Badiou in French Philosophy', in Peter Hallward (ed.), *Think Again*, London: Continuum.

Bartlett, A. J. (2011), *Badiou and Plato: An Education by Truths*, Edinburgh: Edinburgh University Press.

Bartlett, A. J., and Justin Clemens (eds) (2010), *Alain Badiou: Key Concepts*, Durham and Montreal: Acumen Publishing.

Bartlett, A. J., Justin Clemens, and Jon Roffe (2014), *Lacan Deleuze Badiou*, Edinburgh: Edinburgh University Press.

Bosteels, Bruno (2011), *Badiou and Politics: Post-Contemporary Interventions*, Durham, NC: Duke University Press.

Fraser, Z. L. (2007), 'The Law of the Subject: Alain Badiou, Luitzen Brouwer and the Kripkean Analyses of Forcing and the Heyting Calculus', in Paul Ashton, A. J. Bartlett, and Justin Clemens (eds), *The Praxis of Alain Badiou*, Melbourne: re.press, pp. 23–70.

Feltham, Oliver (2008), *Alain Badiou: Live Theory*, London and New York: Continuum.

Gibson, Andrew (2006), *Beckett and Badiou: The Pathos of Intermittency*, Oxford and New York: Oxford University Press.

Gillespie, Sam (2008), *The Mathematics of Novelty: Badiou's Minimalist Metaphysics*, Melbourne: re.Press.

Hallward, Peter (2003a), *Badiou: A Subject to Truth*, Minneapolis: University of Minnesota Press.

Hallward, Peter (ed.) (2004), *Think Again: Alain Badiou and the Future of Philosophy*, London and New York: Continuum.

Hallward, Peter (2008), 'Order and Event', *New Left Review*, 53 (October): 97–122.

Lecercle, Jean-Jacques (2010), *Badiou and Deleuze Read Literature*, Edinburgh: Edinburgh University Press.

Marty, Eric (2005), 'Alain Badiou: l'avenir d'une négation', *Les Temps Modernes*, 635–6 (November): 22–58.

McNulty, Tracy (2005), 'Feminine Love and the Pauline Universal', in Riera Gabriel (ed.), *Alain Badiou: Philosophy and Its Conditions*, Albany: State University of New York Press.

Meillassoux, Quentin (2010), 'History and Event in Alain Badiou', *Parrhesia*, no. 12: 1–11.

Milner, Jean-Claude (2005), 'Le juif de négation', *Les Temps Modernes*, 635–6 (December): 12–22.

Mount, Madison (2005), 'The Cantorian Revolution: Alain Badiou on the Philosophy of Set Theory', *Polygraph: An International Journal of Culture and Politics*, 17: 41–91.

Norris, Christopher (2009), *Badiou's Being and Event: A Reader's Guide*, London and New York: Continuum.

Norris, Christopher (2014), *Derrida, Badiou and the Formal Imperative*, New York: Bloomsbury USA Academic.

Pluth, Ed (2010), *Badiou: A Philosophy of the New*, Cambridge; Malden, MA: Polity Press.

Power, Nina, and Alberto Toscano (2009), 'The Philosophy of Restoration: Alain Badiou and the Enemies of May', *Boundary 2*, 36 (1): 27–46.

OTHER WORKS CITED

Aczel, Peter (1988), *Non-Well-Founded Sets*, CSLI Lecture Notes, no. 14, Stanford: Center for the Study of Language and Information.

Aloni, Udi (2011), *What Does a Jew Want?: On Binationalism and Other Specters*, New York: Columbia University Press.

Althusser, Louis (2010), *For Marx*, New York and London: Verso.

Aristotle, *Metaphysics*, Oxford: Oxford University Press.

Bell, J. L. (1981), 'Category Theory and the Foundations of Mathematics', *The British Journal for the Philosophy of Science*, 32: 4, 349–58.

Bell, J. L. (1986), 'From Absolute to Local Mathematics', *Synthese*, 69: 3, 409–26.

Brassier, Ray (2007), *Nihil Unbound: Enlightenment and Extinction*, New York: Palgrave Macmillan.

Cohen, P. J. (1996), *Set Theory and the Continuum Hypothesis*, New York: W. A. Benjamin.

Cohen, P.J. (2002), 'The Discovery of Forcing', *Rocky Mountain Journal of Mathematics*, 32: 4, 1072.

Conway, John Horton (1976), *On Numbers and Games*, London: Academic Press Inc.

Cooper, John M., and D. S. Hutchinson (eds) (1997), *Parmenides, in Plato: Complete Works*, trans. Mary Louise Gill and Paul Ryan, Indianapolis: Hackett.

Dauben, Joseph W. (2005), 'Georg Cantor and the Battle for Transfinite Set Theory,' in G. Van Brummelen and M. Kinyon (eds), *Kenneth O. May Lectures of the Canadian Society for History and Philosphy of Mathematics*, New York: Springer Verlag, pp. 221–41.

Deleuze, Gilles (1990), *The Logic of Sense*, London: Athlone Press.

Deleuze, Gilles (1994), *Difference and Repetition*, trans. Paul Patton, New York: Columbia University Press.

Dupin, Jacques (1992), 'Lichens', in *Jacques Dupin: Selected Poems*, trans. Paul Auster, Newcastle: Bloodaxe Books.

Eilenberg, Samuel, and Saunders Mac Lane (1945), 'General Theory of Natural Equivalences', *Transactions of the American Mathematical Society* 58: 231–94.

Engels, Friedrich (1999 [1845]), *The Condition of the Working Class in England*, Oxford: Oxford University Press.

Ferry, Luc, and Alain Renaut (eds) (1997), *Why We Are Not Nietzscheans*, Chicago: University of Chicago Press.

Frege, Gottlob (1960), *The Foundations of Arithmetic*, trans. J. L. Austin, New York: Harper Torchbooks.

Girard, Jean-Yves (1987), 'Linear Logic', *Theoretical Computer Science*, Vol. 50: 111.

Girard, Jean-Yves (2001), 'Locus Solum', *Mathematical Structures in Computer Science*, Vol. 11: 441–85.

Gonshor, Harry (1986), *An Introduction to the Theory of Surreal Numbers*, Cambridge: Cambridge University Press.

Kant, Immanuel (1996 [1781]), *Critique of Pure Reason*, trans. Werner Pluhar, Indianapolis: Hackett Publishing.

Knuth, Donald E. (1974), *Surreal Numbers: How Two Ex-Students Turned on to Pure Mathematics and Found Total Happiness*, Reading, MA: Addison-Wesley Publishing.

Lacan, Jacques (1980), 'Monsieur A', Ornica,r 21–2.

Lacan, Jacques (1987), 'Letter of Dissolution', trans. Jeffery Mehlman, *October*, 14: 128–30.

Lacan, Jacques (1998), *On Feminine Sexuality: The Limits of Love and Knowledge, The Seminar of Jacques Lacan, Book XX, Encore*, trans. Bruce Fink, New York: Norton.

Lacan, Jacques (2001), *Autres Écrits*, Paris: Editions du Seuil.

Lacan, Jacques (2006), *Écrits: the first complete edition in English*, trans. Héloïse Fink and Bruce Fink, New York: W. W. Norton & Co.

Lacoue-Labarthe, Philippe, and Jean-Luc Nancy (1988), *The Literary Absolute: The Theory of Literature in German Romanticism*, trans. Philip Barnard and Cheryl Leser, Albany: State University of New York Press.

Lazarus, Sylvain (1996), *Anthropologie du nom*, Paris: Editions du Seuil.

Lyotard, Jean-François (1988), *The Differend: Phrases in Dispute*, trans. Georges Vaan Den Abbeele, Minneapolis: University of Minnesota Press.

Mac Lane, Saunders (1971), *Categories for the Working Mathematician*, New York, Heidelberg and Berlin: Springer-Verlag.

Mac Lane, Saunders (1997), 'The PNAS Way Back Then', *Proceedings of the National Academy of Sciences, USA*, Supp. 1: 5220–7.

Marx, Karl and Friedrich Engels (1988), *The Economic and Philosophic Manuscripts of 1844 and The Communist Manifesto*, trans. Martin Milligan, New York: Prometheus Books.

Miller, Jacques-Alain (1968), 'The Action of Structure', *Cahiers pour l'analyse*, Vol. 9.

Nietzsche, Friedrich (1990), *Twilight of the Idols and Anti-Christ*, trans. R. J. Hollingdale, London: Penguin.

Panza, Marco, and J.-M. Salanskis (eds) (1995), *L'objectivité Mathématique: Platonismes et Structures Formelles*, Paris: Masson.

Pasolini, Pier Paolo (2014), *Saint Paul: A Screenplay*, trans. Elizabeth A. Castelli, London and New York: Verso.

Plato (1925), *Plato in Twelve Volumes*, trans. H. N Fowler, Cambridge, MA: Harvard University Press.

Quine, Willard Van Orman (1937), 'New Foundations for Mathematical Logic', *American Mathematical Monthly* 44: 70–80.

Rancière, Jacques (1991), *The Ignorant Schoolmaster: Five Lessons in Intellectual Emancipation*, trans. and with an introduction by Kristin Ross, Stanford: Stanford University Press.

Rancière, Jacques (2007), *On the Shores of Politics*, trans. Liz Heron, Radical Thinkers 21, London: Verso.

Rancière, Jacques (2012) *Proletarian Nights: The Workers' Dream in Nineteenth-Century France*, trans. John Drury, London and New York: Verso.

Sartre, Jean-Paul (1956), *Being and Nothingness: An Essay in Phenomenological Ontology*, trans. Hazel E. Barnes, New York: Philosophical Library.

Sartre, Jean-Paul (1957), *The Transcendence of the Ego*, trans. F. Williams and R. Kirkpatrick, New York: Noonday Press.

Zermelo, Ernst (1967), 'Investigations in the Foundations of Set Theory I', in Jean van Heijenoort (ed.), *From Frege to Gödel: A Source Book in Mathematical Logic, 1879–1931*, trans. Stefan Mengelberg, Cambridge, MA: Harvard University Press, pp. 183–98.

Žižek, Slavoj (2008a), *The Plague of Fantasies*, London and New York: Verso.

Žižek, Slavoj (2008b), *The Ticklish Subject: The Absent Centre of Political Ontology*, London and New York: Verso.

Žižek, Slavoj (2009), *The Parallax View*, Cambridge, MA and London: MIT.

Žižek, Slavoj (2012), *Less Than Nothing: Hegel and the Shadow of Dialectical Materialism*, London and New York: Verso.

Notes on Contributors

A. J. Bartlett is Adjunct Research Fellow at the Research Unit in European Philosophy at Monash University. He is the author of *Badiou and Plato: An Education by Truths*, co-translator of Badiou's *Mathematics of the Transcendental* and co-author of *Lacan, Deleuze, Badiou*.

Bruno Besana has taught philosophy at Paris VIII and Bard College, Berlin. He is the author of several articles on contemporary philosophy and a translator from French and English into Italian. He is an alumnus of the ICI Kulturlabor Berlin and of the Jan van Eyck Academie, Maastricht, and a founding member of the Versus Laboratory collective.

Anindya Bhattacharyya is an independent scholar based in London working on the mathematical aspects of Badiou's ontology. His essay 'Set, categories and topoi: approaches to ontology in Badiou's later work' appears in *Badiou and Philosophy* (Edinburgh University Press 2012).

Pietro Bianchi is PhD candidate in Romance Studies at Duke University. His first book, *Jacques Lacan and Cinema: Imaginary, Gaze, Formalisation*, is forthcoming (Karnac).

Louise Burchill teaches at the University of Melbourne. She is the translator of Badiou's *Deleuze: The Clamor of Being*, *Second Manifesto for Philosophy*, among other works. Her forthcoming book is provisionally titled *Badiou's 'Woman': Sexuate Ventures with the Universal*.

Justin Clemens' books include *Psychoanalysis is an Antiphilosophy* (Edinburgh University Press 2013) and, with A. J. Bartlett and Jon Roffe, *Lacan Deleuze Badiou* (Edinburgh University Press 2014). He teaches at the University of Melbourne.

Steven Corcoran is a researcher at the Berlin University of the Arts. He has taught at the University of New South Wales and the Melbourne School for Continental Philosophy. He is the editor and translator of Badiou's *Polemics* and Rancière's *Dissensus: On Politics and Aesthetics*.

Olivia Lucca Fraser is an independent researcher living in Halifax, Nova Scotia, with her four youngest children. She is a participant in several research networks including the New Centre for Research and Practice, the Jan van Eyck Association, the Form and Formalism Working Group, and a feminist writing collective, Laboria Cuboniks.

Agon Hamza is a PhD candidate at the Postgraduate School ZRC SAZU in Ljubljana. His publications include *Repeating Žižek*, *Althusser and the Gospel According to St Matthew* and, with Slavoj Žižek, *From Myth to Symptom: The Case of Kosovo*.

Dominiek Hoens is an ex-advising researcher of the Jan van Eyck Academie in Maastricht (2007–12), co-editor of *S: Journal of the Jan van Eyck Circle for Lacanian Ideology Critique*, and teaches philosophy and psychology of art at Erasmus University College (Brussels) and Artevelde University College (Ghent).

Dhruv Jain is a doctoral student at York University (Canada). He is working on a book-length manuscript detailing the ideological history of the Indian Maoists from 1971–91, with a particular focus on the relationship between conjuncture and revolutionary optimism.

Elad Lapidot is a translator and lecturer of philosophy and rabbinic literature at the Free University and Humboldt University in Berlin. He is the author of *Translating Philosophy* (2012), *Fragwürdige Sprache* (2013) and *'Du, der mit Buchstaben und Beschneidung ein Gesetzesübertreter bist': Paulus und die Grundlegung des Judentums* (2014).

Joseph Litvak is professor of English at Tufts University and author, most recently, of *The Un-Americans: Jews, the Blacklist, and Stoolpigeon Culture* (2009). *Ahmed the Philosopher*, his translation of Badiou's comic play, *Ahmed philosophe*, was published by Columbia University Press in 2014.

Norman Madarasz is associate professor of philosophy at the Catholic University of Porto Alegre (PUC–RS) in Brazil. He is the author of *O Múltiplo sem Um: Uma apresentação do Sistema filosófico de Alain Badiou*, and editor of *O Brasil na sua Estação: Lógicas de transformação. Críticas da democracia*.

François Nicolas is a composer and professor at the Ecole Normale Superieure, Paris. He combines compositions with theoretical reflection on music. He recently completed a vast work, *Le monde-Musique* (4 volumes, Aedam Musicae, 2014).

Christopher Norris is Distinguished Research Professor in Philosophy at the University of Cardiff, Wales. He has written more than thirty books on aspects of philosophy and literary theory, among them *Platonism, Music and the Listener's Share*, *Badiou's Being and Event: a reader's guide*, and *Derrida, Badiou and the Formal Imperative*.

Dimitra Panopoulos has taught at the Université de Bordeaux III and at Université Paris VIII. She is a member of the Centre International d'Étude de Philosophie Française Contemporaine and has worked with Christian Schiaretti at the Centre Dramatique National de Reims, notably on Alain Badiou's plays from the *Tétralogie Ahmed*.

Nina Power teaches philosophy at Roehampton University and Critical Writing in Art and Design at the Royal College of Art. She is the author of numerous articles on European thought.

Ozren Pupovac is a philosopher and social theorist based in Istanbul and Berlin. He teaches at Boğaziçi University, Istanbul, and is the translators of works by Badiou, Rancière and Althusser into Serbo-Croatian. He is the co-founder, with Bruno Besana, of the Versus Laboratory research platform.

Jon Roffe is a McKenzie Postdoctoral Fellow at the University of Melbourne and a founding member of the Melbourne School of Continental Philosophy. His is the author of *Badiou's Deleuze* and *Muttering for the Sake of Stars*, and a co-author with A. J. Bartlett and Justin Clemens of *Lacan Deleuze Badiou*.

Frank Ruda is interim professor for Philosophy of Audiovisual Media at the Bauhaus-University in Weimar and a lecturer at Bard, a liberal arts college in Berlin. His publications include: *For Badiou: Idealism without Idealisms* and *Abolishing Freedom: A Plea for the Contemporary Use of Fatalism* (both forthcoming 2015).

Fabien Tarby is the author of several books, including *Matérialismes d'aujourd'hui*, *Democratie Virtuelle* and, with Alain Badiou, *Philosophy and the Event*.

Tzuchien Tho is research associate at the Berlin-Brandenburgische Akademie der Wissenschaften. He has published on the history and philosophy of mathematics in the seventeenth century and the impact of mathematics on contemporary French philosophy.

Samo Tomšič obtained his PhD at the University of Ljubljana, and currently works at Humboldt University in Berlin. He has published on psychoanalysis and twentieth-century French philosophy. His book *The Capitalist Unconscious: Marx and Lacan* is forthcoming (Verso 2015).

Jan Voelker is research associate at the Institute of Fine Arts and Aesthetics at Berlin University of the Arts and a visiting lecturer at Bard College, Berlin. He is the author of *Ästhetik der Lebendigkeit. Kants dritte Kritik*, and the co-author of *Neue Philosophien des Politischen zur Einführung (Laclau, Lefort, Nancy, Rancière, Badiou)*.

Alenka Zupančič is a research advisor at the Slovenian Academy of Sciences and Arts and visiting professor at the European Graduate School. She is the author of *The Odd One In: On Comedy*; *Why Psychoanalysis: Three Interventions*; *The Shortest Shadow: Nietzsche's Philosophy of the Two* and *Ethics of the Real: Kant and Lacan*.

Index

Note: Page numbers in **bold** refer to main entries.